PHYLLIS SHAND ALLFREY

PHYLLIS SHAND ALLFREY

A Caribbean Life

LIZABETH PARAVISINI-GEBERT

Rutgers University Press
New Brunswick, New Jersey

Published by Rutgers University Press, New Brunswick, New Jersey
Manufactured in the United States of America

Library of Congress Cataloging-in-Publication Data

Paravisini-Gebert, Lizabeth.
Phyllis Shand Allfrey : A Caribbean life / Lizabeth Paravisini-Gebert.
p. cm.
Includes bibliographical references (p.) and index.
ISBN 0-8135-2264-1 (alk. paper). — ISBN 0-8135-2265-X (pbk. : alk. paper)
1. Allfrey, P. Shand (Phyllis Shand)—Biography. 2. Women and literature—Dominica—History—20th century. 3. Authors, Dominican—20th century—Biography. 4. Women politicians—Dominica—Biography. 5. Caribbean Area—Biography. I. Title.
PR9250.9.A44Z83 1996
813—dc20
[B] 95-33061
CIP

British Cataloging-in-Publication information available

To Gordon and little Gordon,
lovers of islands

Contents

Preface
The End of Eden

The road leading from the tiny village of Wotton Waven to the capital of Dominica meanders down the verdant mountains before beginning its steep descent into the Roseau River Valley and the town of Roseau in the distance. In the coolness of the early morning it teems with men, women, and children walking the long kilometers to town on their way to work, market, or school. The few fortunate enough to have caught a bumpy lift on the back of one of the ubiquitous small trucks cry out hurried greetings and messages to the walkers before they vanish around the next curve on the road.

In the early 1980s a bird-thin, quaintly dressed white woman was frequently among the walkers. "Good morning, Ma Allfrey," was an oft-heard welcome.

Ma Allfrey was a fixture of the valley landscape. She was universally known and, although considered a bit odd, equally universally respected and liked. Few of her walking companions may have remembered—many may have been too young to know—that the frail white woman sharing their walk and their poverty had founded Dominica's first political party; that she had written poetry, short stories, a classic West Indian novel; that she had been a Federation minister and had addressed large gatherings in places as far away as Geneva and Lagos; that the precarious existence she eked out was worlds removed from the opulence of her powerful planter ancestors; and that she could have prospered as a writer abroad, but was bound to them and to her island by ties stronger than any others she had known, ties that nurtured her poetry and her prose.

All this had been true, but now she lived as poorly as they did in a small sugar millhouse owned by a former plantation overseer. Her English-born husband, Robert, was ailing and too frail for the long walk to town for food. Her children were gone: her beloved firstborn, Phina, tragically dead in Africa; her son, Philip, in his thirtieth year of confinement in a psychiatric ward; her adopted Dominican children struggling abroad—Sonia and David in London, Robbie—the younger of her Carib sons—away on a training course. She and Robert had very little money; too often they had none.

Her spirit, however, was unbowed. She would comment on their "war of attrition" in a casual, offhand sort of way; their "severe bouts of poverty" being no worse than those of the people with whom she had thrown her lot. Every week had one "D. Day" (Deprivation Day) when food ran out, but she claimed it helped them stay slim and active. She struggled against her poverty with the same quiet dignity with which she had accepted triumphs and defeats. Above all, no degree of poverty could spoil the bounty—"the natural loveliness of Dominica, greatest of all consolations"—surrounding her in her little paradise, the tiny millhouse at Copt Hall.

She seldom looked back, she welcomed no pity; indeed, it would have been misplaced. She had survived the ostracism of the white society against whose interests she had struggled; she had endured the betrayal of the party she had founded, when the demands of black nationalism made it expedient. She had helped found and bring to power a new party, offering greater promise to the poor; she had spearheaded some of the most profound changes wrought in Dominican society in the past thirty years. Her poverty and deprivation, real as they were, could never be the measure of her life.

When Phyllis Allfrey died in 1986, the tiny millhouse was sold and built over to make a small hotel. Its stone walls are now part of a larger building eagerly awaiting much-promised foreign tourists. Phyllis would have grieved for her beloved home; but she would also have savored the irony of the house's transformation from nineteenth-century sugar mill into a writer's idyllic final refuge into a guesthouse awaiting the twentieth century's substitute for sugar in the West Indies—the dollar-bearing tourist from abroad. The inn at Copt Hall is appropriately—or inappropriately—named "The End of Eden."

Acknowledgments

If the enduring love and steadfast loyalty of her friends is any measure of Phyllis Shand Allfrey's life and work, she was indeed graced, for every single one with whom I spoke or corresponded during the writing of this book—even former political enemies whose respect she had to earn—eagerly shared their recollections, letters, contacts, and information, in many cases even generously adopting my project as their own. In the course of it I have been privileged to make many new friends and incurred countless debts to some of the kindest people any researcher could come across. My greatest is to Lennox Honychurch, executor of the Allfrey Estate, for his unparalleled thoughtfulness, trust, and support. He provided steady guidance through the maze of thousands of documents in his archives, a stream of insights and anecdotes, and meticulous critiques of my chapters as they came to him; but above all he urged me to keep Phyllis as alive on the page as he had known her—energetic, contradictory, indomitable, and ever heartened by her love for her island. I am likewise indebted to Polly Pattullo, a staunch friend of Phyllis's in her latter years, for her inspiration, hospitality, and advice, her willingness to share with me her own research—and for the sense of humor that pulled me through many a low point. Rosalind Leslie-Smith spoke to me of her beloved elder sister and of their family with unsparing candor, conveying in her many anecdotes and tales the myriad nuances of a Dominican childhood without which the early chapters of this biography would have been impossible to write. I am indebted to her and to her husband, Commander George Leslie-Smith, for their gracious hospitality through many visits and their thoughtful reading of this text. If I have one regret as this book goes to press it is that Rosalind did not live long enough to see it completed. Adèle Olyphant Emery, "my interested informer," generously shared with me Phyllis's numerous letters and her recollections of a friendship that spanned sixty years; without them I would have been unable to reconstruct Phyllis's years in the United States. Patricia Honychurch's contributions—her graciousness in responding to countless requests for information, her painstaking reading of the manuscript, her hospitality and friendship—can only be adumbrated in these words of thanks.

I am particularly grateful to those who have found the time to read the manuscript and provide extensive and most helpful commentary. Margaret Benge, Ronald Benge, Pixie Foley, Brian Merton Gould, and Dilys Henrik Jones—Phyllis's friends from her years in London—offered frank and constructive criticism of the text in addition to page upon page of precious details on Phyllis's life in England and Trinidad. They have my heartfelt thanks. I am especially mindful of the generosity of colleagues and friends—Andrew Bush, Pierrette Frickey, Elaine Savory Jones, Patricia Kenworthy, Ivette Romero, and Consuelo López Springfield—who took time away from their own work to read and criticize mine. Joan Dayan added to her perceptive comments on the text and unflagging enthusiasm for the project the infinite patience of a good friend.

For their kindness in contributing memories, contacts, information, and correspondence I must thank Arnold Active, Daphne Agar, Robert Allfrey Jr., Sonia Allfrey Adeleke, the Honourable Frank Baron, Rachel Beck, Mrs. Decius Benjamin, Dr. Clair Broadbridge, the Honourable Mary Eugenia Charles, N.A.N. Ducreay, Mrs. Ivo De

Souza, Ramabai Espinet, Arthur and Elizabeth Greenhall, Geoffrey and Joan Guy, Janet Higbie, Sara Honychurch, Peter Hulme, Reverend Clement S. Jolly, Anthony Layng, Emmanuel Christopher Loblack, Mr. and Mrs. Manuel Mercado, Gerald Meyer, Robert Myers, Michael and Josette Napier, Judith Pestaina, Jonathan Pulsifer, Lorna Robinson, Dr. John Saunders, Edward Scobie, Jean Soomer, Rosalind Volney, and Francis Wyndham. For making possible my initial contact with Lennox Honychurch I am grateful to Carol Sicherman.

Among librarians I would like to thank first and foremost the late Olga Torres-Seda, head of the Inter-Library Loan Office at the Lehman College Library and the most gentle and loving of friends. Dean Rogers at the Vassar College Library Inter-Library Office handled my often arcane requests with unflaggingly good humor and admirable speed. Shirley Mattheul of the *Dominica Chronicle* very kindly guided me through the paper's archives in Roseau. The excellent staff at the Colindale (London) Branch of the British Museum Library deserves special thanks, as do those of the London Public Record Office and the Roseau Public Library.

Research on this biography received substantial support from the George N. Shuster Fellowship Program at Lehman College, the Faculty Research Award Program of the Professional Staff Congress of the City University of New York, the Vassar College Faculty Research Program, and the Travel to Collections Program of the National Endowment for the Humanities. In 1994–1995 I received a generous fellowship from the American Association of University Women (AAUW) for my ongoing study, *Race, Gender, and the Plantation in Caribbean Women's Fiction,* a grant that also assisted me in completing this book.

The pressures of getting the manuscript ready for publication were considerably eased by the excellent word-processing skills of Peggy Zering and the computer expertise of Julie Commella, Mike Costello, and Eugene Lugo. Annila Rehman and Maria Walton, generous and patient to a fault, helped with countless faxes, photocopies, parcels, and emotional support. Special thanks are due to Leslie Mitchner, my editor at Rutgers University, for her faith in this project from its very conception and her continued encouragement; and to Susan H. Llewellyn, my copy editor, for a superb job.

My husband, Gordon, has been so perfect in his encouragement and support that there are no words to do him justice. To him, whose love has been "a fountain at my fond heart's door," and to our family—Carrie, D'Arcy, and little Gordon—who so cheerfully followed to London, Dominica, and beyond, my best love.

All chapter titles, and the epigraphs that follow them, are taken from the poems of Phyllis Sand Allfrey. All photographs, unless otherwise credited, are included courtesy of the Phyllis Shand Allfrey Estate.

Part I

DOMINICA, LAST HAUNT OF THE CARIBS

Queen of the Caribbean! Solemn peaks
of jagged mountains pierce your misty sky,
Down the deep valleys rolling thunder speaks
The rain-clouds burst the torrent passes by.
And through the curtain like a bridal veil
The sun peeps forth and all the colours pale
Of soft-hued rainbow splendour, dimmed with tears,
Light up each scene as fairyland appears.

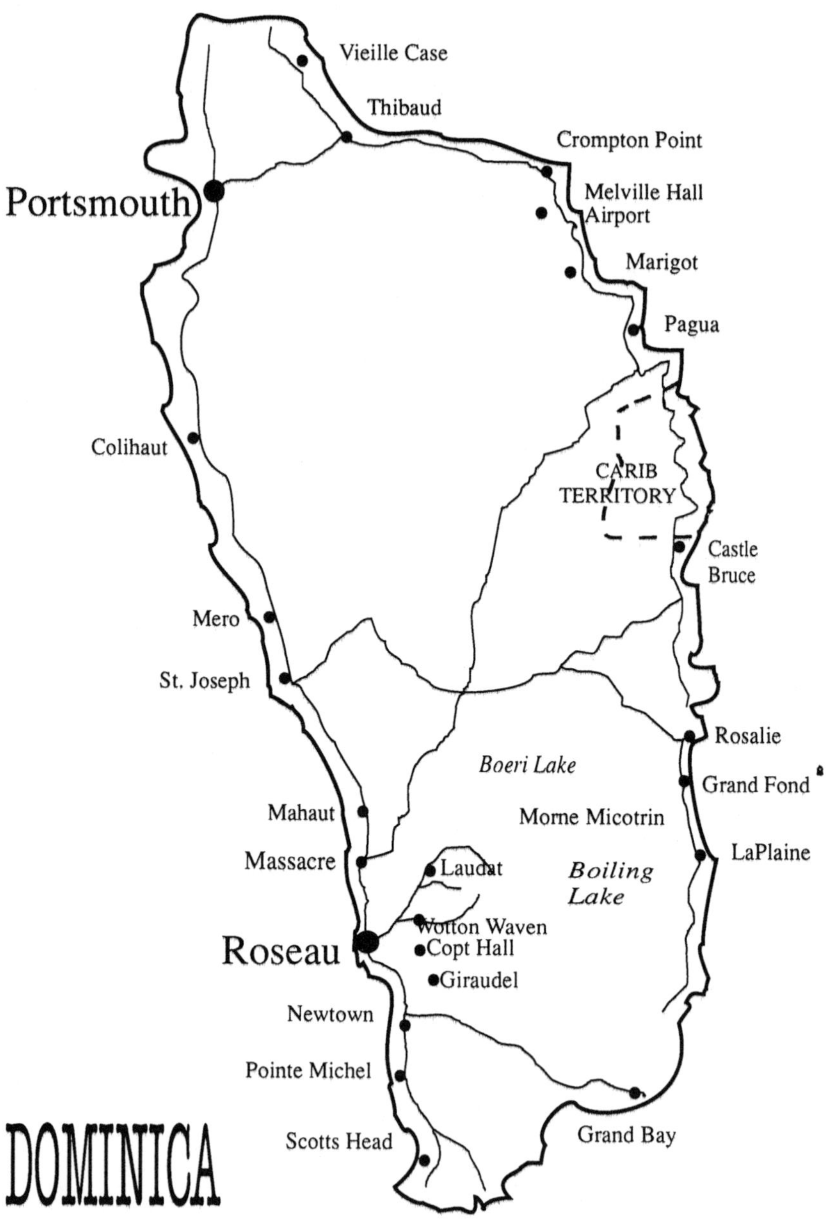
Vieille Case
Thibaud
Crompton Point
Melville Hall
Airport
Portsmouth
Marigot
Pagua
Colihaut
CARIB
TERRITORY
Castle
Bruce
Mero
St. Joseph
Rosalie
Boeri Lake
Grand Fond
Mahaut
Morne Micotrin
Massacre
Laudat
Boiling
Lake
LaPlaine
Wotton Waven
Roseau
Copt Hall
Giraudel
Newtown
Pointe Michel
Grand Bay
Scotts Head

DOMINICA

One

Ghosts in a Plantation House

Strangest of all strange things is the presence of strangers
In the rooms and the haunts and the glades of the dearly known.
Small wonder the slave girl moans and the French Priest talks
And Victorian Doctors stroll out in the moonlight for walks.

Of all the islands of the Caribbean, Dominica—where Phyllis Byam Shand was born on October 24, 1908—is still the most unspoiled. It shoots out of the sea in steep green cliffs, its mountains disappearing into the rain-soaked skies. A land of waterfalls, downpours, and rainbows, with lofty mountains draped to their very peaks with lush vegetation, Dominica can be approached only with fascination and awe. It is an island where all the features characteristic of the West Indian landscape are magnified: The mountains are taller, the rains more forceful, the ravines deeper and more magnificent, the sunlight more piercing. Evidence of the island's volcanic origin is everywhere: in the sulfur springs and boiling fountains, in the mirrorlike surface of Boeri Lake—the crater of an inactive, though not extinct, volcano—and in the ominous resplendence of the Valley of Desolation and its centerpiece, the Boiling Lake. The interior of the island is dense with thick, almost impenetrable tropical rain forests; its shores are the dark gray of moist volcanic sand. Vegetation grows exuberantly in a profusion of greens, prompting Alec Waugh to wonder how "a single colour could have so many varieties of tone and texture, could achieve such an effect of patchwork." The island's vibrant greenery teems with life; lizards, birds, butterflies, beetles, toads, and bats seem to multiply at will, turning it into an eruption of constant birth and rebirth. Undisciplined nature is the true ruling spirit in Dominica.

The island has a complex history. It was one of the sundry territories in the Caribbean granted to the Earl of Carlisle in 1627, but the first successful settlers did not arrive until the mid-eighteenth century, when French planters established sugar plantations. It was captured by the English navy in 1761 and ceded to England by the 1763 Treaty of Paris, only to fall again into French hands in 1778. Despite coming firmly under English control in 1805, it remained, until well into the twentieth century, French at heart. E. C. Eliot, the administrator of Dominica (1923–1931) who married Phyllis's sister Marion in 1927, recalls in his memoirs how adamantly the country people held on to their French patois (or Kwéyol, as it is known today), even though the government schools, to which in any case very few of the peasantry had any access, taught only English. The population of Dominica, about thirty thousand at the turn of the century, was overwhelmingly Roman Catholic, and although the French and Belgian fathers conducted church services in English, it is most probable that patois was the language of choice for sickbeds and house visits. The peasantry looked to the church hierarchy as natural leaders, giving it a powerful hold over island affairs. Such was the power of French language and culture that many English visitors concluded with some bitterness that Dominica was English only in name. But the English influence, if not evident in the language and culture, was manifest in the institutions, the administrative and legislative patterns, the political models, and the style of social life among the community of English settlers. This white community, unlike those of other Caribbean islands, was small and generally not very wealthy. Landowners often allowed their overseers to run their estates, and the island lacked the planter society rooted in grand estate houses that characterized the white upper classes of Antigua and Jamaica.

The island had, in fact, never partaken of the legendary riches spawned by the West Indian plantation economy. The fertility of its soil was legendary, but the plantation economy had already seen its heyday before the collapse of sugar prices in the 1880s virtually wiped it out. Dominica had always been a relatively inefficient producer of sugar. Its rugged terrain and poor communications kept the size of plantations small, and they could not compete with the larger, more technologically advanced plantations on other islands. The topography also made the black population much more independent; there had been, even before emancipation, large settlements of free black and mulattoes who owned land or lived as squatters on abandoned or neglected estates. After the sugar industry's collapse a number of potentially profitable cash crops were tried—cacao, vanilla, and spices; cassava for starch; rubber; Liberian coffee; and limes. The lime industry enjoyed a marked boom during the first half of the twentieth century; since then bananas have provided a source of steady if not bounteous income.

On the eve of Phyllis's birth, Roseau, the island's capital, was a pleasant, unpretentious town in an exceedingly beautiful natural setting; its bay was of the deepest azure, its air transparent, the forest above it a lovelier green than that of any other Caribbean island. It stood on a shallow promontory, its houses arranged in terraces up the hill, the towers of the old French Catholic cathedral dominating the ascending landscape. The town boasted a fort (or its ruins), used then as a police barracks, over which flew the English flag. It was flanked on the north by a public garden built on the edge of a cliff, and on the south by the Carnegie Library, a graceful and airy Victorian building with a broad veranda. Its gardens were a favorite playground of the Shand girls; its contents offered Phyllis a link to the world beyond Dominica so important to her budding ambition. Across the road from the library was Government House, the center of social life, a handsome one story building of solid gray stone, with well-tended gardens and lawns with orange trees, oleanders, hibiscus, palms, and saman trees.

Turn-of-the-century Roseau was a charming, innocent, sun-filled place, its air perfumed by white acacia flowers, sweeter than orange blossom. But for all its surrounding natural beauty, it was not a prosperous town, despite the recent efforts of Hesketh Bell, a young and energetic administrator (1899–1905) who almost single-handedly modernized the Dominican infrastructure. This is the same "Mr. Hesketh" described by Jean Rhys in *Smile Please* as having asked her to dance the first waltz at a fancy-dress ball he gave at Government House. In Rhys's assessment, Bell "improved the roads out of all knowledge and triumphantly carried through his better idea of an Imperial Road across the island so that the Caribbean and South Atlantic sides were no longer cut off one from the other. . . . He arranged for a small coasting steamer called *The Yare* to carry passengers and goods from one end of the island to the other." It was primarily due to his efforts that Dominica had telephone and electric systems by 1909.

At the time of Phyllis's birth, Roseau and its environs boasted seven thousand inhabitants, most of them living in the small hamlets dotting the landscape. Its society was typical of the colonial West Indies in its stratification along class, race, language, and religious lines. Bell, an acute observer of social behavior, found the Dominican people, especially the planters, to be extremely hospitable. The "upper classes," to which Phyllis's family belonged, comprised the proprietors of large estates, the chief officials, and the heads of important businesses. The great majority of these were born Dominicans, with no more than one hundred purely English (that is, white) people, although "the proportion of well-to-do people of light colour and good education was steadily increasing." Social life was firmly within the framework of English colonial life, with fortnightly receptions at which those who had signed the Government House book would be invited. There were, Bell explained, no definite rules about "calling" at Government House, but there appeared to be an unwritten law as to the qualifications that would justify such a course—qualifications that, as in most colonies, were inextricably linked to color and wealth. To write one's name in the visitors' book must, he thought, be a milestone in the life of many a colonial man or dame, and marked a distinct promotion in the social degree. With his characteristic humor, Bell described a gathering that was a typical part of Phyllis's childhood and youth:

> Our fortnightly receptions are usually held in the gardens which are an admirable frame for them. The big shade-spreading trees shelter "birds of a feather" and prevent those sinister rows or circles of chairs which are the bane of a host or hostess. The only drawback to the Government House gardens is the near proximity of the R.C. churchyard. It is only just on the other side of the wall, and the lugubrious intonations of a priest, reciting the Burial Service, have more than once depressed the tone of our parties. Worse still is the fact that, owing to the overcrowded state of the cemetery, the defunct are often not interred at an adequate depth. The result is an effluvium which, when the breeze is coming from that direction, has obliged me, more than once, to send a protest to the Catholic authorities.

Roseau's was a fairly unworldly society, its entertainment "free from all the affectations and pretenses that prevail in more sophisticated places." Amusements fell into a pleasant and placid pattern of small and unpretentious gatherings, with frequent garden parties, dinners, and small dances at which local *jing-ping* bands—a concertina, a steel triangle, a *boum-boum* (or bamboo pipe), and the variously described object they call a *shakshak,* and perhaps a piano or a violin—would play. Musical evenings were particularly popular, with young and old contributing to the entertainment. Jean Rhys, in her autobiography, recalls the allure that Roseau's musical evenings held for her, opening windows onto the world beyond her tiny island:

> Again the whisky and soda and ice, but who'd want to drink when they could listen to Mrs. Wilcoxon singing "When We Are Married Why What Will We Do?" or "The Siege of Lucknow"—that was Mrs. Miller. I didn't know where Lucknow was but I'd get very excited hearing about the sick Highland woman who heard the bagpipe of the relieving Highlanders before anybody else, "The Campbells Are Coming" at the end, and my hands damp with emotion. Before I was old enough to be allowed down during the musical evenings, I would sit on the staircase and look through the banisters into a dark passage. Beyond was the room where the music came from.

This solidly provincial society cradled, within the span of two decades, two of the Caribbean's most admired writers.

Phyllis Byam Shand was born into a well-established Roseau family whose roots in the West Indies dated to the 17th century. Given the questionable social provenance of many of the early white settlers in the Caribbean, the family's illustrious lineage was the source of a profound pride that was an integral part of her upbringing and profound sense of obligation to the West Indies. One of her most cherished possessions was *Antigua and the Antiguans: A Full Account of the Colony and Its Inhabitants from the Times of the Caribs to the Present Day*, an 1844 work which details the genealogy of the Byam-Shand family to that date, and to which she had added in her own hand the names and birth dates of the generations that followed. Historian Gordon Lewis, never a favorite of Phyllis's, once described her as a politician "whose Fabian Socialism [had] not stifled in her an obvious pride in belonging to the 'Royal Family of Dominica.'" She was indeed a woman who, despite her battle against her own class, despite her political campaign against the "bourg high-life," was inspired and sustained by the conviction that her family's deep roots in the Caribbean made her "the First Dominican." She was fond of describing herself as "a West Indian of over 300 years standing despite my pale face" and would look upon her political work—"to have blazed a trail, broken ice, led the way and formed a Labour Government in Dominica"—as nothing but her duty "to pay my obligations to the Dominican people."

Dominican historian Lennox Honychurch tells an anecdote that encapsulates Phyllis's perception of herself as one in a long line in history. Toward the end of her life, he had taken a group of young schoolchildren to visit her, and one of them, in the manner of West Indians accustomed to white people not having lived long in the Caribbean, asked her how long she had lived on the island. "Three hundred years," she replied proudly, symbolically gathering the mantle of history around her shoulders, conscious of being the last of the Byams and Shands in Dominica. The reply was her boast as well as her plea for recognition of her claim to West Indianness, of the fact that despite her skin color and class origins, points of contention throughout her long political career, she was a true West Indian—and the First Dominican. Of the many tributes she received upon her death, she would have valued most Alexander Hoyos's assertion that she had been a valiant woman who had "resolved to conduct her life as a continuum of West Indian history."

Phyllis's earliest ancestor in the West Indies, William Byam, was descended in a direct line, on his father's side, from Caradoch Vraich Vras, Earl of Hereford, Lord of Radnor, and Lord of the Doloreuse, purportedly one of the knights of King Arthur's Round Table. His father, Edward Byham or Byam, having graduated from Oxford in 1604 and taken holy orders, had become vicar of Dulverton in Somerset, a post he held until 1625, when he emigrated with his family to Ireland to take the post of precentor of Cloyne Cathedral. William, his eldest son and heir, was born at Luccombe on March 9, 1622, and attended Lismore School in Ireland before entering Trinity College, Dublin, as "Scholarium Commensalis" on May 34, 1639. After completing his studies, he joined the army just as the tensions between Charles I and Parliament were exploding into civil war. In 1645 young Major Byam was among the Royalist officers imprisoned in the Tower of London after their garrison at Bridgewater had fallen to the Parliamentary army commanded by Sir Thomas Fairfax and

Oliver Cromwell. After several months in the Tower, Byam accepted a pass "to go beyond the seas" and left England with his military companions for a life of exile in Barbados, a fledgling British colony and then a Royalist refuge. There, in the late 1640s, he married Dorothy Knollys, daughter of Francis and Alice Knollys of Standford-in-the-Vale, Berkshire, and stepdaughter of Sir Henry Huncks, former governor of the colony. Marriage into the Knollys family linked William to the first families in England, and even with royalty itself, as Dorothy was the great-great-great-granddaughter of Mary Boleyn, sister to Henry VIII's ill-fated Queen Anne. Soon after his arrival in Barbados, Byam was appointed treasurer of the island and master of the ordnance, and received a large grant of land. He settled down to the life of a pioneer West Indian planter, clearing the tropical forest and fighting against disease and the ever-threatening Caribs. But in 1651, alarmed by the quickly mounting number of Royalist refugees in the colony, and fearing that the increasingly wealthy colony would become a base of operations for the restoration of the monarchy, Parliament sent a fleet to take control of the island. In 1652, after six months of resistance, the Commonwealth navy captured Barbados, and Major Byam and many of his companions were banished to a new Royalist settlement in Surinam.

In 1654 Byam was elected governor of Surinam, a post he held until 1667, when England lost the territory as the result of the Anglo-Dutch war (1665–1667).* In February 1667, a Dutch fleet had laid siege to the Surinamese capital and invited the English to surrender; but Byam informed the Dutch commander that honor obliged him to fight. After a stubborn show of resistance, Byam and his men were forced to lay down their arms. The Treaty of Breda granted the territory to the Dutch, and the English settlement—a thriving one with a number of prosperous plantations and a population of four thousand, slaves included—moved to the island of Antigua. In a letter to a friend in 1668 Byam wrote that he had "deserted our unfortunate colony of Surinam, war and pestilence having almost consumed it. As it is to revert to the Dutch, I have with great loss removed to Antigua, where I am hewing a new fortune out of wild woods." Ever resilient, he was soon named governor of Antigua, and his estates of Cedar Hill, North Sound, and Willoughby Bay, the foundation of the family's fortunes, were returned to him by Charles II's royal patent dated April 20, 1668. Willoughby Bay, reputedly located in the most fertile part of the island, was considered "the best cultivated and most productive" and the "prettiest of all the plantations in Antigua."

Byam, aged forty-seven, died in Antigua in 1669, just a year after the restoration of his lands, leaving his wife, Dorothy; a daughter, Alice, and two boys (Willoughby and Edward), not yet of age. His estate was divided equally between his surviving sons, who would become heads of the two branches of the Byams of Antigua, a family remarkable for its commitment to its West Indian properties and for its almost uninterrupted residence on an island that had more than its share of absentee landlords. Sundry bequests in his will give evidence of the level of sugar production at the Byam plantations in the late seventeenth century, offering a glimpse of the affluence the

*Governor during writer Aphra Behn's sojourn in the colony, Byam led the militia that "savagely" pursued and captured the runaway slaves led by Oroonoko. Behn would narrate the details of the capture and subsequent execution of her noble slave friend in the novel *Oroonoko* (1688). She once described Byam as the "most fawning fair-tongued fellow in the world . . . whose character is not fit to be mentioned with the worst of slaves."

family would enjoy well into the nineteenth century. To his late daughter's child he left forty thousand pounds of sugar and tobacco, "as made on the estate, to be laid out in new negroes out of the shipps [sic]"; to Alice, thirty thousand pounds of sugar and tobacco at age twenty-one; to his four sisters, one thousand pounds each; five hundred pounds to his nephew and two nieces; three hundred pounds each to his doctor and his overseer; and one cow, one calf, and a "yew lamb" to a woman named Eleanor Doyle. His wife was to have a third of all annual produce on the estate.

Willoughby, William's eldest son, became a lieutenant colonel in the army and commanded the bodyguard of the commander in Chief, General Codrington, in the expedition against the island of Saint Kitts in 1690, where he received a mortal wound in the neck. He left three young daughters and two sons: Samuel, who died young, leaving a second Samuel, who married Grace Warner, thus linking the family to another powerful West Indian family—that of Thomas Warner; and William, his heir, a colonel of the army, member of the Privy Council and of the General Council of the Leeward Islands, who married a planter's daughter, Mary, daughter of John Yeamans of Mill Hill, Old Road, Antigua, then lieutenant governor of the island. His eldest surviving son (and heir), Edward, born in 1712, entered Gray's Inn as a junior barrister in 1728, the same year he was admitted as a student to Trinity College, Cambridge. Upon his return to Antigua in 1734, he married his cousin Lydia Byam, daughter of his great-uncle Edward, a courageous soldier and capable administrator who enjoyed a long and successful political career, holding the posts of governor of the Leeward Islands and president of the Council of Antigua, influential positions that helped solidify the family's fortune and contributed to its power and prestige. He was described by John Oldmixon in his *The British Empire in America* as "a man of the best head and fortune in British America" and the most popular man in the Leeward Islands.

The eighteenth century witnessed the full flowering of the plantation economy in the West Indies. It was the century that gave birth to the expression "rich as a West Indian planter," and Edward and Lydia Byam shared in the general prosperity. The extent of their wealth is evident from the legacies in Edward's will, probated on July 20, 1742. Upon his death he left Lydia half the profits of his real estate, six Negroes, his coach and six horses, all his silverplate and "household stuff," all his linen, his Negro Tony, her riding horse, and £30 for the purchase of rings. He also left £2,000 to his son Francis, minister of the local church, with an additional legacy of £290 for the support of an almshouse or hospital for poor sailors or strangers; and £500 apiece to his three daughters, as well as sundry other legacies. He left to the minister and churchwardens of St. George's parish his Negro man and boy "to be hired out, & the proceeds to go towards the instruction of poor children to sing in the church," as well as a bond for £100 for teaching poor children to read and write. The remainder of his estate went to his eldest son, William.

The nineteenth century, however, would see the slow collapse of the family's fortunes, mirroring those of the plantation economy in Antigua. The previous century had closed with personal tragedy. Edward, grandson of Edward and his cousin Lydia, and heir to the family's estates, died at age twenty-eight, leaving an infant son, William. William remained in Antigua, later becoming president of His Majesty's Council and a lieutenant in the local dragoons. Knighted by Queen Victoria in 1859 for his services to the colony, when he died ten years later, in 1869, he had survived his wife and their nine children, and had seen most of the family's land and power slip through his fingers. His eldest son and heir, "a young man of great promise," had been called to the bar in 1850 after his graduation from Cambridge, but in 1853, shortly after returning to his native island, he fell victim to a yellow fever epidemic, dying at twenty-five and leaving his only surviving sister, Lydia, heiress to the family's properties.

Lydia, Phyllis's paternal great-grandmother, had married Francis Shand of Liverpool, a merchant banker from Everton, Lancaster, on March 16, 1837. He was a member of a family of absentee West Indian merchants and shipowners in Liverpool who had before his marriage held several leases on local plantations. His ships brought in British machinery, stores, and supplies for his own estates and consignments of assorted cargo, chiefly of manufactured goods, for local merchants and planters. Through his marriage he became one of the largest proprietors of land in Antigua. By Phyllis's own account, her great-grandfather, like many gentlemen in embarrassed circumstances, used his wife's dowry to pay off some of the vast debts he had incurred, leaving the West Indian estates devoid of capital for modernization. The capital drain on the estates coincided with the changes brought about by emancipation, whose terms Francis Shand had been very actively involved in negotiating with England. There is little to show that he, or the Antigua planters for whom he was often a spokesman, was convinced by any moral argument against slavery; but he argued, in view of the government's determination, that a practical policy to abolish slavery was to expedite emancipation and eliminate the period of apprenticeship. In any event the Byams and Shands weathered emancipation better than most Antiguan planter families. Joseph John Gurney, a visitor to the Byams' Cedar Hill estate in June of 1840, found it in "high order and prosperity." In response to Gurney's inquiry concerning the impact of emancipation, James Bell, the manager, "made an excellent report of it": "It is less trouble," he said, "to conduct the whole concern now, than it was to manage the hospital alone, before Emancipation." (There was a small hospital on the estate for the treatment of leprosy.)

Indeed, given the unavailability of uncultivated lands and the resulting dependence of the freed slaves on estate employment, emancipation had a less severe impact on Antiguan planters than it did on those of other islands. But their inadequate measures to face the new situation—the sale and amalgamation of bankrupt estates, the limited introduction of new technologies, and a new compromise with the working class through the Contract Act—did not stem the collapse of the small-plantation economy in Antigua. Between 1846 and 1887 more than fifty estates, including several owned by the Shands, went out of business, withdrawing ten thousand acres from commercial cultivation. Reported to exceed a princely thirty thousand pounds a year before emancipation, Francis Shand's income fell to about half its former value in the 1840s. Yet in 1852 the Byam (now Shand) family still possessed considerable wealth. The 1852 census listed among their properties a 517–acre plantation at Martin's Byam or Fitches Creek in St. George's Parish; Mount Lucye, a 230–acre estate also in St. George's Parish; Cedar Valley, a 128–acre plantation in St. John's Parish; Harts and Royals, two estates consisting of 206 acres; the 90–acre Blizard estate, and diverse other estates owned or leased by Francis Shand.

Little is known of the fate of Francis and Lydia Shand's thirteen children except for that of their heir, Charles Arthur, listed in the 1885 Colonial Office List as one of twelve elected members of the local legislative council. In the 1870s he married Alice, daughter of Sir Tom Berkeley of Saint Kitts and a descendant of Thomas Warner, with whom he had two boys, Francis Byam Berkeley (Phyllis's father), born on August 11, 1879, and a younger son named Kenrick. The economic forces during the last decades of the nineteenth century had not augured well for the family's continued prosperity. Sugar production in Antigua was falling very quickly into the hands of large firms such as Boddington and Company and Fryer's Sugar Concrete Company. Several well-to-do families, the Byams, Shands, and Codringtons among them, were still able to hold their own, although the Shands struggled along with outmoded sugar machinery, sinking deeper into decay and debt. Some families continued to prosper, even after the arrival in the 1890s of Dubisson and Moody Stuart, the corporation that was to monopolize the industry in the twentieth century; the Shands did not. By the mid-1890s the only property left to the family was the Fitches Creek estate, part of William Byam's original land grant and in the family's possession since the mid-seventeenth century. There, in the 1880s, when Charles Arthur was a young married man, the family entertained the future George V, when he visited Antigua as a midshipman and was invited to enjoy the duck shooting. Years later, visiting Antigua as a federation minister, Phyllis asked to be taken to Fitches Creek, only to find nothing there but a "diminishing pile of grey stones lying in the grass . . . all that was left of the old estate house where a little boy had practiced in the pantry how to hypnotize guests into yawning by making pincer movements with his thumb and first finger." The lands became the property of Dubisson and Moody Stuart. The prince's visit was the family's swan song. The little hypnotist, Phyllis's father, and his brother, Kenrick, were the last of the Byam Shands to grow up on the family's estate in Antigua. They would be the last generation to enjoy the privileges of a rapidly disappearing planter society. When they were still boys, "everything went to pieces." Their father, Charles Arthur, was appointed to the magistracy in Nevis, where he soon died. Francis struggled to gain a legal education in England and returned to the West Indies to work as a magistrate in Dominica. There he met and married Elfreda, daughter of Henry Nicholls and Marion Crompton.

Two

A Birth Between the Palms

. . . a birth between the palms
of a Caribbean mound.
There is a difference
in the diet of spirits,
for some are fed on hurricanes,
songs by moonlight, pomalaks,
coconut milk, yams and the
mysterious granadilla.

Dominica was a place where, in Phyllis's own words, "our roots are less initially gilded but certainly harder [than those of the Byam-Shands in Antigua]." Her grandmother's people, the Cromptons, had been in Dominica for several generations. Her grandmother Marion Crompton belonged, on the maternal side, to a family of French émigrés via Martinique, a connection that Phyllis traced to an uncle of Empress Josephine, Robert-Marguerite Tascher de la Pagerie, Baron Tascher (1740–1806), younger brother of Joseph-Gaspard (1735–1790), Josephine's father. The family belonged to the ancient country gentry of France, with roots in the rich countryside of the Loire. The Martinican branch had settled in Carbet in 1726 but seems not to have prospered, although Joseph-Gaspard's marriage to Rose-Claire des Vergers de Sannois, who belonged to one of the oldest families in the colony, had slowed its steady decline. The family's prestige was enormously enhanced by Josephine's surprise marriage to Napoleon Bonaparte.

The sheer romance of her family's connection to the empress delighted Phyllis. It gratified her romantic nature and deep sense of "family" and nurtured a conviction that her ancestry marked her as someone deeply linked to *history*, someone whose family chronicle could be traced in *books*. It imbued in her a deeply rooted sense of romance and noblesse oblige. It was, moreover, a connection of which she was constantly reminded at home, as one of their central pieces of furniture was an Empress Josephine couch. The allure was strong enough to prompt her later to name her daughter after the empress—the girl's nickname, Phina, was that used by Napoleon for his wife. One of Phyllis's first mature poems, "White Ladies," was inspired by the famous statue of Josephine in Martinique, standing in a circle of palms as a tribute to her romantic destiny.

The Cromptons were also connected to Samuel Crompton (1753–1827), the inventor of the spinning mule, a link that would always be stressed when the Crompton name was mentioned; but the exact nature of the connection is unclear. It is most probable that Joshua Crompton, from whom the Dominica branch of the family descends, was Samuel Crompton's paternal uncle. The Cromptons settled on a small estate on the northeastern coast of Dominica in the early nineteenth century. There, where the estate once stood, is still a lovely crag known as Crompton Point, and Phyllis was told as a child that when Mount Pelée erupted in 1902, the ash blew over to Dominica, destroying acres of crops, including those of the Crompton estate. In 1844 Joshua's great-grandson John Corney Crompton married Marianne Felicité (1825–1863), Josephine's cousin twice removed, with whom he had seven children, three of whom were to figure prominently in Phyllis's life. Her great-aunts Emma Catherine (1852–1923) and Margaret Hannah (1858–1928) were Phyllis's earliest teachers. The Crompton's third daughter, Marion, born in 1857, was Phyllis's maternal grandmother. She married Dr. (later Sir) Henry Alfred Alford Nicholls on September 6, 1877.

Phyllis's maternal grandparents were the equivalent of a Dominican royal couple, their prominence resting on the fame and popularity of Dr. Nicholls, a physician who had come to Dominica in 1877 to further his studies under the mentorship of the renowned Dr. John Imray (1811–1880), a Scotsman who had settled in Dominica in 1832. Imray was a brilliant botanist and physician and owner of several estates, among them St. Aroment, where he revived the island's coffee cultivation through the introduction of Liberian coffee, and pioneered the raising of limes, which eventually provided a solid base for the island's economy. His medical reputation rested on his important discoveries in the nature, causes, and treatment of yellow fever, malaria, and yaws. Nicholls was a worthy pupil. Born in London on September 27, 1851, he was educated at the Universities of Aberdeen and London, graduating with a degree in medicine in 1873. He arrived in Dominica in 1877, having been appointed medical superintendent of hospitals. That same year he married Miss Marion, the shy and retiring third daughter of the late John Corney Crompton. His medical appointment was the first of many he held during his long career: he became medical officer of the public institutions in 1880, health officer in 1897, and senior medical health officer in 1901. He made his most indelible mark in 1891 when, as special commissioner to inquire into the prevalence of yaws in the West Indies, he had written a report, later published and distributed, with the British government's imprimatur, as a Blue Book, for which he had received the thanks of the secretary of state.

Dr. Nicholls wielded a facile pen, and was "ready to express himself both fully and with clarity in medical phraseology that any lay man could grasp." He published, among many texts, a brochure on the prevention of malaria, an article on tetanus, a textbook on tropical agriculture, and pamphlets on the lime industry and the cultivation of Liberian coffee. He was an omnivorous reader who found particular pleasure, as a trustee of the Carnegie Library, in the selection of books. His own extensive private library would be donated by Phyllis to the University of the West Indies. Deeply interested in agriculture and botany, he corresponded with Kew Gardens for many years, exchanging with them plant specimens, and receiving from them many plants for the Roseau Botanical Gardens, which he helped lay out. He was also very active in the local Anglican church. His motto, which could later have easily been Phyllis's, was *Sine Timore,* fearless. He was knighted in 1925 by George V in recognition of his services and died in Roseau in 1926. Upon his death he was hailed as "the Uncrowned King of Dominica."

Doctor Nicholls was a skilled doctor known for his efforts to treat and cure diseases that affected the poor. He served as the model for the Old Master in *The Orchid House*, the novel Phyllis published in 1953, in which she pays tribute to his sympathy with the plight of the poor. "I did not even pay any attention to my own people," Lally, the novel's narrator, muses. "But now I am observing them and seeing how poor they are, and how the little babies have stomachs swollen with arrowroot and arms and legs spotted by disease. That was something which Old Master saw and fought against right from the moment that he stepped onto the jetty in his panama hat for the first time. He never forgot. When he brought his English and American friends who dropped in from their yachts or pleasure cruises to look at his orchids and these gardens, Old Master would say to them seriously, 'Come and see the other side of the picture. Come into the back alleys.'" To Phyllis and his other grandchildren he looked very much the grand man, a typical strict grandfather of the period—"not the type on whose lap you would sit for a cuddle." He was a short, stocky man with a dignified bearing who awed his grandchildren, an awe that did not prevent them from finding him to be the source of some somewhat irreverent amusement. He had a wonderful moustache on which drops of soup would get caught, and the Shand girls would sit, stifling their giggles, waiting for the drops to fall. They were also not blind to the fact that he was fonder of his grandsons than of his granddaughters, and would often call their cousin David, but not them, to his room for a "sweetie."

Dr. Nicholls's country residence, St. Aroment, the thirty-acre estate on the outskirts of Roseau that he inherited from Dr. Imray, was the setting for his agricultural experiments. James Anthony Froude visited it during his voyage to the West Indies in the late 1880s, and found that the chief part of it was planted with lime trees:

> Most of the rest was covered with Liberian coffee . . . growing with profuse luxuriance. . . . [T]he ground about the house was consecrated to botanical experiments, and specimens were to be seen there of every tropical flower, shrub, or tree, which was either remarkable for its beauty or valuable for its chemical properties. His limes and coffee went principally to New York, where they had won a reputation, and were in special demand; but ingenuity tries other tracks besides the beaten one. Dr. Nicholls had a manufactory of citric acid which had been found equally excellent in Europe. Everything which he produced was turning to gold.

He was then on his way to clearing the substantial sum of one thousand pounds a year from St. Aroment, and Froude goes on to call him "the only man in the island of really superior attainments."

As L'Aromatique, "the place of sweet smells," St. Aroment was to become the setting for *The Orchid House*. It was a typical Dominican estate house, built high up on the hills, with shuttered windows and a veranda from which you could watch the bay through a spyglass. It was surrounded by acres planted with limes, cacao, and vanilla. The lavatory, source of great amusement to the girls, was a little house at the edge of a precipice, where you sat with your bottom over the cliff. On his visit Froude commented on Dr. Nicholls's relationship with his black laborers, many of whom he observed working alongside the doctor. "In apparent contradiction to the general West Indian experience, he told me that he had never found a difficulty about it. He paid them fair wages, and paid them regularly without the overseer's fines and drawbacks. He knew one from the other personally, and could call each by his name, remembered where he came from, where he lived, and how, and could joke with him about his wife or mistress. They in consequence clung to him with an innocent affection, stayed with him all the week without asking for holidays, and worked with interest and goodwill." His sympathy for his laborers, however, did not translate into liberal social notions; he was said always to wear gloves when examining black patients. He was a social and political conservative who did his utmost to uphold the prevalent class and color structure, a pointless exercise as Dominica's white population was minuscule, and racial conservatism could lead only to isolation. He tried to hold his family to the same views, but his sons became rather "liberal," which in

Dominica implied a readiness to break the color barriers. In his conservatism he was clearly rowing against the tide, as Dominica had an accomplished colored elite with an increasing hold on the island's economy and government. The stratification of Roseau society along class and color lines was exemplified by his club, the Dominica Club, which until the early 1950s accepted only white men, and very carefully selected white men at that. It would not grant membership to Joseph Jones, an accomplished botanist who created the Roseau Botanical Gardens, because Jones—not quite a gentleman—was not received by his social "superiors." As Stephen Hawys would remark later, the few white people in Dominica at the time were "just numerous enough to be able to refuse one or accept another, according to their unerring perspicacity." His social conservatism and color prejudices notwithstanding, Dr. Nicholls was a powerful role model for Phyllis. He was a man proud of his position as a gentleman, whose link to his adopted home island was rooted in very English notions of propriety and a Victorian-era belief in the middle and upper classes' obligation to serve the poor and needy that would be his legacy to his granddaughter. He was deeply interested in West Indian natural and political history and in the collection and preservation of Carib artifacts. During his lifetime he amassed what was reputed to be the world's finest collection of Carib arts and crafts. He was also interested in genealogy and traced his wife's and son-in-law's family trees in order to document the family's history. Moreover, his sympathy for the poor and his fairness to the laborers working for him at St. Aroment helped lay the foundations for Phyllis's color blindness and her interest in the conditions in which the working classes lived.

The Nichollses also had a town residence, Kingsland House, now destroyed, a fine example of French–West Indian architecture. It was a one-story wood house with broad veranda, a lovely lawn with a well-tended garden, and a clear view of the hills. Alec Waugh, a frequent guest after it was converted into an inn by Maggie Nicholls, loved its restfulness and domesticity: "Mangoes were ripening; the plants bordering the lawn were studded with blue blossom; the tulip tree was still in flower, its bright red mellowing to orange; beyond the convent a poui tree whose presence before I left I had not suspected was now a brilliant splash of canary yellow against the deep green of the Morne; a hen was shepherding four infant ducks beneath the bay tree." It housed Dr. Nicholls's beloved creation, the orchid conservatory that would give Phyllis's novel its title, although in *The Orchid House* it was placed at St. Aroment. She and her sisters, not allowed to touch the flowers, often preferred to play with the barrels filled with little black fish. The novel's old nurse would recall how the Old Master "would stand there under that roof of palms plaited with bamboos, unhanging wire baskets to dip his plants into a tank swarming with tiny fish: the fish were there to eat mosquito grubs. Very often he got paid for his attention with rare flowering things: the poor patients knew his hobby. He would scoop out bits of log and fill the hollows with charcoal, then bind these queer roots with coconut fibre. Hours and hours he would spend there making beautiful labels, and goodness the number of names one spray might have, written in his small script: *Cattaleya crispa purpurea—Bee orchid or golden shower—Madonna or Eucharist or Holy Ghost orchid. . . .*"

Visitors were always welcome at Kingsland House, where Mrs. Nicholls held her "at-homes" every Sunday afternoon. Even perfect strangers never hesitated to call, and important visitors to the island were taken as a matter of course to visit Dr. Nicholls, who was considered not only "the first gentleman of Dominica," but one "whose private life was the model of an English home." Marion Nicholls, the doctor's wife and a favorite of Phyllis's, was a very upright woman whose straight figure belied her age. Undaunted as she was by her husband's personality and fame, it was always said of her that he could not have asked for a better partner. Capable and strong, with the bearing of a grande dame, she had a wry sense of humor that delighted her grandchildren. In her late years she would walk to her daughter Elfreda's home every evening around six for a rum cocktail—and a slice of bread. The cocktail she would down quickly, explaining to her granddaughters that if you drank your rum quickly and followed it with a piece of bread, the bread would act as blotting paper and the cocktail would not go to your head. She had a family of ten children. Odo Imray, her eldest son, was sent away from Dominica for his misdemeanors, purportedly on a holiday, never to return. Her eldest daughter, Elizabeth—redheaded Aunt Liz, the children's favorite—married in 1904 and had a son, David, one of the Shand girls' playmates and close companions. Her second daughter, Margaret—Aunt Mags—was born on May 2, 1881. She would become the Shand girls' teacher and her father's right hand. A second son, Harold, remained in Dominica and had a modestly successful career in politics and business. Elfreda Millicent, Phyllis's mother, was the third daughter. She was followed by a third son, Ralph, the black sheep of the family and without doubt one of the most fascinating characters of Phyllis's childhood. In addition there were three younger daughters: Irene, Gwendolyn, and Dorothy. Their youngest brother, William, known as Willy, was Jean Rhys's childhood sweetheart. His fate followed Odo's, and he was spirited away from the island when his behavior crossed the boundaries of what his family was willing to tolerate.

Elfreda, Phyllis's mother, was a pretty young woman with lovely dark hair and blue eyes, so slim and slight that she was known as "Elf." She was in her late teens when she met Francis Shand, who had arrived in Dominica in the early 1900s to work as an attorney—a handsome, clean-shaven, pale and unsmiling man with sad, penetrating eyes. With his melancholy good looks, solid social background, and the promise of a successful legal career, he immediately became one of Dominica's most eligible bachelors and a favorite of the Nicholls girls. It is rumored—although the story has been categorically denied by the family—that Francis was originally engaged to marry the eldest of the unmarried daughters, Margaret, who had gone away to buy her wedding clothes only to find Dr. Nicholls awaiting her at the jetty upon her return, facing the unpleasant task of telling her that her fiancé was to marry Elfreda.* Utterly bereft at the news, Margaret is said to have thrown herself into the sea in her despair and had to be rescued from drowning. The sisters' lifelong devoted friendship argues against this scenario, although family members concede that Maggie did love Francis Shand deeply, a love manifested though her lifelong devotion to his children. Phyllis recreated her love and dedication in the character of Mlle. Bosquet, the French tutor in love with the Master in *The Orchid House*.

The wedding of Elfreda Nicholls and Francis Shand on March 27, 1905 was Roseau's social event of the year. They married at St. George's, with the church packed to overflowing and Elfreda looking charming in a white satin dress trimmed in chiffon, a

*Elfreda's first-born, Marion, is reported to have been the cause of further heartache for Margaret. Many years later, Margaret, who had remained single, is said to have set her cap at the widowed island administrator, the fiftyish Mr. Eliot, only to lose him to Marion, who married him when she was barely twenty and he almost thirty years her senior.

tulle veil, and an orange blossom wreath. Her four unmarried sisters, in "champagne-colored mouseline [*sic*] de crêpe trimmed with lace," were her bridesmaids. The nurses from Roseau Hospital were present in a body as a tribute to Dr. Nicholls, and there was a guard of honor of the Leeward Islands Police Force in recognition of the groom's legal position. Hesketh Bell was among the guests, as were Francis's mother, Alice, and his brother, Kenrick, who had traveled from Nevis, as well as Francis's dear friend Wilfred Wigley, a barrister from Saint Kitts who acted as his best man. There was a reception at Kingsland House, and the couple honeymooned at St. Aroment. After her marriage Elfreda settled into a matronly life focused almost exclusively on her family. Quiet and retiring, and not very keen on social engagements, she matured into a woman of great inner strength. She would need all the fortitude she could command to hold her family together through the stress of war and the return of a shell-shocked husband. If she was to be faulted for anything in subsequent years it would be for her eagerness to marry off her daughters, or at any rate to send them away from the island as soon as it was feasible; but with the family's dwindling resources and even more limited prospects, she had to secure quickly whatever opportunities presented themselves to her girls. To Phyllis she would always be her "darling mother."

Her sister Margaret Emily Mary was a more openly redoubtable character, known for the hospitality she offered to the likes of Noël Coward, Adlai Stevenson, Alec Waugh, and a procession of other passersby at Kingsland House after she turned it into a guesthouse. Miss Maggie was truly her father's daughter and, like him, left a profound legacy in the island's social fabric. Her services would be recognized by George V with a special Jubilee medal for public service. Reputed to be the brains in the family and a bluestocking, Maggie was an ardent reader with an acute interest in politics. She was her father's right hand, his assistant at his surgery, as well as the real housekeeper at Kingsland House. An avid conversationalist, Maggie was never shy to voice her opinions, a quality with which she imbued her niece Phyllis. Upon her death she was described by the young rector as a *character*—a Churchillian character according to Phyllis—adamant in her conservatism.

"My paternal relations never mixed. My maternal relations were liberal," Phyllis once explained. The "liberality" of her maternal family was exemplified by her uncle Ralph, the black sheep of the Nicholls family, who had scandalized the small white enclave by living openly with a light-skinned woman with whom he had a number of "outside" children. The relationship with his Catholic mistress brought Ralph within the sphere of influence of the Catholic hierarchy, and after many years he was persuaded by the bishop of Roseau to marry his mistress. Phyllis, in her 1981 obituary for her cousin Eugenia Nicholls, Ralph's eldest daughter, alludes to the Shands' isolation from Ralph and his mixed-blood family: "My first memory of Eugenia was when, as a small child straying from my Nurse in the Botanical Gardens, I saw another dark Nurse, dressed in *douillette* [the island's traditional dress], sitting on a bench with a fair infant in her arms. I skipped up near enough to see that the baby was extremely beautiful. Just then, a sturdy young man with reddish hair strode over the grass, sank down beside them, and kissed the baby adoringly. I had no means of knowing then that the child was Eugenia, first-born child of my Uncle Ralph Nicholls and his wife Evelyn"—although here Phyllis is stretching the truth, as Evelyn Royer was not yet his wife. As Ralph's family was not recognized by the Nichollses, the tensions between the illegitimate and legitimate branches were evident. The Shand girls were "the tippest of the toppest" in Dominican society, and when the "other" children would come across the path in their pram, Lally, the Shand nursemaid, would quickly take her charges away. The situation bred competition, and the Shands once received an anonymous note believed to be from the "other" family, saying that now they had a girl blonder than theirs.

As she would do with many episodes from her childhood, Phyllis wrote a thinly disguised portrait of Ralph in an ironic short story called "Uncle Rufus," the same name given to the Ralph-inspired character in *The Orchid House*. Uncle Rufus, Phyllis wrote, was invested with a glamour even his carrot-colored hair and boorish manners did nothing to dissipate. Ralph himself was a bluff and friendly man with a full head of red hair and a hearty sense of humor. He was endowed nonetheless with a fierce temper that would surface quickly if aroused. Like Ralph and his mistress, Evelyn, the fictional Rufus and his mistress, Coralita, speedily accumulated seven children. Dr. Nicholls, who strongly disapproved of fraternizing with the other races, was dismayed by his son's antics, which included not one but three mistresses, with the concomitant trio of colored families. The Nicholls ladies, with the complicity of the servants, made every possible effort to keep Ralph's exploits from his father, helping maintain the illusion that his family stood firmly behind the great pillar of respectability he had erected. But Roseau was, after all, a very small town, and maintaining the deception must have required a large measure of willing blindness on Dr. Nicholls's part.

After Dr. Nicholls's death, there was a brief struggle for Ralph's allegiance between Lady Nicholls and the aunts on one side, and Evelyn and the priests on the other, a contest won by the latter. It is said that Lady Nicholls had been secretly hoping to relax the family's rigid stance, and the veil was finally lifted. Ralph and Evelyn married, and eventually he gained a measure of respectability. "Having married a colored woman," Phyllis writes about the fictional Rufus, "he had thrown in his lot with her people. He was the first white man to shake hands with a visiting trade unionist" (Ralph became a trade unionist himself) and, like Ralph, was a member of the town council and once mayor of Roseau. For all his foibles, and despite the irony she showers on him in all her fiction, Phyllis felt a great attraction and admiration for her uncle—if nothing else—because he was paramount in continuing the family's tradition of service to the island. He would take his father's paternalistic concern for the laboring poor one step further through the founding of the Dominica Trade Union with Christopher Loblack, the very union (and partner) Phyllis would join in 1953 in her efforts to found the Dominica Labor party.

At the center of Ralph's ostracism from his family was the maze of color and class that characterized Roseau society. Francis Shand, like his father-in-law, was adamantly conservative on the mixing of races and likewise tried to keep his family from the colored and black. Phyllis, who repeatedly insisted that she had never harbored any racial prejudice as a child, was nonetheless keenly aware of its existence around her. She had to be. Lorna Robinson, a contemporary of Phyllis's, recalls how, although she saw them in church every Sunday, the Shand girls "kept to themselves," as then "black and white did not mix." In church they couldn't have mixed, even if they had wanted to, as the Anglican church was divided in two parts: one for the whites in front, one for the blacks at the back, with an open space between them. At the end of the service blacks and whites went out separate doors. "I don't think anybody minded this or even noticed it," wrote Jean Rhys in her autobiography. "I certainly didn't. It had always been so, it would always be so, like the sun or the rain." But *they* did mind, and young Phyllis and her sisters knew it well. White, black, and colored in Roseau lived in a never-ending ritual of power plays: Whites tried in subtle and unsubtle ways to maintain their supremacy; blacks struck back by mocking whites—a mockery that could be unsettling. Froude alludes to it in his description of his arrival in Dominica: "Two tall handsome girls seized my bags, tossed them on their heads, and strode off with a light step in front of me, cutting jokes with their friends; I following, and my mind misgiving me that I was myself the object of their wit." The Shand girls, like most whites in Dominica, were frequently the object of teasing. They were once followed down the street by a group of young children taunting them, telling them that their hats looked like chamber pots. They took it in their stride but refused ever to wear the hats again.

Phyllis addressed the racial ambiguities of her childhood society in her fiction. In *The Orchid House* Rufus, for all his mercenary pragmatism, is portrayed as almost radical in his contempt for conservative racial notions. "After all," Joan comments, "white liberal-minded people merely talked against the color bar, Uncle Rufus had taken practical steps to break it down." In "Uncle Rufus," Phyllis writes about the instilling of a consciousness of racial and social superiority into young minds: "Whenever we passed Coralita's bakery on our way to the botanical gardens we would say to our nurse: 'We know whose shop that is, ha, ha,' and she would say: 'Be quiet, children, do. . . . Remember you're white, and think of your grandfather.' But after a while this admonition lost some of its force, for grandfather died." The young narrator of "Uncle Rufus," Phyllis's alter ego, uses her uncle's situation to bring to the fore her own ambivalence about the privileges and limitations their whiteness imposed upon her and her sisters: "We were conscious that being white, and being girls, we would have to grow up properly and correctly, and for these reasons we were bitterly jealous of Coralita, and curious about the assortment of plain and pretty, light and dark babies which she and Uncle Rufus speedily accumulated"—nine in all. Phyllis uses another fictional alter ego, the narrator of "Breeze"—the story of a notorious wild girl—to address a similar theme. In "Breeze" the ten-year-old narrator is whiling away her time reading an old copy of *Tiger Tim's Weekly* (a children's magazine published in London), when she is accosted by Breeze, one of Phyllis's free and uninhibited colored female characters. The character was modeled on a Roseau woman nicknamed Brise (from the French word for "break," *briser*), who had earned her appellation from her tendency to break things. She was one of Dominica's eccentrics, "a kind of hallmark bad child who did not improve with age, but who was extremely rough and resilient, strong as a man, and no respecter of persons." Stephen Hawys, in *Mount Joy*, describes in detail Brise's long career of unbridled criminality. "Brise," he wrote, "was uncontrollable, fearless, indomitable, courageous, free, as no other person in the island—black or white—is free." Phyllis would echo this celebration of Brise's freedom:

> She was the girl who had no home, who lived wild, who was only fourteen but had been to jail five times, who stole, who wore no clothes or at most one garment. . . . She slid down the trunk of the mango tree again, and with

> a single wiggle of her bronze shoulders disposed of the shapeless sack, which had a large neck-opening and no buttons. She stood there before me in maidenly magnificence, and as if the sight of her was not sufficient to shame my puny child limbs, she remarked: "Wouldn't call me skinny now, would you? That's my town clothes. When I live in forest I live free." I gazed at her enviously. "To live free! Wasn't that what every child desired!""

In "Breeze" Phyllis uses subtle irony to unveil the hypocritical prejudices of the Roseau society of her childhood. The convalescing narrator opens her tale with an explanation of the disgrace she finds herself in: "I had been told not to show myself at the front gates. Although innocent of any design on the reputation of the white official class, I was in disgrace. My great uncle, the Colony's medical officer, had issued a statement to the press that the prevalent epidemic was kaffir-pox, a disease which was extremely unlikely to afflict people of pure European blood. Unfortunately, the first white victim of this unpleasant ailment was the Anglican Archdeacon and the second was myself."

Although by the time of her birth her father's family had lost the great wealth it had once possessed, Phyllis grew up in relative affluence. Francis was Dominica's crown attorney, a position that guaranteed the family a comfortable income and social prestige. As such he was a de facto member of Dominica's Executive Council and was dubbed "Honourable." Alice Marion, his eldest daughter, was born in 1906. She was a lovely girl, tall and elegant, with long dark blond hair and a serene, almost dreamy countenance. She drew and painted well and was thought to be the most artistically talented of the girls. She once painted a full-scale portrait of Rosalind, but the only evidence of her talents to have survived is a very lifelike pencil drawing of Phyllis in her early teens. She matured quickly and, although only two years older than her next sister, Phyllis, and a mere six years older than baby Rosalind, she seemed more of a mother than a sister to them. Her father's six-year absence during the war caused her to become her mother's companion and helper, and she always seemed old beyond her years.

Phyllis was born two years later, in 1908, and was given an old Byam family name. Her middle name, Byam, reflected the family's consciousness of its roots. She was physically very similar to her father and had the same melancholy air and nervous energy. Her features, like his, were strong and attractive, although too angular to be considered pretty; she was once described as having an elegant face on the Edwardian style. She would grow up to be slim and willowy with "sharp though frail features" and hands "like little bird claws." She lacked, however, Marion's serene beauty or Celia and Rosalind's soft blond prettiness. From a very young age she also tended to share her father's nature—even in her most charming moments, one would be conscious of something missing, like a thin wispy cloud over her head. Adult acquaintances often described her as "fey." Her childhood photographs reveal a serious, thoughtful child, a deceptively fragile-looking girl. Her seriousness and thoughtfulness, real as they were, could almost instantly be transformed into mischievousness and wit. Her eyes were always very alert and eloquent, her smile quick and contagious. She could be as bubbly and imaginative as she was quiet and pensive, and even into her old age she would be known for her "light laugh that trickled off into a whimsical giggle." She was very skillful at concealing this decidedly impish streak if necessary. Her friends recall how from a very young age she could remain very composed, even when she was up to no good. Only the wicked twinkle in her eye would betray her. Political rivals would later remark how, during the bitterest mudslinging of her political campaigns, Phyllis would remain outwardly calm, but when she was angered her eyes would gleam seconds before she would lash her opponents with her mordant wit.

Many remember her as the odd girl out in her family. From a very early age she was "Labour" in her sympathies and outlook, particularly in her attitude toward racism in her society, but she lived in a family of Tories. She had a genuine interest in poetry, instilled in her as early as her nursery school days, and by the time she reached her teens she already thought of herself as a poet. Her status as the family's poet set her apart from her sisters and gave her the special status she lacked as the plain girl in a group of pretty daughters. Adrien Espinet, a reporter for the *Trinidad Guardian* who interviewed her in 1957, during her first political campaign in Dominica, found her lack of ease with the world of her childhood fascinating. "To the psychologist," he wrote after countless interviews with Phyllis, her "break with her background must undoubtedly provide interesting material for speculation. It is clear that at an early age Phyllis Shand's sensitive and poetic nature rebelled against many things that she found in her great family home—now a good bit dilapidated—standing on grounds at the north end of Roseau."

Her younger sisters had Shakespearean names: Celia Berkeley, born on July 5, 1910, an outgoing and good-natured tomboy, was the most athletic of the sisters. The mischievous feats attributed to Joan in *The Orchid House* reflect her adventures. She could run faster than her sisters and was the best at climbing trees, preferably those of the Botanical Gardens just a few short blocks from their house, from which she would steal fruit. Once, caught in the act, she scampered off, followed by Phyllis, leaving her sister Rosalind to face the caretaker. A complaint was made to their parents, and the girls were not allowed in the gardens for a week. She once pelted the white-clad curator of the gardens, Joseph Jones, with pomegranates after he had caught her red-handed, throwing fruit to her sisters below. The older girls were forced to write letters of apology. Celia was, ironically, to become a most ladylike Tory as an adult, and her relationship with Phyllis would suffer as a consequence. Many acquaintances were convinced that as an adult Celia disapproved of Phyllis's politics and their relationship was severely strained as a result.

The youngest daughter, flaxen-haired Rosalind, was born in "the year there were no hurricanes and the moon was low and the mango tree didn't bear." Delicate and fair, a pretty child with sparkling eyes and a good sense of fun, her sisters often teased her because of her flaxen locks, telling her that she was not a child but an old lady with white hair. Until her death in 1994 "like a gay butterfly, colorful and light," she was Phyllis's favorite sister—the one for whom she would always feel the tenderest regard and to whom she always referred to as "little old Rosalind."

When Phyllis was born the family lived at Moss Lodge, a small house on a stone foundation, which Elfreda had inherited from the Cromptons. But when the family grew they moved to the more spacious Seaview House, which they rented from an Antiguan man immortalized as Mr. Lilipoulala in *The Orchid House*. He was not a drug dealer by any stretch of the imagination, but the girls knew him as "the bad man" because his arrival to collect his rent was dreaded by the entire household and always caused some consternation. His approach was heralded by cries of "The bad man's coming! The bad man's coming!" and the girls would retreat to the relative safety of the top of the stairs and watch through the banisters as the rent money changed hands. Seaview House was located to the south of Roseau, near Newtown, and overlooked the bay. It had a charming garden planted with roses and a view of Scott's Head, the island's southernmost point. It also stood next door to the local prison, of which their father was commissioner. "I could hear the cries of big men being flogged for trivial offences," Phyllis would later relate.

The Shand household was peopled with the models for the characters in *The Orchid House*. Phyllis was never shy about drawing from her childhood experiences and her family history for her writing—she would be, in fact, quite incapable of pure invention in her fiction—and her sister Rosalind confirmed how accurately Phyllis borrowed from their own childhood to create that of the three sisters of *The Orchid House*. Her portrait of Lally, the nurse who would become the narrator of her novel, was as accurate as any she ever attempted or accomplished. A short, plump, brown-skinned woman whose given name was Flora, she was rechristened "Lal" by the children. Like the rest of the Roseau nursemaids, she used her employers surname and was known as Lally Shand. Her own surname has been forgotten. A committed Methodist in a predominantly Catholic society, Lally brought the children the calm assurance that came from strong religious faith. Like her fictional alter ego, she had "come fresh from Montserrat in [her] middle years [and was] an English Negress and proud of her skin, not Frenchy and Catholic and boasting of a drop of white blood." Her commitment to her religion was not without its humorous side; she thought, idiosyncratically, that speakers of patois were heathens. She asserted her individuality and her "foreignness" by shunning the traditional *douillette* in favor of a long black skirt, white piqué blouse, and "tremendous" black leather belt held by a brass buckle. A very proper lady, and proud of it, Lally would never leave the house without her hat. Lally's position in the family, as Phyllis recreates it in her novel, was more that of a family friend than of a servant. From the moment she entered the household to nurse baby Marion, and for the more than twenty-five years she shared her life with them, the Shand girls were the center of her life, as she was of theirs. In *In the Cabinet* she is acknowledged as "the linchpin of our lives." She never married and gave her charges the dedication she would have given her own children. "When I was nurse to the little girls," Phyllis has Lally's fictional counterpart muse in *The Orchid House*, "I had no time to fall ill or to see how beautiful everything was. And anyhow, when you are working for white people whom you love, you can only think of those people and their wants, you hardly notice anything else." Her loyalty to and pride in the family led her to great rivalries with some of the other nurses in Roseau. After a walk through town with her charges she would return to the house and say: "I shan't be able to put that bonnet on that child anymore. The ribbons are not big enough. So and so had bigger ribbons!" Phyllis's portrayal of such devotion has bothered some readers, who have found a white woman's creation of such a loyal black servant problematic. The complexities of textual creation notwithstanding, Phyllis by all accounts succeeded in capturing in her novel the essence of the personality of her beloved nurse. Throughout Phyllis' childhood and adolescence, Lally was the person to whom everyone in the family (except Francis) would go with their troubles. She was the girls' confidante and Elfreda's mainstay. The girls adored her. Their anchor in an often troubled home, she offered love and comfort and a lap to sit on. She gave Phyllis an attentive ear and the benefit of her homespun advice and down-to-earth wisdom. When she finally retired in the 1930s she left her room at the Shands' to move in with her sister, Mrs. Shields, who owned a small house near the Botanical Gardens. She insisted on coming out of retirement, to the extent that her health allowed, to push Phyllis's daughter's pram in the gardens, when she brought Phina to Dominica in 1933.

Less of a comfort, but a constant source of amusement nonetheless, was their cook, Julia, known to readers of *The Orchid House* as Christophine. Julia, like Lally a Montserrat woman, would cook best when she had had a tot or two of rum. On Saturday nights, when she had been to the Hole in the Wall, as the local rum shop was called, you could hear the clang of the pans as she tossed them around in the kitchen. The real Julia, however, was brainier than Christophine and knew the Bible inside out. She could often be heard citing biblical quotations and would come to get her weekly wages asking Elfreda to "render unto Caesar." Julia, fond of shocking the Shand girls with her decidedly unrespectable ways, had a number of children, fathered by different men. Every new child would provoke reprimands and threats from Elfreda, but Julia was always allowed to stay. When she argued on the streets, a not infrequent event, you could hear her loud and clear, demanding to know how her antagonist dared speak to a Shand in that manner. Asked by the girls why she knew the Bible by heart, she was fond of explaining that it was because she suffered from constipation. Asked if she wore knickers under her *douillette*, she would scoff that she didn't favor knickers—without them she could straddle any drain on the street and pee into it anytime she wanted. Most of the patois Phyllis and her sisters learned came from Julia and her daughters, although Phyllis's accent would always be "frenchified." Her father had been adamantly against the girls learning patois; he was a member of the League for the Suppression of French-Patois, and considered its use a "deterrent to progress in the community." But patois was everywhere around them. Phyllis claimed that she was determined to learn it partly because "it was forbidden by the elders of her family" and partly because "her childish curiosity quickly taught her that it was her only hope of finding out all the gossip in town." There would always be traces of the island's patois in her speech. And Elfreda, partly of French descent, did not discourage it. As a child Phyllis would sit with her sisters on the veranda of Seaview House, eavesdropping on the servants as they gossiped in patois about everyone, high and low. It was the start of Phyllis's love of gossip, which she could listen to and gleefully engage in by the hour. However, she always found patois to be a very useful thing, not solely for the love of gossip. "I would never have won the federal elections without it," she later told Polly Pattullo. Her intimacy with the household servants, moreover, gave Phyllis a deep understanding of the servant class. A perceptive friend of Phyllis's found her emotional identification with Lally in *The Orchid House* significant but not surprising. "She really understood *them*," he would recall. "Not the black people in general but the servant class."

Phyllis was only six when World War I broke out—an event that, despite its distance, proved to have a profound impact on her life. On August 3, 1914, the news of the declaration of war in Europe threw Roseau into a frenzy of activity. The twenty-five members of the defense reserve were called into Roseau, and armed police were stationed to guard the harbor, the military storehouse, and the colonial bank. Crowds gathered around the cable office awaiting news. On August 5 came the formal declaration of war between England and Germany, and a small brass band paraded in Roseau, followed by a crowd waving flags and shouting, "God save the King!" Five days later martial law was declared. The Dominicans' loyalty to England was impressive. By mid-1917 the island had sent more recruits than any other colony in the Leewards. Among those joining the English army in Europe were Phyllis's father and her uncle Kenrick, who had volunteered for active duty in the Royal Flying Corps. A photograph taken at the time shows Francis in his officer's uniform with slightly stooped shoulders, a thin moustache that gives his face a new maturity, and premature lines of sadness around his eyes. The excitement and uncertainty of the early days of the war soon subsided. The Defence Force was disbanded, its members required to parade only once a week. The impact of the war on Dominica was felt through the drop in trade and the higher prices of imported food. The supply of flour was uncertain, and there were fixed prices for milk and salt fish. To make matters worse, Dominica was lashed by storms in 1915, 1916, and 1917. The one in 1916 was the most serious: Limes suffered considerably, with cacao, livestock, and peasant crops badly damaged. Dominica came out of the war less prosperous than before: The 1920s saw a decline in the lime industry, and the next twenty years were ones of gloom.

In 1918 the household was shaken by the news of Kenrick Shand's death in combat. More bad news was soon to reach them. Francis, who is believed to have been commissioned in his brother's regiment and to have seen him die, was suffering from a severe case of shell shock. It was uncertain when he would be able to come home. Indeed, he remained hospitalized and did not come home for several years after the war was over. The family kept receiving nothing but the preprinted progress-report cards provided by the English military services. In a tiny society like Roseau's, his prolonged absence was the occasion for much gossip, and many enjoyed speculating that he had another woman and would never return. When he finally did come home the family went through a difficult period of adjustment and never fully recovered its carefree ways. The children had lived through the war in a household of women, supported by their mother's quiet strength, comforted in Lally's bosom, and had grown unaccustomed to the presence of a man—and a troubled one at that. The impact and consequences of his severe case of shell shock were as serious as those of what his daughter described as opium addiction in *The Orchid House*, but he was not the addict depicted in the novel. He returned from the war an emotionally crippled man, however, suffering from turbulent mood changes and frequent fits (for which the family used the French term *crises*), triggered by nightmares. His *crises* could be as violent as they were unpredictable, and, as they frequently occurred at night, they rocked the household, leaving the children shaken. The marked contrast between the violence of his *crises* and his gentleness when he was well puzzled them and made them withdraw from him. He had his meals served to him in his room, and the children both resented this royal treatment and dreaded when it was their turn to take the tray up to his room. To them he was like Dr. Jekyll and Mr. Hyde: courteous, chivalrous, and kind when well, and like a madman when prey to one of his attacks.

Her father's melancholy seemed particularly to have cast a spell on Phyllis, an observant child, who noticed disturbing habits about her father, chief among them his apparent self-medication with alcohol. He had become a man who tended to keep very much to himself. A tall, thin, lonely figure, he was frequently seen pacing restlessly up and down on the veranda at the back of his house, the light from his cigarette visible after night had fallen. Contemporaries remember him as occasionally appearing in court drunk, and he was often seen weaving his way home late at night. Elfreda and her sister Mags took excellent care of him, propping him up physically and emotionally so he could continue working despite his condition. In this they were aided by Dominica's relatively law-abiding society, which did not place too onerous a burden on its crown attorney; in a larger colony he might have had to forfeit his position and relinquish his income. In the figure of the Master in *The Orchid House*, Phyllis recreates her father's pain and frequent despair, leaving glimpses of the gentle man behind the pain. "There was something so love-worthy about the Master," Lally says. "There was such a fineness of feature and speech, a gentleness in him when he was not sick and desperate, and over all the feeling that he was someone who had been hurt, that sometimes it was as easy for us to forget his frightful moods as it was for *him* to forget them." Her sympathetic portrayal of her father in her novel, however, did not belie her disappointment at his failure to take the active role in determining the course of the island's history that she had been taught to expect from the males of her family. He had been barely competent in his position as crown attorney, however respectable, and his role in Dominican affairs had been minimal at best. When Phyllis spoke of him in later years it would be of his family's past glory, of their estates in Antigua, or of his service in the Royal Flying Corps during the war. Of his subsequent life, his failures, and his precarious physical and mental health, her only discussion would be the fictionalized account in her first novel.

One can only speculate as to whether the family "secret" was the cause or the effect of Phyllis's reserve and fervent demands for privacy about family matters as an adult. During the bitter political campaigns of the 1950s she constantly begged her husband not to discuss their differences and virtual separation with anyone, so as not to offer her enemies political ammunition. The tone of her letters suggests how bitter it was for her to have her intimacy violated by gossip. More poignantly, she was to live with another secret by shrouding her son Philip's confinement in a mental hospital and the painful and violent episodes leading to it. Francis's condition made the family's social life something to be approached with caution. It was hard for the Shand girls to partake freely of social engagements in Roseau when they were fearful about their father's behavior. Drink affected him badly; the lightest social drinking could trigger a *crise*. An outburst could be provoked by the most trivial of household activities. The girls could never throw their house open to their friends, and it often felt like living "with the sword of Damocles over their heads." Elfreda managed by pulling a shroud around him, staying home, and arranging small bridge parties for her friends in the afternoon while he was at work. Rather than face distressing scenes if she accepted invitations, she often sent the girls to parties and gatherings in the care of relatives or friends. People did not dare broach the subject of his condition, and the family did not discuss it with him as he didn't seem to remember the episodes in the morning, even on those occasions when Elfreda had to seek aid from the policemen at the nearby barracks to subdue him. Dr. Nicholls set the tone by turning a blind eye to his son-in-law's ailment.

Troubling as their father's emotional state was, the Shand girls had their share of fun, and Phyllis was always to write about childhood in a light, playful tone—not for her the somber descriptions of a haunted childhood we find in Jean Rhys's Roseau memoirs. Theirs was, within their circumstances, for the most part a happy childhood. Although they played only with their own ilk, they enjoyed fun and games, playing rounders, tennis, "scouts," and cricket. Among their playmates were the Archers, a large family with six children who attended the convent school. The Archer and Shand children would meet in the gardens, the library grounds, or other prearranged places, and would play while Lally and the Archer nurses—sisters Minta and Minnie—worked on their needlework or gossiped. The most memorable of the Archer children, Julian, was an extremely good-looking young man—tall and dark-haired, with enormous vitality and a great élan—who would be the model for Andrew in *The Orchid House*. He was "a whiz at dancing" and a great tennis player, and when they played games all the girls wanted to be on his side. As he grew older he seemed to realize he was "smashing," so he played the field, but there was never any indication of an attachment to any of the girls. He was, alas, also consumptive and refused to take care of himself, saying that he would rather have "a short life and a merry one." He would die in his mid-twenties.

Part of the entertainment they made for themselves appears to have been a lot of fighting. One of their most memorable fights, recalled by Phyllis in *The Orchid House*, involved Phyllis and Celia, who came to blows in an argument and fought all the way down the steps. Lally had to douse them with water to calm them down. Their physical and social environment also offered many opportunities for amusement. The most seemingly unauspicious spots were sources of new activities, like the vine in front of Seaview House which was always full of lizards. The girls once decided that Marion was to do a painting of a lizard while Phyllis wrote a poem about it, but they wanted to do this with the lizard's tongue sticking out. As lizards would keep their tongues out as long as someone whistled—or so was their theory—they cajoled Rosalind with promises of their pin money to sit by and whistle for what seemed to Rosalind like hours. Innocent escapades seem to have been common. Once when the girls' dog, Buster, had disappeared, Phyllis, convinced that he had been kidnapped, was bent on investigating. They had already been put to bed for the night when she jumped out and began dressing, determined to go out looking for the lost Buster and his kidnappers. She didn't find him, but Buster, who had been out on a love jaunt, eventually turned up, quite the worse for wear.

And then there was Roseau's gallery of strange characters, like Brise, or the Crookmans—a mother and two sons—who lived down toward Newtown and would often ride into town, the mother ready to strike the boys with her whip if they dared ride ahead of her. The mad girl who lived behind Kingsland House used to make the most tremendous racket. Once—her patience exhausted—Maggie summoned their fat, potbellied, neighborhood policeman, only to see him mirthfully taunted by the girl with cries of "look at the man, always pregnant and never delivered." And once a year there was Carnival, when everyone took advantage "of freedom from self and took two days to run masked and escape from their respectability." The population of Roseau donned a great variety of costumes—"black-dress and corset, the tourists, the hounbaylay, the souswell suwi [carnival figures], indians and red-cloaked cowboys, clowns, men as women, women as men all wearing imported wire masks . . . with pink painted faces, blue eyes and bright red lips. The lighter and thus more noticeable one was, the more one ensured that every inch of skin was covered with clothing, stockings and gloves!" Francis Shand was adamantly against the girls "running mask" with the rabble, but faced with their piteous entreaties, Elfreda would always relent and let them don their masks behind their father's back and join the crowds. Elfreda would wave a red flag from the veranda to signal when it was safe to come back to the house. The Shand girls also took an active part in Roseau's popular musical evenings. Marion and Phyllis both played the piano, and would often play duets to amuse themselves, although duets usually resulted in blows. Mrs. Didier, a friend of the family, would often borrow the girls for the "frolic and funs" she organized for charity. Marion and Phyllis would play their classical duets while the family sat on pins and needles, dreading a public demonstration of the usual conclusion to their playing. The Shands had a musical friend, Mrs. Robertson, a plump lady with an enormous bosom who played the piano with passionate brio. Phyllis and Rosalind would sit by when she played, taking bets on which breast would fall out of her low-cut evening gown first—not that one ever had, or ever did. She took their riveted attention as proof of their interest in music and often congratulated Elfreda on having such musical daughters.

Young Phyllis and her sisters were educated in Dominica. Since they were Anglican, the only private school available on the island—the convent school that Jean Rhys, almost twenty years Phyllis's senior, had attended—was considered unsuitable. Frequent contact with the children's Catholic friends had left Elfreda and Francis unimpressed with their schooling. Their first teachers were Emma and Margaret Crompton, their elderly maternal great-aunts, who ran a small nursery school in their house on Chapel Hill. Their education at the Misses Crompton centered on poetry and arithmetic. Margaret made them memorize and recite poetry and drilled them in their multiplication tables. Emma, who was blind, would sit in a deck chair behind a screen and whisper answers. (When Phyllis wrote her children's story, "Governor Pod," in the 1950s, she had the graying, aging Pod sit at the back of a schoolroom whispering frequently incorrect answers to the schoolchildren.)

After their educational needs surpassed the Cromptons' offerings, their aunt Margaret, with the aid of "a series of tutors, some splendid and some eccentric," took charge of their education, preparing the girls for the School Certificate Examination, now known in the United Kingdom as the GCE O levels. The children called their schoolroom at Kingsland House, where they spent every day from nine to one, Miss Maggie's Academy. Among the tutors were a Mlle. B., their French instructor, who "brilliantly insisted that [Phyllis] read with her Alain-Fournier's *Le Grand Meaulnes*," a book that would have a profound impact on her fiction, and the Anglican rector, Martin Turnell, who expanded on all sorts of subjects, "but could get nowhere with my poor math." Through him, however, Phyllis gained a distinction in religious knowledge in the Cambridge examinations, given locally to ascertain the progress of students educated at home. Their music mistress was Mrs. Scully, Hesketh Bell's sister and Rosalind's godmother, who with her husband owned the estates of Sylvania and Mount Joy. Phyllis remembered Mrs. Scully's anger when she caught her "translating a Beethoven sonata into calypso rhythm at the piano."

Phyllis's love for books developed early. Her father was quite literary, and she used to devour books from his library as well as from her grandfather Nicholls's fine library of books on West Indian history, flora, and folklore. When she was in her teens someone gave her a copy of *The Oxford Book of English Verse,* and she read it from cover to cover. She also remembered reading Rupert Brooke, whose poetry was very popular in the years after World War I and whom Elfreda greatly admired. She was the only one of the girls who continued working toward the Higher School Certificate Examination, or the Cambridge Senior School Certificate, which required two further years of study and was necessary for university admission (now known as the GCE A levels).

One of the things that Aunt Maggie seems to have imparted to Phyllis along with her education was a great admiration for the works of Daniel Thaly, a Dominican doctor who had worked in Martinique and been a friend of Margaret's. Thaly was born in Dominica in 1878. His mother belonged to the prominent Bellot family; his father was a Martinican. He was educated at the Lycée Saint-Pierre in Martinique and studied medicine at Toulouse, graduating in 1905. Although Dr. Thaly was not normally the family physician, as the children were treated as a matter of course by their grandfather, they knew and trusted him. He used to visit, bringing treats and books for Phyllis and her sisters, among them his own books of verse. His poems, full of beautiful images of Dominica, prompted Marion's future husband, E. C. Eliot, to claim that Thaly was one of the few to have discovered Dominica's secret. Phyllis's own poetry would echo many of his themes and motifs. His books, some of them inscribed to Margaret, were among Phyllis's possessions when she died, and she was to use one of his stanzas as the epigraph to *The Orchid House.*

His medical practice was merely a necessary occupation: his heart was really in literature. He had worked as an archivist in Fort-de-France, Martinique, before returning to Dominica and had contributed poems to several Paris magazines, later included in his eight books of poetry. He wrote beautifully about passionate love. Whatever mystery laid behind his bachelorhood puzzled Phyllis. One of her short stories, "It Falls into Place," the romantic tale of a poet "dying almost unrecognized and certainly unappreciated in a hot and barely civilised country," hints at his possible unrequited attachment to one of Phyllis's relatives (perhaps her redheaded Aunt Liz or the unlucky-in-love Margaret). The story's fictional poet, Chrysostome, shared with Thaly membership in the Légion d'Honneur and a "delicate affection for portraits of little girls" in his verses—"children with large brown creole eyes standing amidst waving fronds of palms, gaudy branches of flowers in their frail hands." Chrysostome is said to have adopted one of these girl-children, "the loveliest of them all"; Thaly devoted his affection to Roma, a beautiful "outside" cousin of Phyllis's, one of Harold Nicholls's daughters (Harold followed in Ralph's footsteps and had a girl and two boys with his mulatto mistress), the model for Cornélie in *The Orchid House.*

Phyllis started writing early. She remembered how she used "to sit and write up a tree in her grandfather's garden. . . . My sisters were good at sewing and were better-looking than me. I never put needle to cloth (refused), used to climb into trees and write poems instead." Her first literary efforts were plays she wrote and performed with her sisters in holiday parties she organized for the poor children of the neighborhood. Showing early signs of the tenacity that would serve her so well during her arduous political campaigns in the 1950s, she commandeered her sisters' pocket money to buy little presents for the children—balloons and other trinkets to give them afterward—and would direct the rehearsals and performance with an iron hand. Her first published work also came early, at the age of thirteen. She had submitted several children's stories to *Tiger Tim's Weekly*, one of which was eventually published, earning her a bicycle and enough money to buy a camera. The stories in *Tiger Tim's* were not credited, and a review of the magazine for the approximate period yields no conclusive evidence as to which story is Phyllis's. "The Lost Island," about a young girl who finds a treasure to save her father from ruin and the loss of their house seems by its topic, characters, and setting to be the most likely prospect.

Despite its provincial charms, life in Roseau could be "a monotonous and often dispiriting existence" from which Phyllis and her sisters would escape in the late 1920s. The first to leave home was Marion, who, in January 1927, having just turned twenty, married the fifty-seven-year-old crown administrator, E. C. Eliot. The match, like any between a young, beautiful girl and a man almost three times her age, was the subject of much gossip, the favored explanation being that Marion had married for money and position, with her family's encouragement. It dismayed her younger sisters, who thought that Eliot, despite his relatively youthful good looks, was much too old—older indeed than their father. And despite Marion's obvious love for Mr. Eliot, they felt embarrassed and self-conscious about the gossip and the attention, exacerbated when the wedding was made the subject of a bawdy carnival calypso, "Never Marry an Old Man," just a few weeks after the ceremony. Years later, in a tongue-in-cheek story titled "The Objective," Phyllis would mock people's curiosity about the match while providing no answers: "People keep asking me why my elder sister married the Bishop, and I keep telling them that she fell in love with him on a moonlight night in the tropics, and they don't believe a word of it, they simply don't believe me." Just a few months later, Celia, not quite seventeen, left for England to live with her godmother. Phyllis, who did not have a rich English godmother or a rich and aging fiancé to offer hope of escape, became engaged to a young naval officer named Norman Denning, who had fallen in love with her when his ship stopped in Dominica and had later written to propose. Time and distance eroded the attachment, which on her part seemed based on her admiration for his dashing figure in uniform, and the engagement was eventually broken.* While she pondered her options, she occupied herself in Roseau as best she could. For a while she worked for her father, whose clerk had retired. He had an office in one of the outer buildings at Seaview House, and she managed his appointments and attended to his correspondence and accounts. She later worked as a clerk in the Roseau branch of Barclays Bank, a position she obtained after a former clerk left to marry a young Englishman. But the Englishman jilted the girl, and Phyllis, not particularly enamored of the job, insisted she get it back. (She would not be kind to bank clerking in her writings. In *The Orchid House* Andrew discusses his stint as a cashier bitterly: "They forced me behind the bars of a cashier's desk. That's when all my troubles began. It was dusty there. I was always stooping over ledgers and handling filthy notes.")

In the 1920s visitors in great yachts "dropped anchor in Roseau to pay respects to the white ruling class and enjoy dances on tropical nights." The arrival of overseas visitors was an agreeable break in a monotonous routine. It was with one such

*Phyllis and Norman Denning remained friends for many years thereafter. His brother, the senior British judge Lord Denning, later Master of the Rolls, was a most useful political contact for her in the House of Lords during her ministerial career.

family—that of J. P. Morgan II—that Phyllis left Dominica, on the Morgans' yacht, the *Corsair*. The Morgans had made frequent stops in Dominica during their Caribbean cruises. Morgan had an interest in the Botanical Gardens and kept up a correspondence with Dr. Nicholls concerning it. During one of these visits Phyllis met Jane Norton Nichols, Morgan's daughter, and his sister Mrs. Hamilton Morgan, the women at whose invitation she left for New York in late 1927. Janie Nichols was confident of being able to secure a position as a governess among her numerous acquaintances. "I was adventurous and wanted to see the world," she later said. In the fictionalized account of the meeting that leads to her departure in *The Orchid House*, Stella claims her deep unhappiness as the reason for leaving: "I am very unhappy, I would like to go away, please help me to get away soon," she tells the daughter of the American millionaire who takes her to the United States.

Shortly before she left Dominica, Phyllis met a spirited young woman with an impish sense of humor, Adèle Hammond Olyphant, the daughter of John Henry Hammond of New York—a banker, railroad executive, and successful lawyer—and Emily Vanderbilt Sloane—a beautiful, energetic woman with the soul of a reformer, living "on a golden island . . . [but] not quite comfortable about it." Adèle, reputedly the "most beautiful" of the three Hammond sisters, had been a student at Barnard—the first woman in her family to attend college—and in 1927 married a young Harvard man named Jack Olyphant. In testimony to her adventurous spirit, the couple chose a voyage to the West Indies as their wedding trip. Adèle had been born in 1902, the year of the eruption of Mount Pelée, and a goal of the then-unusual honeymoon was a visit to Saint Pierre. Their ship, the *Nova Scotia*, carried two other honeymooning couples: the chief steward and his bride, and Mr. and Mrs. Eliot, the administrator of Dominica and his young wife, Marion Shand. The couples became acquainted, and friendships blossomed as they shared ice cream sodas in the chief steward's cabin. Their boat was due to stop at Dominica to bring the Eliots home, and the two couples were invited to dinner at the Shands' on the one evening they would spend in Roseau.

Adèle and Phyllis met that evening at dinner. The guests walked to Seaview House from the quay through what seemed to them a sea of the largest fireflies they had ever seen—Dominica's gorgeous *labelles*. Phyllis sat playing a little upright piano by the front door when they arrived. As they sat chatting over drinks in a room where Marion's wedding presents were still displayed in an enclosure by the window, the Olyphants and the Shands discovered that they had many things in common, chief among them their friendship with the Morgans, who had given the two newly married couples identical silver salt and pepper shakers as wedding gifts. Phyllis and Adèle's meeting on the eve of Phyllis's departure for New York was fortuitous. When Phyllis left on her New York adventure, she could look forward to a reunion with Adèle, whose loyal and sustaining friendship would endure to the end of her life.

Part II

EXILES

Living in sunless reaches under rain,
how do the exiles from enchanted isles
tend and sustain their rich nostalgic blaze?

Three

Changeling

The child was not bewitched, but was translated
into a strange and unfamiliar grove
wherein that helpless infant, sad created
fell soft beneath the downy spell of love.

I skipped around the decks like a squirrel . . . yes, I skipped with pleasure as we raced out into the ocean and left all the islands behind. And yet I felt so dreadfully sad to be leaving you all . . . I could have cried myself away and dissolved into the waves. Then I searched the faces on that ship, and they were closed in, with shutters over their eyes. . . . They were the kindest people I had ever met, yet that did not comfort me." Thus, in *The Orchid House*, Stella echoes Phyllis's feelings as the *Corsair*, the Morgans' magnificent yacht, takes her away from Dominica.

Phyllis was undaunted by the prospects before her. She had very little money and would soon have to find work; but she counted on the help of her wealthy New York friends in securing a position and was assured of the comfort of their homes and protection until she did so. Few West Indian migrants have left home under such auspicious circumstances. Disliking secretarial work, and having abhorred her brief stint as a bank clerk, she settled on seeking a position as a child's companion or governess, as employment suited to her painstaking though not overly practical education. There was something quaintly Victorian in the career she had planned for herself—that of the upper-class but penniless governess of Brontëan fiction. She had a penchant for self-dramatization that must have been gratified by this view of herself as a romantic heroine on the threshold of her life's adventure. But she was embarking on this career in a big teeming city where everything—crowds, buildings, noises, weather, even her friends—seemed larger than life and the very opposite of the quiet country manor that coldly welcomed many a Victorian or Edwardian governess. Yet there was indeed something of the heroine about her. Although never conventionally pretty, as she entered young womanhood Phyllis had a pleasant, animated face, quick intelligence, fierce self-assurance, talent, education, courage, ambition, and a passionate, romantic nature as yet unchallenged by experience. She also had what many Victorian heroines lacked—the protection of a powerful family ready to use its influence to aid her.

Phyllis's sojourn in New York formed the basis of the account Stella gives Andrew of her American friends and experiences in *The Orchid House,* a narrative that follows faithfully what is known of her own life during this period. Her friends the Morgans, the "Royal family of finance" as Stella calls their fictional alter egos, belonged to New York's haute bourgeoisie, a tight-knit social world of old families of English descent and Protestant affiliation. They traced their lineage to Miles Morgan of Plymouth Bay, but their fame (some would say notoriety) was of more recent vintage, resting on the legendary exploits of financier J. P. Morgan Sr. (1837–1913), founder of the Morgan banking empire. The family moved in a politically and socially conservative world whose cornerstone was a deeply rooted belief in the "sanctity of property." They belonged to the right clubs and churches, and were active on the boards of well-established charities, hospitals, and museums. Their world was one of strict class boundaries. Their lifestyle, marked by luxury, was rooted on the solid comforts of substantial homes and the best in art, furnishings, food, wines, and cigars. Like their peers, the Morgans were eminently respectable, and Stella, when urged to an opinion, ventures to say that, robber barons though they were known to be, they were "the most upright and moral [robber barons] in the universe."

During her first months in New York Phyllis enjoyed the hospitality of J. P. Morgan II, and the patronage and concerned interest of his sister, Mrs. Hamilton Morgan, and his daughter Janie Nichols. The Morgan clan lived in a series of ample and solid mansions on Thirty-sixth Street east of Madison, in the Murray Hill section of Manhattan, homes embodying "the undemonstrative grandeur of respectable prosperity." Phyllis, fresh from the modest luxuries of upper-class life in her small island, was dazzled by the opulence. She marveled at the velvets, the brocades, the rare works of art on walls, shelves, and tables. She was awed by the surroundings, by the elevator that took her to her bedroom, by the "splendour and dignity" of the Morgans' various homes. "Whenever I think back to them," Stella tells Andrew, "I hear the music of Wagner, I think of my friend Margaret's father as Wotan. . . . Did you ever hear about the palace built for Wotan by the giants Fafner and Fasolt? It was the symbol of his power. Margaret, too, lived in the hall of the Gods. And so did I." Janie Morgan Nichols—the Margaret of Phyllis's novel—was J. P. Morgan Jr.'s elder daughter, an elegant young matron about thirteen years Phyllis's senior. As Janie's young protégée, Phyllis entered a world of rarefied elegance and sophistication far removed from the social and intellectual provinciality of her tiny island. She dined at the Morgans' tables; enjoyed for the first time professional performances in the theater, the ballet, and the opera, visited museums and libraries. The girl who was once scolded for playing Beethoven in calypso rhythm developed a passionate interest in the opera, where she discovered—as she would have Stella describe—how "all the dirt of the struggling world [could be] shut out of [a] gorgeous house with seven floors."

The lavishness of the Morgans' lifestyle, however, made her acutely aware of her own relative poverty. As she would confide to her friend Adèle and later voice in fiction, amid the riches of her friends' mansions she felt like "a beggar-maid among millionaires," alone "in that city of long box buildings pressing skywards. . . . Though I really luxuriated in it, I was never really comfortable there, in my mind. I felt like a modest little governess, somehow or other. Yes, I felt like someone by Jane Austen who had strayed into Wagnerian heights, into Valhalla." Phyllis was indeed an outsider in the Morgans' world. Her upper-class background and British colonial education suited her for their social milieu, but she lacked the connections and property required to claim membership in the top echelons of New York society. Her family, long in financial decline, would be further threatened by the impending economic depression, and Phyllis's meager salary as a governess (once she began working, several months following her arrival) was most inadequate to sustain the lavish style of dress and entertainment of the Morgans' circle. Their continuing patronage, therefore, meant frequent gifts, which came in the form of dresses, some modest pieces of jewelry, tickets to concerts and other cultural events, books, and sometimes money. Phyllis, already beholden to them for their hospitality, could ill afford to be proud, and she learned to accept—and in time to expect—Janie's and the Morgans' generosity.

Phyllis's position in the Morgan household was an awkward one. She was just nineteen and had left her parents' home under the care of Mrs. Hamilton Morgan and Janie, who had placed themselves *in loco parentis,* assuming responsibility for looking after the young woman at least until she found an employer within their circle of friends. Janie, particularly, saw Phyllis as her protégée, and seems to have found a measure of gratification in introducing the somewhat exotic, charming girl to her acquaintances. Phyllis, the fey, alluring Creole, with her poetic ambition, unique background, baronet grandfather, wide-eyed eagerness to embrace her new surroundings—and even her poverty—added a dash of romance to Janie's entertaining, and she relished her role as Phyllis's guide through all the cultural and social wonders New York had to offer. Phyllis had been induced to consider herself a member of the family, and the growing affection between Phyllis and Janie's ten-year-old son, Page, was encouraged. (The two remained friends until the end of her life; he named his youngest daughter Dominica in her honor.) These attentions, coupled with Janie's continued role as Phyllis's patron (even after she went to work), led to certain mutual expectations. Janie required Phyllis to accept guidance and advice; Phyllis assumed that compliance would be rewarded with assistance. From her employers Phyllis would expect very little other than a salary, accepting with great equanimity and submissiveness the conditions of subordinate employment. From Janie she learned to expect more in return for a certain degree of uncharacteristic docility: At her request she would leave her first employer when she was needed by Janie's mother-in-law; under her guidance Phyllis would settle in Buffalo after her marriage; to gratify Janie's wish to be godmother to her first child, she would go against her own wish of choosing instead her dear friend Adèle.

In *The Orchid House,* Stella refers to Margaret's beneficence with a caustic touch of awareness of the burdens it placed on both the giver and the receiver. Seeing that her sister Joan has arrived with barely a dress to her name, she gives her her own dresses, arguing that she will stop in New York on her way back to Maine, "and Margaret will be so ashamed of me and so sorry for my shabbiness that she'll load me up with new dresses. I must see her anyhow." Stella adds, "She is miserable without a romantic docile protégée."

The great disparity in wealth and social position between Phyllis and Janie, coupled with the younger woman's growing independence of spirit, would eventually (one could say inevitably) lead to a severing of their relationship. Phyllis, particularly after her marriage in 1930, led an often hand-to-mouth existence, frequently on the brink of financial disaster, and would occasionally turn to Janie for help out of her "jams." Janie, in turn, would come to feel that Phyllis accepted her gifts and help with too much alacrity, and to resent her constant need of money, particularly after becoming aware of Phyllis's leftist leanings. Despite indisputable tensions, the final blow to their friendship would not come until 1962, when Phyllis attempted to borrow $250 from her to buy the *Dominica Herald* and she replied with a stern letter. Janie once told Adèle that she had given Phyllis up, since whenever she heard from her she always wanted something. Phyllis would feel the sting of the charge for the rest of her life and would refer to it when writing to Adèle on Janie's death in 1982, at a time when Phyllis was nearly destitute. "I learned of Janie Nichols' death," she wrote. "Since she reprimanded me for borrowing a small sum, you recall, I've only written to her once. She replied quite amicably. But I was *sorry* she didn't leave me anything (at one time we were very close; and she was Phina's Godmother). People don't know how hard it is for writers to live and work. However, she has left her property to the U. S. Conservation Society (whatever its name). That is good." At the heart of the tensions between Phyllis and Janie were radically different attitudes toward money and possessions. Phyllis would become rather indifferent to material wealth after her political radicalization, and all too prone recklessly to give away everything she had even when she had little to give. Her friends are fond of telling stories of her often imprudent generosity, particularly about her disregard of her own and her family's needs and comfort when she perceived the needs of others as more desperate. The reverse of this selflessness was her assumption that others acted in the same spirit. She had difficulty, therefore, understanding why those who had so much could be reluctant to part with a little of it. Janie would not be the only person to resent her ready acceptance of help—or her taking for granted that a favor, once done, would be repeated.

The tensions between them, however, were slow to develop, and the early months of Phyllis's stay in New York were punctuated by Janie's generous concern for her guest's welfare and entertainment. Eager to help her settle happily in New York, soon after her arrival Janie asked her for the names of any friend or acquaintance she would like to have them invite to dinner. Other than Adèle and Jack Olyphant, the couple she had met during their honeymoon the year before, Phyllis knew no one. The Olyphants were duly invited to dine, and the reunion led to the blossoming of a warm and long-lasting relationship between Adèle and Phyllis. Although they were to see each other only a handful of times after Phyllis left the United States for England in 1936, they maintained a correspondence that spanned five decades, and she would always speak of Adèle as one of the closest friends she ever had.

When Adèle had met Phyllis in Dominica, she likened her to the heroine of Margaret Kennedy's *The Constant Nymph*, a novel that had enjoyed great popularity upon its publication in 1924. Phyllis, like Tessa Sanger, Kennedy's heroine, displayed "the delicate beginnings of a noble mind, a grandeur of outlook which would well repay development." Like Tessa's, her young friend's character was remarkable for its "naked honesty" and "absence of pretense." Adèle was particularly struck by her new friend's piercing intelligence, and by the lack of arrogance with which she would defend her convictions, while steadfastly refusing to be swayed if she believed herself to be in the right. Phyllis, even then, had a sense of occasion, and in her political career would not be above a bit of grandstanding, but she would give herself to her dreams with "a passionate readiness," with the "singleness of vision" that was her nature. To Adèle, reminiscing more than fifty years later, she was a woman remarkable for having always been "admirably true to herself." The couple had not known her long before they concluded that this talented "footloose child" was "one of the most worthwhile people" they had ever encountered.

Phyllis was indeed fortunate in her friend. Adèle possessed a luminous beauty, still remarkable in her old age, that came as much from her physical attributes as from her openness to embrace and encourage her friends' enthusiasms and dreams. The two friends grew into the habit of spending Monday evenings together while Jack attended weekly meetings of the Boys Club. The Olyphants' home at 103 East Seventy-second Street soon became Phyllis's refuge. She and Adèle would meet for dinner, an outing to the theater, or just a long chat. Phyllis, a good storyteller, would amuse Adèle with stories of the goings-on among her employers. Sometimes they would meet for quiet evenings during which Phyllis would play the piano while

Adèle worked on her watercolors. As the friendship blossomed, Adèle's companionship became increasingly vital to Phyllis. They were kindred spirits, and she was not beholden to her as she was to the Morgans, giving their friendship a frankness absent from her relationship with Janie. Moreover, to Phyllis, virtually alone in New York City, Adèle's unquestioning faith in her and support were invaluable.

Phyllis was later to write a story set in New York, "Parks," which captures some of the alienation she felt in her new surroundings. It tells the tale of Minta, a young West Indian, "a lovely hybrid," who finds herself "white . . . spotless . . . retrieved, in the eyes of her present world . . . growing away from her mother just the degree of breed that lay between them—growing towards the white, leaving a great gulf fixed between the pale coffee-colour and her own ivory." Her life, she feels, is "one ghastly sham." It is a story of contrasts, in which she examines through Minta's brooding, ironically lucid self-exploration the differences—social as well as of landscape—between her island and New York: "Central Park, straggled with ugly young men, helpless nursemaids and darling children, was nearly calm; and beyond its low stone wall New York City flowed like a river of unrest, remote. But the other garden, the tropical one! Its solitary beauty had been too forcibly vivid for complacence. The green of it hurt, the trees wavered like tremulous lips. It had been, in alternation, gaudy and uncompromisingly sombre."

In "Parks" Phyllis uses race as the most expedient vehicle to convey to her reader Minta's alienation from her surroundings, an estrangement based on a perception of difference that is as much cultural and historical as it is racial. For her, precisely because she had grown up as part of the ruling minority in a predominantly black island, race was a central component of the way in which she perceived life, and thus a salient marker of how her new world, with its white majority and less fluid relationships between races, differed from her old. Faced with a world in which they did not belong, Minta and her creator (one because of her hidden race, the other because of her colonial culture) must acknowledge their difference. Minta avows her suppressed loyalties when she dons her Creole costume and ventures to Harlem for an evening at the Trinidad Night Club: "Minta knew she was defying the gods. She was mad. She, so fortunate, so secure of her kind! Her kind . . . ah there was the urge, the tragedy; these were her people, these dark, pulsing natives. In most cases the sensitive coloured outcast strains towards the white race. But Minta yearned for humble brown companionship. . . . [She had] sought wild danger and discovered fellowship." Seeing her new English chauffeur respectfully bowing before her, a quick thought stings her. "'Mason,' she muses to herself, 'in the Island of Spathodia you would be a third-rate planter, perhaps, and I . . . a social outcast. I should crave a smile from you, be grateful for the least gesture of desire. And here . . . you are my servant! Funny, isn't it, Mason?'"

Phyllis was soon to have a little taste of servitude herself as she embarked on her career in child care. Her first employers, George White, a former Harvard football player, and his wife, are remembered chiefly for the graphically detailed stories she told Adèle about their tempestuous marriage and frequent rows, which featured the frequent smashing of delicate china. In the summer of 1928 she moved to another position. Janie's sister-in-law, Helen Slocum Estabrook (nee Nichols), had died unexpectedly in May, and her husband had moved into his mother-in-law's (Mrs. George Nichols) home at 42 West Eleventh Street in Greenwich Village with his three children, Laura, James, and John, who ranged in ages from five to twelve. On Janie's recommendation Phyllis was hired as the children's companion.

Mrs. Nichols, Phyllis's employer, was an austere woman given to quiet philanthropy, who sternly disapproved of the emptiness of upper-class New York social life and ran her home and family with, if not an iron hand, at least a firm grasp. Phyllis joined her household as little more than a servant, and was treated as such. The children were in school and her duties were not too onerous, but they were rigidly scheduled and left her little leisure time. She was expected to be in attendance whenever the children were at home, and was allowed, like the other servants, one day off a week. Phyllis, she of "the Royal family of Dominica," dealt with this with "exemplary patience," and was never heard to complain of her lot. She claimed to enjoy the children, particularly little Laura, and established bonds with them that would last to the end of her life. And she made the best of her limited leisure time, spending her days off with Adèle or her sister Rachel, with whom she would often go to concerts or the theater. Rachel remembers Phyllis as disarming and whimsical. She would make any foray to a play or the cinema doubly enjoyable by the wit and depth of her insights afterward. She could also tell stories about life in Dominica by the hour, droll tales about island life filtered through her characteristic perceptions and penchant for the absurd. This experience of near-servitude, however, was pivotal for Phyllis's political development. Her subservient position in Mrs. Nichols's household nurtured the seeds of a political radicalism that would bloom under the tutelage of Fabian socialists in London in the 1930s.

Her employment led to a friendship with Mrs. Nichols's youngest daughter, Susan Pulsifer. Susan, about thirty-five, was a talented young writer and artist, a passionate sponsor of myriad causes whom Phyllis learned very quickly to admire. Her husband Harold Trowbridge Pulsifer, a well-known poet, was editor and publisher of *Outlook Magazine,* in which he gave their first opportunity of publication to poets like Elinor Wylie and Edna St. Vincent Millay. When Phyllis first knew him, he was president of a group of young writers that met in a teashop in Lower Manhattan and included Edwin Arlington Robinson, Wylie, William Rose Benét, Margaret Widdemer, Eleanor Wilkinson, and Arthur Guiterman. Phyllis, an aspiring poet herself, occasionally met the members of Harold's group at the Pulsifers' Greenwich Village apartment or at Cooper's Bluff, their summer home in Oyster Bay, Long Island, where she, as the Estabrook' nanny, was a frequent guest. Though her youth and subordinate position in the household did not allow for an open exchange of ideas with Harold's other guests, she relished the artistic atmosphere and the intensity of the discussions of her chosen craft. Harold, aware of her literary ambitions, offered encouragement and advice.

A more troublesome attachment developed between Phyllis and Susan's younger brother, William Blake Nichols, a handsome, charming bachelor in his early thirties who was his mother's favorite and greatest intimate. Bill had enlisted in the armed forces after his graduation from Harvard in 1916, returning in 1918 to his childhood home, where he still lived when Phyllis arrived. In the forced intimacy of the house a romance blossomed between them and despite their awareness of the displeasure with which his mother and the friends who had placed her there would have received the announcement of their relationship, they soon became secretly engaged. The romance was not bound to prosper. He was by all accounts mad about Phyllis, but there is no evidence that he had independent means—it is quite likely, being the youngest son, that his mother held the purse strings—and nothing is known about his prospects. She, although the next thing to royalty in Dominica, was, in the Nicholses' conservative circles, with their deep awareness of "family" and connections, just a penniless working girl belonging to an impoverished family from an obscure little island. She was also not by temperament likely to be patient with any situation in which she was perceived to be so clearly at a disadvantage. Proud and self-confident, she would never suffer indignity or affront silently for very long.

They were still secretly engaged in mid-1929, when Celia wrote from London to announce her engagement to Jack Allfrey, a young naval officer she had met during a visit to her godmother's newly married daughter. The wedding was to take place at Holy Trinity, Brompton, in London, and Phyllis borrowed three hundred dollars from Adèle to travel to England for the occasion. A wary Mrs. Nichols was only too happy to see her go, and must have rejoiced at the news that her governess—her own son's many attractions notwithstanding—had fallen in love with Celia's brother-in-law, Robert Edward Allfrey, and was not to return. Their attraction had been mutual and immediate. Phyllis later said that as both she and Robert had been left out of the wedding party, they jokingly proposed getting married to show the others.

Robert, then twenty-three, was a tall, lanky young man with boyish good looks and an ever-present frown that would only intensify with age. A member of the declining English upper middle class (his father was a surgeon), he had grown up at Froxfield House, Roman Crescent, Southwick, Sussex, and had been educated at Tonbridge School. When Phyllis met him he had just graduated from Merton College, Oxford, with a degree in engineering. Phyllis's choice of fiancés was always the source of much speculation among her friends. Robert was universally acknowledged to be "a difficult chap," even by those among her friends who liked him. The difficult aspects of his character may not have been readily apparent to Phyllis, having lived, as she had, with a deeply troubled father. But Robert's flaws were of a different nature. He was very intelligent, with a cultivated but somewhat rigid mind; he was also unambitious, and his resentment of authority, coupled with what some described charitably as a lack of talent for his chosen profession, and socialist leanings that would grow stronger after he joined the British Labour party in 1938, meant he was rarely able to keep a job for very long. His checkered employment career would often lead the family to the brink of financial collapse, leaving the burdens of survival too frequently on Phyllis's shoulders. Worse than all this, many friends would argue, was his being "a horrible bore." It has been said that the unfortunate visitor who got "landed" with Robert would have to endure endless lectures in his "mumbling baritone" on subjects of interest only to himself. Despite his lifelong loyalty to Phyllis, a loyalty she reciprocated, many considered him to be her greatest liability. There were many in Dominica who disliked him intensely, and Lennox Honychurch, who knew them intimately and was like a son to Phyllis in her late years, recalls instances of people sending their regards to Phyllis and directing him not to bring a word to Robert.

When Phyllis met him these qualities were not foremost, however, and she was, if anything, too predisposed to fall in love with someone like him. He was "an English gentleman," with the allure of an education at a well-known English public school and an Oxford degree. Phyllis, who would always be a bit of a snob about "things

English," could not have failed to be enthralled by his quintessential Englishness. Edward, the character in *The Orchid House* modeled on Robert, is described as "an English gentleman . . . in the old conception of the term." His intolerance of authority could easily have passed for manly independence and rebelliousness (especially if compared to Bill Nichols's failure to make their engagement public); his lack of ambition may have been forgotten among talk of his impending departure for India to seek his fortune. But before the romance could blossom, Phyllis left for her six-month tour of Belgium and Germany with an old family friend and her daughter. Her collection of postcards tells the story of her tour: Bruges; the Castle at Marienburg; East Prussia (now Malbork, Poland); Jerome Bonaparte's *Schloss*, at Kassel; their hotel at Bad Wildungen. In January 1930, shortly before their return to England, they were in Hannover, where they attended a performance by violinist Bernard Etté. Phyllis, gushing with schoolgirlish admiration, sent a postcard with his photograph backstage, with a request: "Mr. Etté," it reads. "Please play 'Mean to Me' and 'Dein ist mein ganzes Herts.' Bitte sign your name on this card & give it back to me. Ich bin eine Engländeine" [*sic*]. Phyllis' self-identification as an "Engländeine" gives us a measure of her own "Englishness" when she first arrived in England. As with many other Caribbean writers of her generation, she felt that she was going "home." In time she would come to discover her essential "otherness," to acknowledge an identity deeply rooted in her Antiguan and Dominican ancestry, a process that would inevitably lead her back home. But not before a personal and political odyssey that would begin with her marriage to Robert in May 1930.

Upon her return to England, Phyllis had gone to Sussex to visit the elder Allfreys. Celia and Jack had gone to his posting at Malta, and Mrs. Allfrey, who had quickly grown fond of both sisters, offered her hospitality until she either found a job in England or returned to New York. She arrived in Sussex to find Robert waiting for her at the train station. They had corresponded while she was traveling on the continent, exchanging short notes and postcards. Once reunited in England, "[they] fell in love—that was the long and short of it." Their courtship was short. She had returned in late January 1930; by early spring they were in love; in early May they announced their engagement. The only obstacle to their wedding, warmly sanctioned as it was by both sets of parents, was his unemployment. His scheme of going to India had been an effort to find a job suited to his training, but that idea had been abandoned months earlier. Meanwhile, the U.S. stock market crash of 1929 cast a dire spell over the British economy. No employment was available.

Phyllis was soon busy trying to secure a job for Robert in the United States. She appealed to her wealthy friends, asking for their help in finding her fiancé a job that would enable them to marry. Her marriage plans, however, were not immediately popular in New York. Robert's lack of fortune and prospects lay at the heart of the opposition. Janie tried to persuade her to wait, not to rush into an unwise union, but Phyllis was adamant, and Janie must have relented in the face of her persistence, for Robert was eventually successful in securing a job with the Morgan-owned Niagara Hudson Power Corporation in Buffalo, New York. With a job in hand, they were married in a religious ceremony on May 22, 1930. She had no relatives or friends in England at the time and, in the absence of her father, was given away by Edward Hutson, archbishop of the West Indies, who signed the registry as witness together with Robert's father. It was a small wedding—the party comprised mostly Robert's family and a few friends—but the late English spring day was lovely, and Phyllis, in a long bridal gown and lace veil, looked thoughtfully content. The newlyweds left for the United States after a brief honeymoon, and on July 9, 1930, for reasons probably connected to establishing Robert's legal residence in the United States, were married again in a civil ceremony in New York City.

They could not have arrived at a more inauspicious time. Robert had been hired as a hydraulic engineer, and although his résumé lists his employment at the Niagara-Hudson Power Corporation to have lasted from 1930 to 1936, there were long periods of joblessness in between. The promised employment did not materialize immediately—actually not for almost two years—and they went through trying financial difficulties. They had arrived in Buffalo in the late summer of 1930 and found a top-floor apartment at 472 Ashland Avenue—"three rooms in a large baroque house." Their first winter was to be bitterly difficult. The weather was horribly cold, it snowed incessantly, and there was a dangerous epidemic of influenza making the rounds of the city. They lived on their own meager savings, whatever limited aid their respective parents could send, and on small loans Phyllis got from her New York friends Adèle and Janie. To add to the pressures, she soon discovered that she was pregnant. This first winter in Buffalo was to leave its imprint. The city became the standard by which everything negative was measured and she would, till the end of her life, compare any dismal place or unhappy period to their life in Buffalo. For anything to be "worse than Buffalo" was indeed a condemnation. (A friend in later years recalls showing Phyllis her new kitchen cabinets, only to have Phyllis scoff dismissively, "Buffalo!".) The chief cause of their unhappiness was Robert's inability to stay employed. There, as later in England, Trinidad, and Dominica, he was frequently out of work, and her friends often commented with some tartness that he was incompetent as an engineer, "quite incapable of getting anything to work," and that this failure placed too much of the burden of the family's economic survival on Phyllis's more capable shoulders. Every time he lost a job she had to work doubly hard to make ends meet. But throughout her life she was extraordinarily loyal to him, deeply sympathetic to his plight, and would listen to no criticism of her husband, doing her best to shield him from it. She addressed his frustrations in "Lily" and "I Got Capital," two versions of the same story about an unemployed househusband.

The setting of both tales is "an ugly suburban bungalow" surrounded by "huddled houses" in "a housing estate gone dead," where Arthur Percival—unemployed, dependent on his wife's income, burdened by the ugliness of his surroundings—feels like a "distressed human being, a left-over." References to his being a househusband, "that fatal expression," make him wince. His wife's sympathy and support are further sources of humiliation: "He could see her now, walking quickly between the banks of snow that he had shovelled aside, returning home from her office with the expression of a husband coming home to dinner, half-smiling, a look of tender security, that look which said 'You are mine, and more than ever mine because the industrial world doesn't want you.' No sir, she never nagged him the way other women nagged the men who were forced to lend a hand around the house, doing the cleaning and cooking, the shopping and feeding of the hot-air furnace." In "Lily," Arthur Percival befriends the woman next door, a fellow "left-over," who has just been evicted and whose cat he agrees to keep. In "I Got Capital" the adoption of the cat leads to an almost desperate, drunken sexual encounter, which makes his wife wretched and destroys their marriage. Of the two versions of the story, "I Got Capital" succeeds best in capturing the near despair that must have been Robert's lot during the long days he spent at home waiting for Phyllis to come home from work.

On February 12, 1931, their first child, Phyllis's "snow baby," named Josephine after her Martinican-born imperial ancestor, was born. Phyllis described the event in thinly veiled fictional form in *In the Cabinet:* "That girl, conceived in the old world, travelling to America as nearly full-grown embryo, born on Abe Lincoln's birthday, was supremely beautiful . . . perfect." The baby, "made of eggs and apples and snow," was nicknamed Phina and was christened shortly after her birth, with Janie Nichols standing as her godmother. When the baby was born Robert was still unemployed, and the additional burden of a child worsened their financial situation. As 1931 progressed, they realized that it would be easier for Phyllis than for Robert to find a job, and she decided to take Phina to the West Indies, where she would leave the baby under her sister Marion's care until Robert was back on his feet. There are some indications that the marriage was collapsing under the weight of too many financial and emotional pressures, and that Phina's sojourn in the West Indies was meant to lighten the emotional as well as the financial burdens. (Phina spent almost a year with her aunt.)

Thus, in late 1931, Phyllis returned to Dominica for the first time since her departure in 1927. It would be her last visit before her father's death in 1938 and the one fictionalized in *The Orchid House*. The reencounter with her native island was enlightening. Always sensitive to the waves of change, Phyllis could see the island she knew fast disappearing. The economic and political system that had marked the society of her childhood and youth was changing. The relative prosperity of the century's second and third decades had collapsed under the weight of the worldwide economic depression and the destruction of the lime industry. A hurricane in 1930 had devastated the island's crops. The large estates that had dominated the principal river valleys were now idle and reverting to bush; they could provide little or no employment, and much of the land was parceled out to tenants. The restlessness that characterized the decade was beginning to set in. As the large, white-owned estates were abandoned and white families lost the prestige that accompanies wealth, power continued to shift into the hands of the colored middle class. Phyllis, by her own admission, would not become a "socialist-minded person" until the late 1930s; the Fabian socialism of the political solutions she proposes in *The Orchid House* would come later. But she did not fail to notice the reallocation of power in Dominica, and the whites' much-reduced share. As Joan tells Cornélie in *The Orchid House*, "The coloured merchants . . . are taking the responsibility from us—we are now the poor whites, we have no longer any power." Her own father seemed to embody a long-lost faraway world; his very existence being like that of a haunted ghost from a more prosperous white West Indian colonial past.

He was not the only symbol of the past she was soon bound to lose. Lady Nicholls, the last link to the family's halcyon days in Dominica, was old and ill and died in 1936. Julian Archer, her old playmate and the model for Andrew in *The Orchid House*, was dying of consumption. He died that same year. Most important, Lally, now retired and living with her sister in a small house near the Botanical Gardens, was already ill with the tumor that would kill her. Phyllis had hoped to find her strong enough to come out of retirement and be Phina's nurse (as she was in *The Orchid*

House), but it was not to be. Lally claimed it as her right, however, to push Phina's pram for a stroll in the gardens. For the girls, now grown women, whom she had shepherded through the gardens in her prime, it was a heartbreaking sight.

Phyllis had come to Dominica heavily burdened with her personal woes. What little has survived of her correspondence with Robert during this separation is marked by her impatience, peevishness, and the near-bitter tone of her reproaches to him for not having shipped the proper anticolic nipples for Phina or sending his letters airmail when surface was just as fast. She would leave her infant daughter (only a few months old) to return to the uncertainty of her life with Robert in Buffalo. Barely twenty-three, her future plans vague, the world of her childhood vanishing into memory, she was nonetheless never given to despair, but in 1931 she was severely tried, and she found again in Lally's bosom, albeit for the last time, the comfort her nurse had offered throughout most of her life. What turn her conversations with Lally took, what happened between them, that would prompt Phyllis to assume Lally's voice when she wrote *The Orchid House*, will never be known. But when Phyllis thought back to 1931 in writing her novel, Lally became the repository of the memories of a world gone by. Lally was "the last of the guardians," and given Phyllis's childhood emotional identification with her, she will emerge in *The Orchid House* as the guardian of her past.

Phyllis returned to Robert, and by the middle of 1932 their situation had improved considerably. He was working, she had a part-time secretarial job, and they had rented a small house at number 3 Linview Terrace in Buffalo. Phyllis wanted Phina back, and her youngest sister, Rosalind, not too pleased with the errand, was commissioned to bring the child home. Phyllis and Robert came to New York City to meet the ship and had an overnight stay—their first ever—with Adèle. But the long-awaited family reunion did not begin well. Rosalind and Phina's luggage was missing, and despite frantic efforts the American Express Company did not locate it for several days. Their car, the first of many troublesome vehicles that Phyllis and Robert would own, began to fall apart as soon as they headed home. The "droll" drive began with their going up Fifth Avenue on one cylinder, stopping every now and then, "when the lights were green." The car struggled all the way to Albany, where it finally gave up—Phyllis feared it wasn't salvageable—and they finally had to throw themselves on the mercy of "some magnanimous friends" in Albany to reach Buffalo, one of whom gave up his sleep to drive them and nearly dozed off at the wheel. "Trains for me next time, thank you," was Phyllis's comment. She wrote to Adèle the same day she arrived in Buffalo to thank her for her hospitality, fearing that "the emotions of anxiety, relief and exhaustion [had been] too much for gratitude." Typical of her letters to Adèle, this one sparkles with humor. Rosie had arrived with what Phyllis described as "several extraordinary evening dresses," which she was certain would rot in Buffalo for want of use. She and Rosie had already had "3 violent Shand quarrels ending in near-tears, but she is otherwise comfortable & Bob calms her down & scolds me." They had to borrow a baby carriage from a friend as Phina's had been left behind with the car in Albany. She jokingly warns Adèle that she'd "better pray that this second installment of family life ends happily."

Despite the many problems Phyllis and Robert faced in Buffalo, it was there that Phyllis began to write in earnest, after what appears to have been a hiatus during her early days in New York. "I wasn't writing novels at the time—I couldn't stick it long enough—but there were always poems and short stories." Her earliest surviving poem accompanied a letter to Adèle. Titled "Transfigurations," it is a short, two-stanza work about Buffalo's wintry landscape. There is further evidence of her continuing writing in her correspondence with Adèle, in which she refers to poems in manuscript in her friend's hands. But except for the copy of "Transfigurations" kept by Adèle, the rest of these early texts appear to have been lost. Of the poems included in *In Circles* (1940), Phyllis's first published collection, only two—"The Gipsy to Her Baby" and "White Ladies"—could have been written before Phyllis's return to England in 1936. "The Gipsy to Her Baby," dedicated to Phina as an infant, might have been among these early manuscripts. "White Ladies," Phyllis's first effort to write with the voice of black West Indian women (the second was *The Orchid House*) appears to have been inspired by a stopover at Martinique, either in 1927 when she left on the *Corsair,* or in 1931 when she brought Phina to Dominica, where Phyllis saw the famous statue of Joséphine Bonaparte. But Phyllis would prove to be only too prone to discard manuscripts, and it is conceivable that all the manuscripts once in Adèle's hands were destroyed.

When Rosalind visited in 1932 she found Phyllis and Robert reasonably well adjusted to life in Buffalo. Their most pressing financial difficulties seemed behind them, and Phyllis, with her characteristic energy, had discovered the city's hidden attractions. Always short of money, she had discovered the Polish shopping district, "where you get superb evening dresses for $1.84." And she had made some good friends, foremost among them Bernd and Betty von Arnim, owners of a farm near Buffalo. Bernd, with whom Phyllis appears to have had an affair, would be the model for Helmut, Stella's husband, in *The Orchid House*. Born Henning Bernd von Arnim-Schlagenthin, he was the son of Mary Annette Beauchamp Russell, the enormously popular author of *Elizabeth and Her German Garden* (1898), *The Pastor's Wife* (1914), and *Enchanted April* (1922). Mary Annette, a cousin of writer Katherine Mansfield, had married Count Henning August von Arnim-Schlagenthin in 1891, and had five children during what she referred to as her "wild career of unbridled motherhood." Bernd, her only son, had been born in 1902 and was, by his mother's description, "extremely genial as a child." He grew up in Switzerland, and after an early private education (with Hugh Walpole and E. M. Foster among his tutors), had been enrolled at Eton, from which he emerged as a tall, slim, and moustached young man "with lovely . . . manners and voice." He was also "passionately musical," with a particular fondness for Wagner, which he would instill in Phyllis. After his graduation, given the strength of anti-German feeling in England after the war, his mother had counseled him to eschew Oxford or Cambridge and migrate to America. Bernd, although legally English and educated as an Englishman, had a distinctly German name and a German title of nobility, and considered himself at heart "a German gentleman." He went initially to join his sister and brother-in-law in California but eventually settled on a farm near Buffalo, where he lived with his wife and children when Phyllis and Robert met him in 1932. Bernd was thirty; Phyllis, twenty-four.

It is easy to understand Phyllis's interest in Bernd von Arnim. He was indeed a romantic figure: handsome, well educated, athletic, aristocratic, titled, the son of a popular novelist, struggling with almost pioneer energy in new surroundings, and apparently (there are hints of this in his mother's diaries) unhappy in his marriage. The details of their relationship in the early 1930s are not known, but in 1941, when

Phyllis (by then settled in England) came to leave her children in Maine with the Pulsifers at the beginning of the London air raids, she considered leaving Robert and remaining in the United States with Bernd. At that time she allowed herself to be persuaded to return to Robert in London, and the romance ended. But she would not forget him. Their correspondence would last until the early 1960s, and he would contribute his German ancestry, his Bavarian blood, the daily routine of what his mother called his "slave-life" on the farm, and his deep love of Wagner to Stella's Helmut in Phyllis's novel.

In 1935 Phyllis had a second child, Mowbray Philip, known as Philip, born on April 24. The family had moved to 164 Commonwealth Avenue in Kenmore, a suburb of newly built homes on streets lined with young trees, to be nearer Robert's job with Niagara-Hudson. The house in Kenmore was the pleasantest they were to have in Buffalo. They were relatively prosperous by depression-era standards and could enjoy outings to Niagara Falls and short holidays in Canada. This period, their happiest in Buffalo, was fated to be short-lived, however, as in late 1935 Robert lost his job and they decided to return to England. The transition would not be easy. They had little money and had to save for their fares and moving expenses. Months passed before they had put aside enough to allow them to leave. With two young children in the house, one of them a restless new baby, the wait was long and stressful. They sailed in June 1936 on the *Southampton,* arriving in England in early summer to a most disappointing homecoming.

Upon their arrival Phyllis, Robert, and the children went to stay with Robert's parents in Southwick. The visit did not go well, and Phyllis sent a detailed account of it to Adèle in "Letter to a German-American Laundress," an autobiographical short story (and her earliest surviving narrative). "I will pass over our early days in England," she writes, "by enclosing for your illumination a sort of story, not brilliantly technical as it jumps from indirect to direct and back again, but still—illuminating." It narrates the cold and unenthusiastic reception they received from Robert's parents upon their return. The elder Allfreys were aging and were less than patient with Philip who, barely a year old and always a difficult baby, was agitated by his new surroundings and cried almost constantly. Phyllis, who would never write about Robert's family (except for her brother-in-law, Jack) without a soupçon of tolerant disdain, felt intensely aggrieved and poured her complaints into fiction. In the narrative, after Robert and Phyllis's fictional alter egos had unpacked all their clothes, "and made as if to pay a visit to good friends . . . then the knowledge came to [them] of what [they] had renounced by going away to America; that they had forgotten, and that they did not want [them] any more." The perceived rejection was all the more painful as it came accompanied by the sight of the "blue English skies, heavy with clouds, so low that they pressed down upon us . . . the birds singing more richly than any birds you've ever heard near Buffalo, New York," and the smell of the beautiful garden—all the things they had longed for in Buffalo. But it had all gone wrong, the narrator tells her former laundress; "And so we could not stay, Mrs. Krieger, more than a few days, because it grew worse and worse and a lump came in our throats, and the lovely damp smell of the garden turned rotten, and the voices of the birds became the twitter of English voices, full of emptiness and incomprehension."

Phyllis would never be able to endure disagreeable situations patiently. Out of regard for Robert she tolerated the situation for a week, but her characteristic impatience won out and she left Robert and the children at Southwick and went to London bent on finding a flat and a job. Although very few furnished places in London were available to parents with infants of Philip's age unless they had "a squad of nannies" ("too hard on the bric-à-brac"), she pawned her jewelry and used the proceeds to rent a flat (at 21 Roland Gardens, London S.W. 7.) and buy furniture. She was also able to find a job immediately—within twenty-four hours of arriving in London—as a secretary with the BBC. The job was "infernally tiring" but she was rather pleased with having "*swindled* the stuffy British directors into thinking me a business-like spinster." It was tiresome, but it was a job, and as Robert had to begin at the bottom again, a much-needed one. He had found a job with Wolseley Motors in Birmingham (which he found "*odious*, much worse than Buffalo"), and the family spent the weekdays apart; but she loved London, and after the years of struggle and the disappointment of their cold reception at Southwick, her new life seemed full of promise.

In a letter to Adèle sent shortly after they settled in London, Phyllis left the only surviving record of her thoughts about her children when very young:

> [Phina] is actually beautiful, and this I can say without a particle of fond exaggeration; strong, vivid, sensible,—a face that (unfortunately) makes people in ships and trains and even streets stop to comment or hand over some asinine present. Philip on the contrary is thinner, more 'difficult' and has a rather distant *fey* look as if he had lately come up from a rabbit hole. Handsome, too, but not so sturdy and vital. . . . Phina was ahead in everything—teeth, walking, speech, and self reliance: Philip deliberates before he does anything. He will not smile unless he is really amused; but Phina's eyes sparkle all the time. I love the little man, though, he is so *very* sober and absorbed. Will put all his toys aside and spend hours tying knots in a piece of rope or lacing and unlacing his shoes.

The description of Philip is quite poignant, prefiguring as it does the troubled young man who was to spend most of his adult life in a psychiatric institution.

In 1937 Phyllis's sister Rosalind arrived in England with a contingent of West Indian Girl Guides to attend a camp in honor of George VI's coronation. She arrived initially for a three-month stay but would remain in England for the rest of her life. Her mother had assured her she would be overcome with emotion at her first sight of the White Cliffs of Dover; she found them gray and unimpressive. Neither was she particularly overwhelmed by joy at being in England. She disliked the country and yearned to return to Dominica, arguing incessantly with Phyllis and Celia, who never tired of touting the benefits of England and of telling her that there was nothing in Dominica to return to. (Years later, after both her older sisters had returned to the West Indies, she would remind the two "blooming hypocrites" of their anti–West Indian arguments in 1937.) She moved into Phyllis's flat, where she found life rather different from what she had known at home. They had no maid, and Robert expected his sister-in-law to help with the chores. He taught her, rather impatiently, to wash dishes and peel potatoes; but faced with her blatant unfamiliarity with housework and her (to him) sassy attitude about it, remarked in exasperation that his wife behaved as if she were a princess, but Rosalind thought she was a queen. His exasperation with Rosalind's nonexistent domestic skills echoed his dismay at Phyllis's disinclination toward housework.

Phyllis was never, as a friend would recall, "totally domesticated." She would always be, in fact, a terrible housekeeper, treating housework, if she did it at all, "as if it detracted from life." Robert was fond of saying that he always knew when breakfast was ready because of the smell of burnt toast. It was always left to him, who had a bit of a mania for organizing things into their appropriate places, to do most of the housework. Throughout their married life, especially when they did not have or could not afford domestic help, he was known to do everything from cooking to mending.

Rosalind was still with them when they moved to a "much nicer" apartment house in West Fulham. Not then a fashionable address— Fulham was, in fact, a "vigorous working-class district, . . . [since] gentrified and gone up-market." Parkview Court was on a busy commercial avenue, full of shops and traffic; but their flat, a spacious and comfortable two-bedroom apartment, was in the rear and overlooked Bishop's Gardens park. It was conveniently near transportation and shops and—as its name indicates—had a beautiful view of the park, with its huge wrought iron gates, shaded paths, playground, and aviary, and the Thames beyond.

During Phyllis's early years in England, she sought out fellow Dominican exiles. Her widening circle included her "outside" cousin Roma, her uncle Harold Nicholls's illegitimate daughter, a pretty olive-skinned woman with delicate features and long dark hair who became a close friend. In 1938 she and Roma traveled to France as Paris was preparing for an imminent Nazi invasion, and the two young women helped prepare sandbags to protect the city's architectural treasures. Together they visited the Luxembourg Gardens, a visit that inspired one of the poems Phyllis included in *In Circles*,—"To Roma"—a tribute to Roma's mixed-blood beauty ("child of mixed blood, how exquisite you are") and a celebration of the power of a beauty that "knows no frontier bar," despite the "circling frenzy" of a "world gone mad." Roma also served as inspiration for the character of Cornélie in *The Orchid House*, in which Lally calls her "the most beautiful of all Old Master's grandchildren." She is described there as having "the same small wrists and ankles and thin long neck as Miss Stella, but her eyes were very dark and seemed to float in her face, and her mouth was full and sad."

It was during this period that Phyllis met and befriended Jean Rhys. In 1936, when Phyllis returned to England, Jean had just visited Dominica for the first time since her departure in 1907, where she had learned of her fellow Dominican in England. Phyllis had always been curious about Jean, whom she had heard about at home as the "rather fast" girl who "had let down the Williams family [Rhys was born Ella Gwendoline Williams] by her life as a stage chorine and a wanderer in Europe." Aunt Mags always referred to her as "[t]hat woman who writes those terrible books." Phyllis had read Rhys's *Voyage in the Dark* while in the United States, and had loved the simplicity of its prose, despite its being "a horrible book for a young girl to read. . . . Her style was so pure but she wrote about impure things." Her own fascination with Jean had a touch of the forbidden. Phyllis was at heart solidly respectable, despite evidence of a passionate sensuality that surfaced occasionally and that she almost always managed to stifle. (Her friends in London believed she had several very ardent but extremely discreet affairs.) Jean's life of bohemian abandon held the allure of the suppressed side of her own nature.

When they met, Jean was living in a small flat at Paultons Square in Chelsea with her second husband, Leslie Tilden Smith, a onetime literary agent, and had for many years been declining steadily into chronic alcoholism that often interfered with her writing. Phyllis came to know Jean well but could rarely be drawn into discussing what she had learned about Jean's struggle with alcoholism, her failed marriages, her troubled relationship with her daughter, her arrests for disorderly conduct and assault. She would often speak of her great admiration for Jean's beauty and elegance—unmarred in her eyes by her alcoholism and difficult circumstances—and for the courage with which she battled adversity. Even toward the end of her life, when pressed for an opinion on her friend, she volunteered very little, despite a growing impatience about the constant comparisons of the two of them. Of the early years of their friendship she would admit that she found Jean to be rather moody, "with outbursts of bad temper." She spoke often of a wonderful ballet party Jean arranged for her eighteen-year-old daughter Maryvonne in 1938, and liked to tell the story of what happened when once, during a visit to Jean's flat, she had been asked, "How were the white people now in Dominica." Conscious of the profound changes undergone by Dominican society, Phyllis replied that they were now "of the common variety, the Smiths and the Browns," and Jean, incensed by the remark, told her that she, too, was a Smith, and then refused to speak to her for the rest of the visit. Phyllis, who had been invited to dinner, had to cook the meal.

In March 1941 Jean was in desperate straits, living in "dreary digs" in Norwich. Her marriage to Leslie was collapsing; Maryvonne, who had been staying with Jewish friends in Holland when the Nazis invaded, had disappeared; and Jean, who had already been feeling suicidal, learned of the death of Lancelot Hugh Smith, her greatest love. She turned to Phyllis for help, and the latter, through her broad network of altruistic, generous leftist friends and acquaintances, contacted an idealistic clergyman from Norfolk whom she had met a year or two before, the Reverend Willis Feast. Feast agreed to help. He visited Jean, arriving during an air raid, and invited her to stay with his family in his country vicarage in the village of Booton. Jean accepted the invitation, too much in need of help to see the unsuitability of a vicarage as a home. The stay bordered on the disastrous. After the war, Phyllis, engrossed in her political work, saw less of Jean. They corresponded sporadically—Phyllis sent her a copy of *The Orchid House*—but in the early fifties they lost touch. It would not be until 1973, when a film crew visited Dominica to explore the possibility of filming *Wide Sargasso Sea*, that Phyllis again wrote to her and their friendship was renewed.

Four

Comrades

Meeting me in the road, he greets me: comrade.
Rough music in that word, rude magic
In grip of clenching fist on willing hand.
This is our barricade against the tragic
Creeping decomposition of our land.

E. M. Forster once wrote—reminiscing on the cultural climate in London in the year that opened with the fall of Barcelona and closed with England at war against Germany—"1939 was not a year in which to start a literary career." But that was precisely what Phyllis attempted. In 1938 she had answered an advertisement in *The Times* for a part-time secretary. The ad had been placed by Naomi Mitchison, the radical aristocrat known for her historical fiction and political activism. Mitchison had established herself as a writer with the publication of *The Conquered* (1923), and had solidified her reputation with numerous works, including her most recent, *We Had Been Warned* (1935), a novel that explored her uneasiness about the direction taken by the Communist party in the Soviet Union. Her writings were known for their sexual explicitness and open references to contraception, and she had helped establish one of the earliest birth control clinics in London at a time when birth control was a remarkably divisive issue. Phyllis was delighted with her new employer. "I loved [Naomi] immediately," she later said. "She was like an Indian squaw." She would work for her until 1939, when Mitchison moved to Carradale, her estate in Argyllshire, Scotland.

Phyllis claims not to have been a "socialist-minded person" until she met Naomi, and indeed their meeting marked the awakening of her political drive and initiation into grassroots politics and community work. Her education in community activism began with the case of a poor woman facing repossession of her furniture because she did not have the one pound she needed to meet her payment. Naomi suggested that Phyllis and some like-minded activists should accompany her to the woman's house to circumvent the removal of the furniture: "We'll sit on it and they won't be able to take it away," Naomi had proposed. And that they did, "But the men said they'd be back. It went on for five days like that. In the end we won and eventually the law was changed. We proved something. Yes, Naomi was a good socialist. I learnt a lot from her." However, their relationship, despite shared political ideals, was not that of friends. Naomi, her socialism notwithstanding, had deeply entrenched class notions and never considered Phyllis to be her social equal. As a matter of fact, she wrote quite condescendingly about the numerous secretaries that came in and out her door through the years: "I had a succession of young and pretty secretaries, probably ill-paid," she writes in her memoir *You May Well Ask*, "but they seemed to enjoy themselves and I always found myself sympathetically involved in their love lives. They also helped with domestic problems." Phyllis's work routine very likely followed the pattern described by Naomi: "When the current secretary turned up, probably around ten, we chatted, perhaps about the progress of her love affair, and dealt with letters; there were always a lot which could be answered by someone else or to which I could dictate a quick answer. . . . There were all sorts of arrangements to be made, trains to look up and people to get hold of."

There is evidence, however, that Phyllis stood out from among this bevy of lovestruck secretaries. There are several references to her in Naomi's published diaries and autobiographical works—the only one of her many secretaries thus singled out. She could not have been blind to Phyllis's keen intellect and aspirations as a writer, or to her upper-class upbringing and her resulting disinclination to assume a secretary's role of social and intellectual inferiority. Indeed, Naomi remembers Phyllis as too prompt to give advice, even making suggestions for changes in her letters. This breach of secretarial etiquette must have half amused, half irked Naomi, as it was her foremost memory of Phyllis more than fifty years later. She did, however, once invite the Allfreys to her house in Hammersmith, West London, for her annual Oxford & Cambridge boat-race party, known for bringing together an "explosive mixture" of people—the likes of Wyndham Lewis, Michael Foot, Margaret Cole, W. H. Auden, Victor Gollancz, Stafford Cripps, Aneurin Bevan, all of them leading politicians, and writers of the British left, and once Nehru and his daughter Indira.* Phyllis described the party she attended as a "social and socialist occasion." Her job with Mitchison also gave her a first opportunity to watch an established writer at work, as she followed the writing and publication of three books Naomi published in 1939: *Kingdom of Heaven, As It Was in the Beginning*, and *The Blood of Martyrs*. Not that Naomi, whose literary productivity was bolstered by servants, cooks, nannies, and numerous "rooms of her own," was a very good role model for an aspiring writer living in a small apartment with a husband, sister, and two children. Through her, however, Phyllis first had access, albeit indirectly, to London's literary world, and made her first useful contacts. Naomi was a personal friend of some of the foremost English writers and intellectuals of the day—Auden, Cole, George Orwell, Stevie Smith, Harold Laski, Stephen Spender, and countless others whom Phyllis either met in the course of her secretarial work or later through her involvement in the Labour party and *Tribune*.† It was most probably through Naomi that she first met Aneurin Bevan, a brilliant but volatile Welsh MP, whose newspaper *Tribune* would accept some of what

*Lewis (1886–1957), best known as a painter, wrote iconoclastic essays and novels. Foot (1913–), then active in the Fabian Society, would enter Parliament in 1945 and have a long and distinguished career in the Labour party, whose leader he was from 1980 to 1983. Margaret Cole, a writer and scholar, had a long association with the Fabian Society, whose history she would write. Auden (1907–1973) was Phyllis's most admired poet. Gollancz was leader of the Left Book Club and founder of Victor Gollancz Ltd, an influential publishing house. Sir Stafford Cripps (1989–1952), a respected statesman who held various ministries during his long political career, was, at the time Phyllis met him, about to be expelled from the Labour party for urging a united front with the Communists. Bevan (1897–1960), a former coal miner and trade unionist, then a vocal and outspoken MP, was to Phyllis in 1938 "everything a politician should be," although many years later she would complain of his "iniquities."

†George Orwell, the pseudonym of Eric Arthur Blair (1903–1950), best known for his prophetic novel *1984* (1949), had published in 1938 *Homage to Catalonia*, a book that Phyllis, in her ardent enthusiasm for the Republican cause in Spain, would recommend to all her friends. Smith (1902–1971), a novelist and poet with whom Phyllis would strike up a brief acquaintance, had published her most admired work, *Novel on Yellow Paper*, in 1936. Laski, a respected political scientist, served then on the executive committee of the Labour party. Spender (1909–1995), a close friend of associate of Auden's, had recently published the latest of his numerous volumes of poetry, *The Still Centre* (1939). Phyllis admired him as much for his poetry as for his social and literary criticism.

became Phyllis's first published pieces.* (She could also have met him through Edith Summerskill, the Labour MP on whose campaign Phyllis worked in 1938 and who was also a close friend of Bevan's.)

There is no denying Phyllis's admiration for Naomi and the transformation that she helped set in motion. When they met Naomi had just published *The Moral Basis of Politics*, a copy of which she inscribed: "To moral Phyllis from sometimes moral Naomi," in acknowledgment of Phyllis's curiously strait-laced morality. She had hurried through the book—"feeling it was essential for social democrats to have strong rocks to hold to in the hurricane"—and Phyllis read it with great care, marking favorite passages throughout. It served as her primer on political philosophy. Naomi's exploration of political morality led her to a consideration of the dichotomies and contradictions faced by people considering political action. Among the questions raised were: What constitutes a political vision? What is the role of violence in effecting political change? What alternatives are open to pacifists? What are the dilemmas and choices—of loyalties, religion, truth and propaganda, economics—that must be resolved before a moral politics is possible? For Phyllis, inexperienced in politics but eager for guidance, the raising of the questions was in itself an education, and the pragmatism of Naomi's answers, her recognition that humanity was imperfect but must nonetheless do its best within its limitations, went to the heart of her own down-to-earth idealism. There was in this analysis perhaps less of the romantic élan that Phyllis would bring to her own political vision, but enough of Naomi's moral certainty, of her conviction of the rightness of her own views and of the belief in the benefits of energetic action, to find an echo in the younger woman's budding political consciousness.

Politics were unavoidable in 1938. The depression had politicized even the most indifferent; the Labour party debacle in the 1931 general election had shocked the working class and its supporters; the rise of fascism and communism in Europe and the Civil War in Spain pushed many workers and intellectuals to the left of the political spectrum. Phyllis threw herself into grassroots politics with boundless enthusiasm. She would describe herself many years later as a "loyalist who learned Party discipline the hard way." As an apprentice she had "the task of sticking leaflets into letter boxes out of doors when it was cold, although [she] was not accustomed to the temperature or the climate." Her first project in politics was helping Edith Summerskill win her first parliamentary seat. Summerskill built her constituency in West Fulham by stressing the need for government to guarantee the family's basic needs: food, housing, employment, and security in old age. Phyllis worked tirelessly on her behalf, distributing leaflets, canvassing voters, and staffing the campaign office. It was a hard-fought campaign. Women candidates were at a disadvantage in 1938, and Summerskill, an ardent feminist who had kept her maiden name, and an outspoken supporter of birth-control crusader Marie Stopes, was considered radical even for the Labour party. Moreover, her Conservative opponent was the very popular and good-looking local coal merchant Charles Busby, whose coal carts, emblazoned with his name in large letters, filled Summerskill and her supporters with apprehension. The

*Always the focus of controversy, Bevan would give his name to the Labour party's radical wing, the Bevanites. As minister of health in Clement Attlee's Labour government in the late 1940s he would be responsible for developing housing programs and for establishing the National Health Service (NHS). He was also considered one of the finest orators of his time.

race was tight—Phyllis even pushed people in wheelchairs to get them to the polling stations—but Summerskill was elected to Parliament.

Phyllis, in turn, had found her element in grassroots politics. She loved the speeches, the meetings, the marches, the canvassing—even the mudslinging and the intrigue—the entire *commesse,* as they would call it in Dominica. She took to leftist politics with the fervor of the converted. Soon she was among the most committed and active of the party members in the neighborhood, volunteering for all sorts of tasks, however modest. Her enthusiasm was contagious, and Robert eagerly followed. Guided by the more politically experienced Mitchison and Summerskill, they adopted the tenets of Fabian socialism. Naomi and her husband, G. R. Mitchison, were very active in the Fabian Society. She had contributed essays to the Fabian Research Bureau's publications; he had been among those who had revitalized the society in the early thirties and was then vice-chairman of its executive committee. In 1939 the Fabians had drawn up a new constitution that reaffirmed their commitment to the "the establishment of a society in which equality of opportunity [would] be assured, and the economic power and privileges of individuals and classes abolished through the collective ownership and democratic control of the economic resources of the community." It sought to secure these ends "by the methods of political democracy," primarily through its affiliation with the Labour party. The society believed in "equal citizenship in the fullest sense," and stressed its being open to all persons, irrespective of sex, race, or creed.

The Fabian Society had provided a transition to the Left for many High Tories such as Mitchison, responsive to its credo of noblesse oblige and its belief that reason would eventually bring everyone to acknowledge the rightness of its views. It would have a similar impact on Phyllis, who had often heard the rationality of unfettered capitalism questioned by friends during her prepolitical depression years in Buffalo, but had never been presented with a coherent political philosophy that could explain with clarity of thought the precise steps that could be taken to achieve a more equitable distribution of wealth. Phyllis and Robert also joined the Socialist League and the pacifist branch of the Labour party—two groups closely associated with the Fabians—fully sharing their belief that no capitalist government could be entrusted with the workers' welfare and that the Conservatives did not have the working class's best interests at heart in making or threatening war. These connections led to her work with the Popular Front, the coalition of socialist and communist groups united in their aim to save the Republican army in Spain. In her political enthusiasm, Phyllis made herself a socialist-red skirt she would wear with a black silk petticoat for demonstrations and rallies. She would slip out of it when the arrival of the police was imminent, and they would always find her in a sedate black petticoat.

The political connection with Mitchison and Summerskill also helped defined her feminism. She eagerly embraced the feminist concerns supported by the Society—birth control, a closer attention to women's health issues, women's access to employment and property, and the defense of women's rights to equal political participation. She became an avowed feminist; a political rival in Dominica who knew her in London would deride her as "always big on the woman thing." Her feminism was bound up with her socialist ideals and emphasized women's responsibility to work actively for a political and social revolution that would transform people's (and hence women's) lives. Her newfound feminism also appears to have transformed her marriage to Robert. Her activism meant that she was frequently absent from home, and she insisted on his taking a more central role in the children's care; she increasingly asserted her right to her budding literary and political career. More important, it led them to reassess the nature of their commitment to each other, from which they emerged with a more sexually "open" marriage. What exactly this entailed can only be infered from their subsequent behavior: "Flings" were acceptable, provided they were extremely discreet and did not threaten their marriage (consequently their friends usually suspected but never knew with any certainty whether either of them was involved in an affair); liaisons with close friends (particularly mutual friends) were out of bounds; their needs as a couple, and those of the children, would always come before any other relationship; and, unless absolutely necessary, their outside relationships would not be discussed between them.

Phyllis's politicization was most obvious in the passion with which she supported the Republican army during the Spanish civil war. The movement perfectly suited her romantic idealism and hands-on political talents. She joined Fulham's Aid-to-Spain committee, one of more than a thousand throughout England, and helped organize meetings and marches, collected food and money, printed and distributed leaflets, and applied pressure on Summerskill to embrace the cause. (Summerskill, like most Labour MPs, was reluctant to openly support the Spanish Republic, a stand that led to profound divisions within the party.) Because of her writing and social skills, Phyllis was in demand for writing letters, designing handbills, and making telephone calls to MPs and other notables. During the campaign to save Spain, her apartment was always full of what to Rosalind seemed odd people coming in and out, at a heightened pitch of excitement, with leaflets and news. Like most members of the British Left, Phyllis was deeply stirred by the fascist threat in Spain. The ideals behind the Aid-to-Spain movement—the protection of the rights of oppressed peoples, the outrage over armed foreign intervention, and the defense of a people's right to determine its own destiny—evoked a special mixture of consternation and enthusiasm among millions of people around the world. To the British Left, the Republic was a legal, democratic government under attack by reactionary forces controlled by fascist allies. Their campaign to aid Spain had been "the biggest movement of international solidarity in British history." In England the battle lines between the Right and Left were drawn around Neville Chamberlain's Non-Intervention Agreement. The United States had passed the Neutrality Act, which embargoed arm shipments to any potential combatant. But in Europe, Germany and Italy joined in calling for neutrality while maintaining a steady flow of arms and men to support Franco. France, with a Popular Front government led by Léon Blum, was sympathetic to the Republicans, but under British pressure was forced to restrict its aid, leaving the Soviets as the only ones openly supporting Spain's legal government.

To the British Left the Non-Intervention Agreement had swiftly become "a pious hypocrisy," and they focused their efforts on pressuring the government to resist the Axis blockade of the Republic, to try to get all foreign "volunteers" withdrawn from Spain, and allow the Republic to buy the arms necessary to defend itself. A fascist victory, in their opinion, would endanger British and French interests by allowing Germany and Italy control of the Mediterranean. As Aneurin Bevan argued, "Should Spain become Fascist, as assuredly it will if the rebels succeed, then Britain's undisputed power in the Mediterranean is gone. We shall be too weak to offer any formidable resistance to the Fascist Governments of Germany, Italy and Spain who will form an alliance. We must form an alliance with France, Spain, Russia and Turkey so as to become so powerful that we shall never have any fear of the Fascists breaking the peace." The British government's continued refusal to aid the legal, democratically elected government of Spain constituted for many on the British Left a betrayal of democracy. By early 1939 it was becoming increasingly clear that Barcelona, the last Republican stronghold, would fall unless emergency supplies and aid reached the Republican army immediately. On January 25, with Franco's armies in the suburbs of Barcelona, Phyllis attended a huge "Arms for Spain" meeting. She listened to speeches by leaders of the International Brigade and the Miners' Federation; by Victor Gollancz, Stafford Cripps, and Aneurin Bevan; and by others who believed that a political breakthrough in Britain might still be possible. After the meeting Phyllis was among the hundreds who marched to 10 Downing Street in a last-ditch effort to pressure Chamberlain into lending the emergency support needed to save the Republican army. She and Rosalind sat in the cold and pouring rain loudly singing "Hey ho, hey ho, old Chamberlain must go." Phyllis described the frenzy of that evening in the unpublished story, "Sitting Around in London." Tom Davitt—a guilt- and debt-ridden Oxford man modeled on Robert—joins his Popular Front comrades in the fictional borough of West Walham on an eleventh-hour march to protest Chamberlain's policies toward the Franco regime. The story captures the pathos of the moment:

> At ten-forty-five people with grave religious faces began pouring out of Queens Hall, carrying with them Ethel, Mrs. Howley, Ynyr, Christine and Tom Davitt. There was no sign of the other West Walthamites; Ethel looked forlorn, and when Ynyr suggested falling in behind the returned men of the International Brigade she shrugged her shoulders and tramped forward with the rest. The rain, sleet and hail had ceased but the feet of the marchers sloshed through thick brown mud. On the way to Downing Street the demonstrators were joined by after-theatre crowds, and the policeman who trudged along beside Ynyr was humming the Spanish Republican anthem too. 'You're wasting your time—the old boy's at Chequers,' he observed in a friendly tone between the verses. Tom Davitt looked up at spacious lighted windows, and to him they were all club windows, and in every club there were gentlemen up above writing out cheques payable to General Franco, each cheque canceling out months of agonizing hard work . . . months of collecting pennies from door to door, old clothes, tins of milk, lint and iodine. 'Here we are, shuffling around in the mud,' said Ynyr, bitterly and ferociously to Ethel, 'while the gentlemen up above. . . .'

Although not entirely autobiographical, the story offers glimpses of Phyllis's life in Fulham and of the people surrounding her: Tom, whose life, like Robert's, "was a network of debts, spiritual and material . . . whose every pennyworth of ambition and financial gain was mortgaged months in advance"; Christine, modeled on Phyllis herself, "ready for action, wearing her red woolen skirt with the slit up the side . . . it was legend that when she saw the Police coming she would slip off her skirt and there she would be, dressed in a jacket and a black silk petticoat"; Ethel, their MP, modeled on Edith Summerskill, agreeing to lead their demonstration in the pouring rain only if they guaranteed a good turnout ("I'll risk catching my death for the sake of Spain, but it embarrasses me to lead a demonstration of two or three stragglers"); and quickly etched portraits of various comrades—a man with the Party loudspeaker canvassing the district and calling members to rally, women quickly sewing a banner, an old couple rushing home for their raincoats and umbrellas—all to no avail. "In the end," a character announces gravely after news of the Republican defeat in Barcelona had reached them, "the demonstration was like a funeral. A sort of barbaric military funeral for our brothers who are being buried alive." On February 27 Phyllis was among the thousands at a Labour party demonstration in Trafalgar Square to protest the government's intention to recognize Franco's government. It was a wasted effort, as Chamberlain was to proceed with recognition the very next day. Bevan, whose radical ideals and working-class perspective best mirrored Phyllis's own at the time, called this day "the blackest page in British history. . . . We have seen the ideals of our movement and the gallant workers who have fought for them harried and slaughtered all over Europe, and we have not helped them to victory or succoured them in their defeat." The downcast British Popular Front then had to watch helplessly as Franco, despite his assurances that reprisals were "alien to the Nationalist movement," unleashed a horrific vengeance that broke the spirit of the British Left.

Still reeling from the blow of their defeat in Spain, Britain's leftist coalition began to worry about the imminent war with Germany. Hitler had marched into Prague, and Chamberlain had announced both his government's pledge to protect Poland, Romania, and Greece against aggression and his Military Training Bill (in essence a conscription measure). England began to prepare for war. In 1938 scores of European refugees began arriving in London seeking sanctuary from Hitler's onslaughts in Germany and beyond. Phyllis and Robert gave shelter to a German Communist, Walter Jahnecke, who spoke little English. Edward Dudley, a member of the Labour League of Youth and a friend of the Allfreys, used to take him home for meals or out for a walk or a game of volleyball. Walter used to express his alarm at the way Labour party members did not take their own security seriously. "*Immer vorsichtig*"—always be cautious—he used to warn Edward. On September 1, 1939, German troops marched into Poland. Two days later, on September 3, war was declared. Chamberlain made his announcement on the radio shortly after eleven o'clock in the morning. An air-raid warning soon followed. After listening to Chamberlain's broadcast, Phyllis told Rosalind to put on her coat because they were going to the House of Commons to listen to the debate. As they reached the bus stop by the Putney Bridge a warden directed them to return home. The war had started, and they were not safe on the streets. Phyllis, to Rosalind's amazement, started back obediently, only to stop as soon as they turned the corner, watch until the warden had left, and run back to catch the bus. They made it to the House of Commons, where they listened as the MPs applied themselves with dispatch to a series of emergency measures, the most important being the institution of compulsory military service for males between the ages of eighteen and forty-one. It was nearly eight o'clock when Neville Chamberlain entered the chamber to a rousing cheer. Phyllis and Rosalind listened as he condemned the invasion of Poland and declared the war a reality.

The beginning of the war threw Phyllis into a whirlwind of activity. Her Labour party branch all went "underground." Like many radical leftists, Phyllis thought the war would bring the Conservative government to crisis and open the way to a socialist revolution. Caught in the frenzy of the air raid precautions (ARP), the wardens, and the blackout, they even adopted secret passwords. Naomi Mitchison, whom she visited in Scotland shortly after the war started, commented somewhat sarcastically on her description of a "tremendously thrill[ing] meeting," at which they "discussed secret business . . . whether they could dare to hold their annual bazaar." Immediately following the declaration of war, Phyllis and Robert engaged in a great deal of "heart searching" about the necessity of removing the children from London. A number of evacuation schemes had been devised during the painstaking preparations for war. From the very first day, thousands of London women and children had been sent to the English countryside, to Scotland and Wales, or abroad to Canada or the United States. Naomi's estate, Carradale—a forty-five-acre farm with a stately home and a fishing river with abundant salmon—had become a refuge for children sent away from London and Phyllis considered that a possibility for her own. Thus, on September 9, she traveled to Scotland by train with Phina and Philip. There, away from the bomb raids and wardens and hysteria, she spent several weeks strolling on the farm, sleeping soundly, and playing records in the library with her children and the Mitchisons'. Naomi found her "a bit jumpy, but not so much so as the last crisis [the fall of Barcelona]; I think she finds all this security rather irritating, as perhaps anyone from the real world is likely to—unless they can accept it as something apart." She returned to London several weeks later, leaving Phina with Naomi for the school term. Philip, too young to be left behind (he had just turned five) returned to London with his mother. The Scottish arrangement, however, soon soured, and she started exploring other options for the children. Naomi claimed that Phyllis, "because the war was not turning out to be the revolutionary success that her anarchist group had planned for with themselves leading it, really took it out on [her]." (One is left to imagine what transpired between these two strong-willed women, one ready to brave the worst of the war in London, ardently involved in the politics of it all; the other trying to withdraw from its expected horrors, fearing for those of her children old enough to go to war, and sick of politics and war talk.

Coincidentally, Susan Pulsifer, Phyllis's friend in New York City, was very active in the movement to evacuate children to the United States. She had led the foundation of the Women's Mercy Ship Committee, organized to press the government to send ships to England to transport children seeking refuge in the United States. Deeply committed to the effort, Susan took a number of children into her own home; at one time her household included seven British children, several of whom were later adopted by American families and remained in the United States after the war. Hearing from Phyllis about the dangers to which Phina and Philip were exposed, she offered to take them in, fearing—justifiably given the fate of the neighborhood during the war—that the Allfreys' flat in London was too vulnerable to German attack. It was soon arranged that Phyllis would bring Phina and Philip to the Pulsifer's Maine farm. The decision was a difficult one for Robert and Phyllis, who often felt "miserable and mistaken"—as she would write in her unpublished tale "Babes in the Woods"—fearing that "what had been a choice between life and death had spun itself out into a termless separation." Phina and Philip joined the Pulsifer children, Jonathan and David, and divided their time between Little Ponds farm in Maine, the Pulsifer home on Long Island, and Susan's childhood home on Eleventh Street in Greenwich Village—the very same house where Phyllis once worked as a child's governess. Jonathan, then about ten, vividly recalls meeting Phyllis when she brought the children from England. Then thirty-one, she had matured into a striking woman with very sharp facial features. Gone was the baby-fat roundness of her young adulthood, replaced by an elegant slimness. Never considered pretty, she had grown into her own brand of beauty. She wore her long hair (which she had begun to let grow in London and would never again cut) pulled back in a way that accentuated the angularity of her features and the "piercing intensity of her eyes." "Once you met her," Jonathan would recall decades later, "you were unlikely to forget her." The strength of her socialist ideals, with their decided Communist bent, also left an indelible impression. The friend Susan remembered from earlier days had become a leftist, grassroots politician arriving in the United States fresh from the disappointment of a failed campaign to save Spain and passionately committed to a workers' revolution against a warmongering capitalist system.

Phyllis's ship back to England was sailing from New York, and she arrived a few days before her departure to see Adèle. She was deeply distressed. After leaving Maine she had been reunited with Bernd von Arnim, her friend from her Buffalo days. Their former attraction was rekindled and Phyllis was torn between her love for Bernd and her loyalty to Robert. She was contemplating a separation from Robert and a new life in the United States with her lover. What led her to this crossroads we can only surmise. Bernd's attractions were many, and he had powerful arguments on his side. If she were to stay she could be with her children, free from the dangers of war; she could have a new life and a new love. The timing of this second crisis in her marriage is not surprising, given Phyllis's growing realization of her literary and political talents and the new outlets to her creativity opening up around her. In 1940 she was entering her prime. She was coming into an awareness of her beauty; she was about to publish her first collection of poems; she had found a purpose in political activism. Her own budding success must have led her to confront Robert's incompetence and lack of professional accomplishments. Faced with an alternative, she wavered in her commitment to him. She was to have other "temptations," she once told Robert, but Bernd was the most serious.

An insightful friend of Phyllis and Robert's saw him as fitting into the West Indian pattern of the "weak" male, dependent on his stronger, more independent wife. It is indeed the pattern she re-creates in *The Orchid House*, and one must wonder whether part of his appeal to her was precisely his unwillingness to eclipse her—his readiness to make her career his own. It would become increasingly difficult for him as her political career blossomed, but she was always eager to give him his due. "It was always difficult to reconcile home and work if one is a very strong-minded woman and I think I am that," she once explained. "I was the one who used to be in the limelight. Robert was always so quiet but, you know, in the background he did so much research and was such a help to me but he never had any recognition." Aware of how his apparent weakness left him open to disdain, she "defended" him in her literary portraits by maiming him. In *The Orchid House*, Edward's lack of success is attributed to the fingers he lost fighting in the Spanish Civil War. (Edward was Robert's middle name.) In *In the Cabinet*, the injuries included the lost fingers and a smashed foot (Robert badly smashed his foot in 1953 when he climbed a tree to rescue a cat). Phyllis's use of what Elaine Showalter had called the "blinding, maiming or blighting motif" in her literary portrayals of Robert (as a "left-over" in "I Got Capital" and "Lily," as the awkward and frustrated Tom Davitt in "Sitting Around in London," as the crippled Edward in *The Orchid House* and *In the Cabinet* [her unfinished autobiographical novel], and as a "Lone Cactus" in one of her poems) underscores her awareness of his "flawed" nature, of his penchant for always saying and doing the "perfectly-wrong thing" and antagonizing everyone around him. Like her mother before her, Phyllis tried to build a protective wall around her husband that would allow only his best qualities to come through. She made herself his interpreter to the world. Paradoxically, his need for her may have provided a stronger bond between them than any other factor, except perhaps for their shared political commitment. In "A Talk on China," a story Phyllis published in 1944, a pensive little priest questions Stella—another of Phyllis's fictional alter egos—about her marriage: "'Are you happy with your husband? . . . Tell me—for I am always very interested—what is it that keeps you united to your husband? For I have found that there is a great need in marriage for a common enthusiasm.' . . . A distress amounting to indigestion afflicted Stella . . . 'In our case,' she said, swallowing desperately, 'I expect it is politics.'"

Infatuated or in love with Bernd in 1940, Phyllis found a true friend in Adèle, who understood her dilemma, but counseled that leaving Robert for a married man was a folly that could only lead to Phyllis's ruin. There was another powerful argument against Bernd—he felt himself to be German, and very loyally German at that, despite his British citizenship, a fact that must have weighed heavily on Phyllis's mind as she vacillated between the two men. (There is a possibility, although the only evidence is extremely circumstantial, coming as it does from her fiction, that Phyllis suspected Bernd of some pro-Hitler sympathies. In *In the Cabinet* Helmut, the character from *The Orchid House* based on Bernd is made into a secret member of a German *Bund* in Buffalo.) In later years Phyllis would become aware of his conservative notions in social and racial matters. The arguments were powerful enough to determine Phyllis to return to England. Adèle accompanied her to board her camouflaged ship, its portholes painted over. They had left a bright sunny day outside to enter a darkened boat ready to sail across treacherous seas filled with German U-boats to a land torn by war. As she said her farewells, Adèle feared she was sending her friend to her death. The specter of death haunting this ocean crossing is evoked by Phyllis in "Cunard Liner 1940," one of her best-known poems. It captures the passengers' mundane concerns as they board the ship, and then asks "What would the U-boat's dart, the spurting mine/Mean to each one of us? The end of *what*?" concluding that " . . . for myself? Oh darling for myself/It would be life's most true and fatal end;/It would be the conclusion in my brain/And my most spirited heart and my fair body/Of you—the last rich consciousness of you."

Phyllis, her romance behind her, returned to London to throw herself into the war effort. Living conditions were difficult at best. Families were separated. War work was exhausting. Mail was censored, and there were restrictions on movement and travel. Food and fuel were rationed, and shortages of every sort of commodity were an everyday problem. Taxes were increased to meet war expenses. And then there was the blackout. From dusk till dawn people lived in relative darkness. Activities one took for granted before, from walking the dog to meeting friends at a pub, declined. There could be no semblance of normalcy in an eerily darkened city. A few months after her return, on September 7, 1940, the blitz began. In the early days there were periods of constant nightly bombing that led to a mounting feeling of stress. Life seemed reduced to

> where to shelter when the air-raid warning sounded, the demands of work in the ARP and emergency services, fire watching, trying to do one's ordinary job in buildings with the windows blown out, or with no building at

> all, trying to get to one's job through streets blocked with debris on bomb-damaged public transport, trying to cope with erratic supplies of gas, water and electricity, having to make constant detours because of unexploded bombs which sometimes kept you out of your home for days at a time, and if one had been unlucky, trying to find a new home, preferably in a steel-framed building.

The population of London dropped by a quarter by the end of November. The bombing of London would continue well into 1941.

The war years were, paradoxically, the most financially stable of Robert and Phyllis's long marriage. He had been working for Parnall Aircraft as a production engineer since 1938, and in 1940 he had been assigned to the Ministry of Production in charge of the South London Office for Coordination of War Production. In 1943 he was sent by the Ministry of Labour to BOAC as technical officer for the development of civilian aircraft. Phyllis had found work as a welfare officer for the London County Council. Her job was that of helping families bombed out of their homes find permanent shelter, clothes, and food. She credited the job with helping her develop whatever skills she possessed in social affairs—the area in which she would hold a ministry in the future West Indies Federation, but it was exhausting work. Her charges were exhausted themselves and often hurt, and she "saw then how poor people lived." Families had often slept in Tube stations for months. Resources to aid them were scarce, and any improvement would often hold only until the next bombing. To make matters worse, the winter of 1941–1942 was bitterly cold, just as coal production had declined and distribution had become uncertain.

The West Fulham district was among the most heavily bombed during the blitz. Phyllis and her neighbors would listen to the broadcasts from Germany of Lord Haw Haw, the notorious William Joyce—later charged with treason and executed—who had lived in Chelsea and Fulham and would warn the neighborhood on the radio that on a given night this or that area of Fulham would be hit. "Families were bombed out time after time and we used school halls to accommodate them during the night," Edith Summerskill recalled. "As I walked among them, old women, who had been completely dispossessed perhaps for the third time, would shout, 'Are we downhearted?' and the answer would come back in a roar, 'No.' Never at any time did one person suggest that we could no longer 'take it.'" In Phyllis's apartment house people slept in the long corridor on the ground floor during the raids. Children and the elderly slept in the basement. Despite the dangers, the atmosphere was often almost festive as people tried to put the bravest face on the ordeal by sharing stories, jokes, gossip, food, and drink. In *In the Cabinet* she described it thus:

> What I learned during my WW II occupational risks was an excellent training for the harsh realities of politics, and it gave me an insight into welfare organisation which I could not have gained so quickly otherwise. I learned to endure incredible hardships and horrible food, and the only thing which nearly smashed my morale was groping about on broken glass in pitch darkness, but that again gave me an immense sympathy with the helplessness of the blind. The noise of crashing bombs was sufficiently like the holocaust of hurricane to seem like a major childhood nightmare, and bearable.

Rosalind, who was still living with Phyllis and Robert, fell in love with a young and very likable naval officer, George Leslie Smith, stationed in the south of England. Braving the blackout, they would board darkened trains to meet halfway and spend a few hours together. The normally short trip often took long hours, and Phyllis worried constantly about her sister's safety. Once she didn't return till morning. She had fallen asleep on the train and, awakened by the conductor long past midnight, could find no way to return home. They were married in October 1940, out of Phyllis and Robert's apartment in Fulham. They had feared an air raid that would have forced them to be married in a bomb shelter, but all was clear and the couple emerged from the church to a lovely sunny day and a naval guard. Shortly after their marriage Robert and Phyllis rented Edenbridge, a small house in the Sussex countryside, where the younger couple remembered picking mushrooms in the fields. It would be the first of Phyllis and Robert's country retreats, where they would gather their friends and she would write. Edenbridge, Phyllis would complain to Jean Rhys in 1941, "has no water to wash in now and the mosquitoes sting like Dominica! The worst of it is that Bob and his friend swat them dead all over the newly whitewashed walls."

In 1940, Phyllis published her first collection of poems, *In Circles*. The small book, published by the Raven Press of Harrow Weald, Middlesex, was dedicated to Phina and Philip. It included thirteen poems, most of them written between 1936 and 1939 and thematically and technically quite varied. "The Gypsy to Her Baby," speaks of Phyllis's joy at Phina's birth. "Decayed Gentlewoman," a harsh poem in which a request is addressed to winter to "drain the clot/Of sap from the decaying tree,/Fell it straight and let it rot/For other lives' fertility," was reportedly inspired by the bitterness she felt at her mother-in-law's cold reception upon their return from the United States. That visit may also have inspired "House of Today," written to a house "standing secure and still,/Snug and escapist in/the little curve of the hill," enjoying the life of wood and stone "but not the ardent life/of blood and bone." The collection included her two most frequently reprinted war poems, "Young Lady Dancing with Soldier"—written for her sister Rosalind—and "Cunard Liner 1940." Together with "To London," a poem that decries "all that shines to make a war surpass/the ordinary decencies men feel," and "Salute," in which she voices her growing socialist consciousness, they evidence the fusion of the personal, the political, and the nostalgia for the fleeting and the lost that characterizes her best poetry.

Three poems in the collection address her West Indian heritage. In "White Ladies," inspired by the famous statue of Empress Joséphine, she assumes the collective voice of black West Indian women to confront the class and race differences sustained in the name of empire. In "To Roma" she seeks to bridge the gulf between white and colored women through the celebration of the exquisite beauty of the colored girl. The untitled poem that begins "These people are too solid/for my frail self . . ." is her first attempt to address the withering away of those "fed on hurricanes, songs by moonlight," when they are away from their native soil. She will return to this theme in the "Stella" section of *The Orchid House,* in which Stella contrasts the beautiful but "sterile" landscape of Maine with the teeming, sustaining, green world of her island.

The collection attracted little notice. There were no reviews, as it was distributed privately to her friends, but it did bring her to the attention of a few in her leftist circles with the means of helping her, and her literary career began to gather some momentum. In late 1941 Aneurin Bevan assumed the editorship of the weekly *Trib-*

une, the newspaper of the Labour Left he had founded in 1936. He and his literary editor, John Atkin, began using Phyllis's reviews, poems, and stories in the newspaper. It was the first time her work had been sought for publication.

Phyllis's lifelong pride in her connection with *Tribune* serves as a gauge of her political opinions in the early 1940s. The paper had been founded by Bevan and his wife, Jenny Lee, also a member of Parliament, with the financial support of Stafford Cripps and of Bevan's friend and fellow leftist politician George Strauss. Its basic propositions were that socialism meant "shaking capitalist society to its foundations"; that "the values of capitalist society are profoundly evil and therefore must be profoundly changed"; that only socialism could "ensure the enlargement of freedom of the individual and his or her enjoyment of the beauty and all the best things in life"; and that a socialism that spurned, or neglected to protect, freedom of thought, speech, and association was "no Socialism at all." The paper waged a sometimes virulent campaign against the Conservatives' failure promptly to address the problems of economic depression and unemployment at home and the spread of fascism abroad. Angered by the Labour party's acquiescence in Neville Chamberlain's nonintervention policy and the free rein it gave to Franco's Nazi-supplied battalions, *Tribune* had used its influence to support the British Volunteers to the International Brigades as well as to promote the views of publisher Victor Gollancz's anti-fascist Left Book Club in its advocacy for the Loyalist cause. Fed by a "strident grass roots radicalism," *Tribune* had lashed out against the government's repressive policies in the West Indies, India, and colonial Africa, its failure to address the problems of unemployment and hunger at home, and its lack of concern for the needs and rights of women and children. It offered loud support for Marie Stopes's campaign for birth control, and during the war served as Bevan's platform from which to pillory Churchill, whose policies he believed (mistakenly, as it turned out), might result in British defeat or at best a problematic stalemate with Germany.

Tribune's literary pages soon acquired a reputation for offering new writers a chance to reach a wider audience than that of small magazines. Regular contributors to the literary pages were such new writers as Naomi Mitchison, Stevie Smith, Arthur Calder-Marshall, Alex Comfort, Julian Symons, Elizabeth Taylor, Rhys Davies, Daniel George, Inez Holden, and George Orwell, who became literary editor in 1943. Phyllis joined the impressive list in November 1942 with the publication of "Colonial Soldiers," a poem about West Indians—those "who were born and breathed in open spaces"—who had joined the British forces in the war. The first of her poems to address the burdens of the West Indian colonial situation, it fitted perfectly into *Tribune*'s agenda of criticism of British imperial oppression. "Colonial Soldiers" and "Colonial Committee" (which appeared on November 19, 1943) bolster Phyllis's claim that she had been an anti-imperialist of long standing ("from my childhood") by the time she became a Federation minister. "Colonial Soldiers" addresses the senselessness of West Indians dying for a cause not their own: "That brown face lifted to the argent sky / to watch the birdlike swoop, with flowering mouth / parted in wonder, spatters out to die / for things uncomprehended in his south." In "Colonial Committee," written "in fact, in Committee Room 13 of the House of Commons once [during a meeting of the Fabian Colonial Committee] when [she] sat with other West Indians of all varying shades," she writes of the careful dance between "the hunted and the hunter," their goodwill like lianas from which descend "the little restless apes of compromise and cavil": "Framed on a northern wall, the oily eye / of noble Lord looks trustee-wise upon / the olive and mahogany and white / of the assembled faces, but no frown / hints at the terminating trusteeship / or at the adolescence too prolonged; / for in this civil jungle scarce a snarl / or yap of pain attests the deeply wronged."

"Uncle Rufus," a short story about her childhood in Dominica, based on the travails of her Uncle Ralph Nicholls, followed in December. It was her first published short story. "Beethoven in the Highlands," an antiwar poem inspired by her playing a recording of Beethoven's Fifth Symphony during her visit to Naomi Mitchison's estate at Carradale, appeared in April 1943. Using the "listless, irresolute seas" of the Argyllshire shore as a motif, she writes of the "unrhythmic grief" that "assaults her throat": "The great deaf German sings to deafened / ears / And darkened minds anticipate the shriek / Of anti-aircraft guns and loyal cheers. / Stop the offensive! Let adagio speak. . . . " She was deeply interested in the situation in Asia, and her reviews of books on the topic—including *Japan's Dream of World Empire, Report from Tokyo*, on development in East Asia and the Japanese menace—appeared periodically throughout 1943. These, and poems like "Lone Cactus," a tender attempt to redefine Robert's characteristic "prickliness" ("Your apartness is but a waiting / Your silence the crouch of strength / Your thinking a hope in struggle") gave her a frequent presence in *Tribune* in 1942 and 1943.

The 1940s were Phyllis's most creative decade. Writing constantly she produced most of her thirty-five to forty stories during these years, in addition to the poems included in *Palm and Oak* (1950) and significant portions of the manuscript that would become *The Orchid House* (1953). Robert's long period of sustained employment and her children's absence (however distressing) gave her a measure of leisure she would only enjoy again briefly during the period in which she finished her first novel in 1952. She was reasonably successful in placing her stories in magazines and journals, particularly as she worked without an agent until 1950. *The Windmill*, a well-regarded magazine, published "A Talk on China" and "The Tunnel," the latter a lightly somber satire of the "ravens and vultures" who controlled British industry. For the detailed portrait of Mrs. Orme, personal secretary to Mr. Lomax, managing director of Railway Sidings Ltd, Phyllis draws on the intimate knowledge of office bureaucracy she had gained in a decade of off-and-on secretarial work. Mrs. Orme's social conscience and quasi-revolutionary outlook ("nothing for it but to change the system") is pitted here against a world dominated by small minds ("Was this the moment in which to speak . . . of the underprivileged to a little woman who as yet knew only of canine miseries?"), confident of their hold on society: "That was the trouble about these people: they enjoyed their enemies; it was hopeless trying to get the better of them while they had pearls and whisky and directorships and a sense of humour." "Breeze," a tale of her childhood in Dominica, appeared in *Pan Africa*. "The Objective," the story behind her sister Marion's marriage to Dominica's administrator, appeared in an unidentified collection. A story titled "The Raincoat" was published in the highly respected literary pages of the *Manchester Guardian*. Years later in Dominica, she still considered it one of the best tales she ever wrote, a "sad and eerie" "short-short story." After reading it, she claimed, a writer on the staff of Geneva's *Genfer Echo* had written asking if he could come to London to interview her about the thousand-word tale. He had done so, and had gone back to write an article about it much longer than her story.

Among the unpublished stories dating from this period are "Babes in the Woods," a poignant tale about Phyllis's separation from her children during the war; "Scraps of Paper," the story of a young man returning to England from the United States to trace information about his dead mother; "Sitting Around in London," about the fall of Barcelona; "Dancing with George," a story of misunderstandings and conflicting cultural and gender values concerning a young American soldier and a married but lonely young Englishwoman; "The Spirit Portrait," a lighthearted tale (subtitled "A Wartime Anecdote") about a psychic friend who tried to make a living by painting portraits of the dead at seances; "At the House of the Countess," the story of two little girls forced to leave their stately home, which is being converted into a nursing home; and perhaps the best among them, "Tea with the Bishop," the richly nuanced and heart rending portrait of an aging and frustrated social worker with her problematic charge. It is interesting to note that her most successful fiction, if judged from the point of view of publication, was that firmly centered on her West Indianness and hence marked by what was otherwise her marginality. In the mid-1940s, when West Indian fiction was not well known—and fashionable only to the extent that it was regarded as exotic—her choice of subjects, the literary themes that were so closely dependent on her childhood in Dominica, and her peculiarly colonial sensibilities, marked her as an outsider, a writer on the periphery. The writers with whom she shared the pages of *Tribune*, on the other hand, were solidly rooted in their Englishness. They were for the most part middle- and upper-middle-class young men and women who had joined the socialist branch of the Labour party in the early thirties in reaction against the social decay and economic injustice of the postwar period. Phyllis lacked these class-bound English roots; in many ways she spoke another language. Her passionate, impatient character was not English; the past that nurtured her best prose belonged to another land and climate. If she had aimed to "belong" to the English literary establishment, she would have been doomed to be an outsider, a hanger-on. But she does not seem to have tried. Her relationship with Naomi had gone sour, and she either did not pursue, or was unsuccessful in developing, links to the writers she met through her or through her work with the Labour party. She admired Auden from afar and knew Stevie Smith well enough to have received a copy of *Novel on Yellow Paper* (1936) from her, but the acquaintance never prospered. George Orwell would be the literary editor of *Tribune* during part of the period of her contributions to the newspaper in the early 1940s, but under his editorship her contributions became less regular and eventually ceased. Stephen Spender, whose poetry she and Robert greatly admired, moved in their political circles but was not among her friends. The closest of her friendships with established authors were with celebrated short-story writer A. E. Coppard (England's best, according to critics) and James Pope-Hennessy (known for his insightful travel writing), who, partly on the strength of her passionate descriptions of Dominica, would visit the island and write a book about its society. She shared with all these writers a "collective experience of a specific set of emotional and economic conditions," but she was beginning to realize that, as a writer, she belonged elsewhere.

In 1943 Phyllis had begun her collaboration with the Fabian Colonial Bureau, joining the West Indian Committee, one of its several long-standing working groups. The Colonial Bureau had been founded in 1940 to address the liberation and transformation into self-governing states of British colonies throughout the world. It proposed to achieve this by bringing together knowledgeable and experienced socialists in discussion forums and conferences and by setting up committees of inquiry into the situation in the colonies. The bureau compiled a library of current journals and press clippings and became a research center for those interested in colonial affairs. The standing committees soon drew the interest of various leftist MPs willing to be briefed by the bureau and bring its concerns up for discussion in the House of Commons. The bureau also established contact with leaders of nationalist movements in the colonies and met with any important visitor or delegation to England from colonial territories. These meetings, held in the House of Commons or at the town house of Lord Farringdon, a strong supporter of the bureau's efforts, gave Phyllis an opportunity to meet the leaders of West Indian liberation movements with whom she would work during the Federation. These contacts were invaluable to her in the 1950s, when she often required aid and guidance from fellow island politicians during the founding of the Dominica Labour party (DLP) and the Federation campaign. It also allowed her the opportunity to establish relationships with anti-imperialists in England who would later offer their support to the DLP—people like Marjorie Nicholson, who became the bureau's secretary in the 1950s; Harold Laski, the anthropologist Margaret Mead; Lord Listowel, later governor-general of Ghana; John Dugdale, former minister of state for the colonies; and Leonard Woolf. The war years were busy ones for Phyllis. She complained to Jean Rhys of being awfully tired "from working hard and trying to give myself out in small portions to committees and people and god knows what. And holding my breath over Leningrad as I did over Madrid, only with more hope." But her concern over the issues that loomed large was tempered by her enjoyment of the political *commesse*. "The Communists collected £1,250 at a street meeting last Sunday," she writes with obvious glee. "Agreed the smart alecs are frights—I endure them in a surprisingly Christian way—hangover from the Anglican Church Roseau?"

During the first year of the war Phyllis met Pixie Foley, a young woman whose personality had "a modern De Falla ring," whom Phyllis would always count as one of the best friends she ever had. During the war the two women would often go to pianist Myra Hess's celebrated lunch-hour concerts in the National Gallery, a symbol of Britain's "cultural resistance" during the war. Pixie was fascinated by Phyllis, with whom she shared political and literary interests and whose flat in Fulham Road was always filled with a "great and varied collection of friends."* Sometimes when coming to visit, Phyllis would turn up with an unexpected friend such as Jacques Arouet, a great-grandson of Voltaire, a very amusing fellow with a rather chaotic history, whom Phyllis introduced as an old friend of the family. Phyllis's friends, Pixie soon noted, would eventually turn up as characters in her stories or novels, as did a French girl who stayed with them for a while in the early fifties and whom Phyllis wanted to involve in a romantic liaison with Philip. The matchmaking did not work, but that did not stop Phyllis from developing the romance in one of her unpublished novels—

*She also developed a "warm and sisterly regard" for Robert, worth noting because most of Phyllis's acquaintances found him to be so difficult. She saw him as "a big shambling bear, always ready to express his views on the topic at issue, but basically very gentle, with an engaging smile and a lovely sense of humour, which no doubt helped him to deal with Phyllis's sudden flashes of anger or changes of plans. . . . In his relationship with Phyllis he was protective and tolerant, as well as being a dependable source of information and worldliness to cushion her characteristic flights of fancy."

Dashing Away—in which the French lass and the protagonist's son die in a tragic suicidal blaze after the girl goes mad. Life with Phyl, as Pixie called her, was never dull, as she "always dreamed up some funny aspect of life or something to be involved with." The relationship was the more precious for them both because it existed "against a background of hyped-up excitement and uncertainty in which such friendships . . . were important rafts in the flooding sea of disintegration." Phyllis's appeal to Pixie came from the curious combination of determination and whimsy in her character. She could be dazzling and stimulating, yet "always seemed to hold herself a little aloof—not preciously but aware of her responsibility in any situation." Once, standing on the steps of the National Gallery in London before one of Myra Hess's lunchtime concert, Phyllis made a comment that had seemed to Pixie to summarize her quandary: "I'm for the people," she had said, "but not of the people."

Pixie shared Phyllis's interest in developments in Asia and worked with her as an active fund-raiser for the Aid to China Campaign, to which Lady Cripps, Sir Stafford's wife, had lent her name. As a socialist, Phyllis had followed with intense concern the course of the Chinese revolution and the Chinese people's tenacious resistance to the Japanese invasion. She was intensely interested in the country's progress toward a socialist society. As the war progressed and Japan continued to conquer most of Britain's empire in the Far East threatening even India and Ceylon, she read everything on Asia she could acquire, often reviewing the books for *Tribune*. Her interest in China extended to attempts at learning Chinese, and Pixie recalls how, "millions of years ago," they sat in the garden of Mayday Cottage in Kent, a retreat from city life Phyllis had discovered—"a small isolated little haven in the middle of the fields"—studying Chinese poetry. Phyllis often raised money for the Aid to China Campaign by giving lectures on China to students and community groups. Her experiences inspired one of her first published stories, "A Talk on China." In the tale Stella—a character very much drawn on Phyllis herself—answers the door of her flat to a little Catholic chaplain in Allied uniform just back from her island as she is rushing out to give a lecture to the girls at a progressive school. She invites him to come along. The richly nuanced story moves from the feminist message of Stella's lecture on Chinese girlhood ("this is new China, where girls are becoming free and equal at last . . . as good as any boy, and as brave") to the soul-searching little priest's confession of his hopeless love for Stella's colored cousin Mirabelle. Phyllis self-mockingly recalls with some dismay the voices of those who teased her for her blind enthusiasms ("After all, Chiang is only another dictator—almost feudal . . . the women in the interior are not even liberated yet"), echoed in Father Grolier's green eyes, "which said as clearly as possible that some girls would be happier embroidering dragons than struggling for equality." But the story also captures her romantic disregard for the negative aspects of the causes she embraced; she could remain single-mindedly focused on the ideals of the Chinese revolution despite her rational understanding of its imperfections in practice, as she remained blind to the Republican army's own ideological contradictions and abuses during the Spanish Civil War. As Father Grolier comments to Stella, "When you spoke to those children you seemed to be in love with a whole country—with the Chinese people—with the world. When I heard your voice—sounding so much in love with the great masses of unknown people, I thought to myself Bon Dieu, she may be in love with the masses, but I am in love with an individual, with Mirabelle."

During the war Phyllis kept open house for the many Dominicans who had come to England to help in the war effort. Her apartment became a gathering place for homesick islanders who had joined the army, Royal Air Force, or ATS (Auxiliary Territorial Service). Among them was another Dominican poet, Edward Scobie, then in the army, a close friend of her cousin Alexis Nicholls (one of Uncle Ralph's sons), with whom he would often stay at Phyllis's flat. These gatherings kept Phyllis abreast of developments at home and made her somewhat of a leader of the fledgling Dominican community in London, since she had the contacts, through her Labour party membership and her affiliation with the Fabian Colonial Committee, to persuade MPs to take up matters of interest to the island in the House of Commons. Throughout the war she eagerly awaited letters from home. Sandwiched between Guadeloupe and Martinique, both of which had been forced to accept the Vichy government, Dominica was increasingly isolated. Fearing that German submarines were refueling in the French islands, Allied or neutral countries were afraid of putting their ships into port there. Dominica, a British possession, had to honor British policy toward French refugees and accepted several thousand people fleeing Martinique and Guadeloupe. The newcomers' demand for a daily meal of meat, for which the Dominican peasantry was generously reimbursed, led to the slaughter of most of the cattle on the island, with devastating consequences for the island's agriculture. Kingsland House, now run by Maggie as an inn, became the headquarters of the Antillean Free French troops. Their sojourn, as described by Maggie in her letters, was recorded by Phyllis in a short story entitled "Proserpeena and the Colonel," a charming tale of a servant girl who gathers together an "army" of refugees for a forlorn French colonel stranded in Dominica without a command.

In November 1943 Robert wrote Phina a long Christmas letter in which he carefully explained why, although quite a number of children had returned to England from America, she and Philip were to remain with the Pulsifers a while longer. Schools were in disarray because most male teachers had been called up, they expected the Nazis to blitz London again, and with him and Phyllis working all day there would be no one to look after them. Added to these was the fact that though children could come back as far as Lisbon fairly easily, from there on transport was very difficult. "In any case you are well and happy, and getting on so well in school that it would not be fair on you to uproot you from your present life. I expect you realise how wonderful it has been of Uncle Harold and Aunt Susan to have you and look after you as if you were both their own children." The letter sheds light on aspects of life with the children of which he and Phyllis had deprived themselves by sending them to the United States, especially those concerning Philip. "You can probably tell us more about Phil than anyone so do try and give us an impression of what sort of a boy he has become. Tell us if you can skate, ski, ride horseback or do any of those things and how well? . . . You see what a lot of things we want to know? What books have you read lately and what subjects do you like best at school? . . . I can tell you that you are never for one moment forgotten, we are full of love for you both and looking forward and working hard towards the day when we will all be together again."

Her separation from the children left Phyllis "bereft." In 1941 she had written to Jean Rhys that she "miss[ed] her children *so* much that [she] could not write to them anymore." It troubled her that Philip called Susan "Mother"—Phina had to keep reminding him that his real mother was in England—and she anguished over ever seeing them again. In "Scraps of Paper," an unpublished short story, she imagines what it would be like for a young man like Philip to return to England to trace scraps of information about his dead mother. The young protagonist, a seventeen-year-old boy with "the taste of New England cream and wild strawberries" in his mouth "and on his cheeks a slap of Maine salt," had been too young to receive any real letter from his mother and had nothing left from her but picture postcards and little presents in matchboxes. (While the children were in the United States, Phyllis and Robert used to send them diminutive presents in matchboxes "a whole collection of those . . . [a]nimals of glass and sometimes wood . . . [a]bout half-an-inch big.") The boy's search for his mother leads him to "one of the ugliest parts of London," where two kindly librarians had saved the scraps of paper his mother left in her borrowed books. They hold the key to the character of "the most impatient young woman" they ever saw, one who "could hardly bear to wait for anything: a new book of poems, or the end of the war, or the warm weather . . . or seeing [him] again." She would blow into the library "like a warm wind on a winter's day . . . and . . . would cry, 'oh how much longer will *everything* take!'" She had sent him away because "she wanted [him] to be world-minded. . . . to have the very best of the new world and of the old. She was very greedy on her son's behalf."

In "Babes in the Woods," perhaps the most autobiographical of all of her stories, she voices her grief at the children's absence: "She had wanted Mark to grow as fast as a poplar tree, and now that he was wolfing down all that American cream and butter it became unbearable to see from the pictures how his knees knubbled out of his babyish trousers." Phyllis's jealousy of Susan's relationship with Philip is seen here in full force. Glancing at a photograph of the American foster mother and the children, Mrs. Pennley ruminates: "The foster mother's dress was black velvet, well cut; she had what English people call a fair amount of money. But no fortune could justify the sums that she had spent on Stella and Mark, trying to give them everything to make them happy, that they would not miss their home, and that they would grow up fine and strong. Tonsils and adenoids were the only things which were lost; everything else was gained: playmates, books, music, food, toys, clothes—a new full life in beautiful surroundings. But all that the foster-mother did for the children made her seem more formidable, more someone to be feared for her giving as well as loved." Her palpable grief over what she saw as her loss of Philip to Susan is responsible for the story's most poignant passages. "But there was that look—there was that look between Mark and the American mother, an unpurchasable look of trust so exquisite that it was impossible not to shake clear of personal grief and think into the future: what about the days when the children leave *her*? What about that other dreadful day? The long sweet regard between Mark and his new mother could not be annulled by parting." She had indeed lost precious years with her son, and this separation would haunt her for the rest of her life. As his mental illness progressed in his late teens, and because of the limited understanding of schizophrenia at the time, his separation from his mother would be blamed for his troubles. It would leave Phyllis with an almost unbearable burden of guilt. Philip's peculiarities, already evident when he was a toddler, became more pronounced in the years he spent in the United States. They may have contributed to Susan's protectiveness toward him, especially as he had grown into a little boy with many likes and dislikes, such as distinct and idiosyncratic aversions to certain foods. He would readily eat his meat and dessert, but no threats would prompt him to eat his vegetables or drink milk. No one thought of him as ill, then, but as rather "peculiar," odd, and withdrawn. Easily distracted and often in a faraway daydream, he was still marked by the musing, distant quality Phyllis had observed when he was a small child. But he grew to share two of Harold's loves, trout fishing and chess, which Harold taught him to play and to which he took very enthusiastically. It was the only thing at which he would ever excel; after his return to England he was to become a junior chess champion in London.

"Babes in the Wood" also addresses Phyllis's relationship with Phina, depicted here as "a little girl whose portrait-face was already infused with the marvelous quality of becoming a woman, wise and poised and surely beautiful beyond her years." Staring at a photograph of her daughter, Mrs. Pennley "realise[d] acutely that she was missing a link in the most objective relationship possible—the relationship between a mother and her daughter." The six-year separation from her parents had not been Phina's first; she had spent close to a year in Dominica as an infant without her parents. While she was with the Pulsifers, Phyllis kept up a "stream of letters," but they were a poor substitute for a parent's presence. It could be argued that these lengthy separations allowed Phina few opportunities to bond with her parents, but despite Phyllis's concerns, the girl was by all accounts a very happy, well-adjusted, and secure child. She had many friends, did very well in school, and grew into a bright, self-confident, and very pretty adolescent. Her surviving letters from the United States speak of a very tender, solicitous regard for Robert and a warm affection for Phyllis, mingled with a recognition of her mother's livelier personality. She seemed to identify with Robert's position as the overshadowed half of the parental pair. Her early "autobiography" (begun in Maine—at her father's prompting, as a record of her life when they were apart—when she was ten) offers glimpses of her relationship with her parents: "When you look out of my window you see a big garden in the square far below [she is describing their apartment in Fulham], and at night the square is lined with twinkly lights. . . . I stand on my bed and cool my nose on the window pane and stare at those curtains. Beds and furniture and houses mean a great deal to Daddy and me, but Mummum likes books and views better." And later—"I mean to write a little short chapter called 'The early life of my father' and another much longer one called 'The early days of my mother'. The reason for the difference in the chapters is that Mummum talks more about her early days than Daddy does. This is because Mummy was born on an island, while Daddy was just an English schoolboy. People who are born on small islands generally have lots and lots to write and talk about."

The children returned home in early 1946. Philip was almost eleven; Phina, fifteen. Susan, Harold, and their children drove them to Montreal, where they were met by Robert. The trip was an ordeal for Susan, who was very fond of both children, particularly of Philip, whom she had had in her care since he was five. After dropping them off at the train station, Susan went back to her hotel and wrote a very long letter to Phyllis detailing Philip's many idiosyncrasies, and exhorting her to take care of him. Susan thought, justifiably, that Phyllis would welcome any details that would help her cope with a child as troublesome as Philip had become, especially after a six-year separation. But her close relationship with Philip was obviously a thorn in Phyllis's flesh, and Susan got a very stiff letter for her pains, one that indignantly reminded her old friend that she did not need to be told how to take care of her own son.

The children's adjustment to London was difficult. The Pulsifers were rich, and they came back to working parents whose ways they were unfamiliar with and to a neighborhood so bombed out that it was "close to a slum." Phyllis got them two kittens, Winkles and Michelle, to help them settle in, but they seemed poor consolation for all they had left behind in the United States. In the best middle-class English tradition, Phyllis and Robert placed their hopes for their children in their education. Phina, always a good student, went to the prestigious Godolphin Day School, possibly on a partial scholarship, where she thrived; but Philip, who attended the local council school, was "miserably unhappy." As he entered adolescence it became increasingly obvious to Phyllis that her tall, slim, handsome son was fighting demons she knew nothing about. He was not very communicative and she could read very little from his absent look and lack of interest in things around him, but his very silence troubled her. He kept everything bottled up—his troubles at school, his fears and angers, his emotional turmoil—until the pressure built to bursting point and he would have fits of incoherent rage. Phina's adjustment was complicated by the fact that she returned to England an adolescent, in a state of rebellion against authority, parental authority foremost. It manifested itself in a deepening of her relationship with her father, the weaker parent, and a mixture of love, anger, and rivalry toward Phyllis, the stronger-willed one, and the one who loved her most possessively. Writing *In the Cabinet* shortly after Phina's premature death, Phyllis addressed the stresses of her relationship with her daughter (called Andrina in the text): "I had wanted her to be and do the things which I lacked. I was born with a brain and a quantum of beauty; she had a marvelous brain and a superabundance of beauty. I had no true education; she had a classical one. What she needed was protection, for her gifts to grow slowly in grace. But protection she seldom had—not in her diversified and poverty-handicapped childhood, her adolescence (though perhaps that was more protected), nor in her marriage." Edward observes that Andrina's decision to work in Africa after her graduation from Oxford stemmed from her desire to be free of them because of her "great rivalry" with her mother, called Joan in the text. "She wanted to shake off comparisons," he says. "You may well be right," Joan replies. "I remember clearly the day she invited those Cambridge men to tea, and asked me gently whether I could possibly go to the cinema! Which I did, of course. And when I was halfway over the Thames bridge, I heard running footsteps and she flung her arms around me, saying: 'Oh Mummum, oh Joan, don't go to the movies! Come back! Be witty! Be devastating! Spoil my teaparty! I love you!'" Phina, by all accounts a beautiful, intelligent, and polished young woman, often found it painfully frustrating to be continually overshadowed by her mother, despite her own greater beauty and academic accomplishments. Her mother, however, now in her late thirties, had the allure of the unusual. She added to her exotic background a gift for storytelling; literary talent; a passionate, romantic idealism captured in her movements and in her "perfectly modulated voice"; and more than her share of energy and élan. Phyllis overshadowed her daughter as she overshadowed Robert. He took his invisibility in his stride; for a young woman coming into her own—even one as self-assured as Phina—it was a more difficult task.

If anything, Phyllis would become a more formidable rival in the years to come. In 1946, when Phina returned from the United States, her mother was busier than ever. After many years in the beleaguered opposition, the Labour party had finally managed to win the general election of 1945 and formed a government with Clement Attlee as prime minister. Her friend Dilys Henrik Jones, a fellow Labour supporter, remembers "the sense of Euphoria when the Attlee government came to power; we all had a Wordsworthian feeling [that] 'Bliss was it in that dawn to be alive'." Phyllis found work as a secretary to various Labour MPs in the House of Commons. She wrote in *In the Cabinet* about how she used to dash through the Underground approach to the British House of Commons used by members and staff of what was her favorite London institution:

> At one time I had a permit enabling me to enter the House through a sort of catacombs arch: I did a part-time job for a Labour M.P. there. It was a privilege to cut through that tunnel with the great roar of traffic above, studying the gait and expressions of M.P.s who went about the nation's business. Twice I walked solemnly along in imitation of Lord Attlee, who was a few yards ahead and had a newspaper in his overcoat and his hands clasped behind his back. The Policemen then in the House knew me well by sight and one (who was a stamp collector) used invariably to ask: "how's that island?"

The job was the source of many useful contacts in the Labour party, which would be helpful in the foundation of the Dominica Labour Party. The familiarity with the MPs at the House of Commons and their staff gave Phyllis a status as unofficial lobbyist for her Fulham neighborhood and the Dominican community in London. Through her Labour contacts, Phyllis had also been appointed a school governor in the Borough of Fulham, an appointment that was not a complete success, given her impatience and lack of familiarity with the typically conservative and snail-paced school bureaucracy. She was to refer, rather humorously, to her experiences as a school governor in "Governor Pod," a story for children about an island child who, after many years in England, returns home to be elected governor. In England Pod had been made a school governor: "The school-children loved having Pod as a Governor, and wrote all their demands to him. Some of their wishes were not very sensible, and soon Pod found himself having quarrels with other Governors. There was one Lady Governor who tried to get rid of him. . . . And finally the Lady discovered the awful truth that *Pod had never been to school*! So she told everybody, 'how can we have a School Governor who isn't even *educated*?' And poor Pod got a letter asking him to quit being a governor. He was terribly sad!"

After the war Phyllis's involvement with the Colonial Bureau intensified as discussions of independence for the West Indies became foremost. Her connection with the Colonial Bureau afforded her an early education in the social problems the developing nations of the Caribbean would confront in later years. It also placed her in an enviable position of influence and authority in the Dominican community in exile, from which the idea of playing an active role in the political transformation of her native colony would emerge. After the new Labour government took office in 1945, the bureau's influence increased significantly. It was generally agreed that through the Colonial Bureau, the Fabian Society "could claim that in affairs colonial its influence had played no small part in formulating policy which was actually carried out." This position left it open to criticism from those who wanted to go "faster and farther" to meet the demands of colonial territories than the bureau was prepared to move. Its gradual, evolutionary approach made it vulnerable to charges of being "the home of inevitable gradualism" and "hopelessly reactionary." These charges notwithstanding, it was generally praised for its diligent efforts to provide a framework for decolonization in Africa and the West Indies. To Phyllis it was the source of an invaluable political education that was to pay off during the early 1950s.

Shortly after the children's return, in August 1946, Phyllis's family had a reunion in England. Her mother, Elfreda; her Aunt Mags; her oldest sister, Marion; and Marion's three sons—David Eliot, Mark, and Henry Bradshaw—rented a house in Hurst Green, Sussex, for six months. From there they went to visit Rosalind and George at Cob Cottage before returning to Dominica. It was the family's first reunion since Phyllis's visit to Dominica in 1932, and it offered the three sisters in England some respite from the tensions they had lived under during the war. Rosalind, whose husband, George, was a naval officer, had spent most of the war fearful for her husband's safety. So had Celia. Her husband Jack, Robert's brother, also a naval officer, had had a very strenuous war, serving as personal secretary to Lord Fraser of North Cape, commander in chief of the British North Atlantic fleet during the last stages of the war. (The strain on Jack had been enormous, and he developed a serious heart ailment from which he would die a few years later, following an operation.) It was a joyous reunion for the grandchildren, of whom there were now eight: Phyllis's two; Celia's son, Francis; Rosalind's young daughter, Wendy, and baby son, Anthony; Marion's sons David, five-year-old Mark, and fifteen-month-old Henry. The visit was partly intended as a diversion for Marion, who had recently divorced her second husband, Wilfred Bradshaw, whom she married after E. C. Eliot's death, and whom everyone considered to be "below her." Phyllis called him "the wicked brother-in-law" and felt that Marion had had a "dreadful life" with him. Bradshaw reputedly abused her—or so Phyllis hinted in a letter to Adèle—and Marion had left him while her youngest son was still an infant. Marion's unlucky marriages were in sharp contrast to her sisters' more fortunate unions. Rosalind's young marriage was thriving; she had found in George a congenial, agreeable companion, as gregarious as herself. Phyllis and Robert—his peculiarities and lack of professional success notwithstanding—were reputedly devoted to each other. Celia had been very fortunate in Jack, who was universally acknowledged to be "the nicest of men," accommodating, lively, and always entertaining. Their happiness cast Marion's troubled marital history in a poignant light. Phyllis, who had not seen her sister for years, was to find her very changed. She drank more than was advisable and seemed "a bit crazed by it all." Phyllis, characteristically, would eventually write a story about her sister's troubles, "The Untanglers," in which she revealed the lurid details of a marriage gone dreadfully wrong. She claimed that she had toned down the story quite a bit, feeling that "if [she] had written the tale as it really was, no one would have printed it." She made sure that Marion never saw it.

In 1947 Robert found a job with the Parker Pen Company, where he was responsible for bringing the technology for the ball-point pen to England. It was the most promising job of his career, and their friends thought it could have made his fortune. That year, while traveling on company business, he visited the Pulsifers in Maine. Jonathan, the older of Susan's two sons, remembers him from this visit as an "odd stick," a man with the greatest facility to antagonize people. He had often heard him described by his parents as a man who had had good jobs and had always managed literally to talk himself out of them. He was soon to talk himself out of his present one, again because of his intolerance of authority and his insistence that things should be done his way. Harold was to broach the subject with Robert at least once during his visit, taking him to task for a lack of diplomacy that sometimes bordered on brutal frankness. "I'll say what I please," was Robert's characteristic reply. During the course of the visit Susan asked if Philip was eating enough, a question prompted by the child's idiosyncratic problems with food—she remembered well how he would only eat foods of certain colors on specified days. Robert, "with his usual knack for antagonizing people," replied that "Philip was certainly eating well, as England now had a Labour government to take care of those matters." The Pulsifers visited England shortly after Robert's return. For Susan and Harold it would be their last trip abroad—Harold had only one year to live. Phyllis's political ardor was to supply one of Jonathan's most indelible memories of the trip. She came to see them one afternoon bringing with her what to Susan seemed a heavily slanted Labour party paper (most probably *Tribune*). When Susan commented that the paper's opinions were very strong, Phyllis, impulsive as ever, jumped up and ran out of the house, coming back shortly thereafter with a copy of the *Times*, as if to say that perhaps there she could get a balanced opinion. To Jonathan, Phina and Philip complained that Phyllis continued to be an avid protester and dragged them to demonstrations, whether they wanted to go or not.

The final years of the decade were marred by the first indications of Philip's developing mental illness. By 1948, when he was fourteen, he had begun to show signs of the psychological problems that would lead to his eventual confinement. Phyllis's pride in his success as a chess player was mingled with growing concern about his stability. Harold's unexpected and premature death from a heart attack came as a major blow, severing a vital link to what was perhaps the most tranquil period in his life. That year he spent part of his school holiday at Cob Cottage, Rosalind's home in the quaint seaside village of Old Bosham, in West Sussex. Despite his dreamy absentmindedness she asked him to keep an eye on her young children while she ran some errands, but she returned earlier than expected to find that he had left the house, leaving the children alone. At the end of the visit she put him on the train to London, and seeing him so absorbed in daydreams, asked the conductor to keep an eye on him and make sure he got off at the proper station. Philip overheard her and never forgave her. Phina, on the other hand, was thriving. She had done extremely well in school, and upon graduation in 1949 had been granted an interview for admission to Oxford, Robert's alma mater. Phyllis was thrilled, and drove her almost insane with good advice, following her around with a clothes brush saying things like, "Now don't forget it is more important to get into High-house than it is to get married, for if you marry a bad man you can always leave him, whereas the influence of High-house will be with you all your life." She also warned her not to go "gadding" with girls she knew at Oxford. Phina was admitted, despite her faulty Latin and having arrived three and a half hours late to her interview because she was in fact "gadding" with her friends. She would graduate with second- rather than first-class honors because she "fooled around rather a lot, climbing the wall to attend balls."

After the war the London public libraries formed a Readers' Circle, which met once a month for a literary talk or discussion. Two of Phyllis's friends, George Horner and Dilys Henrik Jones, were on the committee at the local library, and Phyllis was frequently called on, as a local poet, to participate, either as chairman or speaker. In 1949 she took the chair for Walter Marsden, a young and very promising local writer who had just won the Somerset Maugham Award and whom Phyllis greatly encouraged. She also acted as chair during a poetry reading by John Betjeman, then not as widely popular as he would later become, but yet the object of a devoted cult following, which guaranteed a large audience. Phyllis did not care for his work, which she thought "trivial and lightweight," and after the meeting had told Dilys that she had been "astonished to realise from his expression that the emotion in [his] love poems was deeply sincere." Very often the Readers' Circle meetings ended with a small reception at Phyllis's flat. The only one she remembered as having drawn party crashers was given in honor of C. P. Snow and his wife, Pamela Hansford Johnson, when the flat became so crowded that they had to drink their Irish whiskey in the kitchen with their backs against the walls. A particularly entertaining one, as Dilys remembers, was given in honor of Patric Dickinson, producer of poetry programs for the BBC. Phyllis had asked him if he knew anything about the latest row at the Poetry Society—then and since liable to cataclysmic literary quarrels. Dickinson, who had been called in as peacemaker at one point, enlarged on the happenings, which centered around the then-little-known figure of Muriel Spark, who as editor of the magazine had selected works on merit rather than picking those by the committee's friends. His version of the events was "vivid and probably libellous."

One of the Readers' Circle guests was a close friend and probable lover of Phyllis's—A. E. Coppard, considered by many to be England's best short-story writer. Coppard, born in 1878 in humble circumstances, left school at the age of nine and pursued an early interest in literature, painting, and music. In his late thirties he resigned his job as an office clerk in Oxford to pursue a career as a writer. His first collection of stories, *Adam and Eve and Pinch Me* (1921), appeared to wide acclaim when he was forty-three. He went on to publish various volumes of short stories and poetry distinguished for their poetic feeling for the English country landscape and amusing depictions of rustic characters. Phyllis had read his work in the early 1940s and been so impressed that she had taken what she thought was an unusual step in writing to let him know how much she enjoyed his work. As she told Pixie, "Writers must enjoy hearing how people have reacted to their work." Pixie still recalls Phyllis's excitement at the initial meeting with Coppard, from which flowed "a long steady intellectually supportive relationship" and almost certainly a love affair. Flynn, as he was known to his friends, a ruggedly handsome sixty-three-yer-old, joined her circle of friends and became her mentor. It was the first and only time that she would have as a friend a professional writer who could guide the development of her writing skills. The thrust of his advice was for her "to be more ruthless and selfish in her private life if she wanted to succeed as an author." To Robert's discomfiture, they became frequent companions, often traveling together, visiting friends and relatives, or enjoying Phyllis's retreat at Penhurst. Once they toured England's Lake District. The scenery, as she would recall later, "did not stir the poetry in [her] half as much as was expected." In comparison to the splendid mountains of Dominica, the English mountains seemed "bare and craggy." Their friendship lasted till his death in 1957, despite a serious "falling out" in 1953, when she announced that she was returning to Dominica. She burned his letters at his request, leaving the exact nature of their relationship in doubt. When writing her second (to-this-day-unpublished) novel, *Dashing Away*, in 1953, Phyllis modeled the character of her protagonist's elderly lover on Flynn Coppard, thus adding to the speculation of many of her friends that they were romantically involved. When he died at 79 in London in 1957 she was devastated.

In the late 1940s Phyllis and Robert purchased Penhurst, a dilapidated old country house near Battle. Built in stone, the cottage was a rather rambling, broken-down nineteenth-century-style English farmhouse, a "large long low collection of more than one building" surrounded by brambles and weeds, "way in the wild," and completely inaccessible by road. It could be reached only through the courtesy of the local farmer, who let them leave their car at his farm and walk the three-quarters of a mile or so between the road and the house over his fields. One made one's way from the road "slithering and sliding down the muddy path to the pond and then scrambling up the bank" where one found more mud before "the mellow grey house emerged from the stark trees silent, still and watchful." After fighting one's way through the "primary forest of the garden, in which the brilliant yellow daffodils and the white and orange narcissus, and the primroses and emerging blue bells shone and lightened the browns of the dry grass and dead vegetation," one would squeeze through the narrow gap in the box hedge and step onto the veranda. Installing oneself in the cottage often took several such trips through fields and woods on foot to fetch food, drink, and luggage. Water came from a well, there was no electricity, and one had to search out and chop wood for the fire. They had bought Penhurst for next to nothing, but it needed many repairs and they never had the money to do them properly. The cottage, however, had a decided charm, and Phyllis developed an almost mystical attachment to it. Friends like Ronald Benge, a Fulham librarian who was a frequent guest at Penhurst, found it to be a "fascinating place in the best Phyllis 'romantic' tradition." His then wife Margaret still remembers it as idyllic, a place she regretted not being able to buy when it was offered for purchase. Phyllis called it "a wonderful old haunted house" and made much of the resident ghost, an old lady allegedly burned to death. Ronald suspected that she had made up the legend of the ghost, but he would allow, with Margaret's corroboration, that there was often an inexplicable smell of burning in the night, particularly on the front terrace. Phyllis's poem "The Hidden Hamlet" captures the magic she found in this "house that does not wish to be found," with its lintel "smothered in a pall of wild white roses." She saw the dilapidated buildings as crouching "into the ground/that dwarfish trees may hide them." At Penhurst she would write *The Orchid House*.

Part III

HOUSE OF TODAY

Ah, but house—
Standing secure and still,
Snug and escapist in
The little curve of the hill—
That is the life of wood,
Of wood and stone,
But not the ardent life
of blood and bone.

Five

Return

Coming back to my house
from which I had been absent
so long, so long,
I found it ravaged of all
save you, my shrine and my song.
Savage the winds rake:
yet the bamboo does not break.

Phyllis's most cherished ambitions—literary and political—crystallized in the 1950s. It would be her decade of toil and triumph. She would write and publish *The Orchid House*, found the Dominica Labour party, run two arduous yet ultimately victorious political campaigns, and become a minister in the West Indies Federation. Yet all her triumphs would be overshadowed by pain and loss. Her son would be committed to a psychiatric hospital for life, her literary career would founder under the pressures of her political work, her marriage of almost thirty years—threatened by her passionate devotion to her party—would nearly come to an end. As the 1960s dawned, the Federation would collapse and she would face expulsion from the party that had been to her "like a firstborn." She would realize her dreams, only to see them dissolve like salt crystals dropped into water.

Yet the decade opened auspiciously, with her being awarded second prize in an international poetry competition sponsored by the Society of Women Writers and Journalists. Vita Sackville-West, a writer connected to the Bloomsbury set, whom she greatly admired, had been among the judges. The prize, modest as it would seem, was to make *The Orchid House* possible. The prize winning text, "While the Young Sleep," had appeared in her recently published *Palm and Oak* (1950), which gathered the poems she had written in the late 1940s, plus one, "Colonial Committee," published in *Tribune* during the war. Like *In Circles* ten years before, this second collection was published privately and attracted little notice outside her circle of friends and acquaintances. It was a slim volume that nonetheless marked an important shift in her poetic themes and approaches. Its title, *Palm and Oak*, represented the two strains of her ancestry, "nordic and tropic," the tropical being foremost. Two of the poems address the theme of exile, an increasingly important personal and political issue for her, as the first wave of West Indian immigrants to London in the late 1940s forced her to confront her own status as an expatriate. The poems reflected the growing importance of her work as the unofficial social worker for the fledgling West Indian community in London. *Palm and Oak* opened with a poem titled "Exiles," her meditation on how, while "[l]iving in sunless reaches, under rain/. . . the exiles from enchanted isles/tend and sustain their rich nostalgic blaze." The subject is echoed in two other poems: "The True-Born Villager," in which she encapsulates the philosophy of life of those who, transplanted to a new world, have the "alchemy to turn flats into cottages!"; and "Changeling," in which she captures the bewilderment of a child "translated into a strange and unfamiliar grove" where she "mimicked [her watchers'] hereditary ways" while yearning to return to her familiar abode: "Yet always lurked the fear that in a snatch/the changeling child would vanish as she came;/within that secret grove her friends could catch/the trivial echoes of an earth-bound name."

Palm and Oak contains some of her best and most mature poetry. It is also the most introspective of her poetry collections, one clearly assembled at an impasse at which she questions the relevance of her political work ("Resistance"), explores the futility of lifeless art ("The Ivory Rose") and the inner agony of poetic creation ("Poet's Cottage"), and probes the ambivalences of her maternal love ("While the Young Sleep"). The unifying motif of the collection is precisely the questioning of those tenets that she had held dear and that in the late 1940s—her daughter nearing adulthood, the intensity of her political work ebbing, the consciousness of herself as an exile escalating—seemed no longer to sustain her or give certainty to her life. In "Resistance" she questions her "living outside [her]self," braving "other men's dangers, terror and defeat," stirring unwillingly to read "the grooved frown which speaks divided loyalty." In "Ivory Rose" she writes of the freezing of love into an ivory rose, "chiselled to wear at the breast" like a "silent swan effigy on black silk lake," "being carved beauty . . . fractured by ripples like a star in mud/over which human shadows cross and waver." In "Poet's Cottage" she writes of Coleridge and Wordsworth as two opposite poles of creativity, one craving the bright and healthy, but seeing "flowers as weeds and weeds as opiates," the other escaping "into the yellow sunshine, having claimed the daffodil and daisy as his own." The disparities between them are built in the poem upon evocations of the domestic sphere, where "children were begotten cozily/while the huge mind embraced another love," and where Wordsworth wrote "heedless of clamour and of cooking smells from the dim dungeon kitchen," while Coleridge's spirit "still lingers . . ./bitterly envious of domestic bliss." The poet's ambivalence toward the domestic is central to her prize winning poem, which is excellent in conveying a mother's eager withdrawal into the "marvelous freedom of a lonely room" when her children at long last fall sleep. Its power stems from its interweaving of the mother's contradictory emotions: her love for her children, vividly conveyed in the tenderness of the descriptions of their sleeping bodies and of the "tangled débris" of their books, toys, and clothes; and the exhilaration of her escape "from heights of your demands/into a vale where it is still and warm":

> Marvelous freedom of a lonely room,
> treasures at handsreach dormant, all the past
> in the slow downsweep of a silver brush
> through burnished hair . . . banished the lively fume
> of growth and challenge, now at this languid last
> comes self-remembrance in delicious hush.

As the decade opened Phyllis seemed "pulled between the role models of Virginia Woolf and Beatrice Webb," one an exacting craftsperson known for the "intense excitement and effort" she put into her work, the other, with husband Sidney, a pioneer in British social and economic reform and a leading spirit of the Fabian Society. Phyllis favored Webb's role, while yearning for Woolf's meticulous attention to technique and total dedication to her art, attributes she also admired in Rhys. But Phyllis was very unlike the latter: She could not distance herself from life—and life always meant politics. "She had politics in her veins" and an overpowering need to be "a part of everything" that ran counter to a writer's thirst for isolation. And she held everyone to the same standards. On one occasion she reproved her friend George Horner, "a completely apolitical fellow whose loves were theatre and film, for preferring art to life." Yet during the late 1940s and early 1950s Phyllis had begun to focus her attention and energies on her literary career. The political lull of the relatively prosperous postwar years, with Labour in power and a growing economy, had meant a respite for the British Left, weary of the intense struggles of the 1930s and 1940s. Her contributions to the Readers' Circle kept her literary persona in the foreground and opened opportunities for building a network of contacts with other progressive writers. Her membership in the Writers' Guild and Society of New Authors suggested ways in which politics and literature could be integrated. The Writers' Guild brought together an odd assortment of professional and amateur writers of Leftist persuasions—reviewers, children's story writers, reporters, poets—all sharing an interest in meeting in a friendly spirit to discuss one another's work and offer support. The group would often gather at her Fulham flat and occasionally visit Penhurst. It had even formed a small press to publish members' work. Phyllis's "The Untanglers," the tale of Marion's marital woes, was published as a booklet under the auspices of the guild.

The award for "While the Young Sleep" brought her a level of recognition that had previously eluded her. Although her short fiction and poetry had appeared in well-known and respected newspapers and magazines, she was virtually unrecognized as a writer outside of Fulham. She still worked without an agent and had herself borne the cost of publishing her two volumes of poetry. This was all to change. The awards were presented at a ceremony at the Lord Mayor's Show (then as now, an annual event showcasing the best London has to offer), and there she was approached by a woman she remembered as a "bleached blonde lady" from the Curtis Brown literary agency who wanted particularly to know whether Phyllis had ever written a novel. She acknowledged that she had indeed for some time been trying her hand at a novel about home:

> The idea of *The Orchid House* had been simmering in my heart for several years. The big leap was transferring it from my heart to the mind, and then to paper, without damaging the simple emotional language of the narrator, a "book-taught English-speaking negress." Every time I began a new day's work I had to vault the Atlantic Ocean and land in the Caribbean Sea, and I had to jump out of my own skin and into the heroine, Lally's. It was easier to leap the Atlantic Ocean, as part of me had clung with tenacity to the sights, sounds and smells of my birthplace. I had only to close my eyes to be there in an instant; and the rich, oily scent of a squeezed lime would evoke a whole trail of images and possibilities.

Yet readers who have delighted in *The Orchid House* can not envision how close the novel came to not being written at all. Like those portentous events that depend on almost serendipitous alignments of the stars, *The Orchid House* needed the convergence of myriad factors to emerge from reams of notes into a text. But the stars were propitious: Philip was in school,* increasingly unstable but not yet obviously psychotic; Phina was at Oxford, happy, in love with the man she would shortly marry, not spectacularly successful academically but coming into her own; Robert was employed; and, most important, there were no political crises or national emergencies to draw her toward her first love, politics. "Politics ruined me for writing," she would wistfully write in her poverty-stricken old age; but in 1950 there were no politics for her, and she blossomed as a writer. Robert urged her to seize the moment, and she began writing in earnest, spending long periods at Penhurst diligently working and reworking the text. She "slogged away at it until she finished it."

Phyllis's letters, writings, and interviews gloss over the period during which *The Orchid House* was written. Sketchily outlined, in retrospect, the process seemed simple enough. There was peace and therefore time to be homesick; she was homesick, therefore she wrote a novel about home. But as is true of such things, the reality was more complex. Her continuing work at the Fabian Colonial Committee drew her thoughts continually toward her island home. As the West Indies began their slow quest for independence, countless political and economic possibilities were proposed and considered by the bureau. And she was steeped in detailed knowledge of the concerns facing the region, whose most progressive political leaders she counted among her friends.

Through the bureau she met all delegations from the West Indies and participated in ongoing discussions and negotiations. She worked often as part of the bureau's liaison to the House of Commons. She had a detailed grasp of the forces that were transforming Caribbean politics—the shifting of the balance of power toward the working class; the central role of labor unions in the formation of party politics in the region; the evolving plans for a West Indian Federation, of which she was a steadfast supporter; the difficulties awaiting the colonial territories in establishing independent economies after attaining dominion status; the increasingly resonant calls for full independence. Politically Phyllis was committed to working toward a meaningful independence that would guarantee workers an influential role in the new autonomous governments ready to step in to replace the bureaucracy of empire. A dream of seizing the moment and reestablishing her family's name in West Indian affairs slowly began to take hold during this crucial period in Caribbean history, and she began seeing herself increasingly as playing an active role in these approaching changes. Yet another side of her held to a romantic ideal of the world she had known in childhood, a world that in her eyes had possessed a rare beauty, and that provided the links to West Indian history so important to her sense of self. That world—she well understood its evils—had to give way to the politically just society she was determined to struggle for. This contradiction she resolved in a Janus-like work that combined her nostalgia for a life about to disappear and the process through which the death of that

*In an interview about the writing of the novel, Phyllis mentions that he was at a boarding school, but there is no evidence that this was so. Not having been to school herself, and proud of Robert's education at Tonbridge School, she was wont to equivocate about the children's education. At one time Rosalind accompanied her and Philip to tea with an acquaintance who, upon asking what school Philip was enrolled in, was told by Phyllis that he went to Westminster, leaving it to be understood that she meant the prestigious public school. Philip interrupted, explaining, with some exasperation at her snobbish subterfuge, that he went to a school *in* Westminster (the school district to which Fulham belonged), and not to Westminster School.

world could be expedited. "I wanted to write a book about an island," she once explained. "The island is the real hero. It was probably nostalgia. It's a life that's gone now." But that nostalgia was not necessarily regret, and the novel, its lyrical celebration of the island's beauty notwithstanding, will look to the future. It will not be Stella's romantic attachment to the landscape and the past but Joan's proposed alliance between the working class and the sympathetic remnants of the white upper class that will offer hope in the end.

Despite Phyllis's productivity as a poet and short story writer, her literary fortunes, for better or worse, have risen and fallen with those of *The Orchid House*, her only published novel and the only work for which she is known. This is perhaps as it should be; she once told an interviewer that she had thrown her all into the novel: "love, politics, religion, tragedy, and a few gleams of fun." The novel, as narrated by the old nurse Lally, tells the story of three Creole sisters who return to their native island (undoubtedly Dominica, although it is never so named) after years abroad. Stella, attached to the lush tropical landscape by an impassioned yearning, had been pining away in the United States, where she felt trapped in a troubled marriage to a German-American farmer; Joan had lived for years in England, having married a political activist and undergone a thorough education in grassroots politics with the Labour party; Natalie, a wealthy man's young widow, had been living a hedonistic existence abroad. Their childhood, the focus of the first part of the novel, had been a happy one until their father returned from World War I with a severe case of shell-shock that left him dependent on drug-laced cigarettes for stability. He lives for the arrival of his supplier, the ominous Mr. Lilipoulala, and is sustained by the devoted care lavished on him by his wife and Mademoiselle Bosquet, the girls' former French tutor, who has loved him hopelessly for years. His dependence on drugs depletes the family's funds, and they teeter on the brink of financial disaster until Natalie's money restores to them their old estate, L'Aromatique.

Stella, the first to arrive, is profoundly disturbed by the apathy with which her mother and Mademoiselle Bosquet accept her father's drug-induced listlessness, and by the similar passivity with which her childhood friend Andrew wastes away from consumption without the will to seek help. Lally, likewise, accepts the tumor ravishing her body as another natural phenomenon that must do its fatal work undisturbed. Rebelling against this, Stella murders Lilipoulala, oblivious to the fact that the opium is not the underlying cause but a manifestation of her father's condition. She also seeks to provoke Andrew to live for her, bringing her into conflict with her colored cousin Cornélie, Andrew's mistress, and with the priests who had been trying to prevail on Andrew to submit to his fate with Christian resignation and make an honest woman of Cornélie before his death. Soon, however, fearful of growing suspicions of her role in Lilipoulala's murder, Stella returns to the United States, defeated in her purpose of bringing about change, and leaving behind the prospect of despair when her father's current supply of cigarettes runs out. Joan, the second sister to return, comes to assist Baptiste, the son of the family's longtime cook, Christophine, in organizing a labor reform movement in the island. Phyllis modeled the character of Baptiste on that of Christopher Loblack, the energetic Dominica Trade Union organizer of whom she had often heard throughout the 1930s and 1940s and whom she had finally met in 1949, when he had represented Dominica at the International Confederation of Free Trade Unions, held in London. Joan's pragmatic political vision contrasts sharply with

Stella's oversentimental view of the island as a wondrous garden of beauty and decay. Where Stella sees only the astounding resplendence of vegetation in profusion, Joan sees poverty, corruption, exploitation, and the mere shifting of power from white to colored elites without a significant change in the underlying system. She can see the family's predicament not as a manifestation of lack of will, but as a direct result of sociopolitical and economic changes on the island. But her political efforts soon draw the wrath of the Catholic authorities, and she is blackmailed into relinquishing her political work under threat of disclosure of evidence linking her sister Stella to the murder of Mr. Lilipoulala. Having promised the priests to dedicate herself henceforth to her husband and child, she summons the former from England to carry on her political work. Natalie, the youngest of the sisters and the last to arrive, brings her characteristic nonchalant vivacity and the money to expedite change. "Ah, it's essential to be rich," she argues. "All these drippings and dronings and reformations, they don't get you anywhere without good solid cash!" She whisks Andrew away to seek treatment for his consumption and tries to spirit her father away, only to see him die on the airplane taking him from the island, desperately clutching young Ned, Joan's son and the repository of the family's hopes for a continued vital role in island affairs. Natalie's money, moreover, pays Edward's passage to Dominica, making possible the continuation of Joan's efforts at reform.

Phyllis—quite incapable of pure invention in fiction—never wrote anything that could not be traced to an episode she had lived or witnessed herself, or to characters she had known, hated, or loved. But in *The Orchid House* she came closer to her own autobiography than in any other work. In the story of the three daughters of a once powerful but now impoverished white family she recreates her own family's history, interweaving it with the history of Dominica in the twentieth century. Nor had she ever attempted such a sweeping exposition of her own understanding of the Caribbean historical process. Everything in her experiences in the early 1950s, personal and political, pointed to a crossroads: her own as she begins to sever her emotional ties to England and become acutely conscious of her exile; the Caribbean's as the region moves from colonialism to autonomy and beyond. *The Orchid House* is set at this crossroads, and is suffused with Phyllis's recognition that both she and her novel stand at the intersection of West Indian political history, where the colonized take over from the colonizer the direction of local governments, where the black masses take over from their former white and colored masters the reins of political control. *The Orchid House* is thus the story of a society at a turning point, an exploration of the past that aims at dissecting the forces that led the society to its present predicament and at suggesting options for its redirection. In this respect the narrator, Lally, the symbolic repository of a past the island is rapidly leaving behind, becomes a seminal part of her exploration of Dominican history, a living reminder of the path that society has trod. Phyllis was fond of claiming that "*Lally ç'est moi*," a statement she never explained, and one that—her deep emotional attachment to the real-life Lally notwithstanding—is very difficult to take at face value. Lally, if one is to accept the evidence of those who knew both the original and her fictional counterpart, was no one but Lally, a true-to-life portrait of the Shands' old nurse. In choosing her as the narrator—or heroine, as Phyllis repeatedly referred to her—of her novel, she opted for a spokesperson solidly grounded in the status quo, one who serves as a sounding board against which she plays several fictional recreations of her own self, mirroring her and her society's evolution. In Lally she had a static repository of her own and her family's history, an old-fashioned servant, emblematic of a world gone by, who could serve as the standard against which the characters' and the society's changes are measured. Lally can recall the various fictional versions of Phyllis's self to their roots, while she witnesses, at times in bewildered acceptance, what their society have become.

Much has been made here and elsewhere of Phyllis's use of her and her sisters' childhood experiences in the writing of the novel; but while the fictional sisters' myriad adventures were modeled on those of the Shand girls, the characters of Stella and Joan were modeled on two aspects of Phyllis's own personality. Thus Stella, to whom she apportions her own experiences in the United States, becomes the pre-political Phyllis, the one firmly entrenched in the Dominica of the past, thoroughly one with the landscape, passionately connected to its nature, but oblivious to the sociopolitical changes taking place around her, wishing nothing more than for everything to return to what it had once been. Stella, the character closest to the prepolitical Phyllis that Lally knew, is arguably the latter's favorite among the girls. Joan, the English Phyllis, a Stella transformed by politics, understands that a return to the past would be both immoral and intolerable, and that a legitimate role in their home society is only possible for the family if they embrace the people's efforts to take charge of their own political and economic destinies. Throughout the novel she underscores what had become a central tenet of her political thoughts about the Caribbean: that profound changes must take place in the power structures of Caribbean societies to bring social justice to bear, and that those who persevere in seeking to revive the past are doomed. Lally, as a politically unschooled observer, gave her the perfect foil for the presentation of the world she was attempting in the novel—that of the struggle between a nostalgic yearning for a world gone by and the pressing need to do away with the old. Her choice of Lally as a narrator would become the focus of critical controversy. Early reviewers would question the choice because it resulted in some awkward technical difficulties as she tried to maintain the narrative within Lally's limited scope. Later reviewers, most of them West Indian, would take her to task for daring to appropriate the voice of a black woman for her narrative. One of these, Anthony Boxill, once wrote: "Lally's character, is . . . embarrassing. She is too slavishly faithful to her employers, and too sentimentally portrayed to be quite credible."

The Orchid House, given the anticolonial, African-centered ideology that dominated Caribbean criticism in the 1950s and 1960s, was read "racially"—that is, its author's whiteness guided its reading and determined its early fortunes. Hence Stella's passionate romanticism and Lally's obdurate resistance to join the wave of change are seen as emblematic of Phyllis's "conservatism"; Joan's proposed solution to the political impasse, solutions that echoed the author's own and at whose core was the growing movement towards unionization and labor-controlled political development in the region, get lost in early (and even in recent) readings. And Lally—whose perspective as a Montserrat woman and thus a foreigner in Dominica, a Methodist in a Catholic island, an educated black woman who speaks English in a country peopled by a patois-speaking illiterate peasantry, and "the last of the slaves" in a novel about the empowerment of the black population, is that of the quintessential outsider—becomes "a representative of the black race" who "on occasion sound[s] a bit like a colonial lackey longing for the good old days of the Empire." Lally, however, was central to Phyllis's story, despite the technical difficulties she poses as a narrator, because she represents those notions which Joan must help dispel if working class Dominicans are to transcend their present state. Above all, Joan feels, she has to struggle for a relationship of equality with those who, like Lally and Baptiste, had grown too accustomed to treat whites as their social superiors. Joan must struggle against the privilege of whiteness that Lally still holds dear and that prompts Natalie to refer to her in jest as "an early-Victorian white spinster." It is through Joan's political perspective that Lally begins to question the truth of her own social and political notions. Her entry into the novel breaks the family's isolation, revealing its links to the society at large. Her political activism brings to the fore aspects of the society that the family had been oblivious to in its isolation: the corruption that rules the economy and political life of the island, the hypocrisy of the press, the repression of the estate workers, the unyieldingness of the church, the remnants of empire. The impact of her calls for a labor union and political participation by the masses is shown in their power to crack, however slightly, Lally's conservatism: "Sooner or later those words would come through to me. . . . All the same, the meaning behind the talk would never come into my possession—nor would their intention. It was no good my craving to be beside them as they strolled away. The things they so often spoke about were outside my understanding. Only later, when their words had turned into acts and results, would I feel the full thunderclap of my ignorance."

Trinidadian critic Kenneth Ramchand, writing about *The Orchid House* and Rhys's *Wide Sargasso Sea*, speaks of the novels as examples of the "terrified consciousness" that is the "natural stance" of the white West Indian: "The White minority's sensation of shock and disorientation as a massive and smouldering Black population is released into an awareness of its power." Given his prominence as a critic, his commentary has provided perhaps the most influential guide to a reading of *The Orchid House*. But to read it so is to misread it, particularly in the light of Phyllis's life and political views. The "terrified consciousness" he describes is the product of alienation, of a failure to "belong," and the Shands and Nichollses were always certain they "belonged." Moreover, they were a family acutely aware of their position in Dominican society, whose members were guided by a profound albeit paternalistic love for its people. The Nichollses' zeal was for social service, a zeal driven by a deeply entrenched belief in noblesse oblige, which drove Phyllis's commitment to the island and which was modeled on her grandfather's life of service. When she writes in *The Orchid House* about people flocking to Joan's political meeting out of a sense of obligation and deep respect for the memory of the Old Master she is uncannily chronicling her future: Only two years later thousands of Dominican peasants would gather at the Market Place to hear her launch her political party, and she will interpret their enthusiasm as a mark of respect to the memory of Dr. Nicholls.* Forty years later, an old peasant leaning Cerberus-like against the crudely made sign that marks the start of the old Chemin L'Etang at Grand Fond—the most important mountain footpath before the construction of a road, and one Phyllis traveled often during her

*Lennox Honychurch recalls that Phyllis would allude constantly to Dr. Nicholls in her political campaigning, "so as to place herself in the reflected aura of his philanthropy." But his contributions to Dominican society had been made at the turn of the century, and by the 1950s only older people would have had memories of his work.

political campaigns—would pay homage to that Nicholls tradition of service: "Ah, Mrs. Allfrey," he would say, "she was a great lady. She worked hard for the people."

The Nichollses were a family particularly disposed to compromise, to meet Dominica on its own terms. Ralph certainly was, which is why Rufus, his fictional counterpart, in all his mercenary pragmatism, is so important to the text. Offensive to the Nichollses as the character would be, he offers an indispensable link in the novel's portrait of island society. Rufus has given himself to the island, and mercenary and unprincipled as he may seem, has renounced the privileges of whiteness for himself and his children, bridging the racial gap and giving up some of the prerogatives in the island's racial hierarchy that would naturally have been his as a white man. As Joan insists, the whites are no longer the enemy, they have no money and consequently no power—some of them are not even interested in remaining white. Their social world has slowly given way under the siege of the aspirations of the colored elite, but that has not meant an improvement in the peasantry's lot: "The coloured merchants, the educated people," Joan tells Cornélie, "are taking the responsibility over from us—we are now the poor whites, we no longer have any power. But I don't notice any greater tenderness in their attitudes towards those landless, shoeless devils." Rufus would be a particularly sympathetic character—he is rendered with a heavy dose of affection—were he not so willing to serve the true though unlikely villain of the piece, Father Toussaint, a character modeled a bit too realistically, in the opinion of some, on Bishop Moris, the Roseau prelate who had spent close to fifty years in Dominica. Phyllis was fond of attributing Dominica's ills to the tyranny of "300 years of Catholic morality," and in *The Orchid House* the church emerges as the most conservative and powerful force in Dominica. "The gentlemen over in Whitehall believed that they were governing our island," Phyllis writes. "That was not the case. Father Toussaint and Master Rufus were the real rulers. People challenged them now and again, but those people always lost." In Father Toussaint she creates a character remarkable in his jesuitic awareness of his power to control lives and societies. The pivotal confrontation in the novel between him and Joan—"the two cleverest people in the island"—reveals in a masterly way Phyllis's awareness of the complexities of Dominica's power structure. The jesuitic bargain struck in the priest's shadow-filled room—in which Joan "promised not to engage personally in political activity in the island . . . and to devote [herself] to [her] husband and child," a promise she means to fulfill "to the letter" by having her husband assume her political work—is defended by Joan as politically expedient: "Lally, can't you see that unless people like Father Toussaint and Baptiste and me come to some sort of rough understanding, there's no hope for the world?"

The Orchid House, when seen in the light of its author's biography, seems like an extraordinarily prophetic work, a blueprint for her own preembryonic political career. A few years later, with Phyllis busily engaged in electioneering in Dominica, her friend George Horner commented in amazement that she seemed to have fallen into the plot of her own novel. That it would seem so attests not to any gift for divination but to the clearsightedness of the novel's analysis of the Dominican historical crossroads. The novel demonstrates with great lucidity that by 1952, while still in exile in England, she had her finger firmly on the pulse of her island's political and social ailments.

If the nature of the political solutions offered in *The Orchid House* owe everything to Phyllis's profound understanding of the changes undergone by the society of her youth, the novel's evocative aura and sensory texture reflect the impact on her writing of Alain-Fournier's 1913 novel *Le Grand Meaulnes*. Phyllis had been prompted to read this neoromantic work—"the most delicate rendering so far achieved . . . of the romantic adolescent consciousness"—both by her French tutor, Mlle. B., and Martin Turnell, the young Anglican rector who tutored her in religion and mathematics. The novel—till her death one of her most beloved texts—recounts the adventures of three young friends as they search for lost love and lost time in a style reminiscent of medieval quest narratives and fairy tales. It is characterized by "a sort of poetry of regret for lost innocence and vanished enchantment." Its influence on *The Orchid House* is felt as much on the structure as on the style. Like Phyllis in her novel, he had sought to come "as close as he [could] to his own personal life" in his work, as a review of his biography and correspondence demonstrates, creating characters to embody various aspects of his own self. Many critics have seen his protagonist, Seurel, as "only one aspect of an ideal protagonist formed by three persons: the memory-haunted narrator Seurel, the Quixotic Augustin Meaulnes, and the enigmatic Frantz de Galais." Interestingly enough, Martin Turnell would in time publish an extensive critical article on *Le Grand Meaulnes*, usually included among the definitive studies of the novel, in which he examines Alain-Fournier's use of "doubles" and the curious mixture of romantic evocation and down-to-earth realism of the novel, a study that points to the tantalizing speculation that he may have discussed these issues at length with her pupil, aiding young Phyllis toward a deeper understanding of *Le Grand Meaulnes* than even a perceptive young reader would have reached on her own. His assessment of the novel underscores aspects of form and style that Phyllis would replicate in *The Orchid House*. "We find in the novel what the French call *dédoublement*," Turnell wrote, "which means we are looking at life simultaneously under two different and usually conflicting aspects. It is the story of a great adventure in which we move at times in an enchanted world, but we are conscious all the time of a sense of fragility an underlaying menace. Once a peak has been passed the atmosphere becomes more and more threatening as the magic is gradually dissipated by the sense of disenchantment, the fading of dreams and hopes, the sudden plunge from an earthly paradise into something like an earthly hell."

Le Grand Meaulnes, like *The Orchid House*, is a novel dominated "by memory, and the continuance of sensations which were most deeply held in childhood" but have to give way to the realities of adulthood and history. It is also a book dominated, as Phyllis's would be, by the persona of the storyteller, by the unifying voice of a narrator attempting to explain things beyond his understanding and clinging to the past as the only comforting and safe space. Seurel, like Lally, is a "thorough-going nostalgician; like Stella, he is "hypersensitively attuned to the beauty, the mystery, and occasionally, the menace, of natural landscape." Phyllis celebrated the seductive aspects of Dominica's undisciplined nature; but she was keenly aware of the horrors it could harbor. "Beauty and disease, beauty and horror: that was the island," Lally will ruminate in *The Orchid House*, echoing the young protagonist of her creator's favorite work.

Phyllis had begun writing *The Orchid House* in early 1951; by early 1952, with the novel nearly completed, the carefully balanced set of circumstances that had sustained her through its writing began to collapse. Philip, then just eighteen, had become prey to disturbing and violent attacks of rage. His behavior at home—confrontational, erratic, delusional, and out of control—bewildered his parents. His grasp on his reality became progressively more tenuous, and he began to show symptoms of what was termed paranoia. They were actually characteristic of schizophrenia in its early stages, and it is conceivable that his behavior was caused by hallucinations, a characteristic initial manifestation of the disease, where the sufferer is prompted to act in disturbing ways by "voices" only he hears. Schizophrenia was little understood in the early 1950s. The disorder, since shown to be caused by a combination of biochemical and environmental factors, was then thought to be exclusively the result of psychological trauma.* And in Philip's case, the search for psychological trauma yielded plenty: He was said to be, despite his intellectual ability and his brilliance at chess, unable to cope with the emotional and intellectual demands of school; his psyche, his doctors suggested, already burdened by the early symptoms of mental illness, had sustained a distressing separation from his parents during the war, aggravated by the subsequent separation from foster parents to whom he had grown deeply attached. It was hinted by friends that Phyllis and Robert had put too much pressure on the children to excel and Philip had cracked under the strain, and furthermore, that Phyllis, always devoted to her political and literary pursuits, had put these above her children, causing irreparable damage to her son's sanity. His prognosis was extremely poor, and his parents were given very little hope of improvement or cure.

Drug therapy for schizophrenia was in its embryonic stages, and psychotherapy, although since proven to be of limited or no value without medication, was then the primary treatment for the condition. The illness, shrouded in misconceptions, brought with it the stigma of tainted heredity as well as dogmatic Freudian notions of the mother as the root of all psychological evils. Phyllis was torn by pain and guilt; the medical profession's focus on the role of the mother in psychiatric pathology, coupled with the taint of her own father's psychological frailty, meant that she felt singled out as the culprit in Philip's worsening mental illness. "Blame the mother" was indeed the norm in both psychotherapy and the popular imagination at the time, and Philip's pivotal physical attack on his mother (he was said to have tried to kill her) only seemed to confirm the centrality of her role in his disease. Tragically for her, very few understood at the time the inevitability of Philip's fate: Triggered as his illness was by a genetic predisposition, even the happiest of circumstances and the best parenting might not have prevented its onset.

Phyllis had, moreover, reason to question whether she had been a good mother to her son. Aside from her guilt over having sent him to the United States during the war, she wondered whether her deep attachment to him and passionate involvement in every aspect of his life had harmed him. Her friend Pixie remembers her as perhaps

*Dr. John Saunders, a U.S. pioneer in the development of medication to treat psychiatric illness, sees a possible genetic link between Philip's schizophrenia and his grandfather Francis Shand's "shellshock." Both prone to mental disease because of their genetic makeup, Francis could have lived his life through without any symptoms of illness except for the trauma caused by his war experiences, which triggered the first manifestations of a milder, more manageable form of mental distress. Once precipitated, however, the manifestations could not be reversed. In Philip's case, a different genetic makeup led to full-blown schizophrenia.

too deeply attached to her son; she used to write poems (none of which have survived) about her "alabaster boy" and the umbilical link between mother and son. She did not believe that Phyllis ever really let him go. Pixie, whose intimacy with the family allowed her insights few others were permitted, felt that Phyllis lacked a suitable background experience of families to help her in bringing up her children. Hers—a strong personality given to managing others—gave her family little leeway. When it came to the children, as with everything else, Phyllis was absorbed and impassioned; Robert, as was his wont, was more "laid back," and relied more on well-reasoned arguments. Phina had been strong enough and determined about her rights, and had gone on to develop her own interests and skills. Philip did not have the same forcefulness as Phina and "never really became an independent person."

Phyllis and Robert, overwhelmed by what they saw as the loss of their child, and faced with the widespread misconceptions regarding his condition, responded by growing increasingly silent about him. Phyllis, who often dealt with acute emotional pain by retreating into silence, could not bear to speak about it. His illness would eventually become their secret, a secret so well kept that even people who counted themselves among their closest friends in the more than thirty years they lived in Dominica were not aware that they had a son, least of all a living one. An illness that would become the anguished focus of their lives throughout the 1950s and beyond was rarely discussed outside the family—and in Dominica not at all. Phyllis responded to Philip's condition as her mother had to her father's—by shrouding him in a cocoon of silence. Later this secrecy would work to protect her from political enemies who would have stopped at nothing to ridicule and harass her. Knowledge that she had a mad son would have been invaluable political capital in her enemies' hands. Her mad son, however, would remain for a very long time her secret tragedy, a deep and festering, though concealed, wound. As with many parents of schizophrenics, who tolerate the aberrant behavior until the patient loses control, Philip remained at home until he made a violent attack on Phyllis, at which point he was committed to an NHS mental hospital in the suburbs of London, where he remains today. Phyllis and Robert refused to discuss the incident with relatives or friends, despite obvious evidence of injury to her, and different versions, born out of conjecture, circulated at the time. Some say it was merely a blow; others claim it was a beating. Celia told the Honychurches after Phyllis's death that Philip had tried to kill his mother with a kitchen knife. Philip, on the other hand, was reported to have apologized poignantly to Phyllis during one of his weekend visits to the flat for "hitting her."

Philip's mental illness—and the pain it inflicted on his parents—cannot be separated from the writing of *The Orchid House*, whose recreation of Francis Shand's struggle against his own inner demons was too closely mirrored in the young man's erratic, at times violent, behavior. The hopelessness of Philip's gradual descent into madness could not but reinforce her despair of ever finding the strength and endurance needed for survival in the male side of her family. The women who inspired the various female characters in the novel—Elfreda, Maggie, Lally, Julia, Rosalind, Celia, even Marion despite her myriad troubles, and, of course, Phyllis herself—all emerge as strong and vital figures, while the men—Francis, Julian, Robert, Uncle Ralph, Philip—are depicted as physically or morally weaker, mutilated, or prone to despair. Nonetheless in *The Orchid House*, finished before Philip's first major breakdown, the character modeled on him is the repository of the family's hopes. Young Ned, brought up in London in poverty and fed on politics, is the only character capable of awakening his grandfather, however briefly, from his drug-induced apathy. He is, as well, the one on whom rest the hopes of restoring the family's vital links to the land and of defining a meaningful role for the former masters in the new social order. But after Philip's commitment to a psychiatric hospital this was not to be, and years later, when Phyllis begins the continuation of the family's saga in *In the Cabinet*, we learn that Ned had been murdered shortly after the period at which *The Orchid House* concludes in retaliation for Stella's murder of Mr. Lilipoulala. By then Philip, "extremely withdrawn and deluded," had spent close to thirty years in a hospital for the insane.

During this same period, Phyllis's good friend George Horner—himself the author of a series of lovely poems about Devon, where he grew up with his paternal farm-laborer grandparents—was facing serious psychological troubles of his own. When she had met him he was the Fulham reference librarian—one of her "beloved librarians"—a well-read man "keen to communicate his encyclopedic knowledge of the arts, particularly novels, film, theatre, to all comers, especially the underprivileged." George, a man tortured by his own sexual ambiguities, was also at that period extremely frail physically and psychologically. A self-avowed "classic case of mother attachment," he had been horrified into a state of asexuality by the social ostracism imposed on homosexuals in England in the 1950s, something about which he wrote poignantly and quite frankly to Phyllis, often joking about his temptations to indulge in "illegal activities" and the friends he fantasized about bringing to the flat. When relaxed by drink he might touch or stroke another man's buttocks, but repressed to the point of impotence, he shrank from doing more. The strain had led to several breakdowns. His physical health, undermined from his wartime work as a fire warden at Fulham Town Hall, had been further weakened by two bad bouts of tuberculosis, after the second of which he had attempted suicide. Robert and Phyllis, already burdened with Philip's illness, shouldered a great deal of the responsibility of helping George recover his physical and emotional health. They offered him sanctuary after he attempted suicide, and he moved into their flat at Parkview Court. They did not like leaving him alone, fearing that he might give in to his despair again and hurt himself.

Despite the heartache and complications of Philip's illness and George's suicidal episodes, by mid-1952 *The Orchid House* had been sent to Juliet O'Hea, her literary agent at Curtis Brown. Phyllis's first choice among publishers was Constable, and the manuscript was sent to them at her request. O'Hea had warned her that she must not mind waiting for a long while for Constable to make a decision, but to her amazement, twenty four hours after the manuscript had reached them, O'Hea called to say they had accepted it. In later years Phyllis would often explain that the writing of *The Orchid House* "drove her towards [her] home island," but it was actually the novel's *publication* that set in motion the chain of events that would lead to her return. Her advance from Constable was used, among other things, for two holidays: a tour of Yorkshire and a visit to Dominica, her first since 1932. The highlight of their travels in Yorkshire was a visit to the Brontë house in Haworth, where she was moved to pity and wonder for the "melancholy of those narrow forbidding rooms where the spirited girls were boxed up by a stern father," by Charlotte's "pathetic dress with its fantastically narrow waist (no wonder she died in childbirth); [by] the sad wind-swept moors where Emily, no coward soul, found liberation and insight, [and by] the grim tombstone in the adjoining churchyard." After their tour of the house they had stopped at a pub across the road for "a tankard of beer," and sat opposite a very old man who looked to Phyllis like the "ideal Victorian gaffer" and told them anecdotes he had heard about the Brontës, about how "wild Branwell" used to drink in the pub and his sisters would have to fetch him home. The trouble with all of them, he said, was that they wrote books, upon which she confessed that she too had written a book, and shared with him her misgivings about her autobiographical novel's probable reception in Dominica. He attempted to reassure her by telling her, as he had been told, that "when Bran drank here and them girls wrote at the rectory, every squire hereabouts thought he was Heathcliff." But *The Orchid House*, she feared, was to cause "more commotion in the confines of Dominica than its far greater forerunners did at Haworth."

The trip to Dominica in October 1952 was prompted by the news that Elfreda was facing an operation for cancer. Phyllis, for once with ready cash, sailed home with Robert to be with her mother. While in Dominica, Robert saw an advertisement for the position of engineer at Bath Estate, a lime plantation and processing plant owned by L. Rose and Company, where Rose's Lime Juice, the popular cocktail mixer, was produced. The company, established in the nineteeth century and still Dominica's largest employer, was seeking an engineer to reorganize the plant, modernize the machinery, and oversee the training of workers to operate the new equipment. Phyllis and Robert saw the Rose position as a godsend. In one move they would have the financial security that had eluded them; she would be back in Dominica, where she increasingly felt that she belonged; and they would have a tranquil, bucolic haven where they hoped Philip, sustained by the "sunshine and lack of city cares," could get well. Robert applied for the position, stressing that it was "the desire of [his] wife and [him]self to settle in Dominica, the land of her birth," and was hired on the spot. Phyllis was to return to London to care for Philip, handle the final details of the publication of her novel, pack their belongings, and join Robert in Dominica a few months later. But upon her arrival she had to face her son's confirmed diagnosis of schizophrenia, which brought to an end any plan of bringing him to Dominica and made it impossible for her to return as soon as they had planned. She would not rejoin Robert until August 1953.

The ten months she spent alone in London were painful ones. She would capture some of the uncertainty of this separation in *Dashing Away*, the novel she had begun during that period, a time when "everything she had tucked away, shelved and postponed," as she would write of her main character, Alice, "spilled itself out," and she could feel "the shadow-stripes of separation closing in." Phyllis, always discreet about her personal life, left no record of her thoughts during these months; but her fiction always mirrored her life, and although not always autobiographical in the strictest sense of the world, it was always "autoreferential." So, though it would not be advisable to jump to any conclusions about the lovers Alice is juggling as she prepares to join Gally, Alice's thoughts about Gally could be said to mirror Phyllis's as she prepares to join Robert:

> Fog, fog. . . . The light fades out of the bright world. That was Jem's voice, deep and ruthless. It spoke to her of death—perhaps it was Jem who was dead? But no, he would not die so, though he had a thirty-year advantage

> over her. Seagrave was young—too young; through tenderness and excitement she had taken him into her arms; Gally was her seemly one, the person who so nearly matched her in time and character (for all her partisanship of rebels Alice was fundamentally sensible). Yes, Gally was the one; she had promised the rest of her life to him, and they would build up stone by stone . . . [a] bulwark against meanness and mediocrity.

As Phyllis prepared to depart for Dominica she was torn between her responsibility to Robert and her children's needs, feeling, like Alice, that she was going "too soon, before all the ends [were] tied up." It was wrenching having to plan her departure knowing she was leaving her mentally ill son in the care of strangers. While she did so she wrote poignantly in her new novel of two mothers, one losing her young and talented son in a fire, the other fighting her beautiful daughter's commitment to an insane asylum after she had set the fire that killed her young lover. She poured her own grief into their portraits while she arranged a complex relay of friends and relatives, all centered around George Horner, to visit Philip and take him on an occasional outing. Even Robert's immediate superior at the Rose Company's London office was pressed into service.

During this period Phina, who had finished her B.A. at Oxford, married a fellow student, Allan Simmance, whom she had met through the university's Socialist Club. Robert, who was in Dominica, missed his daughter's wedding. Phyllis claimed to adore Allan, finding him "plain but beguiling, infinitely solid but not stolid, an ex-Catholic," and a good companion for Phina. But she was most distressed by the couple's immediate plans. They had secured positions in a development project sponsored by the Ford Foundation in Kenya, right in the heart of Mau Mau country.* She pleaded and cajoled but, determined to go, go they did. As Alice would conclude, facing a similar predicament, "I can't control their destinies . . . [and] I'm so tired. I can't bear any more." Phyllis's correspondence with Robert during this period bears out her emotional exhaustion and resulting exasperation. She was deeply distressed in London: She had to cope with Philip's illness, and sort and pack the belongings they had accumulated in almost seventeen years at Parkview Court, breaking the ties of those many years. Robert, in turn, had thrown himself into expatriate life with a vengeance, writing to her of servants, tennis matches, and cocktail parties—and Phyllis was not amused. It was widely rumored among his acquaintances in Roseau that he had a mistress, a Dominican employee of L. Rose & Co., but she may not have been aware of this.

In early July, within days of Philip's permanent institutionalization, and days before she was scheduled to leave for Dominica, *The Orchid House* arrived in bookstores. The reviews were lukewarm but encouraging. The *Times* found the novel's most melodramatic parts cloying, and the character of Joan an almost Shavian cari-

*The name *Mau Mau* was given to the Kenyan militants who advocated violent resistance to British domination. It was especially associated with the ritual oaths employed by the leaders of the Kenyan Central Association to promote unity in the independence movement. In October 1952, shortly before Phina and Allan's arrival, after a campaign of sabotage and assassination attributed to Mau Mau terrorism, the British government in Kenya declared a state of emergency and began four years of military operations against the rebels. By the end of 1956 more than eleven thousand rebels had been killed in the fighting, along with one hundred Europeans and two thousand African loyalists.

cature. The reviewer concluded that "it [was] difficult to judge Mrs. Allfrey's abilities from this, her first novel." A week later the *Times Literary Supplement* wrote more enthusiastically about the novel, finding that "Mrs. Allfrey convey[ed] very well a sense of tolerant, languid society full of visual beauty but lacking any inner resources of power of resistance to evil; perhaps in her next book she may find a more lively story to put inside this framework." The *Manchester Guardian* found the narrator's omniscience problematic, but liked the novel as a whole. "Mrs. Allfrey's story had both charm and grasp," their reviewer wrote. "But her spokeswoman is a bit of a worry: what earache, what keyhole inflammation, such a devotion implies!" Marghanita Laski, writing for the *Sunday Observer*, reached the "enjoyable assumption that in Mrs. Allfrey we have a new writer of moderate but delightful talent." This was not overgenerous praise, but she liked the novel for its "emotional evocation of an exotic setting, the sensitive handling of original characters who still belong to story rather than reality, and, most distinctive of all, a brisk matter-of-fact way with people of other races, far more effective than any overtentative delicacy." The *Wolverhampton Express and Star* found the novel "convincing and refreshing," and Lally "a remarkable and lovable person" whose narrative has a "massive simplicity." The *Newcastle Journal* called it a "very skillfully written" book which had the "merit of making one feel that its minor events are symbolic of greater ones."

The reviewer for the *Iraq Times* in Baghdad deeply enjoyed the novel, finding it to be a work which "buzzed with life," written by an author with "real talent." George Scott, writing for *Truth*, called *The Orchid House* "a most remarkable first novel": "Mrs. Allfrey has the charm and skill of E. M. Forster to lead the reader wherever she wills without his wondering or worrying where he is being taken. She has a power which may be likened to Rosamond Lehmann [an accomplished stylist, noted for capturing nuances of mood in her novels] for the leisurely revelation of character through snatches of apparently unrevealing conversation and through the novelist's equivalent of a nod and a wink." The influential *Spectator* was just as enthusiastic. It called the novel "a vivid piece of story-telling, touched now and then with poetry," a tale "innocent of false emotion." The technical difficulties posed by Lally as narrator were again a subject of commentary: "It was a mistake . . . to choose as narrator the old Negro nurse of the family, shrewdly conceived though Lally is, since here and there the slackness of design necessarily shows in her recital of events." The overall impression, however, was positive, and the novel was recommended. "The novel as a whole has a taking liveliness and sympathy and reproduces in fond and confident strokes the brilliance of the Caribbean scene." The reviews were quickly followed by an enthusiastic offer from Dutton for an American edition. They had offered an advance of one thousand dollars and a generous schedule of royalties, which Phyllis eagerly accepted. This behind her, she sailed for her new life in the West Indies. Except for a long sojourn in London in 1956, the Caribbean would be her home until the end of her life.

Phyllis returned home in early August 1953 at the age of forty-four. In the twenty-six years she had been away from Dominica the island had undergone significant changes. The large estates that had dominated economic and social life when she was a child had collapsed; the peasantry had reclaimed a substantial portion of the land either through outright ownership, sharecropping, or rental agreements. Their increased participation in the island's economy had led to the founding of the Dominica Trade Union, led by Christopher Loblack and Phyllis's uncle Ralph Nicholls. The DTU had brought considerable pressure to bear on the powers that be, and in 1953 the island was readying for universal suffrage. Despite these crucial changes, below the surface Dominica remained what it had been when she had left: a small island whose struggling economy depended on the viability of its produce, and where the peasantry continued to struggle to eke a living out of mountainous land. Roseau itself was still "scarcely more than a village, an Antillean Cranford [from the eponymous 1835 novel by Elizabeth Gaskell] clustering gracefully on the edge of a blazing extent of water, and overshadowed by steep and enormous hills fleecy with every excess of tropical vegetation."

Phyllis's new home was the main house at Bath Estate, the headquarters of L. Rose & Co. in Dominica, located in the outskirts of Roseau, just north of the Botanical Gardens. One reached the fields and works by crossing the narrow iron truss bridge over the Roseau River, with its creaking wooden roadway, leading to "the trim green world" of the well-kept plantations, noisy and clangy but unforgettably fragrant with the delicate smell of citrus oil stealing up from the valley below. The house, typical of Dominican estate houses, was an airy wood-and-stone building surrounded by vividly colored and fragrant vegetation. Its chief drawback was its being very close to the factory and therefore noisy and lacking in privacy.

On the morning after her arrival, Phyllis wrote to Juliet O'Hea at Curtis Brown concerning the tax complexities of her income from Dutton. (Curtis Brown's legal department was seeking to determine where the Dutton check should be cashed so Phyllis could avoid triple taxation—United States, Great Britain, and Dominica.) Her joy at being home, the familiar newness of her surroundings, spills over into her letter:

> This is a great big airy house, surrounded by vegetation of the most incredible beauty. There is a proper garden which attempts to be formal down below (I have chosen one of the bedrooms as my writing room, so I look down on it as I type). Robert uses half of the old ballroom as his office! In the garden there is an old woman known as the Weeder, whose sole function is to grub up weeds all day long. They grow so fast that she is always busy. . . . If I could hand you a bunch of flowers through the window, you would find in the clump vermilion hibiscus (with humming-bird attached), yellow and flame ixoras, golden alamanda, frost blue plumbago, carmine portulacas growing on the outer wall-top, lemon acacia and pink coralita. The lime factory makes a tremendous whirring sound like [the commotion] of ship or aeroplane engines. The trees and palms are also perpetually shivering and shuddering in the strong hot breeze, so that the scene is extremely animated.

While Phyllis was in London, Robert had been looked after by two young maids, Mona and Winifred, about whom she writes to Juliet O'Hea: "The cook and the maid . . . are both young, romantic, and giggling, they call me 'Mistress' in a sweet Elizabethan way, and they are very happy because I have told them to carry on running the place in the old style, which means the extraordinary meals they have been serving to Robert in the past ten months. The coffee is so strong that it tastes like aloes." Mona and Winifred inspired a short story, "O Stay and Hear," begun as soon as she settled at Bath Estate. It conveys her delight in being home and the process through which she begins to shed her borrowed "Englishness" to regain the soft irony that marks the Dominican character and which she finds in the fictional maid and cook, Melta and Ariadne. Their song, something rather merry and mocking, like a "Shakespearian song [sung] to an Elizabethan air," slowly takes possession of their English mistress, the English *Madame-Là* who pleases them by leaving everything to them. Phyllis, known to cannibalize even the most trivial episode if it suited her fiction, incorporates into her tale her new perceptions of Robert as she observes his renewed physical vigor in Dominica. He, who had taken up tennis quite exuberantly since arriving in Dominica, served as the model for Rodney, *Madame-Là*'s husband, his "sun-browned face" overlayed by "a strange redness," his whole self "steaming with recent energetic action." Phyllis, as usual when she writes covertly about him, cannot but look at him with sardonic fondness. "All her life she [had] been wanting Rodney to be successful and masterful," she has the mistress muse, "and now she is not sure that success really suits him." "O Stay and Hear" captures the nuances of Phyllis's reentry into Dominican society—at the end of the tale *Madame-Là* borrows "an inflection of mockery from somewhere": her realization that her husband, despite his convictions about the equality of the races, has acquired, in her absence, an unprecedented air of power and mastery now that he finds himself in a position of power over black people; the eruption of race as a central factor in her life (the mistress comes to believe, as she thinks of Melta and Ariadne and "their children of light coloration," that "people in this tropical island do not make love for romantic reasons, but as social and evolutionary means"). The story, with its subtly nuanced insights and light irony, was quickly sold to a highly regarded London literary magazine, *Argosy*.

Despite her delight at being home after such a long absence, Phyllis, overwrought after the dreadful months that preceded Philip's commitment, was at her worst when she arrived in Dominica. Aware of a new maturity in her writing, and fresh from the triumph of having sold her first novel so quickly, she was returning home with a measure of success she would not have expected just a year before. She also returned with an acute consciousness of herself as a writer, and was, according to some, quite tiresome about it. She was peevish about their accommodations at Bath Estate and complained endlessly about how the constant noise of the machinery made it impossible for her to concentrate on her writing. Letters flew back and forth between Robert and the London head office of L. Rose, and a move to another house away from the works was proposed to Robert—and rejected. Not content with letting Robert handle the matter, she wrote herself, blatantly interfering between him and his employers in a way soon deemed unacceptable even by Robert's superior at the London office, the mild-mannered and kind J. B. Barker. From the moment of her arrival she began to meddle in Robert's professional affairs, placing herself—opinionated and pushy as she could be when she was unhappy—at the very center of controversy. She disliked everything, complaining about the vapidity of the L. Rose & Co. social set, and most importantly, about the conditions under which the laborers worked. The staff at the estate, particularly the European staff, soon learned to dislike her meddling and were just too pleased to keep the Rose office in London abreast of the dubious connections with trade unionists she soon established, and of her left-leaning political activities.

In many ways Phyllis's return to Dominica as the wife of an English L. Rose employee placed her in an untenable position. Nothing could have been further from her reality as a "Dominican born and bred," a Labourite, and a socialist than this narrow world of expatriate Englishmen and their wives, living in temporary exile in the tropics, where they led self-obsessed, philistine existences centered on tennis, bridge, cocktails, and gossip (chiefly about Princess Margaret and Group Capt. Peter Townsend). James Pope-Hennessy, after a brief acquaintance with these expatriates, concluded that "the people that come out to make a living in such a place unconsciously shrink from exploring its mysteries, and barricaded themselves inside a chintzy security of pink gins, gossip about the Royal Family, out-of-date illustrated society weeklies from London and whist drives." His portrayal would outrage the small enclave, who found themselves accused of "suburbanism, a deliberate effort to reproduce in exotic tropical surroundings all that is most limited and banal in English life." There was something peculiarly offensive to Pope-Hennessy in the incongruity between the "impeccable tea-table laid with all the paraphernalia" dear to the English and his hostess's "discoursing on bastards and coloured mistresses in the same casual tones in which she had previously been speaking of the meat shortage or of Princess Margaret." The gossip and scandalmongering, he thought, were exaggerated in Roseau "to a scale of dementia." It was a world of "rank vegetation, alcohol and heated blood," where conversation was "no longer a discussion of ideas or books, of politics or history, but a whirlpool of mad stories of drunkenness, dishonesty, violence and attempted murder."

As an L. Rose wife Phyllis was expected to join the wives' circle—Mrs. Dick Lewis (herself a Rose and thus the head wife), Mrs. Tommy Coulthard, and Mrs. Tony Brown—in the usual rounds of shallow entertainment. She lost no time in offending them with her refusals to join their parties, her very obvious contempt for the idleness of their pursuits, and her open scorn for their superficiality and ignorance. She often refused to join their activities by claiming she had to write. Once, when the group awaited—with great trepidation—the arrival of a highly placed L. Rose officer from England, Phyllis ostentatiously announced that she had absolutely no time for contributing to the festivities as she had an article to write. Elma Napier, herself a writer of note and an elected member of the island's Legislative Council, remarked that if that was so she should go and do it and cease announcing the fact to a world that did not care. Phyllis brilliantly captured the psychology of her corporate-wife companions in a short story, "Little Cog-burt," which she would complete the following year for submission to a literary contest sponsored by the local radio station. In the character of Moira, a middle-aged woman who obstinately refuses to become a part of the West Indian world surrounding her, Phyllis reveals with excruciating clarity the lack of empathy she found in expatriate women toward the masses of poor black people around them. Forced by her husband to organize a Christmas party for the children of the estate workers, Moira holds herself stubbornly aloof from her guests, "her heart in fact was in a suburban English house and her mind was on a local cocktail party they promised to attend—as soon as the dark children were out of the way." The expatriate world of clubs and superficiality also serves more as a contrast than as a background for another story she wrote during this period and which appeared in *Argosy* in 1957, "A Real Person." In it Walter, excluded from club life during his school holidays because he is too young, yearns to meet the type of "real person" that seems not to exist in his narrow society, the person he eventually discovers himself to have become. "A real person" was always a code in Phyllis's writings and letters for the type of person she herself strove to be, one confident of being "blissfully alive" and "capable of practically anything," one who believed that "in spite of the mysterious and inexplicable conflict of faiths and races in the world, it was still a world in which miracles happened," the very opposite of her British companions.

With her British Labour party training in leftist politics, Phyllis was aghast at the island's paleolithic political system. There were no political parties, and despite the recent introduction of universal suffrage, political participation by the masses was not sought or encouraged. Despite the moderate success of the Dominica Trade Union (DTU) in pushing for protection for estate workers and universal suffrage, these gains had not led to a greater share of political power. All the peasantry's gains were still presented in the guise of concessions granted them by the ruling class, thus perpetuating old social and political configurations. Phyllis felt that this situation ran against the spirit of the times, and, never shy about expressing her opinions, she quickly began to ruffle feathers. She shocked Dominican society by her disregard of what she saw as the island's Byzantine class and race distinctions. Laudable as were her efforts to bring to her island society a full awareness of the perversity and obsolescence of race and class prejudices, her efforts were not widely appreciated. The middle and upper classes were aghast at her going about inviting black laborers to her home for tea, urging them to call her Phyllis, flaunting her disdain for time-honored codes that required a black or mulatto Dominican of the lower classes to address white and light-skinned colored women as "Madam." Some claim that no one dared to do so, but soon most of the white population of Roseau began to find her "very tiresome indeed" and "a complete nuisance," and most of them cut her off entirely. She further scandalized the town by strolling down the streets and through the parks of Roseau in avid conversation with men like labor leader Christopher Loblack, a local mason. Not content with this, she soon began to ask the leaders of the DTU and other politically minded estate workers to Bath House to discuss the workers' need for a bigger say in political matters on the island. These "stirrings of the masses," as the *Chronicle* referred to them, quickly set tongues wagging, and many more began to shun her. Tensions flared with Aunt Mags, who was just a bit inclined to agree with anyone who would call Phyllis and Robert Communists. Phyllis was at this juncture uncharacteristically humorless. She was so doggedly earnest about effecting change in what she saw as a backward, provincial society that she was unable to take anything lightly. So while writing about the Dominican character in "O Stay and Hear," she failed to take it into account in her dealings with others. She did, in any case, fail to take it into account in her relations with whites, with whom she had as little to do as she could. Unsure how much to disclose about Philip, and, most important, challenging the social mores so deeply entrenched in her social milieu, she was, in her first six months back home, almost perpetually on the defensive.

Being back in Dominica also meant plunging headlong into family affairs, and these were tangled and complex. Elfreda had recovered magnificently from the cancer operation of the year before. She, according to her daughter, who thoroughly approved, had given over to the island, was "as brown as a coloured lady, not above speaking patois, and quite broad-minded." She would often be seen around town in an old Ford driven by her faithful servant Ti Bonnet. She lived with Maggie at Kingsland House, but the financial and physical burden of the house was becoming too onerous and they were considering selling or letting the property and moving to a small bungalow being built for them by Celia's husband Jack on the grounds of St. Aroment. In James Pope-Hennessy's otherwise unflattering portrayal of Roseau society in *The Baths of Absalom*, Elfreda and Maggie come in for unqualified praise. The ladies of Kingsland House, he writes, "have inherited a genuine concern for the coloured people, and care strongly about the island in a way both admirable and touching." Their garden, "where the humming-birds quiver about the syringa-bushes," was one "of the few wholly pleasant memories of Dominica which [he] retain[ed]."

In Aunt Mags, Phyllis found the last of the Victorians, "so British [one] wouldn't believe it," and Kingsland House had become, if anything, a more solid bastion of Englishness now that it was the most sought-after guesthouse on the island. Patrick Leigh Fermor, the well-known travel writer, who arrived in Dominica when Maggie was visiting England with the rest of the family in 1948, was struck by its seemingly timeless Victorian aura:

> When we knocked on the door of Kingsland House, a substantial building in a beautiful garden [with] mango trees, an elderly West Indian woman answered the door with an oil lamp in her hand, surprisingly dressed in all the starched and goffered and pleated severity of a mid-Victorian parlourmaid. Behind her, in the lamplight, a strangely English interior materialized. Polished mahogany gleamed darkly, and the panes of rosewood cabinets full of china and cut glass reflected her burning wick. But no, there were no rooms, and Miss Maggie was away in London. The door gently closed on the world of beeswax and starch and soft lamplight, and we were back again among the frogs.

Maggie, like the house, had retreated into a bygone era. The "liberalization" of relations between the races appalled her. Her niece's social and political notions were anathema to her, and she couldn't comprehend the whites' acquiescence in the new state of affairs exemplified by Elma Napier, then a member of the Legislative Council, who claimed that given the size of the "static white population" [which amounted] to hardly more than fifty, "if anything like a colour bar existed in this place, none of us would ever see anyone."

Phyllis was stunned by the changes that her sister Marion's difficulties had wrought in her. She found her somewhat unhinged by her two unhappy marriages and the strain of raising three spirited and not always obliging sons on her own. Just prior to her return to Dominica, she had published a tale, "The Untanglers," about Marion (the "Laura of this tale which I am glad to say she has never seen") and her "dreadful life." Phyllis thought that if she had written the story as it really had been, "no-one would have printed it, naturally." In the story Laura's brother (Phyllis was fond of assuming male personas in her semiautobiographical tales) listens as his sister recounts "the savage onslaughts" she expected even then from her estranged husband, a "regular demon, a man without scruple." Marion, as a result of her troubles, "sometimes seem[ed] to [Phyllis] a bit crazed by it all, and who should wonder." The narrator of "The Untanglers," echoing her feelings about Marion, is shocked on meeting his sister again after a long separation, "by the changes the tyrant had made in her, by the way that a wretched layer of fat or coarseness smudged out her proud fine features; the way in which teeth mattered now more than once soft lips, and eyelids puffed slightly about those grey eyes which had once been so exposed. By obliterating most of the sensitive traits of girlhood . . . the wicked brother-in-law . . . had written his baseness vulgarly over Laura's face for the world to see." To Phyllis, who always thought of "poor, bewildered" Marion in her "touching early grace" against "an aureole of wistaria," the prematurely aged, often-dazed sister she encountered upon her return to Dominica had too little of the companion she had known as a child. Despite her love for Marion, the differences in their interests and circumstances now loomed large between them, and their sisterly affection was more guarded, less often expressed, more burdened with their radically-differing histories.

Family matters, already strained, took a turn for the worse as the scandal of Phyllis's novel swept through the island's tiny white enclave. She had been apprehensive about the novel's reception in Dominica and had asked Rosalind as she was preparing to leave London to "pray for her as she was going into the lion's den." But nothing she could have imagined prepared her for the *commesse* that the handful of novels sold in Dominica stirred up. *The Orchid House* was read as a *roman-à-clef,* and matching the various characters to their real-life counterparts became the most enjoyable entertainment in the island. The family's past and present circumstances became the subject of gossip and innuendo; they were propelled willy-nilly into the very center of controversy. The white and colored populations declared themselves appalled at the practically revolutionary character of the political solutions offered in the novel, Roseau's elite was aghast and some were openly abusive to Phyllis. The Catholic authorities, portrayed in the novel as cold-blooded, politically astute hypocrites, quite predictably did not take kindly to the novel's publication. *The Orchid House* was never reviewed openly in the church-owned *Chronicle*, but within days of the book's arrival, reference was made in the newspaper to the receipt of a nameless book "full of rottenness in the shape of slanders and lies on the Catholic Church" that "could only be the work of a Communist" and whose use of quotations from the Bible was most offensive. Tensions ran extremely high with Ralph Nicholls's family, who had been bitterly offended by the portrayal of their father in the novel. They all declared themselves deeply wounded by the book, feeling that it had been taken from life and the characters, their father and mother particularly, could be easily identified. Ralph's son Alexis, who had been very close to Phyllis, vowed that he would never forgive her for what she had done to his father. He did not find much comfort in the thought of what she had done to her own father's reputation in the novel. Meeting her some time later in London, he dressed her down publicly and roundly. She would later claim she took it all in her stride, commenting wistfully of her Nicholls cousins that they had "allowed the island's society to narrow [their] views." But she had been hurt and grieved by the general attack. Her position was so publicly difficult that, when she met the island administrator at a party shortly after her return to Dominica, he asked her humorously, "Do you think you will last out here?" "Longer than you, Your Honour," she is said to have replied "with equal bonhomie."

Phyllis's uneasy reencounter with her native island was interrupted in November. Robert had climbed a tree to rescue their cat, and "being Robert," fell off and broke an ankle, literally smashing it to pieces. He was flown to the hospital in Barbados, where Phyllis accompanied him, but the Barbadian doctors were not up to the task of repairing the damage, and he had to be sent by plane to England, where the "second-best orthopaedic surgeon in the world," a paratrooper expert, was to operate on him. She remained behind. Robert would be confined to his bed in a London hospital, his foot tied up in a pulley, "suffering hell for weeks and weeks." He was expected to recover, but would be on crutches for a long time and most probably would never play tennis or dance again, just when he had taken to tennis quite ardently again, and Dominica was "a dancy sort of island." The injury would leave him with a permanent limp. By January 1954 it was evident that Robert would not be able to return to Dominica as quickly as they had expected and Phyllis sailed for London to join him.

She had not been idle in the two months she had been alone in Dominica, and had finished several short stories, "O Stay and Hear," "Little Cog-burt," "A Real Person," and "The Eyrie" among them, and most importantly, her second novel, *Dashing Away*. Some of the stories had been dispatched to Curtis Brown in early October; the novel had been sent soon after its completion in December. Juliet O'Hea had found "Little Cog-burt" delightful, and although the story had reached them too late to be placed in any of that year's Christmas issues, she wanted to submit it for a holiday story competition being run by the *Sunday Times*. "O Stay and Hear" had been quickly sold to *Argosy*. She had had further good news in that she would arrive in London in time for the launching of the French edition of *The Orchid House*. Despite a virulent cold caught on shipboard, she was able, soon after her arrival, to attend a P.E.N. Club meeting, where she presented a copy of the newly printed *La Maison des Orchidées*. The joys of literary success and recognition were short-lived, as she soon learned the sorry fate of her new novel, *Dashing Away*. Juliet O'Hea was "bitterly disappointed" in it. She had been "so much looking forward to reading more of Alice," a character introduced in the early chapters Phyllis had sent, "but somehow the whole story seem[ed] to have got out of hand and although there [were] of course many good scenes, as a whole [she] found [she] had lost interest in the characters and belief in their reality." She also dashed any hope of a serial as they thought there were "far too many characters, too many politics, and too little good sound middle-class morality!" Only six out of the manuscript's fourteen original chapters remain among Phyllis's papers, most of these centering on Alice, a character seemingly drawn on Phyllis, as she prepares to join her lover in Africa after many years in London. Juliet O'Hea's misgivings about the novel's morality seem to rest on Alice's vacillating between three lovers and on the provocative but not overly graphic descriptions of lovemaking in the extant text, which includes an account of Alice's affair with her son's best friend. The reader at Constable, Michael Sadleir, wholly agreed with Juliet O'Hea, although his qualms were not of a moral nature. He thought the novel "wouldn't do," fearing that readers of *The Orchid House* would be "disappointed and bored" by what he thought was "coterie fiction in its most extreme form." His assessment nonetheless provides most of the details we have of the manuscript as a whole. The title, *Dashing Away*, had been taken from a song sung by a young man in praise of a girl whom ("with some ingenuity," Sadleir felt) he contrives to watch as she performs various domestic chores from Monday to Saturday. These sections of the text, now lost, most probably centered on Alice's son and his love for a mad French girl. Dashing away with her iron, she captivates him, enchanting him with her grace as she cooks. "The novel," commented Sadleir, introduced the reader to a set of "rather vaguely adumbrated people, playing parlour politics in Kensington or Chelsea." He felt that she had regrettably refrained, "in the manner of the up-to-date coterie-novelist," from any explanation of character or any help in grasping the "tangle of relationships and psychological worries which afflict the book's various personalities." She had, furthermore, deprived the book of narrative interest, possibly on purpose, "in order to make [her] bold experiment in the rendering of atmospheric sensitivity." His advice to Phyllis was clear: She would be wise to shelve the manuscript altogether and to "pass on to a new story of a kind to benefit from the impression made by *The Orchid House* and let lie, for the time being at any rate, this sudden switch into ultra-modern experimentalism in story-writing."

What remains of *Dashing Away* is not particularly experimental, consisting as it does of the progress of Alice's farewells in her old borough (Fulham, no doubt), her relationships with three lovers, and the death of her adopted child in a tragic fire set by his mad fiancée. Judging by what remains of the text, at some point, in anticipation of revising the text along the lines suggested by the Curtis Brown and Constable readers, Phyllis must have set aside those chapters of the book centering on Alice. The surviving chapters follow the early stages of Alice's affair with Gerald's young friend Seagrave and Alice's reminiscences as she burns the love letters she received from Jem, an old lover who was also a noted writer; Alice's farewell stroll along the streets of her old neighborhood; her despair as she arrives at her hidden country house to find it burned to the ground, the body of her beloved son, Gerald, among the ashes; her reencounter with Jem at an artists' conference; and her departure for Africa. The chapters are indeed impressionistic and make a clear (and successful) attempt to convey the nuances of a living neighborhood of people whose knowledge of each other is based on the most concrete everydayness: the linen to be washed, their dreams of scoring higher than ever in a slot-machine game, the subtleties of local politics, the trivial concerns of café owners and shopkeepers. Phyllis had tried, admittedly, "to put something of her feelings of London into her new book," and the surviving pages indeed recreate her impressions of Fulham. But apart from a heightening of sensibility à la Elizabeth Bowen (whom Phyllis had been reading, along with Ivy Compton-Burnett, while she wrote the novel), there is little of the ultramodern in what's left of the text.

As with *The Orchid House, Dashing Away* is a fiction built upon a solid foundation of autobiographical material. From the description of Alice's apartment building—"a large orange building divided into flats" next to the Close, "backing on a row of decayed Victorian stables . . . with a park adjoining which was usually too peppered with bodies to show grass"—to the dangers of the Mau Mau wars toward which her lover beckons her, the plot combines and recombines the various elements of Phyllis's life in the early 1950s. The exploration of madness, the recreation of the pain of separation, the letdown of the diminution of political activity in the early 1950s, and the deterioration of a warm relationship with an old and now famous friend can all be traced to her own life, although stripped of their autobiographical connection. By far the most intense chapters are those focusing on Jem, a character clearly based on Phyllis's friend A. C. Coppard. Jem, "a poet who never ceased to be a backwoodsman," had been Alice's "daemon lover, not quite to be believed in." A man thirty years Alice's senior, Jem spoke to her "of England, the English land and earth." His letters "made her unfaithful to her concept of Gally as England: for they were more rooted, they were earthy-peasant in their tenacity, bluebells and hawthorn in their traceries enlivened them; he was a great man, and a wise man for a foolish woman to love. No wonder that his public, when fame fell on him like a cloud late in their love, strained to catch the sound of the personal through his words, as it caught and held hard that gnarled, knotty and vibrant individuality." There is a compelling tone of confession, "something of heat and urgency" in these chapters, that could tempt the reader into reading more than mere fiction in Alice's relationship with Jem, particularly given Phyllis's well-known incapacity for pure invention and her undisguised use of Coppard as a model. It certainly is suggestive of a longer and more intimate relationship between Phyllis and Flynn Coppard than that for which hard evidence remains, although there is in the few photographs of the two together a touching intimacy that attests to their deep regard for each other. In *Dashing Away*, in any case, the fictional relationship that emerges from the use of Flynn Coppard as a model is one of an intense, brooding love that founders under the weight of jealous fears and the terrors of age and ill health that had blinded him to "the truth that he was an immortal and that [Alice] had never loved him so deeply" as she had when he cast her off.

Phyllis's response to the negative reaction to her new novel was swift and decisive. She wrote immediately to Michael Sadleir, thanking him for his "severe but benevolent" letter. "I will take your advice and shelve the despised novel," she writes, "rather than be a Constable outcast. Please send me back my manuscript . . . right away before it irritates any more people!" Privately, as she wrote to an acquaintance, she felt that the trouble with the novel was that it had broken away from the mold of *The Orchid House*. "It is a fearful sweat, but I have to rewrite the second half of my new book since both agents and publishers detest it. I guess I rushed it too fast, but my private opinion is that Constable hopes that I'll abandon it and write a new 'tropical one.'" The disheartening news on *Dashing Away* was somewhat tempered by the encouraging early reviews of the American edition of *The Orchid House*, which had appeared in early March. *Library Journal* liked its character drawing and had recommended it. Booklist had not; its reviewer called it an "unimportant tale, notable chiefly for the descriptive writing, and for details of life among the island's Negroes, as narrated by the old nurse Lally." The *New York Times Book Review* liked the "exotic" novel's "languorous, Baudelairian way with [its] décor," and the *New York Herald Tribune* found that the novel was "[w]ritten with great restraint" and "evoke[d] the beauty and pattern of Island life, while gently unfolding its story of decay." Phyllis was to receive her best American appraisal from the *Saturday Review*, whose reviewer wrote eagerly about Phyllis's recreation of "the haunting magic of [the island's] lush beauty, the exuberant and vivid colors, the violence, the decadence, the passion, and the terrible enervating quality which lurks in its warm tropic airs." The review addressed the technically problematic choice of Lally as narrator considerably more positively than had others:

> Mrs. Allfrey is sometimes hard put to keep the events of the narrative logically in Lally's scope, since it requires an omniscience and an omnipresence which are occasionally difficult to maneuver, but she manages to make Lally so consistently alert and attentive in her love and in her love's near-second sight that the reader does not cavil too much at the device. . . . *The*

> *Orchid House* has great charm and atmosphere, and the character of Lally herself is moving and memorable. The author's distinction of style, the poignancy and simplicity of Lally's telling of the story overcome to a large extent the occasional weaknesses of the plot. It is a first novel of considerable accomplishment and promise.

The fate of *Dashing Away*, nonetheless, hung heavily over Phyllis, and when she and Robert returned to Dominica in early April, the impact of her disappointment with the novel's reception was manifested immediately, as she threw herself wholeheartedly into her political work and social activism. She lacked the single-minded commitment to her writing of a Virginia Woolf or a Jean Rhys. She felt politics, not literature, to be her true calling. And she did not know it then, but when she returned to Dominica in April 1954 the best of her literary work was behind her. She allowed the ill fortune of *Dashing Away* to thwart her as a writer—the book would never be sent to another publisher—and except for her autobiographical work about her Federation experiences, *In the Cabinet*, and a handful of short stories and poems, her writing would never again rise to the level of her best work in the 1940s and early 1950s. What she opted for, instead, was to live the life she had invented for Joan in *The Orchid House*.

Six

The Great Days

Those were the great days! Yes, and these are great.
For who has his majority today
and rises to full stature, with the breath
of scientific dragons on his cheek,
he is as great as any hero born
in any century; greater perhaps:
having discarded cloth of gold and shield,
a faery faith and weapon mystical,
armoured in his frail envelope of flesh
and careless of transfiguring rewards,
he stands within the nimbus of his times.

Phyllis and Robert sailed back to Dominica in late April 1954. Mr. Barker of L. Rose & Co., ever attentive to their needs, had arranged for them a pleasant holiday at sea, marred only by Phyllis's unexpected bout of seasickness, which spoiled her previous perfect seaman's record. Despite the enjoyable crossing, her mood soured perceptibly as they approached the Dominican coast, and she arrived peevish and cross. The circumstances of their arrival were not calculated to improve her state of mind: they had to wait two hours to disembark as no launch had been sent to meet them at Portsmouth. (The company's two launches had been out of commission: the governor was being shown around in one, and Dick Lewis, the L. Rose's manager in Dominica, and the man who had spread rumors that they were Communists both in Dominica and in London, had crashed the other onto a reef.) The two-hour delay turned the pleasure ship into a prison, as the crew shut cabin portholes to paint the sides, and the decks had been boiling hot. Phyllis lost no time in writing to Barker, purportedly to thank him for his many kindnesses, but most manifestly to do a little denunciation of her own. Somewhat uncharitably, she lays before him Lewis's most recent misdeeds: "And while being confidentially frank," she oozes, "Dick is in a ghastly state. Everyone is glad that he is going away for a change, especially his key workers whom he insults when drunk. They do not have to tell us so, though they do, since he shouts so loud the whole neighborhood can hear. I hope that nothing tragic is impending." They arrived home to find the Dominican white enclave in an uproar over Pope-Hennessy's *The Baths of Absalom* and its wholesale condemnation of their tight-knit colonial milieu. Phyllis's response to the collective dismay was not geared to endear her to the local expatriates. She was often heard to comment that their indignant reactions to the book only seemed to confirm his "not so generous conclusions." Her venom betrayed the spitefulness to which of her too-close association with colonial corporate mentality had reduced her; but she would soon escape these marginal concerns through politics, and before long she would be too deeply engulfed in the founding of the Dominica Labour party to spare the likes of Dick Lewis much thought.

At a loss for occupation—the disappointment of *Dashing Away* still loomed large, and she felt too discouraged to write—she returned to her dream of a political party. When she had returned home not quite a year before, she had gravitated to the

DTU as the organization whose aims were closest to her own. She felt certain that the party system offered the surest path to worker power in the newly opened electoral process, and that the DTU was the ideal vehicle from which a party—Dominica's first—could emerge. She had reached out to DTU president Christopher Loblack, and "a historic partnership [had been] born." In Loblack, Phyllis found a political soul mate, quick to agree with her on the necessity "not just for a 'Labour Union' or a 'Labour Party' but for a Labour *Movement*, such as the relationship between the British Labour party and the T.U.C. [the Trade Union Council] had made possible." In the West Indies, as she saw it, "Unions had taken upon themselves to be parties as well, not just to affiliate by choice and contribution to the party most likely to raise the workers' standards." Consequently she thought that a party could emerge out of the DTU with enough widespread support to spearhead a revolution in Dominica's political power structure. Christopher Loblack would come to share her dream wholeheartedly, and together they would forever change island politics.

Phyllis had first met Loblack in 1949, when he had represented Dominica in England at the International Confederation of Free Trade Unions, and had availed himself of the opportunity to discuss Dominica's labor and political problems with the Colonial Office. He was then in his early fifties, an energetic, wiry, ebony-skinned man with bright probing eyes and a keen sense of humor who, as DTU president, commanded a great deal of influence among Dominica's workers. Loblack's personal history was poles apart from Phyllis's. Born Emmanuel Christopher Loblack in the southern village of Grand Bay in 1898, and fatherless from the age of five, he had experienced at a young age the harsh conditions under which Dominican laborers toiled. As a master mason with the Public Works Department he had been greatly influenced by the development of trade unions and workers' associations throughout the West Indies. In the late 1930s, when economic conditions worsened in the wake of the Great Depression and labor unrest swept through the Caribbean, the British government had sent a delegation—the Moyne Commission—to visit the British colonies and investigate the circumstances surrounding the disturbances.* Loblack's impassioned testimony before the commission consolidated his leadership role in the struggle for better working conditions and reforms in the laws that restricted the

*The bloody disturbances began in 1935 during a sugar strike in Saint Kitts. A strike in the oil fields in Trinidad and a subsequent hunger march followed in February. There were strikes and demonstrations throughout the year in British Guiana, Saint Vincent, Jamaica, Barbados, and Saint Lucia. Trouble was widespread again in 1937, with numerous deaths as strikes and demonstrations degenerated into riots. The disturbances brought into the political limelight a new breed of leaders identified with working class aspirations: Grantley Adams of Barbados gained prominence after the 1937 riots as legal counsel for some of the men arrested; in Jamaica, Alexander Bustamante and Norman Manley became known in 1938 as founders (respectively) of the Bustamante Industrial Union and the People's National party; Albert Gomes of Trinidad became a popular political speaker during this period and was elected to the Port of Spain City Council. The royal commission, headed by Lord Moyne, visited all the British territories in the area between November 1938 and February 1939. Their report pinpointed the outdated land-tenure structure and the remnants of the plantation system as the chief culprits in the economic crisis facing the West Indies, and recommended the federation of all the West Indian colonies as "an ideal to which policy should be directed," beginning with the federation of the Windward (Grenada, Saint Vincent, Saint Lucia, Dominica) and Leeward (Antigua; Saint Kitts–Nevis–Anguilla; Montserrat) Islands. It rejected, however, the idea of immediate independence and the introduction of universal adult suffrage, both of which featured among the workers' demands.

workers' economic, social, and political rights. It also led to his being urged by one of its members, Lord Citrine, to form a trade union "as a means of effecting necessary change." Heeding this advice, Loblack (aided by Phyllis's uncle Ralph Nicholls), would lead the grassroots effort that resulted in the founding of the DTU in 1945. The DTU had grown rapidly—within six months of its foundation there were twenty-six branches throughout the island—and had moved quickly to introduce legislation to reduce the working hours of laborers and domestic workers and to protect tenant farmers, who only had a right to two weeks' notice before eviction without compensation. The DTU had soon entered the political arena, with demands for universal adult suffrage, a representative government, and an expansion of citizens' rights. Before a new constitution was granted in 1951 in response to workers' pressures, Dominican voters had to meet income qualifications, which barred most of the DTU members from participation in the electoral process. The 1951 constitution brought about major changes in the political system: Dominicans over the age of twenty-one received the right to vote, prior qualifications for suffrage were dropped, and an elected representative majority was created in the legislature. Elections had been held in 1951 under the new constitution, but "the style of politics and politicians [had] not change[d] immediately, and there were still no organised political parties" to represent particular constituencies.

The movement's possibilities of success rested on the friendship between Phyllis and Loblack, a relationship solidly grounded in mutual admiration: hers for his pioneering work with the DTU against tremendous odds; his for her grassroots savvy, her impressive contacts in England, and the solidity of her political agenda. There was in their collaboration an element of mutual dependence, as each saw in the other a path to fulfilling their ambitions. Phyllis needed Loblack as a main entry into the working class—estate laborers, fishermen, farmers—a sector she could never have broached by herself. He, in turn, needed her intellect and contacts to make up for those educational and social requirements he knew he lacked. In countless ways they were kindred souls, alike in the intensity and passion with which they pursued their ideals, and not burdened by any willingness to mold their dreams to what seemed feasible. Polar opposites as they would seem at first glance—she a bookish, sometimes snobbish white woman, he a semiliterate, fiery, and unsophisticated black laborer—they were nonetheless birds of a feather, both understanding politics as founded upon personal bonds between like-minded people, both well suited for the rough-and-tumble of political work, both earnest and able to find gleeful gratification in ruffling feathers. Their friendship and political collaboration would endure for decades.

While in London Phyllis had contacted an old friend, Hugh Gaitskell—then just months away from becoming the leader of the British Labour party—seeking his advice about the formation of a Labour-affiliated political party in Dominica. Gaitskell, whom she had met during her years as grassroots political worker, helped her draft a constitution modeled after that of the British Labour party, which upon her return to Dominica became the centerpiece of her negotiations with the DTU. When they first broached the idea of founding a party allied to the DTU, Phyllis and Loblack ran into "some ferocious opposition" from union leaders who distrusted her personally as an upper-class white woman, a *béké,* and were suspicious of her political agenda, fearing that the DTU would become a pawn of the party and they would find their influence much reduced. She, in turn, was distrustful of those she saw as wishing to use the union for personal or nonsocialist ends. The parameters of the relationship had to be carefully negotiated, especially as in 1955 Loblack was beginning to lose his hold on the union and was facing challenges from a new generation of leaders. A great deal of infighting ensued about the "voluntary and tolerant nature" of the relationship between the DTU and the as yet nonexistent party, and she was often hampered in her efforts by Loblack's frequent "fierce utterances." He had never been known as a measured speaker, and his sallies tended to "rend the gap" wider between the DTU factions. She soon found herself in an "internecine struggle," and "there were incidents like the padlocking of the Union Hall and the young 'General Secretary' of large proportions who declared [that she] had attacked him at his desk with an umbrella." But in the end they prevailed, and the bulk of the DTU membership embraced the idea of a party.

Rumors of a possible political party along Fabian socialist lines soon drew the concerned attention of Catholic officials, who saw in the coalition of socialism and the DTU the specter of communism against which the very Catholic *Dominica Chronicle* ranted continually. The island's elite was as virulently anti-Communist as its counterparts throughout the region, and the weekly newspaper speculated endlessly about possible Communist infiltration in Dominica spearheaded by the rabble-rousing (but as yet unnamed) Phyllis. Soon the considerable resources of the church were aimed at discouraging the establishment of a political party. The Dominican Catholic Church was led by the Reverend James Moris, bishop of Roseau, a capable administrator who two years before had celebrated the fiftieth anniversary of his arrival in Dominica. Moris, although unquestionably a man of faith, was known for the keen eye he kept on the church's worldly interests in Dominica. Little of import happened in the island to which he was not privy, and he had used his considerable influence to consolidate the church's hold on more than the souls of the population. Phyllis, perhaps unwisely but certainly spiritedly, lost no time in openly challenging the church. The opportunity was handed to her on the proverbial platter in the form of the church's petition to the Island Administrator for a portion of Botanical Gardens land adjacent to the Convent School to expand classroom space and build a playground for the girls. Phyllis, to whom the gardens were the people's patrimony and her grandfather's legacy, was aghast, and immediately began to circulate a petition to pressure the administrator into denying the church's request. She persuaded Aunt Mags to write a letter to the administrator explaining how the terms of the original land grant would be violated by the transfer of the land to church ownership. In her determination to thwart the bishop she left no stone unturned, collecting signatures, writing to influential politicians in England, making a veritable pest of herself, and earning the enmity of the church authorities in the process. The affair became known among her friends as "Phyllis' war against the Convent girls," and she pursued it relentlessly, recruiting supporters from across the Dominican social and political spectrum. Her open challenge to the church was a clever though risky strategy: The affair widened her sphere of action, allowing her budding political movement some degree of independence from the DTU, and helping her to solidify connections; her willingness to challenge the Catholic authorities enhanced her reputation with the people, winning her a reputation for fearlessness and tenacity that would serve her well when she began trying to sell her notion of a party in the countryside. The Botanical Gardens affair gave her fledgling movement its first major public issue and a great deal of publicity; but it was tantamount to a declaration of war, and during her two electoral campaigns, nuns and priests would wage an energetic, often vengeful crusade against her.

In mid-1954 the church's efforts were concentrated on removing her from the scene, and they saw Robert's employment as her Achilles' heel. It took just a few well-timed letters to company headquarters in London about her activities to bring matters to a boil. By late September, Robert's relations with the London office were severely strained. The company chairman had heard from more than one Dominican source that Phyllis's political activities were "apparently taken very seriously in some quarters," and some alarm had been expressed about the possible spread of "disaffection and even of seditious influences." They professed themselves dismayed at the prospect of members of their staff engaging in local political affairs of a controversial nature. "As officials of a Company," they wrote to Robert, "it is our duty to steer clear of politics and to render ourselves immune from adverse criticism so far as we are able." Phyllis, in Robert's defense, had fired off several letters to L. Rose officers, some apparently containing excerpts from her diary, leading company officials to instruct Robert to have all "personal correspondence on any subject connected even indirectly to the company's affairs or members of its staff" cease immediately. Robert replied with an expression of his hope that the prohibition on personal correspondence applied equally to those who had "transmitted exaggerated or false statements" about him and his wife. The only political action he had ever taken in the island—he dissembled—was that of signing his name to the Botanical Gardens petition Phyllis had organized, listening to a cross-section of local political speeches, and cabling their friend and MP, Edith Summerskill, to congratulate her on her election to the Labour party chairmanship. He was in no position to proclaim the truth—that he was his wife's most intimate adviser and supporter in political matters. His continued employment at L. Rose & Co. was vital to them, as they wished to remain permanently in Dominica, where employment opportunities were rare. Thus, despite his outrage, he acknowledged the "warning" he received: "I have respected and supported the Chairman's point of view about trade unions and politics in this island," he wrote in a carefully worded response. "My wife and I deeply resent suggestions from any source that we are capable of the spread of disaffection and even of seditious influences when we are firm believers in constitutional principles and methods and loyalty to the Crown whichever British party may be in power."

But that was as far as he would go. And—given the energy and single-minded determination with which Phyllis had embarked on the foundation of a political party, and the virulent local response to her "subversive" activities—it was really as far as he *could* go. Her political work, he acknowledged, was as much out of his control as it was beyond the command of L. Rose & Co. "Some Catholic authorities do not like my wife and nor do certain white ladies here," he protested. "This is reciprocal and is a matter over which I have little control. Nor I think can L. Rose & Company. But one can never be utterly immune from adverse criticism in a parochial place like this. It would not be human." The pressure mounted until he felt compelled to remind them that if it was indeed the case that the chairman considered that his and Phyllis's "open and legitimate membership in the Labour party" was "an acute embarrassment to the Firm," it was his privilege to ask him to resign his position forthwith. But he wanted him, in such a case, to state the reason in writing as being a political one, "since I may fairly claim to have fulfilled my duties as an engineer, an employee of the firm, and as an individual without reproach." The resignation was not requested, and the storm subsided. Phyllis had made the struggle as public as possible, until there were few in Dominica who had not heard of it or taken sides. Her efforts left company officials in a quandary. She repeatedly depicted her husband's "persecution" as evidence of the fear instilled in the authorities by the prospect of a party of the people. His dismissal would have given the movement its first martyr and guaranteed L. Rose & Company the labor strife they were striving to avoid.

In the waning months of 1954, Phyllis's attention was diverted by a land-purchase scheme she had devised to entice her Fulham friends to leave "cold wet London" and settle in Dominica, a plan typical of her impracticality. She had arranged for their purchase, for an investment of £25, of one acre of land each in an area of Morne Micotrin known as Morne Macaque, in the Fresh Water Lake District, 2,500 feet above sea level, in one of the most inhospitable corners of Dominica, with rainfall averaging 260 inches a year. It was an alluring opportunity, for those who knew nothing of the land in question, as Dominican land was not readily available for purchase by foreigners. George Horner had quickly sent his money, and found comfort in "the thought of owning a piece of land in a tropical paradise when [he] was stuck in the tube at Finchey Road." Francis Reid, an old friend from the Borough Council, was full of dreams of growing vanilla in his little plot and keeping canaries, parakeets, rare birds, goats, mountain sheep, and "goodness knew what else," as well as of having unlimited supplies of limes and West Indian marmalade. Dilys Jones was tempted, but felt that she could never live happily in a place with no seasonal changes and declined.

In early 1955 there was also enough spare time and energy to enjoy Dominica's traditional ole mas' Carnival celebration, Phyllis's first since she had left Dominica in 1927. She dressed in jodhpurs, black dinner jacket, brown felt hat, a black nylon veil inside her mask to conceal her face, and red gloves. Her wire mask had a little Don Carlos moustache, giving the effect of "a Dali-esque huntsman." On the first day of Carnival, as she dressed in a small borrowed room over a shop, the sound of drums, raucous songs, steel bands, and strings filled the streets below. One of the calypsos that year was "exceptionally and crudely vulgar, and that of course was the best one for humming and singing." For a short while she watched from the veranda: "people in fantastic costumes followed by a crowd of unmasked persons surging the narrow road below, singing libidinous calypsos." Accompanied by a Fulham friend, in Dominica on a visit, Phyllis sneaked out the back door and flung herself into the tumult. They were soon surrounded by some dazzling harlequins, fibrous monsters, and men covered all over with colored rags. They got caught in a "hot panting stream of chipping masqueraders, and the fascinating terrifying sensation of claustrophobic heat closed in." The sun was very fierce, and as they "ran mask" they could see the English expatriates and American tourists watching from balconies. They let themselves be dragged along, jumping and jigging. On Tuesday she wore a new costume: white tights with red-and-yellow pantaloons, a long-sleeved white shirt, and a beret of Robert's, out of which streaked her long hair with flounces of mosquito netting twisted into it, making it look like streams of coconut fiber. This time she set out on her own, venturing into a little hotel, where she danced with a friend who had no idea who she was. Then she went into the DTU hall, where they had their own tiny steel band, but at first they would not let her in, yelling (Chris Loblack among them), "Dismask!" and she had to unglove her hand, which they recognized, before they let her dance around the hall. It was nearing six o'clock when she left the hall—no masks were allowed after that hour—and the crowds were getting drunk. By then some of the *békés* were on the street, "running" a bit cautiously and self-consciously. Phyllis retreated to her borrowed veranda and watched the police assemble for a mild charge at curfew time before going home.

In the early months of 1955 Phyllis intensified her political work. She had begun traveling to near and remote villages, explaining to gatherings of DTU members and supporters the manifest advantages of allying themselves to a party committed to furthering the workers' socioeconomic agenda. Despite all its newness, the notion was beginning to take hold among the peasantry. Her efforts continued to worry the authorities, and the *Chronicle* stepped up its warnings against "communist activity" and the "spread of class-hatred, mob inspiration, [and] destructive activities." The government of Dominica, they warned, should take notice of the present atmosphere and try to curb the spread of these seditious movements. Phyllis, undeterred, countered by filing a lawsuit against the administrator and the bishop, co-signed by political activist Alison Stewart-Boyd and Daniel Green, a DTU officer, in connection to what the *Chronicle* described as "a small portion of land intended to be used as a play ground for the pupils of the Convent High School." Having gotten nowhere with her petition, Phyllis resorted to the courts, thus escalating her feud with the church.

On April 23, Elfreda Shand died unexpectedly, felled by a stroke as she was sitting down to lunch and dying a few hours later without regaining consciousness. Maggie, whose companion she had been for so many years, was "utterly bereft." Elfreda had been universally liked, and a great number of tributes from every sort of citizen of the island soon began to pour in, describing her most often as "gallant" and "gracious," comforting thoughts to Phyllis, who found these to be "the most appropriate words about [her] Mother." She was buried on April 24, and as it was Saint George's Sunday, a national holiday, and all the flags were flying, Phyllis comforted herself with the thought that her mother was having "a national funeral." Seeking comfort, Phyllis wrote to her former lover, Bernd von Arnim, after a silence of more than ten years. But his reply came as somewhat of a jolt. Divorced and remarried since Phyllis had seen him last, Bernd had left the Buffalo farm to embark on a career as an insurance agent in Boston. When he received her letter he had just returned to the United States after wintering in the West Indies to recover from a coronary, and had been as near to her as Antigua. His comments on his Caribbean experiences jarred her egalitarian, socialist sensibilities. "What a lot of wonderful history there is in those islands," he wrote. "What a responsibility rests on one's shoulders the minute one is called 'Master' or 'Mistress'—and what wonderful expressions the natives use—'dessert' pronounced 'desert'—'mistress has gone to St Kitts to make her baby'—the wonderful graceful movement of the women with their loads on their heads. I felt in singular rapport with the British natives" [that is, the white Creoles]. He added, "Your political activities sound intriguing. There are going to be such changes in the islands now that the airplane has made them accessible. Do you get up and make speeches to the natives and what do you tell them and how much do they understand? The intelligent ones are so intelligent—but so much needs to be done to raise the level of education—hence intelligence." After this Phyllis did not reply. Bernd, the aristocratic hero of her fantasies, had unequivocally revealed his feet of clay. She would not write to him again until 1958, when, separated from Robert (who had refused to return to Dominica with her) and in dreadfully low spirits, she wrote to tell him of her appointment as federal minister. He replied immediately, congratulating her on the "thrilling" news and hoping he could soon travel to the West Indies so he could see "the Hon.(ey) whenever she is not making a speech or dealing with something vital." In the old flirtacious tone of intimacy that marked all his correspondence with Phyllis, he wished he "could be sitting with [her] and talking to [her] about all [her] projects and plans—you were always my idea of the ideal woman." It would be his last letter to her, as his health continued to deteriorate and he would soon die of a second coronary. Phyllis, perhaps hoping to give Robert (then having an affair with an old friend of theirs) a dose of his own medicine, forwarded the letter to London.

On May 1, 1955, in a public display of the Labour movement's growing power, Phyllis led the DTU in Dominica's first-ever May Day celebration. Before a large crowd assembled in the Market Square, waving banners, Loblack, as the island's acknowledged labor leader, spoke of the importance of trade unionism to the Dominican worker. Phyllis followed, recounting her experiences with May Day celebrations in England. These May Day festivities were but a dress rehearsal for the gathering three weeks later that marked the founding of the DLP. The party was launched on May 24 (then celebrated as Empire Day and therefore a holiday) from the porch of the DTU Hall, a modest wood building on a stone foundation in the Lagon neighborhood of Roseau. Before a large crowd assembled on the street, blocking all traffic, with Phyllis and Loblack as principal speakers, the party constitution was unveiled, printed copies were distributed, and speakers rose to toast the new era opening for the Dominican worker. Phyllis's many months of tireless efforts had borne fruit, and Dominica had its first political party. "Those early apprenticeship days!" she would later write. "They were days of struggle and shortage. If anyone asked me upon what funds the Labour Party of Dominica was founded, I can truthfully answer 'on my small housekeeping allowance and the pennies of the poor,' and it is a fact that no member of the wealthier classes came forward with even a single donation. They seemed genuinely afraid of the new thinking posed by the growing Labour Party and were further scared off by malicious rumours." But now the DLP constitution—her "brainchild"—would guide a new era in Dominican politics. Its platform proposed to "secure for the workers by hand or by brain the full fruits of their industry and the best obtainable system of popular administration and control of each industry and/or service; generally to promote the political, social, and economic emancipation of the people and more particularly of those who depend directly upon their own exertions by hand or brain for the means of livelihood; to unite the forces of labour within the territory and to secure the return of Labour Party representatives to local government bodies, territorial Legislative Council and the planned Federal Government of the West Indies." The party subscribed "wholeheartedly to the declaration of human rights as defined by the United Nations Organization" and pledged itself to foster those ideals. It sought to "guard and cherish the natural benefits and advantages with which the island of Dominica has been so lavishly endowed by nature, . . . to promote skilled workmanship in all its forms" and to encourage the creative arts as well as "free and original thought and expression." Phyllis was proud of two innovations in the party's constitution she had personally introduced: its promotion of artistic creativity and its emphasis on ecological conservation. She proudly reminded friends years later that her party had been the first in the Caribbean—possibly in the world—to include ecological conservation in its platform. The *Chronicle* ignored the mass gathering; there was not a word about the large meeting and its import, although it did allow itself a pointed admonition against "those who take upon themselves the role of leader" and are thus responsible for "making the members distinguish the right from the wrong, the good from the evil, the wise from the foolish." "Leaders," it sententiously concluded, "must be men and women of the right type, regarding their followers not as means to their own advantage or advancement, but as fellow-men and women to be trained for leadership."

N.A.N. "Alec" Ducreay, a young businessman who would join the DLP in 1957, remembered the founding of the party as Dominica's "political awakening," a watershed moment in the island's history, whose significance may have been lost on the upper and middle classes but not on the peasantry and working class. While the upper class concentrated its fire on questioning Phyllis's political sincerity and harping on her being a Communist, Ducreay observed, the poor were happy—"drunk" with the feeling she had helped instill in them that "the day of the underprivileged was at hand." Watching from the sidelines in 1955 (barely twenty-three and trying to build a small lumber business), he shared their certainty that Phyllis was motivated only by her deeply felt desire to advance the cause of the workers.

Within days of the launching of the party, Phyllis wrote to Mr. Barker in London in an attempt to counter the possible damage to Robert's career inflicted by the news of her recent activities. The party, she contended, did not represent a threat to the company's operations in Dominica. There had been, after all, no real industrial or labor trouble of any sort in the island for the last several months despite the intensity of her grassroots efforts to draw members to the party. She had, moreover, reached a "gentlemen's agreement" with the DTU: There was to be no meddling with the Bath Estate, which was to be respected as her private home and her husband's place of business, and hence a site where no politics could be discussed or conducted. Her protestations, as she should have realized, would be to no avail. The founding of the DLP sealed Robert's fate with L. Rose. In early May it was emphatically suggested that he go to England on holiday, taking Phyllis with him, and he had no choice but to acquiesce. They sailed for London in late June. Bishop Moris was rid of Phyllis for the time being.

Phyllis and Robert's two-and-a-half months in London was far from being a carefree time. Worried about their financial future, and once again sharing Philip's difficulties daily, they felt demoralized. Just as it was becoming abundantly clear that their sojourn on the island was coming to an end, Phyllis wanted more than ever to remain in Dominica. Consequently she did not allow herself much time to rest. She worked indefatigably to renew political acquaintances who could help the party in the 1957 general election and lobbied for funds for equipment and materials for the coming campaign, chiefly from the Fabian Society. She contacted her agent at Curtis Brown with the idea of a possible series of tales about the Untanglers, a society dedicated to the discreet investigation and solution of tricky personal problems. (Agatha Christie had created two similar series, and Phyllis hoped that hers would provide enough income for them to remain in Dominica if Robert was fired, as they were anticipating.) The response was not encouraging. While in Dominica she had completed enough poems for a new collection entitled *Contrasts,* her third, which she had printed in Barbados shortly before leaving for London. She now made some halfhearted efforts at distributing copies among her friends and acquaintances, leaving a number of copies to be sold for Writers' Guild funds at a forthcoming meeting.

Contrasts is a volume of twelve poems—most of them apparently written while Phyllis was still in England—and a handful inspired by her reencounter with her native island. It is the weakest of the three collections she had published by them, gathering some poems left out of her earlier *Palm and Oak* (1950), presumably because she had not found them good enough for publication then. Texts like "The Hidden Hamlet," "Bazaar," "Nocturne," "Christmas at the Seaside," and "Fugitive Hummingbird" offer haunting and vivid descriptions of places and landscapes dear to her, echoing a need to crystallize in poetry both familiar English locales she had left (Penhurst and the bazaars she had roamed since her Buffalo days, where she is said to have bought all her clothes) and the newly rediscovered Dominican landscape. "Fugitive Hummingbird," for example, captures the "aromatic," "citrus dark" of her surroundings at Bath Estate, while in "Nocturne" Phyllis recreates the enchantment and "warm white pallor of a tropic night." A second group of poems—"Turn the Leaves," "With Time a Threatened Currency," and "The Nights"—may have been inspired by the latter stages of her relationship with A. E. Coppard, one that, whatever its nature, appears to have come to an end during the months she and Robert spent apart in early 1953. "The Nights" uses imagery ("my ormolu darling, my opaline one," "your grey eyes are aloes and monticoline") Phyllis had used in *Dashing Away* to describe her friend and possible lover. "With Time a Threatened Currency" is a wistful meditation on how "with time a threatened currency and space/an indefensive citadel, enough/ransom is paid for the beloved face/to jeopardise the solvency of love." It shares with "Turn the Leaves" (a disarming ode to a journal recording a couple's "chronicle of a concord strange and deep") an elegiac tone of anticipated nostalgia for something held very dear that is about to be lost. "Gentleness of Friends," a poem that was among her favorites, celebrates friendship as a "wine milder than milk," "honey of talk, healing," "cooling unguent juice distilled from lips blistered with private grief." "Andersen's Mermaid" gives a happy ending, distilled in irony, to the well-known fairy tale. But the booklet reads like a collection of hastily assembled texts, and the poems lack the élan that gave her earlier collections their appeal. *Contrasts* also includes Phyllis's best-known and most memorable poem, "Love for an Island," in which she voices her absorbing yearning for the island of her birth. Writing of her love for Dominica as "the sternest passion, . . . pulsing beyond the blood through roots and loam," she portrays lovers of islands as consumed by a "rapacious craving for a possession rude and whole," driving their stakes to plunge "in the heat of earth and smell the stars of the incredible vales." "Love for an Island" finds an ideal counterpoint in "The Great Days," a poem that conveys the compelling drive that bolstered her struggle to found the DLP. Writing of "The Great Days" as peopled by heroes who, "having discarded cloth of gold and shield" and "careless of transfiguring rewards," sally forth in pursuit of their chimeras, Phyllis encapsulates the ideals that fed her dreams, dreams now threatened by the uncertainty that clouded their future.

As Robert awaited clarification of his status at L. Rose & Co., tensions mounted between him and Phyllis. His proposed solution to their dilemma was to abandon politics, give up their London flat, and settle into a quiet and inexpensive life at Penhurst, where she could write and from where he could seek work as a self-employed industrial consultant; hers was to find some way to return to lead her party to victory in the coming election. They were kept in suspense until mid-August, when Robert was summoned to the company offices and officially dismissed, citing as justification completion of the reorganization of L. Rose's operations in Dominica and its no longer needing someone with his level of qualifications. The dismissal was shrewdly planned and executed. Realizing the awkward position in which it would be placed by dismissing the husband of the founder of a new political party with broad worker support, the company had brought him to England on the pretext of a vacation, with the intention of not allowing him to return. Having succeeded, however, they could afford to be generous, trying to forestall any possible political repercussions. Robert's period of notice, which per his contract was to be three months, was extended to six, during which he would receive full pay; he was allowed continued use of the company car; and they would arrange for Phyllis's passage to and from Dominica to pack the family's belongings. Consequently, in mid-September 1955, struggling to overcome her profound disappointment, Phyllis embarked for Dominica. Her too-brief sojourn on the island was over, and she could not foresee a quick return without an income. As the husband of a "subversive" party leader, Robert was virtually unemployable in Dominica; as the subversive, so was she. The forthcoming elections, which offered a glimmer of hope, were not scheduled until mid-1957. How would she even gather the funds for her return passage to the island and the expenses of a campaign? The triumph of the founding of the party had been short-lived indeed.

Phyllis sailed home in the *Colombie*, a French liner, and from the first moment she stepped on board was immersed in the West Indian colonial world of her youth. Among her fellow passengers was a very old lady, Mrs. McDonald, who had known Phyllis's father and her Shand grandparents, and was full of anecdotes of their life at Fitches Creek in Antigua during the last years of the family's ownership of the estate. Phyllis, always eager to hear more about her family's history, greatly enjoyed her company, particularly as Mrs. McDonald had flattered her by remarking that she was the very image of "the old Shands." There was also on board an old Dominican friend of hers, Mona Branch, who had known Julian Archer and "most of the young ghosts of the past." Phyllis spent her days pleasantly on deck gossiping about the old days and reading Simenon mysteries. The crossing was haunted by an eerie accident off the Spanish coast, near Vigo. The *Colombie* rammed a little fishing trawler in fog, drowning five of the small craft's crew of ten. Phyllis had stood on the A deck watching the wreckage drift by with the wounded and dying, some of whom struggled within reach; but the *Colombie*'s crew had been very slow in launching lifeboats, and once launched, it was discovered that the only motorized one had no fuel. One poor greenish corpse floated around in circles with his eyes open—a terrible sight, Phyllis had thought, "like a Goya or Henry Moore shelter figure." For weeks after the accident she could not get the green drowned face out of her mind. As a result they had to return to Vigo, where they were delayed for nearly two days by the investigation. Although the crew said the *Colombie* would still call at Dominica, she was anxious lest, in order to make up time, they would refuse to stop there after all, leaving her stranded on another island seeking passage home. She was also having anxiety dreams about the Botanical Gardens case, probably because the ship was loaded with nuns and priests who had been chanting dolorous requiems for the fishermen drowned or injured in the accident.

By mid-October, however, she was at last settled at Kingsland House. Good news had been awaiting her: she had won first prize in a literary contest sponsored by the local radio station, for "Little Cog-burt," her short story about the unsympathetic expatriate woman. The recognition was worth much more than the twenty pounds' prize money. The story would be broadcast repeatedly throughout the Caribbean. Within days of her arrival, "between intervals of moonlit drizzle," the party held its first big public meeting in the Market Place. The crowd had numbered between 2,500 and 3,000, an enormous gathering for an island with a total population of less than 60,000, and it filled the market to overflowing. The meeting had gone very well, a quality of festival had presided over it all, and "everyone [had] behaved splendidly, though tensions were high." The party leadership had listened to the complaints of the men about to migrate to England in search of jobs, about 240 of them (as Robert learned to his horror when Phyllis wrote to ask him to give them a hand.) People called out "*Mwen evek ou*" (I'm with you), from time to time. Phyllis could indeed imagine that she had stepped into the pages of *The Orchid House*. On the very next day quite a number of people, many of them Caribs,* had joined the party.

Phyllis's political movement had generated an enormous amount of interest among the Caribs, whose territory on the inhospitable eastern coast of the island, with its treacherous beaches, lack of safe ports, and mountainous terrain, was virtually cut off from ready communication with the rest of the island. The things she promised—roads, schools, true representation on the council, medical care, and access to markets for the goods they produced—were the things they desperately needed. The Caribs had quickly adopted her as their spokesperson and sought to send her as their emissary to the queen, with whom they felt they had the right to deal directly, having nothing but scorn for the Legislative Council. Phyllis quickly amassed a "huge roll of communications" from them detailing their many grievances, and they became some of the staunchest DLP supporters. Once, learning that she could not visit their territory as expected, they sent a messenger to ask her if she would like them to come to town "in a body!" Phyllis was to repay their trust, professionally and personally. She had always had a profound respect for the Caribs, whom she felt belonged, more truly than anyone else, to her beloved island. Their history fascinated her, particularly as she felt that it was so closely connected to her family's own through Thomas Warner, the founder of the Antigua colony, who had "married" a Carib princess. She had placed the Caribs' needs high on the party's list of priorities, and once the DLP came to power in 1960 the process of opening the Carib territory to the rest of the world began in earnest. (A road was cut through the area in 1970; electricity and telephone

*The remnants of the Carib tribe that once peopled the Lesser Antilles—easily recognizable because of their skin tone and facial structure—live in the Carib Territory, 3,700 acres of Dominica's rugged northeastern coast. The land, planted in bananas and coconuts, is owned in common by the members of the tribe. The territory, created in 1903, was governed by an elected chief until 1952, when a Carib council chaired by the chief was created. The Caribs' strongest link with the past is their waterproof larouma-reed baskets—whose brown, white, and black designs are handed down from generation to generation—sold in small shops thoughout the territory.

service followed in the 1980s.) She would be indefatigable as a Federation minister in promoting the export of Carib baskets and coordinating visits of tribe representatives to the queen, and would eventually adopt two Carib boys.

The weekend following the Market Place meeting she traveled to Portsmouth, Vieille Case, Grand Bay, and Pointe Michel, making "a vast effort" to visit the Caribs, if only for a couple of hours, by going through Castle Bruce Junction. It had been an exhausting undertaking as the villages she visited were scattered all over the map and a great deal of the traveling had to be done on foot or horseback. It took both extraordinary energy and an iron resolve not to shy from the ordeal. Her goal was to capitalize on the impact made by the Roseau meeting, explain the party's program to village elders, and encourage the founding of branches in the countryside. The party's political agenda, passionately and indefatigably outlined by her in these and many other remote villages, spoke eloquently to the peasantry, cut off from the capital and the rest of the world. Travel to the markets or doctors in Roseau involved miles-long treks across treacherous and slippery mountain tracks during the night, on paths dimly lit by makeshift torches, in order to reach town by early morning—or else equally dangerous sea voyages on unsafe launches and canoes. The transportation difficulties meant that peasants could bring to market only what they could carry, severely limiting economic opportunities and income. Very often they would lose their cargo; all too frequently lives would be lost. In her speeches Phyllis addressed the lack of roads, the substandard conditions of the few roads that did exist, and the lack of running water and clinics and their impact on people's health. She advocated birth control for women as a means of lowering the alarming incidence of unsafe abortions and was passionate about two children-related issues: the high rate of infant mortality and the woefully inadequate access to education. She laid great emphasis on the need to provide equal educational opportunities to all, deploring the fact that many of Dominica's youngsters, regardless of ability, could not get a good job or a scholarship. The message was "clearly socialistic, . . . centering on how no one should be victimized because of race, class, or geography."

In these early days of party politics in Dominica, Phyllis "presented something new for the people, not only the idea of voting, but of educating the people as to what it meant to have a parliament." Her central argument was that the election of an independent candidate guaranteed them nothing, but the election of one committed to the party's program would assure them accountability—the simple but new notion of a government responsible to its electorate. She would bring her point home by offering Howell Shillingford—a wealthy planter who had represented the people of the North Western District for twenty-five years—as an example of all that was wrong with the nonparty system. The people of the district he represented—which included Portsmouth, Dominica's second largest town and busiest port—had no road connecting them to Roseau to bring their produce to town, and were forced to travel to the capital via sea launches or on foot. Yet there was a modern state-built road leading to the Shillingford Estate. In these early days, when the concept of party loyalty was in its most primitive stages, the person—the individual—was still everything, and Phyllis had to build confidence in the party by personally gaining the people's trust. Her greatest advantage was her personal appeal. She was the granddaughter of Sir Henry Nicholls, whom some of the older peasants remembered with fond gratitude; she was a member of the former ruling class on an island where old habits of deference to class and race had died hard; she was the niece of Ralph Nicholls, who had been instrumental in the founding of the DTU; and she claimed to have come to help open the way, on their behalf, to a new concept of politics. Her being a woman, a factor that would have been of primary importance on any other island, mattered far less on Dominica than her race and class origins. Dominicans seem more at ease with women politicians than other West Indians. Although often taunted for harping on women's issues and being "big on the woman thing"—Dominican males are more tolerant of women as leaders than of avowed feminists—Phyllis did not often feel that just *being* a woman played a significant factor in her political life. Moreover, she had followed in the footsteps of another white writer and politician, Elma Napier, who had been very active in local political affairs and had been a member of the Legislative Council for many years. They in turn would be followed by another woman party founder and popular politician, Eugenia Charles, a onetime foe whom Phyllis joined in the foundation of the Freedom party in 1968.

Phyllis's strongest asset, according to many of her early political associates, was the genuine affection for the people that marked her actions and speeches. She was by all accounts deeply troubled by their condition and addressed their problems with a down-to-earth, convincing simplicity that moved them to rally around her. When she campaigned, many remember, "it didn't matter if a place or person was dirty, she would go over," shake hands, chat, reveal her unfeigned curiosity about people's lives and needs. Some would look askance at the sight of a white woman betraying her race and class, professing to want only to help "the people," but most soon came to respect her honesty even when they disagreed with her views. Frank Baron, then the island's most influential legislator, saw Phyllis's concern for the poor as hypocritical and opportunistic. She was, in his opinion, above all a politician, ready to do "what was convenient at the moment to get what she wanted." Her intimacy with the laborers—insincere and manipulative as he believed it to be—particularly irritated him. She had to be aware, he was convinced, of the profound propaganda impact—in an island where race and class divisions had been strictly observed—of the sight of Dr. Nicholls's white granddaughter sitting comfortably in a peasant's hut, eating out of his pot, and eschewing the expected marks of respect due to her solely on the basis of her race and class. She was forever kissing babies, hugging women, heartily shaking calloused hands, listening intently to complaints, offering sympathy and kind words, throwing her arms around people Baron would not have touched for the world.* But what her enemies saw as hypocritical opportunism others saw as uncontestable proof of her sincerity. And even Baron granted that neither she nor her closest associates ever seemed eager for self-aggrandizement.

*The protagonist of Phyllis's "The Bodyguard," a female political candidate who is founder and president of her party, distresses her associates with behavior similar to Phyllis's own:

> Linard . . . found that he was expected on Wednesday to accompany La Présidente on a canvassing tour of a slum area. "We must maintain *touch*," she explained sweetly—but Linard shuddered to see her take the sickly infants of voters into her arms. Worse, she expected him to do the same, and to shake the scaly hands of their parents; her clear eyes quickly detected evasion and compunction. "Do you want us all to die martyrs?" he asked in exasperation when she showed no sign of flagging and the slum became filthier and more degraded. "No, but a politic[ian], like a novelist, must suffer with the people," retaliated Sylvie.

Her personal appeal was bolstered by the absence of racism in her nature. Arnold Active, who worked closely with her during many political campaigns, claimed that she was "colour blind," aware of race but unwilling to give it any significance. This, he believed, was why she "wasn't liked very much by her family"—because "she was a down-to-earth person . . . who never acted as if she had returned to the island to claim her birthright as a white woman, but rather to help the Dominican dispossessed claim theirs." She was also, her friends and enemies alike claim, "Dominican to the core": She "thought, felt, and acted with a tremendous passion for the island" that came through in her addresses to the people. She was, moreover, able to switch with ease from English to patois in her speeches. The use of patois, her political enemies suggested, was a hypocritical last-minute adoption, another opportunistic ruse to bamboozle the electorate. Phyllis, who had always lapsed easily into patois when speaking with her Dominican friends or her sisters, felt the sting of the accusation acutely, and once inquired impatiently of a reporter: "Do you think I could ever conduct a political meeting here without knowing patois?" Phyllis's patois, however, was one of phrases with which she peppered her predominantly English speeches, rather than fluency. Interviewed on the patois *Esperiance Kweole* radio program in 1982, she justified her rather French-laden patois to her Dominican audience by describing it as *patois parisien*! These early days of her campaign in the countryside were not without their humorous side. She was fond of telling her London friends how once, having arrived at a place where the people were suffering from an unusual drought, she was asked what they should do. "You can only pray," she had replied. They had taken her quite literally, the rains had come that very night, her reputation was enhanced, and the number of party supporters had increased. She was also not above rallying the peasantry with "signs and portents." One night, when an apparently inexplicable shower of feathers had descended upon a party meeting, she had immediately seized her opportunity, and they had become "the holy feathers"—a "sign from heaven."

On the first of November she was still in Dominica, writing to Robert on a very hot All Saints' Night, "with the factory going full blast and the candles lit in the cemetery," about the massive exodus of Dominicans who had just left for London in the *Auriga*. She wanted him to meet the boat. "If you could do that, you will be doing an immeasurable service for them and me (us), for they fully *expect* to see you at Paddington Station, as events [that is, his dismissal] have turned you into a national hero." He was becoming a little leery of her commissions, however. She had recently led him on a wild-goose chase after two adventurers who had absconded with five hundred pounds won at the horses by Boy Dupigny, a Carib just back from London. He had left the money with his landlady to be sent to Dominica in a postal check, but the money, and the landlady, had disappeared, and Robert had played detective fruitlessly for several days.

In early November she was unanimously elected as president of the party, and soon afterward announced her decision to contest the Western District, then held by J. B. Charles, Eugenia's father. As she had but a short time left before she was due to leave Dominica she organized a meeting at Laudat, a village in her chosen constituency, to found a party branch and unveil her plans for the district. The news had to be broken to Robert, a necessity that filled her with apprehension. She had fallen into the habit of presenting unpleasant news to him very gingerly, as if he were a child who needed to be cajoled into drinking something "nasty." Her present packet of news would be distasteful indeed, as he was expecting her to give up politics and live a life of semiretirement at Penhurst; therefore she slipped her momentous announcement into a chatty description of her recent activities—she had made some visits, packed their china and silver, been reelected president of the party, gone to a church bazaar, and committed herself as a candidate for election. "So that's that. I shall have to come back from time to time; and I intend to enter politics at 1957 elections, and become a Minister." Then she quickly moved on to other news: The village of Massacre (so named because it was the site of a seventeenth-century massacre of Caribs) now had a DLP branch, and Portsmouth's, where she had spent the weekend, staying in a laborer's tiny household, had grown to be as big as Roseau's; and, more important, she had been "promoted"—the peasantry no longer called her *Madame-là* (a patois appellation used for outsiders), but *Madame-noûs*, the clearest mark of her acceptance. Meanwhile, a Mr. Scarlett, "a nice little man" from the Colonial Office, was visiting Dominica, and Phyllis and Loblack had hauled him to the gardens to show him the site where the playground was to be built. Later they had taken him around the slums and given him a list of "moans from people all over the island, mostly asking her to 'do something for our misery'. It was scroll upon scroll." They had also taken up the cause of some stowaways in the *Master of the Leeward Islands* who had been ill treated by the shipmaster. (It was illegal for a ship's crew to punish stowaways.) The "poor devils" had been caught among the bananas after five days at sea. This, they told the hapless Mr. Scarlett, was the result of the "England fever" running through the islands. "One tells them the snags," she sighed, "but to no avail."

In mid-November, her packing all done, Phyllis began saying her farewells. She had just established a party branch at Grandbay and had one more meeting awaiting her before her departure to solidify the branch at Laudat. On her last evening at Bath House she invited the "Estate folks" to a "goodbye Barbadine punch," a "sort of last supper, [with] everyone getting a little souvenir in the way of a cup or a dish left over from the inventory." She gave Mr. Rolle, Robert's former assistant, his paper knife and clothes brush, "as travelling by air [as far as Barbados] she had to "jettison even some useful objects." She was carting their "lovely [painting by Raoul] Dufy" with her, and all their records, so, flying into Barbados, she would have to wear all her winter clothes on boarding the plane to avoid excess baggage charges, which she could ill afford: "Agonies!" All her friends in Dominica, as she said her farewells, had been "full of drippy sentiments," but they felt sure she and Robert would both come back some day. "I have worked like hell to put my Party on its feet," she mused as she left, "and I'm sure it will not die while I'm gone. Too many enthusiasts for that."

Seven

Now in Our Times' Frugality

Now in our times' frugality, who will stand
patient in dragnet crowd
to purchase measured bounty, and who will break
an easy-gotten loaf between his proud
and simple friends? Oh who will value more
even than bread the life to him allowed?

The year and a half that Phyllis spent in London before her return to Dominica to contest J. B. Charles's seat in the Legislative Council was a crucial period in the protracted negotiations to establish the Federation of the West Indies. Phyllis, a committed Federalist, followed the process with eager interest. The Federation movement, led by Andrew Cipriani of Trinidad and T. A. Marryshow of Grenada, grew out of a desire for self-government, a conviction that the territories would have a greater chance of success in making demands from the Colonial Office if they acted together, and the assumption that "the islands could not hope to become self-governing unless they first federated." In October 1932, at the invitation of the Dominica Taxpayers Association, the political leaders of the eastern Caribbean met for the first time to draft a detailed plan for the establishment of a West Indian Federation bringing together all British colonies in the region. Little progress was made toward federation in the 1930s, however, until the appointment of the Moyne Commission to investigate the disturbances that arose out of the deterioration of economic conditions during the depression. In preparation for the commission's arrival, West Indian political leaders met in British Guiana in June 1938 to establish the British Guiana and West India Labour Congress and draft a proposal to place before the commission, headed by a draft bill for a federation on the basis of full internal self-government with adult suffrage. But the Moyne Commission—doubting the readiness of West Indian public (that is, middle- and upper-class) opinion to accept federation, and aware that while the islands of the eastern Caribbean were solidly united in their desire for federation, the notion had not taken hold in Jamaica—recommended a federation of the Windward and Leeward Islands as a first step in the process.* With this recommendation came another for a large annual grant that led to the creation of the Colonial Development and Welfare Organization, an administrative unit which behaved generally as if the West Indies were already a single entity and became a "working symbol of Caribbean unity." Its success played a significant role in preparing the islands and the Colonial Office for federation.

The 1940s brought fundamental changes in the political process in the West Indies, the most important of which were the shift in the balance of power from the

*In 1938 the notion had progressed much further in the eastern Caribbean than in Jamaica. While political leaders in the smaller islands had concluded many years before that federation opened the surest path to self-government and economic development, Jamaica was only beginning to explore it as one of many options. When the Federation was created, "It was for the Eastern Caribbean the fulfillment of the political ambitions of forty years, backed by much sentiment and propaganda, whereas in Jamaica it was still a recent and strange idea, hardly a dozen years old, which had not yet sunk into the popular consciousness."

middle to the working classes, the election of popular radicals to the legislative councils in the various islands, and expansions of the electoral franchise. There was as yet no universal adult suffrage, no full internal self-government or ministerial system, but power resided with the elected members sitting in the Legislative Councils, and these councils now included leaders like Grantley Adams, Norman Manley, and Alexander Bustamante, men who had built their political careers on their defense of the then radical notions of self-government, universal adult suffrage, and a defense of the aspirations of the working classes. Many of the new leaders were committed federalists, and could no longer be ignored by the Colonial Office. In September 1945 the British Guiana and West India Labour Congress, now renamed the Caribbean Labour Congress, earnestly urged "the development of the Caribbean area as one economic entity as the only way of creating a stable and self-supporting economy." As a result a conference was convened in September 1947 at Montego Bay, in which a Standing Closer Association Committee (SCAC) was established to draft a federal constitution based on the reductive principle of each unit retaining complete control over all matters except those specifically assigned to the Federal government. It set a rocky path for the Federation, one which "trammeled [it] from its birth," by concluding that it was "unnecessary to secure equality of constitutional status in each unit before effecting Federation," leaving each island to secure what constitutional advances it could on its own.

The recommendations of the SCAC (as modified by the London Conference of 1953), set the parliamentary structure for the Federation. It would have a bicameral legislature, with a House of Representatives elected through universal adult suffrage and a Senate appointed by the Council of State or cabinet. The executive power of the Federation would be vested in the governor-general, with the Council of State (to be selected by the prime minister) as "the principal instrument of policy." Representation in the House on the basis of population had been rejected on the grounds that this would allow Jamaica virtual control, and a plan was adopted for a House of forty-five members, of which Jamaica was allocated seventeen seats, Trinidad ten, Barbados five, and the other islands two each, with the exception of Montserrat, with one. "Dual membership" was not favored—any member of a unit legislature or executive council had to resign that seat on appointment to the Federal House. Crucial matters, however, remained unresolved. The choice of the capital of the Federation was not finalized, although Trinidad appeared to be the preferred site. The territorial legislatures continued to push vigorously for the immediate granting of dominion status to all units, while the smaller islands continued to insist on placing "movement of persons between units" under exclusive federal power despite strenuous opposition from Trinidad. This was a potentially divisive issue, since it could lead to unrestricted movement of people from poorer units with high unemployment to richer units.

In the five years that elapsed between the 1953 conference and the starting date for the Federation, substantial changes took place in West Indian politics. In 1953 individual islands had not yet received internal self-government with ministerial status, and local leaders had not yet been able to run their own local affairs. By 1958 these rights had been granted to all participating units and there was an increasing unwillingness on the part of local leaders to endow the Federation with powers that would diminish those of the local legislatures. In 1955 a fiscal commissioner was appointed to prepare a comprehensive analysis of the Federation's financial and fiscal structure, the *Caine Report*. It proposed an initial period of consumption taxes (customs and excise) on gasoline, cigarettes, beer, rum, and other spirits as an interim measure until an income tax could be established, in addition to the profits on a Federal currency issue. The report was bitterly opposed by a conference of delegates in London in February 1956, and a compromise was reached through the acceptance of a proposal for the Federation to be financed through a fixed contribution from each unit (the "mandatory levy") and through the profits from its currency issue. The decision was politically expedient, as most West Indian leaders attending the conference were facing elections later in the year, but it was to prove disastrous later, as it deprived the Federal government of a revenue source it could control, placing it in a virtual financial straitjacket. The Federation was not two months old before the issue formed the subject of bitter charges and countercharges across the floor of the Federal House of Representatives. This issue resolved, the delegates authorized the British government to pass the necessary legislation, and a Standing Federation Committee was named with authority to settle final details and assemble a staff.* The Federation in which Phyllis was to play a leading role was reality.

Phyllis, who had found part-time work at the Fabian Bureau soon after her return to London, followed every development of the conference with trepidation. Her days were consumed with seeking reports, meeting with political leaders, staff members, and reporters with any information to impart on the proceedings. As a Fabian Bureau staff member, she used her credentials to contact British politicians willing to ease matters for the delegates, and her house was open to any political acquaintance needing a place to stay. Dominica's delegate was Phyllis's rival Frank Baron, at best a lukewarm supporter of the Federation, which he saw as "a bunch of politicians getting together, aided and abetted by the English who wanted to get rid of them"; but faced with support for the Federation at home, he participated actively in the efforts towards its formation. But the Federation that emerged was as weak as he would have desired. The Federal government would have little power and little money and would include neither internal free trade nor freedom of movement of persons. Yet, severely limited as it would be, the Federal government would have to impress itself on the popular mind so as to consolidate itself, must demonstrate to the British government its fitness for independence, and conciliate divergent interests in the units with little power to impose solutions. Such a Federation would have required the participation of the best and most experienced political leaders the islands had available, but the conference had finally rejected dual membership in Federal and unit legislatures, forcing leaders to choose between powerful home governments and a weak and penniless

*The committee drafted a constitution, agreed upon "West Indies Federation" as a name, selected a Federal coat of arms, a motto (To Dwell Together in Unity), and flag (white waves across a blue background), and chose Trinidad as the Federal capital. Its most important resolution, one that would prove disastrous, was a change in the time at which review of the constitution might be held, from *during* the fifth year to *no later than* the fifth year (which meant *at any time* during the first five years). A governor-general, Lord Hailes, was appointed, and the first election was set for March 25, 1958. The committee last met in October 1957 to fix salaries for various posts, resolving that the salaries and allowances for ministers needed to exceed those paid to their unit counterparts in compensation for their relocation, loss of local income, and increased expenses. The salaries and free housing, chauffeurs, and garden allowances were later to be the butt of public jibes.

Federation. Baron would choose to remain in Dominica, where he would soon become the island's first chief minister, as would Manley in Jamaica and Eric Williams in Trinidad, leaving the Federation devoid of the kind of political leadership needed to overcome its structural weaknesses.

Baron was to return home to form his own political party, the People's National Movement (PNM), hastily founded with the collaboration of Clifton Dupigny, a political and business associate. The PNM was, by Baron's own admission, less a party than a coalition of liberal, moderate, and conservative politicians whose principal aim was to counter the more radical DLP with at least a semblance of an organization. Baron particularly felt that the foundation of the DLP, with its openly socialist goals, left them no choice but to attempt to present to the populace a coherent policy around which their own constituency could rally. The PNM claimed similar goals to those of the DLP—an adult education drive and the improvement of health care headed its list—but it differed substantially in "the manner of execution." The PNM "appealed to the educated mind, while the DLP appealed to the uneducated—what they called the working class." In 1955 Baron, Dominica's leading minister, thought that what mattered most was not rhetoric but the capacity of the individual to get a job done well, and he counted on his excellent relationship with the colonial authorities to give him an edge against the DLP in the coming election.

After the completion of the conference, Phyllis dedicated herself to strengthening the DLP financially and morally from a distance. In the year and a half she would spend in London before her return to Dominica to contest the 1957 elections, she became the most dependable unofficial social worker for Dominican immigrants, who would leave for England with the confidence that "as long as we get to London, Ma Allfrey will take care of us." In these early days of the great migration rush, before West Indians established communities in England, the immigrants had very few places to go, and Phyllis, as President of the DLP, was thought of as a natural source of work, lodging, and security. Some of the migrants, she thought, confused the British Labour party with the Labour Exchange, "and had to be gently disillusioned." She and Robert had an old car, a Ford van named "Cagey," which he had converted into a rough station wagon with makeshift seats. Freshly arrived West Indians would telephone from the railway station, more often than not at dawn, and Robert would sally forth in "Cagey" for Victoria or Paddington Stations, returning home with a car full of "brave but underequiped [*sic*] West Indians, mostly Dominicans."* At first they had some difficulty with the owners of their block of flats because of the influx of colored people. The manager threatened to turn them out, and they received stern letters from the owners. But Phyllis was not to be deterred; she ignored the letters and they finally ceased to come.

During this "time of the migrants," their flat was open to any Dominican needing a place to celebrate a wedding or christening fete or just a place to stay for a few days or weeks, and it became a bit of a command post where Dominicans would

*Despite his efforts to help, efforts that often entailed considerable personal sacrifice, Robert was not generally liked by the newcomers. His uncompromising frankness and lack of tact often overshadowed his generosity. He occasionally made comments that were at best thoughtless and at worst left him open to charges of racism—as when he observed, upon seeing a group of dark-skinned Dominican girls wearing makeup, that they should know better than to wear lipstick, as it had not been made for them.

gather informally, or where they came when they knew a friend or relative was arriving by boat and would need some warm clothing. Phyllis was forever collecting sweaters and coats from just about everyone she knew who could spare something. In fact, she was a bit too prone to give away everything she had—and everything Robert had, including his only coat. He once complained that he soon would not be able to go out, and friends and relatives learned the hard way to hide their clothes when Phyllis was about. Once, on a cold winter's night, coming home chilled to the bone, Robert asked mildly, "Where is my polo sweater?" and Phyllis could not admit that she had given it to a citizen of Roseau who had turned up one icy afternoon clad in a nylon shirt and flannel trousers. Robert then began to check his wardrobe methodically, and soon remarked, "in less of a reproachful than a statistical tone," "Well, it is a good thing most of the migrants are a lot shorter than I am."

Throughout 1956 Phyllis worked indefatigably to find employment for her charges. Her sister Rosalind, then living in Old Bosham after many years abroad, received frequent calls asking if she or any of her friends needed household help. Once Phyllis almost sent her a consumptive woman, whom, on discovering that she was suffering from tuberculosis, Phyllis and Robert nursed at their flat until she was fit to work. The girl had arrived on their doorstep at two o'clock in the morning wearing a gauzy scarf and a thin dress as her only protection against the cold, and looking seasick. She was coughing horribly, and Phyllis surprised her in her room crouching over a basinful of blood. The doctor they called pronounced her case to be advanced and "at a very contagious stage," but they would not send her away until a bed was found for her in a country sanatorium. She went on to recover completely. Another time they had given shelter to a girl from Giraudel who had stayed for a few days before joining her brother at his boardinghouse and finding a job at Selfridge's (the manager being a "liberal-minded man prepared to give coloured people a break"). Phyllis was thus doubly surprised to come home for lunch one day to find the girl in her living room, dressed only in her panties and hat, holding an umbrella and chanting hymns. Robert, alone in the flat, had sent for her brother, who arrived with an "official-looking man." When Phyllis arrived, the three of them were attempting to get her to take some pills. Seeing Phyllis, she seized her in a "terrifying bear hug," screaming, "Let there be light!" until, soothed by her softer, comforting voice, she relaxed a bit and agreed to take the pills—which she believed to be poison—if Phyllis would lick them first. Waking up from the effect of the tranquilizers at the hospital, she attacked a nurse—she bit two chunks of flesh out of her arm—but soon recovered and eventually became a trained nurse herself.

Francis Reid, Phyllis's friend on the Fulham Borough Council, was eager to hire a Dominican woman recommended by Phyllis, although he, too, echoed the discomfort some people—even those of leftist persuasions—felt about race in those early years of Caribbean migration to England. "I am wondering how dark skinned she will be," he writes to Phyllis of the proposed employee, "for she would have to share the bathroom with my schoolmaster tenant downstairs, and if he has racial feelings, it might cause a riot." Perhaps most helpful to Phyllis in her efforts to find work and homes for Dominican immigrants was Col. V. Paravicini, a wealthy patron, active in the food industry, for whom Phyllis worked occasionally as part-time private secretary. The colonel had been a prisoner of war in Germany and had later organized the distribution of food for POWs. He had connections in industry able to provide decent wages for unskilled work, and his social contacts were extensive enough to be a steady source of housekeeping work for the increasing number of Dominican women leaving the island.

Arnold Active, a founding member of the London branch of the DLP, later to become a minister in the first DLP government in Dominica, saw Phyllis as a social worker at heart, deriving a great deal of satisfaction from her relentless work on behalf of the fledgling Dominican community in London. Once, realizing that most of the party members had never been out of London, she organized for them an August Bank Holiday outing to Penhurst that turned into a lively calypso party with plenty of music, pepper sauce, and rum punch. There were enough musicians among them to form a small band, which accompanied itself with Phyllis's beat-up old piano and responded to requests of "something hot man, play something hot" with calypso after calypso. The party gathered the core members of the party branch in London, founded not too long before at a meeting in Phyllis's flat. The partygoers even composed a special calypso for the occasion: "Mrs. Allfrey, she's all right. / She make our lives plenty bright." They rocked the peaceful Sussex countryside and merited a story in the local newspaper.

Phyllis made sure Dominicans and other West Indians understood and made use of the British political system to their advantage. Members of the London branch of the party were often treated to visits to the House of Parliament and private interviews with MPs she knew well. Active's first initiation into politics was under her guidance, and he rated her an "excellent political trainer." In 1957, when Phyllis was invited by Hugh Gaitskell to represent the DLP at a Labour party conference, she took Active with her, providing him with an "eye-opening" experience rarely available to newcomers in politics.

In 1956 Phyllis, eager to return to Dominica permanently, was most concerned about the possibility of Philip's accompanying them. This hope flew in the face of all medical opinion they had received and against their knowledge that there were no facilities for the treatment of psychiatric illnesses in Dominica. Although still hospitalized, Philip seemed to have made some progress since the onset of the disease in 1952. He often visited Parkview Court on weekends, and behaved to all appearances thoroughly normally, wandering about the flat, looking into the rooms, helping with the washing up and doing other chores without any prompting. Phyllis and Robert drew great comfort from his ability to do simple tasks, yet Philip claimed he had no memory, found it hard to concentrate, and lacked confidence. He was well enough to discuss his treatment, "prospects," and chances of working at some job, but not well enough to follow these discussions with action. Robert, with the quaintness of the fragmentary knowledge of schizophrenia that characterized the mid-1950s, explained to Philip that he was suffering from "an original nervous strain due to something buried in his subconscious in the past [which] had probably caused oversecretion of a gland. His 'tablets' were now able to cancel the oversecretion but to get to the root of the cause required psycho-analysis which should then stop the oversecretion altogether." He advised his son to take up gardening or some other joblike task to train himself for his discharge.

During the period Phyllis spent in London, she resumed writing. She was working mostly on short pieces, but had begun at least one novel, possibly *Three Cups of Tea*, which remained unfinished. A manuscript of that title, approximately 110 pages long, was filed with the rest of her unpublished fiction. It consists of three fully drafted parts and a synopsis of the last three chapters and follows a young woman's life from her youth in the days preceding World War I to her middle age in the early 1950s. More chronicle than novel, the extant text lacks Phyllis's characteristic subtlety and could have been a very early draft submitted to her agents to gauge its marketability and later set aside. Thematically it follows closely her interests: her antiwar feelings, her dread of totalitarianism, the labor unrest of the period between the wars, her faith in the Labour party, and her own personal brand of feminism, which permeated every area of life. Her most significant literary accomplishment during this period was the reading of several of her recent works on *Caribbean Voices,* the influential BBC radio program that helped launch the careers of some of the best-known West Indian writers: Edward Brathwaite, V. S. Naipaul, George Lamming, Samuel Selvon, Derek Walcott, and Earl Lovelace among others. Phyllis's "Andersen's Mermaid," a poem she had included in *Contrasts,* was read in May 1956, "The Search," a short story (now apparently lost) was read in April 1957. "Joybells for Robe-in," another lost story, was broadcast in March.

Phyllis's determination to return to Dominica to run for a seat on the Legislative Council put a severe strain on her relationship with Robert. He most earnestly demanded that she stay; she just as earnestly insisted on going. He balked at paying for her passage. She prevailed on Paravicini to lend her the money. Robert argued that Philip needed her, that she had no chance of winning; she countered passionately that Philip was in good hands and she wouldn't know if she could win unless she tried. He finally relented and saw her off, wishing wholeheartedly as she went that she would lose and soon return. She, in turn, devoted the weeks before her departure to arranging everything for him as competently as possible, so he would have few reasons to complain about her absence—bedclothes, meals, even a replacement for the broken clothesline at the cottage were arranged for his comfort. She sailed in June, a couple of days before Phina's arrival in London for her master's degree ceremony at Oxford, her absence only kindling the embers of Robert's vexation. His first letter to her after her departure told her reproachfully of how he and Philip had gone *alone* to see "Phine-Phine looking very sweet, exchange her white fur BA hood for a Red Silk MA one."

This time Phyllis traveled on a freighter, the *M/S Bonita,* in much less opulent style than that of her last crossing. They left Dublin in rough seas, and her cabin mates, a mother and baby, proceeded to be "sick all over the place." At the "sight, sensation and sound of everything [she] became frightfully sick herself" and felt "quite self-disgraced." The *Bonita*'s cabins were stuffy and the living quarters "nil," so "confinement and stuffiness prevailed." The chief steward was a "horrible unkind twerp" who told them straight away that he hated passengers and would do as little as he could for them, a threat he proceeded to put into effect "very capably." Phyllis became convinced that he hated women as well. To make matters worse, he had been given a catering concession, so that he could make a profit on most things "except the very dull generalities of diet"—and they had, "alas!" an English cook. The quantity and quality of food were so deficient that she became almost obsessive about it. The crew mounted a food strike within days of sailing, and one morning the handful of passengers saw a procession of them heading for the captain's cabin, led by a burly Norwegian carrying a cold plate with two pancakes that looked "like squashed slugs." They rapped on the captain's cabin door and after a short harangue "solemnly waled [*sic*] to the side and pitched the slugs overboard."

Phyllis was to lead a revolt of her own. After a week at sea, the passengers had wanted clean sheets but the steward would not change them. So she and her Irish companion (the baby's mother) stripped off theirs and marched to the captain's cabin and left them there. They had some clean linen "pronto." When not engaged in such activities, she wiled away her time reading a book she thought would be invaluable to her in Dominica, Peter Archer's *Social Welfare and the Citizen*. "It gives one the whole works about all social and state responsibilities, inc. education, landlord and tenant etc.," just the book she "had been hunting for absolute ages." But other than her reading there was not much to interest her and she wrote to Robert of absolute "trivialities"—a white hat she bought in Dublin, a dress she was making for herself—as she "had been leading a rather female existence" on board. On June 15, two days before arriving in Dominica, she had a "dip in the temperate waters of the Saragossa Sea . . . the part when one begins to see seaweed in the water, and it gets warm and blue, and it seems that there should be land ahoy but there isn't." The water was piped up to a little bath on the passenger deck—and "very pleasant it was." Her "very vacant existence aboard" was coming to an end, heralded by this contact with the Sargasso Sea, "so marvelous, a very dark thick blue, just whipped by waves." Suddenly she felt exhilarated and energized. There was moonlight and the Plough (Ursa Major) was brilliant, and she imagined she could already see the Southern Cross. She was almost home.

She arrived in Roseau on June 18. The *Bonita* had been expected at Portsmouth a few days later, and Loblack had been in the north rallying people to give her a hearty welcome; but she arrived in Roseau to be greeted by Veronica Nichols, the party secretary, the members of the executive committee, and some old stragglers who happened to be on the jetty. Aunt Mags and Marion had come in the old Ford to fetch her. Aunt Mags, to her relief, seemed "genuinely delighted" to see her and treated her to a lunch of *crapaud* (the local edible toad) and fruit salad with coconut cream, which in Dominica is "the ultimate in guests welcoming." But Kingsland House was full, and she had its worst room—hot, stuffy, small, and dreadfully noisy. She felt surrounded by the shrill of interminably blaring radios, and the sound of the most banal practicings of the Music Lovers' Society, and was getting ready to "launch an attack on anti-social noises very soon." Her attention was absorbed immediately after her arrival by the news of Bishop Moris's death. "I guess my return was too much for Bishop M!" Phyllis is known to have said. Word soon spread that her homecoming had been too hard a blow for the old man to bear, and he had given up on life. "Who killed Bishop Moris?" became a staple joke during the campaign.

During her absence the party had "languished and almost disappeared," and now, not willing to waste any time, she soon called a meeting of the Executive Committee for a "sharp-shooting session." They needed to decide on the date and nature of their first public meeting, the way they would conduct their countrywide campaign, and most importantly, the selection of candidates. She had to move quickly to settle, at least for the time being, the growing strife between factions within the DTU. Tensions between the union and the DLP had grown in her absence, and the rift "was very bad indeed." But she was encouraged by a belief that the PNM seemed anxious for a good clean fight. Within days of her arrival in Roseau she received a letter from Robert telling her how low and depressed he felt, as usual "when [he] was abandoned." Absence, poverty, and opposition, she mused, affected them both very differently: "It makes me fighting mad and unwilling to admit defeat, but it sometimes makes you cave in." It particularly worried her that relations deteriorated between him and other "bods" when she left the precincts—his letter had been full of grievances against George Horner and other friends. "I wish only that you try and maintain some sort of *status quo*," she wrote to him in mild exasperation, begging him not to quarrel with "dear old George," their "mainstay." At the bottom of this was the inescapable fact that in the matter of the elections they were of two minds. "It is strange being determined to run for you," she writes him, "and your hoping I'll lose." But she particularly wanted him not to "egg at her" to come back yet, since she had barely arrived. "I am on to something big," she pleads, "and moreover, I can tell you that without my timely—but almost too-late—intervention, the Labour Party & the DTU would have torn each other to pieces." Her impatience betrayed her exhaustion and weariness. On that very day she had visited Laudat and Morne Prosper, and was preparing for her first big public meeting in the Market Place on the following day. She had by then gotten a driver's license in order to use the Jeep donated for the campaign by the Fabian Society, and had gone to Pointe Michel—a frightening thought given the conjunction of her very limited driving skills and the precarious conditions of Dominica's roads in 1955. (She was once described as driving around in the Jeep "with not much skill, but a great deal of *brio*.") "Write me soon," she exhorts Robert, "and tell me that you are better, less tired, more fortunate!"

The first task awaiting her was that of identifying candidates for all the constituencies they were to contest. This was a daunting task in a politically unsophisticated island where she was struggling against old-time electoral traditions. She was particularly impressed with two young potential candidates, Edward O. LeBlanc and Alec Ducreay—they were cousins, as Phyllis was later to learn—whom she hoped would be "prototypes of the new kind of politicians in which the West Indies was [then] relatively deficient . . . politicians whose nationalism would not fall within the narrow confines of race or little-kingdom pride but would be based on those United Nations principles which had been written into [the] Party constitution." Ducreay and LeBlanc were "fairly well-educated" young family men who assured her that they were not entering politics for mere personal ambition nor to become Ministers, but because they wanted to "serve the people." She thought of Ducreay as "a promising young recruit, a real gem." Confident and self-assured, he would become one of the party's best speakers and most active campaigners.

LeBlanc was an agricultural extension officer; as a banana inspector he had become well known across the island as he traveled from village to village on his motor scooter to carry out his work. Phyllis saw him as a "good young man" with a promising future in politics, and liked him immensely. At this period of his career she had nothing but praise for his ability and skill. But he was to prove an unlikely partner for her in her political enterprise. Despite his superior abilities, he was a victim of the system. He had wanted to be a veterinarian but had lost a scholarship to the countless prejudices of the Roseau elite against country people. He had persevered in his education, taking correspondence courses and eventually passing the university entrance exams, only to see opportunity after opportunity go to the less-qualified children of the Roseau elite. The slights left a deep imprint on him, and he would always feel that people, white people particularly, were trying to keep him down. He was wont to be resentful of Phyllis's "paternalistic" attitude and of her occasionally imperious manner when she was impatient or annoyed. Resentment would breed hostility, and there would always be in his animosity toward her a deep-set class and racial rancor against which she, in the wide-eyed naïveté of her boundless enthusiasm, failed to protect herself. He would eventually become her bitterest opponent within the party.

By early July, Labour had chosen candidates for all areas, though this was to be kept a secret for a while longer—"as far as secrecy went in Dominica." They were Ducreay for Roseau North; Leopold J. Charles for Roseau South, running against Frank Baron; Phyllis had the Western District, held by J. B. Charles; LeBlanc for Portsmouth; Austell James, the party treasurer, for the Eastern District, where they had the feeblest hopes of all; R. P. St. Luce, the only member of the party already in the council and "a dead certainty," for the Southern District; Edney O. Prosper, "a poor man who had failed twice but who may win with Labour support," for the North Western. Phyllis had felt that only Loblack could have been a sure thing against Howell Shillingford in the North Western District, but Loblack would not stand. The only district unnominated was Marigot-Carib, but there were three Labour hopefuls for it—one of them, to her satisfaction, a young Carib. She wished she herself had been allotted somewhere simpler, "but I daresay they thought no-one else could crack that lot." She feared Robert would get his wish and see her back in London at the end of August, since the opposition—both independents and the PNM—seemed determined "to stop at nothing to prevent [her] from standing." The one encouraging note at this early stage of the campaign was the assurance of support from the mayor of Roseau, G. A. James, who was also editor of the *Chronicle*. He had paid her "a state call" in early June, stunning her with his profuse apologies for the attacks on her by the newspaper in the past. He had joined the DLP *sub rosa*, he claimed, and was prepared to defend her right to stand for election. Whether his newly gained freedom to support her stemmed from his no longer being under Bishop Moris's tutelage he wasn't saying. But it was welcome news nonetheless, as the support of the *Chronicle* could prove immensely valuable in the election.

Robert, less despondent but nonetheless still unenthusiastic about her decision to run for office, alternated between sending sound political advice and discouraging her from continuing. His advice was pragmatic: "Has anyone taken up the question of the insignia 'the hand' for the party," he inquires in one of his letters. "That I consider most important for people who are illiterate and think in symbols so much. How about local village agents and house to house canvassing working from the registers—is anyone doing any organised work? Or is everyone just thinking that it can all be done by making lots of lovely speeches. They are not all such babes in arms, you know, some do a bit of thinking." He was as quick to send useful suggestions as he was to point out the snares to which she would be prey if elected: "Honey," he replied to one of her many blissfully hopeful letters, "it is very lovely and flattering for you but keep your perspective—when you cannot do everything they hope for they may turn—so look ahead six months to dullness, intrigue, hate, fear and greed. Boring minutes and the drudgery of opening bazaars daily." She didn't have to wait long for the "hate, fear and greed." As Labour's fortunes rose the campaign got nastier. The three salient themes of her vigorous campaign—the establishment of government-run schools, the spread of birth control information, and the adoption of the principles of "tropical socialism"—were precisely those that most irked people in an island that was more than 90 percent Catholic. She avowed quite honestly to Robert that the "underground machinations, the lies, the tricksy goings on, [had] to be heard at first hand to be believed. . . . If I were to tell you of the plots and counter-plots, the lies, the strange treacheries, the total lack of *probity* . . . you would have a fit, though not of surprise. Yet the curious thing is that Labour is leading in spite of all." Dominicans, Hesketh Bell had once observed, are "adept in the art of abuse, and their inventive capacity, in the way of picturesque invective, is phenomenal." He had heard terms of abuse exchanged between Dominicans, apparently with little or no effect, which could have raised blisters in others. This Phyllis had been ready for. She was as capable as anyone at dishing out *mépuis* (as patois-speakers called the vituperative give-and-take that characterized Dominican politics, from the French *mépris*), and her gift for mordant witticisms always came in handy. But she was not so sanguine about other campaign tricks, such as her letters being stolen from the post office and made public at her enemies' rallies. On several occasions details of her correspondence with Robert had been read, something that went against her intensely private nature and deeply mortified her. She repeatedly begged him to put "cellotape over every cranny" of his letters; "It is important for me to keep up a good morale and I don't want any more sorrowful news [about Philip, their disagreements about her career, their finances] read out." She also begged him not to tell any Dominican in London that he was not coming to join her because it might be used against her.

On July 7, "one of the hottest nights in the world," she attended two meetings—the first one at the DTU Hall, where she was again needed to contain the inner squabbles. She herself was increasingly coming under attack by the church for her involvement with the union and claiming union leaders as personal friends. Charges had been made that one thousand dollars were missing from DTU funds, and fingers were being pointed simultaneously at Loblack and Daniel Green, who by now had declared his candidacy against Phyllis for the Western District. The second meeting was a rally for Baron at a Roseau school, the evening before his departure for England seeking financial aid and votes from Dominicans abroad. Phyllis had sent in a question, but he refused to let her speak. Pandemonium ensued, with the roomful of swearing people practically unanimously yelling, "Let her speak!" She had to sneak out with Chris Loblack and Leo Charles before things got worse. She found it all pretty exciting, and despite the *commesse*, pretty safe.* At the meeting in question,

*Phyllis offers a romanticized account of a party president attending an opponent's rally in "The Bodyguard":

> Saragot the speaker, a dark short man, could be seen swaying behind the microphone: he was directing his oratory to and against the pale young woman in sandals and a white dress who leaned slightly now towards one and then towards another of her companions. Her light rose-pink lips were curled in a derisory smile, her eyes were half closed. Now and again Saragot would raise a groan from the crowd by referring to the bodyguard as the *royal party* . . . "La Présidente! La Présidente . . ." "It is true," he declaimed, "that she is the president of her party. But she will never be the President of our island republic. It is not only that she is a woman, and this is a land where women are kept in their proper place until some accident of nature, some aberration one might almost say, produced this *lady* who looks so weak and who acts like a tiger. Ask yourselves" (he threw up hands in appeal) "whether it isn't against nature, against God, to have a woman stepping out of her class and her looks and her reasonable behaviour to set herself up as the leader of a party. . . . La Présidente they call her, but I call her Sylvie though they had me to nominate her *Mamselle* when we were both walking on different sides of the street . . . this street used to be an invisible line drawn down the middle and La Présidente Sylvie walked on the one side and people like you and me walked on the other."

Baron had made public some correspondence that showed that he "definitely had jaundiced [Norman] Manley against the [DLP]." When appealed to by Manley, as Dominica's leading minister, for an evaluation of the DLP's application for membership in the West Indian Federal Labour party (WIFLP)—the loose-knit group of West Indian Labour parties (most of them in power in their respective islands), organized as an umbrella party to contest the Federal elections—Baron had called the DLP an irresponsible party whose leadership, however sincere, preached class hatred. The DLP, he had argued, appealed to the uneducated and irresponsible and should not be trusted with the reins of government. Despite Baron's efforts, however, the DLP would be admitted to WIFLP in October.

The day after these meetings Phyllis set out in the loaded Jeep to Pointe Michel to counter a PNM gathering. It was one of her favorite electioneering practices to show up at her opponents' political rallies to rattle the speakers and force discussions of issues. She arrived at Pointe Michel ready to go on the offensive and, taking them by surprise, had her say while the PNM supporters remained too stunned to think of questions to ask. "But they were mad!" she gloated. She loved this aspect of campaigning, as did Loblack; it seemed to satisfy an impish, childlike sense of politics as play, which left them both exhilarated and gay. They both found in the intrigue, gossip and innuendo, conspiracies, plots, and counterplots of the campaign, however tiresome, something of the mirth children display while in the middle of a game. She was known to race against her opponents on the Jeep to secure the best spot in a village for an open-air meeting, or "raid" their meetings to challenge them to a debate. After successful forays she would relax with a self-satisfied "That was good fun!"

On July 17, a warm, crickety night, she had decided to skip the evening's meetings just to stay home and rest. She had just returned, weary and hoarse, from a long campaign trip to the Northern District that had begun with her sailing on the *Princess Mariana* to Portsmouth with Veronica Nichols, the party secretary, and Ducreay. From Portsmouth they had traveled on to Wesley, Marigot, and the Carib Territory, and had returned to Roseau partly on foot by walking almost across Morne Bois Diable to rejoin the Transinsular Road. As the walk literally meant countless miles of trekking across mountains, streams, and dense forests, they had needed a Carib guide.* Phyllis and her companions had been at the Carib village of Salybia for the feast of Saint Peter, when there was supposed to be a blessing of the boats by the French priest. But

*Phyllis described a typical mountain trek in "The Bodyguard":

> At this point on the route further progress by wheel came to a dead halt. The rough asphalt road suddenly pinched into a clay track striking off into jungle depths of lavish and frightening beauty. . . . Cadette soon found that she had chosen a track in which streams abounded: practically every major turn was a small stream or river. . . . Overhead, lianas of gargoyle shape dripped on his head; great rope vines tripped him, and when he put out his hand to save himself he got stung by malignany hairy leaves. Sylvie seemed hardly to brush the pitted and irregular track. . . . And for what was she making this testing and hazardous journey? Just to interview the member for Eastern and hearten her country supporters? . . . "Why anyone should make all this effort just to shake hands with a halfwit in a village, God knows," said Cadette during the return journey. He was not speaking to Sylvie but to one of the voluntary guides who bore bottles full of spirit-soaked sugarcane as flaming brands.

the priest had been angry with the fishermen over their negligence of religious duties and had refused to bless the boats (which had been decorated with flowers and bottles of rum and smuggled liqueurs tied to the masts). So the fishermen threw the flowers into the sea and opened up the bottles and caroused godlessly. Later they sobered up and attended her meeting, during which she tactfully urged them to apologize to the priest. This they at first refused to do, though afterward the chief and councillors went to the presbytery to make peace. The Caribs had agreed to accept the Labour party candidate, a Mr. Telemacque, a rather dignified and elderly man, a nominee from Marigot, as their candidate in opposition to Lionel Laville, who held the seat for the district. During her absence from Roseau, a letter Phyllis had written to the editor of the *Chronicle* on the subject of medical care had appeared in the newspaper, drawing yet more fire toward her. In it she lamented Dominica's deplorable doctor-patient ratio and the fact that most island doctors practiced in Roseau, making it almost impossible for the peasantry to have access to medical care in an emergency. From the earliest weeks of the campaign she had focused on the lack of health care for the poor, underscoring the party's intention to establish free health clinics and make possible more widespread access to primary care.

The week that followed found her once again crisscrossing the island in the trusty old Jeep. That weekend she visited Laudat, Pointe Michel, Mahaut, Massacre, Roget, Portsmouth, Marigot, and once again the Carib Quarter. It was a lot of ground to cover, and she was exhausted but nonetheless encouraged by the degree of local cooperation she was encountering. By then the party had twenty-six substations in the Western District alone—Mahaut, Massacre, Roger, Laudat, Trafalgar, Pointe Michel, Morne Prosper, "and God knows what other inaccessible villages." She could count on local officers to arrange meetings and provide a bit of a meal, accommodations, and very often guides to villages inaccessible by car—and although this made campaigning quite a lot easier, it also meant that they would all have to have an observer during the elections to ensure fair play. The logistics of campaigning on very little more than whatever allowance Robert sent her from his own meager resources were beginning to be felt.

She was weary. In fact, she thought, "the whole place was one good old seethe of corruption," worse than ever before. And she felt overwhelmed by both petty and major concerns. She continued to be ostracized by the white community in Roseau and was not seeing any *békés* at all. None but "dear old" Miss Elsie Lockhart and Dr. Steiger had telephoned or called, and she had run into Colonel Humphrey, at whose house they had often dined when Robert was with L. Rose, who had been kind enough to stop and shake her hand. It was so rare that she would receive such a mark of recognition from a white person that any such occurrence was worthy of being mentioned in her letters to Robert. Aunt Mags was also nagging her "horribly" to relax, but she "simply couldn't until [she] knew what was going to happen to her nomination." Her main worry was of being disqualified. She was particularly concerned about J. B. Charles's threat that he was going "to issue a caveat against [her] when [she] put up as a candidate." There was the issue of her residency, among others that could be raised by her enemies, and this weighed heavily on her. And then there was Robert, depressed by his own hardships and burdened by Philip's ordeal and their precarious finances. He was working as a consultant, and his income was neither steady nor plentiful. He wanted her back; she, in turn, wanted "to play the whole thing out." "I am getting my forms signed and filled out. The only way I can lose is to be disqualified: then I will return to England. I am just curious to know how the dice will fall. The odds are in favour of MY coming to *you*, but I'm holding my peace about that. . . . I'd like to be there to lift your burden and to tell you a few jokes too . . . and other things."

On July 18 the party held a meeting in the Dawbiney Market to boost Leo Charles's lackadaisical campaign against Baron. Phyllis, the first to speak, gave Leo her strongest backing—"A vote for Leo is a vote for the Party and a vote for me," she told the large audience gathered at the market. She went on to underscore the party's intention of making housing for the people their top priority if they were returned, as was the policy of Labour governments everywhere. The promise of a road for the Carib people was reiterated, and she argued vigorously that the deal to build an airstrip at the old Melville Hall Estate on the northeastern coast had little to do with Baron's efforts—funds had been secured from the Federation's foundation grant—and could not be claimed as an election triumph. Her speech, the *Chronicle* hastened to point out, was "devoid of personal insinuations, though she referred to the PNM as Scribes and Pharisees." Leo Charles, for whose benefit the meeting had been organized, summarized the party's goals of agricultural development and an expanded system of education, and ended by declaring his firm friendship for the "barefoot man." Loblack rocked the market with some "broad touches of humor," especially when he referred to the candidate as the least of three evils and launched into roaring descriptions of what those evils were, in English and patois. Ducreay, who had emerged as one of the party's most vibrant speakers, defended Phyllis against the "whispering campaign" that she was a Communist, stating categorically that she was a socialist and that socialism was the only hope for the people of Dominica.

The campaign continued to gather momentum. July 25, 1957, was nomination day and "everyone was agog." Phyllis and her companions had worked so hard and covered such "a hell of a lot of terrain," that even in the "backwaters of the island" the Labour party's name "was slick on the tongue, though many people still had no idea what it meant and often called it the 'neighbourparty.'" As she prepared herself for her nomination, and to gather the required signatures, she had gone to a *bram* (local fete) in Siboulie, a slum of Pointe Michel, where she had at first danced with Ti Bonnet, her mother's old driver, but later, finding that half the hall was dancing solo, she did the same, as the crowd was rather rough and dirty. In an encouraging sign, Bath Estate had shown itself tremendously loyal to her. She had been able to gather "over and above" the required number of signatures on her nomination papers from among Robert's former employees and several "Bath Estaters" had since joined the party. On the next morning, Sunday, after high mass, she had spoken at a meeting at the Pointe, an open-air meeting as were nearly all of their assemblies—at her request. Then she was off to "crummy old Loubiere," where they took a stand by the water hydrant and had "a good show." After Loubiere, a Labour stronghold, they drove to Roget up the Imperial Road, and there, as she did not like driving the Jeep up mountains at night, they had hired a chauffeur to take them to a schoolroom meeting at Giraudel. The day had left her completely exhausted, but Sundays were the best days for campaigning in the country as on weekdays most people were in the fields until at least six o'clock.

The PNM was campaigning heavily in Salisbury and St. Joseph while Baron was in London handling the ongoing negotiations for an airstrip at Melville Hall. The possible airstrip was an important campaign coup for the PNM as it would be Dominica's first. While Baron was in England, Robert had written to Phyllis with "some fine gunshot" about the PNM, Norman Manley, and Eric Williams. He had met the Jamaican and Trinidadian leaders at the House of Commons and had ascertained that despite its being modeled on the Trinidadian PNM, the Dominican party did not have their endorsement or support. Their allegiance, Robert assured her, was with the Labour party. Phyllis called a public meeting to read Robert's report, and there was a great crowd. The bell ringer had gone around town yelling: "Revelations! Revelations! Hear all what Mr. Robert Allfrey have heard in the House of Common[s] from Manley and Eric Williams!" PNM supporters had parked cars "two-deep to get the shock," and she was sure "they hadn't liked it."

During the days preceding nomination, Phyllis had a young reporter from the *Trinidad Guardian* in tow. Adrien Espinet was enthralled by the political situation in Dominica, which he found to be "the most fascinating among the smaller islands at this turning point of politics when an attempt is made to introduce the Party system." He found her to be the "strangest figure" in Dominica's political scene. It puzzled him that a woman who claimed "to be a real politician, should come to Dominica, such a backward place," bent on introducing "party politics of the most modern variety" to "an almost untutored electorate." "What other colonies achieved by more or less gradual stages," he argues, "Dominica is striving to do in one breathless jump," being practically pushed into it singlehandedly by "the wizened bird-like figure of a middle-aged (fortyish) woman who is the founder and leader of the colony's fledgling Labour Party." Phyllis, an "ageless woman" who seemed to have been battered by life "into a sort of timelessness," was conducting an unrelenting campaign "[i]n the teeth of the strong, if unspoken, opposition of members of her own family, and of social ostracism by the class known to patois-speaking Dominicans as 'bourg high-life.'" He was struck, above all, by the manner of her campaigning. "No rabble rouser, she is essentially the dreamer-poet and carries this aspect of her personality unabashedly into her politics." No other politician in the world, he was convinced, "would have thought of opening a meeting in Dominica, of addressing a crowd largely composed of illiterates and near illiterates lost in the dark crevices between two broken languages," with a quotation from W. H. Auden's poetry. "They loved it and understood it," Phyllis happily reported to Espinet, but he was tempted to believe that the people cheered "only because it seemed the thing to do." "On her platform," he concluded his assessment, "Mrs. Allfrey preaches her socialism uncompromisingly, and naturally, this has led to the charge from many quarters that she is a communist. In more enlightened and less prejudiced quarters her idealism is unchallenged and her program so basically sound that even her enemies are willing to admit that, if given a chance, she will 'probably do the country some good.'"

Two days before nominations she went to "a most singular and exciting place" she had never visited before: Morne Prosper. Because the road bordered a precipice, they had engaged a DTU driver, but he turned out to be a worse driver than Phyllis herself—something quite difficult to imagine—and worked the Jeep so hard that although he just panted downhill, the starter was wrecked. In the middle of the meeting, the "able brilliant young coloured Portsmouth candidate," LeBlanc, turned up with a friend and drove them back cautiously. Otherwise they would have been stuck there for the night, "no telephones, no beds, nothing!" The meeting had been held "at the request of the head men of the village in the Morne Prosper Catholic Chapel! . . . It was so strange, speaking there with candles under the shrine, and then the sudden appearance of those friendly faces, LeBlanc and Durban, in the dim chapel, which was packed to capacity with reverent gleaming black faces from as far away as Wotton Waven." Phyllis, the ultimate romantic, was rapturous about that night when she was rescued by her gallant knights. It was a measure of her fervor for her political movement that she was often to describe her evenings of campaigning in those quasi-mystical, passionate tones; it was a measure of her deep-set romanticism that she was to project her notions of chivalry and gallantry onto her companions, Edward LeBlanc foremost among them. She would feel after such evenings "full of magnificent fortitude," and would describe at least one of her moonlit speeches as "a masterpiece and a poet's delight."

On the eve of nomination they had a big meeting at the Roseau Boys School opposite Seaview, her childhood home. All their island candidates spoke for a few minutes each. Leo Charles being the candidate for that district, they had concentrated on his campaign against Baron, who, according to Phyllis, "really was a dastard" and had been playing along with both Conservative and Labour, both in Britain and Dominica. If they could "crack his seat wide open (rather vulgar that sounds!)" they would be in an immensely sound position. Leo, however, had many detractors (he was a heavy drinker), and she thought "only her personal aura could protect him from the slurs." The day following the nominations she spent "a most exhilarating day" in Colihaut, Mero, and Dublanc—Howell Shillingford's strongholds. She had found the experience invigorating enough to feel her "first real intimation that the Labour Party would win the election." Shillingford had chased the group from point to point in a motor boat (they had to visit two of the three places on the schedule by sea), glowering at them as he listened to their speeches. At the last meeting he had asked to be allowed to comment and delivered what she considered to be a conciliatory appeal to their audience. He spoke of himself as a man of charity, to which she replied by comparing charity to public welfare and reproaching him for his vast acres of unused land. "He dared not make a row with us," she recounted, "so [he] just acted like Papa Howell and gave a pacific handshake all around." She had returned to Roseau very tired, salty, and hungry after all this, having had nothing but penny breads and canned meats all day and "being so much in the public eye that [she] could not even relieve the call of nature behind a coconut tree."

While she anxiously waited to see if her nomination was challenged, Robert was growing increasingly despondent about their separation. He was convinced that no one would dare challenge her nomination "for fear of a public rumpus" and she would be "stuck out there" for years. As he saw it, if the DLP got in with sufficient votes to make her a minister, she would be encouraged to run in the Federal elections and "we shall end up never seeing each other for years on end except for scurried visits. . . . I know that it will fulfill your ambition, so naturally all I can do is to encourage you, but all the same feeling terribly virtuous and unselfish doing it and rather scared that you will not be able to handle either the administrative side wisely or be able to cope with the machinations of the other politicians." Though it seldom worked (and did not this time), it was his habit when downhearted thus to seek to undermine her confidence. Then Robert played his trump card—Philip's health. His next few letters were full of negative news about their son. Philip, he reported, was categorically refusing to come to the flat for a visit, something that "[struck] a cold note of guilt" within Phyllis. The news was the more disturbing because it followed upon what had seemed like progress. Just a few weeks earlier she had received her first "little script" from Phil, and it had been "like inheriting a gold mine . . . It had made [her] so happy, so very happy, in its text and tone. Seemed to show a definite maintaining of progress, and even an advance." But now Phil was said to be troublesome, more withdrawn. She found these new developments disconcerting but was quick to demand to be told what the doctor said, fully: "With me the situation is this: for the cause of Phil's health, I would return to England, but only for *that*, for I still have great hopes that both he and you will be able to join me, even if only for spells. However, I must first lead my Party to victory, and I wish to stay if I possibly can. There have been all sorts of smirchings, such as, I will take the £1000 and beat it to England. I will not give up prematurely save for a crucial, heart-breaking family reason." His only reply to this was a two-week-long silence.

Meanwhile the accusations against Loblack were gathering momentum, becoming a factor in the campaign. On July 27 there was a noisy meeting at the Union Hall to discuss the alleged money theft. Loblack, backed strongly by Phyllis, defended himself energetically. Baron, who had been away attending meetings to discuss the possible use of the U.S. naval base at Chaguaramas, Trinidad, as a site for the capital of the Federation government, was back in Dominica, just in time to use Loblack's situation and the inner strife within the DTU to his advantage. But as the election approached her hopes were high. She desperately needed money and wrote to Robert to ask if he could spare a little; perhaps their banker in Fulham would allow an overdraft on her account, if he knew that she was "practically certain to get in, and more certain to be a Minister, the leading Minister, when she did." The party now had the full support of the police, who were with her "wholesale." One of Labour's feeblest candidates, Telemacque, was the father of a young police corporal and, in typical West Indian fashion, the connection had led to the party getting full police cooperation. She received "all saluting honours already." Because of their allegiance, and probably because she was a woman, they had been very protective—unnecessarily, she thought, since whatever trouble there had been had been against their opponents. Shillingford, for one, had been forced to flee the hall at St. Joseph.

Her assessment of the situation as August began was that the opposition's aim was to try to "wipe her out with the vote." She had four candidates running specifically against her, and they were all going around patting each other on the back and slandering her. The "tricksters" were "crazily at work" trying to stop her from getting in. Her "only and big advantage" was that none of the others had overall appeal. Daniel Green had Canefield and Wotton Waven. Elkin Henry (the most menacing of her opponents,"a very dangerous neo-Labour man" put up by the priests), had Mahaut and Massacre, two tough strongholds. He was a young and disgruntled trade unionist "posing as a Labour man" but fiercely opposed to Loblack. Murray Williams was an unknown liberal quantity. She felt she had strongholds too—La Coudrai, Laudat, part of Trafalgar, part of Pointe Michel, most of Goodwill—but was conscious of having drawn one of the most difficult districts, one that needed all her fortitude and strength and was "a hell of a district to cover." She was furthermore burdened by the fact that, at a time when other Labour candidates were depending on her to run their campaigns, she was down to financial bedrock.

As election day approached, she challenged the church on two issues that dominated the latter stages of the campaign: education and birth control. In her speeches she had deplored the woeful inadequacy of the few existing rural schools, arguing that a free, quality education was the right of every citizen regardless of race, class status, or income, and promising widespread reforms and expansion of the school system as part of the DLP platform: Education was to her one of government's top priorities. The church went quickly on the attack, accusing her of being against Catholic schools and intending to force parents to eschew a religious education in favor of government schools, "as communists are wont to do." Phyllis thus had to defend her "radical" view that education was a "national responsibility" that did not preclude the existence of denominational schools. "We regard denominational schools," she insisted, "as complementary to Government Schools, and not rivals." Discussions of birth control were even more fraught with peril in a heavily Catholic island, but she was resolute in her defense of birth control practices. She had, after all, been trained in politics by two vigorous advocates of birth control—Naomi Mitchison and Edith Summerskill—and it was an issue on which she was thoroughly informed. "It is a Labour Party principle that all the benefits of science should be available to people," she would argue. "Scientific methods of birth control are among those benefits, especially in vastly overcrowded and poverty-stricken and famine areas. We should not seek to impose this knowledge upon a Catholic community in an underpopulated island such as ours. However, the abortion rate in Dominica is appallingly high. The question arises: whether it is not better to use birth control methods." The church countered with lengthy articles in the *Chronicle* laying down the law on "Catholics and Family Limitation" and arguing that "historically speaking, the school owes its existence, not to the State, but to the initiative of the family and the Church." The Catholic clergy was instructed to make these teachings the substance of their sermons in the weeks remaining till election day. Drawing nothing but opposition on these issues, Phyllis was therefore pleasantly surprised in early August by a *Chronicle* editorial—the editor, at least, was on her side—commending her highly "for this new awakening" of political interest in the island, calling her "the one woman in the picture who has gallantly taken the situation in hand and helped to bring about a renaissance in keeping with the political growth of Dominica and the rest of the West Indies. . . . [Mrs. Allfrey] has definitely made a contribution to the political atmosphere here by a series of indefatigable excursions in the course of which very instructive addresses have been delivered with very good praise and grace."

On August 12 she finally learned that her nomination, as Robert had feared, was unchallenged. The judge who had to adjudicate on her qualifications (he turned out to be an old friend and lawyer of Marion's) had arrived and approved her candidacy. "At least he is a Protestant," Phyllis commented when she learned who he was, "and white, so he would not prejudge." As Robert had advised, she picked a hand as her symbol. (Symbols were necessary for the printed ballots because the high level of illiteracy made it impractical to rely solely on printed words.) At the crack of dawn on the day following the announcement that her nomination had been accepted, she left for the north and the Carib Quarter. The election was nearing its final "desperate" stage. As if on cue, the rainy season had arrived with a vengeance. It was "fabulously" warm and damp, and it often rained torrentially as they made their way, usually on foot, from constituency to constituency. The uncertainty and the rain were getting to Phyllis, who was feeling increasingly disheartened as the election approached, her mood shifting easily from exhilaration to despair. She was aware that although Labour might win, "the curious thing is that they are all so afraid that I will personally get in as the leader, they will do *anything*, fair or foul, to prevent me." Her own district was so "widespread and mysterious" that the results were impossible to predict. The "darned place [is] corrupt," she wrote to Robert. And she blamed the corruption on "300 years of Catholic morality." The Catholics, in turn, had escalated the campaign against her, now widely perceived as the front-runner, and were engaged in "some last minute flank attacks" about education and birth control.

John Hatch, the Commonwealth officer for the British Labour party, arrived in Dominica a few days before the election and bolstered the party's chances for victory by holding what was described as "the best meeting that has been held in Dawbiney Market" during the campaign. He had landed in Portsmouth, where he addressed an unexpected public meeting in the square leading to the jetty in support of the DLP and Edward LeBlanc, whose district it was. In measured but forceful terms Hatch outlined the work the DLP was doing and intended to do in Britain for the working classes. At the conclusion of the speech, Loblack told the crowd that if, after hearing what Hatch had to say they did not vote for Labour, "they would be committing a crime against themselves. . . . As a young man I used to play cricket," he told the crowd in his homely drawl. "Whenever you put in a bowler and you see he is not getting any runs, what do you do?" "Change your bowler," the crowd responded, and that became the slogan that went around the Portsmouth Electoral District on election day. Hatch's timely visit was credited with tipping the scales in favor of LeBlanc. From Portsmouth he traveled to Roseau, where—in an attempt to educate his audience and counter the PNM's attacks—he carefully explained to the audience gathered at Dawbiney Market the differences between socialism and communism. Phyllis's own defense against the taunts that she was a Communist was to argue that "the rambling broadminded structure of the British Labour Party was the maximum discipline to which an individualist nature like mine could submit, just as the tolerant Anglican Church, with its ritualistic variations and exquisite poetic liturgy, remained my neglected *Mater Religiosa*. The big joke was that in those early founding days of the Dominica Labour Party, the accusers and mischief-makers were types who would easily (in my view) have fallen victims to authoritarian ideology which I would have resisted to the end. For one thing, they had no sense of humor; for another, I could not imagine them suffering in the cause of liberty."

On August 15, election day, she rose early to write an anxious note to Robert—from whom she had not heard in two weeks—and see Hatch off in the Goose. She was optimistic. Her last two speeches before the election—at the Market Place and Newtown—had been "brilliant." But despite a terrific upsurge of sympathy for the party, the outcome was still very much in doubt. As people began going to polling stations across the island, she felt as puzzled as the rest. If they won—if *she* won—then the "Jeep [was] really the winner. . . . That poor little jalopy was stacked against every single higher-up car in the island." But as she stepped out to fetch Hatch in that very same Jeep, she felt that whatever the outcome, she had done the job she had come to do—"the Labour Movement is all set even if we lose."

By early evening the streets of Roseau were jammed with cars blowing their horns and people crowding the sides of the road awaiting the results. The tallies for the Roseau-South Electoral District, Baron's, were soon in. He had won. Excitement awaited the results from Phyllis's district, Western, but these didn't come in until after eight o'clock, and when they did, it was a crushing blow: Elkin Henry, the candidate put up by the priests, had won; Phyllis had received 555 votes to his 889. J. B. Charles, who had held that constituency for many elections, had 627; Daniel Green, the renegade DTU officer, had 260. Phyllis had arranged with Robert to send a cable announcing ELECTED or DEFEATED and adding the number of Labour seats. The cable was duly sent. The *Chronicle* was to claim next morning that the news of the defeat of the DLP leader had been received with great satisfaction by the crowd, many of whom even expressed their disappointment when they heard that she had received enough votes not to forfeit her deposit. But the crowd's reaction had not been so "accommodating" of the *Chronicle*'s viewpoint. Labour supporters, especially the women, on learning of her defeat, were heard to wish that Dominica were a republic so that they could go down and shoot every voter from Massacre to Colihaut for not voting for Mrs. Allfrey. The political trickery, Phyllis concluded in her dejection, had been too much. Late into the night on the eve of the election, canvassers had gone about in her district telling people that the hat was her symbol, when it was actually the hand; nuns and priests had rapped on doors at Pointe Michel until midnight, whispering to startled citizens, "Don't vote for the woman."

When the national results were in the Labour party could claim that it had at least held its own. It had secured three seats: those of Leblanc, Ducreay—at twenty-six Dominica's youngest councillor ever—and St. Luce. The PNM had won only one seat in addition to Baron's. The three remaining seats had gone to independent candidates. With a majority needed to form a government, a coalition would be needed to determine who would govern, and Phyllis lost no time in approaching Clifton Dupigny, as leader of the PNM, to negotiate a union against "the truly dangerous independents." He was not disinclined, but Baron was adamant against a union with the DLP. The two parties had been "vigorous, even violent adversaries," and any conciliatory statement now was more than he could take. As he saw it, with only two seats, the PNM would be dominated by the DLP. Considering a coalition with the independents the only viable alternative, he dispatched someone to Marigot to get a commitment from Lionel Laville, who had retained his seat and committed himself to Baron in the hope of a ministry. Laville's position was that he had joined the PNM with the understanding "that it was being organised to counter the Labour Party, certain members of which were known to hold extreme socialist views," and that he would never be party to a coalition with them. Baron also got the support of L. C. Didier, a former DLP member, to complete his coalition. They banded together as the Dominican United People's party (DUPP). It was rumored among DLP supporters that the message Baron sent to both Didier and Laville assured each that he already had the other's support and that his own support would consolidate the coalition, securing himself (by duplicity if the story is to be believed) a majority. The DLP's socialism had been the primary obstacle to a union with the PNM, which wondered "how close the Labour Pink [was] to Communist Red." On August 24 it was announced that the PNM and the independents had united to form a government, with Baron retaining his leading minister position. Phyllis declared in response that the PNM had become so "virulently anti-socialist" that after a twenty-four hour truce further talk was impossible. LeBlanc, given the upper hand in his silent struggle against her by his electoral victory, had insisted that he preferred to stay in the opposition rather than work with people he could not support. The DLP soon announced that it intended to challenge Baron's election on grounds of bribery, but that came to nought. "It is a defeat. Let's face it," Phyllis wrote to Robert, "and Dominica remains the most backward island in the Caribbean." She could only hope that the party's supporters could stay loyal for the five years it would take for new elections to be held: "It is almost too much to expect."

It was not only a political defeat, but the collapse of her most personal hopes. She had seen the elections as providing her with a role—and a job—that would help the family get out of the "rut of insecurity" in which it had lived for the greater part of twenty-five years. The days following were bitter ones: Phyllis was all too aware that her enemies were celebrating her defeat. But she soon rallied. Rather than return immediately to London, she opted to remain in Dominica for a few months, finish the Untanglers tale she was working on, "resist the impression of defeat," and stand for the Federal elections when the Labour party would have an overall symbol. In retrospect the confusion over the various symbols seemed to have been one cause of Labour's defeat, as was the lack of money and canvassers to counter the opponents' tricks. She was heartened by the renewed interest in the party as a result of the election: "Since the results, more people have joined our Party than ever before. Those who voted against us are largely sorry, realise the tricks, and are lamenting. . . . But it's too late."

On August 19 the DTU held a demonstration at which disgruntled voters got an opportunity to voice their chagrin at having been "cheated." Pandemonium ensued until Phyllis rose to speak—"cold (hot) comfort." The opposition saw the Labour defeat as a chance to smash the whole union movement. No sooner had the election results been announced than the struggle for control of the union began. Chris Loblack was waging "a huge war" for control, but it was one he was destined to lose. He was ousted and replaced by an Acting Secretary General, an ex-policeman, "a very nasty type put in by the Bulletin Office and the Baron crowd." Phyllis feared that the Union "would soon be in Police and Government pockets." Loblack, seething from his ouster, had filed a lawsuit against the general secretary and the DTU Executive Committee for slander over the allegations that he and Daniel Green had taken one thousand dollars said to have disappeared seven years before. No one had ever shown proof that the theft had even occurred, but as an election smear it had been effective and had helped diminish Loblack's substantial influence and Phyllis's own votes. Now the union was in disarray and she was despondent. "Our minority of three in the Council (which hasn't been sworn yet) remains loyal," she wrote to Robert, "but would they last out five years, being Dominican, being human?"

By early September, discouraged and without money, Phyllis felt she had no choice but to return to London. She was living on Labour party takings owed to her, but her funds were very low and her financial situation precarious. If she were to return she would have to get her passage on credit. "I will come, though," she wrote Robert, "not only for your sake but for my own. . . . I love you and I long to be in Penhurst." While she waited for a booking in one of the banana boats, she left for the country to stay in a little shack lent to her by Miss Alice Dumas, a DTU trustee, to do some writing, as she had found it impossible to do "a body of work with the multitude around [her]." She had been sporadically working on a story for her planned

Untanglers series, and felt that if she managed to finish that, "would not the great adventure here have been worth something? More to old George [Horner] perhaps than the winning of the elections!" She was also finishing a story with a Dominican theme, "which might do for *Argosy*," most likely "A Time for Loving," a charming tale of gypsy lovers from enemy tribes who elope and seek the help of a would-be woman preacher who has for a long while sought permission from the island administrator to perform marriage ceremonies. Swept away by the aura of romance, he grants her request, and the lovers can be married and spirited away from Dominica. She found Myo Estate, where she was staying, "a happy place for writing," at least during the days, which were "truly marvelous in their beauty." The nights were typical of the Dominican countryside, full of huge squirreling rats and "squeaky and troublesome" bats. Her isolation was broken by frequent visits from Robert's former assistant, Mr. Rolle, who came by almost daily with news, including the unexpected announcement of her sister Celia's impending marriage to "a Cable and Wireless type called Frost." Aunt Mags reported him to be "not bad, pleasant, sporting, but not up to Jack in quality." "I should think not!" Phyllis wrote to Robert, ruefully sighing over Celia's "great love" for Jack—"I am damned if I'd ever console myself for you—no, never." By the time she returned to Roseau in late September her depression had vanished, and she began working in earnest to build the party membership in preparation for the Federal elections, now scheduled for late March. By the time she left in mid-November the party had secured its own hall and had increased its membership to more than one thousand. She had been elected general secretary of the union on September 28, despite (perhaps because of) her resolute support of Loblack against the theft accusations. Upon hearing the news a political enemy had taken a hacksaw and smashed off the padlock of the hall, occupying the premises and barricading the president's office.

In early November 1957, as she prepared for the DLP's Annual General Meeting, she held talks with the governor of the Windward Islands to discuss the departure of so many skilled younger workers, which she described as "an exit strike against the government." The meeting took place on November 15, days before her scheduled departure for England, and as expected, she was reelected president. She and LeBlanc, moreover, were nominated as candidates for the Federal elections. This secured, she left to spend the Christmas holidays in London, planning to return to Dominica in January. Once again she got passage on a freighter, and arrived in early December, exhausted and weary but hopeful. Robert, as she expected, was deeply displeased with her plans to contest the Federal election, but the London branch of the DLP, sharing her hopes, threw her a welcoming party at Fulham's Harold Laski House.

Part IV

THE HUNTING OF THE SMIDER-SNARK

T'was pathetic, no doubt, when the Smiders found out
That the Unit they thought of as swell
Had only one notion—to give them the ocean
And a bad reputation as well.

Yelled the Captain and Crew as the schooner hove to
(For Smiders are sailors of boats):
"Look out, loving friends, and take care what you do.
We Smiders have Federal votes!"

Eight

With Time a Threatened Currency

With time a threatened currency, when once
a beatific interval is given
wise fools indulge themselves as in a trance
jealous lest any dividend be riven.

"You were told often enough my feelings about your going back"—Robert would remind Phyllis after her insistence on returning to Dominica in February 1958 for the Federal elections brought their marriage to its worse crisis ever—"but towards the end you paid no attention at all to my protestations, you were so single minded that you just argued and then did not listen so that in the end I just said nothing."

Phyllis's two months in London before the election were the most tension ridden of her twenty-eight-year marriage. Robert was dumbfounded when he realized that she had committed herself to contesting the election, and positively exploded when he discovered she had had election leaflets printed "behind [his] back or without telling [him] that she figured in them as a candidate." At the heart of their increasingly strident disagreements were their differing outlooks on how to face their bleak economic prospects. Robert was exploring a chemical-spraying venture she deemed unwise and dangerous. Frantic at seeing him "restlessly combing through job after job," she wanted him to try his hand at teaching, a career choice that would allow him to follow her to Dominica, and on to Trinidad if she won the election. But he felt that at his age (fifty-two) he could not break into a new field or uproot with impunity. She, in turn, argued that politics was not only her calling but the means of assuring herself and her family an income. She had, she claimed, "no ambition at all," but felt the "aridity" of "becoming a typist all over again when [she] had qualities of leadership and inspiration." She had carefully considered their debts, their son, the "lovely house and land in which [she] above all had caused [them] to invest and mortgage [their] future on," but could see "no hope of contributing in a big way in London."

Her contradictory assertions that she had "no ambition at all" yet saw herself poised on the brink of "contributing in a big way" in Dominica encapsulate her dilemma. She had always sought to defer to Robert, to preserve his dignity and self-esteem in an era in which men felt entitled to such deference. But never during their life together had his needs and hers come into so sharp a conflict as they did at this juncture. He wanted her to retire to Penhurst to write and live the sparse life so typical of the impoverished English middle class. But she saw herself as having barely scratched the surface of her political possibilities. Moreover, by now she had given up every dream of making a living from writing—the need to do so had become obvious, she declared, when her "latter-day writing" had been rejected. "The time was not right for me in that line," she explained. "But it *was* right for me with Dominica, and I *knew it innately*. I had such faith in your faith. It seemed to me that you had bourne [*sic*] so much, you could stick out (surely) the last hurdle, so that at last we could make things secure." In many ways their impasse brought to the fore the cultural differences they had managed to bridge so effortlessly during their long marriage. It was a struggle between his quintessential Englishness and her own particular brand of West Indianness. Burdened as they were by their financial difficulties, he proposed

"English" solutions that clashed with the ambition she denied. Phyllis did protest too much about her lack of ambition, but she could never be brought to see her aspirations as such. Ambition was individualistic, personal—and she saw her goals as bound up with the needs of the Dominican people and her family's history.

They argued bitterly about obtaining the money she would need for her return home. He was adamant against incurring any more debt, but she prevailed on him to request a loan from Elizabeth Wilson, a well-built, well-off friend with whom Robert, in his dismay at Phyllis's "leaving" him, would go on to have an affair. He had felt "secretly terribly glad, glad, glad when she refused." Phyllis, undaunted, appealed to two friends, Bill Pedder and Arthur Hyde, who agreed to lend her the money she needed if Robert had no objections. He, with a heart "so heavy," lied to them so she could get the money she was so determined to have; but he was heartbroken by her perseverance, feeling that she had chosen Dominica and her career over him. "I tried to capture you this Christmas," he would lament, "but my impoverished mold was not enough."

The turmoil preceding her return home caused many delays, and she finally left London with little time to spare, risking not reaching Roseau by nomination day, set for March 1, 1958. As it happened, it was to take something "little short of a miracle" to reach Dominica in time. Traveling by air "cheap rate" as far as Barbados, she had to jettison her packed clothing because she could not afford overweight. The printed leaflets Robert had found so objectionable, "two thousand stacked in a rucksack," and two cotton dresses was all she could take with her. She arrived in Barbados, exhausted and jittery, five days before nomination day. But there her inquiries about air transport proved fruitless, and she spent the day after her arrival pacing up and down the schooner pool in the scorching heat looking for a boat traveling north to Dominica. All were bound south, she was told. Unconvinced, she stubbornly watched one boat after another up-anchor and head slowly southward. In the late afternoon, hearing of a plane leaving for Saint Lucia in a matter of minutes, she grabbed her few belongings and raced in a taxi through the airport barriers as the aircraft door was shutting. She had to be lifted into the airplane.

In Saint Lucia she was again marooned. Immediately after her arrival she contacted Carl La Corbiniere, the prominent Labour leader soon to become Federal minister of trade and industry and deputy prime minister, and he generously took time from his own campaign to hunt for something seaworthy to take her home in time. Phyllis spent the next two nights in his book-lined guest room, playing with his young children and trying to subdue her worry. He worked unflaggingly, seeking private yachts, sailboats, trying unsuccessfully to persuade launch owners to risk the brief unpredictable passage. "Miraculously," at dawn on the last day of February, the day before nomination day, when Phyllis had despaired of success, a banana boat of the Van Geest line, speeding north to pick up bananas in Dominica, was alerted by radio. It was not due to stop at Saint Lucia, but the captain agreed to slow down sufficiently to allow her to board. Awakened before daybreak, she dressed quickly, gathered her parcel of leaflets, and boarded a fast launch. With the banana boat moving, she staggered up the emergency gangway, to be greeted by Mr. John van Geest, who kindly vacated his cabin so she could rest. Six hours later, in blazing sunshine, she was awakened by the rattle of the anchor at Fond Colé and the voices of the shoremen. She put on the straw hat that was her party's electoral symbol and boarded another launch for

Roseau and Customs. At Roseau she stepped ashore to find an informal political meeting in progress near the bayfront. A speaker was hissing out: "And look at how that white woman has let you all down! Didn' she promise—didn' she say . . . didn' you all believe her! And looka how she didn' even come home in time! Just wanted to take your money and spend it abroad! Even her patois was learnt in Paris! I'm telling you, friends, I can assure you, the election is won awready!" Phyllis "lifted [her] hat from [her] face and said in *patois—moi veeway*—I have arrived." Her supporters crowded around her, laughing, jumping, and cheering. The women hugged and squeezed her, their eyes filling with tears. "Yeah boy," they said to the speaker good humoredly. "You said right. *Belle parole*. Election won awready." That night, after she had settled at Kingsland House, she felt "in her bones a creeping of exhausted elation and apprehension." The next day, her nomination papers in place, the campaign went into full swing.

From the start it became clear to the DLP leadership that only Labour could win the election. It was to be Dominica's first islandwide election, one that would go to the party with broadest mass appeal. Only a handful of politicians—Phyllis, LeBlanc, and Baron—could count on massive support, but Baron, not a great admirer of the concept of Federation and secure in his position as chief minister, would not run for a seat in the Federal legislature. There would be seven candidates for the island's two seats, Phyllis and Edward LeBlanc among them. The brief campaign—there were scarcely three weeks between nomination and election days—was dominated by the Labour party. Phyllis and the party leadership had learned from the mistakes of the year before and had planned their campaign accordingly: They had secured and briefed house-to-house canvassers; their two candidates would share the symbol of the hat; both would once again visit village after village in a personal appeal for voters' support. Her two thousand precious leaflets—bearing for the first time in Dominica's history photographs of the candidates, the party's electoral symbol, and its platform—were an enormous success. On an island where the peasantry had precious little access to anything else to adorn their walls, they soon took pride of place as home decorations and were still to be seen years after the Federation was gone.

The physical demands of the campaign wore Phyllis out. The emotional strain of her visit to London, the tensions and uncertainties of her voyage home, the intensity of the effort to travel far and wide in scarcely three weeks, the unhealthy diet of dry bread and coconut water eaten on the run brought her thin body to the point of emaciation, her legs fragile from clambering up the mountains. But the DLP went on to what the *Chronicle* called "an overwhelming victory." Of the nearly 13,000 votes cast for the team of two, Phyllis received 9,860 and LeBlanc 9,471. They won in 135 out of 138 polling stations, gathering a staggering 77 percent of the vote. Their nearest competitor received a mere 1,859 votes. She was ecstatic. "They had voted for the Federal Team of two in their thousands," she would write, "giving me the largest majority the island had ever known, although I was a descendant of colonists, although hecklers had urged them—don't vote for that white woman! She learned her patois in Paris! She has come here to take your money and spend it outside. The manifest confidence, strong enough to override any question of race-origin and all kinds of libel and slander strengthened my own innate confidence in the ordinary people." Privately she would write to Robert of how surprised she had been "to over-reach Eddie in votes & public feeling. . . . I am so grateful to whatever Gods there be at the outcome of all this. It's all rather *Fatima* isn't it." She believed that even some of her enemies voted for her. Indeed, they may have in the belief that if elected she would have to leave the island, clearing the field for her political opposition to gain a firmer hold on island affairs.

In contrast to her own overwhelming victory, the "stunning surprise" of the Caribbean-wide election results came as a shock to her. Like everyone else she had expected WIFLP (which comprised, with the exception of Saint Vincent and Dominica, all the parties then in power in their respective islands and was moreover led by Manley and Williams) to "score a sweeping victory." But WIFLP had secured only twenty-two of the forty-five seats contested. The Democratic Labour party, the hastily formed "scratch team" led by Alexander Bustamante and Albert Gomes, won twenty. In Jamaica the Democratic Labour party secured twelve of the seventeen Jamaican seats; in Trinidad it won six of ten. In Barbados, the government party, the Barbados Labour party, returned four of the five island seats, with the fifth going to an independent candidate, Mrs. Florence Daysh, a wealthy plantation owner prominent in social work. In the Leewards and Windwards, Antigua, Dominica, Saint Kitts, and Saint Lucia each returned two seats for WIFLP; Montserrat's one seat went likewise. Only Saint Vincent gave its two seats to the Democratic Labour party. WIFLP's tenuous victory (and two-thirds of its parliamentary strength) therefore came from Barbados and the Leeward and Windward Islands; the opposition's strength consisted entirely of members from three islands—Jamaica, Trinidad, and Saint Vincent. The resulting imbalance was to have important consequences, the most obvious one being that the three independents, two from Grenada and one from Barbados, "carried the fate of both sides in their hands." WIFLP's "narrow and insecure" lead was bolstered by Florence Daysh's support. During her campaign as an independent she had repeatedly stated that she would support Prime Minister designate Grantley Adams, "so long as his policies were in the interest of Barbados and the West Indies," and she would be true to her word, occasionally serving as the "casting vote" on important decisions. As a result the government faced the formal inauguration of parliament with a virtual, if not absolutely dependable, majority of three over a redoubtable opposition.

On March 28th Phyllis and LeBlanc celebrated their victory with a rally at the Market Square, which was so packed that men were hanging perilously from the rafters and she "could not keep from worry in case of dry rot." The ovation was terrific. The day after their victory celebration she and LeBlanc were received by the island administrator, Mr. Alexander Lindo, at Government House, and a ceremony of official recognition of their electoral victory was held at the courthouse. She arrived flanked by Aunt Mags and Marion, who had persuaded her to go despite Chris Loblack's advice (given in a lugubrious tone) to keep away or she "would get *squeezed*!" In the days following her victory, Lindo had "bombarded" her with masses of printed material regarding the lavish plans for the inauguration, arriving in large envelopes, inscribed in his hand, "The Hon. Mrs. Shand Allfrey." The first time she had been so addressed she "could not keep back a sardonic chuckle." Loblack had a "wonderful rendering" of the title—"the Honourable Comrade Phyllis!" The inauguration, she wrote to Robert, was being turned into a giant spree. Frank Baron and Elkin Henry, the Lindos, Howell Shillingford, and "all sort of horrors" were attending at government expense. Lindo had even offered to pay all Robert's living expenses in Trinidad if he chose to come, but this she declined, arguing that her husband would hardly consider the "idyllic but wasteful proposition," feeling nonetheless that everyone would have somebody there except her. She would have friends there—former Secretary of State Arthur Creech-Jones, LeBlanc, Adams, and Manley among them—and hoped not to feel "too marooned, except for the empty husband-seat." Meanwhile, she was savoring her victory, relishing the "lovely tributes" from perfect strangers she had been receiving, which included a letter of warm congratulations from the Caribbean Women's Association, headquartered in Trinidad.

The cable announcing her victory, however, was the last straw for Robert. Furious at a victory that proved her right in her stubborn perseverance and committed her to a prolonged residence in Trinidad, he fired off a letter declaring himself separated from her and informing her of his new liaison with their friend Elizabeth Wilson. It was a letter that would bring Phyllis intense pain for years to come. "Please do not feel *guilty* about leaving me," he had written.

> You chose a career and Dominicans instead and you must not now change horses in mid-stream. . . . One thing you must see, darling Phyllis, is that for my own self-respect, I cannot just tag on behind you. And another thing, I have not the zest that I can chop and change my surroundings at my age and my ties to England are as strong or stronger than yours to Dominica. I am being selfish for once and am going to form a pattern of life for the next 18 months which does not include you. . . . A price to pay. When you come back to England in 2, 3, or 5 years time there may be more to pay, since the pattern of my life may have hardened into a mould that does not bear your imprint so firmly and you will have to fit my mould instead of me yours! . . . I had a hell of a rough and unhappy time in the last twelve months. I am not a weak character, I just do not happen to be as strong as you or as single-minded.

On April 3, 1958, a Holy Thursday, with "the gloom of Good Friday [already] settled on the island," the weekly Grumman Goose brought Robert's letter, "dropping so innocently out of the square promising envelope." It "settled like a black cloud over [her] brow and heart." She went through her work for the day without betraying her pain, thinking she could not bear anyone knowing how "overcome" she felt. In the afternoon she had "crept into the Anglican Cathedral, sat in a side pew, and wept fountains." The letter brought down upon her the whole weight of her "utter loneliness." She found "nothing to quarrel with" in it "if looked at from the husband-angle," only that it contradicted and "made hypocrisy" out of the "king-consort" letter he had sent her to read to the people, in which he claimed that everything his "beloved wife" did was done with his "support and consent." After that, "How then can I declare myself separated from you," she would ask him in reply, "thrown to the wolves so to speak?" His affair with Elizabeth Wilson she haughtily dismissed, as it was "uncontaminated by a true early friendship between herself and me." What disturbed her about the affair was its public nature—Robert's intention of "going around" with her—and his threat of "form[ing] a pattern of life" that would include Elizabeth but not her. In her unhappiness, she became convinced that people had gotten at him by "referring to [her] *ambition* as if any success of [hers] belittled [him]"; it was "a smart undermining trick." They had, in any case, succeeded, making it impossible for her to enjoy "the fruits of [her] victory." "What is it but dry dust if you take it in that bitter manner."

Having gone to bed in a state of dejection, she woke "with a sickening anxious start" at two-thirty in the morning. The cocks were crowing in the neighborhood as she reread his letter, stopping in fury at his final words—"press on and do a good job. I shouldn't love you but I do." "You shouldn't love me?" she scribbled at the end of her letter to him. "You should never love me more. I need your love and faith very badly if I am to be the sort of superwoman my present situation demands. And I dare not fail, for everybody's sakes, yours and Phil's first." His closing remarks about their income taxes added to her rage—he knew well enough that the clerk in charge of that office was a political enemy of hers. "If you think I shall put on my income tax *separated* and give my enemies a chance to say again what they wish to happen and have been lying about all along, you are crazy. . . . I've had enough trouble already with people saying you don't care for me (they *know* I care because they can see my face while they insinuate.) I may put something like separate establishments necessary while husband winds up his affairs, but *not separated*. It is a word I refuse to tolerate."

Robert was stunned by the intensity of her reaction and replied in tones considerably more conciliatory than those of his first letter, tones that nonetheless did not bear a shift in his basic position. "You took my letter much too hard . . . ," he told her. "It seemed from your reaction that I must have said something very ambiguous and cruel-sounding." The filing of separate tax returns, he explains, "does not infer that they are legally separated." As to Elizabeth, he will continue to see her, but she "should not be worried that E. will displace you in anyway. I shall be 'going around' with her a bit, but no-one is going to think any the worse of you or me for that." As for his mode of life, he writes, "I want to develop myself and strengthen my ability a bit. You are a stronger personality and you have, without realising it, done things *your* way so much—often I have wanted something a bit different and said nothing because I knew you would [overcome] me and cause dissent. I want now to balance that side of our relationship up a bit and will take advantage of the next years." To this Phyllis never directly replied. Her letters to him following this softer restatement of his position were full of gossip and chatty details of the coming inauguration celebrations. For months she studiously avoided the topics of tax declarations, Elizabeth Wilson, and Robert's newfound independence.

The weeks between the election and her departure for Trinidad were spent in hurried preparations. She had been nearly driven to distraction by a list she had been sent of the things she needed for those receptions involving Princess Margaret, deciding finally to ignore most of them. She had had her seamstress, Sésé (Alexandrina Jean-Baptiste)—a young woman who would follow her to Trinidad—fit her with a couple of "inexpensive but charming" new dresses and alter some of her old "long and loopy" ones. All she lacked, she remarked, was a tiara, a few rings, long black and white gloves, "and a de Maupassant necklace!" Phyllis, who rarely gave what she wore much thought, found the effort of putting together a successful politician's trousseau most mortifying. She spent her last evening in Roseau sitting on the little family veranda with Aunt Mags, having their scheduled cocktail and chatting idly about whether there was any possibility of her being offered a ministry.

On April 16 she left for Barbados in a charter seaplane with Edward LeBlanc,

1. Sir Henry Nicholls. (*Courtesy of Commander George Leslie-Smith*)

2. Francis Shand, 1914. (*Courtesy of Commander George Leslie-Smith*)

3. Kingland House. (*Courtesy of Commander George Leslie-Smith*)

4. Elfreda Shand at Seaview House, 1920.

5. The Shand girls—Marion, Phyllis (*top right*), and Cecelia, with their cousin Jack, 1914. (*Courtesy of Commander George Leslie-Smith*)

6. Young Phyllis, as drawn by her sister Marion, 1920.

7. Phyllis at Seaview House, 1926. (*Courtesy of Commander George Leslie-Smith*)

8. Adèle Olyphant, 1927. (*Courtesy of Adèle Olyphant Emery*)

9. Phyllis and Robert's wedding, 1930.

10. Phina, Philip, and Phyllis, 1937. (*Courtesy of Commander George Leslie-Smith*)

11. Phyllis at Niagara Falls, 1932.

12. Phina, Philip, and Rosalind, 1938.

13. Phyllis, Phina, and Philip in Maine, 1941.

15. The family reunited in 1946.

14. Phina in the United States, 1945.

16. Penhurst, near Battle, Sussex. (*Courtesy of Mrs. Margaret Benge*)

17. Aunt Maggie, Celia, Henry Bradshaw, Elfreda, Francis Allfrey, Mark Bradshaw, and Marion, England, 1946. (*Courtesy of Commander George Leslie-Smith*)

18. Phina's wedding, Phyllis (*second from left*), Alan, and Phina.

19. Phyllis and Flynn Coppard at Cob Cottage, 1948.

20. Phyllis, 1954.

21. Federal election leaflet.

22. The Federal House of Representatives.

23. Phyllis with Robert Bradshaw during Federal inauguration ceremonies.

24. Phyllis and Robert reunited in 1958.

25. Phyllis in Geneva following the ILO walkout against South Africa.

26. Phyllis at Radio Trinidad broadcasting the Jamaican referendum returns.

27. Phyllis visiting Barbados as Federal minister. (*Courtesy of* Barbados Advocate)

28. Phyllis and Robert in Trinidad, 1960.

29. Sonia, David, Robert, and Phyllis in Trinidad, 1961.

30. Sonia and David in Trinidad, 1961.

32. Lennox Honychurch. (*Courtesy of Polly Pattullo*)

31. Robert, Phyllis, Robbie, and an unidentified staff member at the *Star* office, 1974. (*Courtesy of Adèle Olyphant Emery*)

33. Robert, Robbie, and Phyllis before the Federal flag. (*Courtesy of Lennox Honychurch*)

34. Phyllis at the Copt Hall mill house, 1984.

35. Phyllis, 1984. (*Courtesy of Christopher Cormack*)

"Mrs. Eddie," Frank Baron, and "the despicable Elkin Henry," the man who had defeated her in the 1957 elections. In the plane she had on her knee a wonderfully resigned three-year-old boy from Castle Bruce who had swallowed a large nail and was being taken to Barbados for an operation. In Barbados she met Florence Daysh, WIFLP's "saviour," a "very light coloured woman, known as Brown Sugar," who was "Stevie Smith's double in look and voice" and had a past background "exactly the antithesis" of Phyllis's. Daysh's grandfather had lent cash to impoverished sugar estate owners at about the same time the Shands were losing their lands in Antigua. Her grandmother, "having grown rich on the sugar paupers," had "bought her way in almost to the Government's top by copious donations to charities, etc." And yet, Phyllis concluded, Daysh "might have gone in with Bustamante and Gomes, so we should be grateful."

As soon as she settled in at Queen's Park Hotel in Port of Spain, Phyllis contacted an old friend, Donna Read, an American UNICEF officer. On her first Sunday in Trinidad, the day in which Grantley Adams was due to announce his ministerial selections, Phyllis and Donna went swimming at Chaguaramas, a lovely area, with a sparkling cove and huge orange groves, and the site of the American naval base under discussion as the possible location of the Federal capital. Phyllis drove there "out of sheer inquisitiveness," having first heard of Chaguaramas during the war, when the agreement with the United States to build the naval base had been finalized.* She had thought it a "bad bargain—war or no war": fifty old warships for a fine piece of land, a harbor, and a ninety-nine-year lease was "a terrible deal."

Although Phyllis claimed—not altogether believably—that she had "never received the slightest hint" that she was being considered for a ministry, she was nonetheless not oblivious to the meetings taking place in Port of Spain. When Donna urged her to stay at Chaguaramas for tea, she declined and insisted on returning. As she entered the hotel lobby, covered with sand and salt, she found V. C. "Papa" Bird, the Antiguan Labour leader, impatiently waiting for her. He took her by the elbow and marched her to the lift: "Where have you been all day?" he demanded. "The Prime Minister is waiting for you. There's a meeting going on in his suite." He wouldn't even let her put away her bathing suit and brush her hair. "It is a meeting of Ministers," he announced.

When she entered Adams's suite she found a gathering of nine Federal representatives. Adams greeted her perfunctorily and immediately started reading from his list, beginning with Robert Bradshaw of Saint Kitts as minister of finance. Carl La Corbiniere was named minister of trade and industries, W. A. Rose of Trinidad was chosen to be the minister of communications and works. F. B. Ricketts of Jamaica was his choice for minister of natural resources and agriculture, and A.G.R. Byfield of Jamaica was named leader of government business in the Senate. There were three ministers without portfolio, J. L. Charles of Saint Lucia, V. Vaughan of Barbados, and J. Liburd of Saint Kitts. He finally got to Phyllis's name, almost casually mentioning that she was the obvious choice to be the first Federal minister for labour and social affairs. It was, as she would later tell Robert, "a big surprise." After the appointments

*The building of the American naval base at Chaguaramas was funded by the U.S. Lend-Lease program, authorized by Congress in 1941 to aid any nation whose defense was deemed vital to U.S. security.

were announced they all went to the governor-general's house for coffee and brandy before taking the oath. Phyllis, "being *A* and the only woman," was first. "Another big moment—The first woman Minister of our Nation and the First West Indian Minister of Social Affairs." While the others were drinking, "not un-soberly," as they all had "rather a grave sense of mission," she stole away to write a note to Robert for the first morning mail. "My honey," she asked, "how do you like what you by your political closeness and many sacrifices have helped to achieve? Do you truly feel now that it is absolutely right?" The following morning, recalling that her letter would not reach him for days, she sent a telegram: YOUR PRESENCE MY ONLY LACK, DARLING, MINISTER OF SOCIAL AFFAIRS.

It was widely held that the Council of State, as the cabinet was called, "was not generously served by the results of the general election, either as to experience, or the 'field' from which Ministers could be selected." Apart from Bradshaw, formerly chief minister of Saint Kitts–Nevis–Anguilla, and La Corbiniere, who had been a member of both the Legislative and Executive Councils of Saint Lucia, no one in Adams's pool of prospective ministers could claim any experience of ministerial responsibility, close contact with government management, or the external regard and respect that came from long-established political careers. The appointments were thus met with barely concealed misgivings and some open derision. (He was caught in a classic catch-22 situation. Prevented by the constitutional ban on dual membership from drawing upon the region's most experienced statesmen, Adams was chastised for relying on polical neophytes.) Jamaica and Trinidad felt "grossly underweight" in cabinet representation: "the 'tail' of eight Ministers from Barbados and the smaller Eastern units, looked ominously like wagging the Jamaica-Trinidad 'dog' with three novitiate Ministers." Phyllis, "the sole lady," was seen as a political neophyte who had been chosen because "her eagerness to produce some new message to the women of the West Indies must have impressed Sir Grantley." Not that her feminism was likely to have gained her any respect or admiration in the misogynistic inner circles of Federal politics. Never specifically targeted for criticism or antagonism in Dominica *as a woman*, Phyllis would be slow to grasp how the mere fact of being female would leave her open to ridicule and derision in Trinidad.

Grantley Adams himself was fiercely attacked by Bustamante, who made a statement deploring his appointment as prime minister, calling him an "insular man who lacks sufficient imagination" and asking how he could ever "do any good for the ten federated States, having ruled over pauperised Barbados for so long, obviously without realizing the state of poverty there?" The comments were circulated widely and provoked violent outrage, particularly because of their injustice to a man with a long career as a labor leader and a history of effective leadership in his own legislature. Adams and his friends, Phyllis among them, were deeply hurt by the personal attack, and the wound festered, but no protest was published so as not to invite an ugly dispute that would mar the inauguration festivities. The long-term effect of the Bustamante-Adams incident was to introduce "a pattern of invective in the airing of personal animosities, which was to become the fashion of exchanges, sometimes even between political allies."

On the evening after the ministerial appointments Adams, in "an affectionate command," asked Phyllis to take a stroll with him round the Savannah, the huge roundabout—the largest in the word, Trinidadians claim—that houses the sports grounds and racetrack. As they set out he asked her about her husband, and Phyllis answered that he was abroad: "I didn't know the PM well enough to answer, '[H]e got sick of my giving him up for island politics and I believe he has another woman.'" They talked of how the gentle people of the world steep themselves in literary murders, of English schoolboys, of cricket, about which Adams was enthusiastic but she loathed. (Later he would joke that, had he known she despised cricket, he would never have made her a minister.) It was only as they approached the bright lights of the hotel that Phyllis noticed how the prime minister lagged, almost limping from the painful foot ailment that would soon lead to damaging speculation about his health. At the lift he took her hand to wish her "Goodnight, my child." "Goodnight, Sir," she replied, and he stopped the lift with a gesture to the operator. "Don't call me *Sir* again," he admonished her, only to have her reply, "I can't help it. You are the only man I've really enjoyed calling Sir."* He smiled and lifted a hand deprecatingly. As the lift doors closed, she turned to look at a middle-aged Canadian or American tourist sitting in the lobby, who had murmured "disgusting" as she had come up the steps with Adams, and who seemed disappointed when the lift swallowed up "a solitary bowed figure."

The inauguration of Parliament by Princess Margaret was the highlight of a week of lavish festivities that celebrated the theme of a "kindred and colourful West Indian history and culture." The unifying accent prevailing over its gaiety and merriment was the islands' consciousness of a common destiny and their determination to move together to full independence, underscored by numerous festivals of drama, music, and dance, exhibitions of paintings and history, carnival troupes, and military parades. The whirlwind of activity included countless lectures and receptions honoring the many distinguished guests of the government, among whom Sir Grantley moved with an "urbanity and distinction" that succeeded, at least temporarily, in establishing him as a symbol of unity and conciliation. Prince Aly Khan, Adam Clayton Powell Jr., Vice President Nixon, Arthur Creech-Jones, C.L.R. James, and the venerable Federalist Albert Marryshow were on the long list of "legendary personalities" attending the festivities. Phyllis had become "very matey" with Guyanese leader Cheddi Jagan and his wife, and had dined with Paul Robeson Jr. and his young wife, socialist activists she had met in London. Mrs. Robeson had given a lecture on the eve of inauguration, after which Phyllis addressed the gathering in patois, receiving "a tremendous ovation." After the lecture she had returned to her room—one of the worst in the hotel—in a reflective mood. Burdened as she was by personal debts, she saw herself as truly representative of the poor Federation of which she was a minister, "rich only in land beauty and land fertility, good human potential and healthful sunshine." The "lavish flash and bang" of the inaugural celebrations reflected a confidence in the Federation's permanence that she was far from sharing. Such large sums had been expended on bringing VIPs from abroad and on entertainment to celebrate the debut of a Federation that was perhaps fated not to last that it appeared to her on the eve of the "debutante's ball" that they would have been "better advised to wait for independence to make merry." She was due to move the next day to an air-

*Phyllis's hero worship of Adams often led her unconsciously to imitate his accent at cabinet meetings. Once he leaned over and said (with the "foxiest of smiles"): "Look out de wind doan change and you doan tark dat way forever."

conditioned room up above, among the other ministers, a move symbolic of her changed status. Ministers with portfolio received salaries of twelve thousand BWI dollars plus allowances, a free furnished house, several passages to visit their constituencies, and funds for entertainment. In the meantime she had to be careful about her few clothes and the jewelry she had borrowed from Aunt Mags, which included an old family locket inscribed in tiny gold lettering with the words *Virtute Duce Comite Fortuna*. Her Uncle Ralph used to say that it was an antidemocratic motto, and should be translated: "The virtue of the Dukes is the fortune of the Counts." Phyllis preferred a different translation more in accordance with her political philosophy: "The virtue of the leader is the fortune of the community." She went to bed wearing Aunt Mags's pearl necklace for safety.

Inauguration day began with the ministers being introduced to Princess Margaret at the airport. The princess was "very fetching" and, with her big blue eyes, reminded Phyllis of Phina. She found her to be "a proper little Madam who [prior to the evening reception that closed the momentous day] had kept the dinner guests waiting, standing in a ring of roses while she had her hair altered." Aunt Mags's advice on how to hold a conversation with the royal visitor had been simply "not to talk politics," suggesting instead that she describe how her Shand grandfather had entertained the royal grandfather in Antigua when he was a midshipman. But when she raised the subject with the princess, who was sitting on a sofa after dinner between her and the Roman Catholic archbishop, Margaret asked promptly, "Whatever was my grandfather doing there?" On being told he had been duck shooting she muttered a disappointed "Is that all?" and "averted her marshmallow pink cheek." She then asked Phyllis some "pretty sharp questions" about historical events and dates. Luckily the archbishop began to compare their inaugural rockets with the fireworks of Versailles, and anyone could see that the princess "was partial to Archbishops and enjoyed his conversation far more than [Phyllis's]." Margaret might have liked her better "if she had ignored Maggie's advice and talked about West Indian politics."

The inaugural ceremony had begun for Phyllis with an annoying taunt from Minister of Finance Bradshaw, whose misogynist antipathy toward her was blatant and who never wasted any opportunity to sneer at her. Seeing her—her knee-length hair elaborately braided for the occasion—come down in the hotel lift to join him for the procession, he derisively commented, loudly and publicly, that she "should have done something to her hair." Phyllis, Frank Baron declared, "almost died." The procession was saved by a telegram of congratulations from Robert, handed to her as she joined the line, a touching gesture she quickly wrote to thank him for—"perfect timing again!" One of her most vivid memories of inaugural day was leaving the "uproarious rostrum" to lay a wreath on Andrew Cipriani's grave. Having once heard the name "Cipriani" used to frighten children much as the name "Boney" was used in Napoleonic days, she found the small gathering by the quiet grave very moving. It marked the first and last occasion on which she saw with her own eyes "the three big rival leaders of the West Indies—Adams, Manley, and Williams—standing together in evident unanimity of emotion."

On April 23, the festivities over, she set to work. Her office was a charming private room opening into a garden with palms and wisteria. The desk was immense, "as was the work ahead," since her ministry covered labor, higher education, health, social services, housing, and building. Her duties comprised such dissimilar subjects as sports, the Red Cross, Alcoholics Anonymous, the International Labour Organisation (ILO), and UNESCO. From the point of view of position, however, her office was the worst in the building, just as her parking spot was the worst in the alley behind Federal House. She could be aggressive for others but not for herself, and usually got "the left-overs." She therefore had the "hottest, noisiest space for my Ministry." But she was determined to prove wrong "those who had said that [she] would embarrass the Government by being a woman and expecting concessions and delicate treatment." Her colleagues treated her "without gallantry, as one of themselves. . . . Sometimes indeed they treated [her] indirectly and perhaps unconsciously as the least of themselves. That was an historical *volte face* which [she] had to expect and endure" as a minority white woman in an "all-coloured, near-Negro cabinet":

> My type was more Scandinavian than creole, and this served me well and ill. It was bound to serve me some ill because of the legacy of colonial rule in our islands, and even further back, of slavery. But it also served me well, since I was a symbol, a symbol of tolerance. I was a living recognition of the fact that we were a mixed community. . . . It was not so much that the white citizens, few in number, looked to me in hope in a world of emergent Afro-Asian nationals—for some of them disliked me very much. It was just that the ordinary people, the black peasants and labourers, accepted and loved me.

The many problems facing Adams's precarious government were not manifest during Parliament's brief "running-in" session in late April, whose highlight was "the Speech from the Throne," read by Governor-General Hailes to the Joint Houses on April 30. As a first statement of the government's policies, the speech offered assurances of the British government's awareness of the "sensitive areas of conflicting territorial interests" and of its intention of addressing them with patience and caution. After a review of matters on which it intended to proceed studiously and purposefully—the formulation of a regional housing plan (one of Phyllis's central responsibilities), the creation of an efficient interisland passenger and freight service, the reconciliation of various territorial policies on industrial development, the continuation of the Customs Union study in progress, and further discussion of the principle of Freedom of Movement of Persons—it plaintively outlined the harsh financial realities facing the Federation. The budgets for defense, the University College of the West Indies, and the shipping service would consume nearly 60 percent of the mandatory levy, leaving "only a slender margin" for the tackling of other problems.

This first session of the Federal legislature was over in early May, and Phyllis immediately left Trinidad for Montserrat—her "first official port"—and on to Dominica. She was hoping to use her four-week break to revise a television script of *The Carib's Revenge*, based on an early episode of the island's history, which fellow Dominican poet Edward Scobie was interested in broadcasting in London. She was still making an effort to continue her writing, although her most recent story, "The Bodyguard," had just been rejected. "I am not surprised neither am I disappointed now that *Bodyguard* was returned," she wrote Robert when he forwarded the news, "and in fact I am somewhat relieved at this stage as it might have been thought to reflect directly on my triumph which was a victory for sweat and democracy."

She arrived in Montserrat on May 5, 1958. The island, which she knew only from her nurse Lally's descriptions, was "a little Jane Austen colony planted in vegetable gardens and cotton." A general election was scheduled for the following Sunday, and after a special "punch session" at Government House, she was expected to help promote the Labour candidates: "slightly coloured" Clifford Wall, an old acquaintance and the "nicest" richest man in the island; and Rose Kelesick, "that unusual thing, a young coloured well-to-do girl who is on the side of the barefoot people." Mr. Bramble, the MLP leader, a groom in earlier life and a "Chris[Loblack]-like character," thus dragged her to three "interminable meetings" on their behalf. She went on to Antigua, where she met with the governor and toured the mental asylum and the general hospital. Her host, Papa Bird, an "absolutely magnificent 6 ft. 4 light Negro," paid her every courtesy and even went so far as to show her around social spots in his car. She thought he was "absolutely grand—respect-worthy in the Manley-Adams tradition, with a contemplative manner which is *so* English!" He drove her to see her old godmother, Mrs. Lena Henzell, who told Phyllis about how when they were little she and Francis Shand met at the crossroads of their adjoining estates and rode their ponies to school together, and of how they had a great crush on each other which never diminished and had made a pact that they would be godparents to each other's children if they did not marry. Afterward Bird showed her all the old Shand/Byam estates—Fitches Creek, Cedar Hill, Martin's Byams, Cassava Valley—and Parham Church, a "most beautiful church" with a very high vaulted roof and wall memorials to both Berkeleys and Byams. Like the houses, it was in "a state of decrepitude." She had not even felt too sad at the thought of the family's decayed glory, for as Bird had told her, "If you had grown up like the Henzells you would not now be a Labour leader." By May 14 she was back at Kingsland House, pressing to clear some electoral business that took her on quite a trek, mostly on horseback, into the hinterland—Dieper, Tranto, Goodhope, Rosalie, La Plaine, and Grand Fond. Her horse, Charlie, hated women, and she had been advised to keep silent, which she did while the rain fell and fell and she and Charlie were practically blinded by it. He finally "dumped [her] off" at La Plaine, "after shying off at every goat and cow on the way." She went on to Grand Fond, feeling that as Adams had especially given her leave to thank the voters (as in fact they were all obliged to do in the various islands) she felt she had to push on "weather or no weather."

During the few days intervening between her return to Trinidad and the reassembling of the House on June 9, she settled in her new bungalow at Federation Park. Her first week in the house was disastrous. All the plumbing went wrong, no chairs were delivered, the telephone had not been installed, and Adams had to resort to motorcycle messengers to contact her. She quickly set about organizing her housekeeping, hiring a Dominican housekeeper, Lucy Fregiste, "a superior Party member, rather too educated," and arranging for the arrival of her friend and seamstress Sésé. Once settled in the house, the three women felt "luxurious." None of them had ever before inhabited a house with two baths, three showers, four lavatories, three sinks, and four washbasins. "Never mind that the authorities turned off the water nearly every afternoon in dry weather, so that we had to squeeze driblets out of the garden tap. We felt rich." To complete her staff she reached an agreement with Nicholas, "a nice hire-car man" who had come to see her, announcing he was a Dominican and would be "her friend, her bodyguard, her loyal adherent." It was to prove entirely true. His presence in "the wicked big island comforted her inordinately."

Federation Park was a place not unlike "a tropical edition of Commonwealth Avenue, Buffalo . . . more luxury building, of course, but the same feeling of waste land." The compoundlike park faced the great savannah, an area well-known for brush fires, which presented a riveting spectacle licking their way through the scrub-land, scorching to death flowering shrubs and the few trees in its path. Robert was later to paint a realistic landscape of such a fire—"flames beating up to a tiny Hindu house with its prayer-flags, one white and red, stiff in the Sirocco breeze, and the family rushing to drag out the bedstead." The painting hung for years on their wall at Copt Hall "like a scene from an adventure story." The parkland surrounding the bungalow, however, had been a concentration camp for aliens during World War II and was devoid of trees. Phyllis, accustomed to the mountains and profuse vegetation of Dominica, found herself inordinately homesick and depressed and was "trying desperately to learn which are the fastest growing trees and shrubs." One day, after an excursion to Maracas Bay, Phyllis and Sésé took from the side of the road a pail of rich earth and a few *bois flot* roots. (The *bois flot*, or balisier as it is better known, was the emblem of the Federation's host country, a tree with "banana-ish leaves and a wonderfully mounted red and yellow plume.") They stuck the wet earth by the porch, and within a year the tree topped the roof. Phyllis's nearest neighbor, Richard Byfield, was alarmed by its rapid growth and feared it would attract snakes, undermine the foundations of the house, spoil the timber front, block the roof gutters, and cause trouble with the host government, which had built the house. It would blow down in a storm and smash the casuarinas and the electric wires. He was utterly shocked when Phyllis replied to all this: "I would rather have my tree than the house. If it can last as long as I hold office, I'll be happy; let the next Minister cut it down. How would you like me to undo a miracle—you a religious man!" But he said he was a Baptist and "did not go for that troublesome sort of miracle."

While getting her house in order, Phyllis was also establishing a working routine that would soon leave her exhausted and disheartened. She was in her office every day by 9:30 A.M., and her mornings were taken up with dictation, a daily meeting in the prime minister's sitting room, and an early lunch, followed by meetings of Parliament in the afternoon, which sometimes lasted till 9:30 or 10:00 in the evenings. In between she had to squeeze "rather dreary social engagements," and she was often so tired that she slept during her lunch hour. Since her return it had been "one cabinet meeting after another"—the major issue being Chaguaramas, about which she could not "on account of State discretion, say anything [to Robert], but there's far more behind it than meets the newspaper eye."

In the early days of the government the cabinet met at the governor-general's house—a noble gray stone mansion set amid spacious lawns—in a large dining room, air-conditioned to the point of frigidity as Hailes suffered intensely from the tropical heat. He also disliked the casual unpunctuality of many West Indians, and Phyllis remembered an occasion when, to his annoyance, Grantley Adams was alarmingly late, arriving nearly three-quarters of an hour after the scheduled meeting time, walking very slowly and looking unabashed. He apologized in his "courteous, deprecatory voice," announcing that he had been to the funeral of a former schoolmaster who had died very poor. Phyllis took off her glasses and turned a melancholy gaze on the prime minister as she heard him add in a sad aside: "one of the best teachers I ever knew." The scene, set against the background of Hailes's British "foreignness," embodied for her a concept of "universal love which overshot limitations of race, social status, and personal discomfort."

Adding to Phyllis's growing depression was a realization of the virtual powerlessness of the penniless ministries. Her ministry was particularly limited, charged as it was with overseeing areas that were rigidly bound by the bureaucracy of colonial administration, a structure she would be unlikely to change single-handed. She and Byfield, her closest friend in the cabinet, often confided in each other their frustration at feeling "ambushed within a Ministry whose walls were made of paper, with grave responsibilities but hardly any authority." Every day was a battle, often against the "arch-frustrator" of her new existence, Robert Bradshaw, the minister of finance. As her ministry had no funds allocated for special use she had to go to him for everything, and he—who never disguised his contempt for her as a white "lady"—seemed to her to delight in keeping her waiting, humbling her by causing her to "renew her supplications in several approaches," and often writing "nearly rude replies" before crushing her hopes with a no. At one point matters came to such a pass that she obtained from England a paper setting out the duties of the chancellor of the exchequer in the hope of finding some loophole through which she could assert her rights. But she soon saw that when it came to her ministry, Bradshaw was virtually omnipotent. She was appalled that he used his fiscal powers to interfere in the conduct and policies of other ministries, but she had no recourse. In all his dealings with her he was strictly correct. If he denied her funds or injured her projects by delays or deprivations, he did these things according to protocol. She could seldom appeal to Adams. Her obvious admiration for him had led to particularly nasty rumors that she was attempting to seduce him, and any intervention by Adams on her behalf only fed the rumor mill and was ascribed to her having offered him sexual favors. She was, alternately and contradictorily, either portrayed as a scheming seductress or ridiculed as an old and unattractive hag. Overwhelmed and frustrated as she often felt, she shrugged off the rumors as being one of those things that must be endured with patience by those who lead a political life.

On June 9, the very day the House reassembled for its first full session, obviously nervous and ill at ease, Phyllis rose to give her first speech, a rambling affair that did little to quell her detractors' sneers. Having risen to reply to a speaker's objections to her appointment as minister, she made a statement on her ministerial projects that was marked by a note of almost incoherent defensiveness. Her speech was vague and disconnected: "I call my Ministry the Ministry of the Humanities," she told the House. "That is how I read it and that is how I study it. I am now in the planning stage. Though initially handicapped by very slender resources, we are preparing a series of plans which will be put into operation as soon as, not only funds, but all the other things that go with plans, are available." Her characteristic eloquence seemed to have deserted her, and she was her usual self only during a brief, impassioned promise to improve housing conditions throughout the region. "[I]t was borne out to me in Dominica that we can never hope for a good citizenry, until people, sheltered from the sun and rain, can make dwellings fit for human habitation. This is a most practical problem that we have pledged ourselves to undertake." She had barely sat when her opponents rose to renew their attack. W. B. Williams, representative from St. Catherine, Jamaica, took her to task for the manner in which she, rather than telling of her research and proposals, had only been critical "and has left us worse off than when we started." Adams, ever the gentleman, "highly commended" her maiden speech, which was described by someone as "not a maiden over but a maiden wicket." She did not understand cricket and presumed it was said in praise, as indeed it was, being the equivalent in baseball of getting a hit the first time ever at bat. But she knew it had not been a success and sank even further into an uncharacteristic depression.

During this first full parliamentary session the opposition lost no time in challenging the government and setting a pattern of unpleasant personal attack as a mode of operation. One of Adams's greatest fears—a dread Phyllis shared wholeheartedly—was that the opposition would use the strength of its numbers and talented speakers to attempt to embarrass the home governments and their leaders. The government lacked the sort of formidable parliamentarians the opposition boasted: men like Ashford Sinanan, leader of the opposition and deputy leader of the Trinidad Democratic Labour party; Albert Gomes, a well-known Trinidadian author with an outstanding political career; and Morris Cargill, deputy leader of the opposition, a solicitor with extensive experience as a radio and television commentator. They and their closest political allies—Roy Josephs, Ken Hill, Robert Lightbourne—had all been ousted from high office in Trinidad and Jamaica by the victories of Williams and Manley, and had since lingered in political obscurity.

The session had scarcely begun before the opposition began exploiting the ministers' sensitivity to accusations of being a mere puppet cabinet controlled by Manley and Williams. Sinanan quickly charged that both were attempting to treat Adams "like some glorified yo-yo," and urged him to repudiate "back-seat driving." Gomes denounced Manley and Williams as "people who had a positive genius for chronic error and egregious stupidity." Adams made every effort to repudiate the personal attacks, which became increasingly biting as the session progressed. Phyllis addressed the House to "deplore not only the parochialism but the personalism that people are trying to reintroduce into West Indian politics. I am, in fact, we are fighting for principles now." The opposition's strategy succeeded only in damaging the Federation's reputation. In establishing from the outset a pattern of using the House "as a whipping block on which to flay political adversaries," they sabotaged "the prestige and effectiveness of the Legislature as a forum of conciliation in the difficult days ahead."

The government's first crisis came during the June session. The Federation's claim to the American naval base at Chaguaramas as the site for the Federal capital had by the time of the inauguration become a symbol of West Indian nationalism. But the report of the joint commission of American, British, and West Indian technical experts appointed to study the request to release the base had found that "on strategic and military considerations, the Gulf of Paria was the best location for a Naval Base in the Eastern Caribbean," and that not only did "the present base fulfill . . . strategic and military requirements" but "a phased programme of expansion by the U.S. Navy was already planned." The report, which presented the cabinet with its first fiasco barely a week after the lavish inauguration, was greeted with "bleak silence." The initial reaction was to "play it slow" while the ministers looked around for a "tenable face-saving move"—a strategy that backfired when the British government announced, with "execrable timing," that "Her Majesty's Government would not ask the United States to move their base and would not consider making any contribution to such an operation." The Federal Labour party leaders—principally Williams, Manley, and Adams—now faced a new barrage of jeers from the press, and the opposition took the report as license to embarrass the government in the House. Outraged, Phyllis nonetheless followed Adams's example and displayed nothing but restraint in public. Not so Manley, who launched a scathing attack upon "the usual arrogance and contempt of an Imperial power," calling the British statement "an insult and an outrage to the people of the West Indies and the Federal Government." Discussions between Manley, Williams, and Adams produced an agreement for a united regional response: The report would be rejected by all the West Indian governments involved on the basis that the committee had had only fact-finding functions; talks in London should be resumed; and a conference of representatives of all the units should be convened to decide on the next step.

But, after a special meeting of the cabinet, Adams issued a statement that gave Williams and Manley "twinges of uneasiness." The government, Phyllis wrote Robert (swearing him to secrecy), had decided—for an indefinite period—to do without a capital but "to make do and mend" in loaned buildings. This would be economical and "please a large section of the (destitute) population who disapprove of luxury spending." It seemed clear to Adams that to continue to call for a surrender of the base would only lead his government "to the catastrophe of a first-round defeat" in the House. Consequently he rejected the report and called for resumption of the London talks, but shifted away from Williams and Manley's militant stand by recognizing the military essentiality of Chaguaramas and ignoring the agreed proposal for a territorial conference to plan the next move. With the opposition poised for a debate on Chaguaramas on June 16, which they expected would prove devastating to the government, Adams and his cabinet agreed to a British-American proposal assuring the government that the release of Chaguaramas would be reviewed in ten years' time. The cabinet held the acceptance of the agreement in the strictest secrecy, and Adams was able to deliver his prepared statement—to the opposition's consternation—at the opening of the House proceedings on June 16.

The government had survived, but the costs would prove enormous. To Williams, locked in a violent test of strength with his own opposition over the base, the agreement was a cynical "stab in the back" from Adams. Both he and Manley felt that the Federal prime minister had made a separate "surrender" to their joint enemy. Adams and his ministers were branded "traitors" and were subjected to public expressions of contempt from Trinidadian ministers and the press. Relations between the three leaders would be marked from then on by "shadows of distrust and bitterness." The "seed of dissension" had been sown among the three most prominent personalities in Caribbean politics.

Phyllis watched the deterioration of relations between Adams, Manley, and Williams with deepening concern. It had all seemed so different to her just weeks before—in the "days of the Princess"—when all the island leaders stood on the rostrum and addressed a cheering crowd of thirty thousand under the trees. In those "great, sparkling, delighted public days, they did not need to delve into human motives. We just spoke, laughed, acted according to our lights, and straightened our newly bowed shoulders." But by early July the ministers were all having "rather a bad press," especially concerning the increased allowances voted in the closing minutes of the June session—which not only increased but extended those for local and constituency travel, upkeep of gardens, and chauffeurs—and which had been vigorously opposed by Williams, who had protested their being "extravagant and too fat." The repeated innuendos of the regional press in the early days of July succeeded in placing the ministers charged with feathering their own nests in a very bad light. Phyllis was "holding [her] own on all fronts," although she was often described by the press as "the Firebrand!" and had become "easily cartoonable because of her hair" and "matchstick" arms and legs. Her irritation with the press burst out in response to one of Robert's "moral lecture" letters: "You get me all wrong," she told him, "like the Press."

Life in Trinidad for the Federal ministers was also full of minor irritations. "Although the ordinary people treated them warmly and well," Phyllis would write later, "it was obvious that they were not entirely welcome in Trinidad, a large, competitive and populous island where there was already one set of rank-proud Ministers." There was constant jostling for precedence between Federal ministers and their Trinidadian counterparts; there were petty squabbles over the flying of flags on Federal cars. Adams would later complain of feeling "spied upon" at Federation Park. (In 1962 he would sadly inform the House that he "must have done something criminal in a previous life to be punished by having to live in Trinidad.") Phyllis, in turn, felt that Trinidad was "as full of spies as Lisbon in wartime," believing that the Queen's Park Hotel and, later, Federation Park were nests of "intrigue, pressmen, opposition M.P.'s, people who wished the new nation to fail or to make a fool of itself." She was aghast at the attacks on Adams, at the rumors of his drinking, and at the way some had latched on to the injured-foot story, which ended up in newspaper headlines as IS AILING PRIME MINISTER CAPABLE OF STEERING THE NATION TO INDEPENDENCE? In those days when they "were building a nation brick by fragile brick as rapidly as they could," she recalled, state secrets leaked "at an alarming rate." The ministers had barely reached their cars after private meetings before the radio emitted excerpts from their confidential papers. (Phyllis carried hers jealously in her locked portfolio until they became too numerous, and then she stored them in her house in a locked steel cabinet.)

The main debate of the House's first full session was on a motion by Ken Hill, the member for Surrey (Jamaica) calling for a review of the constitution. Earlier drafts of the Federal constitution had prescribed a review process *during* the Federation's fifth year in order to give it time "to grow roots" before returning to the matters on which the units were divided. The final text had casually been altered at the last moment (in 1957) to *no later than* the fifth year, leaving the door open for review at any time and laying the stage "for battles which rocked and finally wrecked the Federation." Hill's motion called for a joint committee of the House to be appointed to formulate proposals for dominion status for the Federation "at the earliest date," arguing that the "ineffectiveness of the Government flowed from lack of powers to manage its own affairs." The ministers, angered at the slur upon their effectiveness (absurd as it was, as an accusation against a government not yet two months old), and not ready to put the government's voting strength to a test, proceeded to "parley with the Opposition and juggle with the language" of the motion. Adams offered a proposal that a series of committees should be set up in the territories to make recommendations, a proposal backed by Phyllis: "I would welcome the suggestion of the PM," she argued, "that Unit Territories should hold discussion groups to examine the flaws in the present Constitution. We all admit there are flaws in it. And I would also welcome the suggestion that no useful purpose would be served by the appointment of a Select Committee comprised of both sides of the House. The more the Constitution is aired and discussed in the Units the more the general public would know about it, the more universally and democratically will such flaws as exist in this document—now a public document and worthy of being discussed by the public—be challenged in the near future."

Phyllis's reference to the common people's ignorance of the constitution drew a cheap shot from Sinanan, who claimed that he must "pause at this stage and point out to the Minister for Labour and Social Affairs that she need not have reminded us that her constituents were ignorant, because more people might argue that her presence here was proof of that." Ultimately, after "some of the most unseemly episodes . . . ever to take place in the Federal Parliament," the government succeeded only in delaying the conference for twelve months. The debate ended on an acrimonious note with the first threat of secession from Hill, who declared that if the government persisted in its present policy of annoying public opinion in Jamaica, "it would in fact be negotiating the secession of Jamaica from the Federation." Adams mocked the remark as "a display of bad behaviour by little boys in village cricket—we bat first or no game," assuring the opposition that "Jamaica could leave and the other units would remain." In this climate of attack and mistrust, Phyllis continued to press on with her ministerial work. The bulk of her budget, and time, during the first months of her ministry, was allotted to future plans for expansion of the University College of the West Indies. By virtue of the Federation agreement, UCWI had come under the purview of the Federal government, consuming almost half its budget, and had been placed under Phyllis's ministry. Her efforts on UCWI's behalf through 1959 would focus on securing the funds necessary for the expansion of the university prescribed by a commission appointed to review the nature and scope of the curriculum, the appointment and promotion of West Indians on the staff, and its relationship with the University of London. Questions arose in June about the need for a school of dentistry, a plan hampered by "the limiting factor of finance," and about the extension of the curricula and programs, a matter in which she assured the House that "the Federal Government [would] be guided by the voice of the University Council."

In August 1958, Phyllis called together a regional conference of chief medical staffs that earned her the grudging respect of a good number of her colleagues. Competently organized and flawlessly carried out, the meeting gave her a first showcase to demonstrate her talents and capabilities. Gracious as a hostess and at greater ease as a minister, she displayed in her opening address to the participants a poise and self-assuredness she had not been given credit for in the House of Representatives or the press. She had grown as a minister since her appointment in May, learning above all to consult others more knowledgeable than herself and to choose judiciously from among the various courses suggested to her. She had established an easy working relationship with her Federal medical adviser, and his advice had led to the outlining of a coordinated program for basic medical care in the region, which it was the conference's aim to discuss and amend. "Disease," Phyllis told the gathering, "is no respecter of the sea between territories . . . each island would have to coordinate its inoculation, vaccination, and other health precautions so that disease would not spread between the states." One of the resolutions passed proposed that regional treatment centers be established and that certain specialists travel among the islands to provide medical and surgical services not then available in those territories.

In the West Indies in 1958 there was only one doctor for every four thousand people, far short of the international standard of one for every one thousand. Phyllis's staff had calculated that it would require an increase of one hundred doctors per year for fifteen years to bring the units to a rate of one doctor for every two thousand people, and they had begun efforts to double UCWI's medical faculty to speed up the training of medical personnel. For years Phyllis herself had been acutely aware of the shortages in medical care in the region, and had made the issue one of the centerpieces of her political campaigns in Dominica. Medical care, however, was a unit rather than a Federal responsibility, and she would attempt to have it placed on the concurrent list (the list of issues over which Federal and local governments shared jurisdiction) during the Constitutional Conference in 1960, arguing that "in any nation there must exist in some central body the necessary machinery for the control of disease and the promotion of health, and that the placement of Health on the Concurrent List, as well as the formation of a Council of Ministers of Health to determine Federal health policy, is desirable."

In late June Phyllis had written to Robert, wishing she could describe to him the "acute mental and physical loneliness which [had] afflicted [her] for the last couple of weeks—to such an extent that [she] dared not write to him because [she] was in the mood to jump into a plane and quit the whole gruelling show." She was exhausted by the pace of her work, by the obvious resentment and distrust of her male colleagues, by the bad press she and the Federation were receiving, by the dreariness of her surroundings at Federation Park, by the fact that she found the white Europeans in Trinidad "much like the ones in Dominica—mainly bores." In Trinidad she lived "in a goldfish bowl and [she] long[ed] for [her] own personal private intimate life." She had felt tormented by a "peculiar psychic-physical feeling of being part estranged" from Robert, who had written to announce that he was going to the French Riviera on a holiday with Elizabeth Wilson, who owned a house there. Phyllis gave the voyage the approval Robert seemed to be asking for—"I want you to be happy, and if it causes me to be somewhat unhappy, I live such a peculiar dedicated life that I take unhappiness in my stride now." But she had no vocation as a martyr, and ended her letter with a statement of her true feelings: "I am the most influential woman in the West Indies but I have no one to love, no one I can really talk to. . . . Try not to abandon me too far out of self pity. We really do belong you know. When one reviews the whole of our lives . . . what struggle, but what high times too! I had many temptations, but in the end it was always *you* who won, and I hope it may be so with you, but every man's life is his own, and I suppose there comes a limit to sacrifice, and perhaps Shakespeare was wrong when he said Love is not love which alters when it alteration finds."

Throughout the summer she had been particularly concerned about the possibility of losing Penhurst. Robert's business ventures had not prospered, and she was frantically weaving schemes to help him financially and secure their property. Her "big aim" was "to help Phil and keep Penhurst." She offered to take Donna Read in as a lodger to help with expenses and send her savings to him for Penhurst repairs.

"Let Penhurst be *ours*. Leave it alone. Let it be bush. It's *too* valuable to sell for a song. When I quit politics I'll *need* it, honestly. I *adore* it. Ease the strain, don't go there, shut it up save for occasional visits, but keep it *please*!" Often she held up to him the hope that with a majority of one the government could collapse at any point and then she would "come back right away, live at Penhurst, quit politics (secret)." "Honey," she attempted once more to explain, "it isn't that my heart is in my homeland. It is that I *had* to prove myself capable of the highest, I *had* to help you and Phil, I *had* to follow my star. I've done that, and could give it all up tomorrow without much regret."

Under the weight of the mounting pressures, she felt an increasing longing to have him with her. She felt she had to "submit to the most terrible of deprivations. [She] had no one to love, [she] had no time for love anyway, and Auden's lines kept coming to [her] head . . . the lines about 'What every human needs/not universal love/but to be loved alone.'" She yearned for his company and sorely missed his advice in the conspiratorial environment of the Federation. "I don't mind being a Minister at all," she wrote in June, "but there's a hell of a lot of reading attached to it. There will be quite a bit of travelling and probing, some desk work, and callers . . . it's hard to plan my time. Wish I had you to tell me!" He had always been her most trusted adviser, and he continued to be generous with his advice in his letters, but they were no substitute for his actual presence. Throughout their separation she kept up a gentle but steady pressure on him to join her. As the summer progressed and his business ventures failed to thrive, he began to relent; his arguments against joining her became less forceful, focusing on trivialities like the quality of Trinidadian food: "Personally I don't think you would get bowel trouble in Trinidad," Phyllis countered. "The food here is not like Dominica food at all, more like English. . . . I think your stomach trouble is affected by your worries too, don't you?"

Philip, after some moderate improvement, had almost completely withdrawn into himself and was back in the hospital, his prospects bleaker than they had ever been before. Robert's proximity to their son, his principal argument for remaining in England, therefore lost its force. Thus in early August Phyllis was overjoyed to receive a telegram announcing that he would join her "if she would have him." In response, she declared that there was nothing she wanted more dearly, having discovered "in those lonely nights that the thing she loved best about [him] was his strong gentleness, his Englishness," and vowing to "no longer to dominate him, just to let him go his own way, knowing that the role of a consort would not please him."

Phina received the news with relief that the "very great distress Mum-mum was obviously suffering" would come to an end. She had known about her father's relationship with Elizabeth Wilson, calling it a "sensible idea" except for two "snags": "When once you have been married to a very unusual person it must be difficult to settle down with someone rather more ordinary"; and "The Robert/Phyllis syndicate" was "far too strong, despite occasional appearances, to be dissolved." Robert's mother, having prayed fervently for the restoration of her son's marriage, sent him off with her warmest blessing. "You and Phyllis had a very beautiful wedding," she wrote, "and you took your vows to each other with great love & hoping you would both be faithful to them . . . & I pray that may be the case now." Phyllis, Aunt Mags had assured her, could "do great good in making conditions better for the West Indians if she has her husband at her side as a real help-mate, someone she can *trust* & who will keep his mouth shut and never repeat confidences or make criticisms that may be repeated and do *her* damage or rather her 'cause.' For a man to have his wife in a big position & have to play second fiddle advising, helping, forwarding her work will be a very unselfish job but oh how rewarding!'' At the airport on the day of Robert's arrival an enterprising photographer took a candid closeup of him kissing Phyllis. To his annoyance the rather glamorous photo was in the *Trinidad Guardian* the next morning. But Phyllis was radiant. His arrival, following her successful medical conference, opened new vistas for her embattled ministry, and his steadiness and support gave her the strength to face the task ahead with fresh vision.

Nine

The Roads

And do the roads wind uphill all the way?
—Yes, to the very end.
But if they need more finance, who will pay?
—England, my friend.
How many votes are there to half-a-mile;
—That would depend
On peasant sense and smart speech making style.
—Just guess, my friend.

Fate was to grant Phyllis but a short spell in which to enjoy success as a West Indian politician. During the eighteen months between her reconciliation with Robert in August 1958 and the triumph of the Dominican Labour party in the January 1961 elections, she lived her role as a minister to the fullest. These months tested what she called "the essential quality of the politician-apprentice, the capacity to suffer and remain unshaken—"One must be prepared for the financial squeeze, the shocking insult, the startling treachery"—but they also offered her generous rewards. The Federal government, however threatened, went hopefully about its work, while she traveled abroad and spoke to international gatherings about her ambitions for her fledgling nation, made lasting new friendships, and lost herself in meaningful paid work for the first time in her life. Throughout these months and beyond—as even her political enemies would grudgingly agree—she "did a good job." Her success was in great measure the result of Robert's presence and advice, and it was with boundless pleasure that she introduced him to the crowd gathered at the Dawbiney Market when she returned to Dominica for a constituency visit in October 1958. It was his first visit since his dismissal from L. Rose and Co., and Phyllis treated it as a the return of the prodigal son—his presence being both a reaffirmation of her marriage and a vindication of her political dream.

After her visit to Dominica she traveled to Paris for the annual UNESCO conference, the first of several foreign trips as minister and one she had anticipated with almost girlish glee. She would come to enjoy official travel immensely, darting in and out of New York and London en route, seeing old friends, indulging in a bit of modest luxury, and relishing the pomp and circumstance that surrounded her as a ministerial visitor abroad. The conference, moreover, had the added appeal of marking the Federation's admission as an associate member of UNESCO, in "an interim recognition of [their] new nationhood before [they] attained the full privileges of membership." She arrived in Paris on November 5 to find the city "deep in an unusual peasoup fog." She was suffering from a "dreadful cold," coughing so horribly that the night before her speech the hotel maid thought she should go to the hospital. Unwell, weary, and wearing a black turtleneck sweater out of which her profile emerged wanly, "with a strong resemblance to Madame Curie on the verge of a great discovery but also at the point of death," she nonetheless gave a rousing speech that was greeted "with loud and prolonged applause." It was the first time she had addressed such a distinguished audience—hitherto her speeches had been confined to peasant villages and small groups in Trinidad—and she had worked on her text painstakingly, seeking to convey eloquently her vision of the Federation as "a new nation which could set an example for racial harmony and peaceful coexistence." She saw herself—she assured the international gathering—as "living proof of this promise," her election and ministerial appointment giving testimony of the "triumph of tolerance over skin-deep differences, and even over historical prejudices, a triumph of tolerance over creed as well as race":

> We may well be able to provide a laboratory for the art of living together, without prejudice and partiality. We have already begun to do so, all the races in the West Indies save the Arawaks and the Caribs began as strangers—*déracinés*. To us nationalism means something other than race. It means an ideal of a country. It means the words that we have inscribed beneath our national emblem: "To dwell together in unity." That is our text. Now in our nation of a few million people, so varied and so vital, scattered in little islands as different as our physical types, human beings can mingle free and tolerantly.

Years later, while writing *In the Cabinet*, Phyllis would reread this speech with "wonderment. . . . Did I really believe what I said at those times?"—she asked herself—"Was I deceiving a multitude or—more pitiful—deceiving myself? My words seem to tremble with passionate conviction. The answer is that I did believe them, I did believe that the quavering little Federation, so poor that Port of Spain City Council had more money to spend in one year than the near-nation was allotted, would surpass in its capacity to blend in harmony and beat down the follies of prejudice, the rancours of historical injustice, and the stale false doctrine of race superiority, any other land."

The British minister of education, Sir Edward Boyle, congratulated her warmly on her address, calling it "the best Commonwealth speech of the session." He was one of the contacts Phyllis had come to Paris to pursue. One of her fundamental goals as minister was to pave the way for the development of an independent educational system in the West Indies, and she was seeking aid and technical expertise from UNESCO for that venture. While in Paris she initiated particularly promising connections, and on her return to Trinidad via London she paid calls at the Colonial Office and consulted with the heads of the West Indies Section and the Education Department. By November 17 Phyllis was back in Trinidad—that "kaleidoscopic, microcosmic, scorching and fabulously interesting place . . . lovable in its diversity and hospitality, swarming with incident and intrigue"—to be greeted by a parliamentary discussion of the "tremendous benefits which can accrue to the housing situation throughout the West Indies by use of the newly-invented CINVA-RAM Block Press." Phyllis, by now in complete command of parliamentary procedure and language, could reply in full ministerial babble: "The minister . . . is informed that several types of machines are in present use by Unit government Housing Authorities for the manufacture of stabilized earth blocks. . . . The minister welcomes the attention which has been drawn by the honourable Member to the use of machinery for housing construction and expects that territories with housing programmes will give their attention to the use of machine-made stabilized earth blocks."

Robert's presence was the stabilizing force she needed to take firm hold of her ministry. The support he offered was more than emotional—he made it his business to research the issues facing the Federation and quickly became her unpaid right hand. Whatever it cost him to have swallowed his pride and joined her in Trinidad, he seemed to have made the best of it. As he wrote to his attorney in London: "I am not, so far, gainfully employed but spend much time in committees, lecturing on Business Management, teaching Art at the Mental Hospital and as an arbitrator in Trade union disputes—all this besides acting as P.P.S. [parliamentary private secretary] to my wife and attending the innumerable boring cocktail parties for visiting celebrities etc." He was invaluable in helping Phyllis turn her vision into policy and in showing her how to pilot that policy through "the salt water of acrimony" that flowed between the units. The results were evident almost immediately: She ceased feeling and appearing flustered and disorganized, and her own agenda began to emerge with coherence and clarity.

As she gained greater command of her ministry—which occasionally made her feel "like a very humble prototype of the Hindu God, Shiva, with five heads, several eyes and several hands"—her list of priorities became better defined: education, housing, employment and migration, medical care, and child welfare became the focus of her work. Her ministry seemed perpetually under attack, but her initial defensive posture had turned into firmness. She had been back in Trinidad but a few weeks when the mere existence of her ministry was again challenged in the House. Sinanan charged that there was no need for her ministry as its responsibilities could easily be allocated to others. Now, however, she could respond with something bordering on humor: "I also incidentally rise to respond amicably but firmly to the slightly bickering remarks made by the Opposition and to congratulate them also on one or two phrases. . . . I very much enjoyed hearing the Member for St. Thomas . . . use the expression 'masterful inactivity' which I think is delightful. I was trying to find the antonym, and came up with 'ineffective restlessness.'" Her multiple ministry focused on human resources, the greatest natural wealth of the fledgling nation: "They are greater even than agricultural and commercial riches. It is useless to have roads, harbours, airports and other commercial undertakings if the people who walk those roads and ascend the gangways at those harbours and airports are illiterate and diseased."

Under Robert's guidance Phyllis made education the core of her work throughout 1959 and 1960. Constitutionally the provision of educational facilities at the primary and secondary levels was a unit responsibility, but Phyllis looked upon a Federal educational philosophy as "the thing to cement the Units." Every new nation, in her view, "must ultimately formulate [its own] national education policy." She thus focused her efforts on the "embryonic project" to wrest the School Certificate Examination from overseas control and replace it with one "to suit our own rational circumstances," with the necessary standards set by the UCWI. She directed her staff to begin devising "text books with a West Indian flavour," declaring in the Federal House: "The days when we taught children to sing 'Bonny Banks of Loch Lomond' at the age of five in the West Indian schools have passed." Her office had also started devising a certificate for qualified teachers that they hoped would someday be acceptable throughout the West Indies. She had recently sponsored and chaired a seminar on teacher training for the Windward Islands, and negotiations were proceeding to put into operation a Federal scheme for educating young teachers. She had made sincere efforts to establish good working relationships with teachers throughout the territories, particularly through the Caribbean Union of Teachers, whose Silver Jubilee Conference she addressed in Barbados: "Teachers, and particularly the Caribbean Union of Teachers, combining in their organisation the solidarity of a Labour Force and the tradition of the teaching profession, really do believe in a West Indian federal tradition and culture. It is their aim and goal." The cornerstone of Federal education policy, however, was the UCWI. Phyllis's functions as minister in charge were mostly budgetary, consultative, and occasionally ceremonial. Her office did not interfere with the college's academic affairs, which were conducted almost entirely through the UCWI Council, but she had pledged her efforts to "keep UCWI at a high level and not allow it to degenerate into a superpolytechnic," as it was "fast becoming a great University in the best European tradition." Her concerns regarding UCWI were accessibility and expansion. "More people in the West Indies want education today than they can either afford to get or are getting," she told the House, "and it is our job . . . to see that each term more students get a University education." She was committed to making possible a "greater intake of women students."

Phyllis's efforts throughout 1959 and 1960 centered on the expansion of the university's colleges prescribed by the *Cato Report*, which advised the incorporation of the Trinidad College of Agriculture into UCWI. On August 1960, three years ahead of the mandated schedule, she was able to announce that they had merged to become the Faculty of Agriculture of the University College. The Federal government had also accepted the report's recommendation to establish a Faculty of Engineering at UCWI, and as early as mid-1959 steps were being taken to provide funds for its establishment. (The Engineering Faculty would eventually be based in Trinidad and would be accompanied by a Faculty of Arts and Sciences, to become the St. Augustine Campus of the University of the West Indies.) The university's progress by late 1960 had been impressive. A Faculty of Social Science and a Department of Economics had been established. There had been a 50 percent increase in the Medical Faculty. The Institute of Economic and Social Research, which had received large grants from a number of foundations, had by then "an enormous programme of research in economics, political and sociological matters in hand."

The report had suggested the award of thirty scholarships to allow students from the units to attend UCWI, a matter that occupied much of Phyllis's time, occasionally becoming "the main day to day work" of her two advisers. The difficulty, as with everything her ministry envisioned for the new nation, was "simply hard cash." Very limited funds were available, and Phyllis, in frustration, turned her energies toward securing scholarships abroad, particularly in technical areas in which the West Indies needed better-trained personnel. "We are also laying a great deal of emphasis on this technical education question," she would explain, "because we do not want our migrants even to go away from their islands lacking the skills which they should have to give them a better chance of getting employment." Her ministry had secured scholarships for technical courses of four to twelve months' duration in forestry, farming cooperatives, broadcasting, agriculture, and economics in the Federal Republic of Germany, Ghana, Australia, and the United States. The process was slow and tedious, as her office had to await replies from the units before the selection of candidates for scholarships could be made, a process they strove to follow "very carefully and in a proper democratic manner."

As part of her ministerial responsibilities toward UCWI, Phyllis accompanied

Princess Mary, the Princess Royal—who had been instrumental in raising funds for the founding of UCWI and was UCWI honorary chancellor—on a visit to the new university campus in Trinidad. The "darling old Princess," a great-granddaughter of Queen Victoria, was the very one who, believing that "you can't put those lovely brown skins into black gowns," had chosen instead a "beautiful shade of crimson" for the university's academic robes. Strolling with her on the campus, the princess had asked Phyllis which university she had attended. "I'm afraid, your Royal Highness," she had replied with a blush, "I never went to a university. And I didn't go to school either." The "little Royal lady" gave her a "delicious" description of her German governess before confiding "in a tiny murmur": "Don't you think it preposterous that both the University Chancellor and the Federal Minister of Education have never been formally educated?"

As if the multifaceted issues of elementary and higher education were not enough to overwhelm her small staff, as 1959 dawned she came under intense criticism for what the opposition saw as her "too positive attitude towards trade unions." At issue was an application for the West Indies to have regional (rather than unit) representation at all future conferences of the ILO. Federal representation meant the elaboration of a regionwide labor policy, which, given Phyllis's—and the ILO's—socialist leanings and strong prolabor stance, could only mean a broader role for the unions than the opposition was willing to countenance. Her "ministerial relations" with regional labor organizations, she conceded, were "very good," and she was "dealing personally with labour and with social welfare matters." The unions had been "prepared to give us the benefit of their advice," and she hoped, as she told the House defiantly, "to make use of this friendly co-operation whenever necessary. We should not dream of instituting major changes in industrial policy without consulting the Trade Union's leaders." It had been argued "that our duty was to make the workers work until it hurts. I do not see that as one of the functions of my ministry at all. How would it look to people if we went around to the Trade Union Congress and other Labour organisations and told them that their workers would have to work longer hours every day? That would certainly not be in accordance with our harmonious relationship." In forthcoming ILO meetings she would strongly advocate the establishment of the Caribbean Congress of Labour (CCL) as a "noteworthy step in the progress of trade union solidarity and solidity, for without good trade unions one could never achieve good arbitration." When the CCL had its inaugural session on September 14, 1960, she was, appropriately, its keynote speaker.

The House's final meeting before the 1958 Christmas break brought a bit of respite, as discussion focused on the comparatively innocuous topic of the Federal mace. On December 3, fresh from the barrage of questions she had faced in the House on education, labor and housing, she had attended a state dinner at the governor-general's house in honor of the visiting United Kingdom parliamentary delegation, which presented a new mace—a gift to the Federal Parliament from the House of Commons—that would replace their old West Indian–made mace. Phyllis rose during the December 11 meeting of the House to propose that both be displayed on exhibit, praising Ken Moris, the West Indian artist who had "toiled with far less suitable instruments and . . . gave us a beautiful piece of art." Phyllis, who saw herself as a defender of West Indian creativity, then quoted proudly from the constitution of the Dominican Labour party—"We intend to promote skilled workmanship in all its forms and stand for the encouragement of the creative arts and of free and original thought and expression"—challenging the House to guess where the words had come from. "From Russia!" came the voice of opposition leader Sinanan, rising to the challenge, only to be silenced by her assertion that it was "the fourth clause in the Constitution of the DLP—from the Constitution of that party of which I am president." She would later exasperate him further by arguing that it was "a great sadness" that the Federation had no "rousing, first-class and absolutely acceptable patriotic" national anthem, proposing that they choose "a tune with a light calypso rhythm" as an anthem, as calypso was "more or less our national tempo."

In late March 1959, with the legislature back in session, Phyllis chaired a regional conference on social development in the West Indies, an event she would always count among her proudest ministerial achievements, and one that entailed numerous weeks of earnest preparation and culminated in the formulation of a number of important resolutions: the setting up of voluntary councils of social services in each territory, the introduction of Community Development Services in urban areas, the establishment of a Federal prison system, the planning of a conference of senior prison officers, the interchange of personnel between unit governments, and the drafting of social security legislation. During the first half of 1959 her ministry came under increasing pressure from the opposition to explain "what steps had been taken to alleviate the rising unemployment in the Federation." Most of the employment schemes then under consideration involved migration. She had recently raised the issue of admission of West Indians into Canada for purposes of employment with the Canadian commissioner and a senior official from the Department of Citizenship and Immigration in Ottawa. A 25 percent increase in admissions of female domestic workers into Canada had been granted, and she had negotiated the admission of near relatives of the girls into Canada under conditions laid down by the Canadian government. She had deplored the necessity of young girls' leaving the Caribbean at the ILO conference, where she told the assembly that "when the quota for [Canadian] jobs was raised in 1959 from 200 to 250, enthusiasm was embarrassingly high, and hundreds of young women applied for places." She was also exploring an increase in the number of West Indian workers admitted into the United States, where a farm labor program in which thousands of West Indians participated had been in operation since 1951.

In the last week of May 1959, as Phyllis was preparing to leave for the ILO congress in Geneva, she became embroiled in a literary debate in the House with Albert Gomes, himself a novelist of note. He had read some of Phyllis's poetry in a local newspaper, and it had prompted him to propose a motion on "the desirability of providing scholarships for West Indian writers with the view to enabling these writers to preserve their contacts with the West Indies." He felt that his motion had "a very good chance of success" since the minister responsible for this area "is not only a patron of the Arts but is indeed, in her own way, a poet of sorts." He argued eloquently that it was to the creative writer that the West Indies must look "for the nationalism that will be of lasting value to the West Indies." Apart from the calypso and steel bands—"still the two main reasons for our popularity abroad"—it is the young West Indian novelists "that are putting the West Indies on the map today throughout the world." Phyllis found the proposal worth pursuing. "There are two types of civic attitudes towards writers; one that is that better writing is produced in starvation and the second is that a certain degree of assistance, if not pampering, may be necessary," she countered, "I do not have to tell you which side I'm on . . ." But having written *The Orchid House* in exile after decades away from the Caribbean, she took issue with his arguments about the relationship of proximity to literary quality. "A return to source is essential sometimes, but if a writer lives away from home, that does not mean that the quality of his work suffers."

An animated debate on political commitment among writers followed, in which Gomes heatedly defended those writers "engaged" with their nation's sociopolitical reality. "The honourable member spoke as if all authors could be divided into political and non-political ones," Phyllis retorted. "I do not share his opinion about this absolute cleavage. We know that Jane Austen took no notice of the wars or even the revolutions of her time—her outlook was that of the parish. But she was a great writer." She concurred with Gomes nonetheless in that, given the importance of West Indian literature to "the recent growth of national consciousness," the Federation must view with shame the writer's need to emigrate "in order not only to be recognized but even to exist," an urgent concern at a time when "the West Indian art forms are beginning to take shape." She therefore submitted a motion to sponsor a congress of artist and West Indian writers. "Not only will they derive intellectual stimulus and moral uplift from the contact with one another but they will also be brought into contact, into relation, with the new society which is now springing up in the West Indies."

Within days of this debate, following a broadcast marking the anniversary of the inauguration of the Federal parliament, Phyllis left for the 1959 ILO conference in Geneva, where she addressed the meeting on June 11, her speech a blueprint for the challenges ahead for the West Indies. The chief exports of the islands of the Caribbean, she deplored in her speech, are migrant labour and agricultural products,

> because they have never had the equipment to turn their own natural resources into finished goods, nor sufficient technical schools to turn their intelligent unskilled workers into trained technicians and craftsmen. Much of this may be attributed to past neglect by governments and the shortsightedness of certain employers who have not ploughed their profits back into benefits for human advance. . . . I have heard us described as a bunch of arrogant mendicants, but I can assure delegates that we are trying hard to climb out of our impoverished past. . . . For about 300 years we have hobbled along on one foot—and that foot was a bare one, and the roads were stony and thorny. Then we went forward on two feet, but we were wearing borrowed shoes. What we want now is the chance not only to progress boldly on our own two feet wearing our own shoes but to produce those shoes (as indeed we have begun to do) and to produce the means for a rising standard of life for our people . . . we must press forward with social development or we shall break faith with our people.

In *In the Cabinet*, she will speak wryly of this address as a prototype "for begging speeches which our poor island leaders will have to make for years after I have ceased to function."

A few days later Phyllis received news that her sister Marion, while traveling by boat to London via Port of Spain for her eldest son's wedding, had died in Trinidad.

Robert had gone to meet her and her younger son, eighteen-year-old Mark, at the dock, but she had been too ill to be moved and had died on shipboard—"of long drawn out alcoholism," as Robert insisted, "which her family and friends had tried to cover up for 12 years." Robert, alone in Trinidad and having to cope with the funeral arrangements and a bewildered Mark before Celia's arrival from Barbados, managed to alienate everyone with his harping on Marion's alcoholism. Celia, exasperated and confounded by his behavior, had finally barred him from the funeral and a rift had ensued. Phyllis received Robert's account of Marion's death and the "strange upside-down affairs" he had been involved in with barely concealed annoyance. She wanted him to "obliterate" from his mind "all those happenings and entanglements," and embarked on an angry tirade against Celia, of her three sisters the least like her in temperament and tastes. They were poles apart in their political inclinations (Celia was a committed Tory) and most dissimilar in their social attitudes. The differences had not led to close sisterly regard, and the latent tensions flared once again in Phyllis's reaction to her sister's behavior after Marion's death: "You would never believe me when I told you that Celia [was] cruel and unkind and does not like us," she wrote to Robert from Geneva, "I was not even there so it cannot be attributed to a sisterly hate alone. It is her character. Mean and jealous." She was philosophical, almost dispassionate, about Marion, concluding, "People should not outlive their souls and their sense of responsibility. It is too sad."

On June 25 she was back in England. Exhausted and belatedly grieving over Marion's death, she had spent a day with Phil at the hospital before going to Penhurst for a few days of rest. She returned to London for a whirlwind of meetings and visits. Before leaving for Kenya on a brief visit to Phina, Allan, and the baby girl they had just adopted, she spoke to West Indian nurses at Bethnal Green Hospital. She also met Grantley Adams, in England for meetings related to the Constitutional review. She is said to have visited him in his hotel room to pressure for some project that needed immediate funding (Frank Baron insists it was for funds for a cocktail party), only to find Adams politely asking to postpone the meeting as he was not properly dressed and did not even have shoes on. To which Phyllis replied by taking her own shoes off and saying "Well, there, neither do I. Now we can talk comfortably." As Baron told the tale when he returned to Dominica, Adams finally threw up his arms in exasperation, exclaiming, "Oh give the damn woman her money!"

This period of Phyllis's life in Trinidad included frequent social engagements. "[If] I ever become an old woman reduced to name-calling," she wrote in *In the Cabinet*, "I'll simply flip those diary pages, and out will fall the names of those whom I entertained so simply, or who met me by request": Philip Habib, the longtime U.S. State Department officer; Princess Mary, the queen's aunt; French-American coloratura soprano Lily Pons; West Indian pianist Winifred Atwell; and Trinidadian novelist V. S. Naipaul. She established some deep friendships during this time, one of them with C.L.R. James, the well-known Trinidad author, and his wife, Selma, with whom she often attended evening poetry parties and other literary functions. As a minister Phyllis was often asked to meet prominent visitors to the Federation and dined at the governor-general's house with Harold Macmillan, "tall and courteous" (who turned out to be "so much nicer than they British Labour party socialists had expected") and with "beloved Hugh Gaitskell" (then next in line to become Labour prime minister of Britain, shortly before his unexpected and premature death). She and Robert were invited for dinner at Hailes's house when Winston Churchill visited Trinidad. Seated besides Lady Hailes at dinner, Phyllis overheard him ask, "Who is that little man across the table?" as he pointed to Eric Williams. Learning he was the prime minister of Trinidad, he asked him if he had visited Blenheim, his family's estate, while at Oxford. Williams had not. "What!" Churchill gasped. "You were a student of history and never visited Blenheim!" Williams claimed that he had been too busy. "Too busy to visit Blenheim! A sheer fragment of English history . . . ," Churchill exclaimed, looking "really upset." Phyllis, whose dislike for Williams was ever growing, loved to recount the anecdote. All this dining led to reed-thin Phyllis gaining a few pounds. She had been particularly bony when she arrived in Trinidad, and her fleshier appearance after a year of good eating did not pass unnoticed in the House, where Gomes observed "that the minister is becoming very expansive in more ways than one." A comment months later on how she had "sometimes tried to exceed my slender constitutional power" provoked mirthful laughter from the House.

Phyllis also reestablished friendships that had begun in London, chiefly with a former Fulham librarian, Ronald Benge, and his wife, Margaret. Ronald had come to Trinidad as a "wandering tutor attached to the Regional Public Library in Port of Spain," and he and Margaret became Phyllis and Robert's most frequent companions, frequently lunching at the Allfreys', where they were invariably served Trinidad rum punch. Phyllis, Margaret remembers, was "an interesting, entertaining hostess, very efficient and a woman with enormous 'drive.'" She was small, "fragile almost," fair, and blue-eyed, "with a normally soft pleasant voice which belied her determination, energy, the iron will, the confidence and managerial qualities she had": Phyllis had "what perhaps everyone needs who is to get things done in a political, economic, or social field, a fierce belief in the *right-ness* of her own values and standards and the *confidence* to impose her will on others—in matters big and small. This meant sometimes, on a personal level, she made one supremely uncomfortable when watching/hearing her *organizing/manipulating* lesser mortals." To Margaret, however, she was always "very kind." When she and Ronald married shortly after Robert's arrival in Trinidad, Phyllis gave her the hat she wore for the ceremony as well as an original painting of a shantytown in Port of Spain by the popular Trinidadian watercolorist and landscape artist Noel Vaucroisson which had hung in the Allfreys' house in Federation Park and which Margaret had admired. Robert she remembers as having "his own aura and presence": a tall, rangy type, "and in a way quite physically attractive." He always used a cigarette holder "in a rather theatrical sort of way" and was a good talker, "if a bit patronizing and pedantic on occasions." He took his usual "back-seat" role—"a foil and behind-the-scenes manager for the minister."

Robert and Phyllis, who liked to think of themselves as "patrons of the arts," also took under their wing a local artist, Dermot Louison, whom Robert had met through the Port of Spain gallery where they both exhibited their work. (He had taken up painting while alone in London and continued to paint in Trinidad, where he also became active in artists' circles.) Some of their friends thought that Robert and Phyllis truly "patronized" Dermot, but the relationship was close enough for him to eventually spend prolonged periods painting in Dominica, where he saw the Allfreys constantly. Dermot's marriage was often cited as evidence of Phyllis's penchant for manipulation. He and a young woman, Basilia Ramirez, had a baby out of wedlock in 1961, and she absolutely insisted on and arranged their marriage, as she had earlier organized the christening of the baby, whom the Benges later adopted.

In 1960 Phyllis and Robert themselves adopted a twelve-year-old Afro-Dominican girl named Sonia, the granddaughter of Edith Matthew of Laudat. Edith's house was on the footpath to Rosalie, a route Phyllis often took when walking to the east side of the island on campaign visits, and where she often slept when she was too tired for the long walk down to the east or west coast. Sonia had lived with her grandmother since she was eight months old, when she had been "dumped" by her parents, from whom she received no parental care since. Phyllis got to know Sonia well during these visits to Edith. The girl's intelligence and straightforwardness must have appealed to her—Sonia was, even at her young age, a direct, no-nonsense personality with a strength of character that matched her own. Phyllis grew fond of sitting with her and discussing the ills of racism or why the system was unfair to black people, workers, and women. She never explained what prompted her to take charge of the young girl by legally adopting her. It could have been any of the reasons her acquaintances have offered—her undeniable love for the child, a manifestation of empty-nest syndrome, an acknowledgment of the need to compensate for the loss of Phil to mental illness, an unacknowledged desire to prove through the nurturing of another young person that his illness was not her fault, the desire to establish a closer and public link to the Afro-Caribbean population to whose interests she was devoted, or the realization that Edith, then well into her eighties and suffering from high blood pressure, would not be able to care for the girl much longer—or a combination of all these factors. Whatever her motives, in 1960 she asked Sonia if she would like to go to Trinidad with her, and she eagerly agreed. Sonia adapted quickly to a life that was luxurious compared to the one she had known in Laudat. They had a big car and chauffeur, a comfortable home with a housekeeper and maid, stimulating company, and many friends. And there was Phyllis, to whom she developed a fierce loyalty that was closer to that of friends and equals than mother and daughter. She would come to respect and appreciate Robert, whom she remembers as the "domesticated" one who kept a semblance of order in the household (after the Federation's collapse, when there was no one else to do it, he did most of the cleaning and mending); but her affection seemed reserved for Phyllis, the more difficult character of the two, and the one with whom Sonia would always be in more conflict, but also the one who loved her unreservedly. She soon learned to understand her in ways that she would never know Robert. The luxuries of their life in Trinidad, for example, which brought such a material change to the family, mattered very little to her new mother. They had a car and driver, "but somehow Phyllis's car always had to be pushed to get it started . . . [but] people would go and see her if she lived in a kitchen for other things she had to offer."

Phyllis's appointment as a Federal minister had not entirely put an end to her literary career, and she attempted through 1959 and early 1960 to regain her stride, albeit only when her busy schedule allowed. In an interview with the *West Indian*, she would comment ruefully that she had put aside any thought of further publication "just now. . . . At the moment I am too busy helping to make a nation to complete a book to my satisfaction." She had been inspired by the tossing of a bottle by her onetime gardener at Queen's Park Oval—her only connection with cricket—to write "The Man Who Pitched Bottles," a wry satire about the defeat of a longtime politician by a savvy grassroots candidate (the former gardener, whom he had rescued from jail after being arrested for throwing a bottle after a cricket match.) The story appeared in the

Manchester Guardian. She had also published "A Real Person" in *Argosy* and had started an autobiographical account of her career as a minister, *In the Cabinet*, chapters of which she soon sent to her agent to gauge interest in the project. The response was encouraging, and she continued to work on the text on stolen moments. A handful of her poems appeared in the Trinidadian press during this period, all of them previously published. Her only original poem was "The Hunting of the Smider-Snark," a parody of Lewis Carroll's *The Hunting of the Snark*, which she completed in March 1960. It satirized the rampant prejudice and discrimination against small islanders she found in the "big island" of Trinidad, a unit adamantly opposed to "freedom of movement of people" across the territories. She tried to publish it in the local press, but, as she wrote to Edward LeBlanc, to whom she sent a copy, "They were frightened to put her poem in the newspapers in case it should prevent the census people from doing their jobs!" She had discovered the power of witty, irreverent poetry as a political weapon and used it here to throw barbs at opposition members who had "scolded" her for her use of the term "Smider" in the House. Gomes had declared himself irritated by her use of the expression "small islanders," and had asked for a ban on the four syllables "once and for all from this House." "My use of the expression 'small islander,'" Phyllis countered, "is due to an obsessive pleasure in those words, so much so that I not only call myself a small islander but I have also abbreviated it to *Smider*. But after hearing that it is hurting the feelings of the non-insularist members of this honourable house, I will delete this expression from my vocabulary while addressing this house."

On May 27 Phyllis left Trinidad for London on her way to the 1960 ILO conference. She arrived in Geneva on June 1, "exhausted but triumphant after the compressed 2 months of events [she] crammed into 2 days in London." She had visited Phil, who had seemed "patently glad" to see her despite being "off" his new doctor and feeling neglected and left out. His doctor had told him that all he needed to do was "to make an effort to conquer [his] illness" since he had a fine brain, to which he had replied, "Oh dry up, won't you!" She was overcome with "love and pity for our darling," as she wrote to Robert, but assured him she had not felt sad upon leaving her son, "although up to now his poor eyes haunt me." Her speech at the ILO—an eloquent description of how the West Indies Federation was trying to climb out of its impoverished past—showed her detailed command of the central issues at the heart of the labor and social situations in the West Indies. It focused on industrialization and price stabilization in order to achieve the reasonable standard of living and return of capital needed to stem the "drifting away of young people" to England and America. She cited the lack of technical education and "adequate and varied employment" for young people as the "prime cause[s] of the outward flow of workers." Though their remittances were in many ways responsible for the improvement of living conditions of families in the West Indies, she was encouraged by the return of many West Indians with increased skills and education obtained abroad to enhance the Federation. The achievement of dominion status, for which the Federal government was struggling, would bring "a national upsurge and concomitant opportunity [which] will both attract and keep many workers with special talents 'back home.'" At the core of her philosophy for achieving full employment in the West Indies was a return to the land, and she praised the faculty of agriculture of UCWI's Trinidad campus as instrumental in this effort: "An attempt is being made there to instill that love of the land from which all too many of the young in every country turn in apathy or boredom: as my favourite poem says, the city 'beckons with a crooked finger to the farmers' children.'"* She pondered the housing situation at length, stressing inadequate housing as "probably the most immediate and observable" factor in the health of youth: "The matter of slum clearance is a bottomless pit from the financial point of view, and in little countries it can only be tackled little by little and with the utmost encouragement and assistance from international agencies. . . . We are however trying hard to help ourselves, not only by self-aided housing schemes but through the efforts of local Governments to promote low-cost housing and in some cases to advance housing loans." The problem was as serious in the city as in the countryside: "We desperately need more rural housing, in order to keep our agricultural workers on the land and to raise the quality of village community life, which is uneven in its development."

The ILO conference was made memorable for Phyllis by her participation in the first walkout against the South African government, staged to underscore opposition to apartheid in that country. A group of Africans, West Indians, and other sympathizers walked out of the meeting room as J. F. Hannah, South African secretary for labour, rose to speak. Phyllis had seen it as "symbolic of the position the new Federation was gradually acquiring in the outside world—even while it was being undermined from within" that the African and Indian Labour delegates should specifically seek her out to ask for her support. Knowing the unanimity of the Federal delegation, "with polite reservations from the employers' side," she gave them "an unqualified *yes*." They also asked her if she would be prepared to speak on their behalf in a committee session. As a nonindependent representative it was unlikely that she would be allowed to address the meeting, but she said she would try. She sent her name to the chairman, who initially acquiesced in her request, but at the last moment, after "some whispering around the chair," permission was withdrawn, to the vexation of her African and Indian colleagues. A European minister drew her aside afterward to rebuke her; the Federation's British sponsors and their American counterparts also made their displeasure clear. But she remained unmoved, certain as she was that the protesters were right: "The South African worker delegates did not represent the toiling suffering millions of their country. How could they, when those people had no voice?" (The following year, at the forty-fifth ILO conference, a resolution was passed with overwhelming support condemning the racial policies of the government of South Africa, expressing "the utmost sympathy" with those South Africans "whose fundamental rights are suppressed by . . . apartheid," and calling on South Africa to withdraw from the organization.)

On the day after the walkout she was told that some South Africans wished to speak to her in the lobby of her hotel. She went down to face a group of "well-mannered gentlemen" who tried to point out how wrong she was. They argued that "to squeeze South Africa out of the ILO would do more harm than good to the workers," but she "did not give an inch." Finally one of them warned her: "You are flattered because these people seem to trust in you, but one of these days when they have

*Phyllis was misquoting the last two lines of W. H. Auden's "The Capital" (1938), in which the city is addressed as a place "Where, hinting at the forbidden like a wicked uncle, / Night after night to the farmer's children you beckon."

climbed on your shoulders as high as they can go, these Negroes will turn and kick you to death." To which, "with cool confidence," she replied: "Never." (In 1963, when she was expelled from the Dominica Labour party, she would have occasion to reflect "lugubriously" on the words of that irate South African. The event nevertheless "did not make [her] bitter or change [her] mind in general." She had long before come to the conclusion "that perfidy and ingratitude [were] not singular to any particular race," a conclusion strengthened "by the way in which the average man and woman in Dominica felt dishonoured by [her] unwarranted expulsion from the party [she] had created. The modest voters of Roseau gave the answer not just to a small clique but to the South Africans and to the world.")

If Phyllis ever tired of the burden of handing out prizes at school award ceremonies she never said so. As a minister she was compelled to deliver countless speeches "to mark a special occasion," including several "On Public Speaking." The most important assets of a good speaker, she advised, were imperturbability, wit, "a curfew of half an hour on any address whatsoever," and "a sense of consumer reaction"—"those who ignore the obvious boredom of their audience do so at their own peril." The most important thing of all, however, "is to believe in what you are talking about. If you really care for the matters you are discussing you will find that a ring of vitality comes into your words and gives your speech just that touch of authenticity which makes the people in the hall, market place, campus, or wherever it may be, whisper to each other—'just what I was thinking.'"

Within days of her return from the ILO conference she was again off to give another such speech at the Boys' Secondary School Awards Ceremony at St. George's, Grenada. It typified hundreds she gave as a minister: "And what shall I say to those whose prizes are yet to come perchance next year, or even later? Everyone expects them to persevere and read hard, and I will tell them, in case they don't know it, of a character in Thackeray's 'Rose and the Ring,' Prince Giglio, for whom the Fairy Blackstick wished 'a little bit of bad luck.' It was this magical creature's opinion that humans need a little bit of bad luck now and then to stir them to greater effort, and make them independent and persistent. But I hope that it will only be a little bit of bad luck, for the delayed winners, and that it will soon change to good."

In early September 1960, as the House prepared to reassemble after the summer recess, Phyllis made a radio broadcast to announce the establishment in Antigua, Dominica, Grenada, Saint Lucia, and Saint Vincent of technical training centers funded by the International Cooperation Administration (ICA). Scheduled to open in mid-1961, the centers would train students in woodwork, machine shop and sheet metal work, house wiring, motor winding and repair, gas welding, masonry, electrical appliance repair, and auto and diesel engine work. The centers had led Phyllis into quite a bit of ministerial trouble. Despite her belief that those wholly pledged to Federalism "had to exact the strictest impartiality of themselves" and "were bound to see the needs of the islands on a broad scale and not to press for special benefits first for our own constituencies," she had written to Grantley Adams threatening to resign if Dominica did not get one of the technical wings for the Roseau grammar school. Only three such centers had initially been offered by the American donors, and five islands had submitted applications. Adams complied, but the incident left her open to criticism and feeling ashamed enough to return to the American representatives to persuade them to stretch the gift to five. They eventually did so, but not before she received an "extremely rude" letter from one of her Federal colleagues, charging her with unfairness. She would be present for the opening of the first such center in Grenada, telling the assembled teachers and students that the school was not to be a place for "left over students who fall behind in their academic work," but one to provide "early specialist preparation for a good career in industrial arts" preparatory for an important role in their "increasingly industrialised society."

On September 24, 1960, Phyllis left Trinidad for the Nigerian independence celebrations. Not part of the Federal delegation, she had nonetheless been invited as a Federal MP and "a member of the greatest, or shall I say, the most powerful trade union in the world—the working women's trade union." She arrived in Nigeria determined to have a splendid time. On her way to Lagos she had visited Phina, who had lent her two beautiful dresses and a crimson velvet "rather Garbo-ish" hat that made her feel, for once, "stylish." She had been allocated a "magnificent" room in the newly built Federal Palace Hotel "with a view of the harbor and the Nigerian ships, the quiet water and soft lights at night." Lagos was brimming with visitors. "The whole world seemed to be there," as she wrote to Robert, and it all struck her as being "*Out of this world!*" Her path occasionally crossed that of the West Indian delegation, headed by Grantley Adams and the opposition leader, Ashford Sinanan, both of whom had come to Lagos with their wives. The Federation, it turned out, was the only nation other than Cameroon to bring its opposition. She had never been in favor of doing so, but she declared for public consumption that it exemplified "magnanimous impartiality." Sinanan, she reported privately, had been "glued" to the prime minister night and day, "making private mischief," and "using to the fullest Adams' popularity in Africa."

Phyllis truly enjoyed the festivities. A perennial royal watcher, she admired the "brilliance not only of the diamonds in Princess Alexandra's * hair and dress—so dazzling that she seemed to be catching on fire in the House of Representatives—but also the brilliance of the cottons worn by the working women in the streets of Lagos." Among the events Phyllis attended was *The Song of Unity*—a play performed at the race track—a "racy satire with a political moral" about the emancipation of three wives (the three regions of Nigeria) from their husband (the British Empire). She was most impressed—at least officially—by the tolerance displayed on the eve of the inaugural ceremonies, when the leaders of the Anglican, Roman Catholic, and Muslim faiths all stood together on the same platform and prayed in turn, with thousands of Nigerians chanting their responses. Her spirits refused to be dampened even after the fiasco of the colossal opening garden party for official guests at Government House, interrupted by "hurricane rains" that threatened to "drown us all out." Only hours before, Sir Hugh Foot, an old acquaintance of Phyllis's, had commented on the marvelous weather, saying it was "too good to be true—nature will intervene." There had been "a terrible failure of public relations" when the downpour started, no one thinking of broadcasting regrets to the guests, or inviting them inside, and they all had to shelter, damp and discouraged, in galleries and verandas, "without a drop to drink other than rainwater." The outdoor buffet was washed away. As Phyllis's chief mission in Nigeria concerned women, she invited as many of the "redoubtable" Nigerian women leaders as she had met to her hotel for an informal talk and to deliver a "simple but heartfelt message" from the Caribbean Women's Association. On her

* The princess, a cousin of Queen Elizabeth II and wife of Sir Angus Ogilvy, was then among the most popular members of the British royal family.

return, however, she would report that regardless of what had been said about the advantages of African countries over the West Indies, "we . . . can still teach the people of the Northern regions of Nigeria something about the emancipation of womankind."

In early November, Phina arrived in Port of Spain with her baby for an extended visit (she planned to stay until after Carnival). Phyllis was overjoyed and planned countless social engagements to introduce her daughter to her friends and colleagues. She insisted that she attend a session of the House and spoke to one and all of her beauty and accomplishments. Her friends, however, differed in their opinions. Many found Phina's reputation for beauty exaggerated, finding Phyllis more charming and attractive than her daughter. Others found Phina "supercilious" and "more like her father in character and manners." She was, one of Phyllis's friends remembers, "very brilliant and witty with a little mean streak which she must have gotten from her father." But nevertheless they all agreed that she took Trinidad by storm, and that the men were "gaga." Having lived for some years amid the rather free Kenyan society, Phina lost no time in scandalizing the more provincial, even Victorian Port of Spain elite. "In no time at all" after her arrival, an acquaintance recalls, "she was in bed with a Trinidadian poet/surveyor." Phyllis chose to ignore Phina's behavior. Writing about the visit in *In the Cabinet*, she contended that "[her daughter] had swiftly made so many friends, all of whom were in love with her, [that] she was out most of the day." But Phyllis was, as one acquaintance in Trinidad phrased it, "incredibly good" at "knowing nothing" when it did not please her or was something "rather inconvenient or uncomfortable to acknowledge." Phina's conduct was the sort of thing that was "never, ever acknowledged or recognized outwardly by her, but she must have known if she knew anything about her daughter at all."

In the final months of 1960, housing dominated Phyllis's agenda. Her housing adviser, an expert in the field of housing finance on loan to the Federal government for a year, had visited most unit territories and prepared a five-year housing program for the Windward and Leeward Islands. He had assisted the Trinidad government in the revision of its housing legislation and had been instrumental in the establishment of a Housing Mortgage Loan Board in Jamaica. Her ministry had also sponsored two competitions for low-cost housing designs, with prizes donated by Canadian banks and a private firm. They had been building up a collection of designs for modestly priced houses that were available to the public at nominal cost. In November she had submitted a report on a housing grant that she had secured for Dominica from the Caribbean Development and Welfare Fund as an example of what could be accomplished "even with limited funds." For a cost of BWI $123,800, an estate in Goodwill, near Roseau, had been laid out with roads, water, and a sewage scheme for more than 700 houses, of which more than 350 had already been built. In addition five new industries were either complete or under construction. A part of Goodwill had been set aside as overspill for a slum clearance scheme in adjoining Pottersville, and "thirty houses were already available for rent by families displaced through street widening and a thinning out of congested housing." Just a few days later—her ministry under severe attack from the opposition during the budget debate—she wished in exasperation that she had the power "to tear down the slums in the West Indies and build homes for humans to live in. But unfortunately I do not run a ministry of wishful thinking."

The December 1960 session of the House brought additional acrimonious debate and an angry outburst from Phyllis, declaring that her ministry had been "crippled by the Constitution from inaugurating the social legislation for which I long and for which the labouring man, unprotected as he and his family are, longs and prays. If I have been frustrated, not only by knavish tricks, in my dreams and ideals, the fetters and shackles were forged (perhaps in an unintended manner) by others, before my accession to ministerial rank; and they have been strengthened by chains added to those shackles by the enemies of the Federation." Her anger was followed by a plaintive "confession" that "as a Minister I have not done enough. I have not done enough! That is a fact. . . . I have not been allowed to do what I wanted to do and what I still intend and wish to do—not enough for the poor, the disadvantaged (that is a new word I learned at ILO), the underprivileged, the people who have not spoken yet. And this hurts . . . genuinely hurts me; because (although this word has not yet fallen from anybody's lips in this honourable house) I am and always will be a Socialist." Thus Phyllis—by her own admission "not by nature a consultative type" but "a doer, a shifter and a social revolutionary"—expressed her sense of frustration at being thwarted in her effort to "leave no stone unturned that they may earn their bread under decent and worthy conditions." The budget debate—accompanied as it was by Phyllis's near-tears outburst—gave ample evidence of the constant harassment she was often subjected to as a woman in an overwhelmingly male legislature. Throughout her career as a politician in Dominica, her gender had been secondary to her race as a political factor. What had made her different and controversial had been the combination of class and race factors, exemplified by her unlikely political partnership with Chris Loblack. In Trinidad the climate was distinctly different. Her gender and race—and the scarcity of women in the House—made her an easy target for the unforgiving political misogyny that West Indian men often assume when faced with women opponents. And since race was a far more explosive issue to raise in a beleaguered Federation, gender became the focus of attack. Alfred Gomes, for example, delighted in calling her "the minister *in labour*." In the midst of the budget debate, having announced that she had her "hand waiting to go to the money bag" after she had been promised additional funds for a cherished project, she was accosted by a comment from Gomes—"Spoken like a housewife!" She replied that she was indeed not "ashamed to be a housewife and a minister—and a good cook to boot!" Earlier in the debate she had expressed her gratitude to the honourable member for Westmoreland for addressing her as a "Lady Minister," since moments before another member had hinted "that it was the duty of a Lady Minister to be a hermaphrodite or something similar." The gender-related bickering during that debate had reached such proportions that when Phyllis deplored the "mistake" of the Federal founding fathers in not having "a single founding mother among them," the House gave her a resoundingly mocking "Hear! Hear!" Once, during a discussion of people's lack of recognition of the Federal flag, she had told the House how, upon arriving at the airport in Jamaica with her own sizable flag, she had been accosted by people exclaiming, "Look at that! My! What's that? and things of that sort. They couldn't really understand what the peculiar object was." Gomes rudely asked her if she was sure "it was the flag they were talking about?" but she proceeded with her comments without missing a beat. "Being a politician," she wrote in 1961, "is not an easy role for anyone," but it was still less so for a woman, "since we seem to be more vulnerable to insults, slander, mockery and the minor disgusts of political life than men. For a politician, like the novelist in Auden's poem, is expected 'to be among the filthy, filthy too/and in her own frail being, if she can/must suffer dully all the wrongs of man.'"

Throughout 1959 and 1960, as the possibilities of an islandwide election in Dominica became more distinct, Phyllis made increased efforts to visit her home island often. As early as October 1958, when she made her first visit with Robert after his return to the West Indies, she had begun to focus on the campaign to force the government into early elections. "The DUPP proved themselves to be two-faced," she had told her audience then. "They cannot serve the people as socialists and at the same time be anti-socialist. No man can claim to be a Christian if he is not a socialist." The "bosses" of Dominica's government were "intransigent," she argued, and she made her point by narrating how LeBlanc had gone to the administrator to inquire whether a development program had been devised, only to be told "to prepare a list if [he] had any suggestion." Never losing sight of the fact that the party's victory in the Federal elections had meant no change in the balance of power in Dominica, she kept agitating for broader popular participation in the political process. "The only way to bring up the standard of the district was for the people themselves to help the government by forming their own governments through Village Councils," she told the crowd that had congregated to greet her. Her speech addressed a concern that LeBlanc had shared with her after working on organizing party branches for several months: The people supported the party, he had told her, but they did not seem "ready to take the responsibility to manage those branches."

Her comments on the interchangeability of Christianity and socialism, as was to be expected, drew a forceful rebuttal from the *Chronicle*, in which she was also taken to task—her loyalty to Grantley Adams being well known—for his published advice to Dominica to use its "backwardness" as a way to attract tourism. Adams's misguided comments soon took on a life of their own. Elkin Henry greatly enjoyed prancing around deprecating the prime minister's statement, and Phyllis could only wince every time the comment was repeated to her. LeBlanc, who did not share her admiration for Adams, would become livid with rage. He had warned Adams that such a statement might cause turmoil in Dominica and wrote to Phyllis that the prime minister had "better be ready" to refute "the many pernicious inferences which are being made by our opponents."

She was back in Dominica in January 1959 to visit La Plaine, Point Michel, Vieille Case, Portsmouth, Colihaut, and the Carib Territory. As had become the pattern in her speeches to the Dominican people since Federation, wherever she went she explained the Federal government and her role in it, emphasizing that the Dominican government was not Labour and therefore did not truly represent the people. It was a point she lost no opportunity to make, even on the floor of the House, especially as she knew that her speeches in the House and other public statements were invariably published in the *Chronicle*. In May she told the House that "the government of Dominica is not, and has never been, a Federal Labour government and the blame for the backward conditions of Dominica, past or present, does not therefore fall on the shoulders on her Federal representatives in this house." The statement had followed a series of attacks from Dominica, where Baron and the DUPP had "badmouthed" her "so viciously" in absentia that Loblack had felt called upon to offer a spirited defense in a public meeting of the Dominica Labour party. He could not understand, he told the crowd then, "the hatred that exists towards her among certain Dominicans." Although the nature of the attacks seems almost silly from our vantage point, they were cleverly suited to influence the populace against her. Baron claimed that she had no gardener (she did) but collected a fifty-dollar-a-month gardener's allowance and gave half of it to Robert; that she had no chauffeur (she had Nicholas) but collected the appropriate allowance and paid Robert a tip for driving; that the Federal travel allowance had been increased and she traveled around in luxury. The DUPP charged, more seriously, that the Federal government was but "a Communist praesidium" seeking emergency powers that would make it possible for them to "send troops to shoot Dominican people down if they go against Fed[eral] policy." In early March A. F. Joseph, a disgruntled party member, had published a "scurrilous" letter in the *Chronicle* "full of vitriol" against the party. Phyllis contemplated an action for libel, but chose instead to reply through an open letter answering the charges one by one. The details of the accusations appear trivial in retrospect; she was accused of intending to build a "tourist guest house at the Lake!" and of being disloyal to Loblack. ("All of my friends are fully confident that I have remained loyal to Chris Loblack through his vicissitudes, while reserving the right to criticise him—and *any* other member of my party—in his own hearing.") Phyllis was most mortified by the charge that she "dictated" to the party: "All those who know me in the Party are aware that I do not dictate. My only worry is that I allow the Party to run itself too much, and cannot now give enough time to it. But I have confidence in the Party's executive."

During her visit it had become clear to her that the DUPP had gained an edge over the DLP in some constituencies by the simple advantage of having access to a public address system. She returned to Trinidad determined to obtain one for the party, but, failing to find a donor, finally purchased one out of her personal funds and sent it as her gift. It prompted a letter of thanks from LeBlanc, who noted that because of her generosity and "other philanthropic ventures" (it was well known that Phyllis sent monthly contributions of between five and twenty dollars to needy party members, Chris Loblack among them) she would "end by walking over the hill to the poorhouse." The party held its first "amplified" meeting in Roseau in June.

In October 1959 she heard, with great concern, from Alec Ducreay, then in Trinidad himself for medical reasons, that Edward LeBlanc, then in his late twenties, had been ill with two mild heart attacks. The news came as a shock to Phyllis, who wrote immediately to urge him to be cautious and not to attempt "any strenuous mountain climbing by jeep or on foot for the time being," whatever the cost to the party's present efforts to solidify its position with the peasantry. "You look so strong and tough that it seems impossible for the old ticker to cause you any trouble, and I hope that your natural resilience will come into play and keep away any future attacks." He had fully recovered when she visited in January 1960 to tour the prison and the Princess Margaret Hospital. After an inspection of a guard of honor of prison officers she visited the lunatic asylum, the female prisons, the security block, and the officers' quarters, declaring herself impressed by the general cleanliness and orderliness of the prison. As the mother of a mentally ill son, however, the poignancy of the location of the asylum in the prison was not lost on her, and she wrote to Robert that the visit helped to reconcile her to Philip's remaining in London.

Throughout 1960 Phyllis continued her frequent visits to Dominica, sometimes staying for just a couple of days, in order to keep up a steady pressure on Baron and the DUPP. In April she chaired a mass meeting at the Dawbiney Market, at which she denounced the South African government's treatment of colored people as "shocking and horrible." After stating that "no racial prejudice existed within her party," she forwarded a resolution on behalf of the Dominican population expressing their "horror and disgust" at the treatment meted out to colored South Africans. The resolution pledged Dominica's support for the worldwide boycott of South African goods "as long as the iniquitous policy of apartheid was enforced," and called upon the governments of Canada and the West Indies "to offer help to the victims of South African persecution." It was passed unanimously by a show of hands, and copies were forwarded to the secretary of state and the governor-general of the West Indies. A minute of silence was observed "in respect for the colored victims of the South African outrages." In July 1960 the DLP finally forced the government into an early election through the resignation of all its elected members from the Legislative Council and that of two DUPP members who had switched their allegiance to the Labour party. The strategy to force the election had been under discussion as early as March of the previous year, and had led to some tension between LeBlanc and Phyllis—particularly as LeBlanc, always thin-skinned when it came to her reputation for having a keener intellect, felt that she had mocked his tardy realization that they had had an opportunity to strike in March 1959. He had sent her a "raw-nerve" letter in which he admitted that he had "tortured" himself "with all sorts of mental agony for [his] dullness," claiming nonetheless that he was "satisfied that if the brainwave caught me at the eleventh hour it was not too late." It *had* been too late, however, and the party had to wait fourteen months for their next opportunity. When it came and the DLP Legislative Council members resigned, Phyllis moved quickly to forestall any possibility of support for Baron's plan of holding five by-elections "as a stalling-off measure"—which would have been "indeed wasteful of funds and of the people's patience"—by meeting with Hailes and writing to Adams: "If any Federal member of the W.I.F.L.P. is forced into the unnatural position of propping up an unpopular Government in Dominica, it will damage the federalist attitude of the people and of their next Government." She insisted on a general election being held immediately: "One of the clauses of the new constitution is that elections should take place if 'conditions warrant them.' It is the view of the Dominica Labour Party and the populace that these conditions now prevail even more blatantly than ever before, and that an election should take place this year. The Baron government has been defeated by Parliamentary tactics and no amount of propping up can disguise the fact that it does not exist."

In August Phyllis was again in Dominica for a whirlwind tour of her constituency. She joined the "Touring Team" of party officials crisscrossing the island visiting potential voters, traveling from place to place on foot carrying the Federal flag, sometimes wrapping herself in it for warmth. The first item on her agenda was a meeting at Loubiere where she heard the villagers complain that they were neglected between elections. She visited Pointe Michel, addressed a Village Councils Conference, held a public meeting at the Market Place, visited La Plaine and Grand Fond, and attended an open house at Government House. During her visit she was chastised in a published letter to the editor of the *Chronicle* from L.F.C. Royer, general secretary of the DUPP, for saying in an interview with the *West Indian* (Grenada) that the liberal government of Dominica was undemocratic because it "is a government without opposition." On August 23 the party held a mass meeting at the Market, where Phyllis gave a brief account of the ILO walkout. She predicted a DLP victory, claiming that general elections would come soon and be won by the poor and the friends of the poor. "There has been too much merchant domination," she claimed, "and Labour's first job would be to give a true sense of national being and to promote social justice."

On September 3, days after her return to Trinidad, a young Dominican girl, Mersula Benoit, the daughter of one of her constituents, arrived in Port of Spain, seriously ill with an undiagnosed brain ailment. Phyllis took her in, sending her to the best brain specialist in the region for a life-saving operation. She and Robert nursed her after her discharge from the hospital, and she was soon well and fit to return to Dominica, from where she wrote gratefully of how proud she was to share with her people how good she and Robert had been to her, "because I never thought I would fall in the hands of someone like you to be like a mother to me, most people are taken back when I tell them how nice you and Mr. Allfrey were to me." Mersula's loyalty to Phyllis would be lasting, and it would be shown primarily through frequent letters in which she detailed Dominica's petty political squabbles. She was particularly fond of sending Phyllis reports of Elkin Henry's iniquities: "Mr. Henry," Mersula wrote in November,

> told the Public you don't let them know what is happening, you only stay in Trinidad giving Cocktail Partys all the time, and when you come to D/ca you put on a dungare dress and go down to the Market making promises which is never fulfilled. He further went on to say you took the people like dam fools and made them march up to Government House without consulting with somebody or the other (I can't remember the name he said). He still went on to say (because he couldn't say six words without mentioning your name) when he was in Trinidad, a certain man said to him, "what kind of person you all sent here to represent Dominica?" . . . I feel if I could go up there and give him a good shaking it would satisfy me . . . He even said you promised the people houses and up to now you haven't told them a word."

Phyllis's generosity to Mersula was in no way unusual. As had been her practice with her flat in Fulham, she made her house in Federation Park, her money, and her resources available to countless Dominicans traveling to Trinidad. Several months earlier she had aided a young man from Vieille Case to extend his stay in Trinidad, where he had come looking for employment. His cousins were LeBlanc's schoolmates, and he wrote to Phyllis of his satisfaction at seeing that "Robert finds theirs a decent family, and to assure him that they come from respectable and genuine parentage." His irony was not lost on Phyllis, who could detect the veiled sarcasm against Robert mixed with the appreciation for her efforts, but who in cases like these chose to attribute it to Robert being misunderstood by Dominicans, and not to LeBlanc's competitive relationship with her. Given the "cornflicks within the Party"—as a DLP member once put it—even Phyllis's generosity would be subject to inner-party squabbles. "I must say I was treated as a member of a family rather than a guest from our party," Arnold Active once wrote thanking Robert for his and Phyllis's kindness during his stay in Trinidad—"though Leo [Charles] has spread a wide propagand[a] saying that I was not well treated in Trinidad by the Allfreys, but at a public meeting last night I made a statement how I was treated while in Trinidad."

In September Phyllis wrote to Vivian Grell, a British official who had frequently advised her on political matters, to share with him her impressions on the DLP's prospects in the coming election. "I am of the opinion," she writes, "that we shall certainly win 7 seats, we *may* win 9, but 2 or 3 are very doubtful . . . If we lose seats in this election it will be because we have thrown them away ourselves by talking nonsense or some other defect—the people of Dominica are solidly behind our Labour party." In early November, back in Dominica and with elections on January 17th now a certainty, she led a march of poor people to present a petition to the Administrator seeking improved housing. Baron immediately denounced the march, calling it "stupid" and stressing that "housing on a big scale was a matter for the Federal Government and that the Federal Minister was neglecting Dominica and its housing problems." She replied to these allegations without delay, telling a meeting at the Market that the chief minister "was severely fooling the people on the subject," reiterating that she was "always willing to lead a march to draw government attention to the plight of the people," and explaining that housing was "a territorial affair and that the Federal Government could not legally tackle housing."

The inner-party squabbles grew more hostile as the decision neared as to who would lead the DLP's election slate. Federal ministers, having left their islands to embark on work that often led them into conflict with their constituencies, had endangered their careers at home. Indeed, with almost no exceptions, Federation ministers saw their careers come to an abrupt end when the Federation collapsed. The greatest danger Phyllis faced as a minister was losing direct touch with the people and being undermined in her absence. LeBlanc, as a member of the House, had a freedom and mobility Phyllis lacked, and he used it as much to strengthen his position as to weaken hers. His shrewdest move was to create a new position in the party executive, that of "political leader," which he assumed himself. Phyllis retained her title of president and founder, sharing the latter with Loblack, but the political leader's functions threatened to reduce the president's role to something quasiceremonial, similar to the relationship in Britain between the prime minister and the queen. Whether LeBlanc—his antiwhite feelings being well known—played the racial card in his struggle for supremacy within the party no one will discuss openly even today, but there are indications that he did avail himself of the increasingly Afro-Caribbean emphasis in political movements throughout the region to weaken Phyllis's position within the party. Slowly yet clearly the party leadership and membership began to define their allegiances to one or the other. Her supporters went as far as to put pressure on Robert to settle himself in Dominica "to keep the party in line for her," a proposal he would not consider, feeling that it "might exacerbate Eddie's power hunger instead of making things better." Phyllis herself was of two minds. On the one hand it rankled her to see LeBlanc slowly gaining the upper hand in their struggle for party leadership; on the other she was committed to the Federation and felt that her chance to be Dominica's chief minister might come after her stint with the Federation was over. In any event, she was soon to learn that the decision was out of her hands. In late November he was asked to relinquish his Federal seat to lead the party in the coming election. The party, Ducreay would explain years later, "felt they should invest all their resources in that election. The choice as to who to put forward as their main candidate was debated, but the feeling was that Phyllis would remain in the Federal government and the choice would fall between LeBlanc and [himself]." Her being a woman, or being white, for that matter, "played no role in the decision," except perhaps for the fact that the campaign was expected to be a dirty "rabble-rousing affair" for which a "man of the people" was best suited. Arnold Active defended the selection by arguing that she would deal directly with the issues, but the campaign needed someone ready to dole out a little bit of "not very nice language" here and there to drive the points home, and she "would not deal with that type of thing." On the day she received the news, she wrote to Active to assure him that she would support the party wholeheartedly. "Rest assured," she tells him, "that everything I can do to help our party win the forthcoming elections will be done. Please kill any ridiculous rumours stone dead. The Labour party was founded by me and I shall not abandon it." She also wrote to Mersula and others, asking them to help in dispelling any rumor about a falling out between her and the party because of LeBlanc's nomination for office, rumors "which are nearly always invented for the purpose of making mischief." Within weeks she was back in Dominica to see how the party was faring in "the toughest political campaign in Dominica's history."

A few days before Christmas the party held a mass meeting at the Market, at which Phyllis replied to a number of DUPP allegations against her and the DLP. She informed her audience that she had ordered samples of a vegetable protein food that could prove helpful in alleviating the undernourishment of children in Dominica and the West Indies. She stressed the need for a tuberculosis ward and for an islandwide campaign to help combat the disease, and voiced her distress at the now-certain disintegration and collapse of the DTU. Replying to those who said that she was not interested in helping Catholic institutions, she assured them that she had "always maintained scrupulous fairness to Catholic institutions," and had helped Catholics in their youth groups and dinners for the poor. "I am careful to be as impartial and generous to Catholics as President Kennedy will, I am sure, be to Protestants in America." On the eve of the election, Elkin Henry harangued a crowd from his mother's veranda. Speaking in patois, he asked them if they knew who had caused the election to be held this year. "It is an old white woman called Mrs. Allfrey who is a damn dog [*sacré shein*]." The crowd demanded to know what harm she had done him and taunted him to stop his cursing if he claimed to be a respectable man. He then took a hat (the DLP's electoral symbol) from a "wayward child" and, while exhibiting it to the public, said repeatedly, "Hat, I command you to speak," remarking before the hat's silence, "Just as a hat can't talk so are Labour Candidates useless." He promised that the following evening, "when the Baron's candidates would have win, [they] will dress eleven monkeys (which [he] already had made arrangements to get) with hats on their heads, will drive them along the road in a parade, with the slogan 'Go on, LABOUR, Go on.'"

On January 21, 1961, the election results were in, and, as Phyllis had predicted months earlier, the Labour party had received a majority of the votes, winning seven out of the eleven seats, with three going to the DUPP and one to an independent candidate. Edward LeBlanc was chief minister. At the mass celebration in the Market Square, she stood beaming on the platform, basking in the glow of her party's long-awaited success. If she felt a pang of jealousy or disappointment at seeing him rise to the post of chief minister, the very post she always aspired to, she never even whispered so much as a word.

Ten

The Perfection Seekers

Torn from the monolith
granite of memory
all the frail ivy-green
tendrils of pleasure.
All the fair kindness,
the laughter, the feasting,
the miracle-sharing
was never, was not;
all good is forgot.

Labour has secured seven seats out of eleven in the Legislative Council, and for this God be praised!" proclaimed W. S. Stevens in the *Herald* on January 21, 1961. The victory, the newspaper blazoned, augured "a new era in Dominican politics." As the peasantry took to the streets in exultant celebration, the new chief minister vowed that Dominica would "at last with pride and prestige take her rightful place and make her full contribution towards the West Indies Nation." As the revelry subsided, however, the staggering challenges facing the party leadership surfaced massively before them. Their promises to the electorate had been moderate—in this Phyllis had been adamant—but meeting even their modest stated goals would require large amounts of cash (whose source was unclear) and a tremendous mobilization of resources. The party's development agenda centered on road construction and the promotion of agriculture and industry. Heading the list were the construction of a western coast road linking Roseau to Portsmouth, the opening of feeder roads connecting the "productive hinterlands" to arterial roads, and the reconstruction of the Roseau–Sylvania road linking the west and east coasts. The DLP proposed the construction of a permanent jetty at Portsmouth, the opening of post offices and installation of telephones for all out-of-the-way hamlets and small villages, the building of an islandwide electrification system, the securing of water service for all citizens, the replacement of dilapidated school buildings around the island, and the establishment of thirty health centers and the building of five cottage hospitals. In the early months of 1961, when the Federation's continuity still seemed assured, the party trusted to the Federal government, and to Phyllis, to secure funds to bankroll these projects.

For Phyllis, ironically, the victory she had worked so hard to achieve signaled the beginning of public marginalization in Dominica Labour party politics. Her inner party marginalization had begun months before, as she, wrapped in the affairs of the threatened Federation, lost increasingly more ground to LeBlanc in local matters. Her correspondence with members of the party executive during the months leading to the election revealed her recognition of her growing isolation. "My views are not asked for before hand," she complained to Alec Ducreay in September, "and the majority have a right to disregard them." Grateful for suggestions for improving a speech, she declares herself to be "more modest than some colleagues in Dominica, who don't want to refer to their old president for anything!" "Yet," she asks self-pityingly, "what are we older politicians trained for if not to offer a little advice now and then?" Approaching her fifty-second birthday, her political and administrative skills just reaching their full flowering, she was regarded by the youthful party leadership as belonging to another era. And she was becoming increasingly aware of a new racial element entering the political equation, a card LeBlanc was beginning to put into play and against which she had no defense other than the fact that she had always endeavored to struggle against those who had traditionally oppressed Dominica's black population. During the campaign his antagonism toward her became quite obvious to the party leadership. Arnold Active tells of an incident in the Carib Territory in which she held a dirty child while she spoke to the mother. Minutes later, coming to a stream, she washed her hands. It was, Active insists, just what everyone else would have done after a long trek down a muddy forest path, but LeBlanc, choosing to interpret it as a reflection of her disgust in having touched the dirty child, chided her. "Phyllis," he told her scornfully, "if you knew the child was dirty, why did you pick him up?" Sensing that the limelight was quickly moving away from her and toward the increasingly popular LeBlanc, whose "meteoric rise to power" was confirmed by his overwhelming margin of victory, she placed herself at the center of an electoral to-do when interviewed by the *Trinidad Guardian* upon her return to Port of Spain. "Most of the [DUPP] attacks" during the election had not been against Labour candidates, but against herself as President of the Party." "Racial and religious issues" (which would have applied to her only as a Protestant and a white) had been exploited very little "except in one or two out-of-the-way pockets of parochialism." Her claim that the people "were exhilarated but so tired they could hardly jump up" after Labour's "famous victory" seem to reflect more her own growing dejection than the "extreme good humor," the frantic rejoicing, "excessive" in some cases, exhibited by DLP supporters. She, not they, "had worked so hard" she was "completely fagged out," and was returning to Trinidad with the conviction that she was being edged out of Dominican politics, and that her sphere of power and action was narrowing. She was becoming conscious that her political star was tethered to the Federation just as the latter was following a course of action that would inevitably lead to its demise.

Back in Trinidad, as Robert had once warned her, her life seemed increasingly reduced to the "drudgery of opening bazaars every day." As the only woman minister, she did more than her fair share of openings and celebrations. (She later told a friend that "in many ways her role was that of a 'gracious hostess.'") Quite often her remarks were mere words of greeting—as in her "Message for Commonwealth Youth Sunday," in which she spoke of how being a mother "is a long, difficult job . . . essential for a good nation," and one for which "[mothers] seldom get thanked." Occasionally she was given an opportunity to address issues closer to her heart, as she did when she gave a feminist address to the Caribbean Women's Association, of which she was vice president: "If women decide to act in unity," she told the membership, "they are *quite invincible*. The only thing is that men know this too, and their counteraction may be summed up in these words: Flatter and divide, and above all keep women in their proper place. Of course, it is up to individual women to decide what that proper place is; but fewer and fewer of us nowadays will accept anything less than absolute equality with joint responsibility. Our demands are quietly and (I hope) graciously expressed, but the answer we expect from the men of the Caribbean is an unequivocal YES."

As the Federation's future clouded she spoke more and more often to women, urging a message of responsibility and empowerment that she thought might be her most lasting legacy as a minister. Addressing the Indian Women's Cultural Association at Fyzabad, Trinidad, she exhorted them to work in earnest to better their sisters' lot: "Some of the hardest-working women I know are the womenfolk of agricultural workers in Trinidad who glean rice and care for their livestock, setting us an example of thrift and devotion. I have sometimes wondered why more is not done for these women by their more fortunate sisters to help them attain a higher degree of leisure and enlightment." She admonished the young members of the St. Augustine (Trinidad) Girls' Alumnae Association that "sensitive, strong and able young women with a good education can make a tremendous impact on their society," but only if they directed their efforts at "the communal society of all classes with emphasis on underprivileged peoples, of whom we still have so many in these islands." She used her visibility as a minister to exhort young women to challenge tradition ("that gently hampering restriction which is so much harder to throw off than downright tyranny") and "seize the many opportunities which are gradually opening out."

Aware of the storm clouds gathering around the Federation, Phyllis nonetheless continued working on her busy agenda. Her efforts at the ministry were focused on full employment and migration issues, particularly on countering the increasing threats from Harold Macmillan's Conservative government in Britain to ban migration of West Indians after independence was achieved on May 31, 1962. The British government, obsessed with its own financial problems, had focused on a ban of migration from its former colonies as a means to appease British voters. The Federation, Phyllis vowed, "would resent bitterly any attempt, legislative or oblique, to deprive the brave, industrious and eager for knowledge among us of opportunities abroad." Her recommendations on how to approach the threatened ban were not always popular, as became clear some months later when the Federal House held a debate on migration. West Indian demands for reassurances from the British government had been growing increasingly more strident by the day, and she made an eloquent plea for a more enlightened way of approaching demands on British reception of migrants:

> *But* remember this when you add a few bars to the beggars opera:—The majority of people who pay taxes in Britain today are not the descendants of those who profiteered out of the early days of the West Indies. They are descendants of the industrial revolution and were themselves pathetic wage slaves a couple of generations back. . . . Therefore, if we are going to demand generous treatment from those people we have to do it in a manner befitting our national dignity and our innate decency. . . . I think it would be much wiser for us to emphasize the splendid talents and capacity for work of our nationals, and to underline our confidence in the open door liberal policy which Britain has hitherto maintained and which she surely would not dare foreclose on at this moment of heightened national and race consciousness and anxiety about the future of human rights. . . . We are a multiracial, multi-religious, traditionally tolerant community, and now is the time for us to set a good example which should make us respected and welcomed everywhere in the world.

In July 1961 Phyllis went to Geneva for the last time as leader of the West Indies delegation, stopping in London to see Philip in her "once-a-year pilgrimage of love-anguish." The visit left her "*flattened*." He had been happy to see her and had "smiled a lot," but had not said much, although the little he had said was "sensible." The doctors continued to offer little hope. The drugs that had proved most helpful were also the ones that "might physically kill him," so they were at a loss as to how to proceed. She had found the strain overwhelming and burst into tears during her meeting with his doctors, leaving the hospital "so teary I had to wear my dark glasses." On her way to Geneva she stopped in Paris for meetings with the director general of UNESCO on the tentative plans for the formation of a West Indian National Commission "in preparation for full membership in UNESCO as soon as Independence had been achieved." While in Paris she was the guest of the French government and had "a proper VIP time," having at her disposal an official car and a suite in the Pavillon Henri IV. But she arrived in Geneva "shockingly anxious," overcome by "a great sadness," and in "a state of deep underlying depression." She wrote to Robert, "I can tell the 3 causes, you, Phil, the fate of the West Indies. All seem in doubt and one is overcast by absolute tragedy. It seems as if I live with the three anxieties." Her busy schedule in Switzerland, however, left her little room to brood. Shortly after her arrival she was to host a reception at the Palais des Nations, and was to attend a conference on immigration convened by the World Council of Churches at Leysin, at which she and Pastor Martin Neimöller of Germany were to be the principal speakers. The council chairman, in introducing her, described her rather gauchely as "the hors d'oeuvre"—Neimöller being presumably the main course—and she graciously admitted that it had indeed been so, as his speech, "exquisitely written in English in his German script," was "as strong and *right* as the man himself—cut across all creeds." She had moreover to "rake her brain" to prepare her ILO speech. "It just *sticks* and doesn't get started," she complained bitterly. "How can I write a speech about a nation that refuses to act nationally." Her subject was social security—something "barely known in some islands of the West Indies Federation." Invoking "the anxious thin faces of those who do not know how or where their pensionless old age will gradually filter away," and those to whom "an annual fortnight's holiday with pay still seems like an unexpected miracle," she made her case for an economic program centered on full employment.

Soon, however, these concerns would be pushed to the background by Jamaica's setting a date for holding a referendum to decide whether the territory would remain in the Federation. Jamaica's uneasiness with the concept of Federation had come initially from its own growing confidence in achieving independently "the self-sustaining economic growth that would lead her eventually into the ranks of the 'modernized' and 'developed' countries." Believing itself capable of independent political and economic development, the island did not relish saddling itself with eight impoverished little islands over which it "assumed a superiority corresponding to their size." Jamaica had reached an agreement with Esso in 1958 to refine oil, an accord that placed it on a collision course with Trinidad, the traditional supplier of oil products in the region. The Trinidadian government sought to block Jamaica's request for Federal approval for a consumption tax on Trinidadian oil imports into Jamaica, a concession that would restrict the free movement of goods within the Federation. It took no time for the issue of the refinery to become linked to the feasibility of the Federation, the animosity escalating through a "cross fire of statements" punctuated by threats of secession from Jamaica's representatives to the Federal parliament (most of them members of the opposition) and resulting in a Jamaican proposal for a Constitutional Review Conference "to decide whether it would be best to end the present tragic farce of federation and await a time when the West Indies could have a real federation internationally, intellectually, and spiritually."

Grantley Adams, ever incautious about statements to the press, would in October 1958 push Jamaica closer to secession by assuring journalists that the Federal government "would seek to get agreement . . . to bolster Federal revenue before the end of the five year period" stipulated by the constitution and that it "could levy its own income tax, after five years" and make it "retroactive to the date of Federation." Coming less than six months before general elections in Jamaica, the incendiary statement, coupled with what was perceived as Federal interference with Jamaica's right to establish its own industrial development accords, played perfectly into Bustamante's campaign against Manley, making the Federation a central point of the campaign. Phyllis and her fellow ministers watched helplessly as the storm was unleashed. Never having been consulted by Adams before he made the declarations that had "stirred up the hornet's nest," they felt "ridiculous and helpless" but, bound by loyalty, "kept a morose silence."

The 1959 Inter-Governmental Conference charged with reviewing the constitution proved to be "very provoking and irritable," as Phyllis wrote LeBlanc, with the ministers reduced to "more or less acting as referees and keeping ourselves quiet." Bustamante quickly issued his own proposals for a "handcuffed Federation," painting a "fearsome picture" of the reduction of Jamaica to "Parish Council Status," and publicizing a list of *conditiones sine qua non* Jamaica would be forced to withdraw: the rewriting of the constitution so as to make it impossible for the Federal government to impose taxation on the units without prior unit approval; representation in the Federal House on the basis of population; and assurance that any customs union agreement would not hurt Jamaican workers and economy. Manley, under pressure from the opposition, demanded that the constitution exclude the possibility of Federal control over industrial development and tax levies. He suggested instead a constitutional formula that would enable the units to entrust the Federal government with a greater or lesser range of powers according to their needs. The conference achieved little beyond making it clear that "all continuance of the federal union would depend on the possibility of the other Units coming to terms with Jamaica."

In January 1960 Manley led a delegation to London for meetings with the colonial secretary, seeking guidance about minimum requirements for dominion status. Having received assurances from the Colonial Office that it would not block a request for independence from Jamaica—assurances seen by Adams and his ministers as "a callous violation of the spirit of the Federation"—an emboldened Manley announced that Jamaica would not remain in any Federation "which had the right to take over all the economic controls of the area as soon as it becomes independent. . . . If we cannot reach early agreement [with the other units], Jamaica will leave Federation and will seek independence on her own." A few months later he announced his government's decision to submit the issue of Jamaica's continued participation in the Federation to a referendum, with a date eventually set, after some delays, for September 19, 1961.

In March 1961, while on a visit to the West Indies, British Prime Minister Harold Macmillan, in a speech delivered to both houses of the Federal parliament, had underscored the British government's trust in the success of the Federation and his hopes that by early 1962 it would become an independent state. Heartened by this, and setting aside the obvious rifts separating its members, the Federal government decided to go ahead with the planned Inter-Governmental Conference in Port of Spain and the London conference in May–June 1961. Just prior to these meetings historian Gordon Lewis earned Phyllis's everlasting wrath for declaring the Federation "doomed" during a visit to Trinidad. No other federation of nations had ever succeeded, he argued, and the West Indies version was not about to break the pattern. Phyllis would often refer to him after that as "this little man who thinks he knows everything." But he would prove to be only too right. Both meetings were dominated by Jamaica's threats. Eric Williams remained isolated and could muster little support for his proposals for a strong federal government.* As the *West Indian Economist* commented at the end of the London conference: "The Federation has now been pared down to what Jamaica says she wants. It is up to Jamaica to accept it. If anything is wrong with the federation now, Jamaica is to blame."

But by then there was little hope of the Jamaican people supporting even the much weakened Federation that had survived the London meeting. For over a year Bustamante's Jamaican Labour party had been waging an all-out vigorous anti-Federation campaign, concentrating on rural areas, while Manley and his party pursued constitutional revisions favoring Jamaica. When he finally turned his attention to the referendum issue, Manley would "[lay] his political life on the block" only to lose that vote, and, as a direct result, the general elections the following April (1962). The opposition exploited familiar factors such as unemployment, poor housing, high cost of living, all of which may not have had any relation to federation, but were nonetheless linked to it by political demagoguery. All of these conditions would get worse "while we continue to send millions to Trinidad." The campaign slogans made the most of this disingenuous link: "We want work, not Federation"; "Free me from federation;" "Federation is Slavery." According to Phyllis's friend F. A. Glasspole, Jamaican minister of education, "The propaganda that was carried out in the country was vicious." The opposition had gone so far as to tell people in the countryside "that Federation meant slavery and that they had seen the chains on the 'Federal Maple' which were intended to put slavery into effect." The "poor people in the rural areas" had been caught "flat-footed and fell the victims of a fear campaign." Manley had made "valiant efforts to counteract this flood of propaganda," but he had very little assistance from his ministers, and failed to make the complex issues—particularly as they concerned the cost to Jamaican taxpayers of continued membership in the Federation—clear to the peasantry. On September 13 he wrote Phyllis to thank her for her contribution to the referendum campaign funds and to tell her that it was going "as well as I could hope." He would not attempt any forecasts "because a terrific struggle is being waged and I just prefer to keep on campaigning rather than to talk about what will happen." The campaign had by then entered its final crucial stage

*Trinidad's position, outlined by Williams in *The Economics of Nationhood*, was that the Federal constitution should be based on securing the objectives of independence, the basic human freedoms, and the economic development and integration of the region. It advocated strengthening the power of the Federal government against that of the units, giving it, particularly, powers of taxation in all fields and final word in legislation on matters affecting planning and development.

and he was not very sanguine about victory. As Jamaicans went to the polls, Phyllis sent him a telegram of encouragement, which simply read: TRUSTING IN VICTORY.

On the evening of referendum she had agreed to join the broadcasters of Radio Trinidad to cover the election results, the first of which came from the ten constituencies of the corporate area of Kingston and St. Andrew—the traditional strongholds of Manley's People's National party. Although there was a clear lead in favor of the Federation, it fell ominously short of expectations. The tide turned steadily after that. By early evening returns showed a huge "no" majority, placing defeat beyond doubt. With only 60 percent of the Jamaican electorate participating, 54 percent had voted against continued federation. The atmosphere at the station was "like a wake." Manley conceded defeat shortly before midnight, speaking briefly on the radio. In a voice tense with emotion, he conveyed his regrets to the rest of the West Indies, declaring: "Tens of thousands will grieve at this defeat of all their hopes for the future, and I share their sorrow." The referendum had been determined by the rural population. Farmers were distrustful of new and unknown solutions, which could greatly change their lives, and were inclined to listen to Bustamante's "demagogical warnings." Phyllis, who had been asked to comment on the results, said that "the consequences of this decision are too grave for comment without profound thought. But to me it is the triumph of the little kingdom mentality over the spirit of sharing and community kinship. Brave men and women were involved in the struggle and I do not think they will lose their courage overnight. I salute our friends the losers of Jamaica." The very next morning she wrote to Manley, calling the defeat "the most discouraging moment in our history . . . more I will not say to add to your burden of grief." He did not reply until a month later, hoping she would understand "how hard pressed I have been." He "hoped and pray that the nine islands will now get together and form a stronger Federation. Maybe history will justify the ways of 'foolish people.'" But by then he had accepted the "mandate of the people" and proceeded to take the necessary steps that would bring independence to Jamaica at the earliest possible date.

The reaction throughout the West Indies was one of dismay. TRAGEDY HITS THE WEST INDIES FEDERATION declared the *Herald* in Dominica. In a broadcast the day after the referendum, Phyllis called the Jamaican decision "a decisive blow to the hopes and aspirations [of West Indian nationalists] for a united West Indies in physical terms as we understood it as far back as 1947." But she also vowed that it would be "sheer folly to think of turning back at this stage." In a talk she delivered on September 26, an address punctuated by numerous quotations from the poetry of Robert Bridges, Dylan Thomas, W. H. Auden, Emily Brontë, as well as her own, she spoke of the "darkness of spirit" that had fallen over the West Indies: "the sense of being abandoned by trusted friends." In the trying days they had just lived through she had turned to poetry "for consolation, prophecy and reassurance," hoping "vaguely for inspired words to burst like shooting stars through the dark night of the soul." Addressing the Labour party conference in Dominica two months later, Phyllis attributed the decision "to the failure of human relations and public relations," but trusted that the future shape of the federation would be "hammered out in the next few months."

It became clear to Phyllis during this visit that her influence with the party leadership was waning, and that she was being sabotaged from within. Just after the referendum the party discussed a resolution reaffirming its full support for the Federation, regarding it as "the only safe road for Dominica notwithstanding Jamaica's decision to secede." The executive, however, defeated by a narrow margin a second paragraph of the resolution "placing implicit confidence in the ministerial system of Government" and condemning "the acceptance of the unitary system of government" by Jamaica. LeBlanc had openly vowed to struggle to "scrap the Ministerial system in the Federation." Phyllis nonetheless continued to use her limited Federal powers to help the political effort in Dominica. Robert Bradshaw had a scheme, which she "strongly support[ed]," to get seven hundred thousand dollars from the United States for roads in those territories of the Federation which had not benefitted financially under the hand-over of bases. She was hoping Dominica would get "a goodly whack," and was keeping "on the mark" about it. When the funds came through she wrote to L. C. Didier, the relevant minister in Dominica, informing him confidentially of the grant in advance of the official announcement, and expressing her hope, though she knew the list was long, that "a little bit of it" could be assigned to the village of Good Hope for making "a rough improvement of those poor people's byway." She had gotten a "pathetic letter enclosing a petition" from Boyd Berkitt, the village council leader and an old friend.

As usual she was bending over backward so as not to seem to interfere in local affairs, sensing correctly that LeBlanc was extremely sensitive to any appearance that he was under her guidance and control. In September she wrote him, addressing him as "My dear Chief Minister" (gone was her usual "My Dear Eddie") and trusting that he would not regard her letter "in any way as interfering," but asking for an increase in the small stipend of $280 per month allowed three nursing sisters attached to the staff of the Princess Margaret Hospital. As members of a religious order they were not expected to have expenses as heavy as those of lay employees, but she thought that the stipend, which the three shared, was "not sufficient to maintain a decent standard in view of the present cost of living." He appears to have ignored her request. But as president of the party she did feel she had a right to act on the party's behalf, and did so, not always with his approbation or support. She had encouraged the formation of a Women's Guild within the party, headed by Mabel James, an old political crony of hers and a "valiant fighter," and was encouraging the formation of a guild for youth, "whose attitude and welfare require special attention." LeBlanc had frowned upon the Women's Guild, which had begun with great élan—Mabel wanting to use its influence to take "the winds out of the sails of Baron's ship." The group gathered together politically and socially, and their activities (most of them gender-bound) varied from cooking the banquet that celebrated the party's annual conference to singing carols at Christmas, something that got them "in a cheery merry mood" for the holidays. Phyllis had arranged for the guild's admission as a member of the Caribbean Women's Association. In January 1962 the guild's women led a "hell-fire counter demonstration" against the DUPP, which had protested against the new taxes passed by the Labour-dominated Legislative Council. The women had prepared twelve placards: FACE THE FACTS AND PAY THE TAX; CAESAR AUGUSTUS MADE A DECREE THAT ALL THE WORLD SHOULD BE TAXED; AND MARY AND JOSEPH WENT TO BE TAXED; LITTLE MAN, LET BIG MAN FIGHT FOR HIMSELF; TAXES MUST BE PAID; ROADS CANNOT BE BUILT WITHOUT MONEY; WE WANT BETTER HOMES, BETTER SCHOOLS, MORE ROADS; WE WANT A BETTER DOMINICA; LITTLE MAN IS PAYING, BIG MAN MUST PAY; HEAVEN HELP THOSE WHO HELP THEMSELVES; TAX THEM, BROTHER, TAX THEM; WHEN YOU PAY ONE CENT BIG MAN PAY DOLLAR. They had returned to the office "quite satisfied."

She was often seen by LeBlanc as keeping too close an eye on local politics. He scoffed at her entreaties to Alec Ducreay in October 1961, exhorting him to embark on an "all out *Grow More Food Campaign*," an initiative she was eagerly promoting. Every Dominican should be encouraged "to plant ground provisions, if even for their own consumption to break the grip of high grocery prices." This Federal campaign, her brainchild, stemmed from her belief that the vast importation of food in the West Indies was "an unwarranted luxury." No "tinned-food government," no "canned-food government" could hope to survive as "no child brought up on tinned food will survive healthily." The recommendation was put forth in the House as an effort both to address the needs and deficiencies of people's diets and the massive trade imbalances caused by the amount of resources spent in the importation of foodstuffs which could be grown locally or substituted by others locally grown.

In November 1961 the party held its Annual General Meeting at Wesley, in the north. In her address Phyllis said that the party had "moved northward in a historical gesture" to indicate "that all were in it together and that Roseau was not the only center of political activity and importance." It was the first general meeting since the DLP's triumph in the January election, and Phyllis spoke of the people's role in that victory and of the party's need for their continued loyalty if it was to persevere. Loyalty, she told them, was a first essential, as without it,

> neither family nor Government could endure and prevail . . . I believe that everyone here present contributed in some way to this victory and rejoiced in unison. It was the first time that a Government springing from the very grassroots, an avowed socialist Government, had taken over from people who called themselves Independents, DUPP,—all sort of names—but whom *we* knew as "the old gang." . . . You may think that having gained these two great prizes the Labour Party might afford to "take it light," go easy and consolidate its gains for the good of the people, unmolested by malice or sabotage. Of course, such a thought could only be a pious hope in Dominica, where the wicked forces of the reaction, enraged by their defeat, are working like wood-ants and termites to rot and destroy *your* legally elected, popular Government. . . . In every political set up there are people waiting under cover to take advantage of the dissatisfied . . . suppose you are one who expected miracles from the Labour Government . . . a road . . . a clinic . . . a school. You see other things being done and you are not prepared to wait. This is the time the enemy can dump poison in your ear. But if you, by encouraging discontent, help them get back into power, it is not your road, clinic, school, scholarship they will be concerned with—it is their own private interest. Make no mistake. This is a struggle of the *public good* versus the *private gain*.

As usual her constituency visit was not without its aggravations. So violent were the feelings she awakened among some sectors in Dominica that a nursery school teacher of a different political persuasion had vowed she would throw away a shipment of toys that Phyllis had obtained from the United States and had delivered to Good Hope during her stay. Upon learning of the incident she wrote back in characteristic fashion, declaring herself not insulted at all by the violent rejection of the gift, but underscoring that the teacher was being unkind "to those good American people who sent the present of the toys in my care." But she would not interfere. "She is a voluntary teacher so it is not my business to interfere with her work. The people of Good Hope can settle the matter for themselves." A more serious matter arose when she was rebuked by W. S. Stevens, Dominica's new minister for labor and social services, a member of her own party, for granting a half-day holiday to the staff and the pupils of the Morne Prosper Government School "without the courtesy of prior reference to, or sanction of the responsible local authority." Her "impropriety" was noted in an official letter of censure sent "with regret by this Government and in accordance with their advice." Just a few weeks earlier she had had a bitter argument with Stevens when she brought up at an executive meeting of the party a complaint she had received from a junior teacher about inadequacies in some local schools (which fell under his jurisdiction). He had replied indignantly, charging that her attitude clearly showed that she had come to pick a quarrel with him and had singled him out for criticism, accusing her in the process of having lied about receiving a complaint. In any case he felt himself responsible to the people of Dominica and not to a Federal minister in Trinidad who could "never know the facts." He excoriated her further for constituting herself a recipient of "irresponsible gossip." Her only response to this barrage seems to have been to move to another topic.

Stevens had been apparently causing more serious mischief, albeit indirectly. Some months earlier a representative of Radio Trinidad had asked Phyllis to recommend a correspondent in Dominica. She had given him two names, one of them that of Pat Stevens, the minister's son. Stevens had gotten the assignment, and from that day on "false 'news items'" about her had been coming through, broadcast by Rediffusion Barbados in advance of the Trinidad recording. While in Dominica in December she had tried to find out who had been doing "the mischief," but had not gotten very far except by a process of elimination. In December, Radio Trinidad had issued a report on a rumor that she was going back to Dominica to depose the chief minister. She had had to issue a denial, declaring herself "amazed" at the report and stating that she had "no plans at the moment beyond remaining with the Federation, and continuing my work, which embraces the people of Dominica as much as the other people of the West Indies." In January 1962 a news item was broadcast stating that she was to address a meeting in Roseau Market Place at a time when she was sitting at home in Trinidad. She guessed that it had been "deliberately done to draw a crowd and disappoint the population."

As the Federation neared its dissolution after the Jamaican referendum, a segment of the party leadership began to fear that her return to Dominica would lead to a power shift within the party, just as LeBlanc and his supporters were entrenching themselves at the party and government levels. As a result Phyllis began to be pilloried from within. Damaging stories, some traced back to her party colleagues, were circulated about passages in *The Orchid House*, which led to a near riot at St. Joseph in January. Excerpts from the novel, taken grossly out of context and presented as reflecting her views on black laborers and political relations, were quoted in meetings and circulated widely prior to her arrival at the village. Numerous excerpts from *The Orchid House* proved useful to her enemies when presented to a near-illiterate audience unable to ascertain what meaning (other than that inferred through political demagoguery) they had in the text. Phyllis had arrived with Didier, the minister of communication and works, and two other members of the Labour party, to find a hostile crowd awaiting, and accepted police protection. While they were setting up their loudspeakers in a shop, an opponent addressed the fairly large crowd in an inflammatory impromptu speech whose "whole theme . . . was race hatred." He alluded to a passage in the novel "about the true relationship of government and people being a 'father-children' bond" and denouncing the idea of "any parent, however bad, feeling it necessary to come among his children under the protection of policemen." He urged the people not to listen to Phyllis, after telling them that although the police were under orders, "beneath their uniforms beat good black hearts." Just as the local Labour party chairman was helping to fix the public address system, a large rock was hurled at the platform, hitting the roof. This was followed by a few others. Phyllis had taken refuge in the shop, but after a while, as a considerable number of people still waited in the street, she stepped into the lighted doorway and made a brief, calm speech, telling them that her book "was written for and not against negroes."

In a statement about the incident she published a week after the events, Phyllis wrote that she was

> sure that there are a great number of people in St. Joseph who deeply regret such violent behavior, and I send them my kind thoughts. It is to be hoped that racial antagonism, which is causing so much suffering throughout the world and against which we have consistently fought, will be firmly discouraged in Dominica by all people of good will. We may reflect that our friends and benefactors in the Commonwealth, the United States and the United Nations are, like West Indians, persons of many shades of complexion; and we may also give a mind to the welfare of our migrants in Britain who are trying bravely to resist another form of prejudice.

Just a few days after the St. Joseph incident, at a DUPP meeting in Roseau conducted from Frank Baron's veranda, "aspersions" had been cast on Phyllis as a white woman. Speaker after speaker "only kept referring to race," inciting the people to "racial prejudice." Letters to the editor of the *Herald* came to her defense the following week, however, deploring this "uncalled for behaviour [which would] tend to destroy the possibility of our ever having a tourist industry established in this island." Of Phyllis personally a writer would say, "Perhaps not many Dominicans have written books, but they do speak with their mouths, and they don't speak well of the poor all the same. . . . If members of the Dominica United People's Party . . . can love their countrymen, then why can't Mrs. Allfrey whose native land is also Dominica?"

Phyllis returned to Port of Spain from these troubles to face the crushing blow of the dissolution of the Federation. After the Jamaican referendum, the center of attention had shifted to Trinidad and Eric Williams. Some had assumed he would now seize the opportunity opened to him by the power vacuum left by Manley to rebuild the Federation along the strong central lines he had repeatedly advocated. But many also remembered his many declarations that if Jamaica were to withdraw, Trinidad could not be expected to carry the entire burden of Federal leadership. After the referendum he had kept everyone guessing. He had faced a general election within a month of the Jamaican vote and maintained that Trinidad's membership or withdrawal from the Federation was an issue his government would decide afterward. During the campaign, however, he had made his intentions quite clear, threatening that if in the coming election Trinidadians were to support the revised West Indian constitution as it stood after the London meetings, he would withdraw from public life. It was his opinion that Trinidad had "only too long taken part in this tomfoolery." It had become obvious to all that after the Federal government's kowtowing to Manley in London, Williams would have nothing to do with a Federation ruled by Adams "and his company." After Jamaica's successful attempt at defining independence in its own terms, Williams seemed more interested in leading a unitary state.

Grantley Adams and his ministers had consequently prepared themselves for the fatal blow. But Phyllis steadfastly held to a belief in Williams's earlier support for a strong Federation, hoping that it would prevail over other concerns. Just weeks before Williams's announcement, while on her constituency visit to Dominica, she had reasserted her confidence in the Federation's survival. Addressing a crowd at the Market she told them that she "believed that the Federal concept in the West Indies will persist out of sheer necessity for the national union of small territories in the world of today. I expect there will be much rethinking, revision of attitude after re-forming. Trinidad is a vital factor, and I trust that the leaders there will be generous and wise. The future is rather unpredictable because so much of West Indian politics is still founded on personal relations. Nevertheless, my confidence in the necessity for and the desirability of Federation is firm." But on January 27, 1962, Williams announced Trinidad's withdrawal from the Federation, explaining that it was the inevitable consequence of Jamaica's secession.

Williams's decision had come in the wake of meetings in Trinidad between Reginald Maudling, head of the British Colonial Office, and the chief ministers of the units, at which it became clear that if Trinidad were to secede, as it seemed certain to do, the remaining islands, the "Little Eight," would attempt to form a new federation. By January 23 the Federation appeared to be doomed, but a meeting between the chief ministers and Grantley Adams was scheduled for January 24, at which a final decision would be made. Hours before the scheduled time, however, Adams's secretary received a telephone call from another secretary intimating that the chief ministers had already been meeting that morning drafting the constitution for a new federation and would not be keeping their appointment with the Federal prime minister. Adams would not receive even the simple courtesy of a final visit from the chief ministers who helped bring his Federation down. It was "a tragic moment" for him and he had sat in his office "pathetically mumbling to his Ministers who themselves had little heart to comfort him." With little recourse, Maudling, meeting with the Federal cabinet on January 25, informed them of his intention to recommend to his government that an enabling act be passed in March, under which dissolution of the Federation would become effective in April by order of council. An interim commission would take over to administer the assets and liabilities, disengagement procedures, and a scheme covering relocation and compensation of officials. The members of the cabinet, Phyllis among them, were too stunned to remonstrate. There was no discussion or protest. With the "odor of failure" hanging heavy in the room, the prime minister had slumped forward, "staring dejectedly at one spot on the table before him, at the end stirring himself to mutter thanks to the Secretary of State." Twelve days later, on February 6, 1962, Maudling announced in the House of Commons the British government's decision to dissolve the Federation of the West Indies. On that day Phyllis wrote to her friend Mabel James, telling her that she was living under intense pressure, "like someone condemned to extinction!"

At the February 14 House meeting, Trinidad's secession and the possible continuation of the Federation with only "the Gallant Little Eight" were debated. A motion had been submitted to appoint a delegation "of both sides of the House to proceed immediately to England to represent the case for the continuance of the Federation." Phyllis was undecided about her support for the preservation of a Federation from which "others have—I nearly used the word 'absconded'—seceded. Trinidad for us is somewhat like the Trojan Horse: We have been betrayed from without and from within." She was doubtful "how useful this exercise will be," and had had to be persuaded to speak in favor of the motion for continuation of the Federation: "I support it unwillingly, hesitantly, loyally . . . for the simple reason that I fear it may be misinterpreted as an effort on our part to prolong a life which many of our friends think ought to be sinking into the grave."

Adams's delegation, meanwhile, proceeded to London, where they would receive treatment universally described as shameful. They scarcely had a courteous welcome. No Colonial Office official met them at the airport, and Adams had to wait five days before Maudling consented to see him. By then he had had the "excruciating experience" of attending the House of Lords session at which the Federation was dissolved.* Then came two "shattering embarrassments." The chief ministers of the Little Eight, then meeting in Barbados, had dispatched a telegram to the secretary of state desiring to record "in the most unequivocal manner that the present Federal Mission to London has not been authorized to speak or negotiate on behalf of the Leewards, the Windward Islands or Barbados." More devastatingly, without prior consultation with Adams, the Federal cabinet's financial powers were summarily withdrawn. At the February Federal House session the 1962 appropriation bill had been considered. At first it included merely token amounts for compensation and disengagement of civil servants and ministers. But before the bill was passed, the minister of finance, under pressure from House members, had substituted an amount of BWI $352,000 to pay compensation to Federal ministers and legislators. The enormous figure was intended to cover payments to each minister of one year's salary, their approved allowances, and the expenses of repatriation. All MPs and senators would similarly receive six months' salary and allowances. This was claimed to be reasonable compensation for politicians who suddenly found their income stopped without any opportunity of seeking immediate reelection. But the governor-general considered it a scandalous business, and after conferring with London, refused to give his assent to the bill. He referred the matter of ministers' compensation or pensions to the unit governments.

The Dominican government, under LeBlanc's guidance, passed a resolution expressing its "shock and indignation at the recent action of the Federal Government in voting ex gratia allowances for Federal Ministers and Members of Parliament." The resolution deplored the "egoistic" action as one "directly contrary to the established principles of Parliamentary Democracy," and one to be contradicted by "the consensus of world opinion." He used the incident to pillory Phyllis, as one additional piece of evidence of her greed and her desire to feather her nest. Rather than discuss the

*The second reading of the West Indies Bill (1962), dissolving the Federation, took place in the House of Lords on March 7, 1962. (The House of Lords had been chosen for this second and final presentation of the bill in order to accelerate the process.)

allowance of the small pension in his cabinet, he chose to chastise her and the Federal government in a public meeting, excoriating her for her rapacity. After getting the crowd riled he asked for a show of hands to indicate its disapproval of the request for a pension. This was Dominica's "vote" on the issue. Phyllis, when she learned of this, wrote to a friend that "such behaviour [had] made me very angry, and I am going to speak about it to the people when I return. All good people here are disgusted by this action." To another friend she wrote that the executive had sent word to the governor-general "to refuse money to Mr. [Archibald Angelo] Bellot [elected to the Federal House on LeBlanc's resignation] and myself (and others) so that we would have to go back to our homes without a cent, but please continue to have faith in God. I do not think our miseries can last forever." The reason for this unwarranted attack on Phyllis seems clear from the minutes of the party's executive meeting of February 23, 1962. The "future of the president" had been discussed, in the face of the threatened dissolution of the Federation, and the executive had given "the assurance that if there was to be an election, she would be the selected candidate for the candidature."

The press in Trinidad and throughout the Caribbean quickly seized upon the incident. Exaggerated reports on the amounts the legislators were proposing to vote themselves were published, and the incident soon became known as the "Federal payola." The ministers were publicly ridiculed. British reaction was as swift as it was extreme. On March 14, without any formal consultation with Adams, who was still in London, or the cabinet, an order in council was signed amending the constitution and releasing the governor-general from the obligation to act on advice from the Federal ministers, and the minister of finance in particular. Bradshaw immediately broadcast his intention to resign, but given the disparagement to which the ministers were being subjected in the press, he received no public sympathy. Privately Phyllis would describe the manner in which power was wrested away from him as "a very mean and treacherous thing." Adams was treated even more shabbily. He had learned of the British government's decision to oppose the appropriation bill in a hurried interview with Maudling. Not a word was said to him of the order in council removing financial powers, and he had to read the news in the London newspapers that night. In a letter to the British Colonial Office, he described the conduct of the British government "as a step backwards in the history of the West Indies, an arbitrary action, too hastily undertaken, and incompatible with the spirit of the federal constitution." In the House Bradshaw was to denounce another aspect of the "fishy" manner in which the "notorious" order had been issued. Advance local copies had been printed the very day of the announcement in the Federal Printery, a few yards away from his office, without him or any other minister having the slightest inkling of what was afoot.

Phyllis returned home in a state of frantic rage after the House adjourned. Her sister Rosalind, who had come for an extended visit during Carnival, did her best to calm her down. Contributing to her fury was the fact that Lord Hailes, whose role in the whole affair had been so pivotal and damaging, and his wife, whom Phyllis liked and respected, were scheduled to come to dinner at the Allfreys' the very next day. Livid with wrath at what she saw as treachery, Phyllis vowed to everyone who would listen that she would refuse to receive him, finally sending him a curt note telling him that he had not done enough to save the Federation and disinviting them. She told Rosalind as she dispatched the note that he had been "weak and wishy-washy." In reply Hailes sent his chauffeur with a gracious note declaring that they would not be "the slightest bit hurt if you thought it better for us not to dine" with her. But he pleaded their own heartache—"You must not think that [we] do not suffer too"—having also devoted themselves to the Federation "as best we knew how. . . . It is the West Indian people, with all their splendid qualities, which matter and which must cause anxiety." She relented and sent Nicholas, her driver, over with yet another note asking them to please join her for dinner after all, but warned Rosalind to stick to the British weather as a topic of conversation.

A week later Phyllis addressed the Federal House in a heartfelt eulogy on the collapse of her beloved Federation. "We Federal Members of Parliament and Ministers of the Federal Government," she proclaimed, her voice full of emotion, "are now numbered among the insulted and injured of this earth." The destruction of a nation, she declared, was "an abnormal catastrophe, and what has happened is that those who remained loyal to the idea of patriotic brotherhood have been monstrously engulfed and deliberately humiliated, while those who looked after their own interests and promoted selfish individualism ducked away from disaster." England was singled out for blame in the debacle, as a nation ready to spend "millions on armaments and in other devious stratagems to maintain the peace of the Commonwealth and the world," but too stingy to allocate $352,000 West Indies dollars for legislators

> who have been defrauded not only of their terms of office but of their nationhood; too high a price to pay for a dignified funeral service! . . . It would be well for everyone in this chain of islands with their mixed economies, mixed races, mixed feelings and mixed motives to reflect that the greatest struggle in the world today is centred around the equality of races. The Migrants Bill in Britain, the Order in Council, the tenseness in British Guiana and sometimes even in Trinidad, the forthcoming electoral struggle in Jamaica, the hideous murders in Algeria and the Congo are all a part of this desperate combat between the peoples of the world for egalitarian recognition. The West Indies appeared to be the nursery of a civilised and enlightened solution to a virtually intractable problem. Just as I am the symbol of tolerance which emanates from the grass roots of the people, so also in a deeper sense the Prime Minister is a symbol of tolerance to the world. One thing is flashing clear. An emergent nation may be destroyed, but the patriot's spirit, once aroused, overrides all boundaries of superficial difference. I am on the side of the affronted Minister of Finance and of the Prime Minister in this matter. We and our colleagues in the Cabinet and in the House of Representatives do truly represent the homogeneous peoples of the West Indies. They may strip us Federal Ministers and Members of honourable dues and even tie me to the stake in rags, but no one can deprive me of the signal and irrevocable honour of having been the first woman Minister in the first Federal Government of the West Indies. Let the rains fall on dry lands and holy feathers drop from the sky—the traces of our passage will not be obliterated.

On April 9–11th, 1962, the Federal Legislature held its final session. Sir Grantley Adams had insisted on one last meeting and had had to promise the governor-general to make it brief in order to save further waste of dignity and money. But the session opened with two-thirds of the members' seats vacant and a mere dozen curious spectators in the gallery. There was nothing of much substance to discuss other than the old record of recriminations and bitterness. Some found comfort in the news of Manley's defeat in the Jamaican elections the day before. Phyllis was not slow to join in, pointing the finger of blame at England. "The British Government has displayed a lamentable lack of understanding of the myriad-minded attitudes of our people," she would argue. "They have not tried to understand us. . . . They got tired of us and they put their money on the two so-called viable fragments of the whole, then they threw us overboard to sink." The one important thing salvaged from the debacle, she reminded her dwindling audience, was UCWI, which on April 2, 1962, became, by royal charter, an autonomous body to be known as the University of the West Indies (UWI). Since the Jamaican referendum, the location of the main campus of the university in Jamaica had become a source of concern for the Federation, and for Phyllis's ministry in particular. In the House's last meeting on April 11 she argued that the university was as of that moment still on nonrepublican terrain and there was yet time for the two campuses (one in Jamaica, the other in Trinidad) to be declared extraterritorial lands, as in the case of the United Nations. She would find comfort in years to come in the survival and expansion of the university she had helped build. Her final words in the House were in a tribute to the speaker of the House. "As the only woman on the Front Bench, and as the only female in this depleted House today, I should like to say how much I have appreciated your subtle directives in the conduct of this Honourable House and moreover those occasional touches of asperity and witticism delivered in the form of asides."

Phyllis's grieving for the Federation was a long process. In March, addressing young players at the opening of their cricket season, she had pleaded for a return of the brotherhood and fraternalism of "those who have awakened to the wider national idea . . . In politics as in sport the players in the match have to learn how to be good losers. They must never give up until the last possible moment, and if they are beaten, they will rise to prove the strength of their spirit and future intention." In her 1961 Christmas broadcast, with the writing on the wall plainly legible, she would give her most eloquent paean to the Federation, building on the symbolism of the pelican, the heraldic bird on the Federal coat of arms:

> There is a legend that the pelican restored to life its young ones destroyed by serpents by pecking at its own flesh and reviving them with its blood. As a born symbolist I was enchanted to see a Pelican in the waters of Chaguaramas last Sunday. . . . There are some who call the whole federal concept a failure. Are they not passing judgment too soon? Perhaps we West Indians did not begin humbly enough; perhaps we celebrated prematurely. And so . . . I stand with restraint in the high garden of the spirit and watch the Pelican, the bird of charity, floating in the waters of the future. Is she just searching for fish, or will she remake the disturbed nest and give her lifeblood for the brood of eight?

Some hope remained for the concept of Federation, although not perhaps for Phyllis's career as a Federal minister, in the ongoing negotiations for a Federation of the Little Eight. As she wrote to Mabel James, "a Federation of the Eight [was] better than no federation at all." Since the January meetings with Secretary of State Maudling, negotiations had progressed and definite proposals had emerged from a meeting of delegates in Barbados in late February. If plans proceeded as scheduled, the new Federation, whose capital would be in Barbados, would come into being and receive its independence as early as January 1963. The British government, however, remained very cautious, and it would take several months before London would become convinced of the feasibility of the proposals. Agreeing to the new scheme, the Colonial Office stated that the Federation's new constitution ought to grant the central government appropriate powers and that the Federation would have to achieve economic and financial stability before claiming sovereignty. Debates, meetings, and conferences started anew. The next meeting of the heads of local Caribbean governments with Maudling took place in London on May 9–24, 1962, and the basic governmental principles were settled on and sent to local parliaments for approval. A regional council of ministers was set up, presided over by the governor of Barbados and comprising the local chief ministers. The council, as was assumed, could later on become the basis for the future Federal government. These efforts however, would collapse in 1965, and the Federation of the Little Eight would never come to be. But even in 1962, when the new Federation appeared a certainty, it seemed very clear to Phyllis that she would have no role in this new scheme. In May she would write with remarkable prescience to her friend Marjorie Nicholson in London that she had "no further Federal elections to look forward to in the larger sense. I exclude any opportunities which the Little Eight may offer, since I think they will reject the old Feds. In other words, we shall return home labelled as failures, whether we have done good jobs or not, and it may be four years before we make a comeback."

Throughout the Federation's slow collapse, Phyllis struggled to maintain a semblance of domestic normalcy in a household that now contained two children. Sonia was thriving in Trinidad, and though her grandmother, in great financial need, hoped she would earn some money to help the family in Laudat, Phyllis had done everything to forestall the moment when Sonia would have to do something to make her living. Although barely fourteen, she had reached the age at which a poor West Indian girl was seen as fit to work. But she seemed happy in school and was a promising student, so Phyllis sent word to Edith that she was exploring part-time employment opportunities for her, but she "must not expect Sonia to earn a lot of money at first because . . . she is too young to do a full-time job [and they] had just spent thirty dollars equipping her with clothes and shoes. She now has three beautiful new dresses (made by Sésé), black shoes, underwear and so forth. In fact, she looks a very pretty young lady! I will encourage her to save when she starts earning, so that she can send a little money back to Laudat regularly." But by then Phyllis was in the process of legally adopting Sonia, and meant to give her, as far as she was able, the opportunities she gave her own Phina: an education, leisure, and support.

A few months later, while on a constituency visit to the Carib Territory, Phyllis had met the six-year-old Carib boy who would become her second adopted child. David, the son of Mr. and Mrs. Decius Benjamin of Bataca, had been chosen to hand her a bouquet of flowers, and she, charmed by the flowers and the boy, thanked him warmly, wishing she had a little boy just like him. Mrs. Benjamim, a warm, motherly woman with a brood of children, replied half in jest that she could have him along with the flowers. Phyllis took her at her word, and before the visit concluded ascertained that she would indeed place him under her care. It was all arranged quite casually, so that when she returned to Trinidad she took the boy with her. There as with Sonia, she and Robert would begin the process of legal adoption. There now dwelled together under one rooftree, as Phyllis would state during a December 1961 broadcast, "persons of varied ages, four religions, and three or more races. This is our personal solution to the world's strife—learning to treat your neighbor as a real friend or as a child of the house. Mere theorising is not enough." As she had done with Sonia, Phyllis worked hard at keeping the bonds between the child and his biological family strong, assuring Mrs. Benjamin that, as soon as David could write real letters, "I will encourage him to write to you both." She wrote to Mrs. Benjamin as soon as she and the boy arrived in Trinidad to reassure her that he was well and cheerful and had done nothing but smile and laugh. Phyllis had bought him a toy airplane, a ball, a boat, and books to write and draw in, and he was to sleep in the same room as Sonia, so he wouldn't be lonely. David, a sensitive, soft-spoken boy, would develop a close relationship with Robert, a bond begun when he took the child, within days of his arrival, for a thorough medical examination and to have two sores on his feet treated. She was soon writing to friends to tell them that David was going to school and had met a lot of children. "His conversation is splendid, and when we return to Dominica, we will certainly continue to keep him with us and educate him." She kept his parents abreast of his progress, writing in April 1962 that the child could now write his name and was learning his letters. He was learning to play cricket and knew "quite a few prayers and songs."

As the Federation collapsed, Phyllis began to rethink her literary career. She had not published any new poetry or fiction since 1960. But now, as she examined the options open to her after she left Trinidad, writing seemed the most viable path. On March 21, 1962, "the day of my probable resignation as a Federal Minister," she sent a partial manuscript of *In the Cabinet*, the autobiographical account of her experiences in the Federation, to her agents at Curtis Brown. "It looks as if I shall have plenty of time in which to finish that book soon," she wrote, and "I hope to be able to send you a few more [sections] from Trinidad before I go into exile." There was soon little left to do but to pack up and leave. In April, Phyllis and the other ministers had to submit to inventories of their household furnishings and appliances. A secretary from Dominica who worked in the Information Office of the Federal government later told her of how she went into her section while it was being "cleaned out" during the change-over from Federal House to Trinidad House. With "hot tears pour[ing] from her eyes," she had seen "stacks of files ceiling high, into which months and years of her own hard work had gone," being dragged out to be burned, hardly being sorted "for historical treasures." To add to Phyllis's disappointments, she was to have been made a chevalier de la Légion d'Honneur, and the French consul general had already made the announcement, but the governor-general had inexplicably vetoed it as he had the right to do. Hailes may have felt it to be counterproductive to have one of the Federal ministers so honored at a time when the Federation was being dissolved; but the circumstances were not conducive to her listening to his explanations. Within days of his decision the consul general—with whom Phyllis, as president of the local branch of the Alliance Française, had become very friendly—died unexpectedly, adding grief to her anger and disappointment. On May 10 there was a somber, tearful good-bye gathering at the prime minister's home. Representatives and ministers mingled even as the packing of Adams's personal belongings proceeded.

On May 16 Phyllis and her family left Trinidad. She did not know upon leaving whether she would return to Trinidad before the dissolution of the Federation in June, but as she wrote to an acquaintance, "Demain-jour ça c'est un jour douleureux." She was indeed devastated. The Federation "had seemed to legitimise her own sense of West Indian-ness" and given her the chance to be "a little bit great." Now she was returning home as "an endangered species": still "a romantic spirit, squeezed between her own colour and class and the sense of social and economic justice that drove her to politics, an idealist," but now politically "homeless," deprived of the "brief lodging" her internationalist brand of politics had found in the "doomed West Indies Federation."

Part V

AFTER GOD IT'S THE LAND

Apres Bondié c'est la Ter,
said the boy to his mater.
Apres sisserou *[the parrot on Dominica's crest]* c'est crapaud,
said the cow to the buffalo.
Apres Bondié c'est la Ter,
said the boy's gloomy pater.
But he paused for a drink
and fell over the brink,
to the depth of the crater.
It is later than you think.

Eleven

For Theirs Is the Power

The kingdom can never belong
To just one man and his throng:
The kingdom, so secret and rare,
Is yet a republic to share.

In early June 1962 Phyllis, Robert, and the children left the former Federal capital by the ancient French liner *Colombie*, sailing into "a State of Obscurity." Her "name-calling days" were over. The dismantling of their "struggling little nation" had been "a sad affair." "[A] dispiritedness had fallen over the old scene" as friend after friend retreated in defeat, and she spent the days on board laying in her bunk musing over the final weeks while Robert entertained the children on deck. On their arrival in Roseau they were met at the bayfront by Aunt Maggie, Chris Loblack, and a small group of faithful political friends. They had staggered up the St. Aroment hill in a rumbling hired car—the old private drive was now a public road lined with houses—to their new home at Baobab House, which Celia and Jack had built for Elfreda on the grounds of St. Aroment. They had reached an agreement to share the bungalow with Aunt Mags who, now in her eighties, was ill and frail after two serious heart attacks. It was an arrangement that would soon turn sour. Phyllis insisted that "despite her old racial prejudices" Aunt Mags had taken quite a liking to Sonia and David and had grown very fond of them both. But when writing *In the Cabinet*, she would charge that her old aunt had immediately begun to treat Sonia as a "sweet little superior maid." They complained to all and sundry about their "utter lack of privacy" and the constant reminders that Baobab House was not their home. There were also myriad petty annoyances: The hedges were cut without consulting them; they could not take a shower without being overlooked by the tenants in St. Aroment; when they sat on their own veranda they overlooked another neighbor's bathroom; they were reproached if they rearranged the furniture. Aunt Mags's persistent reminders of their subservient position in the household seemed to them a deliberate attempt to undermine their authority and consequently their ability to discipline the children. It was all "too much strain." After three far from blissful years they declared the situation intolerable and reached a compromise with Celia to move to the old boiler house at the estate, from where they could keep an eye on Aunt Mags while maintaining some degree of independence. The ruined boiler house was very cool, shady, and pleasant, but not the best place when it rained—and in Dominica it rains often—as the two ends of the roof were full of large holes that flooded the floor below. The children slept in relative dryness upstairs, while Phyllis and Robert slept in an annex, but they had no proper living room, and their books, ornaments, and papers were "all around getting damp and full of cockroaches." All the joints of the rafters, beams, posts, and joists were rotten with either termites or damp, and Robert feared the whole lot would come down at the first hurricane lash. But at least they had their privacy.

It took some time for all the strains leading to their move to the boiler house to surface, however, and in the weeks following their return to Dominica, finding herself settled so near her old familiar home, Phyllis could not conceal her excitement at being back, declaring herself to be "as happy as [a] skylark." Robert, who had been "rather miserable" in Trinidad, was "luxuriating in the cool sunny climate, the swimming, and the general atmosphere." In those first few weeks he would hike in the hills gathering wildflowers "with great zest," guided by some old notes left in small leatherbound notebooks by her grandfather Sir Henry Nicholls. Phyllis, in turn, was quite sanguine about the future, fully expecting to be a candidate at any forthcoming by-election or at the very latest at the next general election, scheduled for January 1966. If successful she assumed she would be appointed to a ministerial post, perhaps even that of chief minister.

In the meantime they were poor, having received no "golden handshake or pension" from the Federation, and the children, Sonia particularly, felt the change acutely. Phyllis remembered these "marvelous nostalgic lines" from a letter her daughter was writing to her English pen pal: "Once we lived quite grandly, and Dave and I had tea with Lord and Lady Hailes, but Dave refused to ride their donkey, as Caribs don't like donkeys, they like boats." Now they lived in a small bungalow on the old family estate and had "an antique fridge." Phyllis and Robert were no less aware of having stepped down in the world. Aunt Mags would remind them constantly of their folly in saddling themselves at their age with two young children they could barely support, and more than once Phyllis had been pestered by questions about the children from friends and acquaintances. She had been particularly miffed when her old friend Mabel James suggested "rather rudely" that now that they were so poor they should return them to their homes. Mabel had gotten a tart reply for her pains.

Phyllis and Robert had returned to Roseau with little in savings and no job prospects. Soon after their arrival, therefore, they both gratefully accepted part-time teaching jobs at Wesley High School, teaching fifteen- and sixteen-year-olds "for a pittance." Phyllis taught literature; Robert, geography and mathematics. The young girls soon declared him to be "an unbearable bore," as "non-descript" a teacher as she was "effervescent." She was "almost mesmerizing"; he was "her shadow." One of her young students, Judith Pestaina, remembers her as "tiny and full of life," . . . "very effusive about everything she said, [and] totally taken up with literature." In class she would get carried away by her topic, bringing literature and literary characters to vivid life, putting "her whole self" into her work. Phyllis indeed relished her task, and would invite the girls to her house for tea—"like something out of the nineteenth century, like playing a role"—where they would discuss Wordsworth and Keats, Daniel Thaly (the Dominican poet she had known since her childhood), Dante Gabriel Rossetti, and her old favorite, Auden. She would always boast that her girls did extremely well: "All my girls have gone right to the top."

Within weeks of Phyllis's return to Dominica the Labour party celebrated its seventh anniversary. She was present for the festivities although no longer as the principal speaker. Relegated now to the quasi-honorary position of president and founder of the party—the real power resting with LeBlanc as political leader—she gave a brief speech asking for a minute of silence in memory of her recently-deceased uncle Ralph Nicholls, "without whose pioneering activities on behalf of trade unionism the Labour movement in Dominica could not have advanced." It would be her last hurrah with the party she had founded and nurtured. Just over three months later she would find herself expelled.

Phyllis's return to Dominica had been the cause of much uneasiness among a party executive committee eager to consolidate its power. Young, male, and race conscious, LeBlanc and his supporters "wanted to make sure their leadership was trenched." Phyllis, still a popular political figure despite the "Federal fiasco," represented a very real threat to their power, as she "could always have appealed to the Party membership and [LeBlanc] would have had to relinquish his position." To LeBlanc, reputed to be "anti-white" and "not comfortable with or in favour of white people," the prospect of surrendering his power to a white woman must not have been a congenial one, particularly as he had begun to use race as a political issue, often denouncing in his speeches the continuing power held by whites on the island. (The argument was as effective as it was disingenuous, as Dominica had a tiny and not particularly prosperous white population. Real power had for many years rested with the *gros-bourg*.) He had begun an inner-party campaign against her many months before, and his efforts to marginalize her only intensified after her return. She was not far off the mark when she told a friend that "the [officers of the party], unknown to [her], had plotted to get rid of [her] by a *putsch*, and tried hard to make an excuse." She would hand them the reason they so eagerly sought through her connection with the *Dominica Herald*, the newspaper whose editor she became shortly after her return.

Phyllis and Robert had been back in Dominica but a few days when they learned that the *Herald*, to which she had had the first subscription when it started publication in 1955, was in great difficulties, lacking financial stability and an editor who could "draw." The former they could not remedy, but they felt capable of supplying the latter; thus, when the offer came, they accepted it "not gladly, but with relief." Phyllis took on the editorship for "nationalistic reasons," sensing that if Robert had done so she would have left herself open to accusations of having made it possible for an Englishman to influence public opinion. "No one could really touch me," she once explained, "such as deporting me if they dislike my editorials etc.—because I *belonged*, and my people landed in these parts before the Africans." Robert, however, as she confessed to all, did most of the work of editing and management, while she provided two little editorials weekly, "and—alas—got most of the credit." The editing of the newspaper had been like a gift from heaven, offering her a forum for public commentary and placing her prominently in public life after the debacle of the federal enterprise. Financially, however, it was not a wonderful opportunity as it paid Robert a paltry BWI $35.00 a week, while Phyllis worked for $1.00 a year. In *In the Cabinet*, she would write: "There began a totally distasteful life for Joan, who detested journalism and had to nerve herself to correct poor contributions and to listen interminably to radio news. Three years of that! How did I bear it." To Polly Pattullo she would explain that journalism was "a different experience to writing" for her; it was not "romantic enough." "When I edited Dominica's little paper, *The Herald*, it revolved around very petty, small-island politics, and after the politics of the federation, it all seemed rather tame."

The *Herald* was a struggling biweekly owned by J. Margartson Charles, a blind old man who ran the paper out of a building which also housed his rum shop. It had a circulation of 1,750 copies per issue (Robert felt that the number could be increased to 2,500) and was in considerable debt, owing about BWI $2,500 (a considerable debt, as a copy sold for five cents). The paper operated "in a sort of chicken coop with five hand-setters of type, and Phyllis had a sort of "matchbox editorial office," which was always full of people; but her dearest hope was that one day she and Robert "would entirely own the little press." Then—Robert often joked—he would be "a bloated capitalist like everyone else!" Phyllis quickly managed to use her editorial forum as a path to controversy. She had been at the helm of the *Herald* only a few weeks when she had sprung to the defense of a "rather timorous" young English schoolmaster accused of kicking a black boy who had pestered him in the classroom. In the early 1960s, with the reverberations of the American civil rights movement reaching the Caribbean, the "shocking matter" of the young white teacher's assault on a black boy quickly became a cause célèbre. Phyllis was quick to jump into the fray, declaring publicly her belief that the young man acted "spontaneously and out of anguish" and that he was being "most unjustly treated." It was a situation that "[could] not be allowed to pass unnoticed." The "very lovely and kind outcome" had been that all the teachers in the grammar school—"from ebony to coffee"—manifested their support for the English "victim," "which shows that there is some multiracial spirit of justice around." Privately she confessed that she had never defended "a more despicable person."

The editorials she wrote for the *Herald* provided her with a biweekly forum to address issues that dominated political and social debate in Dominica. Foremost among these were the racial tensions that were beginning to dominate the climate of island society, a deplorable state of affairs that she placed solidly on LeBlanc's shoulders, spearheaded by what was generally seen as his antagonism to whites and his using race as the means of polarizing the electorate and solidifying the DLP's support. One of her outspoken editorials would play perfectly into LeBlanc's hands and result in her expulsion from the Dominica Labour party. In August 1962 the Labour-controlled legislature had passed a law imposing a 15 percent tax on all banana cargoes leaving Dominica. Phyllis, in what was otherwise a rather mild editorial, questioned the wisdom of a legislature imposing an export tax on what was principally a peasant crop. The editorial, entitled "Green Blood," underscored the advisability of building feeder roads to facilitate the movement of banana crops to market ("heading" was still the most common method) and of choosing better fertilizers to increase productivity and more effective plant-disease control methods. It was fairly innocuous except for a phrase the party would find extremely offensive: "Government might finish with the old foolishness, practiced nowhere else in the world, of taxing exports."

The party executive did not immediately declare the editorial objectionable; they would in fact not react for almost a month, not until after opposition jibes had brought it repeatedly to their attention and Phyllis had submitted to the party leadership a document charging that the DLP was "falling down on basic principles, as well as organization, in particular over their attitude to human rights." The opposition jibes furnished LeBlanc with the opportunity he had been awaiting since her return to "put . . . an end to her political aspirations"; her critical document of September 20, with its clear references to her objections to racial polarization, reminding him all the while that she represented an obstacle to his complete control of the party's policies and direction. Under Clause V, Subsection 6, of the party's constitution—"Any member who breaks the rules of this Party or offends against its constitution and policy will be liable to immediate expulsion by the officers of the Party"—Phyllis had left herself open to dismissal.

Word of the expulsion, broadcast by West Indies Broadcasting System (WIBS) news in the early evening of September 25, "struck the citizens of Roseau like a thunderbolt." It was front-page news in all the island newspapers for that week. Phyllis was, after all, one of the best known politicians on the island, not to mention the founder and president of the party from which she was being banished, the Party then in power. In the midst of the storm she remained calm, not believing that the party's executive committee would go along with such a harsh punishment for such a mild offense. Not that she had been naive or blind to LeBlanc's purposes. Soon after her return to the island she had written to a friend that she and Robert had to be "very wary" as "several people are trying to trap us into doing something wrong—don't ask me *what*!" But she had not thought that such a "state of siege" could last forever, nor had she estimated correctly LeBlanc's success in undermining her prestige and authority with the executive, many of whom she had brought into politics and trained as politicians and could not believe would pay her back with such disloyalty and betrayal. In a state of disbelief she fired off a letter asking the party secretary, Arnold Active, to call a meeting on September 28. He replied, almost insultingly in her eyes, that "the tenor of your letter proposing a date for a meeting is unacceptable and *ultra vires*. If you so desire you may appeal in writing to the Executive who will appoint a date for such a meeting." He sent a copy of the letter to the *Chronicle*, which quickly bannered a LABOUR PARTY PRESIDENT SNUBBED: APPEAL NOT DISCUSSION ASKED across its front page. She did appeal, and a meeting was scheduled for October 5. "Mrs. Allfrey's expulsion has been received with mixed feeling, and several supporters have criticized it," heralded the *Chronicle* sententiously in its announcement of the forthcoming meeting, "on the other hand there are those who view it as a move in the right direction and as a party prestige booster." The appeal process would be condemned by Chris Loblack as "undemocratic" and "decided in advance." LeBlanc's supporters had calculated very carefully their assured votes and those they expected would go to her from among the fourteen members of the executive, and had planned their strategy accordingly. LeBlanc himself would be "off-island" when the meeting took place. He had excused himself from attending with the claim that, although he had not signed the letter of expulsion, he had authorized it. It was widely rumored at the time that he had escaped to Barbados so as not to be present when the final decision was taken, but had informed the executive before leaving that if they listened to any argument in her favor he would resign the chief ministry, and the government (and their jobs) "would break up." Knowing that the chair would not be able to vote except in the case of a tie, the leadership of the executive, "in the interest of fairness," appointed Party Secretary Active (whom they believed would support Phyllis) as chair, effectively neutralizing his vote. They had also discussed in advance plans for riling Loblack, whose tendency to storm out of meetings when infuriated was well known, as further assurance that they would have the votes required to dismiss her.

After a discussion of the case, lasting one and a half hours, Phyllis was called in to present her appeal. She argued that she had not attacked the party, and that, in fact, in the last paragraph of her editorial she had praised the island's political stability. The officers of the party, through her expulsion, had brought the government into far greater disrepute. The editorial's real attack, she claimed, was against the "old colonial foolishness" of imposing any export tax at all, such imposition being "a disincentive to production." She conceded that the editorial could have been better worded, since it had implied a minor criticism of the government in the use of the word "foolishness," something she regretted. But it was an unheard-of thing for the founder and president of a party to be expelled "without preamble of courtesy, prior discussion, or warning," especially as she had repeatedly been elected president by the membership and such a move should have been preceded by a resolution to be discussed by the executive and the Annual General Meeting of the party. The officers' behavior amounted to "shockingly unkind and inhuman treatment of the first friend the Party ever had." She spoke of freedom of the press, pointing out that the salaried MPs in England were quick to publish minor criticism of their party and the government in the press without retaliation. She held no such position. To bolster her arguments she quoted a letter she had received recently from Dominica's public relations officer, which assured her that it was not the policy of the government to interfere with the running of a free press. She appealed for the "mending of broken good relations" for the sake of the party and the people, reminding them that "this sordid expulsion" would lead to lack of trust and damage not confined to Dominica alone. Finally she had asked the executive to compromise by withdrawing the expulsion decision in favor of a mild vote of censure "since no one was superhuman or perfect." Her arguments, however rational or convincing, were bound to fall on deaf ears as the editorial had been but a pretext for LeBlanc and his followers to gain absolute control of the party. During the heated discussion that followed her departure, Chris Loblack, as anticipated, allowed himself to be taunted into a fury and stalked out. Without this "blunder," Arnold Active believes there might have been a tie, and he as chair would have voted to allow Phyllis to remain in the party. But that was not to be, and the decision went overwhelmingly against her with a vote of nine in favor, one against, and three abstentions.

She took the decision "very badly." It would not have been like her to do anything disparaging, and she did not, but from that moment on she kept herself entirely away from the executive. Her feeling of betrayal was evident to all; she would never speak to most of them again. She had put a lot of effort into the creation of the party, Ducreay recalls, a "bold, very courageous decision" that had left her "open to abuse" and had required "great bravery." To have that courage repaid by expulsion had been heartbreaking to her. At the time he had pushed for her expulsion, believing that "once she'd done her share [the party had become] a public thing" which she could not have hoped or expected to control. But he had known even as it was being set into motion that had she remained in the party she would most likely have been found to be "the person most fit to lead" at the following elections. The expulsion had not been about the editorial but about control of the party, and—given its tremendous following in the early 1960s—about control of the government and of the political direction Dominica would follow in the coming decades. It had been, her erstwhile enemy Edward Scobie remembers, nothing but "an act of treachery" motivated "quite simply by a jostling for power. The clear alternative had been that at the next election she would have become the prime minister." LeBlanc and his supporters had operated throughout "as if the party could not tolerate this white woman coming from England to be Prime Minister"; but in this they were willfully misreading what the party membership was ready to accept. "She was always accepted by the electorate," Scobie recalls; no rejection of her as a leader ever surfaced among the people.

In order to undermine her as a leader LeBlanc had waged a multiflanked attack.

The DLP, Scobie recollects, "played dirty" and "crucified her in the eyes of the people." They would ridicule her looks, her age, her mannerisms. They accused her of a mania for power, of wanting to control the party to suit her needs, needs that revolved, according to her enemies within the party, around a continuation of white power. They exploited her occasionally patronizing airs and remarks as evidence of her conviction that she still belonged to the Royal family of Dominica. The most serious challenge came in connection to her ability to lead and govern. Despite the fact that she had proven her leadership abilities in organizing and bringing the party to power barely six years after its creation—her more than creditable performance as a minister in the Federation notwithstanding—they presented her to the executive and the people as not capable of sustaining a government. They adopted her old political rival Frank Baron's contention that she lacked the "strength of character to lead a country . . . [that] she didn't have the gumption to do what was unpopular." In Baron's opinion she was, "like Jimmy Carter" some years later, "too ready to do what the populace would like."

The expulsion from the party was to stay with her for the rest of her life. Scobie once remarked that one of her faults was that "she would never forget any wrong," and indeed this was one she would never bring herself to put behind her. It would to her dying day be like an open sore. LeBlanc himself she could never forgive. She and Loblack had made him what he was, hence her rage "at having their creature turn against her." His betrayal would always stand as the most flagrant example of perfidy and treachery she would come to know. From then on she would tell "anyone and everyone" that Edward LeBlanc "[had done] her dirty," and he would be the butt of many a stinging remark about his policies and leadership. All those who remember the events leading to her expulsion and beyond—Alec Ducreay, Edward Scobie, Arnold Active, Chris Loblack, Lennox Honychurch, Eugenia Charles—believed that she "harbored her resentment about the expulsion into everything she did subsequently, from the founding of the *Star* to the creation of the Freedom Party." Of the party she had founded she would write in *In the Cabinet* that it had been "*damned* because they got it for their own ends . . . and turned it from a broad social democratic movement into something approaching nationalist Black Power." Phyllis was left with the cold comfort of believing that throughout the very public and often humiliating affair the electorate had sided with her. This to her had been proven true when Roseau had a town council election immediately after the expulsion and "the poor old decapitated Labour Party" had lost every seat, handing over control "to a bunch of so-called racketeers." And this, she claimed, because the electors abstained from voting "to show their displeasure at the way [she has] been treated." The whole thing had been "a fearful blow," and she had thought of what the white South Africans had said to her at Geneva: "Wait until those people get on top and they will turn around and kick you. . . . But every day I would see the loyal dogged faces of the laborers in the street, and hear the little asides they said, and after the town council election, I know they had their own way of making amends for a minority. This made me feel very happy and grateful."

In the months following the expulsion, Phyllis repeatedly published supportive letters to the editor in the *Herald*, keeping her dismissal fresh in the eyes of the readers. "The ordinary members consider the loss of you as a betrayal," wrote "A Native of Roseau" in November. "They have made a very bad mistake," wrote another supporter. An "Ex-Minister of Government from Barbados" argued that it had not been the result of something she had done "but a question of colour. Unfortunately there is a group in our West Indies who still cannot accept people different from them in colour regardless of how liberal the white person may be." In November she wrote an editorial titled "The Absentee," in which she addressed her absence from the Labour party's Annual General Meeting, or rather the absence of the spirit of their early crusade "founded on fraternal kindness towards all mankind." Efforts would be made at the convention, she prophesied, to change the very nature and structure of the Party, and it would never again be what it was meant to be: "a socialist party founded on the pursuit of the brotherhood of man and equality of the races and the sexes. . . . If that is missing what is left save opportunity?"

After the expulsion Phyllis's efforts were focused on raising funds to buy the *Herald*. With the prospect of a political career vanishing now that she no longer had a party to support her, ownership of the newspaper was becoming "a matter of future or no future" to her and Robert. Not wanting to borrow any money, she hoped to raise the necessary funds (BWI $800, just under US $500) by appealing to her American friends Adèle Olyphant and Janie Nichols to help her arrange for the sale in New York of her small collection of jewelry, consisting mostly of not-very-valuable pieces she had received as a Federal minister (a Canadian official, for example, had presented her with a gold maple-leaf brooch). It was "desperately important to do so quickly" as there were forces "trying to wrest the paper from [them]." By late 1963 the paper, although not free from debt, was struggling out of the morass of the years before. The circulation had "more than doubled," and advertising revenue was increasing. But there were threats to their continued tenure as editors, and she had focused on Edward Scobie, her old friend from the war days, as the source of most of their troubles. He had returned home at LeBlanc's invitation to organize a national festival, and, once in Roseau, had been approached by Margartson Charles with the suggestion that he become the paper's assistant editor. Phyllis and Robert seemed to have greeted his arrival with cool grace, but tensions quickly surfaced between them, particularly about politics. She was particularly annoyed, especially after her estrangement from the Labour party, at Scobie's frequent assertion that LeBlanc was "the only true politician in Dominica," and watched his growing intimacy with Margartson Charles with apprehension. Charles was "easily influenced on most matters," particularly by the patrons of his rum shop, where he himself "imbibed quite a bit." To Adèle she would say that "a regular Black Muslim agent [Scobie] had crept in, drank a lot with the old blind man—and all was wrecked." Scobie, who had frequently reported on the American civil rights movement, was very conversant with the rhetoric of racial struggle beginning to ensconce itself in Dominican political discourse. Phyllis and Robert saw him as a supporter of the island's burgeoning black power movement, and saw behind his actions against them the specter of racial tensions that LeBlanc had so dangerously roused. Robert would comment to a friend that Scobie seemed to be "living up to the black shirt he always wears: some of his diatribes sound like Black Muslim stuff."

Her anxieties over the newspaper were exacerbated by complications arising from her falling-out with Edward LeBlanc. The *Herald*'s major creditor was Margartson Charles's adopted son, "*not* a reliable man," and in fact "the brother-in-law of my worst political enemy [LeBlanc], the perfidious Chief Minister whom I helped to power on United Nations principles, but who immediately used this power to destroy my influence and persecute white people." Hence the urgency with which she appealed to Adèle and Janie for their help: "If you could advance me [U.S.] $250 and Janie the same I would be *rescued*." Correspondence between the three friends in the early weeks of 1964 was frequent, almost urgent, as Phyllis tried to keep them abreast of a rapidly changing situation. The efforts had left her "exhausted and strained (as if I'd made a public confession of impoverished failure)": "All the talk about how the *Herald* can't make a big profit has made me somewhat low in spirit," she wrote to Adèle in January, "and alarmed me about borrowing any money for its sake just now. It would be better if you did not lend us anything under present circumstances, and just let us continue to struggle along as at the moment." Adèle and Janie, however, had already sent their checks when this last letter was dispatched, and Phyllis accepted the money "with bashful feelings of gratitude," despite the fact that Janie's check was accompanied by a note chiding her for her continued requests for help. But the battle over the *Herald* was ultimately lost, and they walked away from it without a chance of recovering the BWI $900 they had invested in it. The break had been precipitated by a letter from Charles to Robert concerning the expenditures of the *Herald* for 1964—when the paper sustained a loss. This "unhealthy state of affairs," he argued, "cannot not continue indefinitely," and he informed him of his decision to take control of the cash and accounts as of July 1. "Under the circumstances I shall inform the Manager of the Royal Bank of Canada that all cheques drawn on the *Herald*'s account shall no longer bear the signatures of yourself or that of your wife as was customary in the past." Robert, livid at the public humiliation the withdrawal entailed, refused to countenance the implied insult, which they believed had been the direct result of Scobie's scheming. They both resigned in protest. "Had we just lain down and kept quiet (the simplest thing)," she wrote to Adèle, "we would have been untrue to hundreds of West Indians who think this colour hatred is trash, as well as untrue to our whole life's work."

If Phyllis felt any desire for revenge on Scobie she got her opportunity a few months later. He had returned to Dominica with his two young daughters, five and three, leaving his English wife behind in London. The latter, "driven by her anxiety over the well-being of her daughters and a longing to have them in her care," armed herself with an order from the British courts giving her custody of the children and engineered a daring "rescue": She flew into Dominica, hired a car, presented her papers at the courthouse, drove to the children's school, put them into the car, and drove straight back to the airport, whence they returned to England. Phyllis narrated the dramatic events on the front page of the *Dominica Star*, the newspaper she started shortly after leaving the *Herald*, calling it the "Drama of the Week." "For those gentlemen in Dominica who tend to underestimate the power and capacity for effective planning of a woman," she concluded, "the message is clear. A woman's determination, fired by love and grief, will overcome all obstacles. . . . We regret the whole tragic business. But we are also very glad that Harriet and Amanda are with their mother again."

Phyllis's immediate response to her expulsion had been to seek to found a new political party, the Star, a step motivated, as she would admit quite frankly, by "sheer revenge on a perfidious group of bastards!" She wondered all the while whether she was "trying to commit suicide or to salvage something magnificent"—"a persistent pursuit of [her] vision of the good life." She had taken steps to register the star as a political party symbol, but it had been kept off the electoral list "by a policy of negation." Having been advised by counsel that a simple legislative act could add it to the list, Chris Loblack had submitted a motion to that effect in the legislature. But it had found no seconder and had not even been debated. Foiled in her efforts to register the fledgling new party, in 1965 Phyllis decided to run as the independent Labour candidate for the Roseau North District. With elections scheduled for January 7, 1966, she campaigned heavily, speaking repeatedly throughout Roseau on issues such as the situation in Rhodesia, the DUPP, and "her present day opinion of the Dominica Labour Party." During the campaign, Scobie, who had replaced her as editor of the *Herald*, had published an article by Wallace W. Plenderleith, "Power Politics in Dominica," from which he had deleted a number of positive references to her. She mischievously printed sections of the original version in the *Star*, underscoring the portions Scobie had omitted:

> Time, energy and planning was devoted to the formation of this [Labour] Party, *and by a very capable woman, too. She started from scratch, came along step by step over the trying years. The obstacles in her way were many. Humiliation was great. She did not quit. She was determined to have good representation for the people. Good Government by the people. Her intentions were honest, her sincerity sound: above all she was capable. A leader one could look up with admiration.* Supporters grew slowly, mainly from the lowly man. The so-called ELITE would not join. Alas! At their first general election the Party lost out. *Saddest of all,* the Political woman leader herself was not returned at that election. The Labour Party is divided among itself now. It is in a state of chaos. They have no leadership *since the founder and original leader was dropped for voicing her views (and rightly so) over the 15% surtax on the exportation of bananas. But was she really and truly dropped for this reason? Oh no. It was bright as day. The West Indies Federation was a flop; she returned home to Dominica to pilot and guide her own Party forward to higher heights. This could not be—'she must be kept out of this now. Her usefulness is over! The child is ours now. She will teach the child to walk in righteousness for Dominica's sake. We don't want this to happen. We must manage the child our way'—some Labour Executives demanded.*

In a front page editorial in the *Star* she also addressed the incessant accusations by her former colleagues that she was a Communist. "In Catholic Dominica," she argued:

> Communist means anti-God, anti-religion, anti-anything that is decent, established and respectable. . . . The Editor of the *Star* intends to take part in the general election. If anyone dares to call her a Communist, she will not only call them back mischief-making communist types who wish to disturb the peace, but she will take rapid, spectacular action, and can call upon two British Cabinet Ministers and one retired West Indian Prime Minister to vouch for her political integrity—which resources will not be available to her detractors. We advise anyone else who may suffer from similar insults not to 'take it easy' any more. Not in Dominica. Not today."

Phyllis's campaign efforts would be swept away, like those of virtually all other candidates, in the Labour party's landslide victory in the 1966 elections. Of the eleven seats in the legislature, only one was secured by the opposition. She was mortified at the overwhelming triumph, especially since she had pulled out all stops in her efforts to disparage LeBlanc. In one of her last editorials for the *Herald* as the country was preparing for the elections, she had likened him to Hitler and Mussolini. LeBlanc had startled her by declaring that "there [had] been no corruption" in Dominica. When Lord Acton had said "power corrupts and absolute power corrupts absolutely," she wrote, he had been referring "to what is known in modern parlance as the paranoia of power-unbalanced politicians": "Hitler and Mussolini were very corrupt men, yet they were constantly boasting what good roads and railways they built and that they were put into power by God. If, for example, we pursue the word corruption in its 'improbity' form, what synonyms do we find? *Perfidy, betrayal, double-dealing, treachery and unfairness.* We ask the public: has Government really fulfilled its claim to have eliminated corruption in our community? If so, we are living in an island paradise."

In 1966, however, LeBlanc was invincible. His populist style of governing, the informality of his attire and manner, "his skills of communication with 'the little man,' in the field, at the bayside, in the street, in the rumshops, became renowned." The early 1960s, moreover, were years of prosperity. Bountiful banana crops selling at high prices and an increase in foreign aid for roads and welfare programs made him "virtually a father figure for the mass of the people." It is true that most of the roads and social programs on which he and his government based their popularity had been planned, and in some cases begun, before they took office, but it was during their first term in office (1961–1966) that they had come to fruition. The opening of the Portsmouth–Roseau road, for example, had been a triumphant event exploited by the DLP for all its worth as propaganda. No opposition party could have prevailed against the fact that "there had never before been such a surge of development concentrated at one time upon a people who, for generations, had lived at subsistence level at the mercy of social and political conditions over which they had had no control." Moreover, as Lennox Honychurch has argued, the Labour party had presented the people "with a form of leadership with which they could identify, speaking in a language and presented in a manner which they could understand." LeBlanc's continuing success was bitter gall to Phyllis. Such was his popularity in the 1960s, such the adulation of which he was the object, that very few were ready to question the wisdom of his policies or challenge the gradual concentration of power in his hands. She found much to criticize—from the party's abandonment of her cherished socialist agenda to the racial polarization that was in great part responsible for his ever-increasing level of approval. Had she lacked a vehicle publicly to vent her frustrations there is no telling what might have happened. But in the summer of 1965 she provided an outlet for herself in the newspaper she had founded, the *Dominica Star*.

Shortly before leaving the *Herald*, Robert had unexpectedly received a legacy of three thousand BWI dollars from a bachelor uncle and invested it in the machinery and the printing press they needed to run a small weekly. Phyllis, Sonia contends, started the paper "as a form of vengeance," an assertion her adoptive mother would not have contradicted. She repeatedly described the *Star* as her artistic and political "weapon" against "petty small island habits," one she wielded from the outset against LeBlanc and his ministers. The paper's very first issue referred to the DLP as the "Tiny Tots Government," in retaliation for the party executive's frequent references to her as an old woman. She was then fifty-seven.

The *Star* did not have the most auspicious of beginnings. Only 300 copies of the first issue had been sold, but circulation had quickly picked up and in a matter of weeks they were selling out a printing of 650. They expected to touch the 1,500 mark by Christmas of their first year. "It will take a little time for the *Star* to show a profit," she wrote Adèle when the paper was scarcely into its second month, "because we don't live in town and have to rent premises; but you will be pleased to hear that the *Star* sells like fresh bread, we can't turn the handle fast enough! It's probably the low price plus 'what is Ma-Allfrey saying?' and Robert runs it with great efficiency since I am hopeless over accounts and machines." By 1974, when John Lent, an American scholar, visited while researching a book on the mass media in the West Indies, the circulation had stabilized at 2,000 on good weeks and 1,600 on slow-news weeks. It would never be very profitable, however, and they would bolster their income by being correspondents for Reuters and the *Barbados Advocate* and accepting commercial and private printing jobs.

During his visit Lent followed Phyllis through a typical press day at the *Star*. After bringing the stencils to their Roseau "depot" to be duplicated, she had given the boy operating the Romeo mimeograph machine meticulous instructions before phoning several reporters who had failed to file their stories. Her printer, she complained, "makes at least one or two mistakes in every headline and if I ask him to correct them, he makes more." They traveled across town in her green dune buggy to pick up a photograph of a beauty contest winner that turned out to be too small to print. From there it was on to her home. On their way, noticing a stalled vehicle on the side of the road, she stopped to offer help, and Lent listened to the greetings and inquiries, "realizing that they were more than just casual remarks, but the gathering of information for the following week's issue." At the mill house (by then they had left the boiler house for an old mill house on what had been Copt Hall Estate) a table was set up on the patio and there, "in the outdoors, with lush foliage and a clear stream only inches away," most of the work of producing the newspaper was done. Robert and Phyllis typed stencils, answered correspondence, laid out advertisements, and discussed island politics and the *Star*. The newspaper, she told Lent, had soon become a thorn in the government's side, and repeated efforts had been made to shut them down. "They'd like to get Robert out but it would be like chucking the prince out of Buckingham," she explained. "I'm one of the few white people here who is indigenous and I have held some powerful positions . . . they cannot get the *Star* out of the way as long as I'm behind it."

In news content the *Star* would never compete with the *Chronicle* or even the *Herald*, as Phyllis was very selective, one could say very personal—in the news she chose to cover. She would, for instance, avoid writing about Vietnam, even while the war dominated news throughout the world. On the other hand, the most trivial news about the British royal family would often find a place on the front page. She was an inveterate royal watcher, fascinated by the goings-on among the royals, and would have loved the Princess of Wales feeding frenzy of later years (the announcement of her betrothal appeared on page one of the *Star*). Her coverage of Queen Elizabeth II's visit to Dominica in 1966 was typical of her approach to news. She greeted the occasion with a dreadful sappy poem printed on the front page. "She steps—the Lady of our delight, / On our volcanic sand: / Her step is delicate and light / As is her face, and hand; / She smiles on us, not from a height / But level with our land." Despite her profound admiration for all things royal, her reports on the visit were nothing if not sardonic. She praised the queen's appearance as "a triumph of understatement, and her expression likewise seemed sometimes rather subdued and serious, brightening at intervals with the world-famous kind and cultivated smile"; but she found most everything else to border on the ludicrous. When the queen replied to LeBlanc's speech of welcome at the Botanical Gardens, Phyllis claimed, "some of us felt a certain twinge of disappointment." Elizabeth had exhorted Dominicans "to be brave in answer to uncertainty," reminding them that the island had "good friends in the world beyond your shores." As Dominica was living through a period of unprecedented prosperity, the call to bravery was puzzling. Impatient at the barrage of platitudes, she wondered if the queen had meant to give them "the gentlest of premonitory brush-offs." With her appreciation for the droll and whimsical, she focused on the absurdity of the proceedings. A Carib boy who had been charged with making a presentation of "armfuls" of Carib baskets in the company of four girls dressed in *douillette* had refused point blank to wear "any sort of fancy Indian costume." He replied to the diplomatic family negotiations in exasperation: "Why do I have to meet the Queen of England? I'm a Carib. Does the Queen want to meet me?" Her report on the luncheon on the *Britannia* (to which everyone of any importance, herself included, had been invited) provided more opportunities for sardonic wit. The queen, despite Prince Philip's declarations that it was "wonderful," refused to taste the local delicacy, the *crapaud* (toad) dish. Some meritorious citizens felt squeezed out of a royal handshake because government partisans were brought up "by the truckload" and given priority. "If royal styles are followed," she counseled the fashionable ladies of Roseau, "the upside-down-flower-pot or wastepaper basket hat is *out*. All the fashion is turban these days with an oriental flavour."

The *Star*'s appeal to readers was in the quality of the writing and in the many voices for which it provided the first and only outlet. People bought the paper for Phyllis's "invisibly scathing editorials," her satiric poems signed by Rose O, Androcles's sharp critiques of the Labour government (written by Loftus Roberts, a retired civil servant), the acerbic appraisals of government policies signed by John Spector (contributed by Robert), Ralph Casimir's militant poetry, and Cynthia Watt's tales of Ma Titine (the half-patois, half-English conversations of a poor Roseau housewife and her friends). The paper was above all a forum for opposition to the government, and her stable of writers grew from among those friends and acquaintances who found no other outlet for their frustrations. Through the *Star* she would encourage and nurture aspiring young writers. She was, as many would insist, "generous to young writers to a fault," believing, as she wrote of Joan in *In the Cabinet*, that "the only useful thing she did as an editor was to encourage talented young [Dominicans] to write." She predicted that "nearly all the good writers of the future, those born in [Dominica], I mean, will have first been published by me." This would be the only thing for which she would be publicly honored in her homeland.

Among those she encouraged was Lennox Honychurch, a young man who served his writing apprenticeship in the *Star* and whom she would come to love like a son. Lennox, the grandson of novelist and politician Elma Napier, was then a promising poet and painter, who in the early 1970s, when barely twenty, would make his mark with an acclaimed series of radio programs, *The Dominica Story*, recounting the history of Dominica from the discovery to the present. (The text of the radio series, the most comprehensive source to date on Dominica's history, would be published as a book shortly thereafter.) In time he would become the island's foremost historian and conservator (and executor of Phyllis's estate). Lennox "cut his literary baby teeth in the *Star*," for which he worked as a reporter and writer while still in his teens. In the early 1970s he became the paper's assistant editor, and Phyllis, who fostered the hope that he would one day take it over, was furious when he accepted a job with the local radio station. In 1975 he would accept the Freedom party's nominated seat in the House of Assembly and become the government's press secretary following the party's electoral victory in 1980. To young Honychurch the *Star* had "a little bit of the flavor of the Hogarth Press, where everyone pitched in." Phyllis herself was "Virginia Woolfish." Printers, newsboys, writers, and friends would congregate in the little office, standing amidst the machinery and newsprint, sharing gossip and off-color jokes. Phyllis and Robert had a "coy . . . attitude about sex" which led to frequent hilarity. At some point Robert had devised a tool they called the pricker to help unstick the printer and laughter would reverberate through the *Star* office every time someone would need to "press the pricker." Phyllis also nurtured her newsboys as if they were family. This was out of both shrewd business sense and personal involvement. The young boys who worked as freelance newsboys for very little commission were crucial to distribution and sales. They would go to the first newspaper whose issues were ready and start selling, and once they got tired they rarely returned to circulate those that had later press runs. Phyllis was very personally involved with her boys and their mothers, listening sympathetically to their problems and baking cakes for them around Christmas.

The burden of producing the little newspaper, however, fell heavily on Phyllis, who spent most of her days gathering news, listening to the radio for news stories, writing reports, articles, editorials, short stories, and poems to fill the pages of the *Star*. She typed the stencils for all contributions and advertisements, often under pressure, if they had been delivered too close to press time. Occasionally, when short of materials to complete an issue, she would publish pieces by writers she had personally known—A. E. Coppard, Harold Pulsifer, and Jean Rhys—or her own poems and short stories.

But work on the newspaper curtailed for the most part her own creative work, other than that meant for the *Star*. "I am always hovering on the brink of writing another book," she once wrote her friend Adèle, but "the beastly little *Star* is a nuisance. Tomorrow seldom comes. There's not enough of the true dedicated artist in me probably." Most of the creative writing Phyllis did for the newspaper was nonfiction, principally portraits of ordinary Dominicans or sardonic verses about the government's latest foible. Shortly after the *Star* began publication she started a column, "Our Favourite People," in which she featured friends and acquaintances. Typical of the Dominicans profiled in the series was Bartholomew Benjamin, her own son David's fifteen-year-old biological brother, a "wayward boy" who had wandered away from his home in the reserve and whose poignant story she narrated in "Death of a Carib." Barty, homeless in Roseau, had died of staphylococcal septicemia after a long night of delirium, and had been sent home "in the back of a relative's car, lying dead on a mattress, shrouded, late that night." David had spoken about having seen him the day before as he himself was climbing into the Rover to go home after school. "He was trembling all over," David said. "I just had time to call out, 'What's the matter, Brother?' But he had not replied other than by a little shrug and had sat down on a stone step." David had seemed nonchalant when told of Barty's death, but little

Robbie, the second of the Benjamin children Phyllis and Robert had adopted, reported the next morning: "You see how Dave's eyes red? Is cry he cried in bed." "So now there is one Carib less in Dominica," Phyllis concluded. "There were perhaps only half a dozen of his precise age group. A being of such rare descent should have had a chance to eat well, to be educated, to be happy, to live quite a good long life—like some of us more ordinary mortals. Yet though it is true that one or two people had a try at reforming and providing for Barty, their attempts collapsed through impatience. As I have said, he was a bit of a wayward boy, an adventurer."

In early 1967 Phyllis and Robert adopted a second Carib boy, David's five-year-old biological brother Robert, known as Robbie. The elder Robert had one day come across Robbie sitting on a doorstep in Bataca, and as it was David's birthday and they planned a celebration, told the boy to come along. He had never left. Phyllis wrote to her friends of how "enormously" she loved Robbie, describing him as "a rare little boy" who was, like David, "handsome and bright." His gregarious personality and occasional impudence appealed to her own strength, and he soon became her favorite.

In 1967 Phyllis had been reading Virginia Woolf's "autobiography" of Elizabeth Barrett Browning's dog, *Flush*, and hit upon the idea of creating a column for the *Star* written by her homely mutt, Rags Twotones, whose photograph wearing her spectacles accompanied his byline. Rags became another weapon she used to satirize LeBlanc, his Government, or any other issue that absorbed her at the moment. In one of his columns Rags "wrote" of Willie the cat's attempts to claw down the nest of brown migrant birds that had settled in a wall hole in the kitchen. The birds had migrated to Venezuela, as they always did in that part of the year, and after the harming of their nest, Rags's mother thought with dismay that they would never return: "Imagine Mam's joy when she came back home [Phyllis had just returned from England], to hear their lovely songs and see them flying high in the kitchen again. They had removed their straws from the old nest-hole and added some extra furniture, including a yard of Mam's hair, placing their new home so high up near the tin roof that no cat in the world could ever jump so far. This is where they live now. It is as if they were saying to Willie: 'Go to the devil! You can't keep us out!' This pleases Mam a lot. She calls them West Indians in Britain." The Migrants' Bill to which Rags's story alludes had caused Phyllis much grief and had received ample coverage in the *Star*. She had called the British Labour Government's 1965 *White Paper on Immigration* "a miserable and squalid apologia," which had not given the true reason for the new restrictive cutting down of immigrant intake. "That is, in our view, the attitude of the British electorate as a whole to coloured settlers, and the uneasiness of Ministers and Members of Parliament over this attitude during tight-rope-majority times." The white paper ran counter to "England's great tradition of extending refuge and hospitality":

> "But before anyone in Dominica starts to *holler* against the English for this piece of meanness, we ask them to re-read the first lines of this editorial ["There is only one way in which the diverse races of the world can ever learn fully to agree with each other, and that is to 'dwell together in unity'"] and ask themselves a few questions. If you were a well-off coloured resident, would you take a poor white child into your home? If you were a West Indian employer, would you give a job to a penniless Britisher? Would you share a loaf of bread with a down-and-out from over-

> seas? If these people's habits differed from your own, would you get vexed? . . . The Immigration White Paper is a miserable and squalid apologia. Criticize it and protest, if you can find a means of doing so. But search your hearts at the same time. Integration works two ways.

By far her most effective weapon in the *Star* was Rose O (a pun on "Roseau"), a writer of satiric verse she had created and through whom she could direct her barbs "against a petty-minded, small-island government." Rose O's verses appeared once or twice a month, and she used them "to satirize the goings on, taking everyone for a ride." Between 1966 and 1981, when the *Star* ceased publication, she would publish dozens of Rose O poems. The conception of this alter ego was proof positive that the anger that propelled the *Star* had not embittered Phyllis, that she could distance herself from her resentment through irony. As she grew older, her friend Daphne Agar maintains, she developed "a great sense of humour about the whole thing" and could have you in absolute stitches about government follies she would have greeted during her earlier political career with stern seriousness. Rose O's poems, modeled on both the traditional English verses she had grown to love through *The Oxford Book of English Verse* and the West Indian oral folkloric tradition (some of them were written in patois), often took mirthful digs at the LeBlanc government and were eagerly read by the populace, whether or not they agreed with her political viewpoint. They were her weapon to add "a nice little *picong* [spice]," to stir things up. In "A Bribe and a Favour," published a mere two weeks after the DLP's victory at the 1966 elections, she charged that the LeBlanc government had bribed the populace with promises of roads, schools and scholarships to secure their votes: "What is the difference, darling Mum, / Between a bribe and a favour? / Well a bribe smells strongly of cash and rum, / But a favour has no flavour." In "Sunday Dinner," which appeared in November 1966, she addressed the high cost of food staples in Roseau through Rose O's dialogue with a little boy eating a piece of meat: "My fadda bought de beef, / costin a whole day pay, / just for our family / to eat one meal dis day / The balance of de week / is dasheen dat we eat; / sometime a little fish, / only on Sunday, meat." A month earlier Minister of Home Affairs Mabel James's proclamation of "Courtesy Month" was mockingly addressed by Rose O in "A Cautionary Rhyme," with references thrown in about the government's decision to seek associated statehood status as a first step towards full independence. "The more independent we get, / (so they say) / the better behaved / we shall all be some day. / Since being cut off from protection, we must / resign our poor future to those we don't trust." At times Phyllis would jokingly censure her creature. "We regret that Rose O's contribution this week was unacceptable to the Editor," she wrote in December 1967. "Aside from lacking the Christmas spirit [it was] distinctly vulgar." Her poem on the subject of the opening of the new public latrine, which began—"Oh, have you been invited to the opening / Of the nice little house by the sea? / If so, have you swallowed your Epsom salts, / Or just castor-oil like me?"—were described by Phyllis herself as hardly ladylike and not up to her usual witty standard.

But Rose O's most sarcastic barbs were saved for LeBlanc personally, whom she once ridiculed in a parody of "Tweedledum and Tweedledee" as "Eddydum and Eddydee." In "Village State" she addressed a brawl between the villagers of Thibaud and Vieille Case (LeBlanc's home village) in December 1966 which left many injured and property burned and looted. He had traveled to Vieille Case to mediate a truce, and of this visit Rose O wrote: "But the Vieille Case people like Vietnamese/firmly rejected the pipe of peace./The moral of this *conte* of heat and hate/is first rule your village,/then rule the state." In "Swine Fever" she came as close to insult as she was bound to, writing about the "sickly swine of Vieille Case" moving to Roseau, jeering LeBlanc, who favored the countryside over Roseau and was often critical of those who had moved into the capital: "You sickly swine of Vieille Case/be careful where you die,/for the veterinary teamsters/were bound to pass you by./Don't emulate your betters/and move to Roseau-town,/or the pig-hog population/will go down, and down, and down."

Despite the burdens of the *Herald*, and later the *Star*, during the 1960s Phyllis was still making an effort to write. While at Baobab House she had taken the maid's room as her writing room and had settled down to complete *In the Cabinet*. She had been "going on with it gradually," but the pressures of journalism and family life with two children (soon to be three, with Robbie) soon put that project in abeyance. She would not return to it until after Phina's death in 1977, when it would reemerge as a tribute to her beloved daughter. Except for her journalistic pieces for the two newspapers she edited during this period and the poems by Rose O, there would be but a handful of new strictly literary texts after the federation. Two formerly unpublished stories had appeared in the *Herald*—"It Falls into Place" and "The Naming"—but these had been written during the 1950s. "It Falls into Place," printed under the pseudonym of Philip Warner, was the tale inspired by the mystery behind Daniel Thaly's unrequited love which so puzzled her as a child. "The Naming" was one of her Fulham tales, stories in which she had sought to capture the elusive qualities of her former neighborhood, peopled with gossipy charwomen, busybody matrons, and frustrated young men seeking love. The naming in question is that of a new community-sponsored arts center by a committee split between eighteenth-century portraitist Sir Joshua Reynolds and Mabel Bourgeoise, an unknown local artist beloved by the neighborhood matrons. The narrator, a young man "in that desperate condition of wanting to be in love but finding no appropriate object for his rhapsodic longings," objects to Mabel's prosaic name on aesthetic grounds but remains curious about the mystery surrounding the dead woman and the "strong waves of emotion in the meeting hall," until he comes face to face with her self-portrait, with "the face which had dazzled the Mayor and come near making the new arts centre a national laughing stock." She also featured a number of her earlier short stories, some previously published, in the *Star*: "A Time for Loving," "A Real Person," "Proserpeena and the Colonel," "At the House of the Countess," "Tea with the Bishop," "The Spirit Portrait," and "The Man Who Pitched Bottles" appeared in the first two years of the publication of the newspaper.

The handful of short stories she wrote in the 1960s were more anecdotal in nature and less polished than her pre-Federation work. Perhaps her best was "The Homeworkers," the tale of a young failed West Indian teacher who sets up a "homework" business in his one room. The "germ" of the story had come from a report in a Paris newspaper about a young man who had been brought into court and charged with doing pupils' homework for small fees. In Phyllis's version the young tutor sees through the croton bushes the young widowed mother of one of his clients, coming to reproach him for doing her son's work. He is visibly alarmed, but then realizes she has not come to spoil his career but to retrieve her son's homework—being lonely and bored, she used to do it herself. When he agrees to give up working for her son, the mother, with sporting instinct, hints: "If you ever expand. . . . " The distilled irony of the story, the quick delineation of character and setting, and above all the story's satiric intent were reminiscent of V. S. Naipaul's earlier work, namely *The Mystic Masseur* and *The Suffrage of Elvira*. So was Rose O's "Las' Lap, Las' Laugh," a story about the accidental revelation of a middle-class woman's fling with a tourist while her husband was away at a commercial conference. It was clear from these and several similar but less accomplished stories—"We Three Kings," "How We Spend Christmas Here"—that her circumstances, be it time, concentration, leisure, were not those conducive to her achieving in this new work the level of maturity and skill of her earlier fiction. No wonder she called the *Star* a "nuisance" and questioned whether there was enough of the dedicated artist in her. Politics and journalism had indeed ruined her for writing, if only to the degree that they had marked a path for her that completely absorbed and expended her energies, leaving little or no room for expressing her creativity through literature. She would return to writing in earnest again when she resumed *In the Cabinet* after "the beastly little *Star*" had become history, but by then she had to wonder whether, as a friend once suggested, "perhaps she had started it too late."

The decade that had opened with the Federation's collapse and Phyllis's wretched expulsion from the party was one of few personal satisfactions. For her it was a decade of dwindling hopes and closing options. In January 1964 they learned that Robert's mother had died in England. Robert had spent the days following the news "writing sad letters" while Phyllis sat in the abandoned servants' room below, her refuge, feeling "even gloomier because [she had] never really liked her." In June 1966 Miss Maggie, one of the few remaining "landmark[s] of the old days," had died in her sleep, marking, as Phyllis wrote in the *Star*, "the end of an epoch." She had been the proverbial pillar of the community and the service had been attended by scores of mourners, many remaining till the end to watch "the last spadeful of earth and the great flashing mountain of flowers cover up Miss Maggie's tiny coffin."

In June 1964 Robert had traveled to England with David for a reunion with Phina, Allan, and the young children (Diana and Stephen) they had adopted after Phina's reluctant acceptance of her inability to conceive (she once told her mother she would mourn her "unborn children" till she died). They paid repeated visits to Philip, who looked physically very well and seemed pleased to see his father after a separation of six years, but took little notice of his sister. He made no conversation, did not want the cigarettes and chocolate proffered, and his replies were "a bit monosyllabic but perfectly intelligent." Robert was never to see him again, as in the years that followed he and Phyllis grew too poor to afford the air fare to London. They also visited George Horner and his flatmate Brian Merton Gould, who remembers David as a "charming shy little boy finding support in his father." The holiday would go awry, however, when, during a visit to Rosalind and George's cottage in Old Bosham, Robert lost consciousness, fell backwards, and hit his head on the flagstones, resulting in a serious concussion. The doctors thought there was just a chance he had had a small painless coronary thrombosis. From the hospital he would write plaintively to Phyllis, asking her to consider the possibility of their returning permanently to England. She, lonely at home, telephoned him offering to join him immediately in England, willing to discuss a permanent stay. But by then Robert had reconsidered. It would mean giving up the *Star* and all their efforts in Dominica, he argued, and in England they would have to live "fairly roughly" and he might have to take "a very lowly non-independent job." Phyllis's response may have been occasioned as much by concerns about Robert's hospitalization as by his efforts, which he had outlined for her in a previous letter, to sell half of Penhurst and rent the other half. Her attachment to the cottage was so strong that the prospect of losing it left her despondent. It was the only thing other than the *Star* they owned after a lifetime of hard work, and she was extremely attached to the land and the cottage, dreaming of it as a refuge if they ever had to leave Dominica.

During his visit Robert had worked on repairs to the house, spending nearly two hundred pounds they could ill afford and leaving everything in reasonable shape, barring the depredations of field mice. But he had been unsuccessful in finding a tenant, as the cottage, being too far off the road and lacking running water and electricity, was not a convenient home for any but the sturdiest. For several more years they struggled to hold on to it, and even hired a caretaker to keep an eye on the property. Hence their shock in April 1967 when they learned from a friend who had thought of making it his temporary home that it had been vandalized. He had found open boxes with the remains of their contents scattered throughout the rooms, mattresses torn, china broken, and books pulled from the shelves and left to rot on the floor. The news was disturbing enough for Phyllis to leave for England in midsummer, largely to see to repairs to the cottage and attempt to let it. She recruited George Horner and Brian Gould to help her tidy up the house, and as they approached it Brian remembers her murmuring "Le Grand Meaulnes" to herself as "a kind of secret, personal message." It would be her last visit to Penhurst, which was sold outright the following March—all but one and a half acres of the original eighteen, which they retained for their use if they ever returned to England. During this visit she visited George and Brian at the flat they were sharing in Chiswick. Brian remembers her sitting on their sofa, "still the same slim lady in a print dress," staring up at the brown overmantel, suggesting gently that, as she was pressed for money, George might relinquish his claim to the small plot of Dominican land he had purchased from her. George and Brian had a pipe dream of retiring there, but being "two drinks behind the rest of the world," they let it go.

The high point of Phyllis's visit was sharing the Parkview flat with Phina and their tenant, a black South African film director named Lionel Ngakane, whose documentary on race relations, *Johnnie and Jemima*, had just won an award at the Venice Film Festival. Phina and Phyllis had arrived at the apartment hoping that Ngakane, an old friend of Phina's, would allow them to stay for a few days. He did more than that, kindly insisting that they stay with him for as long as they remained in England. He soon became a favorite of Phyllis's, helping turn what she had anticipated would be an ordeal alleviated only by Phina's presence into an "enchanting" holiday during which he hosted parties for her old literary and political friends and made familiar surroundings sparkle. One morning she had encountered him in his nightshirt, emerging from what had once been her bedroom, and had told him: "Lionel, I'm a great adopter. And I've never had an African son. Consider yourself adopted forthwith." He had kissed her "with filial courtesy" on each cheek and said that he would like that very much. She was deeply moved by hearing from Phina that during a later visit to Zambia, while being feted like a hero by many, he had told his friends: "Ah, you should meet Phina's mother—the most dynamic woman I know." He was, Phyllis declared, one of the nicest men she had ever met.

One of the highlights of her London visit was a meeting with Edward Kamau Brathwaite and the Caribbean Artists Movement Committee, of which she would write upon her return to Dominica that it was a group any artist, "whether in words or paint or design," should join. It was an organization that "will keep young West Indian intellectuals informed on trends among the brilliant exiles as well as giving them fresh thoughts from the homelands." A few days before her return to Dominica she had spent the night with Brathwaite and his wife, Doris. It had been, as she told him in a hurried note from the airport, "a peak time of my London visit. I had hoped to make contact with kindred spirits, but was full of joy when it actually happened." At the Brathwaites' she had met her old friend C.L.R. James (Nello) and his wife, Selma, "who gave me a lovely welcome, and I felt fortified in carrying on my lonely literary battle by the encounters I experienced within the walls of your home." She returned to her considerably more limited horizons in Roseau feeling like "a snail under a cataract." Roseau, though not an absolute intellectual wasteland, nonetheless offered very little mental stimulation. Books were not readily available, the library's holdings were unimpressive, and news from abroad not plentiful and slow to come, even for newspaper editors. She had been fortunate in finding a friend in Anne Woolfson, a doctor's wife, a sophisticated, bookish, though somewhat pretentious young woman whose literary tastes ran to Pinter's plays and experimental fiction. Like Phyllis, she was not entirely approved of in white circles, and the two women became fast friends, commiserating with each other and sharing books and news. Anne occasionally wrote for the *Star*, and her husband was suspected erroneously of writing the acerbic column of political criticism Robert published as John Spector. But shortly after Phyllis's return from London Anne announced she was returning to England. In fact, she would be in London to greet Sonia when she arrived in May 1968 to continue her training in nursing.

Phyllis's relationship with Sonia, who had been well into adolescence when they returned from Trinidad, had often been stormy. They were both strong personalities and clashed often about friends, school, even politics. Phyllis, Sonia complained, expected you to be the enemy of her enemies and did not like people who had strayed away from the "right" politics. Neither could she bring herself to forgive anyone who had betrayed the Federation. Roseau being such a small town, those restrictions allowed Sonia little scope to establish friendships. Phyllis was, moreover, "in some ways very Victorian" and kept a close eye on her daughter's acquaintances and friends. In fact, she disapproved of most of her companions. Sonia, fearing that if she did not "impose" herself she would ultimately be overwhelmed by her adoptive mother's personality and strength, would finally tell Phyllis that she "would always be loyal to her, but that was *all* she owed her." Phyllis nonetheless came under criticism from friends and relatives who thought that she and Robert, despite their reduced circumstances, treated Sonia like a princess. They devoted a large portion of their meager resources to helping her realize her dream of a career as a pediatric nurse, from the infant nursing courses available in Roseau through their arranging for her to complete her training at a London hospital. The departure was only possible after prolonged legal steps had been taken to validate her right as an adopted child to enter England as an immigrant. The case, which set a legal precedent, was finally resolved through appeals to Phyllis's many friends in the House of Commons, just as it was to be submitted to the International Court of Law at The Hague.

David was no less a concern. A gentle, polite boy who often seemed bewildered by his new life, he was frequently too shy and reticent. Once, when David had broken his arm playing on the cement courtyard of Wesley High School as he waited for his parents to finish work, Robert was deeply disturbed to learn that, unwilling to interrupt them, the boy had crouched beneath a running water pipe until he was picked up at lunchtime. He had been very slow at learning to read, despite Robert's loving efforts. "He has sufficient intelligence that when he gets going he should forge ahead fast," he wrote to Phina reassuringly, describing the young boy as "most troublesome in the most charming way." Robert felt a deeper love for the little boy than he would ever express for Sonia or David's brother Robbie, and seemed to have transferred to him some of the hopes dashed by Philip's illness. He wished to educate David to become a leader among his people and eventually take over the *Star*, giving the Caribs of Dominica, for the first time in their history, direct access to a forum from which to voice their concerns.

Robert had also found a niche of his own in Roseau as president of the Mental Health Association of Dominica, whose primary goal was that mental patients be treated in outpatient clinics or within the framework of the ordinary general hospital. Hitherto mental patients had been housed and treated—if treatment it could be called when Dominica lacked a psychiatrist—in the local prison. Phyllis, in her turn, had founded a branch of the Alliance Française—she had been president of the local branch in Port of Spain—and as a result felt that "Martiniquan and Dominican people were becoming fraternal, exchanging news and views, paying visits, and so forth." Her own command of French had shown a marked improvement. In March 1964, at the invitation of the Fort-de-France branch, she had gone to Martinique to meet General de Gaulle and had been delighted to meet Aimé Césaire, who had given her a volume with "a thrilling inscription": "A . . . la seule béké progressiste que je conaisse [*sic*], et dont la vie est un beau combat pour la fraternité humaine." (To the only progressive *béké* [white woman] I know . . . whose life is a beautiful struggle for human fraternity.)

Her connection to the Alliance Française had led to a warm friendship with Pierre Lucette, a music professor from Martinique she had met in 1962 and enticed to Dominica to study social customs and record vernacular songs. Lucette was a "most flamboyant" colored Martinican "with Chinese blood" who lived with his aging mother and aging aunts in an aging mansion in the middle of Fort-de-France. His standard wear was a large straw hat, a voluminous dashiki, leather sandals, and pajama pants that came down to his calves. He was also the "most incredible chef." Quickly "adopted" by Phyllis, Lucette would come often to Dominica to stay with her, lighting up the house with his flashy ways, cooking, planning some cultural event or other, discussing politics, shocking Roseau with his evident unconventionality. Phyllis felt a deep affection for Lucette, which deepened after he developed a warm rapport with Phina (during her visit to Dominica in 1974 they produced a radio reading of C.L.R. James's *Minty Alley* with Lennox Honychurch). However, her attachment did not keep her from ruminating mischievously on his sexuality. She had what some have called a "smutty" curiosity about sex from which not even her best friends were safe, and frequently wondered whether Lucette "had his eye" on David, a thought that seemed to amuse her and led her to pondering whether perhaps David himself was homosexual. She and Robert had always felt a curious fascination with other people's sexuality, especially keen when it came to homosexual relationships. They had always had very close homosexual friends, but that never prevented their lewd inquisitiveness and ribaldry about possible homosexual liaisons. Once, at a performance in Roseau, seeing Daphne Agar, her friend Mary Narodny, Eugenia Charles, and a woman politician from Barbados sitting in the first row, Phyllis had maliciously drawn Lennox Honychurch's attention to the "row of lesbians." Lucette, who was passionately involved in Martinican politics, kept Phyllis abreast of developments throughout the French islands and beyond. His attitude to politics, like Phyllis's own, often bordered on the conspiratorial, and he was fond of phoning mysteriously from public booths during demonstrations, claiming to be on the run from the police after some illegal political action or another. Phyllis did not give credence to most of his claims, but he often made her feel close to the pan-Caribbean political world, which now seemed as removed from her life as if she had never moved breezily from island to island as the most influential woman politician in the region. Indeed, Phyllis rarely saw any of the prominent friends and acquaintances who had shared her life as a Federation minister. In pan-Caribbean politics her name had been all but forgotten as a new generation of leaders not tied to the Federation had moved into the spotlight. The Federation had indeed ended the political careers of most of those connected with it. Robert Bradshaw had been the only one to rise out of its ashes to assume nearly autocratic control of his island's government. In March of 1968 Guyana's controversial leftist leader Cheddi Jagan and his wife, friends from Federal days, arrived in Roseau for a lecture, providing a rare opportunity for Phyllis to meet former associates.* "They are two of the bravest people I've ever met," she wrote in the *Star*. "They are frank. They are prepared to suffer. They never give in. A lot of what they say is true." But a lot of what they said, in her view, was not. "I believe most of their basic premises are worn out and rigid. And are even the valid ones worth the sacrificing of one or two whole generations?" In the speech he had given while in Roseau he had seemed to her to be looking forward to upheavals in the Caribbean, and Phyllis took the opportunity, as she was wont to do given half a chance, to take another dig at LeBlanc. "Now, let's face it—most of us who are not satisfied with things-as-they-are look forward to the overturning of the dug-in types who seem determined to retain power at all costs; because good democrats believe in the possibility of change. Good democrats believe in the attainment of change by peaceful constitutional means. But outside this fringe there are others who feel that constitutions can be wangled to suit the sitters, that electoral methods are fixed, and that legal frauds are perpetrated." Taunts

*Jagan (prime minister of Guyana from 1957 to 1964, and president of the country since 1992), and his wife, Janet, had advocated throughout the 1950s and 1960s a militant Marxist ideology as "a creative tool" for building a new socialist society. Phyllis would have agreed with Gordon Lewis's assessment in *The Growth of the Modern West Indies* that their Marxism, "filtered through the strainer of Russian Stalinism, was of a rigid and doctrinaire kind and never really faced up to the special dialectics of Guyanese reality, the difficulties, for example, of sovietizing a rice peasantry thoroughly individualistic in its thinking, or of applying the Russian nationalities policy to a colonial polyethnic society neatly balanced between two equal groups."

like these would, in a matter of months, bring Phyllis to her most serious political crisis since her expulsion from the party. In an effort to silence the unrelenting criticism heaped upon him by Scobie in the *Herald* and Phyllis in the *Star*, the LeBlanc government would pass the Seditious and Undesirable Publications Act and bring upon itself a political crisis that would culminate in the foundation of the Freedom party—and would give Phyllis's political career a new lease on life.

In March 1967 a new Dominican constitution had been enacted, granting the island associated statehood status. In administrative terms its impact was more momentous than the attainment of independence eleven years later, as it gave Dominica virtually complete self-government for the first time in its history. Executive authority would rest in the hands of an appointed governor acting on the advice of a cabinet made up of a premier and government ministers chosen from House of Assembly members. The new constitution granted the Dominican government extensive powers in the field of external relations, subject to consultation with its British counterpart; only external defense remained in the hands of the United Kingdom. Dominica would be free to end its association with Great Britain at any time by a vote to that effect ratified by a two-thirds' majority of the elected members in the House of Assembly and two-thirds of the votes cast at a referendum.

The prospect of associated statehood, granting as it did increased powers to LeBlanc and his cronies, was greeted by Phyllis with publicly expressed misgivings. In an editorial she published in February 1966, shortly after news broke of the opening of negotiations toward a change in status, she had stated her conviction that Dominica should never be separated from the British Commonwealth of Nations. Distrustful of the new breed of West Indian politicians with self-aggrandizing proclivities, she found comfort in the possibility of a higher power to which to appeal. She feared that unless Dominica remained part of the Commonwealth, the island may become "a paltry pawn in the Caribbean game of chess." Britain had made "many historical mistakes—the migrants bill is one of them, in our view—but unlike the Dictatorships, she usually admits her errors." Faced with the *fait accompli* of the new constitution in January 1966, she left it to Rose O to voice her apprehension in "A Dose of Independence": "Oh, a dose of independence is superb;/but prepare a notice—PLEASE DO NOT DISTURB:/You may find your state much sicker/from consumption of its dregs,/so do test your head and legs/before you drain that Independence liquour [*sic*]./Oh, a dose of independence suits the soul,/but we do not recommend the bottle whole:/just imbibe with moderation/and a glance at other cases/on a diagnostic basis—viz./Nigerian, Vincentian, Cuban, Haitian." Phyllis's incessant allusions to LeBlanc as a power-hungry and imperious politician were not a mere outgrowth of her bitterness at his perfidious victory over her in their struggle for control of the DLP. They were founded on intimate knowledge of his character and what was generally seen as "his deep-rooted dislike of the traditional establishment, particularly the powerful Roseau-based group of farmer-merchants and professionals usually identified by the DLP as 'the mulatto *gros-bourg*,'" a dislike that "in one way spurred him on and in another distorted his judgment of issues and events." Throughout Dominica's history there had been deeply entrenched divisions between Roseau and the countryside. Before the DLP victory in 1961 the Roseau elite (politicians, planters, merchants, civil servants, and office clerks) had always dominated island affairs. This would change radically in the 1960s; within one decade LeBlanc and his government would succeed in raising rural affairs above those of Roseau society. The transformation would not be a smooth one, but one achieved through a policy of divisiveness and recrimination that would eventually leave profound scars on Dominican society. Old race and class enmities had been conjured to solidify the DLP's mandate and spearhead a movement to wrest power away from the "*gros-bourg*,"a process driven by a militant, pugnacious rhetoric that discouraged opposition.

The absence of a viable opposition disturbed Phyllis deeply. The DUPP, Frank Baron's party, had responded to its overwhelming defeat in the 1966 elections with "a year of quiescence." As the party prepared for its annual convention in 1967, she wrote a passionate editorial exhorting the membership to reorganize its ranks and "once again constitute itself an effective opposition party." Democracy presumed "an opposition able at a moment's notice to take over the reins of Government. The absence of such an opposition party, as all history testifies, leads straight to one or other of the various forms of dictatorship, with dire results for the liberty of the subject." With a majority of ten to one in the legislature and no effective voice—other than that of the newspapers—to rally public opinion against the possibility of arbitrary rule, LeBlanc and his supporters in the legislature and the party executive could proceed with virtual disregard for public interest. It did not take long for the DLP's assured power to attract "a circle of hangers-on seeking to benefit from the spin-offs to political patronage. Several key civil servants, members of Statutory Boards and a growing number of businessmen, including important figures in the Syrian and Lebanese sector, were increasingly using their influence to entrench the party's power and thereby secure their own. Interests of the Party took precedence over decisions of State." It was a situation that had prompted Phyllis to call the Labour government "a petty little group of nationalist islanders calling themselves Labour."

She was not alone in her concerns. Throughout the decade the three island newspapers, the *Star*, the *Chronicle*, and the *Herald*, had shouldered the burden of commentary against the DLP's growing disregard for democratic procedures. The Labour party, as Phyllis's expulsion had demonstrated, had always been wary of criticism. But it was "especially rankling when it came from the trio of liberal, light-skinned, Roseau-based newspaper editors and their associates in their anti-Labour Dominica United People's Party, and later, [Eugenia] Charles' Freedom Party. Further annoying to the government, all three newspapers printed columns by a constantly changing stable of writers who, usually disguised by pen-names, needled the island's politicians, government employees and each other." The *Star*'s blistering sarcasm, expressed through Rose O and John Spector, and the *Herald*'s weekly political scandal column, "Is It True?", were particularly irritating to LeBlanc. Phyllis skirted the libel laws by her use of irony; Scobie did so by presenting his allegations as questions. As a result, government officials had engaged in a policy of harassment against the press. The *Star*, Phyllis told John Lent some years later, had been the subject of the "government's thundering against media on the political platform." But her use of irony made it difficult for government officials to attack the paper. "For a politician to explain to the illiterate common man how the *Star* has done the politician dirt is difficult when the story is couched in irony." They had suffered repeatedly, nonetheless, through the withdrawal of government advertising from the paper. Scobie, on the other hand, had received anonymous letters from government supporters threatening to burn his press building and kill him. As a candidate for office during the preceding election he had been stoned at public gatherings. LeBlanc had threatened publicly to "make the *Herald* inactive" because of its antigovernment articles, charging that Scobie was destroying his public image by talking of government incompetence. He had attempted to close the paper in various ways, after trying to entice him into giving it up with promises of putting him in charge of national radio or commissioning him to write the island's history.

Throughout 1968 the newspapers' criticism only intensified. In May, in an attempt to curtail inflation, the government had imposed price controls on consumer goods despite intense opposition from local merchants and the Chamber of Commerce, who argued that some of the prices imposed were lower than the landing price of the items in question. Shopkeepers had held a protest march widely supported in the press. Shortly thereafter the government had shut the local radio station, WIBS, and demoted a popular broadcaster to a desk job in retaliation for adverse coverage of its policies. Rose O responded to the WIBS incident with a parody of "Silent Night": "Stille nacht . . . /Maybe he's right!/Joshua called WIBS/a le-egeal fight./ Those who steam open notes/or defame,/must pay up/to restore a good name./ Praise the heavenly pe-eace/of Cuba, and Haiti and Greece." In June 1968 the newspapers subjected to intense scrutiny the government's plans to develop the former Canefield sugar estate into a five-hundred-lot housing scheme. The *Herald* charged that sixteen lots had been set aside for relatives of Ronald Armour, minister of communication and works. At the June 26 meeting of the House of Assembly, Armour had brandished a copy of the paper, ranting and raving against the press.

As a direct result of the intensification of criticism from the press, in early July 1968 a bill was introduced in the House "to provide for punishment of seditious acts and seditious libel, and facilitate suppression of seditious and undesirable publications, and temporary suspension of newspapers containing seditious and undesirable matter." In a clause addressing newspapers that habitually contained seditious matter, the bill would give the government the power to "prohibit for a period of one year future publication of that newspaper, and prohibit similarly publisher, proprietor and editor of that newspaper from publishing, editing or writing for any newspaper or from assisting whether with money or material or personal service or otherwise in the production of any newspaper." The government could order every printing press used to be seized by the police and detained for one year, and any person found guilty of an offense under the act would be liable to a fine of BWI $500 or imprisonment with or without hard labor for three months or to both fine and imprisonment. A second offense could bring penalties of a BWI $1,000 fine or six months' jail. The bill, christened by Eugenia Charles the "shut-your-mouth" bill, drew immediate criticism from concerned British MPs and newspaper editors throughout the Caribbean region. The Inter American Press Association called for the repeal of an Act so "shockingly contrary to the letter and spirit of press freedom." The night before the presentation of the Bill, at a mass protest meeting in Lagon which drew a large and enthusiastic crowd, critics of the Bill gathered to condemn its introduction. Speaking from the same front porch of the Dominica Trade Union Hall on Queen Mary Street, from which he and Phyllis had launched the Dominica Labour party in 1955, E. C. Loblack stressed "the backward turn from increasing freedom that the Bill entailed." He was followed by Stanley Boyd (editor of the *Chronicle*), Phyllis, Eugenia Charles, and Scobie.

Early the following morning, on what would become known as "Black Friday," marchers gathered outside the war memorial at Peebles Park, where Phyllis read a proposed resolution condemning the introduction of the "malevolent Seditious Act which is contrary to Human Rights, dignity and freedom and demand[ing] its total withdrawal." It was adopted by a show of hands, and copies were later cabled to the British government and the United Nations. The group then marched to the precincts of the House of Assembly, the eighteenth-century courthouse, led by the newspaper editors, members of the opposition, and a number of Roseau merchants. Wearing mourning armbands and waving placards, the demonstrators greeted the ministers with boos, catcalls, and shouts of "We want freedom" as they entered the courthouse for presentation of the bill. LeBlanc, rumored to be in Montreal or Guyana, was not among them. A number of protesters then crammed into the House chambers, filling the galleries, and taking over the chairs usually reserved for government officials. The debate on the bill commenced amidst calls from the outside of "Put them out! Change the Government!" The two opposition members, Elkin Henry and Anthony Moïse, pressed for "total abandonment" of the bill but were soundly defeated and walked out of the House to the cheers of the crowd. The final vote showed eight in favor, two against, with four abstentions. In a joint statement Phyllis, Scobie, and Stanley Boyd announced their decision to suspend publication jointly and simultaneously if any one of their three papers was suspended under the act.

The three editors, with Eugenia Charles, Chris Loblack, and a small core of protesters, immediately banded together to launch an islandwide petition drive to pressure the government to repeal the act. Throughout the summer the loose-knit group, christened "the Freedom Fighters," crisscrossed the country explaining to the peasantry the provisions of the act and collecting signatures. Phyllis and Scobie, the main targets of the bill, were the group's "spokesmen and propagandists." On Sundays the group would travel to remote villages, set up a loudspeaker in front of a church or school, and present its arguments against the bill. Their receptions varied. In Roseau, the Southern District, and in Chris Loblack's hometown of Grand Bay they drew enthusiastic crowds. Throughout the rest of the island they often met "apathy, suspicion and occasionally, heckling." The campaign brought Phyllis back to ground she had so painstakingly covered repeatedly during the DLP's initial membership crusade, the Federal campaign, and numerous constituency visits, affording her an opportunity to bring their case before audiences with which she was comfortable and familiar. By early September the Freedom Fighters had gathered 3,317 signatures against the legislation.

These efforts culminated in September with a protest march through Roseau and a demonstration in front of the government headquarters. Hundreds of demonstrators had gathered at Goodwill Savannah early that morning and were preceded by a police van, their numbers swelling at every step, accompanied by a booming loudspeaker blasting "We Shall Overcome." In the front line of marchers were Phyllis and Carib chief Jermandois François, wearing his ceremonial sash and carrying his silver mace. At the climax of the protest, the signed petition for repeal was presented to LeBlanc. At this point he emerged on the balcony to defend the act, declaring that the people must accept everything done by a legally elected government till its tenure of office was up. By some accounts LeBlanc also announced forcefully to the crowd below: "We are here to rule and rule we will." His comments had led to the *Chronicle* christening him "Premier Nyet." In immediate and dramatic response, Eugenia Charles pushed through the crowd, grabbed the microphone on the protesters' Land Rover and retaliated "with a vibrant barrage on democracy and constitutional law," vowing that a new movement would rise to end his tenure of office. From then the idea of forming a political party with Eugenia as leader took root. Within weeks Anthony Moïse, Elkin Henry (the political antagonist Phyllis had once described as "despicable"), Eustace Francis (a member of the House), Eugenia Charles, the Allfreys, Scobie, Loblack, Loftus Roberts, and others met to establish what became known, at Scobie's suggestion, as the Freedom party. The name was modeled on that of Ceylon's (now Sri Lanka) Freedom party, which, Phyllis pointed out, was also led by a woman, Sirimavo Bandaranaike.* In a meeting attended by about two hundred people at the old Roseau Grammar School on October 10, 1968, the Freedom Fighters merged with the National Democratic Movement and formally adopted the Freedom Party name. Phyllis, Scobie, Henry, Eugenia, and Loftus Roberts were named to the steering committee, which was in turn charged with developing a manifesto for the forthcoming Roseau Town Council elections which the new Freedom Party meant to contest.

The Freedom party's "Policy Statement No. 1," a one-page document issued immediately after the announcement of the founding of the party, included in its introduction Franklin Roosevelt's wartime Four Freedoms: Freedom from Fear, Freedom from Want, Freedom to Worship, and Freedom of Speech and Expression. In the summary of its objectives and goals, the party undertook to better the living conditions of the people of Dominica, institute a plan for social security, advance the "unity and social harmony of our State by standing against the forces of discrimination," rescind harmful legislation (the Seditious Publications Act foremost), spur economic development (particularly as it concerned agriculture and tourism), provide training for young people, lower the voting age from twenty-one to eighteen, "preserve in every way consistent with advancement and increasing industrialisation, our beauty of landscape and the natural riches [of Dominica]," and strive to meet the needs of the old, the sick, and the frail. It concluded "in a burst of alliteration and populist fervor: 'People Before Power. People Before Politicians. People Before Privilege and Things.'" In *In the Cabinet* Phyllis would write that the document bore "her imprint and her signature." And indeed it was a fundamentally liberal, social democratic manifesto resembling the declared objectives of the Dominica Labour party, which she had written in 1955. Its insistence on conservation and promoting welfare were particularly reminiscent of the earlier text.

Phyllis's association with the Freedom party proved that politics do make strange bedfellows. She would write in *In the Cabinet* that Joan and Edward, "revolted by the destruction of their earlier work and belief in the [DLP] after ten years of frustration had attended by invitation the first meeting of a group of all kinds of disenchanted political people—mostly conservative—in 1968." Anyone daring enough to have told Phyllis in her Labour party days that she would ally herself with the likes of Eugenia, Baron, and Elkin Henry—old political rivals—would have come in for a barrage of abuse. For years to come the DFP would have a "landed-aristocracy image" with the country people that she must have tolerated only because things were

*Upon her party's victory in the 1960 general election, Mrs. Bandaranaike became the world's first woman prime minister.

so bad otherwise. Eugenia had earlier been a political enemy of hers, and although their relationship was to warm up considerably, the two would never see eye to eye politically. Eugenia, once described as "a traditional conservative politician with more than a touch of reactionary sentiments," would "never be sure whether the ideas of the Freedom Party were congenial to Phyllis." She claimed that "Phyllis' heart was very much in the right place, but that she had extreme views" and was "a little bit before her time." Phyllis, Eugenia would grant, had worked hard to develop "a socialist slate" based on a belief that "those who had had to share with those who didn't have" and had been "very keen on the environment" at a time when no one seemed at all concerned with such issues, but these concerns had never been paramount to her own political philosophy. However, Phyllis and the Freedom party needed each other. She was in great part responsible for providing the fire that galvanized the opposition into action and resulted in its foundation. She had, moreover, a proven forum for presenting the opposition's viewpoint. The party, on the other hand, gave her lone opposition voice a resonance it had lacked before. She could no longer be ridiculed as an old woman bitterly ranting and raving in the political wilderness about old wrongs. When she attacked now she attacked as a member of the Freedom party.

The joys of returning to the political fray were not without cost, however. In early October the government retaliated against her by deporting Al Akong, an artist they had met through Dermot Louison (the painter they had befriended in Trinidad) and who had been living with the Allfreys for some months. He had been refused a renewal of his visitor's permit and ordered to leave the island immediately. The government charged that Akong—who had spent most of his time in Dominica roaming the countryside, drawing and painting, and teaching art to children in the Carib Territory—had violated the conditions of his permit by accepting paid employment. He had allegedly painted a mural in a local restaurant, contributed some drawings to the *Star*, painted two large signs, and sold a couple of paintings, one of them to Phyllis and Robert. Phyllis was livid and retorted with a Rose O poem, "The Artist's Departure," a rewriting of her "Smider's-Snark" in which she cautioned the government that "artists have friends/who have votes."

Another unlikely outcome of the political turmoil surrounding the Seditious Publications Act was Phyllis's reconciliation with Edward Scobie. Since the *Herald* fracas their relationship had not been the most cordial. Scobie, as a matter of fact, had once referred to Phyllis as "that pale pink woman with her pale pink paper," a description that stuck and would be often repeated to ridicule her. As a put-down it had effectively addressed Phyllis's race and pink (socialist) as opposed to red (Communist) politics, and the fact that at some point she had gotten hold of a supply of pink newsprint with the result that many issues of the *Star* had actually been printed on pink paper. Their closer association during the years the Freedom party remained in opposition would awaken in him a deeper appreciation of her qualities, especially as he saw her dealing with the Labour party attacks without ever moving out of character. He regarded her, perhaps for the first time in their long acquaintance, as a romantic figure, a "wispy shadow of a woman," almost "transparent," her skin of a whiteness that was "whiter than white, like white porcelain, despite her being always in the sun." As she grew older he would watch her become more and more fragile, "like something you would not like to crush, something to touch gingerly, like rare pink porcelain." And this physical fragility was all the more surprising because of the energy and forthrightness of her character. She may have looked like a rarefied species of endangered flower—once when Scobie visited her at the mill house she picked "the most fragile of fragiles" in her wildflower garden and called it her favorite, "because it needs me the most"—but "there was no ice to break when you first met her." After all the discord they had shared, he found, "You couldn't hate her." After their rapprochement Scobie shared with her his conviction that *The Orchid House* was a book "motivated by a great feeling of love," and she replied approvingly, "You know, you're not a bad chap." All this did not mean, however, that she ceased taking "digs" at him. He recalls that at the time when he was the most exposed person in the Freedom party, she had said to him publicly: "I know you already know exactly what you're going to say. You have structured everything, including your reactions."

Robert does not seem to have been so ready for reconciliation, and was wont to maintain a severe politeness in his public dealings with Scobie while frequently maligning him in private. In October, as they were preparing for the Roseau Town Council election, he wrote to Sonia in London that the Freedom party's campaign had been going well "until Scobie had one of his lost weekends and mucked up the flyer he was supposed to print by putting in a lot of unauthorized *mépuis* on the back without any reference to the Committee." Then he had suddenly reappeared "dead drunk and [had] made some fearful, stupid, libellous and slanderous, dirty-words statements over the mike outside Vics to a middle-class audience before Mum was able to shut him up." Robert's condemnation of Scobie notwithstanding, the Freedom party would go on to a respectable showing in the Roseau Town Council election of November 1968. The party had waged an all-out campaign that had voters in a frenzy by election day. Phyllis was back in her element, holding rallies, running about from meeting to meeting, helping crank out leaflets, speaking to crowds from the platform, immersing herself once more in the *commesse* of party politics from which she had been summarily banished in 1962. She returned from one of her meetings to tell Robert gleefully of a "very hostile reception" at a public meeting which had been "largely due to [Alford] Pressy Benoit paying some old crones and a mad preacher to break [it] up."

But after the votes were counted the six-week-old party had won two seats on the Town Council, one of them going to Edward Scobie. It was just the beginning of a painstaking uphill climb to power that would culminate in the Freedom party victory of 1980. Throughout the 1970s Phyllis would face devastating personal ordeals that would bring her close to despair. But the political crusade in which she was engaged would always offer a purpose, a mission that would spur her on despite loss and pain, and help her "to carry on living."

Twelve

My National Song

Oh they've had it too sweet for too long
Is the theme of my national song.
One hour in the sun for a fish
will spoil the tastiest dish,
while a day in an open tin
will harden the bread from the bin;
when it comes to political man
ten years is an awful long span,
and for most politicians alive
the maximum term should be five.

In July 1969 Phyllis returned to St. Aroment, "the very site of old childish holidays, the place of inspiration." The move had come about quite serendipitously. Celia had flown over to make repairs on the property after her most recent tenants had vacated it, painting the squash court "snow white inside and out," installing new louvre windows, and leaving everything freshly scrubbed. Eugenia Charles, in charge of letting it, had encountered Phyllis at a Freedom party meeting and—"more amenable now"—had offered her the house for rent. "Snap just like that" she had said yes, "Because it [was] really a long dream—coming back to the Orchid House, even for a short while." The rent was ten times what they paid Celia for the old boiler house, an amount they could ill afford, but as it was a spacious, roomy house, with plenty of space for guests, they meant to run it as a modest hostelry. Phyllis "genuinely believe[d]" she could now return to writing, "tucked away in a secret alcove behind our big bed."

They had moved in bit by bit, with their old Mini-Metro car, straining every muscle and temper, but "somehow right away [St. Aroment] had been restored to something of its old look, a colonial country house full of books and pictures." The return satisfied Phyllis's ever-present yearning for historical continuity, particularly as the old estate—now that Kingsland House had been torn down to make way for a supermarket—was the sole standing symbol of the family's continued presence on the island. Her only regret was that it all had come about just after Phina had been there for her first visit to the island since her infancy. She had come from Kenya with her family the previous April and, troubled by her parents' living conditions at the boiler house, had insisted on their looking for some land for her to purchase where they could build a refuge for their old age. Phyllis had quickly found two suitable pieces of land. One in the Reserve itself, which—given the restrictions on ownership by non-Caribs could only be purchased as an investment for David—so there would "be an Allfrey-named boy in the Reserve with his descendants"; the other site perfect for an escape cottage, "a real holiday place for everyone, near to the people who are so dear, the Carib and half-Carib race," with an "exquisite view" of Pagua Bay. Too far from Roseau for them to make it their home, it was only accessible by jeep and needed forest clearing, being "sheer virgin stuff," but it stood right on the boundary of the Reserve, high upon the volcanic cliffs of the Atlantic windward coast. They built a small house on it, a typical one-room Carib house set on a *pilotrie*, or large wooden posts.

Phyllis's happy interlude at St. Aroment was not to last long. The house was well beyond their means, and they were ill equipped for the burdens of running a hostelry. She was indeed never truly domesticated, and the house was in continuous chaos—a "real mess"—and overcrowded with the many stray cats and dogs to which she was known to give shelter. So she and Robert were privately relieved when little over a year later Celia announced her plans to sell the house and grounds, and Phyllis began looking for a home far away from overcrowded Roseau. She soon found just the place, an old stone cottage on the edge of a wild hilly plantation surrounded by moist and leafy undergrowth, near the village of Wotton Waven. Copt Hall mill house, built in 1830, was an idyllic spot, shady and cool, with a small pool fed by a clear stream amidst acres of fruit trees and wildflowers. The air, scented with orange blossom, felt like "hot sunshine through a green veil," and the house was "like a little bird cage," with birds constantly flying in and out, many nesting on the beams or on the old mill wheel, which was part of the interior decor. "Ah," she would say, "birds know a friend." The mill house would be her home until her death, as untidy and undisciplined a home as its natural surroundings and as its occupant.

Phyllis, a notoriously bad housekeeper, was by all accounts unfazed by the considerable "germiness" of her new home. Cats, dogs, and goats strolled in and out nonchalantly. The hens laid their eggs on the chair cushions on the lean-to that served as a terrace, and many a time unwary visitors sat down to the crunching of delicate egg shells. Patricia Honychurch tells of visiting while there were uncleared cat feces in the house and how, because she kept moving her hand to her nose, Phyllis sent her home with some pills for her "cold." Meals at the mill house were concoctions of rice, peas, dasheen spinach, and whatever else might be found around, including some fungi that grew on the trunks of coconut trees and which she had been told were good to eat, all served on plastic plates scarred with hundreds of knife cuts. But housekeeping, never a priority for her, would be the farthest thing from her mind in a tumultuous decade that brought her searing losses and very few joys.

The first loss was that of David, who in early 1973, when he was not quite eighteen, decided to migrate to London. The decision came as a blow to Robert, who declared he would "miss David a great deal, both for his help [he had become a useful typesetter and reporter] and his company." He feared that David simply wished to escape. He had always been a shy and introspective boy whose transition from a crowded home where the father drank and chased the children with a cutlass to a gentler but no less bewildering life with two aging and intensely political white people had been an awkward one. It was rumored that his biological father's outbursts had driven his brother Barty into a rebellious life and an early death; his eldest sister Charlene, a beautiful young girl, had one day walked into the sea and drowned herself. David had plenty of reasons to feel uneasy in the fluid, shifting emotional world bound on the one side by his native village of Bataca in the Carib Reserve and the mill house at Copt Hall on the other; and he lacked the determination and strength of will that had allowed Sonia to take her adoptive parents on her own terms. Many of Phyllis and Robert's friends believed that, eager as they had been to raise David "as a well-brought up son," they had failed to understand the difficulty of his position and how ill equipped he was to manage it well. Aunt Mags, more perceptive and less sentimental than Phyllis, had told her disapprovingly when she returned with the children from Trinidad that "that boy's going to let you down; the girl's a better bet."

David always seemed to them less vital and resilient than his younger biological brother Robbie, though Robert always favored David. Robbie, he would reassure his older son, was "a well-organized self-centred person who never bears a grudge and will drive his way through life pretty successfully, without having much thought for any one else;" but he was "not so lovable as you." He described the younger boy as he entered adolescence as quite an interesting character but "wearying on one's nerves because he must always be the centre of attention and one heaves a sigh of relief when he is not around—one can then do one's own thing. He makes some kind of noise, singing, repeating radio adverts, or simply imitating noises of cars, dogs barking or what have you." To Phina he would complain that Robbie was being "a great trial to us both," "arrogant, rude, untidy, and a nuisance—highly admired by his peers and well-liked by the mothers of his friends in whose houses he behaves with the best manners and sterling rectitude." He would come to fully appreciate Robbie's gifts only after this adolescent period of rebellion had been transcended.

David's departure was not without complications. As they had with Sonia, problems arose about his visa exemption, and Robert had once again to exert himself to prove that an adopted child had the same rights as a biological one. He worried about how the difficulties would affect David's feelings. "Caribs are sensitive proud people" he told a friend at the high commissioner's office, "and to be rejected by my country would be a bitter blow to him." David's flight to London was preceded by Robert's nearly frantic letters to Phina and Sonia urging them to meet his plane ("he must be met"), and insisting that Sonia finalize her wedding plans quickly—she was marrying a Nigerian engineering student named Kola Adeleke—and make arrangements for someone to look after David at their apartment while they were on their honeymoon, as David was "too inexperienced as yet to stay at Parkview alone for more than a couple of days." He had arranged for him to spend some time visiting friends in England—his brother Benjamin (adopted by the former governor of Dominica Geoffrey Guy and his wife); his aunt Rosalind (Phyllis's sister); and Phyllis's cousin Rufus King at Cambridge—before choosing a career or professional course of some sort, preferably some training in the graphic arts and printing that would prepare him for taking over the *Star* when he returned to Dominica.

From the moment David arrived in England until the end of their lives, Phyllis and Robert would live in constant anxiety over his welfare. His life as a Carib in London was a lonely and often bewildering one, and at times he seemed to have been swallowed up by the city. Through the years that followed they would be grieved by various reports of his alcoholism, homelessness, or unemployment, and would often be reduced to pleading with Sonia or their many friends to try to contact David and send news. "We were so happy to get a letter from you at last," Robert wrote once when a letter had arrived after many months of anxious concern, "even though you do not give us much detail on your work, your rooms and your room-rate, what you like doing in the evenings and weekends." Robert's affection for David was manifest in the support and reassurance he sought to impart from afar. "You must not be dispirited because you are not academically brilliant," he once counseled. "What you have is integrity, kindness to others and the true thoughtfulness that makes a civilized gentleman. . . . Forget about big ambitions, do not feel frustrated . . . and if you get really fed up in England you can come back to old Dominica and us and the *Star* and its printery is all yours." But David was not to return. At times his periods of silence would last for months; once they did not hear from him for close to two years, during which he seemed to have vanished as if dead. Phyllis and Robert's hopes of his taking over the *Star* were eventually relinquished, and they learned to live with yet another emotional void.

The tide of black nationalism to which Phyllis's political career had fallen victim rose to flood levels in the 1970s. "There was a problem when I got home [after the collapse of the Federation]," she once explained. The black power movement "had taken root. They were people who had in the past given me support. Now they looked upon me as a white person—and you know I didn't like that very much." The movement had arrived in the West Indies in the mid-1960s, brought home by university students returning from England, the United States, and Canada, who found a receptive audience among the poorer, less educated, unemployed contemporaries they had left behind. Like similar movements across the region, Dominica's responded to a conviction that the island continued to be dominated politically, culturally, and economically by foreigners and a few white and mulatto local families. It vowed to fight for profound socioeconomic changes that would result in the allocation of power to the black masses, and posited African-inspired fashions, hairstyles, music, and food against what they saw as the *gros-bourg*'s Eurocentrism.

Dominica's black power movement flourished under LeBlanc's pro-working-class Labour government, for which it provided the means to solidify political power. The Labour leadership made the rhetoric of the black power movement its own, railing constantly against "the bourgeois exploiters," the "mulatto *gros-bourg*," and "the white oppressors," keeping open "every possible wound between 'gros-bourg' and 'petit-bourg' for political purposes." Phyllis was often a target of these attacks, as she was at a mass meeting of the Labour party in 1971, when Ronald Armour, then minister of finance, had charged her with posing as "a great white angel when she was just a hypocrite." He contended that she was "childless," "only adopted Caribs because they had light color and straight hair," and "never lets negroes into her house." Phyllis, who was almost apoplectic when she heard of this, prompted David to write a letter of rebuttal. In "A Son to the Defence," a text that reads suspiciously like her own work, he offered a spirited defense of his mother's lifelong struggle against racism, underscoring the fact of Sonia's adoption, and that there were three races in the Allfrey family. "No one," he concluded, "should believe ministers who say and spread lies."

The climate of racial discord fostered by such attacks, however, had soon expanded beyond the Labour party's control as parts of its constituency became more radicalized, more distrustful of politicians and organized political parties, and more extreme in their class and racial hatred. As unemployment rose (to levels of above 30 percent), it became increasingly difficult for the economic sector to absorb record numbers of high school graduates, leaving the island's increasingly radicalized youth bitter and angry. The Movement for a New Dominica, the main black power organization on the island, seized upon these frustrations, fanning the flames of radical political struggle during weekly "black power meetings" at the Botanical Gardens and through their newspaper, *Twavay*. Phyllis decried their "racist militant attitude," contrasting it with the more positive negritude movement, then spreading through the French Antilles,* which she saw as fostering not racism but "the accumulation of the civilised values of the Black world." She posited negritude as not just "a racial attitude . . . but *a state of being*: the state of being Black, and proud of it, and eager to dignify that condition." The black power movement provoked her more often to exasperation than to fear. Her printer and some of her writers were members, and she expected "any day for the whole paper to go up [in smoke]." On at least one occasion they had all gone to a black power meeting and had not gotten the paper out on time, leaving a thousand copies unsold.

As the decade progressed a vocal minority among the "black power boys" spearheaded a campaign of abuse against whites, who were openly called honkies, jostled, pushed, at times spat upon and hit with stones. With Dominica's white population the smallest of any island in the Caribbean, tourists became the most frequent targets of abuse, and soon what little tourism the island had enjoyed vanished altogether. In the early seventies, as the influence of the Jamaican Rastafarian movement reached Dominica's youth, Afros gave way to dreadlocks, the cultivation and use of marijuana increased, and more and more instances of attacks against tourists and villagers in isolated areas began to be reported as the "Dreads," as they came to be known, literally took to the hills.

The Dreads, at most two hundred young people from the middle and lower classes, soon were blamed for every social and economic problem on the island. Largely unemployed, they had taken lands in the mountains of the interior, living most often as squatters and subsisting on ground provisions and other vegetables. They advocated a return to the land and a more equitable distribution of the island's resources, opposed the importation of produce and the use of meat, proposed that all clothing should be made locally out of natural materials, and criticized the elitist nature of the educational system and its ideology. As a result of the black power militancy they exemplified, tensions on the island escalated into incident upon incident of racial and class unrest. By Carnival 1974 the situation had deteriorated seriously. The calypso sung as the bands marched through the streets that year was inflammatory: "Black man time is come!/White man had his fun!/Black man stronger than white man!/Black man sweeter than white man!" During Carnival weekend two white couples were slashed, an American doctor suffered a fractured skull in a stoning incident, and on Mardi Gras night a white visitor was shot and killed. As a result of similar disturbances, rebellious youths burned Elias Nassief's Geneva Estate at Grand Bay as well as his store at the old Roseau marketplace. Phyllis's sister Rosalind and her husband, George, who had been in Dominica for Carnival, had been warned that a few black power youths "meant mischief." But Rosalind was still recognized by many and "lashed unruly people with the local patois." The "poor defenseless Americans" were not so lucky. Phyllis, who had built a political philosophy based on an ardent belief in the possibility of multiracial, multicultural harmony, alternated

*Negritude, promulgated by Léopold Sédar Senghor (president of Senegal, 1960–1980), was a pan-African movement that grew out of rejection of French assimilationist policies and advocated the affirmation of the African heritage of the peoples of the diaspora as the point of departure for anticolonial political movements. Phyllis, who had traveled to Martinique to hear Senghor speak in 1964, had been impressed by the absence of racial animosity in his philosophy and by his insistence that the affirmation of African-derived culture need not necessarily lead to racialist struggles.

between fury at the government for fostering racial discord and dejection at seeing her island reduced to "a messy lacerated sore." "It is abysmally sad," she wrote to Adèle, who had recently visited Dominica. "I'm so very glad it didn't happen when you were here, though I do not believe you would ever have run into that sort of danger, with us. I regard it as a temporary phase in our history. There are strong battalions on the other side. . . . So all is not lost; but what a setback." Just weeks before Adèle had landed at Melville Hall airstrip in the northeast corner of the island in the late afternoon, and Phyllis and Robert had gone to fetch her in their rickety old mini-moke. As they drove across the mountains on the lonely Transinsular Road, through the heart of Dread territory, the little car sputtered along until it finally stopped and refused to travel any farther. They were forced to spend the night by the side of the road huddled together against the cold mountain air. Adèle, who knew nothing of the Dreads, slept in peaceful discomfort; her old friends expressed no anxiety or fear. As Phyllis proudly told Pierrette Frickey, a scholar she befriended in the early 1980s, "In spite of the bad publicity about the dangerous presence of Rastafarians in Dominica and their encampment in the hills so close to her mill house, she had never felt threatened. She lived in peace and not in fear on the island."

The accumulation of incidents quickly led to something akin to mass hysteria, with the Dreads—"lazy misfits from whom every right-thinking Dominican should disassociate himself"—as scapegoats. With the population caught in what became a "national paranoia" and demanding "more effective police measures," the government began allowing the police and defense forces to descend upon shacks, garden plots, and homes occupied by the Dreads, search and seize their property, and arrest them with or without cause. These aggressive tactics did not succeed in quelling the panic, and in November 1974 the government passed the Prohibited and Unlawful Societies and Associations Act, which made it illegal to be, look like, or associate with a Dread. Dreadlocks were banned by law, as was supporting, hiding, or conspiring with a Dread, the law going as far as allowing any person to kill any member of the group "found at any time of the day or night inside a dwelling house." The "Dread Act," as it became known, was more successful as "a psychological damper" to people's fears than as an effective piece of legislation. But with general elections only four months away, it had its intended political effect, as people seemed reassured by the tough measures it proposed.

The act met with widespread support from all sectors of society. The *Chronicle* endorsed it, "since it was about time the government did something about the deviant elements in the society." Eugenia Charles, speaking on behalf of the Freedom party, called it "a painful necessity," although she blamed the Labour government for creating the discord that made it necessary. "They are the ones who made rich people hate poor people, poor people hate rich people, white people hate black people, black people hate white people, people in the North hate people in the South." Given the climate of fear reigning in Dominica, few were willing openly to criticize its restrictions on civil liberties. Phyllis did, however, urging its repeal in the *Star*, arguing that "wrongdoers among the dreads could be prosecuted like other suspects under Dominica's existing criminal code." She never got tired of repeating that the "dangers they represented were grossly exaggerated, that they were a convenient scapegoat," and would further anger the government by charging repeatedly that the Dominica Defence Forces were hunting them down like pigs. Once, when a report commissioned by American conservationists had suggested that forest rangers be drawn from the local Defence Force, she had sent Premier Patrick John into a fury by suggesting that the rangers should also be drawn "from the outlawed forest-living young men known as Dreads, who know the tropical rain forest better than most." In 1975 a Commission of Enquiry was appointed to investigate the Dread problem, to which Lennox Honychurch, by then a member of the House, was named. It concluded that the numbers of Dreads believed to be in the hills had been "greatly exaggerated" and that the dissatisfied youth fell into one of three categories: "the peaceful counter-culture group, the political activists and the criminal element." It recommended revising the Dread Act to become a terrorist act, not geared against societies or physical appearance. Finding the report "weak and too conciliatory," the government ignored it, but the scare soon abated. Toward the end of the 1970s only a small group of Dreads, led by Leroy "Pokosion" Etienne, remained active in the south of the island. Isolated incidents continued to be reported, but the worst of the crisis seemed over. The Dread menace would flare again briefly though tragically in 1981, when Ted Honychurch, Lennox's father, was kidnapped from his farm at Giraudel and murdered by Pokosion's group.

Phyllis's cautious empathy with the Dreads stemmed from the passion they shared for the conservation of the island's magnificent rain forests. In the mid 1970s, during the peak of the Dread crisis, and in response to the government's attempts to reach an agreement with British timber firms for the exploitation of Dominica's forest, she and Robert joined Lennox Honychurch and others in founding the Dominica Conservation Society, whose immediate goal was the creation of a Dominican National Park to protect the forests from commercial exploitation. Phyllis's credentials as a conservationist were well established. The 1955 Dominica Labour party constitution had included a clause pledging the party to work toward the conservation of "the natural beauty of Dominica." One of the earliest issues of the *Star* had openly declared Phyllis's love for wild nature. "We love bush. . . . Not for us the lawns shaven like good civil servants ready for the office, the rows of zinnias like the border of a well-made skirt. . . . We respect such landscapes, but we eschew them, because what we enjoy is savage natural luxuriance in plant-life." In *The Threatened Forest*, a manifesto for conservation that she and Robert drafted for the society, they vehemently argued the case for conservation.

> Dominica . . . is in itself one vast national park—a jewel in nature's own crown from which gems of huge forest trees cannot be wrenched without spoiling the whole emerald tiara. . . . The people require jobs, and the Government has given them cause to believe (through public utterances) that among other dreams, the timber industry will be revived, and the great felled giants of the Dominica forest will be sawn up and processed for export, thus providing work for a few, but at what price. . . . [Dominica] could be, with the founding of the national park and the overall protection of the island's beauty, a sort of mecca for natural beauty-lovers who can afford to travel and who want to tread little or untrod paths and explore the glories of "elfin woodland," the tremendous rain forest, multi-coloured hot springs and mysterious lakes, including a boiling one. . . . Let nothing disturb the whole ecology of such a marvelous small land, or Dominica's national park, flanked by acres of stripped hillsides, will within less than twenty years be only a "scientific memento."

Throughout 1974 and 1975, with the forests at serious risk, Phyllis fought fiercely to assure their safety, even recruiting Jean Rhys into the struggle. In 1975, when Premier John traveled to London pursuing the logging accord, she dictated a cable for Lennox, as president of the society, to send to the Foreign Office to coincide with his arrival—THE PEOPLE OF DOMINICA PROTEST THE DESTRUCTION OF THE FOREST. The telegram was immediately brought up to John for discussion, and he had been livid. Upon his return to Dominica he openly abused Lennox in the House, ranting and raving about him and his cohorts being "people against the development of Dominica"; but when the latter went to Phyllis to complain of the predicament she had placed him in, her only response was a gleeful, "Oh very good! That means he got angry."

In February 1973, taking advantage of a visit from a group interested in filming Jean Rhys's *Wide Sargasso Sea*, Phyllis wrote to her old friend after a silence of many years. "Many times I nearly lifted pen to paper to write you a note of joy [on the success of *Sargasso Sea*]," she wrote, "but I believe it was that very success which put me off—was afraid you would think I was one of those acquaintances who just bask." Her news, after such a long silence, summarized the essentials: Phina was in Africa; she and Robert had adopted three children, all "absolutely rewarding"; she had made "the fatal mistake" of getting involved in island politics and becoming a Federal minister, being left "stranded and deposed" when that "scheme" broke up, and now owned "this little paper . . . non-profitable but a useful vehicle and weapon, though it kills us with hard work." Jean immediately wrote back, "delighted" to have heard from Phyllis again after so many years. She was living then in a "pretty cottage" at Cheriton Fitzpaine, Devon, where it was "Too quiet!" but had London holidays, which she enjoyed, and was "keeping her fingers crossed" about the film, feeling pleased that some of it was being shot in Dominica. (In fact, a film of *Wide Sargasso Sea* would not be made until 1993, and would not be filmed in Dominica as she had hoped.) To Phyllis's suggestion that she return to Dominica she replied that "to come back and lay my bones where I was born [was] a splendid lovely idea and I wish I could but whether it'll be possible I'm not sure. We'll have to see. Perhaps."

Thus would start a casual, sporadic correspondence that lasted until Jean's death in 1979, and became her link to Dominica in her final years, helping "to keep fresh in [Jean's] mind the singular ambiance of Dominican life." Phyllis would send the weekly edition of the *Star* with personal notes tucked between the pages; Jean replied in brief, wry, and self-deprecating notes that attested to their closeness and rapport despite the many years of separation. At times the feelings transcended words. "Dear Phyllis," Jean once wrote at the end of one of her notes, "this humdrum letter is not all what I am really thinking. You will probably guess that. But anyway it's to send you my very best love." Often Jean's fancy would touch Phyllis's life in unexpected ways. At one time she had written to acknowledge receipt of several copies of the *Star*—"I do like to read the Dominica news"—and had enclosed a check for an amount she hoped would cover the cost of a subscription. "If any cash to spare," she had added, "do buy a bottle of champagne, wish me luck."

Throughout the years of silence Phyllis had not forgotten Jean. In May 1967 she had reviewed *Wide Sargasso Sea* in the *Star*, calling the book the "strange flowering blossom of a late-flowering tree," stemming from two of Rhys's "great and enduring obsessions—love for the island and the injury which men can inflict on women." (Jean was not a feminist, Phyllis argued elsewhere, but she was "intensely independent and championed womanhood when it was degraded or ill-used by man; she hit back with the most marvelous derision.") Of *Wide Sargasso Sea* she then wrote:

> Jean Rhys has betaken herself through this inspired medium into emancipation times, and thereby her third obsession—the love-hate between coloured and white people, engendered in her memory of childhood nostalgia—takes first place in the Jamaican opening chapters of the tragic tale. But . . . and let us be realistic, perhaps it is because we know how much she is bound to Dominica in dream, myth and reality . . . the Jamaican days and events, wildly dramatic as they are in scene and scope, do not grip a Jean Rhys fan as much as the Dominican days of Part II: that exquisite nightmare of cruelty, mésalliance, and the beauty of natural surroundings. The writer's observation of scene, servants, and the helpless onslaught of mania is infinitely moving, and although this book is not in tightness and construction the best of her works, it is still a marvelous book by Jean Rhys, a song by the late-singing nightingale, causing one reader at least to lay it down and turn at once to Matthew Arnold's poem "Philomena" in *The Oxford Book of English Verse*. That poem epitomizes the life and work of Jean Rhys far better than any reviewer's words can do. "Hark! from that moonlit cedar what a burst!/What triumph! hark—what pain!"*

Phyllis lost few opportunities to remind her readers that in Jean they had a Dominican of whom to be proud. She often decried in the *Star* the fact that the Roseau library had no copies of her work. In "Most Famous Dominican," a piece Phyllis published in the *Star* in January 1968, years before they resumed their correspondence, she had summarized Jean's career and defended "her right to be called a Dominican," a constant theme of hers when writing about her friend. Jean was, like herself, a Dominican "born and bred," "the fifth generation born out here on [her] mother's side," just as she had written in *Voyage in the Dark*. And even though she had left the island at the age of sixteen, "all her books have at times a strong yearning towards the island." As if to prove her point, some months later she reprinted Jean's story "Again the Antilles" in the *Star*.

*In a recording for BBC Radio Three in 1981, Phyllis would reiterate her preference for the Dominican sections of the novel. "My impression is that really it's all about Dominica and the Jamaica part seems, not unreal, but it seems like superimposed Dominica to me, except that the people, the unkind servants and so on, are not like our people." When she moves to describe the Massacre/Mahaut District of Dominica, then it becomes "very real indeed." Asked then if the island "still resembled the enchanted place that Jean Rhys knew as a child," Phyllis had replied that the landscape was very much as Jean had known it. "The hills, blue and green, are still so incomparably beautiful. If you had been able to see this morning's dawn, it was a marvelous morning and still is a gorgeous day, you'd have thought you understood Jean for her obsession." Jean's obsession with Dominica, presented so vividly and movingly in *Wide Sargasso Sea*, had its humorous side. "I'm sure you can guess that I would love to come back to Dominica, and think of it constantly" she wrote in reply to one of Phyllis's frequent entreaties. "You are quite right: I ought to die where I was born." But she did not quite see how it could be managed. She was still "a bit shakey" after a fall, and "don't laugh—I am afraid of cockroaches and other insects. I know this will sound ridiculous but it dates from long ago. However nice people were, I couldn't expect a bodyguard to kill every cockroach, could I? But I still think of it, and try to plan some way of doing more than thinking."

Shortly after they resumed their correspondence, Phyllis had written a short poem dedicated to Jean, "The Child's Return," built upon a line in one of Jean's letters about coming back to "lay her bones in Dominica." It read partly thus: "And one dark day I'll board a boat/When I am ready to die./The timbers will creak and my heart will break/And the sailors will lay my bones/On the stiff rich grass, as sharp as spikes/By the volcanic stones." Jean had quickly replied with her thanks, wishing "something like that could happen." "Strangely enough," she had added, years before she had written a poem about going back to Dominica, which she had titled "Return." In her poem she was dead "but only know it when no one recognizes or sees me." She had written it at Maidstone, just days before leaving her "horrible rooms" and going to live "at quite a nice pub called The Ropemaker's Arms. As soon as I unpacked I realized that I'd left the poem behind and flew back to rescue it." But it had been thrown away and "though I've tried over and over again to rewrite it I've never been able to do so." The lost poem may have planted the seed of one of her stories, "I Used to Live Here Once."

From mid-1974 through the summer of 1975 the correspondence between the two friends focused on Dominica's threatened rain forests and the political instability of the West Indies. The passion for Dominica's natural beauty was one the two friends had always shared, as evidenced by its prominence in both *The Orchid House* and *Wide Sargasso Sea*. Phyllis had often written to Jean of her dread of an economic development threatening to the forests, and Jean had grown progressively more anxious about the destruction of a beauty that had sustained her creativity. Jean had also heard from a woman in Grenada about that island's situation under its flamboyant leader, Eric Gairy, whose nationalistic working-class movement had deteriorated into an almost delusional cult of personality, and felt that was "happening in the smaller West Indian islands [is] a great pity . . . and the fact that no one protests or cares is just as bad." She feared they were "up against complete indifference" but was nonetheless eager to find avenues to bring attention to the situation, speaking to a friend, Francis Wyndham, a young writer for the *Sunday Times*, about publishing an essay by Robert on the threat to the forest in the London press. For months she kept a steady pressure on Phyllis "to write what is really going on for it needs saying badly. . . . Do try & write an article that will stress the other side of West Indian politics. Tell your stories," she exhorted. Jean was becoming so passionate about the issue that she felt that perhaps friends like Wyndham thought her prejudiced. She had told him that most of what was said about the West Indies "both past which I know a bit & present which I guess at, is simply *not true*." In England people "believe all manner of things [about the West Indies] which aren't true at all and seem to regard the truth as something of a joke. I can assure you that I have had lots of people here who are utterly astonished that I am not as black as coal—in fact they don't believe it. I don't know whether it's more funny or more sad."

In January 1977 Phyllis received from Jean a copy of her new collection of short stories, *Sleep It Off Lady*, which she acknowledged in an open letter in the *Star*. "My dear Jean," she wrote, "Of course I love [your book], as I love everything that is yours, that is you. And I think of how many thousands of people in the world just know the name Dominica because of you. . . . Robert and I thank you for going on writing, and writing so wonderfully." But the year would be a harrowing one for Phyllis, and their correspondence would be sparse. Jean had been ill off and on in the early months of the year and had not been able to write without assistance; Phyllis would withdraw after Phina's death in April into the deepest depression she would ever know. By September, not having received the *Star* for many months, Jean wrote, agitated with worry: "I'm getting rather anxious about it, or have you just got tired of sending it to me?" Concerned that perhaps she should have contributed something for all the copies Phyllis had sent her, she said she would call at the London address on the paper and find out how she could send money out of England to her. "It's stupid but I imagine all sorts of things may have happened so anyhow do send a postcard or something to let me know how you are."

In 1978 it would be Phyllis's turn to worry about her friend's long silences. The start of the year had not been "very lucky" for Jean, as she had "stupidly" fallen and had been in a nursing home for some time. After her return home she had been "comme si, comme ça," but was nonetheless making progress on her autobiography, the text that would be published posthumously as *Smile Please: An Unfinished Autobiography*. "I've found it difficult to do for it is long ago, longer even than you will remember. I don't want to argue neither do I want to be too dull so it's a balancing act." Progress would be hampered by increasingly frequent bouts of ill health that required her to return to the nursing home. In March 1979 she wrote that she had been ill again, "cracked up a bit." She was supposed to rest for several months, but "if possible" she would try to write "something as a preface" to a hoped-for reissue of *The Orchid House*. She expected to travel to London in "two or three weeks and it goes without saying will do all I can for the book. I have a copy of it and I am taking it to London with me and am sure I can get it read by André Deutsch. Also, I will talk to Diana Athill [Jean's editor and friend] and she may be able to give good advice. . . . I do wish your book the best of luck."

But Jean would finish neither her autobiography nor her promised preface to *The Orchid House*, for she died in May. Phyllis and Robert learned of her death through Lennox Honychurch. Usually they listened to the BBC "News about Britain," but on Wednesday mornings they listened to DBS, "trying to find out what imbecility the Government of Dominica was up to," and had missed the notice about their old friend's death. Lennox, knowing how close she had been to them, had driven over to tell them. It had hardly come as a surprise, Phyllis wrote later, since Jean was eighty-four and had been so ill for so long. But it was "a serious loss" to Phyllis, as she wrote to Adèle: "For so many years we had been correspondents—I simply put 'slips' into *Stars* (she adored the poor little *Star*, it kept her in touch;) and she wrote (until lately when a secretary typed) in her huge distinctive hand. The last loss was—she was going to write a foreword for a reissue of *The Orchid House*. The last letter I had from her told me she was wondering what to say. I replied 'say I was a West Indian writer who *went back home*.'"

With Phyllis and Robert there were never many dull moments, but in 1974 they must have prayed for boredom as incident after incident seemed to lead them into threatened or actual court cases. In early April, Phyllis had been out for a walk picking wildflowers, when the local schoolteacher, returning home to Morne Prosper, had been bitten on the leg by Jango, one of her dogs. Phyllis had gone immediately to the woman's aid, gripping Jango by the collar, but the schoolteacher weighed some two hundred pounds and had dragged her down to the gravel, nearly cracking a rib, and scraping Phyllis's legs. Jango—thinking the woman was trying to kill her—bit her eight more times. Her husband, a shop steward, was very aware of his rights, and they had threatened to bring a case against the Allfreys, but realizing perhaps that there would be little to gain had not pursued it. It was all complicated by the fact that the husband was the local salesman for the Gestetner machine on which Phyllis and Robert depended to bring out the *Star*. For some weeks Robert had to drive her daily to have her leg dressed.

In September, in what would be one of the most humiliating and mortifying episodes of her life, Phyllis was arrested for shoplifting at Nassief's supermarket. She had taken her glasses out of her bag, while shopping, to read the price on a jar of Nescafé and, in her confusion, had placed the glasses in the wire cart and the Nescafé in her bag. The cashier had apparently noticed it and said nothing, but as she and Robert were approaching their car they were surprised by a stranger coming to tell them that she had an item in her bag she had not paid for. She had returned to the supermarket, where a plainclothes police constable "just jumped in and arrested her" for the theft of a $1.53 jar of Nescafé as she was about to pay. He ordered them to drive him to headquarters, and as Eugenia, Phyllis's lawyer, was away they had to go to magistrates' court, plead not guilty, and have the case postponed. This despite the fact that J. E. (Usief) Nassief, the supermarket owner, who had known Phyllis for years, had asked the police chief to withdraw the case since it was "obvious that a person like Phyllis had no intention of stealing." But Phyllis and Robert decided to "stick it out" rather than have "cries of privilege going around." Radio Dominica had given a midmorning news flash about the arrest, and within hours it was the talk of the town. It did not take long for Phyllis to find out that the arresting constable was a "notorious black power type" known as "Sogo-Fly," and to conclude that he had just seen his chance to embarrass her politically. After she was released he had rushed around town telling "all and sundry" that Ma Allfrey was a thief, and complaining "that the other policemen had given her bail."

Phyllis, quite indignant at being treated in such a shoddy fashion, defiantly reported the arrest in the front page of the *Star*. EDITOR OF STAR ARRESTED, proclaimed the headline. But the arrest was only the beginning of the ordeal. The case was talked about for months—and she was painfully aware that most of the people outside her circle believed that she was guilty, seeing her as a silly old woman who had been caught doing something foolish. Many years later Frank Baron would cite the episode as evidence of the tragic depths of her descent in her old age. Indeed, even her friends were unsure of her innocence. By 1974 Phyllis and Robert were drinking quite a bit—daily, in fact—and many thought that she had been too soused to realize that she had put the jar in her bag. The case was not resolved until the following March, when the court found that there was no case to answer and the charges were dismissed. Robert and Phyllis declared themselves glad that it was over, "both having suffered due to insults and inconvenience," and Phina, who had come over to support her mother through what she feared would be a public embarrassment, said it was worth flying ten thousand miles for that outcome.* Not a word was said on Radio Dominica about the verdict that cleared her of the charges.

Just a few months later Phyllis found herself involved in another court case.

*During this visit Phyllis was made the butt of Labour party jokes for her misguided introduction of Phina at a public meeting as "a princess, a princess from England." It was, her friends pleaded in her defense, just evidence of Phyllis's exaggerated pride in her daughter, but her political enemies chose to see it as evidence of her conviction that she still felt she belonged to "the Royal family of Dominica."

This time she brought charges of libel against *The Educator*, a venomous newsletter the Labour party had launched in 1971. In July 1975, following an article in the *Star* charging the Dominica Defence Force with overly aggressive tactics against the Dreads, in an incident that left two Dreads and a soldier dead, *The Educator* published in "Nothing But the Truth" an article Phyllis considered to be "a horrible attack [that] could not be ignored":

> Evil personified. This is Phyllis Shand Allfrey. A wicked little old woman, living out her last days still dreaming of her return to power in the Labour Party from which she was expelled. Whatever evil Phyllis has wished to others, it appears rather convincingly, that she has inherited. Her life has been a failure, from Politics to feeding herself. Even the false love which she conveniently preaches has been exposed. . . . We fail to see that the Dreads are being hunted down like pigs. We also note that the falling Star newspaper indicated that the armed criminals in the bush should be brought to face the courts. Very praiseworthy. We would like Phyllis and Robert to help. Having such knowledge which could save lives, and refusing to pass it on to the Law Officers is nothing short of criminal. Dreads note: the Star knows how you can be brought in alive, but continues to let you be shot by the Police.

Phyllis was angered and shaken, both by the viciousness of the personal attack—the references to her poverty were particularly galling—and by the risks to which it exposed her and Robert through its malicious references to the Dreads, of whom she was, in fact, more supportive than most. "If I were not extremely resilient I would have a nervous breakdown thinking of the horrible things they have printed about me," she commented. She immediately contacted Eugenia Charles as her attorney, asking her to sue for libel. They would have to answer for the word "wicked," she told her. "As to *old*, writers and some politicians are never too old to exercise their skills, and what they fear about me is that I am too young and tough and creative for my age, just as they like to label childless women as 'worthless' . . . and base all their standards of worth on sexual availability." A letter was sent forthwith to the editor of *The Educator* to indicate that unless they were prepared to publish "in as conspicuous a manner as possible a withdrawal and apology—in terms to be dictated by her solicitor—and to pay her a reasonable sum by way of damages and to indemnify her in respect of the costs she [had] incurred," they would proceed. No apology was forthcoming and a libel suit was filed.

The case provided Eugenia and the Freedom party an opportunity to turn the tables on the antipress Labour party, but for Phyllis it offered a path to a more personal vindication. "The fact is," she wrote to Eugenia in a set of notes to prepare her case, "that I have as you no doubt know a very high reputation both at home and abroad [and] you will see why I am jealous that my reputation should not be wilfully smeared by a posse of maleducated political journalists." Her "whole life" had been far from a failure. She had attained "the highest position ever open to a woman in West Indian Politics—the only woman Minister in a West Indian 10-island Cabinet." Anything else would be a local anticlimax. . . . [and] I need not say how vindictive and absurd it is to say that I am dreaming of a return to power in their dirty old Labour Party." When the case was eventually heard in court, judgment was entered for her as plaintiff, and *The Educator* was forced to pay an undisclosed amount. An overjoyed Phyllis triumphantly announced her victory in a special insert on pink paper in the *Star*.

Toward the end of 1976 Phina, concerned about her parents' poverty and frailty—Robert had turned seventy, and Phyllis was sixty-eight—and by the back-breaking work the *Star* required for little financial return, was insistently urging them to return to England, even if only temporarily. Phyllis argued against such a move. Dominica represented "family background, beauty of surroundings, gentleness of friends, the ability to keep going on next to nothing," and she felt "securely bound" to the island by "love and other ties." Yet, as Phina countered, England offered all those things "in its own way." They could return to Fulham or Penhurst—they could even get much needed dentures through the National Health Service. Among Phina's many arguments to entice them to return to London was Philip's marked improvement. A new doctor in charge of his ward had revolutionized it, and her brother was much better, "not to the point that he is anywhere near cured, but at least he is now a social being, and can benefit genuinely from being visited."

Phyllis and Robert were feeling particularly vulnerable just then, and Phina's appeals threw them into a "turmoil of thoughts." Phyllis had not been at all well during the year, which had opened with a Christmas Eve burglary that had left them poorer and more shaken. They had been in Roseau when thieves had broken into the mill house and stolen their holiday supplies and all their modest gifts. It had been a particularly vindictive robbery, the burglars leaving the house in an indescribable disorder—papers, kitchenware, and clothes thrown on the floor and a bed raked apart in a search for money. This was the seventh time they had been robbed, and in every case the police had been notified. Not one single bit of their stolen property had ever been traced, though the police had "once or twice shown some apparent interest in their recovery." The incident gave Phyllis one more reason to criticize the government, not only for the increase in hunger and poverty that led to such crimes, but for doing precious little to reduce their occurrence. As a result, in the U.S. tourist guides "the fair name of Dominica has been debased."

But 1976 had been, in the phrase later immortalized by Queen Elizabeth II, Phyllis's *annus horribilis*. Her teeth were crumbling, and she had been suffering from a painful skin condition exacerbated by nerves and stress—"a nervous allergy coming out in bumps all over." She had been, as Robert described to Phina, "up and down with all the blows we get." Robert himself had not been well as he had begun to suffer from what was diagnosed as a hemophiliac condition that led to frequent tongue bleedings that had to be stopped by stitches. Throughout the year they had also been concerned about Phina's protracted divorce. In early 1974 she had written to announce that she was divorcing Allan after twenty-three years of marriage. Phyllis, with her strong views on marriage as a partnership not to be dissolved come what may, was not very sympathetic to her daughter's tale of a relationship that had degenerated into boredom. She angered Phina by her references to the breakup being the result of her being "in an acting crowd." (She had some years before joined an amateur playgroup and begun to act and write plays, but Phyllis had never accepted it as "a serious occupation.") She had consequently not been very supportive when she heard that Phina was again in love, with a Col. Edmund "Ted" Dowling, whom she proposed to marry after her divorce. Eager for her parents' approval, she wrote constantly, each letter full of poignant descriptions of her emotional turmoil. She was devastated by her separation from her children, who had opted to remain with Allan, and by their obvious distress. Phina respected their decisions but anguished over not seeing them enough. It angered her that Allan rarely consulted her when matters of importance concerning them arose, and she felt "degraded" from her position as their mother. Amid her marital difficulties she was trying to have the lease to 47 Parkview Court transferred to her in case she needed to return to London, and problems arose between her and Sonia, who had been living in the apartment for some years with her husband and two children. They had been expected to leave for Nigeria shortly after their marriage and relinquish the apartment to David, but had stayed on, and after their first child arrived, David had had to move on. This had not pleased Robert, who favored David and blamed Sonia for casting him adrift, and a break had ensued in which acrimonious words were exchanged concerning their continued presence in the apartment, and even about the furnishings and fittings. It had made Phyllis, torn between the claims of her two daughters, quite wretched.

By March 1977 Phina, happily settled with Dowling in Kenya and awaiting the resolution of her divorce, wrote to her parents enthusiastically about the expected arrival of her twelve-year-old son, Stephen, to spend the school holidays with them. They were planning to drive down to Botswana to spend Easter with Ted's son and his family. She was just emerging from the tumult of the last three years and was bursting with creative energy, having just produced a three-act play for which Ted had done the sets and in which they had both acted, she playing an alcoholic former beauty. Her acting career seemed finally to be flourishing, and she saw nothing but opportunities ahead. But within a month of writing this hopeful letter Phina would be dead, killed at forty-six in a car crash while on holiday with Ted and Stephen in Botswana. The sudden blow-out of a front tire had caused her Peugeot station wagon to swerve off the road and overturn, and she had been hurled out of the front passenger seat and crushed under the car. There were no cuts or punctures, no blood, and she appeared unhurt, but she had died half an hour later without regaining consciousness.

Phyllis and Robert received the sorrowful news from the grief-stricken Ted Dowling, who telephoned the morning after the accident. Robbie, just coming in from town as Robert relayed the news to Phyllis, stood by helplessly as he watched her succumb to a misery she could only express through a persistent, almost unearthly wailing she could not bring under control for an excruciatingly long time. Robert, lost in his own anguish, could not bring himself to comfort her. To Adèle she would write that same evening that she was "in agony." Her alter ego in *In the Cabinet* described it thus: "When *she* was killed, I kept beating my breast like a mourning Jewish or Negro mother and calling out soundlessly, 'Why was she taken and not us? We've lived tremendous lives against great odds. She was just coming into the fullness of her gifts.'" That week's *Star* carried a brief announcement of Phina's death: "Our loss is the world's loss."

Phyllis's mourning for her daughter would last as long as she lived. She had invested so much of herself and of her hopes in Phina, especially after the tragedy of Philip's mental illness, that her premature death seemed to crush her. The death of her daughter, "a beauty in the fullness of her promise," had "smashed" her and Robert, "splintering their hearts more than the bombardment of any hurricane." Her "brightness [had fallen] from the air, exploded," and became "utterly still . . . torn up in moments." Phyllis tortured herself with thoughts of her daughter's body crushed and broken (she had suffered devastating internal injuries), and for many months seemed distraught by the realization that contrary to anything she could have brought herself to believe, Phina had not outlived them. In losing Phina she had lost more than a beloved daughter—she had lost a vital link to the future. "Legacy . . . prolongation," the "great questions of [Phyllis's] life," had been dealt a critical blow. In the days, weeks, and months that followed Phina's death, she tormented herself with searing thoughts about all she had lost: her dreams of Phina coming to live and write in the little house near the Carib Reserve, thereby prolonging the family's history of commitment to the island; her yearning for the grandchildren she would never see again; her guilt at not having offered Phina unequivocal support during her divorce (her retroactive anger with Allan over his treatment of Phina would be such that she would never again use the name Simmance in connection with her daughter); the realization that she was now indeed the last of her line in the West Indies. Her and Robert's only comfort came from Ted Dowling, whose grief matched their own, and whose letters told them that he had valued their daughter as they had. (For a few years after Phina's death he behaved toward them as a true son-in-law, attempting unsuccessfully to purchase the mill house for them and continuing the small allowance Phina had sent them and on which they for the most part lived.) He would travel to Dominica in June bearing Phina's ashes for burial; they would be placed over the threshold of the house in the Carib Reserve until they were buried with Phyllis nine years later.

Phyllis's response to her grief was to withdraw, and friends and acquaintances found it difficult to approach her and offer sympathy. She could seldom be brought to speak of Phina again and could not even face replying to the many people who had written to her and Robert after hearing the sad news, not even to Jean Rhys, who had written in May to tell her how "so very sorry" she had been to read in the *Star* of her daughter's death. It wasn't until December that she finally acknowledged the many notes of sympathy they had received in a brief duplicated letter accompanied by a handful of quotes describing Phina's beauty and brilliance. To a friend she would write much later that "a black depression [had] settled in me . . . because of the total loss of Phina. I just seemed to lose everything, even my confidence." When she had seen that same friend drive away after a visit with her husband and three daughters, she had felt "quite a feeling of envy." Her only comfort would come through her writing, and she would seek to give vent to her grief in a new book, *In the Cabinet*, which was to be "half about Phina, and also about [her]."

Phyllis and Robert were sustained through the difficult decade by a constant flow of visitors who came to them from all corners of the globe seeking information, friendship, and encouragement. "Some came out of loyalty to progressive trends already in motion, although the affluence and most of the influence had been suddenly cut off at our end. Others came because they felt we still had something important to give. . . . They came from all kinds of quarters—the United Nations, the British Government, the United States, even France, and from the various world services concerned with Labour, Health Education and their subsidiaries. . . . An alphabetical list of the things they sought local enlightment on ranged from anthropology and art through conservation and medicine to zoology." Many of the visitors were friends of many years. In early 1974 their old friend Adèle Olyphant visited Dominica for the first time since her honeymoon in 1927, bringing cheer, "beautiful gifts," and "tins of delicious candies which [they] so greedily demolished." She had found the mill house enchanting. The late orange blossom in the vale had been out in full splendor and aroma, and she had basked in the comfortable intimacy of the household, playing Scrabble with Robbie and bathing in the cascade that fed the small pool. Adèle, then seventy-one, had seemed to Phyllis "a bit like a princess thawing out after a long hibernation," awakened by the warmth of Dominica. So much so that Phyllis was not surprised when shortly after her return home Adèle wrote to announce that she was getting married, leaving Phyllis enthralled by her storybook romance. Widowed then for many years—Jack Olyphant having died in the early 1960s—she had had a chance encounter with a former suitor, Jack Emery, who as a young man fifty years before had left for a world tour without declaring his love, only to return to find her engaged. Now, almost a lifetime later, they were in love. "It is great you are in love, a great condition," Phyllis wrote after receiving the news. "The only fault is that the fellow will confiscate you from your friends—we'll never have you to ourselves entirely again! But that's a selfish thought."

Pixie Foley, Phyllis's friend from the war years, came from Australia to find her old friends living frugally "with a limited diet of root vegetables and few other trimmings." As they walked through the streets and markets of Roseau, Phyllis never tired of pointing out that the government "didn't worry about things like curbs and gutters and decent streets but were most interested in the power they could grab." Aware of her friend's interest in politics, she took her to an open-air political meeting at a Roseau crossroads. The speakers, of which Phyllis had been one, had addressed the crowd from the balcony of one of the houses on the intersection. There had been a lively interest in the topics discussed, and the "orderly gathering" had provided "an opportunity for important issues to be brought to light."

Among Phyllis and Robert's new friends was Anthony Layng, "a charming young American social anthropologist" who had been "a great success with the Caribs and other neighbours." They had met him shortly after his arrival on his first visit to the island—having read *The Orchid House*, he had been eager to meet her. They had driven him to the Reserve, where he agreed to rent their small house for the many months he would need to complete his work. Their shared interest in the Caribs cemented the relationship. Phyllis, he soon found, was an avid conversationalist, knowledgeable, passionate, witty, and often fascinating. He would sit to listen to her "in awe," grateful to her and Robert for the generosity with which they would share information and contacts. Robert, though informed and helpful, was eclipsed by her "dynamic personality." She cast a "pretty strong shadow," from which it was difficult for him to emerge. He also tended to be "a little laughable." Once, when they had come for dinner, Layng recalls, Robert volunteered to drain the pot of spaghetti out the door, succeeding only in dropping the whole potful to the ground below. Everyone roared with laughter, but Robert understandably could not be brought to see the humor of the situation and was distraught. Despite her brilliance and charm, however, Layng saw Phyllis as a tragic figure. Even before the heavy blow of Phina's death she would at times reveal an embittered, self-pitying side, and would rail angrily about "her island being run by people she had no respect for and did not respect her."

On those occasions when she allowed herself to wallow in the recounting of the many ills that had befallen her at the hands of ungrateful and treacherous former friends, she became "a pitiful figure," an embittered old woman consumed by disappointment and rage.

Layng was characteristic of the many visitors to Dominica who would sooner or later make their way to the Allfreys' house for conversation and information. As with Dr. Nicholls two generations earlier, visitors interested in learning more about the island's history, culture, literature, ecology, or opposition politics were as a matter of course taken to meet Phyllis and Robert. Many of them, like Layng and American sociologist Robert Myers, would become friends. Others, like Anna Rutherford, editor of the literary and scholarly journal *Kunapipi*, and her colleague Kirsten Petersen, had come seeking insights and information on Jean Rhys after their friendship came to light following Jean's death. In the late 1970s, with interest on Caribbean women writers on the rise and a growing recognition of her role as one of the "founding mothers" of women's literature in the region, a trickle of scholars came seeking insights about her own work. Some months after Phina's death Phyllis met an American scholar, Elaine Campbell, who would do much to assure the reissue of *The Orchid House* after almost three decades out of print. Campbell was visiting friends in Dominica when she was taken to meet Phyllis. They had a brief conversation about her work and the burdens faced by women writers. When she returned to the United States, Campbell had approached Dutton, Phyllis's American publishers, and her agents at Curtis Brown to inquire into the possibility of a new edition of the novel. She exhorted Phyllis to make progress on *In the Cabinet*, reissue *Palm and Oak* and *In Circles*, and gather her short stories into a collection. In her zeal she had even visited Jean Rhys in England and persuaded her to write a preface for *The Orchid House* in the event of it being reissued. Both grateful and delighted, Phyllis only hoped that if the novel were to be reprinted and sold in the West Indies, "it should really be as a paperback, since the people who would want to read it could never afford the high price of a hardback book."

In the summer of 1978 the noted Guyanese writer and literary critic Arthur J. Seymour, in Dominica for a series of lectures, visited Phyllis at the mill house and gave her a collection of his poetry—*Images of Majority*—which she "read in its entirety far into the night." The two had never met before but greeted each other with the warmth of old friends. She was left full of admiration for the strength, love, and friendship he conveyed in his poems; he went away convinced of the wealth of ideas and talent she had yet to offer to a Caribbean readership were she to resume her writing. He wrote to her admiringly upon his return to Guyana, urging her to do so. "You were a name on a page. You were the most mature creative example of the White West Indian that I knew. I had read of your novel in the pages of Ken Ramchand's book, but I had never seen the book itself. So it was a great event to see you, read your poems, run my editorially-trained eye swiftly over your short stories in the magazines you showed me and hear you articulate your thoughts on Daniel Thaly and Jean Rhys. The world of which you spoke is a world that is being lost completely and unless you recount it, however succinctly, it will be no more."

Seymour's advice was one she was wont to heed, as toward the late seventies, impelled by a need to bequeath a legacy to Dominica through her writing—finally acknowledging that politics had brought only temporary triumphs—she was eager to return to fiction. With Phina gone, her path to "prolongation, . . . legacy," rested on the literary work she had almost completely set aside when she became a Federal minister. Inspired by Jean Rhys's dedication to writing despite setbacks and illness, she had in 1973 (shortly after they resumed their correspondence), published *Palm and Oak II*, a selection of her favorite poems from *In Circles, Palm and Oak*, and *Contrasts*, to which she added a handful of new poems: "Trio by Lamplight,"a loving portrait of young David as combining the attributes of Hiawatha, Hucklebery Finn, and Lord Fauntleroy, in which she celebrates the tender bond between Robert and the little boy; "The Child's Return," the poem she dedicated to Jean; and "Ghosts in a Plantation House," a meditation on how the decay of her father's class had not stemmed the race and class acrimony of a former plantation society. "But land is land and the predators are busy," she wrote, "From an enchanted enclave of long days past / Nobody wants to move. Both ghosts and lawyers are waiting / Deep in the shadows: the struggle not yet abating." As evidence of her productivity through the sixties her new poetic work was scanty indeed. She sent copies to various friends, among them C.L.R. James, who wrote to thank her for the book and its kind personal inscription, declaring himself "not only astonished but impressed by the poetic power which shines out in poem after poem." "Turn the Leaves," he thought, was a magnificent poem. But with those kind words she had to content herself, as very little additional notice was taken of the volume.

In 1978, encouraged by Seymour, and having received a couple of "nice critical write ups" in *Kunapipi* and Donald Herdeck's *Caribbean Writers*, she had resolved to write a new version of *In the Cabinet*, a fictionalized rendering of the earlier autobiography, which she intended as a tribute to Phina. But the resumption of her writing career was not without its difficulties. Her primary obstacle, as it had been since her return from Trinidad, was the *Star*, and through it the public role in Dominican affairs that had become "such a part of her identity." The paper was her little "sling shot," and although she acknowledged that it "slowed down [her] creative writing" she could not bring herself to give it up, even though by 1978 it was hardly worth it financially. By then they were keeping it going on a mere four pages and sorely needed advertising—"the lifeblood of any newspaper!" But she was not ready to relinquish it, even if it meant being able to return to her new novel. The *Star* kept her in politics, and it seemed that politics indeed had "ruined her for writing." She was also doubtful as to whether any new creative work would indeed guarantee her a place in the new Caribbean literary "establishment." She aspired to a triumph equal to that of Jean's *Wide Sargasso Sea*, while knowing deep in her heart that any such triumph would have to come to her not in England, but as a West Indian writer *in* the West Indies. Though she had no identity other than that of a West Indian, she doubted whether she would be accepted as such by fellow Caribbean authors so seemingly focused on race. As a white West Indian writer she felt as displaced as she once had felt as a West Indian writer in England.

In February 1979 Phyllis had reviewed the then current issue of *Caribbean Quarterly*, a collection that brought home with full force the extent to which race, though not necessarily racism, permeated every aspect of Caribbean literature. It included Jamaican novelist John Hearn's short story "Snow Virgin," "Sea Grapes," by Derek Walcott (one of her "four greats in poetry—Auden, Dylan Thomas, Walcott, Yeats"), and works by "nearly all the fine names of good West Indian writers"—Martin Carter, Samuel Selvon, Slade Hopkinson, Wilson Harris, and Edward Brathwaite—and was "thick with ideas which open up gates to works which are only half-known in some cases, throughout our islands." But its many negative references to V. S. Naipaul's work on the subject of race left no doubt of the closing of ranks against nonblack writers. He was called "anti-black" by one reviewer, and "elsewhere the horrible word *miscegenation* crops up." Phyllis was not herself a great fan of Naipaul's. She had met him and his "mousey English wife" in Port of Spain—they had come to her house at Federation Park for dinner—during the very return he had described in *The Middle Passage*. She had thought then that most of his conclusions—on Trinidad—had been true; but he had not stayed "long enough or explore[d] deeply enough to find out everything about the others." She was nonetheless troubled by the volume's continuous emphasis on blackness as the only possible source of West Indian literary authenticity. In her isolation in Dominica, with her contacts with other writers limited to an occasional letter from authors she had known in the past, like C.L.R. James, Jean Rhys, or Edward Brathwaite, she had been oblivious of the extent to which racialist approaches (of which she had been aware in Trinidad in their embryonic form) had dominated theoretical and critical discussions of West Indian literary developments. Now for the first time in her life she began to acknowledge her whiteness as a problem. "I sigh, thinking how during Federal days I believed that the West Indies could be the best small nation of *mixed* people in the world. After all, I have been here for 356 years (since Thomas Warner came). *Then* I strolled to the Trinidad Library and found my one novel on a shelf for 'white people's fiction.'"

As had happened too many times during her career, progress on *In the Cabinet* would be sidetracked by politics. Between 1977 and 1980 political developments in Dominica were too tumultuous for even the most indifferent to ignore. The Freedom party had been slowly but indefatigably working to broaden its power base and overcome the perception that its leadership was of the *gros-bourg*, and in the 1970 general election, after two years of working steadily to build up its strength in the southern districts, it had won two seats in the House of Assembly. The party's hopes had been bolstered when a sudden and unexpected rift had divided the Labour party leadership; Alec Ducreay, Mabel James, and W. S. Stevens, along with other members of the Executive Committee, had sought to expel LeBlanc from the party. A dispute over the party name and voting symbol had ensued, and a court decision had granted the rebel members the right to the name Dominica Labour party and the symbol of the hat. Unfazed, LeBlanc had simply formed a new party, the LeBlanc Labour party, retaining the DLP's massive traditional vote. Rose O had counseled a change of leadership in "My National Song," claiming he had had it "too sweet for too long," but LeBlanc had gone on to yet another victory.

The Executive Committee's revolt was but the first of many challenges LeBlanc would face in the years that followed. A questionable accord between Dominica, Grenada, Saint Lucia, Antigua, and Guyana in 1972 to join together as a political and economic unit—the Grenada Declaration, decried by a Saint Lucian leader as "an agreement between sardines and a shark"—in addition to other more local concerns, had led to a sharp rise in political tensions. In 1972 the Freedom party had won the Roseau Town Council elections and had engaged in a petty dispute with the central government over ownership of part of the land on which the new Roseau market was being built. In retaliation LeBlanc sought to dissolve the council and appoint instead an interim commissioner to run the capital. A bill to that effect was to be passed on December 6, but bitter feelings against both this and the Guyana issue exploded into a massive demonstration before the courthouse, during which a crowd burst through the main gate, pouring into the chamber as the House was about to commence its meeting, forcing it to be adjourned. Numerous people involved in the demonstration, Eugenia Charles among them, were charged for their part in the events, so many that Phyllis reported in the *Star* overhearing the following conversation at the Roseau Post Office: "'Got your summons yet?' 'But of course! Got yours?' 'No such luck. I live slightly out of town.'" Though most cases were dismissed, a number of the accused were found guilty and fined.

In July 1974, as the country was readying for elections, Phyllis printed in the *Star* a copy of the famous Federal election leaflet bearing her photograph with that of LeBlanc. "Each leaflet," she told her readers, "was worth at least two votes." It accompanied an article exposing the treachery involved in "How LeBlanc Climbed to Power," a perfidy that included assuming the post of political leader "behind Mrs. Allfrey's back and without even informing her," and her expulsion from "her own Party on a quibble." She had pasted out the word Labour in the leaflet "lest some of our simpler readers take it as an invitation to vote for LeBlanc again or for his party. *We strongly advise them* not *to do so*." But voters would not be given the opportunity to reject LeBlanc at the polls. Within days of the publication of this article, and after more than fifteen years in public office (thirteen of them as head of the government), he surprisingly resigned from politics, citing the "rising dissension in the country" and family considerations. Always thin skinned, LeBlanc had virtually disappeared from Roseau after the Town Council debacle, moving back to Vieille Case and traveling to the capital twice a week for House meetings. Eugenia Charles had taken to calling him "the invisible man." The pressures he alluded to in his statement of resignation included accusations of "autocracy in his dealings with the opposition, the unions, and even with members of his own executive."

Phyllis was elated, as were the Freedom party leaders with whom she had so closely allied herself. ONE DOWN, ONE TO GO, heralded that week's *Star*. He was replaced as premier by Patrick John, a former school teacher and trade union leader whose first major political post had been as mayor of Roseau. His rise to power had been "meteoric," particularly after he had been forced to resign as mayor for illegally borrowing two thousand dollars of Roseau Town Council funds. He nonetheless had gone on to win a seat in the 1970 general elections and had joined the cabinet, ultimately acceding to the premiership after ridding the government of other potential claimants. Riding high on his popularity, the DLP immediately called a general election and launched a campaign centered on John as a man of action at a time of crisis, "young, virile, fun loving, and proletarian." His decisiveness and virulent speeches on platform and radio, backed by a new team of political players, all pointed in their favor. The campaign slogan was "Our new team, the electrifying one," prompting Phyllis to comment wryly in the *Star* that they seemed to have blown a fuse. She was not at all impressed with the often crude young politician, whom she had once described as "one of the potatoes that got spoilt in the bag." John's young team of candidates, promoted as a "dynamic combination," swept the 1974 election, wining sixteen of the twenty-one seats, with three going to the Freedom party (one of them to Eugenia) and two to independents. The large margin of victory gave John the mandate he wanted to deal heavy-handedly with the Dreads, and he escalated his already broad offensive against all those presumed to be associated with the group. The activities of the security forces were intensified, and in November an act was passed for the establishment of a full-time Defence Force charged with maintaining "the integrity of the boundaries of Dominica," and assisting the police force in the maintenance of law and order during civil disturbances. John assumed the rank of colonel in a force that was problematic from the start, seeming to operate at times as his small private army, an undisciplined, substandard group notorious for its sexual laxity (there were countless instances of officers engaging in sexual relationships with female recruits), and led by unqualified officers known to smoke marijuana with their men.

At the Labour party's twenty-first annual convention in August 1976, Patrick John announced plans to seek independence. Preliminary talks were held in London the following March, not, as the government had hoped, to set a date, but to clarify the issues of contention between the government and the Freedom party. The government wanted independence as of November 1977; the Freedom party favored the holding of a general election before its declaration. The opposition supported a republican system of government with a president elected by ballot, an assembly of thirteen members elected to represent the single-member constituencies, and an additional eight to be elected on the basis of proportional representation. The Labour party favored an assembly of twenty-one elected members plus nine nominated members, five chosen by the government and four by the opposition. Having failed to garner any support for their position from the Colonial Office, the Freedom party mounted a public campaign designed to build up opposition to independence in the form sought by the government, insisting on a delay of at least six months "in order that the full implications of independence could be explained to the people." Believing that the prestige of her name would add weight to the Freedom party's petition, Phyllis asked Jean to sign it. "Jean Rhys is a completely non-political person," she underscored in the *Star*, "so Dominicans will realise what a great gesture her signature is. We thank her." Privately, Jean wrote to tell her that she had "signed a thing about the referendum" and hoped "it does some good. . . . [But] it all seems a terrible muddle, and there's a bit of muddle here too if it comes to that. I'm afraid I just drift along and try not to think about it." Independence was finally approved in July 1978 in the form sought by John's government. The official ceremony, attended by Princess Margaret, took place on November 2, 1978; but by then John's hold on the government was tenuous at best.

Just weeks after the "surreal" ceremony marking Dominica's independence, the island was rocked by the disclosure of John's involvement in a planned armed invasion of Barbados by mercenaries hired by a shady adventurer, Sydney Burnette-Alleyne, who had intended to install John as ruler of both islands. John's relationship to the disreputable Burnette-Alleyne dated back to 1975, when the premier had signed an agreement with Burnette-Alleyne establishing a corporation charged with raising funds for the construction of an international-size jet airport at Point Crompton, an oil refinery, and subsidiary industries, including hotels and casinos. In return Burnette-Alleyne agreed to pay fifty million Eastern Caribbean dollars (the currency that replaced the BWI dollar in the smaller islands after independence) per year to the island treasury. The agreement had met with misgivings justified almost immediately when Burnette-Alleyne was arrested and imprisoned in Martinique for illegally transporting arms to Barbados, allegedly to be used in an armed overthrow of the government. Fresh out of prison in December 1978, he had been arrested again for planning this latest attempted coup.

These revelations came at a time of widespread disgruntlement in Dominica. Unemployment was rising, and there was growing discontent on the labor front. The government had failed to control the leaf-spot disease plaguing the banana industry, and the crops were seriously threatened. Several weeks after the Burnette-Alleyne fiasco, Dominicans learned that John had sought to lease forty-five square miles of Dominican land to the little-known Texas Caribbean Southern Corporation for a resort-type development to include hotels, casinos, banks, and radio and television stations. This "free port" agreement met with vociferous protests, and he was forced to bow to massive pressure and call off the deal. John, one observer noted, "does not seem to have realised that independence did not transfer ownership of Dominica from Britain to himself and his government." In response to these dubious ventures, Eugenia led a no-confidence motion against him in the House, a move that, given the DLP's significant majority, was preordained to fail. But the debate that followed, broadcast over the radio, became "Dominica's version of the Watergate hearings" and significantly undermined his popular support.

From then on he would be under relentless pressure to resign. Phyllis eagerly joined the fray. In March 1979, when Eric Gairy was deposed by a relatively bloodless coup d'état led by Maurice Bishop and his New Jewel Movement, she took advantage of the occasion to send a stern warning to the government. Dominica had to learn lessons from the Grenada situation that the patience of the people would not last forever; that free and fair elections must embrace unbiased and open registration of electors; that misuse of power can only exasperate the people and drive them to take desperate measures; that the people cannot tolerate corruption in Government forever; and that if people are denied the effective use of the ballot they will resort to the bullet. "Let us hope Govt. leaders will learn these lessons appropriately—or stand the consequences." In April Phyllis sought to explain to her readers the meaning of the words appearing under the *Star*'s masthead—*Virtute Duce Comite Fortuna* (The virtue of the leader is the fortune of the community). "Every community deserved, though it may not always merit, a virtuous leader," she had written, so it was "with a sense of shame" that many Dominicans had learned that "in this UN Year of the Child," their prime minister had not paid a "black cent" toward the upkeep of his youngest daughter by a Catholic marriage, nor had he made maintenance payments to his divorced wife. A few weeks later she took advantage of Margaret Thatcher's election as prime minister of Great Britain to blazon on the front page of the *Star* that it was also TIME FOR A CHANGE in Dominica, an island in dire need of "A Good Woman Leader. Think of this—fast!"

In May 1979 John's government introduced two bills in Parliament that would serve as catalysts to its downfall. One, amending the Libel and Slander Act, was aimed at thwarting criticism from the press; the other severely restricted workers' rights through changes in the Industrial Relations Act. The amended Libel and Slander Act required editors of newspapers to disclose the identity of any person whose work had been published anonymously, and prohibited the publication of any article that directly or indirectly criticized any person in his or her professional or official capacity.

The new Industrial Relations Act sought to prevent civil servants and other workers in essential services from striking, and to prohibit people from giving any financial assistance to strikers. Response to the bills was immediate and overwhelmingly critical. In the *Star* Phyllis labeled them "sinister" and "punitive and vengeful." "Should this Bill be passed," she wrote of the Libel and Slander Bill, "there will be no newspapers in Dominica, and no news for the people save that emanating from the Government by radio and otherwise. In other words, we shall become a fascist state." On May 29 a massive protest march against the bills was held with a crowd estimated at nearly fifteen thousand gathering in front of government headquarters. The Defence Force had stormed the crowd, bayonets fixed, and—angered by the stones hurled at them by several young protesters—began firing tear gas, choking the crowd. Phyllis had rushed into Patricia Honychurch's flat at Cross Lane, after she had been teargassed, looking "like a Macbeth witch, coughing, and wheezing" but enjoying the moment to the hilt. She kept telling Lennox, "This is so exciting." However, the Defence Force's rampage had not stopped with the tear gas, but had escalated into shooting, first into the air and then at the crowd. Philip Timothy, a nineteen-year-old protester, had been shot repeatedly while standing in an alley near government headquarters. The meeting of the House, in progress despite the commotion outside, continued even after news of Timothy's death reached the members. Eugenia had demanded bitterly that the House be adjourned, but she had been outvoted and had led the Freedom party members out of the House in protest. The meeting had proceeded in the absence of the opposition and the two contested laws were passed without dissent. Meeting later with supporters at the parish hall, the Freedom party leadership had called for a national strike to shut down the island until John resigned.

The following day the young victim of the shootout was buried. Funerals, Phyllis wrote in her account, had been exempted by "our fantastic rulers" from the assemblies and demonstrations prohibited by proclamation. Yet Philip Timothy's funeral had been "the biggest demonstration of the Dominican people's grief and resentment at the shooting by a DDF marksman of an innocent fellow-citizen." Long before four o'clock, when the funeral procession was due to leave his house, the street had been crowded with more than four thousand mourners, many of them trade unionists. Philip had been a steelbandsman in the D Special Band, and the pans led his corpse through the tense streets of Roseau to the Roman Catholic cathedral. It had been very much a state funeral with the mayor of Roseau marching with the mourners wearing his mayoral chain, and Eugenia prominent during the church service. All along the route people had lined the streets to watch the procession go by, many falling in as it passed. It had been "quite unlike the usual decorous funeral march," with "waves of mourners stretched right across the streets of Roseau." On June 8th Phyllis announced joyfully the formation of the Committee for National Salvation, whose aim was "the Resignation of Patrick John and his Government at Once." Dominica, she wrote, was teeming with people determined "to arrest the downslide caused by greed, corruption and slavish-mindedness," people with "warm hearts, strong hands and clear minds—though let us admit that some of those minds only became clear this month." It had taken "criminal stupidity leading to death" to make the revelation. Dominicans were all prepared to suffer and indeed were already suffering for its achievement. "We say to them, as the earliest free critic of corruption in government, the *Star* is with you."

The impact of the general strike on the population was severe. For three weeks there would be no mail in or out, no ships entering port or planes leaving. "We are marooned," Phyllis wrote in the *Star*. "Cut off from the outside world save for its messages of condemnation directed at the Government, still mail-less and many of us virtually foodless (certainly in regard to proteins), with only the good old telephone and electricity still keeping going, we are living in a small, contained, turbulent society." With the banks closed, everyone was penniless. There had been no bread and no flour, and all shops, including food shops, had been closed. Phyllis and Robert had lived through the crisis on the proceeds of a check Adèle had sent just days before the strike began, but given the scarcity of food, they had been near starvation. They had had the wisdom to send Robbie to the Reserve, where he lived on root vegetables and boiled figs, but they themselves had emerged from the strike nearly emaciated, looking "like those fantastic stick insects."

Pressure on John to resign mounted throughout June. One after another the members of his cabinet resigned, leaving the country in "constitutional disarray." On June 11 the Committee of National Salvation unveiled a compromise proposal for an interim government headed by former Minister of Agriculture Oliver Seraphine to guide the country until elections could be held. At a rally in Goodwill on June 12 fifteen thousand people gathered to demand John's resignation. Following his appointment of Sir Louis Cools-Lartigue as president, and the latter's dissolution of the House, looters destroyed shops in town owned by Labour party supporters, sacking the Lartigue bakery after stoning his house and "scaring the family almost to death." Lartigue quickly resigned his appointment as acting president, claiming it had not been officially sealed and declaring his proclamation dissolving the House invalid. On the evening of June 16 the "marvelous old Court House," was "criminally set afire by vandals," destroying all the legal documents, title deeds, birth, death, and marriage records. The loss, Phyllis wrote "can hardly be calculated. It is irreparable." Following the resignation of his two remaining ministers on June 18 John agreed to step down.

The proclamation of the new government at an emergency meeting of the House on June 19 was "charged with excited joy," wrote Phyllis, who had gotten press tickets to attend what she called V day. It had been "one of the most important days in Dominica's history." Strewn around the entrance were charred remains of lawbooks, dragged out of the burned-out walls of the courthouse; inside the chamber every member present rose to pledge his support to Oliver Seraphine's interim government. "There is no doubt that the people of Dominica are on the majority immensely satisfied with the [government's] composition," Phyllis declared in the *Star*, "We certainly are." Rose O's verses for that week proclaimed: "Oh the people of Dominica / are a great and glorious clan: / they have saved their country and coastland / from a cursed barbarian."

Dominica's constitutional crisis was over, but another, more devastating crisis was to shake the island just two months later. On August 29 Dominica was utterly devastated by David, one of the worst hurricanes to strike the Caribbean in the twentieth century. It left the island "bare and brown like a petrified moonscape, . . . all mashed up." Phyllis and Robert had had some advance warning, as Celia, fearing they might drown, had phoned from Saint Vincent the day before, urging them to leave the mill house and move to higher and drier ground. The hurricane's winds, she said, had been reported at three hundred miles per hour before being "seeded" by the U.S. Air Force to bring down the speed. Celia had not been alone in urging them to leave for a safer refuge, but they stood their ground, and indeed their little thick-walled stone house was to withstand the winds better than any other refuge they might have found.

David's onslaught had started in the midmorning with a driving rain and fierce winds, like "an attack by an evil giant on the sleeping beauty . . . punctuated by the shattering noise of gnarled fingers deliberately tearing out the roofing overhead." It was the beginning of what for the frail and elderly Phyllis and Robert would seem like apocalypse. Robbie had gone to the Carib Reserve for his last week of summer holiday, and they were alone except for their pets: two dogs, a father and mother cat with their two kittens, and two goats tethered out in the field. It had not taken long for the sheets of corrugated metal roofing to be blown away, and after a while they had no cover save the thin ceiling board, which began to split. The flood rains came into the house slantwise and soon their bed was soaked, and they were driven to take refuge in Robbie's tiny room, which provided a patch of roof. They had struggled to save the animals and the house, pressing a soaked mattress against the bay window with their dripping bodies to fight the increasing fierceness. The horizontal rain continued to batter them "with a deepthroated roar" and they found themselves surrounded by swirling waters and mud that came into the carport and under their front door. For a brief half an hour in the afternoon, as the eye of the storm passed over them the wind and rain stopped completely. Then with a change of direction, the wind and rain started up again wildly and continued for several more seemingly never-ending hours:

> Then it was daylight. What a sight. We were, it seemed, living in an entirely different land. All the green was gone; the mountains which had seemed so blue and round were now harsh peaks with dead stark trees stripped of leaves. Our stream had changed its course and now ran on the other side of the house, between carport and driveway, which was non-existent—a tangle of fallen trees. Aside from the volumes of water around us the island of Dominica was a petrified island. Yet it was strangely beautiful. The stillness was absolute. Not a bird to be heard. . . . We ourselves could see the unclimbable 80-foot high coconut trees uprooted and lying like strewn giant matches within a few yards of our house. The great 150 year old chimney made of lovely bricks of the ruined boiling-house was destroyed. The ruins stood there bare with their walls breached in one place. Old orange trees were uprooted and avocado trees and breadfruit trees torn up. Everything was brownish, as if denuded by a forest fire.

For the first two days they saw nobody and lived mostly on the things they picked from the ground—oranges, avocados, coconuts, and rather green breadfruit. They spent the first day after the storm bailing and mopping "like shipwrecked people," with little food for themselves and the pets. Their old car, brakes on and in gear, had been lifted by the wind and floods and jammed against a stubborn little bush. Their battery radio miraculously worked, but all island communications—lights, telephone, and local radio—had been cut off. Their only news came from

Radio Antilles, from which they learned that throughout Dominica forty people had been killed, 60 percent of the population left homeless, and 90 percent of the banana crop and most of the coconuts destroyed. And then, on the night of August 31 they had to steel themselves for their second major hurricane in two days—Frederick, whose "wet violence" brought them closer to death by drowning than the "tempestuous David." Floods of rain came in a straight downpour against which they had no protection and they were "damp and discouraged." They bore the floods as stoically as they could, working against the water, longing for morning; but the day dawned rainy. By then they had no roof left and their food was very low. The avocados and oranges, sun-scorched on one side, were rotting. Helicopters had begun to appear and they waved, longing for them to drop just one tiny packet of food. But they flew on to Morne Prosper, Wotton Waven, and Trafalgar. They had heard messages on the radio bearing their names but could not reply.

On the third day after the hurricane Phyllis went to town, leaving Robert behind to work on repairs and guard the house from looters. All along the road as she walked people were searching for roofing. Just that morning she and Robert had begun the back-wrenching labor of dragging galvanized sheets which had flown through the air or flowed downstream. Then she had taken a bath in the rerouted stream before setting off to Roseau in search for food. Her path to town was one of devastation. The numerous houses built on what had once been the L. Rose estate were roofless and looked forlorn. Bath Estate Big House, where they had lived when they returned to Dominica in 1954, was deroofed. All the splendid new houses above St. Aroment had been reduced to nothing. The St. Aroment road was impassable and she would learn later to her distress that the house itself had been destroyed. The sight of Roseau, "looking so broken and threadbare, with piles of junk in the streets and sad hungry people strolling," had wrung her heart. A contingent of British navy personnel had been busily clearing what they could of the debris on the streets, but their efforts had done little to conceal the general devastation. Here and there she found a house miraculously undamaged; Jean Rhys's old home, "with its two coats of new paint and mammoth mango tree," stood unscathed. She had made her way to the damaged post office and sat on a step to write letters to Celia and Rosalind, posting them hastily in a pillar box outside; but unknown to her the post office had been abandoned and the letter box waterlogged. All banks and shops were closed. She went to see her cousin Rosalind Volney, one of Ralph's daughters, whom she tracked to the Red Cross office, where she got a few things to eat and a pair of old tennis shoes for the hazardous walk back to Copt Hall. Outside she could see a long queue of highly respectable people lined up to receive their rations. She walked with great apprehension to the *Star* office to see what if anything remained of their files and machinery. She found it wet yet standing, but their office had been commandeered by the landlord to accommodate homeless relatives, and they would have to drag their bits of machinery to the already overcrowded mill house.

The following day she secured some V-2 U.S. Army rations, "and very nice tasty and gentlemanly they were," and found that if they added rice and dasheen spinach they could make a meal for three or even four out of one little box. Very slowly they began to emerge from the debris and wetness. Nature soon reasserted itself. Within days the birds were back and their Bohinia tree, partly uprooted and lying on its side, began "timidly" to show its orchids. Several partly fallen orange trees were not only in leaf "but bearing orange blossom!" The felled bananas were trying hard to make new shoots, and the mountain slopes were showing "a little tender new green." But the trees, "the huge trees for which [they had] campaigned so ardently," were still "dead looking, blasted." They also soon began to receive help from friends and relatives abroad. Adèle, frantic with worry, had repeatedly inquired through the Red Cross about their fate, and also sent a timely check, which helped fix the roof. Jean Rhys's daughter Maryvonne had written to Diana Athill after hearing the news of the hurricane, asking her to send Phyllis two hundred pounds from Jean's estate. Dilys Henrick Jones, Phyllis's friend from the Fulham days, had heard the disaster appeal in England but thought that rather than just put some money into a general fund she would send what she could afford directly to Phyllis, who had been both surprised and pleased, and had used the money for the sort of items Dilys would not have thought of—replacing Robert's birthday present, which had blown away, getting a new pen for herself, and paying Robbie's grammar school fees. "We live like peasants," Phyllis wrote to her with her thanks, "except that the soil is not producing again. . . . I'm so sick of rice I'll never eat another grain when our island vegetables are 'in' again."

The island—and Phyllis and Robert—had survived the worst, but months of scarcity and deprivation followed. By October the best she could report to her friends was that they had "enough to eat." But their situation, like that of most Dominicans, had improved very little. Everyone was poorer, there was no electricity, no telephone service, no cooking gas. Debris still lined the streets. Worse, to her, was the lack of news; DBS had long stretches of total breakdown. The police had announced that many thefts had taken place, some of the robbers being "high-placed persons"; but there was not a functional court before which they could be charged. Distressingly to Phyllis, "the lovely old Carnegie Public Library" had lost its roof, leaving the books to the elements, and the government had done nothing to fix it. The post office was likewise in disrepair. There was a curfew, called by some victims "the curfew that came too late," and she warned in the *Star* that "nobody should walk around Roseau after 8 pm." The mill house, meanwhile, was terribly cluttered, as they had had to move all of the *Star* equipment—two duplicators, two presses, desks, and tables—to the house after they lost their Roseau office. They had two old cars in the carport, neither of which worked for lack of parts; the pool was choked, their water supply only a trickle. And then rumors had reached them that J. B. Charles had sold the house and grounds, and they would have to leave by the end of April. As there were no houses to let anywhere in the south of the island, where many people were still living in tents, that meant they must get the little house near the Reserve in shape—it had been pushed off its *pilotries* by the storm—and would have to retire completely and live in it, hoping that in time they could give it a more proper foundation and build a living room and kitchen. To add to their worries, they heard that the house had been ransacked shortly after the hurricane struck. Someone had wrenched off the door hinges and taken all the crockery, glassware, pots and pans, mattresses, and anything else portable. Hence in December 1979 Phyllis and Robert announced in the *Star* that they were taking a holiday in order to fix the house, and the newspaper would not appear "for a while."

One positive outcome of the Hurricane David debacle was Robert's growing respect for Robbie, whose help had been so invaluable in repairing the house, helping with the difficult move of the *Star* equipment to the mill house, and publishing the *Star* in the months following the devastation caused by the storm. Now he would write about him to friends in something approximating the note of affection and pride he had previously reserved for David. "Laconic Robbie is not shaping up too badly," he wrote Edmund Dowling in late 1979. "He is keen on his school work and took over Albert-on-the-roof directing him how to do the job properly." His manners "could be improved," but he would be "a great Carib leader with a set of principles one day quite soon."

As if the aftermath of Hurricane David had not been enough of a burden for the Dominican people, they soon had to contend with yet another political crisis. The interim government's response to the crisis had been characterized from the start by "mismanagement, fraud, and partisan patronage." The stakes had been substantial, as Dominica had received in excess of $180,000,000 (Eastern Caribbean) in hurricane relief, roughly three times the island's annual budget. In early October, Seraphine had moved to repudiate the Committee of National Salvation that had put him in power, declaring that Hurricane David had blown away all the prehurricane political "marriages of convenience," and dismissing two ministers critical of his measures. The announcements were protested against strenuously in the *Star,* in which Phyllis charged that at a meeting at Springfield between LeBlanc, Patrick John, and Oliver Seraphine, the latter was said to have been given guidelines by his old Labour party colleagues, including advice to fire the two ministers. "If this meeting is a fact," she declared, "the Interim P.M. should resign and call a general election immediately." Seraphine had further angered those who had trusted him with the prime ministry and charged him with leading a caretaker government until elections could be held by signing the St. George's Declaration in Grenada, which linked Dominica to the "fantastically named" Non-Aligned Movement. He had, Phyllis declared in the *Star,* "absolutely no mandate from the country nor any right granted from the Committee of National Salvation to commit Dominica . . . on any foreign affairs, such as international agreements, borrowing of money at interest or any long-term negotiations. . . . The P.M. would do well to stick to appeals on behalf of his suffering people, and hasten the election." From then on she would keep a tenacious pressure on Seraphine to call for elections at the earliest possible moment. Even in their "impoverished and desolate state," they must have "a properly conducted election and bring into power MPs and Ministers of the people's choice." In her view the interim government should concentrate on feeding the people and pave the way for a general election which would then be the starting point for long-term planning under a properly elected government.

In early February the island was rocked by another investment scandal involving the government. An agreement was disclosed between the government and the shady Los Angeles–based Intercontinental Development and Management Company to confer Dominican citizenship on would-be investors through a network of offices that would serve as Dominican consulates. The passports, which would be available for an investment of ten thousand U.S. dollars, were intended for Iranians stranded in the United States after the fall of the shah. It was but one of the government's numerous improprieties before calling for a general election on July 21, which included the distribution of stores of rice and galvanized sheets by the Defence Force on behalf of government candidates. It was an unscrupulous electoral campaign, during which

Phyllis repeatedly urged her readers *not* to vote for anyone associated with attempts "to sell our Island." LeBlanc, she reminded them, sought to sell the Sunday Island scheme, a plan foiled "by public protest." Patrick John's plan to sell forty-five square miles of land to individual American investors had been "foiled as before by a big outcry from the public." Oliver Seraphine had gone one step further, seeking to sell Dominican nationality at ten thousand dollars a passport. "All these men are Labour men—of a sort. They bear the tag, but do not behave like honest socialists. Now John and Seraphine and their partisans are going up for election. They have committed other governmental misdemeanours, but selling Dominica is the worst of all. . . . Avoid them. *Do Not Vote For Any of Their Crowd.*"

When the people went to the polls on July 21, 1980, they responded to the mismanagement and scandals of the last several years by giving the Freedom party a resounding victory. FREE AT LAST AFTER 19 YEARS OF HARD LABOUR—was the *Star*'s headline—"We Have Overcome!" Eugenia Charles and the Freedom Party had won "a landslide victory," securing seventeen out of twenty-one seats. Two had gone to "friendly independents," two to the opposition. "Hearts which had been beating with anxiety now thumped harder with delight," Phyllis exulted. "At last, at last, after nearly twenty years of misrule by Parties calling themselves Labour, the thrall was broken by Freedom. So now we have the Caribbean's first woman Prime Minister—and what a woman, what a Prime Minister. How we love her!"

Thirteen

Love for an Island

Their passion drives them to perpetuation:
they dig, they plant, they build and they aspire
to the eternal landmark; when they die
the forest covers up their set desire.
Salesmen and termites occupy their dwellings,
their legendary politics decay.
Yet they achieve an ultimate memorial:
they blend their flesh with the beloved clay.

The Freedom party's victory in July 1980 took the wind out of the little *Star*'s sails. The paper, born of rage and fed on a diet "of critical asperity," found "nothing valid to criticize in the behaviour of [their] new Freedom rulers" who had pledged to "wipe out" the class discord between "Haves and Have-nots, Gwos Bougs and Petits Bougs, Black and White" that had stunted Dominica's growth for the last twenty years. If at any time they did anything to offend, "either against our beloved principles of human rights or otherwise," Phyllis promised her readers, it would be pinpointed "in our typical barbed manner." The paper, long since reduced to four pages and subsisting on the publication of legal notices—many times they had nearly given up "save for the pleading of lawyers"—resumed publication shortly after the elections as a monthly newsletter. The anti-Labour-party momentum that had propelled Phyllis and Robert to persevere in its publication despite failing health and increasing frailty vanished with her old enemies' ouster by the Freedom party, and its days were now numbered.

Within days of the elections, and after months of anxiety over the need to leave the mill house now that Eugenia had sold it to her former overseer, they were astounded to learn that he would allow them to stay for as long as they lived. Eugenia, conscious of their precarious finances, had let them live in the house "as a sort of grace and favour residence," and they had feared moving to the small house near the Carib Reserve, given its isolation and distance from the road, for Robert had an enlarged heart and was incapable of the mile-long walk over a rough steep track required to get from the main road to the house. In the *Star*'s "Freedom Victory Issue" Phyllis would publicly thank Eugenia and the present owner for their kindness, which demonstrated "a just and generous spirit in Freedom people."

In the *Star*'s last year Phyllis's reporting—or editorializing, as it should properly be called since she appeared to abandon all semblance of journalistic objectivity—centered on two "dire" events that absorbed public interest on the island: one the tragic abduction and murder of Lennox's father, Ted Honychurch; the other Patrick John's Ku Klux Klan–aided attempt to invade Dominica with mercenaries hired to overthrow Eugenia's government. In early February 1981, on the eve of Carnival, Dominicans had been shocked to learn that following an early-morning police raid that had left two Dread youths dead, Honychurch's farmhouse in Giraudel had been burned to the ground and he had been taken hostage. In return for his release, the kidnappers demanded the freeing of two Dreads sentenced for the murder of a schoolteacher the year before, an inquiry into that morning's deadly raid, and an end to police brutality. Honychurch, a gentle, generous man who had often defended the Dreads, was well liked and respected throughout the island, and the news disturbed Dominicans like no other violent act in memory. Phyllis, who loved Lennox so dearly, reacted to the news with barely suppressed anger, charging in the *Star* that the kidnappers were terrorists "addicted to marijuana—the evil home-grown drug whose sale and consumption are rotting our youth: it puts fantasies in their mind to take the place of education and reason"—and questioning whether they were capable of compassion. "They have debased themselves to the standard of beasts in the fields."* Eugenia immediately declared that no negotiations with the Dreads would take place unless they released Honychurch and surrendered their weapons. Her close relationship to Lennox made the situation all the more awkward—he had been for many years her right hand and was then the government's press secretary. But nothing further was heard from the kidnappers, despite numerous radio appeals for his release from Lennox—"whose love for his father rang in every word"—and from numerous civic, labor, and religious leaders. The Caribbean Conference of Churches was prepared to bring outside negotiators if contact could be established, but the stalemate continued for many anxious months. In May many began to lose hope after *France-Antilles* reported that the four terrorists responsible for the abduction were in Martinique, leading to speculation that they would have disposed of their hostage before leaving. It was sadly to prove too true; shortly afterwards one of them led police to the place where Honychurch's body had been wrapped in a stolen mattress and set alight in the hope of concealing all trace of the crime. He had died on the very evening of his abduction, killed as he attempted to escape. In late April, with Honychurch's whereabouts still a mystery, Dominicans were stunned by the news that undercover FBI agents in New Orleans had been engaged by mercenaries tied to the Ku Klux Klan to invade Dominica, oust Eugenia, and replace her with Patrick John. The group was arrested just as they were about to sail, heavily armed with automatic weapons, Uzi submachine guns, and dynamite. Eugenia had immediately declared a state of emergency and placed the former prime minister under arrest. Phyllis and Robert, upon learning that their names were on a list of persons to be liquidated had the coup been successful, felt "flattered." The most peculiar thing about the failed coup, she commented in the *Star*, was how men like John, "who claimed to love their black brothers and sisters," teamed up with white supremacists and racists, "even with leaders of the dreaded Ku Klux Klan, to wrest power from their own people!" Dominica's Rastas and Klansmen would have formed "an unholy combination." The affair did not end there. The following December a group of his supporters attempted a dawn raid on the prison where he and his accomplices were held, seeking to release him and place him once again at the head of the government. Another group had attacked the police station, seeking to seize and break open the armory. The raids had been foiled by the police, but not without casualties on both sides. The attacks had come during floods caused by singularly heavy rain that had wreaked havoc on roads and bridges and caused countless mudslides. The mill house had been surrounded by water for days, and the nearby public road was nothing but a "series of crevasses—a river bed." One

*During the crisis she planted a reader's letter in the *Star* questioning a poem from *Palm and Oak II*, "Resistance," which showed "strong sympathy with Guerrillas," to which she replied that the guerrillas in question were members of de Gaulle's Free French Movement. "I detest terrorism," she added, "whether it emanates from the PLO, the IRA or certain Dominicans."

of Phyllis's pet goats had caught pneumonia as a result and had to be treated with antibiotics and nursed back to health. By the end of the year Dominica was "truly struggling out of the morass of destruction," but, as Phyllis wrote to Adèle, who had written to suggest a visit, it was not "a land to which one could invite a beloved friend!"

"The so-called indestructible Allfreys" were plagued by debilitating illnesses and accidents throughout 1982. Robert had been diagnosed as suffering from some sort of pernicious anemia—he appeared to have "no bone marrow"—and had been again afflicted with his "hemophiliac tongue." He had needed twice-weekly injections of vitamin B_{12} and careful nourishment and care they could barely afford. He had, moreover, been instructed to give up alcohol, something that upset her terribly since, as she told many of her friends, she could not stop drinking and hated doing it alone. On the matter of their alcohol consumption their friends and acquaintances are in agreement; everyone acknowledges that they drank "quite a bit" of rum, and that they did so daily, but all concur in declaring that they "were never blasted" and were seldom impaired in their work or any other activity by alcohol. Be that as it may, by the early 1980s, plagued by ill health and adversity, they had fallen into a habit of drinking at all hours, not continuously perhaps, but in earnest, often failing to eat properly as a result. Drink had become their solace, a means to dull the pain of Phina's death, forget their poverty, and increasingly, their hunger. She once wrote to a friend that it was "cheaper to drink than to eat in Dominica," and as the decade progressed they had so little money that it was easier to buy a bottle of rum and drink to forget. In 1982 they would realize with full force how near destitution they were. The *Star* would cease publication in January, cutting off their only source of income, however meager. Social security was not available to them; neither of them had been employed consistently enough to have secured a pension. They had little help from their children now that Phina was dead. David and Sonia were struggling themselves and not in a position to offer much help. Robbie was still in school and needed their support. The allowance Ted Dowling continued to send them after Phina's death had stopped arriving without explanation after a while and they heard no more from him. They survived on the proceeds of the reissue of *The Orchid House*, occasional small fees for reprinting her earlier work, and a small monthly allowance from Rosalind and George, supplemented by frequent gifts from Adèle and occasional checks and parcels from friends, out of which they sent what they could to Philip's hospital for cigarettes, chocolate bars, and the occasional magazine.

More troublesome than their poverty were the mishaps and ill health that began to plague them as they grew older. In June 1982, as they were returning home after shopping in Roseau, they had a serious accident. They had drawn up at the single-lane Bath Bridge on a wet day, with a fast car approaching. Seeing them, the driver braked, hit the bridge, and slithered sideways, hitting them head on and smashing the front of their car. Phyllis, thrown forward, crashed her head against the dashboard, her dark glasses broke, cutting her face, and for a while they feared her nose had been broken. She emerged from the wreck of their car with multiple cuts and bruises, a sprained back, and a broken left thumb. Robert, who broke his knee, was unable to walk for a long time and she, despite her injuries, had to nurse him, "among my other jobs." Six months later, with his knee just about healed, he developed terrible abdominal pains that led her to fear that he had been poisoned. Carless since the accident, she appealed to Lennox to drive them to the hospital,* where he was diagnosed as suffering from a twisted intestine and rushed to surgery. With his weak heart and the unsanitary conditions for which the Princess Margaret Hospital was known, it had been "touch and go" and he had nearly died. After the surgery he had been sent home too early as his bed had been needed for an emergency case. Each day a nurse had come to dress "the horrible wound," and Phyllis had been "in terror" of infection as the mill house was "germy and pet-filled." His cure—for he was cured—was said to be miraculous. By February he was quite active and "chirpy," though still very thin and frail. As a result Phyllis had not been to town for weeks, having to depend on friends, chiefly Lennox and Patricia Honeychurch, to bring groceries and medical supplies. She had also been very short of money, so much so that she had not picked up a package from Adèle being held for them at the post office, because she had not known how much duty would be owed. She was rescued from her "apathy" by a one-hundred-dollar check from Adèle—"a godsend"— and had been able to "cheer herself both with the money and the parcel." Later in the year, Adèle, who had set aside the considerable sum of three thousand dollars for Phyllis in her will, decided to send the money right away. Phyllis was astounded at receiving an amount that came to over EC $6,000. It was "the largest sum of money [they'd] ever had in [their] bank since they [had] bought the little machinery for the *Star* . . . and enough to give [them] a lovely feeling of security, which is so good for writing. [She]'d been uneasy off and on for so long." Besides, she told her old friend, they much preferred to have it while Adèle was still as alive as they were. The one other bright event of the otherwise distressing year was the reopening of the Roseau library after its "resurrection" following the damage caused by Hurricane David. Phyllis, a staunch supporter of the library, who had appealed successfully to her many librarian friends in England to send books and donations, was asked to say a few words during the inaugural ceremony and was rewarded with borrower's card number one. During the remaining years of her life she would spend countless hours at the library, reading and occasionally working on the manuscript of *In the Cabinet*.

Faced with health and money troubles, Phyllis and Robert had no choice but to relinquish the *Star*. She had struggled against the decision, but by late 1981 she was too exhausted from nursing Robert and coping with little money and no car to argue any further, and in January 1982 (the month during which he nearly died) the last issue came out. She "felt it dreadfully," as with the little newspaper went a vital part of her identity as a public figure. The *Star* had assured her an active role in island affairs, which had sustained her through the worst of her political and personal travails. Without it she no longer had the privileges of access of the press to question, challenge, and opine. In the painful period after Phina's death and the tumultuous months following the devastation caused by Hurricane David, the paper had given her "a reason to get up in the morning." Her life without it would be reduced to the private realm of her little mill house and her friends—not a lonely life as the latter were many and she had Robert and Robbie and countless pets—but one of a retirement for which she was ill suited. Therefore Phyllis, never one to let grass grow beneath her feet, reverted to her other sustaining identity—that of writer. She immediately announced her determination to finish *In the Cabinet* once and for all. And the

*Lennox recalls Phyllis on that occasion filling out the "marital status" line of the hospital admission form with "a long and happy marriage."

Star's final issue carried on its front page the announcement of Virago's reissue of *The Orchid House*.

Phyllis had learned of Virago's intention to republish the novel in August 1980, when Carmen Callil, its founder and publisher, had written to express her delight. The book had come to her via Phyllis's agent at Curtis Brown, she had read it overnight, and made an offer the very next morning. "I really think it's one of the best novels we shall publish on our Classics list," she wrote. Phyllis was overjoyed at the realization of what had long been a cherished if elusive dream. She had faced disappointment before, when Heinemann had considered a reissue for its Caribbean Writers series, only to decline after a discouraging report from its West Indian office. Elaine Campbell would intimate in her introduction to the new edition that that decision had been racially motivated, prompted by Afrocentric notions of what could properly be considered authentic West Indian fiction, such as those held and promoted by Edward Brathwaite. Privately she would share with Phyllis her apprehensions about the latter being asked for an opinion by Heinemann and offering a half-hearted endorsement that would put an end to their hopes from that direction. This charge Brathwaite has resolutely denied. He respected and admired Phyllis—"such an important WI writer"—and had never "harboured any wish or intent to prevent . . . the publication, circulation, or admiration" of her work.

When Phyllis received her first copies of the new edition in January 1982 she was thrilled. The much-anticipated event enlivened a period of her life when she was "down and out," and lifted her depressed spirits. They arrived when Robert had been close to death from his abdominal troubles and she was exhausted and disheartened, and she propped a copy on a table in the middle of the mill house's main room for all visitors to see and admire, encouraging everyone to praise the appropriateness of the cover, with its orchid, hummingbird, and verdant mountains as a backdrop. The triumph of seeing the novel reissued was marred, however, by her discomfiture when she read the introduction and found that from its opening paragraph it was built on establishing comparisons between her and Jean Rhys. Virago's decision owed much to Elaine Campbell's efforts, for which Jean had paved the way by bringing the novel to the attention of Francis Wyndham and Diana Athill, and Phyllis had been exceedingly grateful. But now she found herself "most distressed" ("rather excited," as one friend described her) at being again placed under Jean's shadow, her own career presented, in her view, as an appendage to Jean's stellar success with *Wide Sargasso Sea*. Despite her affection for Jean, comparisons between them had become wormwood to her. Phyllis felt that as a Dominican writer she had come first—her own *Orchid House* having been published a good thirteen years before *Wide Sargasso Sea*—and, considering her own novel every bit as good as her friend's, was unwilling to take a back seat to one whom she had loved dearly but whose life had fallen short of her own ideal of a "real" life immersed in the events of the world and their island. She came to feel that "she had come first and Jean had gotten all the praise." She believed, moreover, that Jean had "borrowed" elements from her work. She would insist that she had "pinched" character names from *The Orchid House* (Christophine and Baptiste), and would tell her friend Pierrette Frickey during one of her visits, "over the usual tea and crumpets," that Jean had unconsciously taken passages from her novel. Asked whether she had ever mentioned this to Jean, she replied that "she would have done so, but did not want to hurt her."

There are indeed numerous similarities between the two novels—the character names Phyllis often mentioned, the central role played in each by the childhood nurse, the lavish descriptions of an overwhelming and often threatening landscape, the estate house as a focal point of each tale, among others—that justified Phyllis's feeling piqued when she heard Jean's work lionized by the many admirers who wrote or visited with numerous inquiries about Jean and very few about herself. Her own career had had such breadth, she had risked and lost so much in pursuing her dream of being of service to the Dominican people, that in the years following Jean's death she had come to resent the frequent inquiries for information and insights into her old friend's career. More often than not she would leave letters unanswered—Jean's biographer Carole Angier had to appeal to Phyllis's friend Polly Pattullo to get a reply—and would greet visitors politely but reticently. Those interviewers who succeeded in eliciting the most information about their relationship were, not surprisingly, those whose interest was in her own career and writings, like Polly and Pierrette Frickey. Some friends came to feel that "the worst thing anyone could do was to compare her to Jean Rhys."

Grateful as she was for Campbell's efforts to get the book reissued, she saw the comparisons to Jean in almost every review of the novel as stemming primarily from her introduction. Rory Barnes, in the *National Times*, made much of the comparison, concluding that *The Orchid House* was not another *Wide Sargasso Sea*, "but given the pure genius of Rhys' shimmering masterpiece, this is hardly devastating criticism." *The Bookseller* acknowledges the book's original publication in 1954 but still goes on to describe it as "strongly evocative of . . . *Wide Sargasso Sea* by her friend and compatriot Jean Rhys." Even when not dwelling on the Rhys connection, the early reviews were distasteful to her. The brief uncredited note that appeared in the *Sunday Times* was, as the friends who sent it on to her called it, "rather unpleasant." It was not a review in any sense of the word, as it contained no comment on the novel itself other than a perfunctory allusion to Jean's work. It described Phyllis as having been left "broke" by the closing of the *Star*, and intimated that the publication of her novel "may improve her finances, which have never recovered from a hurricane in 1979." Allfrey, the anonymous writer underscored, "speaks with the Cheltenham accent of a vicar's wife, except that she says 'man' at the end of every sentence, like a Jamaican dope-smuggler." She was gratified to learn that J. S. Arthur, an old friend from the British High Commission, had brought the novel to the attention of Princess Margaret during the latter's visit to Barbados—he had reminded the princess that she had met Phyllis on board ship at the Independence celebrations in Dominica, having met her previously at the Federal inauguration—but even privately she could not escape comparisons to Jean. "Both my wife and I think it is every bit as good as Jean Rhys," he wrote, "in fact I would say rather better—the most enchanting work I have read in a long time."

Her chagrin over the introduction severely damaged her relationship with Campbell, whom she had considered until then a warm friend and toward whom she had felt a strong feeling of obligation for making possible the new edition of her book. She had meant to dedicate *In the Cabinet* to her and Robert. But after the debacle of the introduction and the reviews that drew upon its comparison between the two Dominican writers, she would frequently abuse her when speaking to her friends, charging in the years that followed that Campbell was using her to further her academic career, and repeating often that she was trying "to suck her dry." Some claim that in the years that followed she "came to hate the very sound of [Campbell's] name." The latter, however, continued her efforts to promote Phyllis's career abroad, trying unsuccessfully to secure an invitation for her to represent Dominica at a literary conference organized by the Universidad Central de Barcelona, and writing to Eugenia Charles to propose appointing Phyllis as Dominica's literary ambassador. She made numerous attempts to find a publisher for a collection of Phyllis's short stories, but even this would lead to acrimony, as Phyllis claimed that her sole copy of the stories, many of them unpublished, had never been returned to her by Campbell. In this she was not being quite fair to her erstwhile friend—as she had also given copies of her stories to Pierrette Frickey. (The stories, however, were indeed not among her papers at her death, and a new set had to be pieced together from various sources in preparation for this study; but given the vagaries of the Dominican postal services, any parcel from Campbell had every probability of never reaching her.)

The book's reissue had also rekindled the Nichollses' animosity. Mindful of the scandal that arose in Roseau in 1954, she had tried to forestall any renewed enmity in her announcement of the book's publication in the *Star*, telling potential readers that *The Orchid House* was "not a biography": "As Flaubert once said when asked who was Madame Bovary—*Mme. Bovary c'est moi*—this is true of the three sisters and even of Lally the Montserrat nurse, but the author underlines that Rufus in the book is not a portrait of her uncle Ralph nor of her father's cousin Rufus King of St. Kitts." She could have saved herself the ink. Despite her efforts to draw attention away from the novel's autobiographical aspects, Ralph's children (the Nicholls girls, as Phyllis frequently referred to them) were again incensed, especially as this time the novel was readily available for sale in Roseau, and the reading public had grown considerably in the thirty years that had elapsed. Phyllis gave a copy of the book to her cousin Rosalind Volney, to whom she grew very close in her last years, but Rosalind claimed she had thrown it away "somewhere"—she was "not going to read that trash."

But all was not negative. Shortly after the novel's reissue she received an offer of a contract, which she eagerly accepted, for the publication of a Czech translation of the novel. And later that year, thanks to Lennox's efforts, she was made the recipient of the Dominican Government's Golden Drum Award, given to her in recognition of her years of encouragement to young writers. It would be the only thing for which she would be officially recognized by her country. The planned ceremony found her with literally nothing fit to wear in public, and Celia quickly sent a dress, which proved too long and was hastily taken up by Phyllis at the hips rather than at the hem, giving her a slightly "oddball" appearance. (Polly Pattullo once described her as dressing in a "touchingly quaint" way, as if her clothes came from some fantastic "tropical jumble sale.") The poignancy of the moment was not lost on some of her old Labour party associates. Arnold Active would comment later of the Golden Drum Award that it had not been sufficient recognition for the magnitude of what she had accomplished in Dominica. In the end she had gotten "nothing from her party, or the opposition, or those she associated with after the Labour party, after being in fact the person that invented political parties in the island. She had been the *architect* of political change in Dominica, and for this she had never been honoured."

The reissue of *The Orchid House* brought into Phyllis's life two women who would be among her most stalwart friends in the last years of her life, Polly Pattullo and Pierrette Frickey. The two became "like family" to Phyllis; Polly would become her spokesperson to the world, writing frequently about her in the British press and keeping her name alive outside Dominica in this period of Phyllis's deepest obscurity.

In April 1982 Polly, then an assistant writer for London's *Observer Colour Magazine*, wrote to propose a visit for an interview about her political and literary work. Phyllis's gratification was enhanced by this being the first request for an interview she had had in years that did not revolve around Jean Rhys.* Polly had come across a reference to her political and literary work in Gordon Lewis's *The Growth of the Modern West Indies* and had just finished reading *The Orchid House*, which she had found "truly beautiful." The visit would not come about until January 1984, but when it did the two women hit it off extremely well. Polly, a smart, straightforward, politically sophisticated woman with a quick wit and a wry sense of humor, immediately fell head over heels in love with Dominica—which proved to be the quickest way to Phyllis's heart. Her interest in the Federation, and her genuine understanding of the older woman's curious mixture of idealism and pragmatism, led to an outpouring of information and insights. For many years her published interviews and articles would remain the most revealing and informative sources on Phyllis's life and career. She was able to capture in their conversations the fusion of triumph and pathos in Phyllis's pursuits, conveying this through the most seemingly insignificant details of their meetings. "I'm slow at cooking, slow at writing, quick at talking," Phyllis told her during their first visit as she prepared lunch, which they ate "at a battered old whist table cluttered with jam jars of wild flowers, books, papers." The pumpkin soup was served with a "great blackened monogrammed silver ladle."

Polly's first visit came only a few months after the U.S. invasion of Grenada in late 1983—she was also to interview Eugenia Charles, who had gained international fame for her role in the events†—and she found that Phyllis had photos of Eugenia and Lech Walesa prominently displayed, propped on the electricity meter. They were "her people for 1983." At the time Eugenia's popularity was running so high that hardly anyone spoke out against her, and Phyllis did not, declaring her erstwhile

*A few months later Phyllis had been quite interested in an request from an assistant editor at the *Times Literary Supplement* to provide a few pieces for the *TLS*, only to be sorely disappointed at the first book they asked her to review—Selma James's *The Ladies and the Mammies: Jane Austen and Jean Rhys.*

†On October 13, 1983, a hard-line faction of Maurice Bishop's People's Revolutionary Government, led by Finance Minister Bernard Coard, took control of the government, placing Bishop under house arrest. On October 19 thousands of demonstrators marched to his residence, freed him, and helped him attempt to organize a defense at Fort Rupert, an old British fort overlooking the capital, St. George's. Twenty people were killed when Coard's army opened fire, forcing the crowd to flee, and Bishop was seized and executed on the spot, together with five close supporters. A curfew and numerous arrests followed. U.S. President Ronald Reagan, who had mounted a steadily escalating campaign against Bishop since taking office, was eager to intervene militarily—U.S. military forces had in fact, repeatedly practiced invasion procedures off the coast of Puerto Rico. On the day following Bishop's execution, prompted by the American government, the leaders of the Eastern Caribbean met and resolved to request formally that the United States intervene. Eugenia Charles personally delivered the request to Francis McNeil, U.S. ambassador to Costa Rica, at a meeting in Barbados, and hurriedly flew to Washington to press the issue. At the White House she was co-opted into appearing with Reagan on national television when he announced the impending invasion, her presence intended to defuse criticism from opponents of the intervention. In her statement to the media, Charles offered a number of unconvincing explanations: the Eastern Caribbean leaders' concerns about their own citizens living in Grenada; their dismay about Cuban and Soviet infiltration in the region; the absence of a tradition of political violence in the Eastern Caribbean. Her performance before the White House press corps, however, was a major success, and she became an instant celebrity, used by the American government to justify to the country its military actions in Grenada.

political foe to be her heroine, and praising the marvelous job she was doing to pull Dominica out of the morass of the last two decades. Their old antagonisms had worn themselves out long before, and Phyllis was nothing if not admiring. She compared Eugenia to Margaret Thatcher, "lower middle-class with all their faults and virtues—but very brave," and had by then put aside feelings of dismay concerning the American intervention that she seemed to have shared with no one but Lennox. When Eugenia had returned to Dominica in late October after the now famous television appearance with Ronald Reagan, legitimizing the invasion, to a tumultuous welcome from joyous crowds lining the streets cheering her passage, Phyllis had sat listening to the crowds on the radio feeling strangely disturbed by the events. As she dejectedly told Lennox, it did not "ring right."

In 1978, when the New Jewel Movement had toppled the Gairy regime in Grenada, Phyllis had been very sympathetic to the new rulers, and had been quick to denounce in the *Star* the "smug hypocrisy" of the United States vis-à-vis the situation. The Bishop government had restored to the people of Grenada the right to pursue life, liberty, and property, Robert had written then: "Let not the powerful people of America deny the citizens of Grenada their natural rights." Criticism of the United States was a running theme throughout 1979. In April, Phyllis published an essay by Alister Hughes, a Grenadian newspaper editor who was a close friend of hers and Robert's, warning against American threats to his home island. "The world owes us nothing and, in the arena of international politics, even the richest, freest and most generous will squeeze us if it suits their purpose. When we established the West Indies Federation, it was a voluntary move towards political unity. It appeared then that we understood that unity could give us strength. Perhaps the realities of independence will drive us back to the almost discarded concept of West Indian Nationhood." After Bishop's successful coup, Phyllis had watched Grenada's ostracism by other Caribbean nations with deep concern. In their rush to line up to receive American aid and investments, they had turned their backs on Grenada, currying favor with the Reagan government through open expressions of antagonism to the Bishop regime. Still a committed Federalist, she felt that the governments of the Caribbean should have been working in unity to solve the region's problems and not open themselves to American intervention, something unknown in their history. In her eyes American pressure on Bishop and continued interference in his nation's affairs was "wrong." When the revolt that killed him and overthrew his government broke out on October 19, she was filled by a deep sense of shame at what the Caribbean had been reduced to and opposed American intervention as unnecessary. But by the time Eugenia appeared by Reagan's side in Washington to "request" help, Phyllis was torn. For days she had been concerned about news of Alister Hughes's imprisonment—he was generally believed to have been killed—and his rescue by American forces partially reconciled her to the invasion. But to Lennox, who came to see her the evening of Eugenia's triumphant return, she confessed that she could not "link my feelings with those people in the streets."

But what she could share privately with Lennox she would not reveal to Polly at their initial meeting, despite the strong bond that developed immediately between her and the younger woman. In the years that followed they kept up a steady correspondence; Polly sent much-needed parcels of books and magazines, utility knives and forks, an essay on her old employer Naomi Mitchison, and occasionally a check to help them along—for all of which Phyllis was keenly grateful, writing once to her new friend that she was behaving toward them "just like family—just like Phina used to do," the highest praise she could bestow on anyone. "What can I say to this?" Phyllis wrote once upon receipt of one of Polly's checks—she would not buy wine or rum with it now that Robert had been forbidden alcohol, but she would try to buy "things like long-life milk youghurt [*sic*] to make Robert get better and better." In 1984 Polly urged her to apply for a Royal Literary Fund grant, sending the necessary forms and offering every possible assistance, and Phyllis did, although she procrastinated until close to the application deadline and almost failed to send them. She somehow "couldn't bear to fill in the R.L.F. form [which required a full financial disclosure—in her eyes a confession of dire poverty]. Something held me back. Silly pride, perhaps." She received a grant of £1,000, which, with the proceeds of the sale of their car (£2,000) and of the *Star*'s printing equipment (£1,300), constituted the bulk of their income for what turned out to be their most prosperous year in the 1980s.

During this period Phyllis also befriended Pierrette Frickey, a literature professor at West Georgia College, whom she met in 1983 while she was visiting Dominica researching an essay on Jean Rhys. Pierrette had been taking a jeep tour in the mountains when she had seen "a very thin and fragile-looking woman with the bluest eyes, her lovely white hair pulled in a chignon," walking along the road. She had known at once that it was Phyllis, about whom she had heard often and whose novel she had read, and who, overjoyed at the prospect of company and conversation, had invited her to the mill house nearby for the first of many chats, during which they drifted from one subject to another: from Doudou, Phyllis's goat, to the merits of taking baths among the ferns in the waterfall in front of the mill house; from Phyllis's belief that Jean had "stolen" the character of Christophine from *The Orchid House* to her admiration of Jean's "superb craftsmanship" as a writer; from her love of Robbie to the importance of owning the little cottage near the Carib Reserve. She sometimes spoke of Phina, but that loss was evidently so great that Pierrette never pressed for more information when she spoke of her pain. Pierrette, as soft and nurturing as Polly was vibrant and challenging, appealed to Phyllis's romantic, more sentimental side, and to her she would pour out the pain of loss—of Phina and Philip, and to a certain extent, David and Sonia—and of her poverty. Pierrette, hearing of her friend's many burdens, had a very difficult time understanding "the lack of gratitude on the part of some of the ones she held most dear (this included her adopted children and the government of Dominica)." Like Polly, she would do what she could to ease the older woman's hardships, helping enormously during the period Robbie spent in the United States in a teacher-training course. Phyllis had appealed to her then to help him with the warm clothing he would need, and Pierrette had provided that while continuing to send frequent checks and parcels to Phyllis herself.

Encouraged by the reissue of *The Orchid House* and at the urging of new and old friends, in 1982, after a "hold-up" of many months, Phyllis resumed work on *In the Cabinet*. Throughout 1980 she worked diligently on the text, despite complaints that it was "hard tiring work," and had written to Adèle that for months she had been completely dedicated to her writing, so much so that the house was "shabby as hell because since I am deep in writing I don't do any house cleaning and Robert is left with most of the burdens." But she had made no progress on the book since then. The eighteen-month gap had been caused not only by Robert's illness but by "a mental block.'" It is true that for weeks he had been in the hospital "at the point of death," and she had given up "everything—even writing—to try and keep him alive." It had been a "monumental struggle, interlaced with transport difficulties to and from the hospital." But, as she wrote to Adèle, in late 1980 she had reached "such a moving part" she "couldn't bear to write of it." By this she meant the chapters dealing with her relationship with Phina, for the writing of which she had consulted her daughter's childhood autobiography, and a lifetime of letters, school papers, and mementos that are still to be found among Phyllis's papers. But in April 1982, encouraged by the new lease on her writing life offered by *The Orchid House* and with Robert fully recovered from his latest troubles, she set herself a goal of two to three pages per day. If she kept that pace, she hoped, she would be able to finish the novel by midsummer.

The book, however, would never be finished, and it is unclear how much work Phyllis did on the text between December 1980 and the end of her life, since just ten additional manuscript pages are left beyond the six chapters she described to Adèle as having been drafted by that date. The text, more autobiography than fiction, drew extensively on the manuscript of the same title she had started in 1961, numerous excerpts of which she had published in the *Herald* during her tenure as editor. The earlier text had been unquestionably autobiographical and had narrated Phyllis's life from the founding of the Dominica Labour party in 1954, through the "time of the migrants" in London in 1956–1957, to her experiences as a Federation minister. Many of those chapters were incorporated verbatim into the new text, together with many of her ministerial speeches and personal correspondence, also faithfully reproduced. The new *In the Cabinet*, purportedly a fictional text, seeks to continue the story of Joan, the middle daughter of *The Orchid House*, now elderly and frail, as she reminisces on her past as a Federation minister and the loss of her daughter. These chapters alternate with those in which her husband, Edward, and her old friend Baptiste search for the murderer of her son, Ned, killed many years before in retaliation for her sister Stella's murder of the Haitian dope smuggler Mr. Lilipoulala in *The Orchid House*. *In the Cabinet* begins in the aftermath of Hurricane David. The opening chapters, "Why Are We Alive?" and "Love for an Island," draw upon a piece Phyllis had written for *Kunapipi*—"Hurricane David: The Skeleton of a Survival Tale"—and possess an eerie power and beauty reminiscent of her best work. Chapter 3, "Abraham Lincoln's Birthday," summarizes the three sisters' post–Orchid House lives as a backdrop for the birth of Andrina (Phina) in Buffalo. Chapter 4, "Greatness and Secrecy," intermingles new autobiographical material—the fixing of the mill house's roof after Hurricane David, Lennox's arrival with a poem about the devastation of the island, their relief at Robbie's safe return from the Carib Reserve—with the discovery of some sodden Federation files as they are cleaning their home. The discovery allows Joan to reminisce about her days "in the cabinet," her loneliness, her longing for Edward and Dominica (Anonica in the text), the treachery of her colleagues. Most of the material in her recollections came word for word from those earlier excerpts published in the *Herald*. Chapters 5 and 6, "Love for a Daughter" and "A State of Betweenity," are set during Phina's visit to Trinidad in 1961, while her mother was a minister, and explore the strains in their relationship, again drawing extensively on earlier materials, among them Phina's childhood diaries and autobiography, and Phyllis's speeches. In answer to a query from Andrina as to what her mother believes she has accomplished, Joan embarks on a long explanation, interspersed with numerous quotations from her (that is, Phyllis's) own addresses to various groups, chief among them the ILO. A seventh chapter, "A State of Obscurity," narrates Joan's return to Anonica after the collapse of the Federation, and her creation of Rose O as a vehicle to satirize the government's goings-on. In this last extant chapter she seemed to be moving more firmly toward a focus on Ned's murder—the only truly fictional element in the manuscript—as central to the plot.

The text as it remained after her death is too disjointed to be discussed as anything near a finished literary work. Its very lack of coherence loomed dauntingly before her, and she might have been better served by its remaining strictly an autobiography as initially intended, as that would have supplied a natural structure that the manuscript lacks. To the biographer who has reviewed the materials incorporated into the "novel" in their original state, the manuscript of *In the Cabinet* has the feel of pieces collected for a collage, fragmented and showing their ragged edges, awaiting the artistry that would turn it into a harmonious tale. Of artistry there are glimpses, particularly in the first two chapters, a paean to the devastation of the island which finds exhilarating hope in every new leaf and bud. And it is clear that she had begun the process of imposing upon the discontinuous materials some degree of shape. The novel's three thematic strands—the achievements of the Federation, her grief over her daughter's death, and her ever-present goal of leaving a "legacy" behind her—fuse structurally in Phyllis's use of Phina as the novel's audience, the you to whom descriptions and explanations are offered. But this device is not followed consistently, and when used is not altogether successful. Her other textual device, the murder plot, employed subtly in *The Orchid House*, where it was well integrated structurally and thematically, here appears forced and contrived. She was also struggling with the tone and aim of her project, alternating, as her correspondence with Adèle shows, between tragic and upbeat endings: Faced with the island's devastation after the hurricane, Joan and Edward would leave in a suicidal swim to Marie Galante, during which they would either perish or be rescued by a Carib canoe.

From 1982 till her death Phyllis would make repeated efforts to complete the novel, but her heart was not in it, as Lennox and his mother soon realized. She kept searching for interruptions. At first she complained of not having a typewriter and having to write in longhand, a slow and painstaking process that made editing difficult. Lennox, eager to help her, brought her an old typewriter of his as a kind of permanent loan; but after weeks of little progress she claimed she did not understand the machine and could not use it (this despite her extensive experience in secretarial work). Patricia, who had used it to type one of Lennox's books, came to the mill house and patiently explained how to use it; but Phyllis did not seem to be taking it in, as if she did not mean to use the typewriter at all. At one point, Patricia recalls, she had decided on a schedule that would have her at the typewriter for a set period every day. She soon began to rationalize her lack of progress by complaining that a neighbor, a nurse who worked the night shift, would always come around eleven o'clock for a chat. She had "never in her life had so much servant talk," she told Patricia. But when the latter urged her to explain to her friend that at certain times of the day she was going to sit down to write and did not want to be interrupted, Phyllis had replied, "Actually, I like to be interrupted."

Throughout 1983 and 1984 she complained to Polly and Pierrette about the many hardships that interfered with her writing. To Pierrette, whom Phyllis had been expecting to visit in October 1983, she wrote dejectedly of how "dreadfully disappointed" she had been when Pierrette had decided to visit Jamaica instead. "I daresay those more forward islands had much more treasure to unravel," she moaned self-pityingly, but she had hoped that her visit would "revive my writing spirits," brought down by "the little Mill House [being] so much of a sick bay." In August 1984 she had a serious accident, which she claimed caused a gap in her typing of the second half of *In the Cabinet*. She had been preparing for a lunch guest on a rainy morning when, throwing some peelings over the edge of their little pool, she "pitched [her]self over with them." It was a nine-foot drop over rocks, and the fall left her with a severely bruised thigh and rib cage. Luckily the cascade and mud in the overflow saved her legs from more serious injury. Had she fallen headfirst, she told her friends, she might have killed herself. She had clambered back up, finished preparing her lunch, and got into dry clothes, and it had not been until after her guest left that Robert had bound her ribs with strips of white sheets after rubbing on "some embrocation." She had not called a doctor—"a waste of money which [they] didn't have anyway"—and her injuries and lacerations had taken a long time to heal, long enough to sap her energy and keep her from resuming her writing.

A measure of literary enthusiasm would return occasionally when she had a request for the reissue of some of her old work, or when scattered articles appeared about her work. In 1983 she received a request for two old poems for an anthology of World War II poetry from Virago—"Young Lady Dancing with Soldier" and "Cunard Liner 1940." In 1984 Penguin requested two others for inclusion in a poetry collection—"Love for an Island" and "The Child's Return," the poem she had written for Jean Rhys. Some months later she had received a copy of an essay on Dominican literature Elaine Campbell had published in *World Literature Today*, an American academic journal, in which her work had been discussed with Rhys's and Elma Napier's. Polly's flattering article in the *Observer* appeared in 1985, cheering her enormously. "So things are not entirely dead," she commented to Pierrette in the light of these instances of renewed attention to her work outside Dominica. "I must really work very hard on ITC now, get it done and delivered." But this goal would prove to be beyond her—and she knew it full well. To Adèle she would write that she did not seem to have "much more to tell" in her work, and the dwelling on the past entailed by this work of literary reminiscing was never to her taste. The writing of the novel would never be relinquished or declared to be at an end, but she would continue to procrastinate, finding myriad reasons for delay, until it was indeed too late.

If Phyllis and Robert survived the illnesses and poverty of their last years as long as they did, it was primarily thanks to the unfailing friendship and generosity of their friends, chief among them Lennox and his family—his mother, Patricia, and sister, Sara. Phyllis, in one of her favorite poems, had written that "gentleness of friends was a wine milder than milk," and in the Honychurches she had found friends of unequaled gentleness and devotion. Lennox would in all respects behave toward her like a son; he was indeed everything she would have wished a son of hers to be—talented, devoted to Dominica, politically minded, dutiful, and sensitive to her struggles. In these years when she was "down and out" he came to the mill house frequently, often daily, keeping her abreast of what was happening in Dominica, seeking advice, being her conduit to those public affairs from which she had been barred with the collapse of the *Star*. Busy as he was with his many endeavors—as a historian, lecturer, writer, broadcaster, and architectural restorer—he always found time for her. Patricia, kindness itself, would patiently deal with the more pragmatic needs of the often troublesome pair, finding, as most people do when dealing with elderly friends set in their ways, that helping often requires enormous reserves of forbearance. It was left to her to help with errands, lifts into town, mail, and food shopping, tasks not lightened by her feeling that Phyllis took her doing so for granted, as if a favor done once became an obligation.

Throughout these last quiet years they could also look forward to occasional visits from dear friends. Loblack would occasionally wander down the valley from Roseau to talk about the old days. Whenever he complained to her of the fate that had befallen both of them, Phyllis would always seek to comfort him with the same words: "When you work for the rich you get money; when you work for the poor you get hell!" Adèle came to see them from the United States, as would friends from the Federal days like Elizabeth Greenhall, who had been with Phyllis during her broadcast of the Jamaican referendum results and had since returned to New York. Monica Green, who had worked on the Save the Children campaign with Lady Hailes, had come to live in Dominica, becoming one of Phyllis's closest friends. They shared, among other things, a penchant for detective fiction, enjoying "stacks of Dick Francis horsy mysteries." Pixie's daughter came from Australia, returning home "a changed person" after a wonderful vacation during which Phyllis had shared her anecdotes about the writers she had known in England—Doris Lessing, Stevie Smith, Stephen Spender, and Jean Rhys. Once, during "one of the best days of [her] life," Janie Nichols's son (whom Phyllis had taken care of in his childhood in New York) had come with his young wife and small children to spend the day. Phyllis had not seen him for many years and felt "a pang of joy" upon being told that he had named his two-year-old daughter Dominica—"it seemed to express their love so completely."

Phyllis's cousin Rosalind Volney assumed a great part of the responsibility for helping her and Robert in those last years when they were "not on the Government's poverty list but close to it." One of Ralph's younger daughters, she was the child of one of his "outside" relationships, a warm matronly woman who had successfully raised a large family after her husband's untimely death by founding and managing a small tropical crafts enterprise, specializing in beautifully made straw mats. Their relationship flourished despite profound ideological differences. The two had always quarreled about politics; Phyllis was always taking her to task for her deep conservatism. Rosalind was indeed a conservative in social and racial matters—a great admirer of Ronald Reagan (whom Phyllis despised), and, after so many years, still aghast at Phyllis's friendships with poor blacks. When *The Orchid House* was filmed for British television's Channel 4, in 1990, and Joan's political rallies were recreated in Roseau, Rosalind recalls, there were "all kinds of black people agitating on the streets." It had been "just . . . the kind of thing [Phyllis] would have liked. She had liked nothing better than to be with the black people running around and agitating."*

*Frances Barber, the actress playing Joan, would comment on the filming of these scenes: "I started off tentatively, feeling a bit of a fraud, but when I said the bit about the right to education of our children, to medicine, to work, they went wild. I was shaking with exhilaration—I've never had such response from extras. People came up and slapped me on the back—I couldn't sort the fantasy from the reality." Lennie James, who played Baptiste, the character based on Loblack, said: "We were blown away by it. It was like documentary footage." (Interestingly, the filming took place at the time of a general election.)

But there was nonetheless a warm feeling of fellowship between them that Rosalind attributed to a blood connection that transcended the differences between them—despite all their disagreements, they were "family." In the late 1970s Phyllis grew into the habit of visiting Rosalind whenever she went to town. She would take the bus or walk down to Roseau in the morning, run her errands in town—market, visits to friends, the library—and then come to her cousin's for lunch and a nap while waiting for one of Rosalind's sons to give her a ride home in the late afternoon. Sometimes Rosalind would come to the mill house to help Phylis clean up; often she would collect clothes and food for her to take back with her. Rosalind saw in Phyllis's acceptance of her help proof of the affection that bound them. She was "a very proud person who would never ask for help," and would accept it only from those she trusted implicitly. Phyllis, in Rosalind's estimation, was "never very affectionate"; she was "like a person who never got enough love. It was like there was always something missing." But she would kiss Rosalind when she greeted her, "which with her always meant a lot." If there was an obstacle to a perfect understanding between them it was not their philosophical differences when it came to politics and social issues, but Rosalind's absolute contempt for Robert, whom she would always describe as "a pig." He had "never had any time for her"—unlike Phyllis, he could not look beyond their differing social outlooks—and she swore that although she would "do anything for Phyllis, who was family, she would not lift a finger to help Robert." She would tell everyone who would listen (including Phyllis, who would not) that he "abused" his wife. Her accusations, while Phyllis was alive, were founded on his allowing her, despite her frailty and ill health, to bear the burden of providing for the family in their impecunious state, of expecting her to make the increasingly arduous trip to Roseau for food and mail, and of knowingly accepting (or so Rosalind claimed) her going without food to make sure he and Robbie had enough to eat. Rosalind attests that Robert stood by, knowing she was starving herself so that they could eat, and did nothing to dissuade her from thus harming herself. But Phyllis could not be brought to complain about Robert and seemed to derive "great comfort from his presence." She would emphasize instead all the things he did for her, telling friends of how his frequent back rubs, after she had hurt her back when she fell into the waterfall, helped her to get well. She suffered from living so frugally—when Pierrette met her she was "practically starving"—and knew full well that many among her friends blamed Robert for her sufferings, but she was never heard to complain about him, and Pierrette had the impression that she "wanted to be left alone on the subject."

Rosalind's wrath at Robert and all those whom she felt had failed Phyllis would only intensify after her cousin's death. Within days of her passing she learned from Celia that Robert had had a considerable amount of money available to him in England (according to Rosalind, forty thousand Eastern Caribbean dollars—some nine to ten thousand U.S. dollars—although it is beyond credibility that he would have had such an amount) that he had "refused" to claim while he let his wife starve. She was equally infuriated with Phyllis's children. In her estimation—although in this she was not being quite fair—Sonia "had not moved a finger" to help her adoptive mother, but had later come to see Rosalind at Tropicrafts to ask if Phyllis had left her anything. Sonia, living in London and herself burdened with an ailing child, had done as much as she could. Neither had she a good word to say about Robbie, whom she believed got "this money that Robert didn't bring in on time." She saved her respect for David—"very much a gentleman"—for coming by her house (during a visit to

Dominica from London, where he still lives—he is unmarried and works for a caterer) to thank her for what she had done for his mother. Rosalind's abiding rage on Phyllis's behalf, a rage the intervening years have not tempered, is poignant in that it endures as a living testimony of the wrongs Phyllis forbore but never herself dwelled upon.

Young Robbie—Rosalind's disapproval notwithstanding—was a great comfort to Phyllis and Robert, and many of her friends felt "nothing but pride in the young man" for his stalwart loyalty to his adoptive parents. He was particularly faithful to Phyllis, whom he would always consider his "real mother" despite his affection for his biological mother, to whom he had always been close. He remembers fondly her efforts to help him with his schoolwork and the care and attention she paid to assuring him a better future than would have been his lot without her. As Phyllis and Robert became older and frailer, he took upon himself most of the physical burdens of the poor household, producing the *Star* during its last year and taking responsibility for the many repairs the little house needed after Hurricane David. He did his best to supplement their income with his own, even though employment opportunities were not plentiful in Dominica. Phyllis, however, was bent on his having the same opportunities they had offered David and Sonia, although by now they were incapable of sending him to London for any special training as they had the older two children when they were Robbie's age. She therefore strived to secure a scholarship for him, finally succeeding in procuring funds for him to travel to the American Midwest for some teaching training, an opportunity she urged him to take despite their having to do without his company and help during his absence. He would be the only one of the children to return home, and after Phyllis's death would take Robert, by then extremely ill and "with very little notion of where he was," to the Carib Reserve, where he and his biological mother took care of him until he died nine months later. Robert, whose love for the Caribs was one of his most endearing qualities, would be buried in the little cemetery in the Reserve. Phyllis would have been heartened, given her desire to leave "an Allfrey-named boy and his children in the Carib Reserve," to see the grounds around her little house carefully planted by Robbie in ginger and ground provisions and to hear him talking about his plans for the house, his wife and baby, and the fact that he still feels the void of her absence and "think[s] of her every day."

Among Phyllis's dearest friends in the latter years of her life was a young American woman, Ella Maria Mercado—Ria—a nurse who had come to Dominica with her husband, Charles Fisher, a professor of microbiology at Ross Medical School in Portsmouth, and worked as a volunteer training women in hygiene and child care. They had met when Ria had come by the mill house to see if Phyllis would teach her how to operate a short-wave radio. As inevitably happens with anyone compelled to live for any extent of time in Dominica, she fell in love with the beauty of the island and its people. She was herself of Indian origin, and was very interested in the Caribs, whose folk remedies, healing practices, and beliefs she wanted to explore. She was also a budding writer, and Phyllis, who had always enjoyed encouraging young authors, became her mentor. They soon fell into the habit of spending their mornings together, discussing books and sharing their work. Out of these meetings came Ria's first published short story, "The Master Sisserou of Dominica," a conservationist tale about the need to save the tropical rain forest from commercial lumbering, which Phyllis helped her place in a textbook for Caribbean children. Phyllis was grateful for the company and attention; she was then "out of the swim" and feeling unwell, and really appreciated the younger woman's presence and friendship. She brought "a bit of culture" and a "breath of fresh air." Hence her sadness when Ria told her in September 1983 that she was returning to Michigan with her husband to enroll in a master's program in transcultural nursing at Wayne State University. Barely a year after Ria's return to the United States, Phyllis would learn to her horror that her young friend had been murdered in bizarre and mysterious circumstances. As her husband reported to the police, he had been in bed shortly after midnight when he thought he heard her returning from her job at a local hospital. As he made his way downstairs to greet her, he had been knocked out by a blow to the head. Awakening to find himself tied to his own bed, he struggled to free himself and went looking for Ria, whom he found unconscious in the living room, lying face down, her head wrapped with duct tape. She was still alive, but by then she had sustained severe brain damage and died ten days later when her life-support system was disconnected. There had been little evidence of the attack on himself that Fisher had described to the police, and this, coupled with the troubled state of his marriage to Ria—which her parents believed had been the "main and only cause" of her death—led to his becoming the primary suspect. The fatal attack had come two days before her departure for Germany on a visit to a cousin, of whom her husband seemed to be "insanely jealous," after which she had planned to seek a divorce. Aware of the suspicions focused on him, Fisher had refused a lie detector test, as he was within his rights to do, and after weeks of interrogations had declined to continue to speak to the police, leaving Michigan shortly thereafter without indicating where he was going. He would himself write to Phyllis of his grief and his loss, telling her that he was then living in seclusion, devastated by his misfortune and the burden of suspicion he was living under.

Phyllis was shocked and brokenhearted at the news, which brought back with full force the pain she had felt at the loss of Phina. She wrote to Fisher about how she had stood at her kitchen sink grieving for her friend and had composed a poem about Ria, the "girl with the laughing eyes" who had loved them and would therefore continue to live in their hearts, for love was lasting, it remained "like the light on your face / And the light in your heart, / Always, always." In November Ria's distraught parents wrote to Phyllis, pleading for her help in ascertaining whether Fisher had returned to Dominica. Although not accusing him of any crime despite their strong suspicions, they wanted him to return and face any possible charges. She would help them track him down to Ross University's new campus in Saint Kitts, where he was apprehended and returned to the United States. (Since then Fisher has twice been convicted of Ria's murder, but the convictions have been reversed on technicalities, and he awaits a third trial for murder while serving a sentence for obstruction of justice for attempting to persuade two fellow convicts to confess to the crime.) Phyllis, in her dejection, fully identified with Ria's parents—she well knew the devastation of their loss—and came to share their belief in Fisher's guilt. She had found him to be a depressing, "grey," and possessive man, and on the strength of that "evidence" spoke of him to everyone as guilty of her beloved friend's slaying. The tragedy of her young friend's death disturbed her deeply, shaking once more the foundations of her yearning to leave behind her a legacy of work and inspiration. As had happened all too often in her life—most devastatingly with her own daughter—she had again devoted her now dwindling energies to foster a young woman's writing career only to see her life prematurely ended. Ria's sad fate cast a dark shadow over the last year of Phyllis's life.

In October 1985 Phyllis, by then utterly penniless and nearly starving, was invited to a reception with Queen Elizabeth on board the royal yacht *Britannia,* during the latter's brief stopover in Dominica. Phyllis was most eager to go, but such occasions required the sort of dress and accoutrements that were now quite beyond her reach. Hearing from Lennox about the invitation while he was on a visit to Barbados, Celia looked among her evening dresses for one she thought would fit her tinier sister and had it cleaned and pressed for her, sending it with Lennox and writing to ask Phyllis, whose seventy-seventh birthday was just a couple of weeks away, to accept the dress "and extras"—shoes, stockings, evening bag, and costume jewelry—as her present. Phyllis, decked in Celia's finery, attended the gala occasion, amusing Lennox immensely by using her evening bag as a repository for all sorts of hors d'oeuvres and other delicacies to take home to Robert, who had not been strong enough to attend. She spent her last Christmas with Lennox and Patricia, who had just gotten a television set. It had been raining hard, and they had had to come inside after dinner, spending Christmas night watching a broadcast of *Oklahoma!* "What a strange Christmas," she remarked afterward of the prosaic but unfamiliar pleasures of an evening before the television set, "but what fun."

By the time of the *Britannia* party Phyllis, who had always been slim, had become extremely fragile and could barely be persuaded to eat, even when there was any food to be had. She told Pierrette that her stomach seemed to have shrunk. The reason became clear soon thereafter, when she was diagnosed as suffering from colon cancer, as her mother had before her. Her doctor recommended going to Barbados for an operation, and Celia urged her to come as soon as possible and stay with them. But Phyllis procrastinated. Robert had been so ill that she could not believe he would live much longer. She could not leave him for an extended stay in Barbados. The struggle to survive with little money and increasing ill health had undermined them, and she told her sister Rosalind that she did not think she would "bother" with the operation but would "let things take their course." In December, "sick with worry," Rosalind wrote to Lennox for an objective assessment. Worried that it might be money that held Phyllis back, she wrote him that if an operation was advised, it was essential that she have it and to consider them as insurance for the cost. "Please, please," she pleaded with him, "when you get this do let me know as much as you can and if any financial help is needed *now.*" Reassured by that fact that she had friends who had fully recovered from cancer operations, she kept up a steady pressure on Phyllis. She felt powerless to do more than continue to insist that she follow medical advice, and sent her "grateful thanks" to Lennox and Rosalind Volney for taking care of "my brave and much-loved sister." For her sister's sake more than anything else, Phyllis yielded and underwent the operation in early January at Princess Margaret Hospital in Dominica. The procedure was declared a success, and the doctors assured her that she would fully recover.

But on February 1 Phyllis, weak and ailing, was taken back to Princess Margaret Hospital, where Robert was already hospitalized with a degenerative heart ailment she was certain would kill him. What brought her to this condition so shortly after being pronounced to be beyond danger no one purports to understand. Her doctors could have been mistaken about the progress of her malady, or perhaps she lost her will to live once she persuaded herself that from then on she would have to face life without her husband. Whatever the cause, by February 3 she was holding fast to the belief that within days she would be dead. When her cousin Rosalind visited that afternoon bringing food, clean linen, and fresh clothes, Phyllis had a singular request—she had received some money from Adèle and wanted a bottle of champagne with which to commemorate her "long and happy marriage" to Robert. Rosalind did as she was asked, and on the following evening, champagne in hand, Phyllis persuaded the nurses to bring Robert from his ward to spend the evening with her. The bottle was consumed, and it may be that during that night's long vigil they exchanged their words of farewell. She died the next day.

Phyllis had always had a sense of the occasion, and the champagne was her last grand gesture, a gesture of drama. But life in the Caribbean resists such solemnity—its true spirit, as she had always known, is that of comedy. Hers had been, despite its many trials and tribulations, a Caribbean life—and her passing would not fail to partake of the comic. There is in the blazing heat of the West Indies a true urgency about the prosaic matters pertaining to death, of which Lennox was reminded when he came to collect her body in his small pickup truck. With her coffin laying out on the truckbed in the sun, he had to argue with the nurses, who insisted that he go up to Robert, who was "bordering on the comatose" and "pretty much out of it"—the result, perhaps, of too much champagne—unhook his intravenous feeding tubes, put him in a wheelchair, and bring him down to the veranda to see her for the last time, "on account of their having been married so long." While the junior nurses gestured behind their superior not to do so, Lennox maintained that he could not take such a sick man out in such a hot day when he was already late with the coffin for the funeral. Finally disentangling himself, he sped away toward Rosalind Volney's house with his cargo bumping gently in the back.

The honors Phyllis had not received during her lifetime were accorded her after death. Friends and enemies filed past the little coffin she shared with the ashes of her daughter, resting amid flowers on a table in the middle of Rosalind's living room, to pay their last respects. Lennox made sure that as a former Federal minister, political party founder, and Dominica's foremost writer, she had a state-like funeral. Eugenia was away, but the deputy prime minister came in her stead to lead the march, and the crowded procession advanced to the Anglican church with a police escort. Lennox's tender eulogy dwelled on her having been "a romantic" in love with the hills, rivers, and green valleys of their island. He recalled her expulsion from the Labour party as "a wound which affected her for years," but more than anything he spoke of her strength. "And yet through lean years and hurricane she fought on each new sunrise over Copt Hall, and the shades of green along the steep sides of the Roseau Valley seemed to give her strength. But all this life is summed up in the poem of her life love for an island, which to the very last line tells of her love passion for this steep volcanic crumpled mountain in the sea called Dominica." As the mourners emerged into the bright sunshine, the chords of a touchingly appropriate hymn reverberated in the acacia-scented air: "Now the Labourer's task is o'er; / Now the battle day is past; / Now upon the farther shore / Lands the voyager at last. . . . / There no more the powers of hell, / Can prevail to mar their peace."

The coffin, carried through the streets of Roseau to the Anglican cemetery, was draped in the brilliant sun and blue-and-white waves of the Federation flag.

A Selection of Short Stories by Phyllis Shand Allfrey

UNCLE RUFUS

WHEN I READ those terrible words, I thought at once of Uncle Rufus. You may wonder why I thought of him first, when the letter was from my aunt, and the last paragraph said: "For two weeks now we have not had a single slice of bread—there is none to buy. Our people stand looking out to the horizon, searching for the ships which are always overdue. When there is meat, the police are called out to control the queues, which are often violent. We are eating sliced breadfruit with every meal, and pray that it will never go out of season. The ground is rotten with the oranges which cannot be exported. No doubt those in England still think of us as the islands of sunshine and plenty."

You will understand why the look of the word "bread" on paper or even the smell of bread baking which sometimes drifts out into a London street, would make me think of Uncle Rufus: when I was fourteen years old Uncle Rufus married a coloured woman who owned a bakery shop. And Uncle Rufus was the most entertaining and mysterious character of my childhood.

While grandfather was alive, Uncle Rufus just lived with the coloured woman, whose name was Coralita Duboisier, in a secret way, though the secret became rather open when they had a family. Still, even the servants were in a conspiracy not to gossip about Uncle Rufus and his family in the hearing of my grandfather; so when we were in bed they would sit on the verandah steps which opened out of the nursery and whisper about him, and we would strain our ears to listen. As they spoke in patois, we took the trouble to learn that fascinating language from the cook's daughter. In this way we got to know the names of all our illegitimate cousins, their bad and good habits, their mother's extraordinary charm in spite of bow-legs and a squint, and the way in which Uncle Rufus would run through grandfather's allowance and then borrow from Coralita's bakery till. As he was the last male in what was fast becoming a matriarchy, Uncle Rufus was invested with a glamour which even his carrot-coloured hair and boorish manners did nothing to dissipate.

We were conscious that being white, and being girls, we would have to grow up properly and correctly, and for these reasons we were bitterly jealous of Coralita, and curious about the assortment of plain and pretty, light and dark babies which she and Uncle Rufus had speedily accumulated. It was queer, but with the exception of the eldest, Virginia, the light children were the plain ones and the dark children were the handsome ones; it was as though nature had tried hard to be impartial, handing out spread noses and large mouths to those with gingery hair and pale skins, and straight high noses and small voluptuous lips to those whose skin was golden-brown and whose hair was more than curly. But Virginia, the first-born, had all the best qualities of both races: her colour was pale golden, her hair copper brown with soft waves, her limbs douce and oriental, and her eyes brown and innocent.

Whenever we passed Coralita's bakery on our way to the botanical gardens we would say to our nurse: "We know whose shop that is, ha, ha," and she would say:

"Be quiet, children, do." Such a lovely smell came out of the shop, which had great stone ovens, charcoal fed, at the back, and the palms at the gate leaned back towards the roof and seemed to be bending down to sniff the lovely rich aroma. And our nurse would say: "Remember you're white, and think of your grandfather." But after a while this admonition lost some of its force, for grandfather died.

Then there began a brief struggle between grandmother and the aunts on one side, and Coralita and the priests on the other, for the body of Uncle Rufus. I can only say the body, for in those days Uncle Rufus showed small indication of having a mind. But the priests said that he had a soul, and that he was committing mortal sin. And when Coralita was having her seventh baby they told him that she was in danger of dying, and made him promise to marry her. So after the baby was born it was given grandfather's names at a grand double ceremony which was both a christening and a wedding, and the other children were all bridesmaids and pages. Our nurse told us that Virginia looked like one of God's little angels in turquoise-blue satin. We wept angrily into our pillows that night because we had not been invited, and because the aunts would not let us go to the cathedral—not even to hide behind a pew and peep. At about that time the aunts had a consultation and decided that we were growing too old to remain in the island, and that we must go to school in England.

There was no one on whom we could depend for news of Uncle Rufus, for our nurse was not much of a correspondent. But gradually items of news about him crept into the aunts' letters, and we gathered that in some strange way Uncle Rufus was getting respectable. Uncle Rufus had espoused the cause of the laborers. Having married a coloured woman, he had thrown in his lot with her people. He was the first white man to shake hands with a visiting trade unionist. He was in the Town Council. He was a radical. He was getting fatter. He was in the Legislative Council. He was the Mayor. He was nearly as popular as Coralita's bakery.

The aunts even began to mention him in their letters as if they thought we were getting old enough to share a dubious joke with them. "Just fancy, Uncle Rufus has taken Coralita to call at Government House. Virginia is really a very nice-looking girl, considering . . . They say he lives like a sultan, doesn't even take his own boots off. His children adore him and behave like house-slaves. They say he sleeps with a pistol under his pillow, having announced that he will shoot down any white man who attempts to flirt with Virginia." And then, long afterwards: "You will be surprised to hear that Aunt Julie and I have at last called on Coralita. We found her as ugly close-to as she was at a distance, but very kind and quite modest (strange to say). It was odd being in a house full of children again. I must say that they were very happy children, and quite respectful, for they called us Miss all the time. We had a lovely tea, and of course Coralita was very proud of her fresh-baked bread."

One day, when the guns and bombs first began to roar all over London, I stood looking in at a bakery window and beside me stood a little girl and her mother. The guns began snapping in the suburbs, and the little girl said, with her eyes fixed on a tray of cakes, "Is someone angry, to make such a lot of noise? Is someone cross?" She was listening to the din, gripping her mother's hand and staring at the cakes. It seemed to me that everyone in the world was angry or in danger except the people living so safely and happily in that island, except Uncle Rufus living like a sultan in the midst of his growing sons and daughters.

So now you will understand why I thought of Uncle Rufus when I read the letter. For who could have imagined that the ovens in that island would ever grow cold for want of wheat, or that the smiles would die on the golden and brown faces—that Uncle Rufus could possibly get thin, and that people would be angry and violent everywhere, everywhere in the world, even in the street outside Coralita's bakery.

BREEZE

I WAS STRETCHED out on a mat under the impenetrable mango tree in the back garden sucking pear-drops and reading a very old copy of *Tiger Tim's Weekly*, for I had been told not to show myself at the front gates. Although innocent of any design on the reputation of the white official class, I was in disgrace.

My great-uncle, the Colony's medical officer, had issued a statement to the press that the prevalent epidemic was kaffir-pox, a disease which was unlikely to afflict people of pure European blood. Unfortunately, the first white victim of this unpleasant ailment was the Anglican Archdeacon and the second was myself, then a child of ten.

My nurse, finding me on that morning fretful and convalescent, had bribed me to stay out of sight under the mango tree by giving me a bag of sweets and making many promises which I knew she would not keep. My spotty face was spellbound over the English comic strips, and every now and then I would break one of my nurse's don'ts and scratch my legs with the hand which turned the pages and brushed away flies.

I must have been there for over half an hour before a heavy rustling in the boughs above me made me conscious that something larger than bird or animal was about to slide to the ground. It was Breeze, Breeze the wild girl, the notorious creature, who had been studying me in silence, but could not bear to see the last pear-drops vanish into my listless mouth. Leaping down like a panther, Breeze grabbed the bag and then, a pear-drop bulging out of her cheek, greeted me:

"Hullo skinny! Got the kaffir-pox?"

Although I had never met Breeze before and only seen her once in the distance being chased by a policeman, I knew who she was and a great deal about her. She was the girl who had no home, who lived wild, who was only fourteen, but had been to jail five times, who stole, who wore no clothes or at most one garment; yes, she looked exactly the way the elders said she did, crispy hair shaved, face hard and saucy and merry . . . and as if to demonstrate those legs which were as fleet as the wind and which had inspired her name, Breeze vaulted up into the branches again, her shapeless grey garment flapping.

"Oh, do you live in our mango tree, Breeze?" I exclaimed in admiration, ignoring Breeze's insulting behaviour, for having attained a high branch, she leaned down grinning like the Cheshire cat and calling out just loudly enough for me to hear:

"Skinny, Skinny, Poxy, Poxy."

After a while I became irritated by these epithets and muttered back:

"Jail bird, jail bird. Naked jail bird."

"Like to see me naked? Like to see how I get out of this dress when they chase me?" asked Breeze, and I nodded avidly.

She slid down the trunk of the mango tree again, and with a single wriggle of her bronze shoulders disposed of the shapeless sack, which had a large neck-opening and no buttons. She stood there before me in maidenly magnificence, and as if the sight of her was not sufficient to shame my puny child limbs, she remarked: "Wouldn't call me skinny, would you? That's my town clothes. When I live in forest I live free."

I gazed at her enviously. To live free! Wasn't that what every child desired! Not to be fretted on hot days by starched muslin dresses and cotton bloomers! To sleep in trees like a bird! And to be as beautiful a series of round shapes as Breeze, who was what the elders called ominously, "a Big Girl Now."

"Wish't I could be you, Breeze," I complained.

But Breeze said surprisingly, "Rather be skinny. Don't run so fast now I'm grown. They catch me. Wanted to put me to school. Want me to live on cooked food. Want to put me to work. Listen Skinny," she bent down and glared at me terrifyingly, her brown shining face very near, "know what the p'leece want me to be? Want me to be a bucket-lady."

Now although I was only ten I knew well that to be a bucket-lady was to pursue one of the two most ignominious professions in the Colony; the other being designated "huckster," and having something or other to do with meeting ships and trading with sailors.

"A bucket-lady!" I said aghast.

Breeze to empty our privy pail for one-and-sixpence a week or worse—the privy pail of some family of lower social standing! Breeze having to walk carefully with a stinking bucket poised on her turban, sneaking down the lesser streets where no white people lived, towards the sea-dump, on dark nights!

"Don't ever let them catch you and make you a bucket-lady, Breeze!" I cried.

"Oh, I don't mind smells, I sleep in closets on rainy nights," said Breeze proudly, "but I mind walking slow and not living free, I mind doing same things every week. Hey, what you got on your arm, poxy?" she exclaimed, seizing the wrist on which the tight little gold-coiled bracelet, a gift from my great-uncle when I was five, clung like a permanent handcuff. "Gold! Real gold!" cried Breeze, her eyes greedy for the yellow shining thing. "Gimme that. Make me lovely earrings—I got pierced ears. Gimme, or I'll take it."

And as I crouched away from her, not knowing whether to cry or to comply, Breeze made a nearer tiger-leap and snarled in my ear: "You gimme. Take it off or I'll bite it off." While I huddled petrified and fascinated, she added: "And I'll bite your hand off, too."

Hastily, I tugged at the bracelet, trying to part its two thick gold knobs with my left hand; fortunately, I had grown so thin that it came away suddenly, leaving red marks on my wrist. It rolled on the grass and Breeze picked it up and put it in her mouth, where it gleamed like a bit between her ferociously beautiful teeth.

I began to howl with rage and loss, and Breeze, hearing a bustle in the building behind me, snatched up her grey dress and slipped naked into the undergrowth. Yet so strong was my fear of Breeze, and perhaps also my loyalty to her enviable freedom, that I lay howling on the grass with my wrist tucked under my stomach, refusing to say what was the matter.

I never saw Breeze again, and nobody ever found out what had become of my gold bracelet. I heard of her further escapades, of course, and would listen with fascinated horror to tales of how she bit a policeman and sent him to hospital for weeks, or how she kicked the Matron over, jumped the prison wall and disappeared into the hills. While I listened to these anecdotes I would think of Breeze with fond partisanship.

After a while I also became "a Big Girl Now" and left the Colony for the milder savagery of boarding-school.

The other day I met and American Captain at a cocktail party, and he told me how he had visited my Colony just before the war to make water-colour sketches. He told me how when his ship pulled into the bay, a young woman carrying a tray full of terrible beads and junk, her face powered till it looked blue, and her lips painted purple, stepped up the gangway, and oh boy! What a type! She was a walking tigress, and when she swept off that ship she took with her the Chief Petty Officer and half a dozen sailors and a bribe of a pound from the Purser to clear off and quit making a nuisance of herself, for it seemed that even the local police couldn't keep her in order. "Gee, she was a darn beautiful coloured woman, and I'd have given a lot to have seen her with her face washed and as nude as a diving boy. . . ."

THE OBJECTIVE

People keep asking me why my elder sister married the Bishop, and I keep on telling them that she fell in love with him on a moonlight night in the tropics, and they don't believe a word of it, they simply don't believe me. The moonlight was so fierce that night that Cyril, our cock, began to crow immediately after dinner (this was nothing unusual; he always did it when the moon was full). I think it was Cyril who woke me up, because he suddenly got hoarse and stopped crowing, and what with the silence and the smell of jasmine outside my window, I could not sleep any longer. So I got up and went into Natalie's room. I surprised her in a pair of grey flannels and a yellow shirt, with one leg out of her window, which overlooked the low kitchen roof. She frowned at me and said crossly: "Alice, what are you doing at this time of night?"—quite as if it was a perfectly normal thing for her to be out the window in pants when the Catholic church bells chimed midnight austerely in the distance; treating me like a childish culprit, when she knew only too well that I was barely two years younger than herself. So I hung out my tongue and made a nasty eye at her, and she told me I needn't advertise that I was bilious.

"Well, whatever are you doing in Daddy's trousers?" I asked.

"Exploring."

"Oh! Do you do it often? May I come?"

"Not in that horrible nightgown," said Natalie.

"I'll take it off," said I, and did; a simple action, as the neck was very wide and slipped easily over my ribs and hips, which were equally prominent. I stood there in a triangle of silver, feeling naked and gawky. "You may have my purple bloomers," said Natalie kindly. I put on the bloomers and a pair of tennis shoes with no laces and a rust-coloured jersey.

"Before we set forth," said Natalie, changing into her sepulchral voice which was so thrilling, "I must tell you my objective."

"Oh! Do you always have an objective?"

"This is my first," said Natalie, "we have a delicate engagement ahead. You will have to carry the lantern. I'll take the torch. I made a bet with myself."

She paused. She was always making bets with herself, and she faithfully carried out either the penalty or the reward. You would find her giving up cake out of the Lenten season, and at the same time buying ginger-beer for three nights running, on account of a mysterious bet. It was a great honour to be let into one of her bets.

"I bet," said Natalie, pleased with my silence, "that the new Bishop will be bald. You know Daddy and Mother would not let us go down to the Jetty with the Reception, because they said we needed sleep and the ship was late. So I bet. I bet that he was bald, and I swore that I'd find out for myself to-night. And here I go. Follow me!"

She put the rusty hurricane lantern into my hands, and crying "No time to lose!" she vaulted out the window onto the roof below. I knew better than to express amazement or lag behind. In a moment I too had dropped down and scrambled into the back-garden. We unlatched the wooden gate and slipped by the hedges in silence. "Slink along," growled Natalie once; but slinking was really unnecessary, as everybody had gone to bed; people did not loiter in the moonlight, not in this tropical island, unless there was a party, or a lover to meet, or someone was dead. Even the police went to bed. We heard a lot of noises, but they were all quite natural: swishing of palms, the soft crash of the sea before it sucked out through the stones again, a few cocks crowing here and there, and the thud of ripe fruit falling. It did not take us long to slink into the Bishop's grounds. There was an empty sentry-box standing by the gate, for the Bishop's palace had once been the fort. We slunk past it and through the shrubbery to the walls of the old military building. In the big bedroom (we knew all the rooms well, for we had played games in them while they were being done over), there burned a dim lemon light. It occurred to me to ask Natalie how she would have found out the condition of the Bishop's scalp had the room been dark. She was very short with me, and asked me what I thought the torch was for. We pressed close to the rough stone wall and listened, holding our breath.

"Now this is where you come in useful," said Natalie in her most subtle whisper. "Bend down and let me climb on your shoulder so that I can peep in, and after that you can have a turn." I obediently squatted on the ground. The Bishop's bedroom was on the ground floor, in fact the fort was nothing more than an antique bungalow, and everything was apparently easy. But heaving Natalie up to the rim of the window-sill was hard work. She weighed a lot, and I was smitten with envy because her behind was getting so round and fashionable. I sighed, and nearly toppled her forward; but she pressed her hands against the wall, and we achieved it. Of course I could not whisper to Natalie while she was sitting on my neck. And she could not tell me what she was seeing, but in less than a minute she was kicking me wildly in the ribs, and I knew she was dying to laugh or something, so I bent over and let her fall off with a loud flop. She picked herself up, grabbed me frantically by the hands, and dragged me away through the shrubs. Just before we reached the sentry-box she rolled on the ground, giggling and gasping. I felt rather cold towards her. "What about my turn, Natalie?" I asked heavily.

"He smiled at me," said Natalie, ignoring my tone.

I forgot to be angry. "And his hair . . . ?"

"Oh, that!" said Natalie in her most lofty, her most irritating, her most dreamy voice, "*certainly* he wasn't bald. *Of course* I lost my bet. He is young, that is, young for a Bishop. And very handsome. He was reading a book in bed. Such a distinguished man! Far more distinguished than the Governor. I could easily, yes, *easily*, fall in love with him."

"But Bishops always have wives," I said.

"I bet this one doesn't have a wife," said Natalie. "I bet I am the first really beautiful girl he has ever seen, and that is why he smiled. I bet I'll marry the Bishop by the time I am twenty-one."

"Wait a minute," I said, because I was hardly able to bear Natalie's triumph, not having seen the Bishop, having been done out of my fun. "Remember you bet he would be bald. You lost."

"That is a mere nothing," said Natalie. "The penalty is that you and I have to catch thirteen mole-crickets on the tennis court before we go back to bed."

So Natalie and I caught mole-crickets until three in the morning. I did not feel that I was wasting time, because the mole-crickets were chewing up the lawn, and I liked to play tennis on even ground. But the little devils were hard to catch. We baited them with the lantern and a sheet on a pole, and the moon was so bright, they wouldn't rise. Natalie put them in a jam pot and kept them in her bedroom.

Next Sunday we went to the Cathedral to hear the Bishop preach. We heard him preach every Sunday for four years, but I never felt that I knew him really well, and gradually the ladies of the parish came round to the same conclusion too. Anyhow, my sister Natalie married the Bishop when she was twenty.

O STAY AND HEAR

THEY ARE WALKING in the flower-garden, and what are they singing? Something rather merry and mocking; the veering breeze blows up a few words now and then to the ears of a lady behind green bathroom blinds. Now the lady raises a long pale arm and applies a little soap to it, at the same time peeping through the slats without raising from her cool bath-water.

Samedi après-midi,
Madame-là tombait malade:
Voyez, cherchait l'Abbé . . .

The brown girls' arms are intertwined like snakes; yet somehow the plump hand of Melta, who is a maid by profession and fond of arranging flowers, reaches out with a sharp carving-knife and lops off half a bush of crimson roses between one stanza and another; both girls dip in a flying curtsy, and the thinner fingers of Ariadne, eighteen-year-old cook, brush grass and come up with the dazzling spray.

Monsieur l'Abbé venait.
Il dit, Rome Saeculorum.
Madame-là comprend c'est "rhum."

But I thought they said the patois was *common* and that they disdained it, says this English Madame-là to herself, standing on a rush mat and dabbing off rivulets absently. To think of me, me myself, indulging in a cold bath at four o'clock in the afternoon! she comments inwardly.

When she told them about the sudden dinner, they had taken it very sweetly. "A business friend of the Master's." "Oh yes, Mistress: understood." "He is a Director, but has quite a simple appetite." "Flying fish," says Ariadne. "And fried plantains," adds Melta.

"Oh no, I think not fried plantains—too hot. Something green. Perhaps a little stuffed avocado?" "Stuffed with what, Mistress?" asks Ariadne bluntly. "Oh, I don't know . . . perhaps some parsley?' "The hen and the weeding boy have taken the parsley," Melta says. "Then I leave it to you."

They are pleased: they like things being left to them. They take up the carving-knife and go out into the garden. But instead of hunting for a last blade of parsley or a handful of chives, they dance around in the high soft breeze, lopping off roses. Their aprons lift and swirl, and they look like ballet dancers dressed as probationer nurses: the full skirts of their uniforms are covered with a flight of multicoloured wild ducks. Their little song has come to an end, so they begin it again:

Samedi après-midi,
Madame-là tombait malade . . .

It is Saturday afternoon; and if I had fainted in my bath I could have drowned, I could have died, and those girls wouldn't have been in the least concerned, thinks Madame-là anxiously. She is envious of them, because they have each other for gay company. Now they are advancing on the lonely house, using their bouquet to shoo before them a brown hen with well-clipped wings. This is the pullet which had the temerity, in the middle of a sweltering West Indian summer, to lay one egg in a secret place and hatch out a solitary cream-coloured chicken.

The girls drive the hen, the hen cups the chick with her shortened wings, all rush in a giggling, clucking posse towards the kitchen steps, under which the hen and chicken disappear. Something about the hen and chick has a secret power of mirth over the girls: they sit on the bottom step, laps full of roses and arms round each other's necks, laughing fecklessly.

Madame-là has her own method of attracting attention: she leans out of the window with a small brass bell suspended on a string, and tinkles it above the white-capped heads.

"Melta! Ariadne! Don't forget Mr. Whitborough is coming to dinner!"

"Yes, Mistress," says Melta in her deep, harsh contralto. "We forget ourselves. The hen makes us laugh."

But they are speaking to an empty window: Madame-là has slipped downstairs to greet them on the landing. She wants to know what there is about the hen . . .

About the hen? Ariadne starts to laugh again. It is really intolerable. At last Melta says: "It is the hen and her child."

"The hen and her child is like ourselves," says Ariadne, rising to full copper height.

Melta is engaged in slicing off the rose stems, for all the world as if she is going to stuff Mr. Whitborough's avocado pears with the trimmings. Madame-là notices how pretty both girls are, and that Ariadne is the one with the crisp, scornful upper lip.

"She takes pride in her chick, which is of a lighter complexion than herself," volunteers Melta.

"Just as we do," says Ariadne. They both laugh again, to see the amazement and appeal on Madame-là's face. It is giving them great pleasure to satisfy her curiosity tormentingly, bit by bit.

"I have a daughter, of very pale coloration," says Ariadne. "It is a girl. She is named Dolores."

"I also have a child, a boy name Ah-but-not. He is even so light as Adné's child, and born in the same month," says Melta.

"And how old are these children?" asks Madame-là, sounding lost. When she says the word "children" she looks wonderingly at their continuing childish arabesque against a background of roses.

"Two years at Epiphany," says Melta, and Ariadne echoes, "E-pi-phan-y."

"But where are they?"

"Where?" ask the girls together, astonished. "With our mothers in the country, Mistress, naturally."

Ariadne declares, "We were raised up as neighbors. We do everything together."

Madame-là makes an effort, and collects herself. "You must bring the children to see me."

"Yes, Mistress." They undulate evasively.

"But don't forget the dinner. Perhaps I could arrange the roses, to save time?"

Melta lays down the stems reproachfully. To create a diversion, Ariadne exclaims with cunning: "I can hear the Master's step, Mistress."

So Madame-là goes back upstairs and finds that Rodney indeed stands, steaming with recent energetic action, on the upstairs verandah. A strange redness overlays his sun-browned face. "Have you been playing tennis?" she asks him.

"No, darling," says Rodney, turning his back to reveal that his shirt is torn to shreds. "I've been fighting."

All her life she has been wanting Rodney to be successful and masterful, and now she is not sure that success really suits him. Is he, after all, getting *too tough*?

"With the skipper of the *Douce Hélène*," he answers her question tersely.

"Oh Rodney! That poor black man!"

"He nearly made me two thousand pounds poorer, by tipping our new engine into the sea. I had practically to stun him to get it eased back into the boat until we could land it."

She is silent, envisaging the horrid scene, a large lump of tangled steel perilously rocking, and Rodney springing at the skipper's gleaming torso. But Rodney appears unconcerned: he removes his shredded shirt and makes for the bathroom.

To soothe him further, she calls through the netted swing door: "I have a theory about the social aspects of—"

But Rodney calls back: "Oh lord, no theories! Not with Whitborough coming to dinner!"

She is hurt, because really her theory is quite delicate and distinguished. She believes now that people in this tropical island do not make love for romantic reasons, but as social and evolutionary means. She is thinking of Melta and Ariadne and their children of light coloration, and the hen and the chick; it all seems to link up.

Fastening her pearls above the surf-green voile, she sighs, and then she begins to hum the catchy little song the girls were singing in the garden; going downstairs a moment later to see how Mr. Whitborough's dinner is progressing.

If there is any dinner at all, it must be incarcerated in the frightening iron oven. Even the open coal-pot has disappeared. So have the girls.

Madame-là runs back upstairs in distress. "Rodney! I can't find the maids—and the coal-pot has gone, too." She hunts for her little brass bell.

"Don't worry," he says. "They are probably ironing out each other's hair with flat-irons. They always do before a dinner-party. Look out of the back window and you'll see them at it."

He is quite right. Ariadne is stretched on a piece of sacking outside the maids' room; Melta is applying a sizzling iron to her short, crimped hair, pulling as she presses. It is a painful scene, like an operation, and is transforming the girl into a sophisticated Arawak.

"And I can't think," cries Madame-là, "why they should want to have hair as straight as ours, when they *mock* at us so!"

Rodney laughs. He goes to a cabinet and pours out two long frosted drinks, to fortify them against their guest.

Yet, after all, the evening turns out smooth and gracious. Mr. Whitborough does most of the talking; as Rodney has hinted, he is a man of theories. He is a much-travelled man, and makes a good story of how he found an almost untarnished button of his glorious regiment on a high slope in the Himalayas. Once, too, he entered an African chieftain's hut and was surprised to see the pennant of his yacht club fluttering above a four-poster.

"Fluttering?" Madame-là cannot resist exclaiming, thinking of the draught on the dying chieftain—she having imagined African huts as windowless as igloos . . .

"But not the least charming of my adventures," says Mr. Whitborough, over the crimson roses—he is quite handsome for his age, and his quivering nostrils seem to devour the flying fish before he lifts his fork. . . . After all, the dinner is superb, though it seems to have been cooked in ten minutes, and the mysterious stuffing which inflates the yellow-green avocado pears must always remain a secret— ". . . when I visited this island once, not so awfully long ago. My friend Arbuthnot and I went up the Rivière Fantasque: he was trying to net rare birds for his tropical aviary, and I was after edible crabs. We sat there on the river bank, enjoying the scene and contemplating a plunge, when suddenly—" The memory is so sweet, so incomparable, that Mr. Whitborough's nostrils meet his upper lip in an unusual smile.

"Suddenly there was this voice, coming from the depths of what I can only describe as a jungle; and we saw that higher up the river two comely girls, clothed only in a series of patches, were beating some cloth against a rock in the water and singing. At least, one of them was singing: and I am sure you will never guess what the words were."

"A song about a sick lady on Saturday afternoon," Madame-là puts forward, startling Rodney by her sudden vivacity. She has taken advantage of Melta's absence with the emptied plates: but she knows, she is positive that behind the glazed screen two interlinked forms are panting against each other with suppressed giggles.

Mr. Whitborough stares at Madame-là in astonishment.

"And how the Abbé was called in—" she starts to explain.

"Oh no!" Mr. Whitborough states firmly, authoritatively. "Nothing as ribald as that. Something very strange, almost, one might say, moving. A Shakespearian song to an Elizabethan air. We distinctly heard it: *O stay and hear, your true love's coming . . . and the other voice took it up: That can sing both high and low*. I remember how it echoed down the valley. *Both high and low*. It quite put poor Arbuthnot off his game. He dropped the net, and three rare specimen escaped."

"That's a beautiful tale, Whitborough—one of your best," says Rodney.

"And the most beautiful thing is that it's quite true," says Mr. Whitborough.

"*I* believe it," says Madame-là sparkling.

"But surely that's not the end of it?" says Rodney.

"Ah, my dear fellow," says Mr. Whitborough, "I have learnt by long experience as a raconteur that there is a point at which one ends a story. That little tale has an element of pure, unexpected romance. To carry it further would be crude. Since you press me, Arbuthnot went up the river, after his birds or after the girls—I don't know which."

"And did you ever find any edible crabs?" asks Madame-là, borrowing an inflection of mockery from somewhere. She does not expect Mr. Whitborough to reply; besides, Melta has just come in with a crystal bowl full of fruit jelly. The night is so hot that the bright, rainbow-coloured mound wobbles dangerously, on the brink on disintegration.

It looks as if it is shaking—shaking with secret laughter.

A TALK ON CHINA

He pressed the bell with the cheerful boldness of an old friend and stood there beaming behind his glasses: a little Catholic chaplain in Allied uniform, wearing under his military cap the ingratiating smile of someone who is about to beg a favour or tell an impossible story. Stella had seen such an expression on the Nuns' faces when they called to ask for funds for their orphans.

"But I can't talk to you," she said. "I can't talk to you and I can't give you any money, for I am just about to catch a train. I must—I've got to give a lecture to some schoolgirls. Seven hundred of them, in fact. A talk on China."

"But pardon me." The priest inserted into the half-open doorway one of his bony knees, which were encased in khaki breeches. "Do not send me away. I come from your homeland, and have only just arrived in England. I bring you a message from your illegitimate cousin Mirabelle. My name is Father Grolier."

Mirabelle: homeland. The two words rang so sweetly in the chill of the corridor that Stella immediately admitted the clerical ambassador, who followed her indoors to an oval table on which her notes lay pale beneath the three dying daffodils. The sad look on the notes and the accusing hands of the clock reminded her that her urgent problem was one of contraction: how to squeeze four thousand years of mellowing Chinese civilization into twenty-five minutes for the ten-to-twelves and thirty minutes for the twelve-to-fourteens. A more craven spirit would have sagged beneath the enormity of the assignment; but Stella was far more disturbed by the presence of Father Grolier and the condition of the flat which she was about to abandon for the day. Now I shall never have time to tear the beds apart and slap all the dishes into the cupboard, she sighed, her eyes lighting gloomily on the words *T'ang Dynasty. Guerilla factories. Progress of Women.*

"Then Mirabelle. . . ." she slipped one arm into a sleeve of her outdoor coat. Looking straight into Father Grolier's eyes she saw that they were green—as green as the palm-festooned island on which there lived a girl with brown laughing eyes. "But I must hurry!"

"Where are you going?" As he spoke Stella saw on his face a gleam of liberation and the love of adventure. She told him the name of the suburb; he had never heard of it, and she had little idea where it was. "Never mind, we shall find it together, and on the way we shall talk, for I have a great deal to tell you," he said. Together they snatched up notes, gloves and a bag and ran for the bus.

"Shall I tell you about myself first?" They were now in front of the tube booking-office. "Well, may I explain that I have met also your mother, but only in the distant manner of those who participate in cups of tea but do not share a faith. I was very interested to meet her, for being a country priest I had hitherto met in the confessional only those members of your family whose mixed blood adds so greatly to the charm of West Indian types—I refer of course to the illegitimate children of your uncles, your great-uncles, and your great-grandfather."

He paused for breath and to push Stella firmly into a seat, dislodging with courtesy a fat woman and taking up her position. His voice was foreign and clear and had a pulpit attraction for the midday tube passengers, despite the loud whirring of the train.

"People, people, so many people, as thick as the trees in your lonely island! Back in the presbyter, my old housekeeper was deaf, and I had to seek out my parishioners on horseback through a jungle. Imagine, I had come from a lively town in Europe where every scandal, every venal sin even, was a public concern. I loved the beauties of nature and solitude, but after three years of that jungle I seized with joy the opportunity to join our fighting forces over here, for as you see, I am still young." He stooped to pick up Stella's gloves, which had slipped to the floor.

"Thank you. And please may I have my notes?" She took the papers from him and modestly cast her eyes on the words: *T'ang Dynasty. Golden age of Poetry. Comparable—*

"We have a few Indo-Chinese in my unit," said Father Grolier. "Did I tell you that I am assistant censor? It is quite like a continuation of my work in the confessional. Of course the things which interest me most are the problems of marriage and sex. These things are human. They are universal."

Ah, well, thought Stella, I am not keeping my end up; I am cheating the tube public. She smiled and responded in a voice which was more audible than usual: "Did you ever hear the Chinese proverb, 'If a man is unfaithful to his wife, it is like spitting from a house into the street, but if a woman is unfaithful to her husband, it is like spitting from the street into the house'?"

"Very profound, and confirming my personal observations. Is it not strange how often a white man will live in happiness with a coloured women and how seldom a coloured man will remain faithful to a white woman, even though she is said to be his superior? But there is another matter connected with your homeland which has puzzled me for a long while. Why, when there is so much rushing water for electric power in the island, did the Government install a machine running on oil which has to come from abroad? These matters are great mysteries."

The Chinese Industrial Co-operatives create for refugees a new interest in life. Thousands of crippled soldiers and refugees are employed on these projects, read Stella. "And Mirabelle? Is she a mystery too?"

"Mirabelle is the most European of all your cousins," said Father Grolier. "She longs to come over here and join the A.T.S. Actually, that is why she asked me to call. She would like you to get an M.P. to take the matter up in the House of Commons. She does not think it is fair that the boys who volunteer should get free transport to

England to join the forces while she has to teach embroidery at the convent. She is very angry about this. But she is beautiful, Mirabelle! And modern! England is full of Army Captains who are starving for beautiful wives like Mirabelle."

The train groaned into a suburban station. Father Grolier regarded the station clock with pleasure. "We are early. Allow me to take you out to lunch before your lecture. When I take people out to lunch I always patronize the best restaurant, which is generally in the most expensive hotel. Let us go in search of one."

"Oh, no!" cried Stella. "Remember that we have another bus ride—to the school. Besides I always eat at an Express Dairy. I can see one across the street." Disappointed, Father Grolier took her arm and led her to a spotty table. He looked at her hands pensively. "You are married? You do your own housework? You are happy with your husband?"

"I ought to warn you," countered Stella, "that this school at which I am to talk is a progressive one. They will be rather surprised to see me arriving with a priest."

"By progressive," said Father Grolier, "you mean *advanced*?"

"Well . . . I mean progressive," said Stella.

"Are you progressive?" he asked.

"Of course, the expression is a little dated, " she said absently.

"I am not affected by dates," said Father Grolier solemnly. "My calendar is the encyclical of the human soul."

The waitress approached, and he ordered two steak and kidney puddings, adding: "And please bring me a bottle of red wine or two beers."

"I'm sorry, sir, we do not serve intoxicating drinks in this establishment,' said the waitress.

"Then bring us two large black coffees as soon as possible, please." Father Grolier drummed on the table. He returned to Stella, fixing her with his green eyes. "Are you busy this evening? I should like to invite you to the theater. How wonderful it is to see life enacted on a stage! In a moment you are in the interior of a home; you see the domestic tragedy, or comedy. Frequently when I watch these happenings I feel a desire to climb on the stage and give the players a little advice."

Now is he laughing at me or is he really so impossible—asked Stella of herself, saying: "I'm very sorry. But I have to cook the dinner to-night."

"You are a devoted wife." Father Grolier's voice was compound of regret and admiration. "Tell me—for I am always very interested—what is it that keeps you united to your husband? For I have found that there is great need in marriage for a common enthusiasm. . . ."

A distress amounting to indigestion afflicted Stella. She saw China receding into the distance and the mocking palm-girt eyes of Father Grolier coming nearer and nearer. (I shall never get through this lecture. I have forgotten every word of it.) "In our case," she said, swallowing desperately, "I expect it is politics."

Now it was Father Grolier's turn to be distressed. After a pause during which he emptied his coffee-cup, he said: "I am not so sure that it would be a good thing for Mirabelle to take the risk of being interned or running through the U-boats."

They went out to catch the local bus. It was late; when they arrived at the school a little girl ran panting inside to inform the Principal.

The school buildings were stark and new, flung together with occidental haste. Surprised grown-up faces appeared at the windows of the Principal's office; in a few moments introductions were effected, and Stella made a strategic effort to get the Principal into the staff lavatory so that she could explain Father Grolier. "I've never seen him before," she said weakly. "He just arrived—from my homeland—with a message from—"

"Oh, I expect we can squeeze him in somewhere," said the Principal, her face clearing slightly. "You realize, of course, that you will have to give your talk twice. Do you think your friend will wish to listen to both lectures?"

But Father Grolier had already decided for himself. He was in the Principal's office discussing co-education with the geography mistress, a handsome girl with black hair and red cheeks. "After the first talk, Miss Newcombe has kindly offered to show me over the school."

The children were sitting on the floor of the large hall, cross-legged and packed tight. Against the western wall Father Grolier sat on a bench between the Principal and the geography mistress. For a cold moment Stella felt that she was trespassing in Father Grolier's church, that she had stolen his pulpit. Whose was this calm undisconcerted voice speaking to the English young about Young China? Could it be her own? Was she speaking about China or about her homeland? The children were listening, their faces a sea of County Council flowers. "And so, just imagine a girl only a little bigger than yourselves, to whom the whole of life is an adventure," Stella found herself saying. "The Japanese have bombed her school, but she has helped to build it again with her own hands. She feels that she is as good as any boy, and as brave. In a little while she may be in the Chinese army, fighting beside the boys or caring for the wounded. In the olden days she might have sat at home behind the quiet walls of a courtyard doing beautiful embroidery like a girl in a convent. But this is new China, where girls are becoming free and equal at last. . . ."

All the eager faces were Mirabelle's face. They, too, wanted to be as good as any boy anywhere in the world. And though they were more afraid of poetry than of machine-guns, they gulped down a T'ang Dynasty poem like little fishes, coming up with shining wide-open mouths for more. But suddenly Stella glanced at Father Grolier. How mocking were those green eyes which said as clearly as possible that some girls would be happier embroidering dragons than struggling for equality! Stella thought with dismay of the mocking voices of the comrades. "After all, Chiang is only another dictator—almost feudal. Corruption in Chungking . . . struggles in the Kuomintang . . . the women in the interior are not even liberated yet. . . ."

These thoughts were deep behind her words, which had been continuing evenly. She looked out of the window. All around the gaunt school buildings were the chimneys of factories. "I expect," she went on, "that most of your fathers and brothers work in near-by factories or are in the services, and that you think factories must be very dull places. But let me tell you about the most exciting factories in the world, the guerilla factories of China—"

Twenty-three minutes. The talk was over. Some of the little girls had cramps because they had not wriggled. A great rattle of limbs and pennies sounded through the hall; the head girls were bringing up to the platform bags full of their collection for the suffering children of Free China. To Father Grolier the clinking sound must have been almost too reminiscent, for he tiptoed out in the wake of the beautiful geography teacher throwing back at Stella a deprecatory smile.

When the pennies had been transmuted into a cheque for relief and the goodbyes said, Stella walked slowly down the road towards the bus stop. There was only one passenger waiting, half-leaning against the urban bank of grass and dust behind the pavement. Upon this bank he had laid his military cap. (He seems just like a man and not a priest at all! was her thought.) "I waited for you," said Father Grolier simply, "to continue our talk."

Stella was tired; but the peculiar thing was that she was glad to see him. He had come and gone—a temporary disturbing influence—leaving something unfinished. Sitting on the stubbly grass beside him, she said: "But I've talked too much already."

"We've just missed a bus. I expect you think me a nuisance. I talk along certain lines. But yes! I watched your expressions. You see, I feel that I am in a strange country, and can say what I please. It is funny. People must feel like that when they come to me in the Confessional. When I listened to your talk, I thought that you were preaching at me." He laughed, but without mockery. "You seemed like a young priest. You made me think of Mirabelle, too."

Some of the children who had been in the great hall drifted past and stared at them curiously.

"The fact is—" Father Grolier coloured a shy salmon-pink—"the fact is, I feel myself to be suddenly a different person since I am over here, just ordinary. I say to myself, 'Religion? it means different things to various people.' And this is something strange for a priest to admit. When you said *progressive* in the restaurant, your tone was pious. You laugh! But you were giving those children a sermon about a new life. A sermon, but decidedly a sermon. It was just another way of saying 'love thy neighbor.' I could have done some of it better myself. But the part about freedom . . . that's something I could not have done, because I doubt if I have ever been free, if anyone is free, I think if I should ask you, 'Do you believe in God?' you would say, 'No. Certainly not your God.' And if you were to ask me, 'Do you believe in freedom?' I would say, 'No. There is no freedom. We are all slaves to our early memories, our training, our families and our vows.' I *might* have said that, I mean. But listen to my freedom of speech now! I will tell you something, I will make you my confession: I love Mirabelle."

He looked at Stella, expecting her to speak; but as she remained silent, he went on: "I don't know why I speak to you this way: perhaps it is because when you spoke to those children you seemed to be in love with a whole country—with the Chinese people—with the world. When I heard your voice, sounding so much in love with great masses of unknown people, I thought to myself Bon Dieu, she may be in love with the masses, but I am in love with an individual, with Mirabelle!"

The bus was lumbering towards them. They rose and regarded each other gravely. Father Grolier said, very simply, the salmon pink fading from his face, "Yes, I love her as a man loves a woman, and I shall never see her again." They climbed into the bus, and he paid both fares with his earlier hearty flourish. But although Stella expected him to embarrass the passengers with intimate conversation, he remained silent until the moment came for parting.

Notes

Abbreviations Used in the Notes

AA	Arnold Active
AOE	Adèle Olyphant Emery
BMG	Brian Merton Gould
DA	Daphne Agar
DHJ	Dilys Henrick Jones
EC	Elaine Campbell
ECL	Emmanuel Christopher Loblack
EG	Elizabeth Greenhall
EKB	Edward Kamau Brathwaite
ELB	Edward LeBlanc
ES	Edward Scobie
FB	Frank Baron
FR	Francis Reid
GA	Grantley Adams
GH	George Horner
HBA	Henning Bernd von Arnim-Schlagenthin
HD	West Indian House of Representatives Debates
ITC	*In the Cabinet* (unpublished novel)
ITC/DH	*In the Cabinet* (published autobiographical excerpts)
JP	Jonathan Pulsifer
JR	Jean Rhys
JSA	Josephine Shand Allfrey Simmance
LH	Lennox Honychurch
LHA	Lennox Honychurch Archives (Allfrey's papers are held by Mr. Honychurch in Dominica)
MB	Margaret Benge
MEC	Mary Eugenia Charles
NAND	N.A.N. "Alec" Ducreay
PF	Pixie Foley
PFr	Pierrette Frickey
PH	Patricia Honychurch
PP	Polly Pattullo
PSA	Phyllis Shand Allfrey
RA	Robert Allfrey Jr.
RB	Ronald Benge
REA	Robert Edward Allfrey
RLS	Rosalind Leslie Smith
RV	Rosalind Volney
SAA	Sonia Allfrey Adeleke
TOH	*The Orchid House*
TVL	Trevor Vine-Lott

Preface
The End of Eden

ix **Her spirit, however . . .** PSA to AOE, n.d.

Chapter One
Ghosts in a Plantation House

3 **Of all the . . .** Froude, 141. **Vegetation grows . . .** Waugh, 97. **Undisciplined nature . . .** Eliot, 222.

3 **The island had . . .** Eliot, 221.

4 **The lime industry . . .** Cracknell, 84.

4 **Turn-of-the-century . . .** Rhys, *Smile Please*, 89–91.

4–5 **At the time of . . .** Bell, 25, 45. **With his characteristic . . .** ibid., 45.

5 **Roseau's was . . .** Bell, 45. **Jean Rhys, in her autobiography . . .** Rhys, *Smile Please*, 65.

6 **Phyllis Byam Shand . . .** The family history draws from *Antigua and the Antiguans*, Shand family documents, interviews with RLS, and Higham. **Historian Gordon Lewis . . .** Lewis, 159. **She was fond . . .** PSA to EC, n.d.; PSA to REA, n.d.

6 **Of the many tributes . . .** Hoyos, n.p.

7 **In 1654 Byam . . .** Goslinga, 42. **In a letter . . .** Quoted in Gaspar, 66. **Willoughby Bay . . .** Davy, 1854.

7n **Governor during . . .** Quoted by Angeline Goreau, 64.

8 **Willoughby, William's eldest . . .** Oldmixon, 57.

9 **Lydia, Phyllis's . . .** Hall, 143. **Joseph John Gurney, a visitor . . .** Gurney, 64–65.

9 **Indeed, given . . .** Henry, 51; Hall, 145.

9 **Little is known . . .** Stroude, n.p.

Chapter Two
A Birth Between the Palms

11 **Dominica was a place . . .** Stroude, n.p.; Knopton, 4–14.

12 **Dr. Nicholls . . .** "A Brief Memoir of Sir Henry Alfred Alford Nicholls. . . ," n.p. **Upon his death . . .** Menzies, 203.

12 **Dr. Nicholls was . . .** *TOH*, 8–9.

13 **Dr. Nicholls's country . . .** Froude, 164–165.

13–14 **As L'Aromatique . . .** Froude, 145. **As Stephen Hawys would . . .** Hawys, 166–167.

14 **The Nichollses also . . .** Waugh, 128; *TOH*, 42.

14 **Important visitors . . .** Menzies, 203.

15 **The wedding of . . .** "Hymeneal," 3.

16 **Her sister Margaret . . .** PSA, "Obituary: Margaret . . . Nicholls," 4.

16–17 **"My paternal relations . . ."** Pattullo [1985], 23. **"My first memory . . ."** PSA, "Eugenia Nicholls." **The Shand girls were . . .** PH, 11 August 1993.

17 **At the center . . .** LR, 10 August, 1993; Rhys, *Smile Please*, 88; Froude, 144.

18 **Phyllis addressed . . .** *TOH*, 153; PSA, "Uncle Rufus"; Hawys, 171–174; PSA, "Breeze."

19 **Phyllis was born . . .** PF to author, 6 October 1994.

20 **Many remember her . . .** Adrian Espinet, 7.

20 **Her younger sisters . . .** Rosalind was born on July 2, 1912.

20 **When Phyllis was . . .** Adrian Espinet, 7.

21 **The Shand household . . .** *TOH*, 4; *ITC*, 28; *TOH*, 8. **After a walk . . .** RLS, 11 July 1993.

22 **Less of a comfort . . .** Biographical note, LHA. **Phyllis claimed . . .** Adrian Espinet, 7. **"I would never have . . ."** Pattullo [1988], 231. **A perceptive friend . . .** RB to author, 4 April 1993.

22 **Phyllis was only . . .** See Honychurch [1984] for an account of the war's impact on Dominica.

23–24 **Her father's melancholy . . .** ES, 2 July 1991. **"There was something . . ."** *TOH*, 48.

25 **And then there . . .** RLS, 11 July 1993. **And once a year . . .** Honychurch [1988], 69.

26 **Young Phyllis . . .** Pattullo [1988], 226; Campbell [1986], 10; ITC, 81; Pattullo [1988], 226–227; Campbell [1986], 10.

27 **One of the things . . .** Eliot, 222.

27 **His medical practice . . .** PSA, "It Falls into Place." 3, 9.

28 **Phyllis started . . .** Pattullo [1988], 226; Campbell [1986], 10; *Tiger Tim's Weekly* (1921).
28 **Despite its provincial . . .** PSA, "The Objective." **Just a few months . . .** *TOH*, 50.
28–29 **In 1920s . . .** Pattullo [1985], 22–23. **In the fictionalized . . .** *TOH*, 70.

Chapter Three
Changeling

33 **"I skipped around the decks . . ."** *TOH*, 60.
33–34 **Phyllis's sojourn . . .** See Stanley Jackson. **Like their peers . . .** *TOH*, 88.
34 **During her first . . .** Stanley Jackson; *TOH*, 87. **The girl who . . .** Campbell [1986], 10; *TOH*, 88.
34 **The lavishness . . .** *TOH*, 87.
35 **Seeing that her sister . . .** *TOH*, 135.
35 **The great disparity . . .** PSA to AOE, n.d.
36 **When Adèle . . .** Kennedy, 25.
37 **Phyllis was later . . .** PSA, "Parks."
37 **Phyllis was soon . . .** Pulsifer, 28.
38 **Phyllis, she of . . .** RB, 1 March 1993.
39 **When Phyllis met . . .** *TOH*, 150.
40 **Phyllis's self-identification . . . Once reunited in England . . .** Pattullo [1988], 227.
41 **The setting of . . .** PSA, "I Got Capital" and "Lily."
42 **On February 12, 1931 . . .** *ITC*, 29–30. **The baby . . .** *ITC*, 30–31.
42 **Thus, in late . . . As Joan tells . . .** *TOH*, 184.
43 **Phyllis returned to . . .** PSA to AOE, 20 October 1932.
43–44 **Despite the many . . .** Pattullo [1988], 227. **There is further . . .** PSA to AOE, 24 April 1933.
44 **When Rosalind visited . . .** PSA to AOE, 20 October 1932. **She had five . . .** See de Charms.
45 **Upon their arrival . . .** PSA, "Letter to a German-American Laundress."
45 **Phyllis would never be able . . .** PSA to AOE, 27 August 1936.
46–47 **In 1937 . . . She would always be . . .** LH and PH, 3–19 August 1991; RB to author, 4 April 1993.
47 **Not then a fashionable . . .** DHJ to author, 29 May 1993.
47 **During Phyllis's early . . .** *TOH*, 37.
47 **It was during . . . "Her style was . . ."** Pattullo [1988], 227. **Phyllis had always . . .** PSA, "Jean Rhys: A Tribute," 23–24.
47–48 **When they met, Jean was living . . .** Angier, 419, 369. **Of the early years . . .** Frickey, 2–3.
48 **In March 1941 . . .** Angier, 420.

Chapter Four
Comrades

49 **"1939 was not a year . . ."** Quoted by Hewison, 1. **"I loved [Naomi] . . ."** Pattullo [1988], 228.
49 **Phyllis claims . . .** Pattullo [1988], 228; **As a matter . . .** Mitchison [1979], 36.
50 **Indeed, Naomi . . .** PP, 13 January 1991. **Phyllis described . . .** Mitchison [1979], 36.
51 **There is no denying . . .** Mitchison [1938], 171.
51 **Politics were . . .** Hewison, 2. **Phyllis threw . . .** *ITC*, 84.
52 **Phyllis, in turn . . .** See Cole.
52 **She became an avowed . . .** ES, 2 July 1991.
53 **Phyllis's politicization . . .** Firth, 19.

53 **To the British . . .** Quotations from Foot, 219; PSA, "Sitting Around in London."

54–55 **Although not entirely . . . Bevan, whose . . .** Foot, 290, 295.

55 ***"Immer vorsichtig"*** **. . .** Edward Dudley to RB, 27 January 1993.

55 **The beginning . . .** Mitchison [1985], 39–40; Mitchison [1979], 233; PSA, "Babes in the Woods"; JP, 12 September 1991.

57–58 **An insightful . . .** RB to author, 4 April 1993. **"It was always difficult . . ."** Pattullo [1988], 231. **Phyllis's use of what . . .** Showalter, 215. **In "A Talk on China," . . .** PSA, "A Talk on China."

58 **Phyllis, her romance . . .** Hewison, 30.

59 **The war years were . . .** Pattullo [1988], 228.

59 **The West Fulham . . .** See Summerskill, 43.

60 **Rosalind, who . . .** PSA to JR, 19 September 1941, Jean Rhys, LHA.

61 **Phyllis's lifelong . . .** Hill, 7–14.

62 **The 1940s . . .** PSA, "The Tunnel." **A story titled . . .** PSA, "The Short Short Story."

63–64 **In 1943 Phyllis . . .** PSA to Jean Rhys, 19 September 1941, Jean Rhys, LHA.

64 **During the first year . . .** PF to author, 6 October 1994; PF to author, 22 November 1994.

64n **She also developed . . .** PF to author, 22 November 1994.

65 **Pixie shared . . .** PSA, "A Talk on China."

66 **During the war . . .** PSA, "Proserpeena and the Colonel."

66 **In November 1943 . . .** REA to JSA, 24 November 1943.

66 **Her separation . . .** PSA to JR, 19 September 1941; PSA, "Scraps of Paper."

67 **In "Babes in the Woods," . . .** PSA, "Babes in the Woods."

68 **Her early "autobiography" . . .** *ITC*, 62.

69 **Phina's adjustment . . .** *ITC*, 65.

69–70 **If anything, Phyllis . . .** DHJ to author, 29 May 1993. **She wrote in . . .** *ITC*/DH, November 23, 1963.

70 **In England Pod . . .** PSA, *Governor Pod*, 12–13.

70 **After the war . . .** Cole, 281–288.

71 **Shortly after . . .** PSA to AOE, 7 November 1953.

71 **In 1947 Robert . . .** JP, 12 September 1991.

72 **The final years . . .** *ITC*, 63.

72 **After the war the London . . .** DHJ to author, 29 May 1993.

73 **One of the Readers' . . .** PF to author, 6 October 1995. **The thrust of his advice . . .** DHJ to author, 29 May 1993. **The scenery, as she . . .** *ITC*/DH, August 24, 1963, 3.

74 **In the late . . .** RB to author, 4 April 1993; MB to author, 23 January 1993; TVL to REA, 18 April 1967.

Chapter Five
Return

77 **Phyllis's most cherished . . .** AA, 6 July 1991.

78–79 **As the decade opened . . .** DHJ to author, 29 May 1993. **"She had politics . . ."** AA, 6 July 1991. **On one occasion . . .** DHJ to author, 29 May 1993.

79–80 **The award for . . .** Pattullo [1988], 229. **"The idea of . . ."** "The Author's Name Is . . ."; **"Politics ruined me . . ."** Pattullo [1988], 230. **She "slogged away . . ."** Pattullo [1988], 229.

80 **Phyllis's letters . . .** Pattullo [1988], 229.

81 **"I wanted to write a book . . ."** Pattullo [1988], 229.

81 **This is perhaps as . . .** Pattullo [1985], 23.

82 **Phyllis—quite . . .** ***The Orchid House*** **is set . . .** Campbell [1982], xii.

83 **Much has been . . . "Lally's character . . ."** Boxill, 265.

83–84 ***The Orchid House*** **. . .** Wyile, 32. **It is through . . .** *TOH*, 143.

84 **Kenneth Ramchand, writing . . .** Ramchand [1970], 225.

84n **Lennox Honychurch . . .** LH to author, 6 March 1994.

85 **The Nichollses . . .** *TOH*, 194. **Phyllis was fond . . .** *TOH*, 194. **The jesuitic bargain . . .** *TOH*, 234.

85–86 **If the nature . . . Phyllis had been . . .** Quoted in "Alain-Fournier," *Twentieth-Century Literary Criticism,* 11. **The novel . . . recounts . . .** "Alain-Fournier," *Times Literary Supplement,* 390. **Many critics have seen . . .** "Alain-Fournier," *Twentieth-Century Literary Criticism,* 11. **"We find in the novel . . ."** Turnell, 496.

86 ***Le Grand Meaulnes,* like . . .** Paul, 447. **Seurel, like Lally . . .** Gibson, 300.

87 **Phyllis had, moreover . . .** PF to author, 22 November 1994.

88 **Philip's mental illness . . .** Napsbury Hospital to JSA, 26 May 1964.

89 **During this . . . When she had met him . . .** BMG to author, 28 June 1993. **A self-avowed . . .** GH to PSA, n.d.

89 **Despite the heartache . . .** Patullo [1988], 229. **In later years . . .** Campbell [1986], 10. **The highlight of their travels . . .** *ITC*/DH, 20 July 1963, 4.

90 **The trip to . . .** REA to L. Rose & Co., 22 October 1952.

91 **During this period . . .** PSA, *Dashing Away.* **Phyllis claimed . . .** PSA to AOE, 7 November 1953.

91 **In early July . . .** *Times,* 11 July 1953, 8; *Manchester Guardian,* 17 July 1953, 4; *Sunday Observer* (1953); *Express and Star* (Wolverhampton), 10 August 1953; *Newcastle Journal,* 5 August 1953; *Iraq Times* (Baghdad), 29 July 1953; *Truth,* 24 July 1953; *Spectator,* 7 August 1953, 158.

92 **Phyllis returned home . . .** Fermor, 100.

93 **On the morning after . . .** PSA to Juliet O'Hea, 12 August 1953.

95 **In many ways . . .** Pope-Hennessy [1954], 40, 44.

95–96 **As an L. Rose . . .** PSA, "Little Cog-burt," 10; **"A real person" was . . .** PSA, "A Real Person."

96 **With her British . . .** DA and RV, 13 August 1991.

96–97 **Being back . . .** PSA to AOE, 7 November 1953. **In James . . .** Pope-Hennessy [1954], 38.

97 **In Aunt Mags . . .** Fermor, 98. **Her niece's social . . .** Fermor, 98–100.

97 **Phyllis was stunned . . .** PSA to AOE, 7 November 1953; PSA, "The Untanglers," 5.

98 **Family matters . . .** RLS, July 7, 1993. **The Catholic . . .** "News in Brief," *Dominica Chronicle,* 2 September 1953. **She would . . .** ES, 2 July 1991. **Her position . . .** *ITC*/DH, 20 July 1963, 4.

98 **Phyllis's uneasy . . .** PSA to AOE, 7 November 1953.

99 **She had not . . .** Juliet O'Hea to PSA, 4 March 1954. **The joys of literary . . .** PSA, *Dashing Away.* **The reader at . . .** Michael Sadleir to PSA, n.d.

101 **Phyllis's response . . .** PSA to Michael Sadleir, n.d. **"It is a fearful . . ."** PSA to Mr. Barker, 24 April 1954. **The disheartening news . . .** *Library Journal,* 1 March 1954, 449; *Booklist,* 15 April 1954, 320; *New York Times,* 14 March 1954, 23; *Saturday Review,* 20 March 1954, 20, 55.

Chapter Six
The Great Days

103 **Phyllis and Robert . . .** PSA to J. B. Barker, 24 April 1954.

103 **At a loss . . .** See Honychurch [1984], 172–174; *ITC*/DH, 23 November 1962.

104–105 **Phyllis had first . . .** Honychurch [1984], 173. **Elections had been . . .** Honychurch [1984], 176.

105 **The movement's . . .** LH to author, 6 March 1994; *ITC*/DH, 23 November 1962.

107 **In mid-1954 . . .** L. Rose to REA, 21 September 1954; REA to J. B. Barker, 1 October 1954.

107 **But that was as far . . .** REA to Mr. Barker, 1 October 1954.

108 **In the waning . . .** GH to PSA, 17 January 1955; FR to PSA, n.d.; DHJ to author, 29 May 1993.

108 **In early 1955 . . .** *ITC,* 74–77.

109 **In the early . . .** *Chronicle,* 9 March 1955, 6; *Chronicle,* 12 March 1955.

109 **On April 23 . . .** PSA to J. B. Barker, 29 April 1955; HBA to PSA, 30 April 1955.

110 **On May 1 . . .** *ITC*/DH, 7 December 1963; PSA, "The Labor Party of Dominica"; "News in Brief."

111 **N.A.N. "Alec" Ducreay . . .** NAND, 9 August 1993.

111 **Within days of the launching . . .** PSA to Mr. Barker, 28 May 1955.

113 **Phyllis sailed home. . . .** PSA to REA, 17 September 1955, 10 October 1955, and 12 October 1955.

114 **By mid-October . . .** PSA to REA, 12 October 1955.

114 **Phyllis's political movement . . .** PSA to REA, 12 October 1955.

115 **The weekend following . . .** NAND, 9 August 1993.

115 **In these early . . .** AA, 6 July 1991; FB, 9 August 1993.

117 **Her personal appeal . . .** AA, 6 July 1991. **Phyllis, who had . . .** Adrian Espinet, 7. **Phyllis's patois . . .** LH to author, 6 March 1994. **She was fond . . .** DHJ to author, 29 May 1993. **She was also not above . . .** RB to author, 1 July 1993.

117 **In early November . . .** PSA to REA, 1 November 1955; PSA to REA, 9 November 1955; PSA to REA, 13 November 1955.

118 **In mid-November, her packing . . .** PSA to REA, 13 November 1955.

Chapter Seven
Now in Our Times' Frugality

119 **The year and a half . . .** Mordecai, 18, 30.

119n **In 1938 the notion . . .** Mordecai, 30.

119 **The 1940s . . .** Mordecai, 34, 37.

121 **Phyllis, who had found . . .** FB, 9 August 1994.

122 **Baron was to return . . .** FB, 9 August 1994.

122 **After the completion . . .** *ITC*/DH, 7 December 1963; *ITC*/DH, 17 December 1963.

122 **During this "time . . ."** PSA, "The Time of the Migrants."

123 **Francis Reid, Phyllis's . . .** FR to PSA, 7 November 1955.

124 **Arnold Active . . .** Vane, n.p.

124 **In 1956 Phyllis . . .** REA to Audrey Davidson, 16 August 1956.

125 **Phyllis's determination to . . .** REA to PSA, 11 June 1957.

125 **This time Phyllis traveled . . .** PSA to REA, 15 June 1957.

126 **She arrived in . . .** PSA to REA, 18 June 1957.

126 **During her absence . . .** Kunsman, 686; PSA to REA, 18 June 1957; Agenda for DLP meeting, 22 June 1957, LEA; PSA to REA, 23 June 1957; PSA to REA, 7 July 1957; REA to PSA, 11 June 1957; Adrian Espinet, 7.

127 **The first task . . .** *ITC*/DH, 23 November 1962; PSA to REA, 6 July 1957.

127 **LeBlanc was . . .** PSA to REA, 6 July 1957.

128 **By early July . . .** PSA to REA, 26 June 1957.

128 **Robert, less despondent . . .** REA to PSA, 9 July 1957; Kunsman, 685; PSA to REA, 28 July 1957; Bell, 91; PSA to REA, 28 July 1957.

129 **On July 7 . . .** PSA to REA, 7 July 1957; FB, 9 August 1994.

131 **She was weary . . .** PSA to REA, 23 June 1957.

132 **On July 18 the party . . .** "Election Campaigning in Full Swing"; PSA to REA, 25 July 1957; "DLP Candidate—Roseau North—Leo Charles in the Dawbiney Market."

132 **The PNM was campaigning . . .** REA to PSA, 22 July 1957; PSA to REA, 28 July 1957.

133 **During the days preceding . . .** Adrian Espinet, 7.

133 **Two days before nominations . . .** PSA to REA, 23 July 1957.

134 **On the eve of . . .** PSA to REA, 23 July 1957; PSA to REA, 28 July 1957.

134 **While she anxiously . . .** REA to PSA, 22 July and 2 July, 1957; PSA to REA, 8 August 1957.

135 **Meanwhile the accusations . . .** PSA to REA, 28 July 1957.

135 **Her assessment of the situation . . .** PSA to REA, 4 August 1957.

135 **As election day . . .** "Mrs. Allfrey Replies to 'Voter' on Educational Issues"; "Catholics and Birth Control"; "Editorial." *Dominica Chronicle.*

136 **On August 12 . . .** PSA to REA, 8 August 1957.

137 **John Hatch, the . . .** "Visit of the Commonwealth Labour Officer to Portsmouth." Unpublished report, LHA; *Dominica Chronicle*, 14 August 1957; *ITC*/DH, 23 November 1962; PSA to REA, 15 August 1957.

138 **When the national . . .** PSA to REA, 19 August 1957; Kunsman, 684; "PNM-DLP Coalition Fails."

139 **It was not only . . .** PSA to REA, 19 August 1957.

139 **On August 19 . . .** PSA to REA, 19 August 1957.

139 **By early September . . .** PSA to REA, 19 August 1957; PSA to REA, 18 September 1957.

Chapter Eight
With Time a Threatened Currency

143 **"You were told often enough . . ."** REA to PSA, 12 April 1958.

143 **Phyllis's two months . . .** REA to PSA, 12 April 1958; PSA to REA, 3 April 1958; PSA to REA, 31 March 1958; REA to PSA, 17 April 1958.

144 **They argued bitterly . . .** REA to PSA, 12 April 1958; PSA to REA, 3 April 1958 and 31 March 1958; REA to PSA, 17 April 1958.

144 **The turmoil preceding . . .** *ITC*/DH, 9 November 1963.

145 **At Roseau she stepped ashore . . .** *ITC*/DH, 9 November 1963; Pattullo [1984], 23; PSA to REA, 28 March 1958; Baker, 164.

146 **In contrast to her own . . .** Mordecai, 86–89.

146 **On March 28 Phyllis . . .** PSA to REA, 28th March 1958, 31 March 1958 and 21 April 1958.

147 **The cable announcing her victory . . .** REA to PSA, 29 March 1958.

148 **Robert was stunned by the intensity . . .** REA to PSA, 12 April 1958.

148 **The weeks between the election . . .** PSA to REA, 21 April 1958.

148 **On April 16 she left . . .** PSA to REA, 16 April 1958.

149 **As soon as . . .** *ITC*/DH, 31 August 1963, 7; PSA to REA, 19 April 1958 and n.d.

149 **When she entered . . .** PSA to REA, 19 April 1958, n.d., and (telegram) 20 April 1958.

150 **It was widely held . . .** Mordecai, 91, 93.

150 **Grantley Adams himself was fiercely . . .** Mordecai, 93–94.

150 **On the evening . . .** *ITC*, 46; ITC/DH, 6 July 1963.

151n **Phyllis's hero worship . . .** *ITC*, 45.

151 **The inauguration of Parliament . . .** Mordecai, 94. **After the lecture . . .** *ITC*/DH, 14 December 1963 and 6 July 1963; ITC, 52; PSA to REA, 28 April 1958.

152 **The inaugural ceremony . . .** FB, 9 August 1993; *ITC*/DH, 14 December 1963.

152 **On April 23 . . .** PSA to REA, 23 April 1958; *Trinidad Guardian*, 1 May 1958.

153 **This first session of the Federal . . .** PSA to REA, 5 May 1958.

154 **She arrived in . . .** PSA to REA, 5 May 1958; PSA to REA, 10 May 1958. **By May 14 she was back . . .** PSA to REA, 14 May 1958.

154 **During the few days intervening . . .** PSA to REA, 3 June 1958; *ITC*/DH, 29 June 1963.

155 **Federation Park was not unlike . . .** *ITC*/DH, 21 September 1963; *ITC*/DH, 29 September 1963.

155 **While getting her house . . .** PSA to REA, 3 June 1958.

155 **In the early days . . .** *ITC*/DH, 10 August 1963.

156 **Adding to Phyllis's growing . . .** *ITC*/DH, 22 June 1963.

156 **On June 9 . . .** HD, 9 June 1958; PSA to REA, 17 June 1958.

157 **The session had scarcely begun . . .** Mordecai, 98.

157 **The government's first crisis . . .** Mordecai, 116–117.

158 **But, after a special meeting . . .** Mordecai, 116–117; PSA to REA, 3 July 1958.

158 **Phyllis watched . . .** Mordecai, 99; *ITC*/DH, 3 August 1963; PSA to REA, 3 July 1958.

159 **Life in Trinidad . . .** *ITC*/DH, 21 September 1963; *ITC*/DH, 3 August 1963; Mordecai, 99.

159 **The main debate . . .** Mordecai, 101–102; HD, 26 June 1958; Mordecai, 105.

160 **Ultimately, after "some of the . . ."** Mordecai, 105; HD, 30 June 1958.

160 **In August 1958, Phyllis called . . .** *ITC*, 80.

161 **In the West Indies . . .** HD, 6 December 1960.

161 **In late June Phyllis . . .** PSA to REA, 17 June 1958; PSA to REA, 19 June 1958.

161 **Throughout the summer . . .** PSA to REA, 7 June 1958; PSA to REA, 23 May 1958.

162 **Under the weight of the . . .** *ITC*, 43–44; PSA to REA, 19 June 1958.

162 **Phina received the . . .** JSA to REA, 16 August 1958; Mrs Evelyn Allfrey to REA, 7 August 1958.

Chapter Nine
The Roads

164 **Fate was to grant . . .** *ITC*/DH, 23 November 1963. **The Federal . . .** FB, 9 August 1993.

164 **After her visit . . .** PSA, Address to the 10th Session of UNESCO; *ITC*/DH, 17 August 1963, 7.

165 **The British minister of education . . .** *ITC*/DH, 17 August 1963, 7. **By November 17 . . .** *ITC*/DH, 17 August 1963, 7; HD, 17 November 1958.

166 **Robert's presence . . .** REA to Mr. Dews of Wilfred T. Fry, Ltd., n.d.; *ITC*/DH, 14 December 1963.

166 **As she gained . . .** HD, 24 November 1958; HD, 3 December 1958.

166 **Under Robert's . . .** HD, 3 December 1958; HD, 27 May 1959; "Teachers Most Ardent Federalists," *Teachers Journal*, LEA; HD, 19 May 1959.

167 **The report had . . .** HD, 3 December 1958.

167 **As part of her . . .** *ITC*, 81.

168 **As if the multifaceted. . . .** HD, 3 December 1958; HD, 1 December 1960.

168 **The House's final . . .** HD, 3 December 1958; *Trinidad Chronicle*, 4 December 1958; HD, 11 December 1958 and 29 March 1961.

169 **In late March . . .** "Speech . . . ILO conference, 44th Session," Geneva, 1959.

169 **In the last week . . .** All quotations from HD, 20 May 1959.

170 **Within days . . .** PSA, "Speech," ILO Conference, 43rd Session, Geneva, LEA; *ITC*, 71.

170 **A few days . . .** PSA to REA, 19 June 1959.

171 **On June 25 . . .** FB, 9 August 1993.

171 **This period . . .** *ITC*/DH, 7 December 1964; *ITC*, 73–74; HD, 27 May 1959, and 1 December 1960.

172 **Phyllis also . . .** Benge, 95; MB to author, 26 January 1993.

173 **In 1960 Phyllis . . .** Pattullo [1985].

173 **Phyllis's appointment . . .** Stroude, 2; PSA to ELB, 26 March 1960; HD, 21 March 1959; HD, 23 November 1960.

174 **On May 27 . . .** PSA to REA, 1 June 1960; "Allfrey Sees Bid to Wear Own Shoes' "; PSA, "Speech . . . ILO Conference, 44th Session."

175 **The ILO conference . . .** *ITC*/DH, 7 September 1963; unidentified newspaper clipping, LEA.

175 **On the day after . . .** *ITC*/DH, 7 September 1963.

176 **If Phyllis ever . . .** PSA, "On Public Speaking," LHA; PSA, "Notes for Address made at Speech Night of GBSS," LHA.

176 **In early September . . .** *ITC*/DH, 14 December 1963; draft of Speech, LHA.

177 **On September 24 . . .** PSA to REA, 4, 7, and 11 October 1960.

177 **Phyllis truly enjoyed . . .** PSA to REA, 4, 7, and 11 October 1960; "Nigerian Tolerance Impresses WI Minister," unidentified clipping, LHA.

178 **In early November . . .** EC, 7 September 1991; MB to author, 23 January 1993.

178 **In the final months . . .** HD, 28 November 1960. **In November she . . .** HD, 23 November 1960.

179 **The December 1960 . . .** HD, 1 December 1960. **The budget . . .** HD, 1 December 1960, 29 March 1961. PSA, "Women of New Nations," LHA.

180 **Throughout 1959 . . .** ELB to PSA, 26 July 1958; "Federal Minister Speaks. . . ."

180 **Her comments on . . .** ELB to PSA, 29 July 1959.

180 **She was back . . .** *Chronicle,* 13 May 1959, 5; "Points against Minister Mrs. Allfrey," LHA.

181 **During her visit . . .** ELB to PSA, 26 July 1958; *Chronicle,* 27 June 1959.

181 **In October 1959 . . .** PSA to ELB, 3 October 1959.

181–182 **Throughout 1960 . . .** *Chronicle,* 13 April 1960, 4. **In July 1960 . . .** ELB to PSA, 18 March 1959; PSA to GA, 19 July 1960; Kunsman, 692.

182 **In August Phyllis . . .** *Chronicle,* 17 and 24 August 1960.

183 **On September 3 . . .** Mersula Benoit to PSA, 26 September 1960 and November 11, 1960; ELB to PSA, 27 February 1959; AA to REA, 8 July 1960.

183 **In September Phyllis . . .** PSA to Vivian Grell, 6 September 1960; "Allfrey's Housing March Stupid—C.M."

184 **The inner-party . . .** REA to PSA, 10 June 1960; NAND, 9 August 1993; PSA to AA, 28 November 1960; PSA to Mersula Benoit, 28 November 1960; *Herald,* 24 December 1960.

185 **A few days before . . .** Anonymous letter from "A Sincere Labourite," LHA.

Chapter Ten
The Perfection Seekers

186 **"Labour has secured . . ."** "Editorial," *Herald,* 21 January 1961, 4. **The party's development agenda . . .** "Suggestions for Inclusion in the Government's Development Programme, Dominica," LHA.

186–187 **"My views are not . . ."** PSA to NAND, 13 September 1960; AA, 6 July 1991. **"Most of the [DUPP] . . ."** "Mrs. Allfrey Back from Election Win."

187 **She later told . . .** R. Espinet, 34. **Quite often . . .** PSA, "Message for Commonwealth Youth Sunday," LHA.

188 **Addressing the . . .** PSA, "An Address Recorded for the Indian Women's Cultural Association at Fyzabad," LHA; "Address . . . to the St. Augustine Girls Alumnae Association," LHA; "Address . . . to the Trinidad and Tobago Federation of Women's Institutes and Women's Groups," LHA.

188 **Aware of the . . .** PSA to AA, 29 July 1961. **The Federation . . .** "WI to Fight Migration Ban," LHA.

188–189 **In July 1961 . . .** PSA to REA, 8 June 1961. **On her way . . .** "UNESCO Plans for Independent WI," clipping, LHA; PSA to REA, 6 June 1961; PSA to REA, 10 June 1961. **The council . . .** PSA to REA, 18 June 1961; "I.L.O. Plenary Session at Palais des Nations Geneva."

189 **Jamaica's uneasiness . . .** Springer, 19. **It took no . . .** Quoted by Mordecai, 126.

190 **Grantley Adams, ever . . .** Quoted by Mordecai, 128.

190 **The conference achieved . . .** Springer, 23.

190 **In January 1960 . . .** Quoted by Mordecai, 201. **A few months . . .** Springer, 29.

191 **Just prior to the conference . . .** Douglas; LH, 6 August 1991; **Eric Williams remained . . .** Flanz, 97.

191–192 **According to . . .** F. A. Glasspole to PSA, 28 September 1961; N. W. Manley to PSA, 13 September 1961. **As Jamaicans went . . .** PSA to N. W. Manley, 19 September 1961.

192 **On the evening of referendum . . .** EG, 7 September 1991. **Manley conceded . . .** Mazurczak, 104. **Phyllis, who had . . .** Press release, LHA. **Privately she would . . .** PSA to L. P. Delapenha, 23 September 1961. **The very next morning . . .** PSA to N. W. Manley, 20 September 1961. **He did not reply . . .** N. W. Manley to PSA, 21 October 1961. **But by then . . .** Flanz, 102.

192 **The reaction throughout . . .** "Statement by the Minister on the Result of the Jamaica Referendum," 7. **In a talk . . .** "Referendum Aftermath," 2. **Addressing the Labour party . . .** "Labour Party Conference," 1.

192–193 **Just after the. . . .** Resolution presented to DLP's Executive Committee, LHA. **When the funds . . .** PSA to L. C. Didier, 7 February 1961.

193 **In September she wrote . . .** PSA to ELB, 6 September 1961. **But as president . . .** "Labour Party Conference," 1; Mabel James to PSA, 17 May 1961. **The women had prepared . . .** Mabel James to PSA, 1 January 1962.

193 **She was often . . .** PSA to NAND, 14 October 1961.

194 **In November 1961 . . .** "LP Conference: Hon. Phyllis Allfrey—President, Speaks," 1. **"I believe that everyone . . ."** Draft of Speech for the 1961 Dominica Labour Party General Meeting, LHA.

194–195 **Upon learning . . .** PSA to Boyd Berkitt, 8 February 1961. **A more serious . . .** W. S. Stevens to PSA, 12 December 1961. **Just a few weeks . . .** W. S. Stevens to PSA, 3 November 1961.

195 **She had had to issue . . .** PSA, "Statement . . . in reply to erroneous Radio Report," LHA. **In January 1962 a news . . .** PSA to EG, 9 January 1962.

195 **Damaging stories . . .** "Hearing Refused Labour Leader"; PSA, "A Statement"; "Fair-play," "Is It Racial Prejudice?"

197 **It was his opinion . . .** Quoted by Mazurczak, 106.

197 **Grantley Adams and . . .** "Federal Minister on Week-Long Visit . . . ," 1.

197 **It was "a tragic moment . . ."** Mordecai, 448. **With the "odor . . ."** Mordecai, 447; PSA to Mabel James, 6 February 1962.

198 **At the February 14 . . .** HD, 14 February 1962.

198 **By then he had had . . .** Mordecai, 451.

199 **To another friend . . .** PSA to Matilda Maximea, 9 April 1962; **The reason for this . . .** Minutes of DLP Executive Committee Meeting held 23 Feb. 1962, LHA.

199 **The press in Trinidad . . .** Mazurczak, 107. **Privately, Phyllis would . . .** PSA to Marjorie Nicholson, 3 May 1962. **In the House . . .** HD, 14 March 1962.

199 **In reply Hailes sent . . .** Lord Hailes to PSA, 15 March 1962.

200 **A week later . . .** PSA, "A Speech by the Honourable Phyllis Shand Allfrey, Federal Minister of Labour and Social Affairs, 23rd March, 1962."

201 **Phyllis was not slow . . .** HD, 10 April 1962. **The one important thing . . .** HD, 11 April 1962.

201 **Phyllis's grieving . . .** PSA, "Message . . . to the Youths of the County of Victoria on the Occasion of the Commencement of the 9th Annual Cricket Season," LHA; PSA, "The Fourth Christmas," LHA.

201 **As she wrote . . .** PSA to Mabel James, 23 January 1962; PSA to Marjorie Nicholson, 3 May 1962.

202 **But she seemed happy . . .** PSA to Mabel James, 29 July 1961.

203 **There now dwelled . . .** PSA, "The Fourth Christmas," LHA. **As she had done . . .** PSA to Mr. and Mrs. Decius Benjamin, 24 November 1961; PSA to Augustine Charles, 9 April 1962.

203 **On March 21 . . .** PSA to Martha Winston (Curtis Brown), 21 March 1962. **With "hot tears . . ."** ITC/DH, 14 December 1963.

203 **On May 16 . . .** PSA to Mortimer Payne, 15 May 1962; Pattullo, [1992] and [1991].

Chapter Eleven
For Theirs Is the Power

207 **In early June . . .** *ITC* 93–94; REA to Celia Frost, 31 March 1965; REA to JSA, 23 August 1965.

207 **It took some . . .** PSA to FR, 14 June 1962.

208 **In the meantime . . .** PSA to FR, 14 June 1962; PSA to AOE, 3 November 1963.

208 **Phyllis and Robert . . .** JP, 9 August 1993; Pattullo, [1988], 233.

208 **Within weeks of . . .** "DLP Celebrates Seventh Birthday," 9.

208 **Phyllis's return . . .** NAND, 9 August 1993; draft of letter to unidentified friend, LHA.

209 **Phyllis and Robert . . .** *ITC*, 75. Draft of letter to unidentified friend, LHA; *ITC*, 75; Pattullo [1988], 233.

209 **The *Herald* . . .** PSA to AOE, n.d.; REA to Betty Allfrey, 23 January 1965; PSA to AOE, 8 January 1963 [*sic*].

210 **The editorials she . . .** PSA, "Green Blood," 4; PSA, "The Absentee," 4; NAND, 9 August 1993.

211 **Word of the . . .** Charles, 1; draft of letter to unidentified friend, LHA; PSA to AA, 25 September 1962; AA to PSA, 27 September 1962; *Chronicle*, 29 September 1962, 1; "Allfrey Expulsion Upheld," 1; ECL, 5 August 1991; draft of letter to unidentified friend, LHA.

211 **After a discussion . . .** "Allfrey Expulsion Upheld," 1; AA, 6 July 1991.

212 **She took . . .** NAND, 9 August 1993; ES, 2 July 1991; AA, 6 July 1991.

212 **In order to undermine . . .** ES, 2 July 1991; FB, 9 August 1993; LH, 7 August 1991; *ITC*, 18.

213 **The expulsion . . .** ES, 2 July 1991; MEC, 6 August 1991; LH, 3 August 1991. Draft of letter to unidentified friend, LHA.

213 **In the months . . .** "Letters to the Editor," *Herald*, 2 November 1962, 4; PSA, "The Absentee," 4.

214 **After the . . .** PSA to AOE, 21 December 1963; ES, 2 July 1991; REA to Colin Turner, 24 August 1965.

214 **Her anxieties over . . .** PSA to AOE, 8 January 1963 [*sic*]; PSA to AOE, 13 January 1964; J. Margartson Charles to REA, 22 June 1965; PSA to AOE, n.d.

215 **If Phyllis felt . . .** PSA, "Drama of the Week."

215 **Phyllis's immediate . . .** Draft of letter to unidentified friend, LHA; PSA, "Why the *Star*?" 1; PSA, "What the *Herald* Cut Out," 1; PSA, "Name Calling."

216 **Phyllis's campaign . . .** PSA, "On Corruption," *Herald*, n.d., clipping, LHA.

217 **In 1966, however . . .** Honychurch [1984], 180.

217 **Shortly before leaving . . .** SAA, 11 July 1993; PSA, "On Secrecy."

217 **The *Star* did . . .** PSA to AOE, n.d.

218 **During his visit . . .** Lent, 350–353.

218 **In news content . . .** PSA, "The Queen in Dominica I"; PSA, "The Queen in Dominica II"; PSA, "The *Britannia* Luncheon Party."

219 **The *Star*'s appeal . . .** ES, 2 July 1991; *ITC*, 76.

219 **Among those she . . .** ES, 2 July 1991; LH, 5 August 1991.

220 **The burden of producing . . .** PSA to AOE, n.d.; PSA, "The Death of a Carib."

221 **In 1967 Phyllis . . .** PSA, "Rags Twotone Writes Again." **The Migrants' Bill . . .** PSA, "The Only Way."

222 **By far her . . .** *ITC*, 99; DA, 8 August 1991; PSA, "A Bribe and a Favour," "Sunday Dinner," "A Cautionary Rhyme"; PSA, "Rose O Censored."

222 **But Rose O's . . .** PSA, "Village State," "Swine Fever: A Cautionary Rhyme."

223 **Despite the burdens . . .** PSA, "It Falls into Place," "The Naming," PSA, "The Germ of a Short Story"; AA, 6 July 1991.

224 **The decade . . .** PSA to AOE, 8 January 1963 [sic]; PSA, "Obituary: Margaret Emily Mary Nicholls."

224 **In June 1964 Robert . . .** BMG to Author, 28 June 1993; REA to PSA, 6 June 1964.

225 **During his visit . . .** TVL to REA, 18 April 1967; BMG to author, 28 June 1993;

225 **The high point . . .** PSA, "Mr. Lionel."

226 **One of the highlights . . .** PSA to EKB, 6 September 1967; PSA, "Mr. Lionel."

226 **Phyllis's relationship . . .** SAA, 11 July 1993.

227 **David was no less . . .** REA to JSA, n.d.

227 **Robert had also . . .** REA to Jan Van Dyk, 1 April 1964; PSA, "Is Negritude Racist?"

227 **Her connection . . .** LH, 8 August 1991; PSA, "Dr. Jagan: An Appraisal."

229 **The prospect of . . .** PSA, "Stay British—And Live Free," "A Dose of Independence"; Honychurch [1984], 180.

230 **The absence of . . .** PSA, "An Effective Opposition and other Topics," "Editorial"; Honychurch [1984], 181.

230 **She was not alone . . .** Higbie, 86; Lent, 284–285, 264.

231 **Throughout 1968 . . .** PSA, "Silent Night."

231 **As a direct . . .** "Dominica Moves to Provide Punishment . . ."; Higbie, 87; "Governor to be Petitioned."

232 **Early the following . . .** "Government Officials Booed . . ."; "IAPA Criticized 'Press Gag' Law."

232 **The three editors . . .** Higbie, 90.

232 **These efforts . . .** "Premier 'Nyet' on Gag Law"; Honychurch [1984], 182.

233 **Phyllis's association . . .** Smith, 20–31; Higbie, 98; *ITC*, 19; MEC, 6 August 1991.

234 **The joys of returning . . .** PSA, "Al Akong Deported," "The Artist's Departure."

234 **Another unlikely . . .** ES, 2 July 1991.

235 **Robert does not seem . . .** REA to SAA, 20 October 1968.

Chapter Twelve
My National Song

236 **In July 1969 Phyllis . . .** PSA to JSA, 5 July 1969.

236 **They had moved . . .** PSA to JSA, 5 July 1969; REA to PSA, 12 May 1969.

237 **Phyllis's happy interlude . . .** *ITC*, 101; ES, 2 July 1991.

237 **The first loss . . .** REA to SAA, 21 May 1973.

238 **David always . . .** PSA to AOE, n.d.; REA to David Allfrey, 3 April 1976; REA to JSA, 31 March 1976.

238 **David's departure . . .** REA to Tom Puttock, 19 June 1973; REA to SAA, 21 May 1973.

238 **From the moment . . .** REA to David Allfrey, 3 April 1976.

239 **The tide of black . . .** Pattullo [1988], 233.

239 **Dominica's black power . . .** Honychurch [1984], 184; David Allfrey, "A Son to the Defense."

239 **The climate of racial . . .** PSA, "Is Negritude Racist?" "President Leopold Senghor's Speech on Negritude"; Lent, 285.

240 **The Dreads . . .** Honychurch [1988], 165, 188; PSA to AOE, 11 March 1974; PSA to AOE, 11 March 1974; AOE, 11 October 1991; PF to author, 22 November 1994.

241 **The accumulation . . .** Thomas, 78, 81; Honychurch [1984], 188.

241 **The act met . . .** Thomas, 80; Honychurch, [1984], 189; MEC quoted by Higbie, 125; PSA quoted by Higbie, 138; AL, 25 January 1995; PSA and REA, "The Threatened Forest," LHA.

242 **Phyllis's cautious . . .** PSA and REA, "The Threatened Forest," LHA; PSA, "The Simple Life."

243 **In February 1973 . . .** PSA to JR, 8 February 1973; JR to PSA, 23 March 1973.

243 **Thus would . . .** Campbell [1977]; JR to PSA, n.d.; JR to PSA, 23 March 1974.

243 **Throughout the years . . .** PSA, "Wide Sargasso Sea," "Jean Rhys: A Tribute," "Jean Rhys: 'I'll Have to Go on Living. . . .'"

244n **In a recording . . .** "Jean Rhys: 'I'll Have to Go on Living. . . .'"; JR to PSA, n.d.

244 **Phyllis lost few . . .** PSA, "Most Famous Dominican," "Jean Rhys: A Tribute"; Jean Rhys, "Again the Antilles."

245 **Shortly after . . .** JR to PSA, 16 May 1973.

245 **From mid-1974 . . .** JR to PSA, 28 June 1975; JR to PSA, 10 July 1975; JR to PSA, 4 August 1975; JR to PSA, 8 August 1975; JR to PSA, 25 October 1975.

245 **In January 1977 . . .** PSA, "Book Review: Sleep It Off Lady"; JR to PSA, 30 September 1977.

246 **In 1978 it would be . . .** JR to PSA, 4 September 1978; JR to PSA, 3 March 1979.

246 **But Jean would finish . . .** PSA, "Jean Rhys: A Tribute"; PSA to AOE, 6 June 1979.

246 **With Phyllis and . . .** PSA to AOE, n.d.

247 **In September . . .** REA to JSA, n.d.

247 **Phyllis, quite indignant . . .** PSA, "Editor of *Star* arrested," "No Case to Answer—Charge Against Editor Dismissed"; AL, 25 January 1995; LH, 8 August 1991; FB, 9 August 1993; PSA to AOE, 11 February 1977.

247 **Just a few months . . .** "To Our Reader Friends," Note accompanying an unidentified issue of the *Star*, 1975; "Nothing But the Truth."

248 **Phyllis was angered . . .** MEC to the *Educator*, 16 July 1975; "Notes on the Libel Case," LEA.

249 **Toward the end of . . .** JSA to PSA and REA, 23 November 1976; PSA to EC, n.d.; JSA to PSA and REA, 25 May 1976.

249 **Phyllis and Robert . . .** PSA, "Robbery and Ransacking"; REA to David Allfrey, 3 April 1976.

249 **But 1976 had been . . .** JSA to PSA, 9 May 1974; REA to J. P. Walker, Esq., 23 June 1977.

250 **By March 1977 Phina . . .** JSA to PSA and REA, 16 March 1977.

250 **Phyllis and Robert . . .** RA, 10 August 1991; Pattullo [1988], 233; PSA to AOE, 18 April 1977; "Allfrey Daughter Killed in Car Crash, Botswana."

250 **Phyllis's mourning . . .** ITC, 9.

251 **Phyllis's response . . .** JR to PSA, 14 May 1977; PSA to EC, n.d.

251 **Phyllis and . . .** PSA, "Don't Say We Discussed"; PSA to AOE, 11 March 1974 and n.d.

252 **Pixie Foley . . .** PF to author, 22 November 1994.

252 **Among Phyllis . . .** AL, 25 January 1995; REA to TVL, 18 April 1967.

253 **Some months after . . .** EC to PSA, 3 September 1977; PSA to EC, n.d.

253 **In the summer . . .** PSA, "A Visit from Arthur Seymour"; A. J. Seymour to PSA, 6 July 1978.

253 **Seymour's advice . . .** C.L.R. James to PSA, 16 April 1981.

254 **In 1978, encouraged . . .** PSA to EC, n.d.; "A Tribute from Portsmouth."

254 **In February 1979 . . .** PSA, "Review: Caribbean Quarterly"; PSA to AOE, 3 November 1963.

255 **The Executive . . .** Honychurch [1988], 184, 191; *Star*, 7 January 1972.

256 **In July 1974 . . .** PSA, "How LeBlanc Climbed to Power"; Honychurch [1988], 185.

256 **Phyllis was elated . . .** PSA, "One Down, One to Go"; Higbie, 132; PSA, "Premier John," handwritten notes, LEA.

257 **At the Labour . . .** Liverpool, 20–23; PSA, "Jean Rhys Signs Petition"; JR to PSA, 14 May 1977.

258 **These revelations . . .** Smith, 29.

258 **From then on . . .** PSA, "Gary Deposed," "Dominica Freedom Party's Statement of Change of Govt. in Grenada"; John Spector, "Life, Liberty and the Pursuit of Happiness"; Alister Hughes, "The Rich Bully"; PSA, "The Virtue of the Leader Is the Fortune of the Community," "The First Woman Prime Minister of Britain."

258 **In May 1979 . . .** PSA, "Two Sinister Bills," "Jail Jail Jail"; LH, 7 August 1991.

259 **The following day . . .** PSA, "The Funeral of Defence Force Victim Philip Timothy"; PSA, "The People Who Are Saving Dominica."

260 **The impact . . .** PSA to AOE, 6 June 1979; PSA, "Our Island Is Our World."

260 **Pressure on John . . .** PSA, "Our Island Is Our World."

260 **The proclamation . . .** PSA, "Cleaning Up the Mess," PSA, "The People of Dominica."

260 **Dominica's constitutional . . .** The account of the devastation caused by Hurricane David draws upon the following sources: Pattullo [1984], 24; PSA, "Hurricane David"; *ITC*, chapters 1 and 2; PSA, "The Way We Live Now."

262 **The following day . . .** Diana Athill to PSA, 7 December 1979; DHJ to author, 29 May 1993; PSA, "The Way We Live Now"; PSA, "Christmas Greetings."

263 **One positive . . .** REA to Edmund Dowling, 16 December 1979.

264 **As if the aftermath . . .** Higbie, 183; PSA, "Dominica Will Help to Stem the Tide of Socialism"; Smith, 32–35; PSA, "Christmas of Unanswered Questions"; PSA, "The Prime Minister Has No Mandate," "The State of Our Agriculture," "The Choice: United States and Cuba"; "July, Dominica's Fateful Month."

265 **When the people . . .** PSA, "Free at Last."

Chapter Thirteen
Love for an Island

266 **The Freedom party's . . .** PSA, "We Cannot Yet Criticize," "Address to the Nation," "The Prime Minister's Speech," "Events of Our Week," "Shall We Change the Name."

266 **Within days of the . . .** PSA, "We Have Overcome."

266–267 **In the *Star's* . . .** PSA, "Life, Liberty, and Happiness." **Eugenia immediately . . .** PSA, "Ted's Kidnapping—The Appeals." **In late April . . .** PSA to AOE, 24 June 1981; PSA, "The Frustrated Coup"; PSA, "Floods of Rain—And a Second Coup Attempt"; PSA to AOE, 24 June 1981.

267n **During the crisis . . .** PSA, "Resistance."

268 **"The so-called . . ."** PSA to PP, 1983; DA, 8 August 1991; PSA to AOE, 24 June 1981.

268 **More troublesome . . ."** PSA to AOE, 6 April 1982 and 24 June 1981. **As a result . . .** PSA, "The Bright Event of April—Reopening of Public Library."

269 **Faced with . . . troubles . . .** AL, 25 January 1995; PSA, "*The Orchid House* Reissued."

270 **Phyllis had learned . . .** Carmen Callil to PSA, 26 August 1980; Campbell [1982], xv; EC to PSA, 19 November 1979; Edward Kamau Brathwaite to author, 7 December 1995.

270 **When Phyllis . . .** PH, 10 April 1995; LH, 11 April 1995; PP, 12 April 1995; Frickey, 6.

270 **There are indeed . . .** PH, 10 April 1995; LH, 11 April 1995; PP, 12 April 1995; Frickey, 6.

271 **Grateful as she was . . .** Barnes; *The Bookseller*, 6 February 1982; "Indomitable in Dominica"; J. S. Arthur to PSA, 2 March 1982.

271 **Her chagrin over . . .** PH, 23 January 1995; LH 7 August 1991; PP, 12 April 1995.

272 **The book's reissue . . .** Article; RV, 13 August 1991.

272 **But all was not . . .** Pattullo [1992]; AA, 6 July 1991.

272 **The reissue of . . .** PP to PSA, 18 April 1982; Pattullo [1984], 24.

273n **A few months . . .** Holly Eley to PSA, 19 October 1983.

273 **Polly's first visit . . .** PP, 12 April 1995; LH, 11 April 1995.

274 **In 1978, when . . .** John Spector [REA], "Life, Liberty and the Pursuit of Happiness"; Hughes, "The Rich Bully"; LH, 11 April 1995.

274 **But what she could . . .** PSA to PP, 9 March 1984; PSA to PP, n.d. (ca. 1984).

275 **During this period . . .** Frickey, 5; PFr to author, 1 January 1993.

275 **Encouraged by . . .** PSA to AOE, 19 December 1980; PSA to AOE, 14 August 1980.

277 **The text as it remained . . .** PSA to AOE, 6 April 1982.

277 **Throughout 1983 . . .** PSA to PP, August 1984; PSA to PFr, 1 October 1983; PFr to author, 1 January 1993.

279 **Throughout these last . . .** PSA, "A Child Named Dominica."

279 **Phyllis's cousin . . .** RV, 13 August 1991.

279n **Frances Barber . . .** Pattullo [1991], 34.

280 **Rosalind's wrath . . .** RV, 13 August 1991.

281–282 **Among Phyllis's . . .** PH, 23 January 1995. **Barely a year . . .** Manuel O. Mercado to PSA, 14 November 1984; Charles Fisher to PSA, n.d.

283 **By the time . . .** RLS to LH, 30 December 1985.

284 **Phyllis had always had . . .** LH, 7 August 1991.

284 **The honors Phyllis . . .** Funeral address, LHA.

Bibliography

Works by Phyllis Shand Allfrey

Novels

The Orchid House. London: Constable, 1953. Reprint, New York: E.P. Dutton, 1954. London: Virago Press, 1982, 2d ed. Reprint, Washington, D.C.: Three Continents Press, 1985.

Dashing Away. Unpublished.

Three Cups of Tea. Unpublished.

In the Cabinet. Unpublished. There are two manuscripts of this title. The earlier one is an autobiographical account of Allfrey's career as a Federation minister written in 1962–1963. Excerpts of this text appeared in the *Dominica Herald* between June and December 1963 as follows: From chapter 6, 22 June 1963, 4; from chapter 2, 29 June 1963, 3; from chapter 5, 6 July 1963, 5; from chapter 2, 13 July 1963, 7; from chapter 8, 20 July 1963, 4; from chapter 8, 27 July 1963, 4; from chapter 6, 3 August 1963, 3; from chapter 9, 10 August 1963, 4; from chapter 9, 17 August 1963, 4; from chapter 10, 24 August 1963, 3; from chapter 5, 31 August 1963, 7; from chapter 10, 7 September 1963, 4; from chapter 6, 21 September 1963, 6; from chapter 2, 2 November 1963, 8; from chapter 2, 9 November 1963, 8; from chapter 3, 23 November 1963, 5; from chapter 3, 7 December 1963, 5, 6; from chapter 6, 14 December 1963, 6. An additional excerpt appeared in the *Star*, 13 November 1965, 4–5.

The second manuscript is a novel based partly on the autobiographical materials of the original version but which incorporates a substantial amount of new material.

Excerpts

"The Time of the Migrants," *Star*, 13 November 1965, 4–5.

"The Master Comes Home." From *The Orchid House*. In *Her True True Name: An Anthology of Women's Writing from the Caribbean*, edited by Pamela Mordecai and Betty Wilson, 156–163. London: Heinemann, 1989.

Short Stories

"Uncle Rufus," *Tribune*, 11 December 1942, 18.

"A Talk on China." *The Windmill* 1, no. 1 (1944–1946): 52–56.

"The Tunnel." *The Windmill* 1, no. 2 (1944–1946): 105–113.

"Breeze." *Pan Africa* (January 1947); n.p.

"O Stay and Hear." *Argosy* 15, no. 9 (September 1954): 29–33.

The Untanglers. London: Writers Guild, ca. 1958.

"The Naming—A Tale of a London Borough." Part 1, "A Decision." *Dominica Herald*, 5 January 1963, 6, 8. Part 2, "Anonymous Letters." *Dominica Herald*, 12 January 1963, 2.

"It Falls into Place." *Dominica Herald*, 13 June 1964, 3, 9. [As Philip Warner]

"The Homeworkers." *Star*, 7 August 1965, 4–5.

"We Three Kings." *Star*, 24 December 1965, 4–5.

"The Spirit Portrait." *Star*, 29 January 1966, 6–7.

"A Time for Loving." Part 1. *Star*, 12 February 1966, 6. Part 2. 18 February 1966, 6–8.

"Las' Lap, Las' Laugh." *Star*, 5 March 1966, 6–7. [As Rose O]

"A Real Person." Part 1, *Star*, 4 June 1966, 6–8. Part 2, 11 June 1966, 6–7, 11.

"Proserpeena and the Colonel." *Star*, 4 February 1967, 8–11.

"Tea with the Bishop." *Star*, 15 April 1967, 8–9.

"At the House of the Countess." *Star*, 6 May 1967, 8–9.

"The Man Who Pitched Bottles." *Star*, 2 November 1968, 8–9.

"Miss Garthfield's Greenhouse." In *Caribbean Women Writers: Essays from the First International Conference*, edited by Selwyn R. Cudjoe, 116–118. Wellesley, Mass.: Calaloux, 1990.

"Little Cog-burt." In *Green Cane and Juicy Flotsam: Short Stories by Caribbean Women*, edited by

Carmen C. Esteves and Lizabeth Paravisini-Gebert, 5–12. New Brunswick, N.J.: Rutgers University Press, 1991.

Unpublished Short Stories

The following unpublished stories are in the LEA: "Babes in the Woods," "The Bodyguard," "The Carib's Revenge," "Dancing with George," "The Eyrie," "How We Spend Christmas Here," "I Got, Capital," "Letter to a German-American Laundress," "Lily," "Miss Cashamou's Speakeasy," "The Mystery of Ding-A-Ding Hook," "The Naming," "The Objective," "Parks," "The Raincoat," "Sitting Around in London," "Scraps of Paper," and "The Yellow Horse."

Poetry

In Circles: Poems. Harrow Weald, Middlesex, England: Raven Press, 1940.
"Decayed Gentlewomen." In *Rhyme and Reason: 34 Poems*, edited by David Martin, 5. London: Fore Publications, n. d.
Palm and Oak: Poems. London: N.p., 1950. 12pp. Reprint, [Dominica]: Copyotype Company, 1967.
Contrasts. Bridgetown, Barbados: Advocate Press, 1955. 21pp.
"The Roads." *Dominica Herald*, 19 September 1964, 4.
"Poet's Cottage." *Star*, 19 March 1966, 11.
"Trio by Lamplight." *Star*, 21 May 1966, 11.
"The Christmas Stroller." *Star*, 11 December 1965, 7.
"Now in Our Times." *Star*, 2 December 1968, 9.
"Love for an Island." Ibid.
"Exiles." *Star*, 18 January 1969, 2.
"The True Born Villager." *Star*, 18 January 1969, 3.
Palm and Oak II. Roseau, Dominica: Star Printery, 1973.
"Cunard Liner 1940." In *Chaos of the Night: Women's Poetry and Verse of the Second World War*, edited by Catherine W. Reilly, 4. London: Virago, 1985.
"Young Lady Dancing with Soldier." In *Chaos of the Night: Women's Poetry and Verse of the Second World War*, edited by Catherine W. Reilly, 5. London: Virago, 1985.
"The Child's Return." In *The Penguin Book of Caribbean Verse in English*, edited by Paula Burnett, 171. London: Penguin, 1985. Reprint, In *Creation Fire: A Cafra [Caribbean/African] Anthology of Caribbean Women's Poetry*, edited by Ramabai Espinet, 52, 83, 226. Toronto: Sister Vision, 1990.
"The Gypsy to Her Baby." In *Creation Fire: A Cafra Anthology of Caribbean Women's Poetry*, edited by Ramabai Espinet, 52. Toronto: Sister Vision, 1990.
"Love for an Island." In *The Penguin Book of Caribbean Verse In English*, edited by Paula Burnett, 171–172. London: Penguin, 1985. Reprint, In *Creation Fire: A Cafra Anthology of Caribbean Women's Poetry*, edited by Ramabai Espinet, 83. Toronto: Sister Vision, 1990.
The Collected Poems of Phyllis Shand Allfrey, edited by Lizabeth Paravisini-Gebert. Kingston, Jamaica: Sandsbury Press, forthcoming.

Poems by "Rose O" in Star

"Roseau Pa-Ni Gleau," 26 March 1966, 7.
"I Sing of an Island," quoted in *ITC*.
"A Bribe and a Favour," 22 January 1966, 2.
"Tweedledum and Tweedledee: Modern Version," 29 January 1966, 4.
"A Cautionary Rhyme," 8 October 1966, 1.
"National Carnival," 29 October 1966, 6.
"Courtesy Awards Dialogue," 5 November 1966, 2.
"Sunday Dinner," 19 November 1966, 3.
"Village State," 31 December 1966, 2.
"A Dose of Independence," 14 January 1967, 4.
"An A-Pu-Pu-Ironsicle Tale," 21 January 1967, 4.

"Don' Call Awee Small," 4 March 1967, 6.
"Sharpless not Strathmore," 25 March 1967, 3.
"De Donkey Derby," 1 April 1967, 3.
"Jerusalem Aflame," 9 June 1967, 1.
"Swine Fever: A Cautionary Rhyme," 23 September 1967, 1.
"Talkers," 28 October 1967, 5, 2.
"Give Us Jeff and Francis," 2 March 1968, 2.
"Silent Night," 25 May 1968, 3.
"The Artist's Departure," 5 October 1968, 4.
"Electoral Rhyme," 3 January 1970, 3.
"Ghosts on a Plantation House," 2 February 1973, 4.
"Nature Toys of Dominica: The Tree Boat and the LaBelle," 21 December 1973, 3.
"Nature Toys of Dominica: The Palm Horse and The Paw Paw Flute," 4 January 1974, 3.
"On the Death of Clem and Eve," 12 January 1979, 4.
"The People of Dominica," 22 June 1979, 1.

Essays and Other Nonfiction

"A Memorandum for the WIFLP Convention from the President, Labour Party of Dominica." London University: Institute of Commonwealth Studies, 1965.
"The Roman Church and the Dominica B.W.I. Election." *British Weekly*, 12 September 1957.
"Address to the Xth Session of the UNESCO Conference." Paris, 6 November 1958.
The First Year: Six Broadcasts by Ministers of the Federal Government of the West Indies. Port of Spain, Trinidad: Federal Information Service, Federal House, 1959.
"The Day Flames Gutted a Town." *Sunday Guardian*, 5 February 1961, 4.
"I.L.O. Plenary Session at Palais des Nations Geneva." *Dominica Herald*, 8 July 1961, 5.
"Statement by the Minister on the Result of the Jamaica Referendum." *Dominica Herald*, 23 September 1961, 7.
"An Informed Nation—The Role of Community Centres." Opening address by the Honourable Phyllis Shand Allfrey, Federal Minister of Labour and Social Affairs, Trinidad and Tobago Association of Village Councils, 1961 Community Centres Leadership Training Course, 11 October 1961, LEA.
"Address by the Honourable Phyllis Shand Allfrey, Federal Minister of Labour and Social Affairs, to the Trinidad and Tobago Federation of Women's Institutes and Women's Groups, on the Occasion of Their Bazaar." 28 October 1961, LEA.
"The Fourth Christmas." A Broadcast by the Hon. Phyllis Shand Allfrey, Federal Minister of Labour and Social Affairs, 21 December 1961, LEA.
"Statement by the Honourable P. S. Allfrey." *Dominica Herald*, 13 January 1962, 2.
"Message from the Honourable Phyllis Shand Allfrey, Federal Minister of Labour and Social Affairs, to the Youths of the County of Victoria on the Occasion of the Commencement of the 9th Annual Cricket Season—Sunday 11th March 1962." LEA.
"A Speech by the Honourable Phyllis Shand Allfrey, Federal Minister of Labour and Social Affairs," 23 March 1962, LEA.
"Green Blood." *Dominica Herald*, 18 August 1962, 4.
"The Labor Party of Dominica." *Dominica Herald*, September 29, 1962, 2.
"The Absentee." *Dominica Herald*, 17 November 1962, 4.
"The Innocents of Alabama." *Star*, 21 September 1963, 6.
"On Secrecy." *Star*, 6 July 1965, 4.
"Name Calling." *Star*, 7 August 1965, 1.
"Editorial." *Star*, 14 August 1965, 2.
"The Only Way." *Star*, 14 August 1965, 1.
"The Simple Life." *Star*, 4 September 1965, 1.
"Why the Star?" *Star*, 11 September 1965, 1.
"Drama of the Week." *Star*, 9 October 1965, 1.
"What the Herald Cut Out." *Star*, 4 December 1965, 1.
"Obituary: Margaret Emily Mary Nicholls." *Star*, July 2, 1966, 4.
"The Queen in Dominica." *Star*, 12 February 1966, 1.

"Stay British—And Live Free." *Star*, 12 February 1966, 1.
"The Queen in Dominica." *Star*, 26 February 1966, 2.
"The *Britannia* Luncheon Party." *Star*, 26 February 1966, 6.
"Death of a West Indian." *Star*, 12 March 1966, 6.
"May Holiday Caller." *Star*, 7 May 1966, 6–7.
"Our Favourite People: Little Mary." *Star*, 3 September 1966, 5.
"The Death of a Carib." *Star*, undated clipping in LEA, ca. 1966.
"*Wide Sargasso Sea*." *Star*, 13 May 1967, 4.
"An Effective Opposition and Other Topics." *Star*, 30 September 1967, 2.
"Rags Twotone Writes Again." *Star*, 7 October 1967, 10.
"Rose O Censored." *Star*, 23 December 1967, 15.
"Mr. Lionel." *Star*, 13 January 1968, 8–9.
"Most Famous Dominican." *Star*, 20 January 1968, 6, 14.
"Dr. Jagan: An Appraisal." *Star*, 23 March 1968, 14.
"Al Akong Deported." *Star*, 5 October 1968, 1, 2.
"The Artist's Departure." *Star*, 5 October 1968, 1, 2.
"Don't Say We Discussed It." *Star*, 27 April 1973, 3.
"How LeBlanc Climbed to Power." *Star*, 19 July 1974, 2.
"One Down, One to Go." *Star*, 26 July 1974, 1.
"Editor of *Star* Arrested." *Star*, 4 October 1974, 1.
"The Threatened Forest." undated, ca. 1975.
"No Case to Answer—Charge Against Editor Dismissed." *Star*, 7 March 1975, 1.
"Robbery and Ransacking." *Star*, 2 January 1976, 1.
"Is Negritude Racist?" *Star*, 12 March 1976, 2.
"Book Review: *Sleep It Off Lady*." *Star*, 28 January 1977, 6.
"Jean Rhys Signs Petition." *Star*, 1 April 1977, 1.
"Allfrey Daughter Killed in Car Crash, Botswana." *Star*, 22 April 1977, 1.
"A Visit from Arthur Seymour." *Star*, 30 June 1978, 2.
"Review: *Caribbean Quarterly*." *Star*, 2 February 1979, 4.
"Dominica Freedom Party's Statement of Change of Govt. in Grenada." *Star*, 16 March 1979, 1.
"The Virtue of the Leader Is the Fortune of the Community." *Star*, 23 April 1979, 1.
"Gary Deposed." *Star*, 16 March 1979, 1.
"The First Woman Prime Minister of Britain—And Europe." *Star*, 4 May 1979, 1.
"Two Sinister Bills." *Star*, 25 May 1979, 1.
"Jail Jail Jail." *Star*, 25 May 1979, 5–6.
"The Funeral of Defence Force Victim Philip Timothy." *Star*, 1 June 1979, 2–3.
"Our Island Is Our World." *Star*, 8 June 1979, 2–3.
"The People Who Are Saving Dominica." *Star*, 8 June 1979, 1.
"Cleaning Up the Mess." *Star*, 29 June 1979, 1.
"The Germ of a Short Story." *Star*, 3 August 1979, 3.
"The Prime Minister Has No Mandate." *Star*, 12 October 1979, 2.
"Dominica Will Help to Stem the Tide of Socialism." *Star*, 12 October 1979, 1.
"The Way We Live Now." *Star*, 12 October 1979, 2.
"Events of Our Week . . . ," *Star*, 9 November 1979, 6.
"Christmas Greetings." *Star*, 21 December 1979, 1.
"Christmas of Unanswered Questions." *Star*, 21 December 1979, 2.
"Jean Rhys: A Tribute." *Kunapipi* 1, no. 2 (1979): 23–25.
"July, Dominica's Fateful Month." *Star Newsletter*, June 1980, 1.
"Free at Last." *Star Newsletter*, July 1980, 1.
"We Have Overcome," *Star Newsletter*, July 1980, 2.
"Adress to the Nation," *Star Newsletter*, July 1980, 4.
"The Prime Minister's Speech," *Star Newsletter*, August 1980, 2.
"Hurricane David: The Skeleton of a Survival Tale." *Kunapipi* 2, no. 1 (1980): 118–122.
"We Cannot Yet Criticize," *Star Newsletter*, October 1980, 1.
"Shall We Change the Name . . . ," *Star Newsletter*, 9 November 1980, 1.
"A Child Named Dominica," *Star Newsletter*, January 1981, 5.
"Life, Liberty, and Happiness," *Star Newsletter*, February 1981, 1.

"Resistance," *Star Newsletter*, February 1981, 6.
"Ted's Kidnapping—The Appeals," *Star Newsletter*, February 1981, 6.
"The Bright Event of April—Reopening of Public Library," *Star Newsletter*, April/May 1981, 6.
"The Frustrated Coup," *Star Newsletter*, May/June 1981, 6.
"Floods of Rain—And a Second Coup Attempt," *Star Newsletter*, 31 December 1981, 1.
"Eugenia Nicholls." *Star Newsletter*, 31 December 1981, 2.
"*The Orchid House* Reissued," *Star Newsletter*, January 1982, 1.

Children's Literature

Governor Pod. London: N.p. 1951. 23pp.

Broadcasts

The Orchid House. Four-part television adaptation by Jim Hawkins. Directed by Horace Ové. Channel Four (England), 1991.

Translations

La Maison des Orchidées. Translated by Léon Bocquer. Paris: Librairie Stock, 1954.
Das Orchideenhaus. Translated by Bruni Röhm. Reinbek bei Hamburg, 1993.

Works About Phyllis Shand Allfrey

Literary Criticism

Andre, Irving W. "The Social World of Phyllis Shand Allfrey's *The Orchid House*." *Caribbean Quarterly* 29, no. 2 (June 1983): 11–21.

Boxill, Anthony. "The Novel in English in the West Indies 1900–1962." Ph.D. dissertation, University of New Brunswick, Canada, 1966.

Brathwaite, Edward. "The House in the West Indian Novel." *Tapia* 7, no. 26 (1977): 6–8.

Campbell, Elaine. "From Dominica to Devonshire: A Memento of Jean Rhys." *Kunapipi* I (1979): 6–22.

———. "'In the Cabinet': A Novelistic Rendition of Federation Politics." *Ariel* 17, no. 4 (October 1986): 117–125.

———. Introduction to *The Orchid House*, by Phyllis Shand Allfrey. London: Virago Press, 1982.

———. "Literature and Transitional Politics in Dominica." *World Literature Written in English* 24, no. 2 (1984): 349–359.

———. "Phyllis Shand Allfrey (1915–   )." In *Fifty Caribbean Writers*, edited by Daryl Cumber Dance, 9–18. New York: Greenwood Press, 1986.

———. "A Report from Dominica, B.W.I." *World Literature Written in English* 17, no. 1 (1978): 305–316.

———. "The Unpublished Short Stories of Phyllis Shand Allfrey." In *Short Fiction in the New Literatures in English: Proceedings of the Nice Conference of the European Association for Commonwealth Literature and Language Studies*, edited by J. Bardolph, 103–108. Nice, France: European Association for Commonwealth Literature and Language Studies, 1989. Reprint, In *Caribbean Women Writers: Essays From the First International Conference*, edited by Selwyn R. Cudjoe, 119–127. Wellesley, Mass.: Calaloux, 1990.

Carr, W. I. "The West Indian Novelist: Prelude and Context." *Caribbean Quarterly* 11, no. 1–2 (1965): 771–784.

Davies, Barrie. "Neglected West Indian Writers No. 1. Phyllis Allfrey. *The Orchid House*." *World Literature Written in English* 2, no. 2 (1972): 81–85.

Espinet, Ramabai. "Adieu Foulards, Adieu Madras: The Place of the Euro-Creole Woman Writer with Particular Reference to the Works of Jean Rhys and Phyllis Shand Allfrey." Ph.D. dissertation, University of the West Indies, 1993.

———. "A Short Account of the Life and Work of Phyllis Shand Allfrey, 1908–1986." *Bulletin of Eastern Caribbean Affairs* 12, no. 1 (March-April 1986): 33–35.

Figueroa, John J. M. "Some Provisional Comments on West Indian Novels." In his *Commonwealth*

Literature: Unity and Diversity in a Common Culture, edited by John J. M. Figueroa, 90–97. London: Heinemann, 1965.

Frickey, Pierrette. "The Dominican Landscape: In Memory of Jean Rhys." *Jean Rhys Review* 3, no. 1 (Fall 1988): 2–10.

James, Louis. Introduction to *The Islands in Between*, 45–46. London: Oxford University Press, 1968.

Nunez-Harrell, Elizabeth. "The Paradoxes of Belonging: The White West Indian Woman in Fiction." *Modern Fiction Studies* 31, no. 2 (1985): 281–293.

O'Callaghan, Evelyn. "'The Outsider's Voice': White Creole Women Novelists in the Caribbean Literary Tradition." *Journal of West Indian Literature* 1, no. 1 (1986): 74–88.

Phaf, Ineke. "Women and Literature in the Caribbean." In *Unheard Words. Women and Literature in Africa, the Arab World, Asia, the Caribbean and Latin America*, edited by Mineke Schipper, 168–200. London: Allison and Busby, 1985.

Ramchand, Kenneth. "Terrified Consciousness." *Journal of Commonwealth Literature* 7 (1969): 8–19.

———. *The West Indian Novel and Its Background*, 224–226. London: Faber & Faber, 1970.

Seymour, Arthur James. *The Poetry of Phyllis Shand Allfrey*. Georgetown: N.p., 1981.

Williamson, Karina. *Voyages in the Dark: Jean Rhys and Phyllis Shand Allfrey*. Occasional Papers in Caribbean Studies No. 4. Coventry, England: University of Warwick, [1986].

Wyile, Herb. "Narrator/Narrated: The Position of Lally in *The Orchid House*." *World Literature Written in English* 31, no. 1 (Spring 1991): 21–33.

Reviews

Bajan 1, no. 12 (1954): 21.

Barnes, Rory. "*The Orchid House*." *National Times*, 15–21 August 1982.

Brathwaite, Edward. *Bim* 37 (1954).

Brown, Ethel S. "*The Orchid House*." *Library Journal* (March 1, 1954): 449–450.

"Buzzing With Life." *Iraq Times*, 29 July 1953, n.p.

Charques, R. D. "New Novels." *Spectator*, 7 August 1953, 158.

"Enchanted Island." *New York Times Book Review*, 14 March 1954, n.p.

Hay, Sara Henderson. "Island Taint." *Saturday Review*, 20 March 1954, 20, 55.

Laski, Marghanita. *London Sunday Observer*, 19 July 1953, 8.

"Local Colour." *Times*, 11 July 1953, 8.

Nunez-Harrell, Elizabeth. "Beauty from Decay." *CRNLA Reviews Journal* 1 (1983): 97–99.

Booklist, April 15, 1954, 320.

Manchester Guardian, 17 July 1953, 4.

Express and Star (Wolverhampton, England), 10 August 1953.

Newcastle Journal, 5 August 1953.

Library Journal, 1 March 1954, 449.

Booklist, 15 April 1954, 320.

New York Times, 14 March 1954, 23.

Quinn, Maria. "Fight for Rights in Caribbean Classic." *Morning Star*, 6 May 1982, n.p.

Ross, Robert. *Commonwealth Novel in English* 2, no. 2 (1983): 116–118.

Scott, George. "A Hot-House of Beauty and Evil—A Fine First Novel." *Truth*, 24 July 1953, 6–7.

Interviews

Pattullo, Polly. "Phyllis Shand Allfrey's 'Caribbean Chronicle.'" *Observer Magazine* (July 1985): 22–25.

———. "Phyllis Shand Allfrey Talking with Polly Pattullo." In *Writing Lives: Conversations Between Women Writers*, edited by Mary Chamberlain, 223–234. London: Virago, 1988.

Miscellaneous

"Death of a Native Daughter." *Weekend Nation*, 14 February 1986, 6.

Espinet, Adrien. "Pre-Election Dominica: As Seen by an Outsider." *Trinidad Guardian*, 11 August 1957; reprint, *Dominica Chronicle*, 21 September 1957, 7.

Hoyos, Alexander. "The Valiant Woman." *The Vincentian*, 21 February 1986, clipping, LEA.

"Indomitable in Dominica." *Sunday Times*, 11 April 1982, clipping, LEA.
Julien, Valerie. "Phyllis Shand Allfrey: A Very Special Woman." *The New Chronicle*, 7 March 1986, 17.
Lent, John A. *Third World Media and Their Search for Modernity: The Case of Commonwealth Caribbean*, Cranbury, N.J.: Associated University Press, 1977.
"Mrs. Phyllis Shand Allfrey: Obituary." *The Times*, 11 February 1986, clipping, LEA.
Pattullo, Polly. "Allfrey's *Orchid House* Filmed." *Caribbean Contact*, 1991, clipping, LEA.
———. "The Art of Living Together." *BWee Caribbean Beat* 6 (Summer 1993): 78–81.
———. "The Dark Side of Paradise." *Sunday Times Supplement*, 18 February 1991, clipping, LEA.
———. "Phyllis Shand Allfrey: Poet of a Lost Federation." *The Guardian*, 30 May 1992, clipping, LEA.
Peacocke, Nan. "Remembering Things to Come." *The Vincentian*, 14 February 1986, clipping, LEA.
"Phyllis Allfrey Is Dead." *The Vincentian*, 7 February 1986, clipping, LEA.
"Phyllis Shand Allfrey." In *Blaze a Fire: Significant Contributions of Caribbean Women*, edited by Nesha Haniff, 159–164. Toronto: Sister Vision, 1987.
"Political Party Founder Dies." *Barbados Advocate*, 6 February 1986, 6.
"Remarkable Women." *Barbados Advocate*, 6 December 1985, clipping, LEA.
"Some West Indian Novels Face Neglect in West Indies." *Sunday Guardian*, 5 February 1961, 4.
"Stateswoman Dies." *Dominica Chronicle*, 7 February 1986, clipping, LEA.
Stroude, Graham. "W.I. Woman Dedicated to Politics: Pen Portrait of Phyllis Allfrey." *The West Indian*, 21 March 1961, 2.
Vane, Peter. "Calypso Time Down in Sussex." *News Chronicle*, 7 August 1956, n.p.
"Why Not a Monument." *The New Chronicle*, 7 March 1986, 4.

Other Books Consulted

Alain-Fournier. *Le Grand Meaulnes*. Paris: Editions G.P., 1913.
Antigua and the Antiguans: A Full Account of the Colony and its Inhabitants from the Time of the Caribs to the Present Day, ascribed variously to Mrs. Flannegan and Mrs. Lanaghan. 2 vols. London: Saunders and Oatley, 1844.
Angier, Carole. *Jean Rhys*. Boston: Little Brown & Co., 1991.
Atwood, Thomas. *The History of the Island of Dominica*. London: J. Johnson, 1791.
Baker, Patrick L. *Chaos, Order and the Ethnohistory of Dominica*. Toronto: McGill Queen's University Press, 1994.
Bell, Hesketh. *Glimpses of a Governor's Life: From Diaries, Letters and Memoranda*. London: Sampson, Low, Marston & Co., Ltd., 1936.
Benge, R. C., *Confessions of a Lapsed Librarian*. London: Scarecrow Press, 1984.
Cracknell, Basil E. *Dominica*. Harrisburg, Pa.: Stackpole Books, 1973.
Cole, Margaret. *The Story of Fabian Socialism*. Stanford, Calif.: Stanford University Press, 1961.
Davy, John. *The West Indies Before and After Emancipation*. London: Frank Cass & Co., Ltd., 1854.
de Charms, Leslie, *Elizabeth of the German Garden: A Biography*. London: Heinemann, 1958.
Douglas, Karl. "Confederation Doomed—Lewis." *Trinidad Guardian*, 4 April 1961, 3.
Eliot, E. C. *Broken Atoms*. London: Geoffrey Bles, 1938.
Fermor, Patrick Leigh. *The Traveller's Tree*. London: John Murray, 1950.
Firth, Jim. *Britain, Facism and the Popular Front*. London: Lawrence and Wishart, 1985.
Foot, Michael. *Aneurin Bevan: A Biography, vol. 1, 1897–1945*. London: MacGinnon and Kee, 1962.
Froude, James Anthony. *The English in the West Indies or The Bow of Ulysses*. London: Longmans, Green, and Co., 1888.
Gaspar, David Barry. *Bondmen and Rebels: A Study of Master-Slave Relations in Antigua, with Implications for Colonial British America*. Baltimore: Johns Hopkins University Press, 1985.
Gibson, Robert. *The Land Without a Name: Alain-Fournier and His World*. New York: St. Martin's Press, 1975.
Gollancz, Victor. *More for Timothy, vol. 2*. London: Victor Gollancz Ltd., 1953.
Goreau, Angeline. *Reconstructing Aphra: A Social Biography of Aphra Behn*. New York: Dial Press, 1980.

Goslinga, Cornelius C. *A Short History of the Netherlands Antilles and Surinam*. The Hague/Boston/London: Martinus Nijhoff, 1979.

Gurney, Joseph John. *A Winter in the West Indies, Described by Familiar Letters to Henry Clay, of Kentucky*. New York: Negro University Press, 1969.

Hall, Douglas. *Five of the Leewards, 1834–1876*. St. Lawrence, Manitoba: Canadian Universities Press, 1971.

Hammond, John, *John Hammond on Record: An Autobiography*. New York: Penguin Books, 1977.

Hawys, Stephen. *Mount Joy*. London: Gerald Duckworth & Co., Ltd., 1968.

Henry, Paget. *Peripheral Capitalism and Underdevelopment in Antigua*. New Brunswick: Transamerica Books, 1985.

Hewison, Robert. *Under Siege: Literary Life in London, 1939–1945*. London: Weidenfeld and Nicolson, 1977.

Higbie, Janet. *Eugenia: The Caribbean's Iron Lady*. London: Macmillan Caribbean, 1993.

Higham, C. S. S. *The Development of the Leeward Islands Under the Restoration, 1600–1688: A Study of the Foundations of the Old Colonial System*. Cambridge, England: Cambridge University Press, 1921.

Hill, Douglas, ed. *Tribune 40: The First Forty Years of a Socialist Newspaper*. London: Quartet Books, 1977.

Honychurch, Lennox. *Dominica: Isle of Adventure*. London: Macmillan, 1991.

———. *The Dominica Story*. Roseau: Dominica Institute, 1984.

———. *Our Island Culture*. Roseau: Dominican National Cultural Council, 1988.

Jackson, Carlton. *Who Will Take Our Children?* London: Methuen, 1985.

Jackson, Stanley. *J. P. Morgan: A Biography*. New York: Stein and Day, 1983.

Kennedy, Margaret. *The Constant Nymph*. Garden City, N.Y.: Doubleday, Page & Co., 1925.

Knopton, Ernest John. *Empress Josephine*. Cambridge, Mass.: Harvard University Press, 1963.

Kunsman, Charles J. *The Origins and Development of Political Parties in the British West Indies*. Ann Arbor, Mich.: University Microfilms International Dissertation Services, 1963.

Lewis, Gordon K. *The Growth of the Modern West Indies*. New York: Monthly Review Press, 1968.

Lockwood, P. A., ed. *Canada and the West Indies*. Sackville, N. B., Canada: Mount Allison University Publication, 1958.

Mazurczak, Witold. *The Rise and Fall of the West Indies Federation*. Poznan, Poland: Wydawnictwo Naukowe Uniwersytate im. Adama Mickiewicza, 1988.

Mitchison, Naomi. *You May Well Ask: A Memoir (1920–1940)*. London: Victor Gollancz Ltd., 1979.

———. *The Moral Basis of Politics*. London: Constable, 1938.

———. *Among You, Taking Notes: The Wartime Diary of Naomi Mitchison, 1939–1945*, edited by Dorothy Sheridan. London: Victor Gollancz, 1985.

Mordecai, John. *Federation of the West Indies*. Evanston, Ill.: Northwestern University Press, 1968.

Noble, Justice. *A Brief Memoir of Sir Henry Alfred Alford Nicholls, K.B., C.M.G.*. Roseau, Dominica: Bulletin Office, 1928.

Oldmixon, John. *The British Empire in America*. London: J. Brotherton & J. Clarke, 1708.

Pope-Hennessy, James. *The Baths of Absalom, A Footnote to Froude*. London: Allan Wingate, 1954.

Pulsifer, Susan. *A House in Time*. New York: Citadel Press, 1958.

Rhys, Jean. *Smile Please: An Unfinished Autobiography*. New York: Penguin, 1984.

———. *Wide Sargasso Sea*. New York: Norton, 1966.

Showalter, Elaine. *A Literature of Their Own*. Princeton, N.J.: Princeton University Press, 1977.

Springer, Hugh W. *Reflections on the Failure of the First West Indian Federation*. Cambridge, Mass.: Harvard University Center for International Affairs (Occasional Papers in International Affairs, No. 4), 1962.

Summerskill, Edith. *A Woman's World*. London: Heinemann, 1967.

Trollope, Anthony. *The West Indies and the Spanish Main*. London: Chapman & Hall, 1859.

Waugh, Alec. *The Sugar Islands: A Caribbean Travelogue*. New York: Farrar, Straus & Co., 1949.

Other Articles Consulted

"Alain-Fournier." *Times Literary Supplement*, 16 May 1929, 390.

"Alain-Fournier." *Twentieth-Century Literary Criticism* Vol. 6, 1–28.

Allfrey, David. "A Son to the Defense." *Star*, 16 July 1971, 4.
"Allfrey Expulsion Upheld." *Dominica Herald*, 6 October 1962, 1.
"Allfrey's Housing March Stupid—C.M." *Dominica Chronicle*, 16 November 1960, 1.
"Allfrey Replies to Allegations." *Dominica Chronicle*, 24 December 1960, 1.
"Allfrey Sees Bid to Wear Own Shoes." *Dominica Chronicle*, 20 June 1959, 1.
Allfrey, Robert E. "Mental Health Talk." *Star*, 7 October 1967, 6.
———. "Life, Liberty and the Pursuit of Happiness." *Star*, 11 May 1979, 1. [as John Spector]
"A Tribute from Portsmouth." *Star*, 17 August 1979, 5.
Charles, Margartson. "Founder-President of Labour Party Expelled." *Dominica Herald*, 29 September 1962, 1.
"DLP Celebrates Seventh Birthday." *Dominica Herald*, 2 June 1962, 9.
"Dominica Moves to Provide Punishment for Seditious Acts." *Guyana Graphic*, 5 July, 2.
"Dominica Fascinating." *Dominica Chronicle*, 24 July 1957, 2.
Douglas, Karl. "Confederation Doomed—Lewis." *Trinidad Guardian*, 4 April 1961, 4.
"Election Campaigning in Full Swing." *Dominica Chronicle*, 20 July 1957, 1.
"Emmanuel Christopher Loblack: D/ca's Trade Union Godfather." *New Chronicle*, May 19, 1989, 6.
"Fairplay." *Dominica Herald*, 20 January 1962, 4.
"Federal Minister Addresses CCL." *Dominica Chronicle*, 24 September 1960, 1.
"Federal Minister on Week-Long Visit: Re-Asserts Confidence in Federation." *Chronicle*, 10 January 1962, 1.
"Federal Minister Speaks at Market." *Dominica Chronicle*, 24 August 1960, 1.
"Federal Minister Speaks at Meeting." *Dominica Chronicle*, 25 October 1958, 1, 7.
Flanz, G. H. "West Indian Federation." In *Why Federations Fail: An Inquiry into the Requisites for Successful Federalism*, edited by Thomas M. Franck. New York: New York University Press, 1968.
"Government Officials Booed Because of Sedition Bill." *Barbados Advocate*, 6 July 1968, 1.
"Governor to be Petitioned." *Dominica Chronicle*, 10 July 1968, 6.
"Hearing Refused Labour Leader." *Dominica Chronicle*, 6 January 1962, 1.
Hughes, Alister. "The Rich Bully." *Star*, 27 April 1979, 2.
"Hymeneal." *The Dominican*, 30 May 1905, 3.
"IAPA Criticized 'Press Gag' Law." *Dominica Chronicle*, 21 September 1968.
"Is It Racial Prejudice?" *Dominica Herald*, 20 January 1962, 2.
"Labour Party Conference." *Dominica Herald*, 11 November 1961, 1.
"Labour Party Meeting." *Dominica Herald*, 18 November 1961, 1.
"Letters to the Editor." *Dominica Chronicle*, 17 July 1957, 4.
"Letters to the Editor." *Dominica Herald*, 2 November 1962, 4.
Liverpool, N.J.O. "The Politics of Independence in Dominica." *Bulletin of Eastern Caribbean Affairs* 4, no. 2 (1978): 20–23.
Menzies, J. H. "The Uncrowned King of Dominica." *United Empire* 17 (1926): 203–205.
"Mrs. Allfrey Back from Election Win." *Trinidad Guardian*, [21 January 1961], 6.
"Mrs. Allfrey Replies to 'Voter' on Educational Issues." *Dominica Chronicle*, 31 July 1957, 2.
"Nothing But the Truth." *The Educator*, 9 July 1975, 3.
Paul, David. "The Mysterious Landscape: A Study of Alain-Fournier." *Cornhill Magazine* 162, no. 972 (Autumn 1947): 440–449.
"The Philosopher-Correspondent: Eric Sevareid (1912–1992)," *Newsweek*, July 20, 1992, 54.
"PNM-DLP Coalition Fails." *Dominica Chronicle*, 21 August 1957, 1.
"Premier 'Nyet' on Gag Law." *Dominica Chronicle*, 28 September 1968, 1, 9.
"Premier Relates Jamaican History." *Trinidad Guardian*, 19 October 1961, 11.
"Referendum Aftermath." *Dominica Herald*, 11 November 1961, 2.
Rhys, Jean. "Again the Antilles." *Star*, 15 March 1969, 2.
Smith, Linden. "Dominica: The Post-Hurricane 'David' Period." *Bulletin of Eastern Caribbean Affairs* 5, no. 4 (1979): 32–35.
———. The Political Situation in Dominica." *Bulletin of Eastern Caribbean Affairs* 5:3 (1979): 20–31.
———. "Patrick John, Dominica and the Signs of the Time—A Comment." *Bulletin of Eastern Caribbean Affairs* 5, no. 2 (1979) 23–29.

Stevens, W. S. "Editorial." *Dominica Herald*, 21 January 1961, 4.

Thomas, Bert J. "Revolutionary Activity in the Caribbean: Some Notes on the Dreads of Dominica." *Guyana Journal of Sociology* 1, no. 2 (April 1976): 75–92.

Turnell, Martin. "Alain-Fournier and *Le Grand Meaulnes*." *Southern Review* 2, no. 3 (Summer 1966): 477–498.

Radio Broadcasts

"Jean Rhys: 'I'll Have to Go on Living. . . .'" Recorded on April 15, 1981, for Radio Three, British Broadcasting Corporation.

Index

About the Author

LIZABETH PARAVISINI-GEBERT is associate professor of Caribbean and Latin American literature in the Department of Hispanic Studies at Vassar College. From 1981 to 1991 she taught at Lehman College of the City University of New York, where she chaired the Department of Puerto Rican Studies (1983–1988, 1989–1990) and directed the Bilingual Program (1983–1988). Professor Paravisini has written on contemporary Caribbean, American, and Latin American fiction, and on popular culture, for such journals as *Obsidian, Plural, Clues, Callaloo, Sargasso, Cimarrón, Anales del Caribe, Nuevo Texto Crítico, Contemporary Literary Criticism,* and *The Journal of West Indian Literature,* among others. She co-authored *Caribbean Women Novelists: An Annotated Bibliography* with Olga Torres Seda, and has edited Ana Roqué's 1903 novel *Luz y sombra, Green Cane and Juicy Flotsam: Short Stories by Caribbean Women* (with Carmen Esteves), *El placer de la palabra: literatura erótica femenina de América Latina* (with Margarite Fernández Olmos), its English version, *Pleasure and the Word: Erotic Writings by Latin American Women,* and *Remaking a Lost Harmony: Short Stories from the Hispanic Caribbean* (with Margarite Fernández Olmos). Among her forthcoming work is her translation of a collection of short stories by Dominican author Angela Hernández, *How to Gather the Shadows of the Flowers and Other Tales of Awe* (1996) and *Inscribing the Sacred: Vodoun, Santería and Obeah in the Literatures and Cultures of the Caribbean* (with Margarite Fernández Olmos, 1996). She is the recipient of a 1994–1995 Fellowship from the American Association of University Women for her current project, a book-length study of "Race, Gender, and the Plantation in Caribbean Women's Fiction," and is completing a collection of essays, *Writing in the Wake: Women Travelers and the Caribbean* (with Ivette Romero-Cesareo).